The Discourse Reader

Second edition

The Discourse Reader is an integrated and structured set of the key readings representing the diverse field of discourse studies. Focusing on linguistic, interactional, textual, social, cultural and ideological issues, the *Reader* is organised to provide a graded introduction to discourse theory and practice. Readings include:

- influential early papers that laid the ground for the concept of discourse and defined the main priorities for discourse analysis
- discussions of key research methods and resources
- classic texts by leading theorists, highlighting key concepts in different traditions of discourse studies
- papers by contemporary specialists showing what discourse analysis is able to achieve, applied to different social issues and social settings.

Designed as a structured source book for students from introductory undergraduate level upwards, this new edition includes updated introductions to the six sections, study questions and new readings from Roland Barthes, Judith Butler, Deborah Cameron, Nikolas Coupland and Virpi Ylänne, Derek Edwards, Norman Fairclough, David Graddol, Stuart Hall, Anita Pomerantz, Harvey Sacks and Theo Van Leeuwen.

Full list of authors: J. Maxwell Atkinson, J.L. Austin, M.M. Bakhtin, Roland Barthes, Pierre Bourdieu, Penelope Brown, Judith Butler, Deborah Cameron, Nikolas Coupland, Derek Edwards, Norman Fairclough, Michel Foucault, Elizabeth Fraser, Erving Goffman, David Graddol, H.P. Grice, John J. Gumperz, Stuart Hall, Penelope Harvey, John Heritage, Janet Holmes, Ian Hutchby, Roman Jakobson, Gunther Kress, William Labov, Stephen C. Levinson, Bronislaw Malinowski, Hugh Mehan, Elinor Ochs, Anita Pomerantz, Ben Rampton, Kay Richardson, Harvey Sacks, Emanuel A. Schegloff, Deborah Schiffrin, Deborah Tannen, Teun A. Van Dijk, Theo Van Leeuwen, Cynthia Wallat, Virpi Ylänne, Katharine Young.

Adam Jaworski is Professor and **Nikolas Coupland** is Professor and Director, both at the Centre for Language and Communication Research, Cardiff University.

The Discourse Reader

Second edition

Edited by

Adam Jaworski and
Nikolas Coupland

Routledge
Taylor & Francis Group

LONDON AND NEW YORK

First published 1999
by Routledge

Second edition published 2006
by Routledge
2 Park Square, Milton Park, Abingdon, Oxon OX14 4RN

Simultaneously published in the USA and Canada
by Routledge
270 Madison Ave, New York, NY 10016

Routledge is an imprint of the Taylor & Francis Group, an informa business

© 1999, 2006. This collection and editorial matter
© Adam Jaworski and Nikolas Coupland
Individual essays © individual contributors

Typeset in Perpetua and Bell Gothic by
Florence Production Ltd, Stoodleigh, Devon
Printed and bound in Great Britain by
CPI Antony Rowe, Chippenham, Wiltshire

British Library Cataloguing in Publication Data
A catalogue record for this book is available from the British Library

Library of Congress Cataloging in Publication Data
A catalogue record for this book has been applied for

ISBN10: 0–415–34631–2 (hbk)
ISBN10: 0–415–34632–0 (pbk)
ISBN10: 0–203–59707–9 (ebk)

ISBN13: 978–0–415–34631–3 (hbk)
ISBN13: 978–0–415–34632–0 (pbk)
ISBN13: 978–0–203–59707–1 (ebk)

CONTENTS

FIGURES

PREFACE

IN ITS NEW EDITION *The Discourse Reader* is an integrated and structured set of original writings, representing the interdisciplinary field of discourse studies, focusing principally on linguistic, interactional, textual, social, cultural and ideological issues. The book is planned for use as a beginners/intermediate degree-level teaching text, either on its own or as a secondary source-book. The readings are organised to provide a graded introduction to discourse theory and practice. For this reason, we have included several different sorts of text:

- influential early papers which laid the ground for the concept of discourse and defined the main priorities for 'discourse analysis';
- discussions of key research methods and resources;
- reflexive commentaries by leading theorists, highlighting key differences between sub-traditions of discourse studies;
- papers by contemporary specialists showing what discourse analysis is able to achieve, applied to different social issues and social settings.

Since so many disciplines nowadays claim the term 'discourse' as their own, it is inevitably true that we have emphasised some traditions and schools more than others. Whatever discourse is, and however concretely or abstractly the term is used, there will at least be agreement that it has focally to do with language, meaning and context. For this reason we have started with a substantial section of readings on this theme. It is certainly true that discourse is not the privileged domain of linguists and linguists alone. But some appreciation of early ideas in functional linguistics and linguistic philosophy is essential for all students of discourse. Similarly, and although we would resist the idea that discourse analysis is 'a research method' in the conventional sense (see our Introduction to Part Two), it is important to see the broader research enterprise to which discourse analysis contributes. Part Two is, therefore, a collection of readings on methods and resources for doing discourse analysis. It introduces different traditions of social research and questions of research ethics, linked to practical issues of representing and analysing discourse data, and to forms of language analysis.

Parts Three to Six of the *Reader* then reproduce many of the key articles and book-chapters which, over two decades and more, have dealt with specific themes and foci in discourse studies. Despite the need to be selective, we think that a large proportion of the most influential writers and texts are represented. Part Three introduces those approaches most concerned with sequence and discourse structure, tracing links back to ethnomethodology and carried forward in modern conversation analysis and related research. Part Four deals with social and relational aspects of discourse; Five with identity and subjectivity, as mediated by language; and Six with critical approaches to discourse with the main emphasis on ideology, power and control.

One problem for us has been to establish a boundary between discourse analysis and those approaches to language and society referred to as 'interactional sociolinguistics'. In many people's view, including our own, there is no meaningful distinction between interactional work in sociolinguistics and discourse analysis applied to social settings and themes. Several of the readings we include in the present volume would be considered important contributions to interactional sociolinguistics. It would be useful, therefore, to consult the collection of readings titled *Sociolinguistics: A Reader and Coursebook* (1997) and its forthcoming (2007) edition *The New Sociolinguistics Reader* (both edited by Nikolas Coupland and Adam Jaworski, published by Palgrave Macmillan).

We have reproduced all original papers and chapters as faithfully as we have been able to, given the inevitable restrictions of space and the need to produce a coherent and readable collection. We have, for example, maintained authors' original writing styles and conventions, whether they wrote according to British or US norms. In several cases this policy results in maintaining what is thought of as sexist pronoun usage (e.g., Grice's and many others' use of 'man' for non-specific gender, where 'person' would be more usual and acceptable today). Where we have had to shorten texts, '. . .' shows that we have omitted an amount of original material (usually several sentences or whole sections). Sometimes we have added a short summary of the topic or main points of omitted sections. All our editorial comments are contained in square brackets.

ACKNOWLEDGEMENTS

The editors and publishers would like to thank the following copyright holders for permission to reprint material:

J.L. Austin, pp. 63–75, chapter 2 from *How To Do Things with Words*, 2nd edition, Oxford University Press, 1962. Reprinted by permission of the publisher from *How To Do Things With Words* by John L. Austin, edited by J.O. Urmson and Marina Sbisa, Cambridge, MA: Harvard University Press. Copyright © 1962, 1975 by the President and Fellows of Harvard College.

M.M. Bakhtin, 'The problem of speech genres', from *Speech Genres and Other Late Essays*, translated by Vern W. McGee, edited by Caryl Emerson and Michael Holquist. Copyright © 1986. By permission of the University of Texas Press.

Roland Barthes 'Myth today', from *Mythologies*, translated by Annette Lavers, published by Jonathan Cape. Reprinted by permission of The Random House Group Ltd. Translation copyright © 1972 by Jonathan Cape Ltd. Reprinted by permission of Hill and Wang, a division of Farrar, Straus and Giroux, LLC.

Pierre Bourdieu, pp. 66–89 from *Language and Symbolic Power*, edited and introduced by John B. Thompson, translated by Gino Raymond and Matthew Adamson, Cambridge, MA: Harvard University Press. English translation copyright © 1991 by Polity Press. Reprinted by permission of Harvard University Press and Polity Press.

Penelope Brown and Stephen C. Levinson, 'Strategies for doing face threatening acts', in Brown and Levinson (eds) *Politeness: Some Universal in Language Use*, 1987, Cambridge University Press. Reproduced with permission of the authors and the publishers.

Judith Butler, 'Burning acts, injurious speech', from *Excitable Speech*, copyright © 1997. Reproduced by permission of Routledge/Taylor & Francis, Inc.

Deborah Cameron, 'Performing Gender', in Johnson and Meinhof (eds) *Language and Masculinity*, Blackwell Publishing, 1997. Reproduced by permission of the author and publisher.

Deborah Cameron, 'Styling the worker', in *Journal of Sociolinguistics* 4(3), 2000, Blackwell Publishing. Reproduced by permission of the author and publisher.

Deborah Cameron, Elizabeth Frazer, Penelope Harvey, Ben Rampton and Kay Richardson, 'Ethics, advocacy and empowerment', in Cameron *et al.* (eds) *Researching Language: Issues of Power and Method*, 1992, Routledge. Reproduced by permission of the publisher and the authors.

Derek Edwards, 'Narrative analysis', from Widdicombe and Woolfit (eds) *Discourse and Cognition*. Copyright © 1996. Reprinted by permission of Sage Publications Ltd.

Norman Fairclough, 'Global capitalism and the critical awareness of language', in *Language Awareness*, 8(2), 1999, Multilingual Matters. Reproduced by permission of the author and publisher.

Michel Foucault, excerpts from *The History of Sexuality: Volume 1, An Introduction*, translated by Robert Hurley, Allen Lane, 1979, (first published in French as 'La Volonte de savoir' 1976). Copyright © Editions Gallimard, 1976. Translation copyright © Random House, Inc., 1978. Reproduced by permission of Penguin Books Ltd and Georges Borchadt, Inc., for the Editions Gallimard.

Erving Goffman 'On face work', from Erving Goffman *Interaction Ritual*. Copyright © 1967. Used by permission of Pantheon Books, a division of Random House, Inc.

David Graddol, 'The semiotic construction of a wine label', in Goodman and Graddol (eds) *Redesigning English*, Routledge and The Open University. Copyright © 1996 The Open University. Reproduced by permission of the publishers.

H.P. Grice, 'Logic and conversation', from *Syntax and Semantics*, volume 3, Peter Cole and Jerry L. Morgan (eds) 'Logic and conversation', pp. 41–58. Copyright © 1975, with permission from Elsevier.

John J. Gumperz, 'Sociocultural knowledge in conversational inference', from Muriel-Saville Troike (ed.) *Linguistics and Anthropology, Georgetown University Round Table on Languages and Linguistics*, 1977, pp. 191–211. Reproduced by permission of Georgetown Press.

Stuart Hall, 'Whites of their eyes: racist ideologies and the media', in Bridges and Brunt (eds) *Silver Linings*, Lawrence & Wishart, London 1981. Reproduced by permission of the publisher.

Janet Holmes, excerpts from *Women, Men and Politeness*, 1995, Pearson Education Limited. Reproduced by permission of the publisher.

Ian Hutchby, 'Power in discourse' from *Discourse and Society*, 7(4), copyright © 1996. Reprinted by permission of Sage Publications Ltd.

Roman Jakobson, 'Closing statement: linguistics and poetics', pp. 350–77 in Thomas A. Sebeok (ed.) *Style in Language*, 1966. Reproduced by permission of The MIT Press.

Gail Jefferson, 'Transcription conventions', pp. ix–xvi in Atkinson and Heritage (eds) *Structures of Social Action: Studies in Conversation Analysis*, 1985,

Cambridge University Press. Reproduced by permission of the author and publisher.

William Labov, 'The transformation of experience in narrative', in *Language in the Inner City*. Copyright © 1972 by the University of Pennsylvania Press. Reprinted by permission of the University of Pennsylvania Press and Blackwell Publishing.

Bronislaw Malinowski, 'On phatic communion', in Ogden and Richards (eds) *The Meaning of Meaning*, 1946, Routledge. Reproduced by permission of the publisher.

Hugh Mehan, 'Oracular reasoning in a psychiatric exam: the resolution of conflict in language', in A. Grimshaw (ed.) *Conflict Talk*, 1990, Cambridge University Press. Reproduced with permission of the author and publisher.

Elinor Ochs, 'Transcription as theory', from Ochs *et al.* (eds) *Development Pragmatics*, pp. 43–72. Copyright © 1979. Reproduced with permission from Elsevier.

Anita Pomerantz, 'Preference in conversation: agreeing and disagreeing with assessments', in Atkinson and Heritage (eds) *Structures of Social Action: Studies in Conversation Analysis*, 1985, Cambridge University Press. Reproduced by permission of the authors and publisher.

Harvey Sacks, 'The baby cried, the mommy picked it up', in Jefferson (ed.) *Lectures on Conversation*, 1992, Blackwell Publishing. Reproduced by permission of the publisher.

Emanuel Schegloff, 'Talk and social structure', pp. 44–70, in Deirdre Boden and Don Zimmerman (eds) *Talk and Social Letterbox*. Copyright © 1991 Polity Press. Reproduced by permission of University of California Press and Polity Press.

Emanuel A. Schegloff and Harvey Sacks, 'Opening up closings', *Semiotica* 7, 1973. Reproduced by permission of Emmanuel A. Schegloff and Mouton de Gruyter.

Deborah Schiffrin, '*Oh* as a marker of information management', in Schiffrin *Discourse Markers*, 1988, Cambridge University Press. Reproduced with permission of the publisher.

Deborah Tannen, 'New York Jewish Conversational Style', *International Journal of Sociology* 30, 1981. Reproduced by permission of the author and Mouton de Gruyter.

Deborah Tannen and Cynthia Wallat, 'Interactive frames and knowledge schemas in interaction: examples from a medical examination/interview', *Social Psychology Quarterly*, 50(2) (June 1987). Reproduced by permission of the American Sociological Association and Deborah Tannen.

Teun Van Dijk, 'Discourse and the denial of racism', from *Discourse and Society*, 3(1), copyright © 1992. Reprinted by permission of Sage Publications Ltd.

Theo Van Leeuwen, 'Sound in perspective', excerpts from chapter 2, 'Perspective', of *Speech, Sound, Music*, 1999, Palgrave Macmillan. Reproduced by permission of the publisher.

Theo Van Leeuwen and Gunther Kress, 'Visual interaction', in *Reading Images*, 1996, Routledge. Reproduced by permission of the publisher.

Katharine Young, 'Narrative embodiments' in John Shotter and Kenneth Gergen (eds) *Texts of Identity*, copyright © 1998. Reprinted by permission of Sage Publications Ltd.

Every effort has been made to obtain permission to reproduce copyright material. If any proper acknowledgement has not been made, or permission not received, we would invite copyright holders to inform us of the oversight.

Introduction

PERSPECTIVES ON DISCOURSE ANALYSIS

Adam Jaworski and Nikolas Coupland

Discourse: an interdisciplinary movement

DEBORAH SCHIFFRIN'S (1994) BOOK, *Approaches to Discourse*, compiles and discusses various definitions of discourse. Here are three of them, from Schiffrin's pages 23–43:

> Discourse is: 'language above the sentence or above the clause'
>
> (Stubbs 1983: 1)

> The study of discourse is the study of *any* aspect of language use.
>
> (Fasold 1990: 65)

> [T]he analysis of discourse is, necessarily, the analysis of language in use. As such, it cannot be restricted to the description of linguistic forms independent of the purposes or functions which these forms are designed to serve in human affairs.
>
> (Brown and Yule 1983: 1)

Here are some others:

> [W]ith the sentence we leave the domain of language as a system of signs and enter into another universe, that of language as an instrument of communication, whose expression is discourse.
>
> (Benveniste 1971: 110, cited in Mills 1997: 4–5)

> Instead of gradually reducing the rather fluctuating meaning of the word 'discourse', I believe I have in fact added to its meanings: treating it

> sometimes as the general domain of all statements, sometimes as an individualizable group of statements, and sometimes as a regulated practice that accounts for a number of statements.
>
> (Foucault 1972: 80, cited in Mills 1997: 6; see also Chapter 33)

Roger Fowler says that his programme for literary studies has the aim

> to change or even deconstruct the notion of literature so that a very wide range of discourses is actively used by individuals in their conscious engagements with ideology, experience and social organization.
>
> (Fowler 1981: 199)

> 'Discourse' is for me more than *just* language use: it is language use, whether speech or writing, seen as a type of social practice.
>
> (Fairclough 1992: 28)

> Discourse *constitutes* the social. Three dimensions of the social are distinguished – knowledge, social relations, and social identity – and these correspond respectively to three major functions of language . . . Discourse is shaped by relations of power, and invested with ideologies.
>
> (Fairclough 1992: 8)

According to Lee, it is an

> uncomfortable fact that the term 'discourse' is used to cover a wide range of phenomena . . . to cover a wide range of practices from such well documented phenomena as sexist discourse to ways of speaking that are easy to recognise in particular texts but difficult to describe in general terms (competitive discourse, discourse of solidarity, etc.).
>
> (Lee 1992: 97)

> 'Discourse' . . . refers to language in use, as a process which is socially situated. However . . . we may go on to discuss the constructive and dynamic role of either spoken or written discourse in structuring areas of knowledge and the social and institutional practices which are associated with them. In this sense, discourse is a means of talking and writing about and acting upon worlds, a means which both constructs and is constructed by a set of social practices within these worlds, and in so doing both reproduces and constructs afresh particular social-discursive practices, constrained or encouraged by more macro movements in the overarching social formation.
>
> (Candlin 1997: iix)

Other definitions of discourse will appear in the chapters to follow. These, and the ones above, span a considerable range, although a core set of concerns also emerges.

It is this core, and the best-established deviations from it, that we intend to unpack in the pages of the *Reader*. The quotations above consistently emphasise 'language in use'. But there is a large body of opinion (see the later quotations) that stresses what discourse is *beyond* language in use. Discourse is language use relative to social, political and cultural formations – it is language reflecting social order but also language shaping social order, and shaping individuals' interaction with society. This is the key factor explaining why so many academic disciplines entertain the notion of discourse with such commitment. Discourse falls squarely within the interests not only of linguists, literary critics, critical theorists and communication scientists, but also of geographers, philosophers, political scientists, sociologists, anthropologists, social psychologists, and many others. Despite important differences of emphasis, discourse is an inescapably important concept for understanding society and human responses to it, as well as for understanding language itself.

Part of the explanation for the upsurge of interest in discourse lies in a fundamental realignment that has taken place, over the last three decades or so, in how academic knowledge, and perhaps all knowledge, is assumed to be constituted. To put the negative side of this change, we might describe it as a weakening of confidence in traditional ways of explaining phenomena and processes, a radical questioning of how people, including academics, come to appreciate and interpret their social and cultural environments. The rise in importance of discourse has coincided with a falling off of intellectual security in what we know and what it means to know – that is, a shift in epistemology, in the theorising of knowledge (see Cameron *et al.*, Chapter 8; Foucault, Chapter 33). The question of *how* we build knowledge has come more to the fore, and this is where issues to do with language and linguistic representation come into focus.

Academic study, but in fact all aspects of experience, are based on acts of classification, and the building of knowledge and interpretations is very largely a process of defining boundaries between conceptual classes, and of labelling those classes and the relationships between them. This is one central reason why all intellectual endeavour, and all routine social living, needs to examine language, because it is through language that classification becomes possible (Lee 1992). Seen this way, language ceases to be a neutral medium for the transmission and reception of pre-existing knowledge. It is the key ingredient in the very constitution of knowledge. Many disciplines, more or less simultaneously, have come to see the need for an awareness of language, and discourse more broadly, and of the structuring potential of language, as part of their own investigations (see Fairclough, Chapter 9). This is the shift often referred to as the 'linguistic turn' in the social sciences, but it is being experienced in academic study more generally.

All the same, it is not as if linguistics, 'the scientific study of language', has always provided the most appropriate means of studying knowledge-making processes and their social implications. Linguistics has tended to be an inward-looking discipline. It has not always appreciated the relevance of language and discourse to people other than linguists. The dominant traditions in linguistics, one could say until at least the 1970s, were particularly narrow, focusing on providing good descriptions of the grammar and pronunciation of utterances at the level of the sentence. Considerations of meaning in general, and particularly of how language, meaning and society inter-relate, are still quite recent concerns. Discourse analysis is therefore a relatively new area of importance to linguistics too, which is moving beyond its earliest ambition. That was, to put it simplistically, to describe sentences and to gain autonomy for itself as a 'scientific' area of academic study. Under the heading of discourse, studies of language have come to be concerned with far wider issues. Discourse linguists analyse, for example, the structure of conversations, stories and various forms of written text, the subtleties of implied meanings, and how language in the form of speech interacts with non-linguistic (e.g., visual or spatial) communication. Under the headings of cohesion and coherence they study how one communicative act depends on previous acts, and how people creatively interact in the task of making and inferring meaning. We consider some of these main developments, in linguistics and in other disciplines, in more detail in Part One of the *Reader*.

So discourse has gained importance through at least two different, concurrent developments – a shift in the general theorising of knowledge and a broadening of perspective in linguistics. The *Reader* includes extracts from many of the most influential original writings on discourse, both theoretical and applied, which have brought about and benefited from this confluence of ideas. As individual chapters show, language studied as discourse opens up countless new areas for the critical investigation of social and cultural life – the composition of cultural groups, the management of social relations, the constitution of social institutions, the perpetuation of social prejudices, and so on.

Other general trends too have promoted interest in discourse. One is the growing recognition that contemporary life, at least in the world's most affluent and 'developed' societies, has qualities that distinguish it quite markedly from the 'modern' industrial, pre-Second World War period. One of the most obvious manifestations of what Anthony Giddens has called 'Late Modernity' or 'High Modernity' (Giddens 1991), and what is more generally referred to as *postmodernity*, is the shift in advanced capitalist economies from manufacturing to service industries. Norman Fairclough (1992, 1995) refers to one part of this phenomenon as the *technologisation* of discourse in post-Fordist societies (since the beginning of mass production of motor cars and similar industrial developments). Manufacturing and assembly workers working on production lines, isolated from consumers of the items they are producing, have been largely replaced by teams of workers, networked together, involved in communication tasks of different sorts or representing their companies in different kinds of service encounters with clients. Language takes on greater significance in the worlds of providing and consuming services, not least in the promotional language of selling services in the competitive environments of banking, insurance companies, telephone-sales warehouses, and so on (see Chapters 9 and 30).

Rapid growth in communications media, such as satellite and digital television and radio, desktop publishing, telecommunications (mobile phone networks, video-conferencing), email, internet-mediated sales and services, information provision and entertainment, is continually creating new media for language-use. It is not surprising that language is being more and more closely scrutinised, for example within school curricula and by self-styled experts and guardians of so-called 'linguistic standards' (see Cameron 1995; Milroy and Milroy 1999 for detailed discussion of these issues). At the same time language is being shaped and honed, for example by advertisers, journalists and broadcasters, in a drive to generate ever-more attention and persuasive impact. Under these circumstances, language itself becomes marketable and a sort of commodity (Cameron 2000; Heller 2003), and its purveyors can market themselves through their skills of linguistic and textual manipulation (see Bourdieu, Chapter 32). Discourse ceases to be 'merely' a function of work. It *becomes* work, just as it defines various forms of leisure and, for that matter, academic study. The analysis of discourse becomes correspondingly more important – in the first instance for those with direct commercial involvement in the language economies, and second, for those who need to deconstruct these new trends, to understand their force and even to oppose them (see Cameron, Chapter 30).

This *critical* or socially engaged perspective on analysing discourse is apparent in several of the quotations above – most obviously those from Christopher Candlin, Norman Fairclough and Roger Fowler. (Part Six of the *Reader* contains several texts that are critically oriented in this sense, but see also Chapters 8, 9, 13, 26 and 27.) If we ask what is the purpose of doing discourse analysis, the answer from critical discourse analysts would go well beyond the description of language in use. Discourse analysis offers a means of exposing or deconstructing the social practices that constitute 'social structure' and what we might call the conventional meaning structures of social life. It is a sort of forensic activity, with a libertarian political slant. The motivation for doing discourse analysis is very often a concern about social inequality and the perpetuation of power relationships, either between individuals or between social groups, difficult though it is to pre-judge moral correctness in many cases.

As this implies, the focus for a particular analysis can be either very local – analysing a particular conversation between two people or a single diary entry – or very global and abstract. In this latter tradition, the theoretical work of Michel Foucault (see Chapter 33) and that of Michel Pêcheux (1982) has been very influential in introducing the link between discourse and ideology. Pêcheux stresses how any one particular discourse or 'discursive formation' stands, at the level of social organisation, in conflict with other discourses. He gives us a theory of how societies are organised through their ideological struggles, and how particular groups (e.g., social class groups or gender groups) will be either more or less privileged in their access to particular discourse networks. Local and global perspectives come together when some type of discourse analysis can show how the pressure of broad social or institutional norms are brought to bear on the identity and classification of individuals (see, for example, Coupland and Ylänne's analysis of travel agency interactions in Chapter 25, or Mehan's analysis of a psychiatric interview in Chapter 37).

Let us recap briefly. At the most basic level, discourse is definable as language in use, but many definitions incorporate significantly more than this. Discourse is implicated in expressing people's points of view and value systems, many of which are 'pre-structured' in terms of what is 'normal' or 'appropriate' in particular social and institutional settings. Discourse practices can therefore be seen as the deployment of, and indeed sometimes as acts of resistance to, dominant ideologies. The focus of discourse analysis will usually be the study of particular texts (e.g., conversations, interviews, speeches, etc., or various written documents), although discourses are sometimes held to be abstract value systems which will never surface directly as texts. Texts are specific products, or 'sediments' of meaning, which, to varying degrees, will reflect global as well as local discourse practices relevant to their production and reception. Discourse analysis can range from the description and interpretation of meaning-making and meaning-understanding in specific situations through to the critical analysis of ideology and access to meaning-systems and discourse networks. Language and discourse seem to have a particular salience in contemporary, *late-modern* social arrangements.

From this preliminary overview it is already apparent why the study of discourse is an interdisciplinary project. Most disciplines, and certainly all of the human and social sciences, need to deal with the inter-relations between discourse and concepts such as social structure, social relations, conflict, ideology, selfhood, postmodernity and social change.

Multimodal and multi-voiced discourses

It is worth emphasising that discourse reaches out further than language itself in the forms as well as the meanings that can be the focus of analysis. When we think of discourse in the wider context of communication, we can extend its analysis to include non-linguistic *semiotic systems* (systems for signalling meaning), those of non-verbal and non-vocal communication that accompany or replace speech or writing (see Hodge and Kress 1991 for an overview of social semiotics, and Van Leeuwen 2005 for a wide-ranging introduction). Discourse practices include the 'embodied' or more obviously physical systems of representation, for example performance art, sign language or, more generally, what Pierre Bourdieu has called the 'bodily hexis'; see Chapter 32). Other non-verbal discourse modes (although often incorporating aspects of speech or writing) include painting, sculpture, photography, dance, music and film. In this sense, all texts are multimodal (Kress and Van Leeuwen 1996, 2001); speech involves not only words but also intonation, stress and voice quality (prosodic and paralinguistic features), and is normally accompanied by gestures, facial expressions, and so on (non-verbal features). Considerations of written words increasingly involve typography, page layout, the materiality of signs, colour, and so on (see Barthes, Chapter 7; Van Leeuwen, Chapter 12; Graddol, Chapter 13; Kress and Van Leeuwen, Chapter 26).

The idea that discourse is multiply structured has been a dominant one since the earliest days of discourse analysis and its predecessor in functional linguistics (see our Introduction to Part One). Roman Jakobson (Chapter 1), Michael Halliday and others stressed that language-in-use realises many functions simultaneously, for example, an informational function alongside relational/interpersonal and aesthetic functions. The focus on multimodal discourse is in one sense a continuation of this traditional view, especially when it can be shown that different semiotic resources or dimensions (e.g., visual images and linguistic text in a school textbook) fulfil different communicative functions. But texts can be multiply structured in other ways, if they *show multiple voicing* or *heteroglossia* (Bakhtin 1981, 1986; Chapter 6). Texts often reflect and recycle different voices, which may be realised through different modalities or indeed a single modality, and addressing one or many audiences. For example, David Graddol's (Chapter 13) study of a wine label illustrates how the label, as a 'semiotic space', consists of different sub-texts, realised in different visual fonts and layout. The sub-texts are, for example, a description of the type of wine and its qualities, a health warning, and a bar and numerical code. Many of them realise different voices – consumerist, legal, commercial. They address potentially different audiences – consumers, health promoters, retailers – and for different reasons. We might think of these voices as fragments of different discourses – socially organised ways of thinking, talking and writing about wine and food, with value systems built into familiar patterns of expression.

Take another example, a hypothetical TV advertisement promoting a new car, which may embody a number of 'real' or 'implied' voices, addressing viewers in a multitude of roles – as drivers, passengers, car experts, status-seekers, parents concerned over their children's safety, overseers of family budgets, etc. The different 'voices' to be heard (or seen) in this context can be realised via spoken language, perhaps a matter-of-fact commentary on the merits of the car, such as its safety, its comfort or its favourable price. They may appear through written/visual signs, e.g., the company's logo or the advertisement's on-screen small print. Cinematic and musical elements will also be present, perhaps photographs representing selected features of the car's design or its appearance and performance on the road, or a well-known tune with 'fitting' lyrics, and so on.

Some of these voices may be competing with each other or representing conflicting interests or ideologies (e.g., safety vs. speeding). For Mikhail Bakhtin all discourse is multi-voiced, as all words and utterances echo other words and utterances derived from the historical and cultural and genetic heritage of a community and from the ways these words and utterances have been previously interpreted. In a broader sense then, 'voices' can be interpreted as discourses – positions, ideologies or stances that speakers and listeners take in particular instances of co-constructed interaction. Since many and even *most* texts do not represent 'pure' discourses, genres and styles, analysis will have to incorporate a significant element of text-to-text comparison, tracing the influence of one sort or genre of text upon another. This has been referred to as an *intertextual* approach to discourse analysis. The forensic task of the discourse analysis will be to track how various forms of discourse, and their associated values and assumptions, are incorporated into a particular text, why and with what effects.

The layering of social meaning in discourse

Discourse analysis is an interdisciplinary project for many reasons. Most obviously, as we suggested above, many disciplines are fundamentally engaged with discourse as social and cultural practice. But let us accept, for the moment, the least ambitious definition of discourse analysis from the set at the head of this chapter, 'the analysis of language in use'. Even at this level, it is easy enough to demonstrate that discourse is, for example, a thoroughly linguistic *and* social *and* cognitive affair. Consider the following simple instance, reconstructed from a real social event, but with the names of the participants changed. The person called 'Mother' is the mother of the 8-year-old child, called 'Rebecca'. The person called 'Mrs Thomson' is employed as a domestic cleaner by the family in which 'Mother' is the mother; Mrs Thomson's first-name is Margaret. Mrs Thomson has just come in through the front door, having rung the door-bell first, and Mother speaks first, calling downstairs to her daughter. (These brief notes are of course a remarkably sparse account of 'the context' for the talk exchange below, but they will allow us to make some first-level observations on the discourse construction of meanings of various sorts in this episode.)

> ### Extract 1
> (*The front door bell rings.*)
> *Mother*:   Open the door, darling. Who is it?
> *Rebecca*:   It's only Maggie.
> *Mother*:   (looking sheepish) Oh hello, Mrs Thomson.
> *Mrs Thomson*:   (smiles) Hello.

Even this short sequence alerts us to the complexities of meaning-making and the range of resources that both we, as observers or analysts, but also the participants themselves, have to draw on to 'make sense' of what is happening in the sequence, as a piece of situated social interaction. It seems obvious that there is a measure of discomfort in the conversational exchanges here, signalled in our representation of Mother's facial expression as 'sheepish'. 'Sheepish' is, of course, already an interpretation (ours). It is based on a linguistic classification of a possibly complex emotional state. In glossing Mother's expression as 'sheepish', we are appealing to a type of emotional state that we assume is both recognisable to others (in this case, you, the readers of this text), and reasonably applicable to the facial and perhaps postural configurations that we remember as being adopted by Mother. A video-taped recording would in fact be important in justifying our use of the term 'sheepish', if we needed to. But even then, our interpretation that these face and body features properly represent the category 'sheepishness' would depend on others (such as you) making the same or a similar inference.

So far, we have pointed to one small aspect of the linguistic work of classification that is built into the written record of Extract 1. But of course there are very many other classification processes at work here, for us and for the participants themselves. As readers, you may be asking *why* Mother is uncomfortable, and how the discourse — the totality of meaning-making and meaning-inferring generated through this interaction — produces an impression that this is the probable emotional effect. A likely explanation (and the one that led us to choose this bit of talk as an example) is that Mother is embarrassed by her daughter referring to Mrs Thomson as 'Maggie'. She is probably embarrassed further by the expression *only Maggie*, especially (or maybe *only*?) because Mrs Thomson has overheard Rebecca's utterance referring to her.

A linguistic analysis of the usual circumstances under which we use the word 'only' will get us some distance here, when we realise that 'only' often projects an event as being unimportant or unexceptional. Mother may well be embarrassed that Rebecca considers Mrs Thomson's arrival as an event of the sort that might be called an 'only' event. She may also be uncomfortable that her daughter, a child, is referring to an adult by an overly familiar expression — using her first name, all of that being witnessed by Mrs Thomson. In any event, precisely how the different participants are positioned and involved in the discourse is clearly a relevant concern.

On the whole, we have few problems making these or similar inferences. But it is interesting to consider just *how* we are able to make them. For example, they seem to rely, in part, on there being a social consensus about how children usually do talk, or ought to talk, to adults. But is this universally true or just a convention in one particular cultural situation? More particularly, some of the social sensitivity in the exchange hinges on the child using a first name not only to an adult, but to an adult employed as a cleaner. There are particularly strong reverberations of social class and economic power behind this exchange, and they certainly make up an element of its 'meaning'. However, bringing these underlying political and economic assumptions to the surface is a social taboo, and it is Rebecca's unwitting breaking of this taboo that probably also causes her mother's embarrassment.

In the other direction, there is an element of 'understanding' suggested in Mrs Thomson's smile, perhaps implying she appreciates that Rebecca is not fully able to judge the social conventions or rules for addressing adults. The smile may be an attempt to mitigate the discomfort Mother is feeling. On the other hand, Mrs Thomson's smile could also be an accommodating reaction to Rebecca's remark. For her to react in a different way and signal indignation would mean to break another taboo. In any case, note how 'child' and 'cleaner', not to mention 'mother' and 'daughter', are linguistic labels for social categories with culturally meaningful and somewhat predictable social qualities and expectations attached to them. Note that our access to 'the meaning' of the interaction depends on how we hang these labels on individuals, and on particular people's labelling of other people. Note how we have to make inferences about people's intentions, and about how those intentions are perceived and evaluated by others (see Sacks, Chapter 16 on some cognitive processes of categorial work in organising social actors into groups, or 'teams', and attributing specific actions to them).

Another part of what is achieved as meaning in the interaction depends on rather precise timing and placement, which are not at all captured in the written transcript of what was said. As we suggested, Mother's embarrassment may be exacerbated by the fact that, in our reconstruction of it, the *It's only Maggie* utterance is said when all three participants are present together, face-to-face. *Maggie* might well be the usual way the family has of referring to Mrs Thomson when she is not present. Changing the composition of the group by Mrs Thomson's joining the *participation framework* as an unratified recipient, or 'overhearer' (Goffman 1981: 132), of Rebecca's utterance certainly shifts expectations of what are the 'appropriate' forms of expression. In this regard, we might read a particular significance into Mother's *oh*, perhaps as a conventional way of expressing a 'change of state' (Heritage 1984a; Schiffrin, Chapter 19). Mother's expectation that she was speaking with her daughter, and only her, is broken when she sees that Mrs Thomson has already entered the house, and Mother signals this in her talk when she uses the particle *oh*.

There are other, seemingly more mundane, observations to be made about how this interaction is structured, although they are still important from some perspectives. For example, we take it for granted that Mrs Thomson's *hello* is structurally linked to Mother's *hello* in the previous turn at talk. That is, it is not coincidental that both speakers do greeting, and do it through the use of the same greeting word. As conversation analysis has established (see Schegloff, Chapter 5; Pomerantz, Chapter 17; Schegloff and Sacks, Chapter 18, Hutchby, Chapter 36, and our Introduction to Part Three), the second *hello* not only follows the first, but is 'occasioned by' the first; it is the second part of a pair of utterances. Its absence would be a noticeable absence. In more cognitive terms, it is probable that Mrs Thomson feels something of an obligation, however sub-consciously, to match Mother's *hello* that had been offered to her. This is part of what it means to call an exchange of greetings a cultural convention, or a *mini-ritual* of social interaction. Exchanging paired greetings is the predictable or 'unmarked' way of opening social encounters, between either strangers or (as here) people already familiar with each other (see our Introduction to Part Four).

The general point is that, in social interaction, speakers are achieving meaning at many levels. They are exchanging information between them (although very little of the extract under discussion is concerned with transmitting 'information' in the usual sense of 'facts' or 'data'), and negotiating particular relationships between them as individuals. But at the same time their talk is filling out and confirming wider patterns of social organisation, for example in running through predictable patterns of turn-taking, and pairing of utterances. We can say that the structured nature of everyday talk (see Erving Goffman's (1983) concept of *the interaction order*) generates and confirms broader patterns of social organisation (*the social order*). One important facet of discourse analysis is therefore, as we saw earlier, to show how micro-level social actions realise and give local form to macro-level social structures.

Rather than pursue this particular example any further, we can at least summarise those dimensions of discourse that we need to attend to if we want to (begin to) understand how it functions as a discourse event. We have, directly or indirectly, already identified the following aspects:

1   The meaning of an event or of a single utterance is only partly accounted for by its formal features (that is, by the 'direct meaning' of the words used). The social significance of discourse, if we define it simply as language-in-use, lies in the relationship between linguistic meanings and the wider context (i.e., the social, cultural, economic, demographic and other characteristics of the communicative event) in which interaction takes place.

2   Our interpretation of discourse therefore relates far more to what is done by participants than what is said (or written, or drawn, or pointed at) by them. That is, a functional analysis of language and other semiotic systems lies at the heart of analysing discourse.

3   It is important to distinguish between meanings (including goals and intentions) inferred by observers and meanings (including goals and intentions) inferred by participants. Analysing discourse is often making inferences about inferences.

4   All aspects of meaning-making are acts of construction. Attributing meaning to discursive acts is never a neutral or value-free process.

5   Social categorisation is central to these acts of construction. Our language presents us with many categories that seem 'natural' or 'obvious', although they are very probably so only at a given time and place: they may well be culture-specific or idiosyncratic (favoured by an individual).

6   We can only access discourse through the textual data which we collect by observation, audio or video recording. This means that the texts we analyse are always 'filtered' or 'mediated'; they are in themselves a form of social (re)construction.

7   Linguistic expression itself (as speech or writing) often needs to be interrelated with other physical, temporal and behavioural aspects of the social situation, such as body movement and the synchronisation of actions. Discourse is more than (verbal/vocal) language itself.

8   Close attention to and critical reading of particular instances of language-in-use, linked to other aspects of the social context, is a useful way of discovering the normal and often unwritten assumptions behind communication. Although interpretation will always have elements of subjectivity within it, communication is based on linked, subjective interaction (inter-subjectivity). A more formal approach is likely to miss the creative inter-subjectivity of social interaction. (In saying this we do not deny that language is a structured phenomenon, or deny the importance of this fact. Language and other semiotic systems have recognisable structures and the study of these structures as formal systems constitutes an entirely viable, but different, research programme.)

9   Discourse analysis provides a way of linking up the analysis of local characteristics of communication to the analysis of broader social characteristics. It can let us see how macro-structures are carried through micro-structures.

Traditions of discourse analysis

The *Reader* offers a broad and inclusive perspective on the concept of discourse, which is appropriate in view of how many academic disciplines (as we have explained) now see discourse as an important theoretical and empirical focus for them. At the same time discourse, however we define it, has focally to do with language-use. Some approaches remain quite close to the central goals of linguistics, offering detailed linguistic descriptions of texts, spoken and written. At the other extreme, as we have seen, there are approaches to discourse which assume that the most significant sorts of linguistic organisation are highly abstract, and not directly amenable to textual analysis.

We can use this approximate scale of directness–indirectness as a way to organise a discussion of several different traditions of discourse analysis. All of them are represented in the *Reader*, although the following sub-sections (as many taxonomic or listing frameworks do) probably overstate the degree of difference between approaches. In practice, discourse analysts and the analyses they produce do not fall quite so neatly into these types. It is also true that many researchers have taken an inclusive view of discourse studies, to the extent that their work spans most or all of the traditions we survey below. One clear instance is the work of Teun Van Dijk, who has been more responsible than any other person for integrating the field of discourse analysis (see, for example, Van Dijk 1977, 1984, 1985, 1988, 1997; also Chapter 35).

Despite these limitations, it should be helpful to approach the various Parts of the *Reader* armed with a mental map of the principal traditions of discourse studies and their main defining qualities. These general overviews should also be helpful in identifying sources for further reading for students new to any of these fields. We have included at the end of this chapter a list of the main academic journals that print new research in discourse and related fields.

Speech act theory and pragmatics

The study of meaning is at the heart of the discipline referred to as pragmatics. Closely related to semantics, which is primarily concerned with the study of word and sentence meaning, pragmatics concerns itself with the meaning of utterances in specific contexts of use. It is one thing to understand a phrase as far as the individual meanings of its words and its referential meaning is concerned, and quite another to know what its intended and achieved meanings may be in context. Charles Fillmore illustrates the pitfalls of relying on sentence meaning in interpreting talk and disregarding pragmatic meaning of an utterance by recounting two anecdotes concerning the fixed phrase *I thought you'd never ask*:

> It's a fairly innocent teasing expression in American English, but it could easily be taken as insulting by people who did not know its special status as a routine formula. In one case a European man asked an

American woman to join him in the dance, and she, being playful, said, 'I thought you'd never ask'. Her potential dancing partner withdrew his invitation in irritation. In another case a European hostess offered an American guest something to drink, when he, unilaterally assuming a teasing relationship, said, 'I thought you'd never ask'. He was asked to leave the party for having insulted his host.

(Fillmore 1984: 129–30)

Jenny Thomas (1995) distinguishes three types of meaning (illustrated here with our own examples):

- *abstract* meaning (the meaning of words and sentences in isolation, e.g., the various meanings of the word *grass,* or the ambiguity of the sentence *I saw her duck);*
- *contextual* or *utterance* meaning (e.g., when two intimate persons hold their faces very near each other and one whispers to the other *I hate you* while smiling, the utterance 'really' means 'I love you'); and
- utterance *force* (i.e., how the speaker intends his/her utterance to be understood; e.g., when X says to Y *are you hungry?,* X may intend the question as a request for Y to make X a sandwich).

Thomas focuses on utterance meaning and force, which are central to pragmatics, which she defines as the study of 'meaning in interaction' (p. 22) with the special emphasis on the inter-relationship between the speaker, hearer, utterance and context.

The notion of *force* is borrowed directly from J.L. Austin's work on speech act theory (Chapter 2), and his three-fold distinction into the *locution* of a speech act (the actual words used in an utterance), its *illocution* (the force or the intention of the speaker behind the utterance), and its *perlocution* (the effect of the utterance on the listener). Studying the effects of the speaker's utterances on the listener derived from Austin's view of language as a form of *action.* Austin observed that by saying something, we not only communicate ideas, but may also bring about a change in the social environment – a transformation, however small, of social reality. Speech acts which effect such a change through the action of being spoken are called *performative speech acts* (or *performatives).* For example, the act of joining two people in marriage is principally a (performative) speech act involving the formula: *I now pronounce you husband and wife.* Of course, in order for a performative to realise its perlocutionary force, it has to meet certain social and cultural criteria, or fulfil *felicity conditions.* It is clear, for example, that unauthorised individuals cannot pronounce anyone 'husband and wife'. Austin's work gained renewed significance with recent interest in the notions of 'performance' and 'performativity' in cultural criticism and discourse analysis (see Cameron, Chapter 30; Butler, Chapter 34; our Introduction to Parts Five and Six).

Much of speech act theory has been concerned with taxonomising speech acts and defining felicity conditions for different types of speech acts. For example,

John Searle (1969, 1979) suggested the following typology of speech acts based on different types of conditions which need to be fulfilled for an act to 'work' or succeed: 'representatives (e.g., asserting), directives (e.g., requesting), commissives (e.g., promising), expressives (e.g., thanking), and declarations (e.g., appointing)' (quoted from Schiffrin 1994: 57). This taxonomy was one of many, and it soon became clear in speech act theory that a full and detailed classification would be unwieldy given the multitude of illocutionary verbs in English. Stipulating the felicity conditions for all of them appeared to be not only a complex procedure but also an 'essentialising' one – relying too heavily on factors assumed to be essential in each case, when reality shows us that they are variably determined by the precise social context.

An elaboration of speech act theory was offered by Labov and Fanshel (1977) in their examination of a psychiatric interview. Although their prime concern was with the identification of speech acts and specifying the rules governing their successful realization, they broadened the view that an utterance may only perform one type of speech act at a time. For example, the following utterance by a client in their data, reported to have been said to her mother, *well, when d'you plan to come home?*, may be a request for information, a challenge or an expression of obligation (cf. Taylor and Cameron 1987).

Like Austin and Searle, Labov and Fanshel explain communication in terms of hearers accurately identifying the intended meaning of the speaker's utterance and responding to it accordingly. However, given the multi-functionality of utterances, we cannot be sure that the hearers always pick up the 'right' interpretation of an utterance, i.e., the one that was intended by the speaker. At the same time, we might doubt whether speakers always have a clear and singular intention behind many of their own utterances. In general, the problem of intentionality and variability in people's discourse rules precluded developing a coherent framework for explaining communication, beyond producing an inventory of such rules and speech act types. A different way of explaining communication was proposed by H.P. Grice (Chapter 3), whose work was central in the development of inferential pragmatics and interactional sociolinguistics.

Grice, like Austin and Searle, was a philosopher, whose interest in language stemmed from the investigations of sense, reference, truth, falsity and logic. However, Grice argued that the logic of language (or conversation, as the title of his classic paper has it) is not based on the same principles as formal (mathematical) logic. Instead, he proposed a model of communication based on the notion of the *Cooperative Principle*, i.e., the collaborative efforts of rational participants in directing conversation towards attaining a broadly common goal. In following the Cooperative Principle the participants follow a number of specific maxims (conversational maxims), such as *be informative*, *be truthful*, *be relevant* and *be clear*. When the maxims are adhered to, meaning is produced in an unambiguous, direct way. However, most meaning is *implied*, through two kinds of *implicatures*: 'conventional implicatures', which follow from the conventional meanings of words used in utterances, and 'conversational implicatures', which result from the non-observance of one (or more) of the conversational maxims. When participants assume that the Cooperative Principle is being observed but one of the maxims is violated, they seek an indirect interpretation via conversational implicature. To use a well-known example from Grice (see p. 73), if a letter of recommendation appears to be under-informative (violating the maxim *be informative*) and concentrates wholly on, say, the candidate's punctuality and good manners (violating the maxim *be relevant*), then assuming that the author is being in a general sense cooperative, the addressee may infer that the candidate is not suitable for the job.

Grice's impact on pragmatics and discourse analysis in general cannot be overestimated. Although he has been criticised for formulating his Cooperative Principle to suit the conversational conventions of middle-class English speakers, and for not attending to the idea of strategic *non*-cooperation, the guiding principle of inference as the principal means for generating meaning in interaction remains central in most current approaches to discourse. Two areas in which Grice's influence has been felt most strongly are in the theories of linguistic politeness (see Chapters 22 and 23) and of relevance. We will introduce relevance theory in some detail because it is a significant independent model of discourse processing which we have been unable to incorporate as a discrete chapter.

The cognitively oriented approach to communication proposed by Dan Sperber and Deirdre Wilson (1986/1995) makes Grice's maxim of relevance central to explaining how information is processed in discourse. In sharp opposition to the code models of language, relevance theory assumes that linguistic communication is based on *ostension* and *inference*, which can be said to be the same process viewed from two different perspectives. The former belongs to the communicator, who is involved in ostension (a form of 'showing'), and the latter to a recipient, who is involved in inference. Inferential comprehension of the communicator's ostensive behaviour relies on deductive processing of any new information presented in the context of old information. This derivation of new information is spontaneous, automatic and unconscious, and it gives rise to certain contextual effects in the cognitive environment of the audience. The occurrence of contextual effects, such as contextual implications, contradictions and strengthening, is a necessary condition for relevance. The relation between contextual effects and relevance is that, other things being equal, 'the greater the contextual effects, the greater the relevance' (Sperber and Wilson 1986: 119). In other words, an assumption which has no contextual effects at some particular moment of talk is irrelevant, because processing this assumption does not change the old context.

A second factor in assessing the degree of relevance of an assumption is the processing effort necessary for the achievement of contextual effects. It is a negative factor, which means that, other things being equal, 'the greater the processing effort, the lower the relevance' (Sperber and Wilson 1986: 124). The theory holds that, in communication, speaking partners first assume the relevance of an assumption behind an utterance and then select a context in which its relevance will be maximised (it is not the case that context is determined first and then the relevance of a stimulus assessed). Sperber and Wilson also say that, of all the assumptions that a phenomenon can make manifest to an individual, only some will actually catch his/her attention. Others will be filtered out at a sub-attentive level.

These phenomena, which have some bearing on central thought processes, draw the attention of an individual and make assumptions and inferences appear at a conceptual level. Thus, they define the relevance of a phenomenon as follows:

> [A] phenomenon is relevant to an individual to the extent that the contextual effects achieved when it is optimally processed are large . . .

> [A] phenomenon is relevant to an individual to the extent that the effort required to process it optimally is small.
>
> (Sperber and Wilson 1986: 153)

Owing to its cognitive orientation and its initial interest in information processing, relevance theory has been largely concerned with the referential function of language. Due to this methodological and programmatic bias, it has been criticised for being inadequate to account for the socially relevant aspects of discourse, and for insufficient involvement with the interactional aspects of language use. Relevance theory has dismissed such criticisms as misguided, because its primary interest has explicitly *not* been social. Still, in later revisions, its authors have begun to explain the potential of relevance theory in accounting for social aspects of communication (see Sperber and Wilson 1997).

Conversation analysis

The origins and much of current practice in conversation analysis (CA) reside in the sociological approach to language and communication known as *ethnomethodology* (Cicourel 1973; Garfinkel 1974). Ethnomethodology means studying the link between what social actors 'do' in interaction and what they 'know' about interaction. Social structure is a form of order, and that order is partly achieved through talk, which is itself structured and orderly. Social actors have common-sense knowledge about what it is they are doing interactionally in performing specific activities and in jointly achieving communicative coherence. Making this knowledge about ordinary, everyday affairs explicit, and in this way finding an understanding of how society is organised and how it functions, is ethnomethodology's main concern (Garfinkel 1967; Turner 1974; Heritage 1984b).

Following this line of inquiry, CA views language as a form of social action and aims, in particular, to discover and describe how the organisation of social interaction makes manifest and reinforces the structures of social organisation and social institutions (see, e.g., papers in Boden and Zimmerman 1991; Drew and Heritage 1992a; Hutchby and Wooffitt 1998; Chapters 5, 16, 17, 18 and 36). Hutchby and Wooffit, who point out that 'talk in interaction' is now commonly preferred to the designation 'conversation', define CA as follows:

> CA is the study of *recorded, naturally occurring talk-in-interaction* . . .
> Principally it is to discover how participants understand and respond to

one another in their turns at talk, with a central focus being on how sequences of interaction are generated. To put it another way, the objective of CA is to uncover the tacit reasoning procedures and socio-linguistic competencies underlying the production and interpretation of talk in organized sequences of interaction.

(Hutchby and Wooffit 1998: 14)

As this statement implies, the emphasis in CA in contrast to earlier ethnomethodological concerns has shifted away from the patterns of 'knowing' per se towards discovering the *structures of talk* which produce and reproduce patterns of social action. At least, structures of talk are studied as the best evidence of social actors' practical knowledge about them. (Schegloff *et al.* 1996 give an informative account of the early history of CA.)

One central CA concept is *preference* (see Pomerantz, Chapter 17), the idea that, at specific points in conversation, certain types of utterances will be more favoured than others (e.g., the socially preferred response to an invitation is acceptance, not rejection). Other conversational features which CA has focused on include:

- openings and closings of conversations (see Schegloff and Sacks, Chapter 18);
- adjacency pairs (i.e., paired utterances of the type summons–answer, greeting–greeting, compliment–compliment response, etc.);
- topic management and topic shift;
- conversational repairs;
- showing agreement and disagreement (see Pomerantz, Chapter 17);
- introducing bad news and processes of troubles-telling;
- (probably most centrally) mechanisms of turn-taking.

In their seminal paper, Sacks, Schegloff and Jefferson (1974) suggested a list of guiding principles for the organisation of turn-taking in conversation (in English). They observed that the central principle which speakers follow in taking turns is to avoid gaps and overlaps in conversation. Although gaps do of course occur, they are brief. Another common feature of conversational turns is that, usually, one party speaks at a time. In order to facilitate turn-taking, speakers observe a number of conventionalised principles. For example, speakers follow well-established scripts, as in service encounters, in which speaker roles are clearly delineated. They fill in appropriate 'slots' in discourse structure, e.g., second part utterances in adjacency pairs, and they anticipate completion of an utterance on the basis of a perceived completion of a grammatical unit (a clause or a sentence). Speakers themselves may signal their willingness to give up the floor in favour of another speaker (who can be 'nominated' by current speaker only). They can do this by directing their gaze towards the next speaker and employing characteristic gesturing patterns synchronising with the final words. They may alter pitch, speak more softly, lengthen the last syllable or use stereotyped tags (e.g., *you know* or *that's it*) (see Graddol *et al.* 1994 for a summary). Turn-taking is additionally facilitated by the fact that it is most likely to take place in highly predictable, recurring moments in conversation, *transition-relevance points* (Sacks *et al.* 1974). Cues signalling that a turn is about to be terminated (outlined in the preceding paragraph) tend to coincide with the end of various structural units of talk: clauses, sentences, narratives, but they may also be signalled after smaller formal units, such as phrases or single words.

This very brief overview does not do justice to CA's contribution to the description of talk in a wide range of private and public settings. Suffice it to say that its insights are valuable to understand patterns of individual relations between interactants, individuals' positions within larger institutional structures (e.g., Mehan, Chapter 37), and overall societal organisation. What is also important, CA has taken the study of discourse firmly into a more dynamic and interactional realm away from the speaker-centredness of speech act theory (see above).

This is not to say that CA is without its critics. The most contested notion in relation to CA is that of 'context'. Indeed, what CA programmatically assumes to be the sole (and sufficient) source of its analysis is, as John Heritage points out, the organisation of talk itself:

> The initial and most fundamental assumption of CA is that all aspects of social action and interaction can be examined in terms of the conventionalized or institutionalized structural organizations which analyzably inform their production. These organizations are to be treated as structures in their own right which, like other social institutions and conventions, stand independently of the psychological or other characteristic of particular participants.
>
> (Heritage 1984b: 1–2)

The ethnographic critique of CA's disregard for the cultural and historical context of interactions is summarised by Alessandro Duranti (1997). Although he does not dismiss CA's methods and goals *a priori*, he also argues that some of the insights and observations about interaction cannot be accessed without attending to the fine ethnographic detail. (See Moerman 1988; Besnier 1989; Ochs 1988 for examples of studies which combine CA with attention to the cultural detail characteristic of the ethnographic approach. We return to aspects of this critique in our Introduction to Part Three.)

Discursive psychology

An interdisciplinary movement such as discourse analysis is likely to spawn new areas of specialist research, at first on the fringes of established disciplines. Discursive psychology (Edwards and Potter 1992 is an integrative overview) has established itself as a coherent, critical approach to some traditional research themes in psychology such as the study of attitudes, strongly opposing the statistical and experimental methods which have come to dominate research in psychology (including social psychology). Jonathan Potter and Margaret Wetherell's (1987) book, *Discourse and Social Psychology: Beyond Attitudes and Behaviour,* was a ground-breaking critique of established methods and assumptions in social psychology.

Discourse analysts' hostility to the notion of linguistic 'behaviour' (referred to in the book's title, just above) should already be clear from what we have said so far. No approach which treats language as behaviour can come to terms with the strategic complexity and the local and emergent contextualisation of talk, with how talk is co-constructed by social actors, or with how meanings are generated by inference as much as by overt signalling. Potter and Wetherell's position on attitude research is similar. They stress the need to examine contextualised accounts of beliefs, rather than surveying (usually by questionnaire methods) large numbers of people's decontextualised and self-reported attitudes, as social psychologists have tended to do:

> Contextual information gives the researcher a much fuller understanding
> of the detailed and delicate organization of accounts. In addition, an
> understanding of this organization clarifies the action orientation of talk
> and its involvement in acts such as blaming and disclaiming.
>
> (Potter and Wetherell 1987: 54)

Accounts, they go on to argue, can and should focus on variability and even inconsistency, rather than trying to disguise variation in the hope of producing clear and stable patterns. Rather antagonistically, they suggest that variability in discursive accounts of beliefs amounts to 'a considerable embarrassment to traditional attitude theories' (ibid.). They also argue that attitude research tends to reify the assumption that attitudes are held about 'an existing out-there-in-the-world group of people' (ibid.) when most naturally occurring accounts are directed at specific cases rather than idealised 'objects'. A discursive approach to the psychology of attitudes will bring research back to investigating local and specific discourse representations, which are how we produce and experience 'attitudes' in everyday life.

These are powerful arguments, but we should also bear in mind the corresponding limitation of a discursive approach to social beliefs, attitudes and all subjective phenomena, especially regarding its inability to deal with social trends and distributions. It seems necessary to recognise the inherent weaknesses of *all* general approaches, and the most persuasive line of argument is that discourse analysis is able to complement other approaches (such as quantitative surveys) rather than take their place.

Discursive psychology is, however, more than the application of concepts and methods from discourse analysis and CA in the traditional realm of social psychology, even though this was its origin. Much of the most articulate and insistent theorising of *social constructionism* has emerged from social psychology, for example in John Shotter's (1993) book, *Conversational Realities* (see also Billig

1991; Gergen 1982, 1991). Psychology, studying the interface between individuals, cognition and society, needs to theorise 'reality' – arguably more urgently than other disciplines. Shotter's argument, like that of Potter and Wetherell, is that psychology and most social science has tended to seek out invariance, and ignore the processes (the 'ethnomethodological' processes) through which we come to see the world as stable:

> In our reflective thought, upon the nature of the world in which we live, we can either take what is invariant as its primary subject matter and treat change as problematic, or, activity and flux as primary and treat the achievement of stability as problematic. While almost all previous approaches to psychology and the other social sciences have taken the first of these stances, social constructionism takes the second.
>
> (Shotter 1993: 178)

Shotter and his colleagues are therefore keen to reintroduce a *relativist* perspective into social science (see Cameron *et al.*, Chapter 8) and to take very seriously Edward Sapir and Benjamin Lee Whorf's early research on linguistic relativity – the so-called Sapir/Whorf hypothesis (e.g., Whorf 1956; Lucy 1992).

The principle of relativism followed from an early American anthropological tradition (developed mainly by Franz Boas at the beginning of the twentieth century) which argued that languages classify experience, and that each language does so differently. The classification of experience through language was held to be automatic and beyond speakers' awareness. Sapir's and Whorf's comments on social reality are well worth pondering, many decades after publication:

> Language is a guide to 'social reality' . . . Human beings do not live in the objective world alone, nor alone in the world of social activity as ordinarily understood, but are very much at the mercy of the particular language which has become the medium of expression for their society . . . [T]he 'real world' is to a large extent unconsciously built up on the language habits of the group. No two languages are ever sufficiently similar to be considered as representing the same social reality. The worlds in which different societies live are distinct worlds, not merely the same world with different labels attached . . . We see and hear and otherwise experience very largely as we do because the language habits of our community predispose certain choices of interpretation . . . From this standpoint we may think of language as the *symbolic guide to culture*.
>
> (Sapir, originally published in 1929, quoted in Lucy 1992: 22)

That portion of the whole investigation here to be reported may be summed up in two questions: (1) Are our own concepts of 'time,' 'space,'

and 'matter' given in substantially the same form by experience to all
men, or are they in part conditioned by the structure of particular
languages? (2) Are there traceable affinities between (a) cultural and
behavioral norms and (b) large-scale linguistic patterns?

(Whorf 1956: 138; see also Coupland and Jaworski 1997: 446)

One of Whorf's key observations that transfers directly into the domain of
discourse analysis is that a language or an utterance form can unite demonstrably
different aspects of reality by giving them similar linguistic treatment, what Whorf
calls the process of *linguistic analogy*. Linguistic analogy allows or encourages us
to treat diverse experience as 'the same'. A famous example in the area of vocabulary is the word 'empty' in the expression *empty gasoline drums*. As Whorf pointed
out, the word 'empty' commonly implies a void or absence, and conjures up associations of 'absence of threat' and therefore 'safety'. It is as if this expression steers
us into treating 'empty gasoline drums' as lacking danger, when they are in fact
unusually dangerous. Language used to shape cognitive structures can therefore be
referred to as *the cognitive appropriation of linguistic analogies*.

As Shotter (1993: 115) concludes, 'Whorf forces us to see that the basic
"being" of our world is not as basic as we had thought; it can be thought of and
talked of in other ways.' More recent studies in discursive psychology have elaborated on this central point and supported Sapir's, Whorf's, Shotter's and other
people's theorising with textual analysis. Potter (1996), for example, analyses
how 'out-there-ness' is discursively constructed in the writing styles of empiricist
(experimental, quantitative) scientific researchers (cf. Gilbert and Mulkay 1984).
Derek Edwards's (1997; see also Chapter 15) book is a radical reworking of cognitive themes in psychology, for example research on 'ape language' and child
language acquisition, and on the psychology of emotions. He attends to the language
in which psychologists represent and objectify cognition. It is perhaps the ultimate
challenge for a psychologist (even of the discursive kind) to undermine cognitivism,
but Edwards writes that 'one of the reasons for pursuing discursive psychology is
the requirement to re-conceptualize relations between language and mind, and to
find alternative ways of dealing empirically with that "constitutive" relationship'
(p. 44).

The ethnography of communication

In the 1960s and 1970s, the Chomsky-inspired formalism in linguistics triggered
a concerted reaction from function- and action-oriented researchers of language.
Most notably, Noam Chomsky (1965) contrasted the notion of *linguistic competence*, i.e., internalised knowledge of the rules of a language and the defined
object of linguistic inquiry, with what he called *linguistic performance*, i.e., the
realisation of competence in actual speech. Dell Hymes (1972a) also viewed
language as 'knowledge', but extended the object of (socio)linguistic inquiry, or

what he called the ethnography of communication, to *communicative competence*. Hymes's definition of the term consisted of four elements:

- whether and to what degree something is grammatical (linguistic competence);
- whether and to what degree something is appropriate (social appropriateness);
- whether and to what degree something is feasible (psycholinguistic limitations);
- whether and to what degree something is done (observing actual language use).

This far broader conceptualisation of language, and indeed of the purpose of language study, imposed a radically different methodology from Chomsky's linguistics, which was based on introspection and intuition. The object of inquiry for Hymes was no longer the structure of isolated sentences, but *rules of speaking* within a community. Consequently, the sentence was replaced as a basic unit of analysis with a three-fold classification of speech communication (Hymes 1972b):

- *Speech situations*, such as ceremonies, evenings out, sports events, plane trips, and so on; they are not purely communicative (i.e., not only governed by rules of speaking) but provide a wider context for speaking.
- *speech events* are activities which are par excellence communicative and governed by rules of speaking, e.g., conversations, lectures, political debates, ritual insults, and so on. As Duranti (1997: 289) comments, these are activities in which 'speech plays a crucial role in the definition of what is going on – that is, if we eliminate speech, the activity cannot take place'.
- *speech acts* are the smallest units of the set, e.g., orders, jokes, greetings, summonses, compliments, etc.; a speech act may involve more than one turn from only one person, e.g., greetings usually involve a sequence of two turns.

Hymes's model was based on a set of *components of speech events*, which provided a descriptive framework for ethnography of communication. These components were arranged into an eight-part mnemonic based on the word *SPEAKING*:

Situation (physical, temporal psychological setting defining the speech event);
Participants (e.g., speaker, addressee, audience);
Ends (outcomes and goals);
Act sequence (form and content);
Key (manner or spirit of speaking, e.g., mock, serious, perfunctory, painstaking);
Instrumentalities (channels of communication, e.g., spoken, written, signed; forms of speech, e.g., dialects, codes, varieties, registers);
Norms of interaction (e.g., organisation of turn-taking and norms of interpretation, i.e., conventionalised ways of drawing inferences);
Genres (e.g., casual speech, commercial messages, poems, myths, proverbs).

Although the *Reader* does not explicitly address the ethnographic tradition (we deal with it in greater detail in Coupland and Jaworski 1997, especially Chapters 5, 10, 11, 33, and Part VIII; see also Bauman and Scherzer 1974; Saville-Troike 2003), the impact of the ethnography of communication, its methodology and attendance to contextual, historical and cultural detail of interaction is felt across most discourse analytic traditions, especially in interactional sociolinguistics (e.g., Rampton 1995, 2005).

Interactional sociolinguistics

This approach to discourse is inextricably linked with the names of the sociologist Erving Goffman (e.g., 1959, 1967, 1974, 1981, Chapter 21) and Dell Hymes's close associate, the anthropological linguist John Gumperz (e.g., 1982a, 1982b; Chapter 4). Gumperz aimed 'to develop interpretive sociolinguistic approaches to the analysis of real time processes in face to face encounters' (1982a: vii), and this aim has been taken up by various sociolinguists and discourse analysts in a wide range of approaches to social interaction, some of which are represented in this volume (see Schiffrin, Chapter 19; Tannen, Chapter 31).

Goffman summarises his research programme in one of his later papers as being 'to promote acceptance of the . . . face-to-face domain as an analytically viable one – a domain which might be titled, for want of any happy name, the inter-action order – a domain whose preferred method of study is microanalysis' (Goffman 1983: 2).

Although it is hard to find any contemporary approach to discourse that does *not* more or less explicitly refer to Goffman's work, we have included in the *Reader* several papers in which the affinity to Goffman's work is especially clear. (Apart from the chapters mentioned above, see Brown and Levinson, Chapter 22; Tannen and Wallat, Chapter 24; Coupland and Ylänne, Chapter 25; Young, Chapter 28.)

Much of Gumperz's research has concentrated on *intercultural interaction* and especially on the mechanisms of *miscommunication*. For example, in Chapter 4, he demonstrates how seemingly trivial signalling details, such as falling rather than rising intonation on a single word, can trigger complex patterns of interpretation and misinterpretation between members of different cultural groups (see also Roberts *et al.* 1992). These patterns of (mis)interpretation, which he labels *conversational inferencing*, depend not only on the 'actual' contents of talk, but to a great extent on the processes of perception and evaluation of a number of the signalling mechanisms, based on details of intonation, tempo of speech, rhythm, pausing, phonetic, lexical, and syntactic choices, non-verbal signals, and so on. Gumperz calls such features *contextualisation cues*, and he showed that they

> relate what is said to the contextual knowledge (including knowledge of particular activity types: cf. frames; Goffman 1974) that contributes to the presuppositions necessary to the accurate inferencing of what is meant (including, but not limited to, the illocutionary force).
>
> (Schiffrin 1994: 99–100)

Gumperz adapts and extends Hymes's ethnographic framework by examining how interactants from different cultural groups apply different rules of speaking in face-to-face interaction. In his work, he draws heavily on the pragmatic notion of inferential meaning and the ethnomethodological understanding of conversation as joint action (see above).

We have already mentioned the link between Gumperz's contextualisation cues and their role as markers signalling types of speech event, or in Goffman's terms *frames*, which participants engage in. Frames are part of the interpretive means by which participants understand or disambiguate utterances and other forms of communicative behaviour. For example, a person waving his or her arm may be stopping a car, greeting a friend, flicking flies or increasing blood circulation (Goffman 1974). There is a constant interplay between contextualisation cues and what is being said. Framing devices usually form a part of the communicated message but they are used to label or categorise the communicative process itself. Therefore, they also constitute the utterance's *metamessage* (Watzlawick *et al.* 1967; Tannen 1986; Jaworski *et al.* 2004), or its 'message about its own status as a message'. When we look for ways in which frames are constructed and changed or shifted, we try to identify how participants convey their metamessages through various verbal and non-verbal cues (see also Coupland and Ylänne, Chapter 25).

Another concept that links Goffman's work with that of Gumperz is *footing*, 'the alignments we take up to ourselves and the others present as expressed in the way we manage the production or reception of an utterance' (Goffman 1981: 128). As Goffman notes, changes in footing depend in part on the use of specific contextualisation cues, for example, switching between language codes or speech styles.

One of the most significant developments in interactional sociolinguistics was the formulation of politeness theory (Brown and Levinson 1987 [1978], Chapter 22). Penelope Brown and Stephen C. Levinson believe that the phenomenon of politeness is responsible for how people, apparently universally, deviate from the maximally efficient modes of communication, as outlined by Grice. In other words, politeness is the reason why people do not always 'say what they mean'. Politeness theory, which aims to provide a universal descriptive and explanatory framework of social relations, is built around Goffman's notion of face (Chapter 21), i.e., a person's self-image and projected self onto others, and Grice's model of inferential communication and the assumption that people communicating are rational. Brown and Levinson stress the strategic nature of human communication, which is a radical departure from rule-oriented approaches (e.g., Lakoff's rules of politeness as summarised by Tannen, Chapter 31).

The *Reader* carries several chapters on face (Goffman, Chapter 21) and politeness (Brown and Levinson, Chapter 22; Holmes, Chapter 23), so we will not present an overview of these inter-connected theories here. But it is worth pointing out that, apart from Lakoff's approach to politeness mentioned above, there have been several other alternative attempts to theorise politeness. The best-known example is Leech's (1983) approach, based on Grice's notion of the 'Politeness Principle' (analogous to the Cooperative Principle but never fully developed by Grice himself) and a set of corresponding politeness maxims, such as *tact, generosity, approbation, modesty*, and so on. For a recent discussion and reformulation of politeness theory, see Watts (2003).

Narrative analysis

Telling stories is a human universal of discourse. Stories or narratives are discursive accounts of factual or fictitious events that take place, have taken place or will take place at a particular time. We construct narratives as structured representations of events in a particular temporal order. Sometimes, the ordering of events is chronological (e.g., most fairy stories) although some plays, novels or news stories (e.g., Bell 1998) may move backwards and forwards in time, for particular reasons and effects.

Narratives can be verbal (spoken or written), musical, mimed or pictorial, e.g., in children's picture books. Sometimes a story can be narrated in a single visual image, a painting or a photograph, implying a temporal succession of events (e.g., something has happened or is about to happen). Of course, narratives often combine different modalities and many voices in a single story-telling event. For example, recounting a family holiday may involve several family members presenting their versions of events, to which the participating audience may add questions and comments. It may involve showing souvenirs, photographs or a video, or even sampling foods brought home from the trip. This can turn the narrative into a multimodal, multi-voiced text, including the gustatory (taste) and olfactory (smell) channels. Sometimes, different voices are introduced into a story by a single narrator, for example by introducing quotations as direct speech, perhaps marked by changes in pitch or body posture.

The functions of story-telling are quite varied. Some stories are primarily informative, others are used for self-presentation (e.g., during a medical examination, see Young, Chapter 28), for entertainment, for strengthening in-group ties (e.g., gossip), in therapy or problem-solving (e.g., life-stories told in counselling sessions or in problem-sharing among friends), and so on. Although narratives vary greatly in their form (including their length) and function, all verbal narratives share a basic structure (Labov, Chapter 14). William Labov's study of oral narratives was based on data he collected in New York City, in response to the interview question 'Were you ever in a situation where you were in a serious danger of being killed' (Labov 1972: 363; Chapter 14). He formulated the following structural features of narratives (as summarised by Ochs 1997: 195), although it is clear that some narratives do not display all of the following elements:

1   abstract (a summary of what is to be said, for example, 'My brother put a knife in my head');
2   orientation ('This was just a few days after my father died');
3   complicating action ('I twisted his arm up behind him . . .');
4   evaluation ('Ain't that a bitch?');

5   result or resolution ('After all that I gave the dude the cigarette, after all that'); and
6   coda ('And that was that').

One feature that is common to all narratives is of course the plot-line, or what the story is about. Plot is most commonly associated with narratives found in various literary genres (e.g., novels, ballads, fairy tales) and its structure has indeed been extensively studied within literary stylistics (e.g., Propp 1968; Toolan 1988). One example of how this type of work may be applied to the study of non-literary texts is given by Vestergaard and Schroeder (1985) in their study of the language of advertising. Following Greimas's (1966) taxonomy of participants (or as Greimas called them 'actants') in narratives, Vestergaard and Schroeder distinguished the following six, paired roles:

> subject – object
> helper – opponent
> giver – receiver.

The relationships between those roles can be presented diagramatically in the following way:

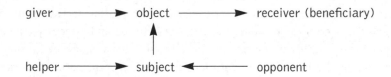

A realisation of this model can be found in many fairy tales. Consider Michael Toolan's 'generic' summary:

> The subject or hero, perhaps a young man of lowly origin, seeks marriage to a beautiful princess (object), in which case the man will also be bene-ficiary (possibly the princess and the country will too). In his quest he is helped generously but with limited success by a friend or relative (helper), but their combined efforts count for little in the struggle against some opponents (wicked uncle of the princess, some other eligible but ignoble suitor), until a sender (better, a superhelper), such as the king or God, or some individual with magical powers for good, intervenes.
>
> (Toolan 1988: 93–4)

Narratives are not inherently objective or impartial ways of representing events, even though they might be *objectifying devices* (ways of claiming or constructing an air of factuality). This is immediately clear with regard to narratives that are works of fiction (fairly tales, detective stories, etc.). But even 'factual' narratives are intimately tied to the narrator's point of view, and the events recounted in a narrative are his/her (re)constructions rather than some kind of objective mirror-image of reality. The first instance of the narrator's subjectivity is present in what s/he chooses to narrate, what s/he finds 'tellable' or 'reportable'. Furthermore, as Goffman explains, the meaning of the narrative is jointly constructed by the selectively filtering actions of both speaker and listener:

> A tale or anecdote, that is, a replaying, is not merely any reporting of a past event. In the fullest sense, it is such a statement couched from the personal perspective of an actual or potential participant who is located so that some temporal, dramatic development of the reported event proceeds from that starting point. A replaying will therefore incidentally be something that listeners can empathetically insert themselves into, vicariously re-experiencing what took place. A replaying, in brief, recounts a personal experience, not merely reports on an event.
>
> (Goffman 1974: 504; quoted in Ochs 1997: 193)

In sum, narrative analysis is an important tradition within discourse analysis. It deals with a pervasive genre of communication through which we enact important aspects of our identities and relations with others. It is partly through narrative discourse that we comprehend the world and present our understanding of it to others.

Critical discourse analysis

In all but its blandest forms, such as when it remains at the level of language description, discourse analysis adopts a 'critical' perspective on language in use. Roger Fowler (1981) is explicit about what 'critical' means for his own research, much of it related to literary texts. He says it does *not* mean 'the flood of writings about texts and authors which calls itself literary criticism', nor the sense of 'intolerant fault-finding' (p. 25):

> I mean a careful analytic interrogation of the ideological categories, and the roles and institutions and so on, through which a society constitutes and maintains itself and the consciousness of its members . . . All knowledge, all objects, are constructs: criticism analyses the processes of construction and, acknowledging the artificial quality of the categories concerned, offers the possibility that we might profitably conceive the world in some alternative way.
>
> (Fowler 1981: 25)

Many elements in Fowler's definition of critical analysis have already come up as hallmarks of discourse analysis in our review – notably its questioning of objectivity and its interest in the practices that produce apparent objectivity, normality and factuality. What we called the forensic goals of discourse analysis re-surface in Fowler's definition, probing texts and discourse practices in order to discover hidden meaning and value-structures. His view of society as a set of groups and institutions structured through discourse is closely reminiscent of Foucault's and Pêcheux's theoretical writings (see p. 5).

There is a wealth of critical theoretic writing behind these general perspectives, which we have decided not to represent directly in the *Reader*. Our thinking is that *critical theory*, while exerting considerable influence on discourse analysis, remains 'theory'. It is a diverse set of abstract and philosophical writing (for example, by Louis Althusser, Emile Benveniste, Jacques Derrida, Umberto Eco and Jacques Lacan) which does not always impinge directly on the empirical analysis of discourse, but is definitely part of the same intellectual climate. (Belsey 1980 provides a useful overview of critical theory approaches; Cobley 1996 is an excellent collection of original writings by several of these theorists.) Those 'theory' chapters we have included – Bakhtin (Chapter 6), Barthes (Chapter 7), Hall (Chapter 27), Bourdieu (Chapter 32), Foucault (Chapter 33) and Butler (Chapter 34) – are ones where theoretical concepts lead more naturally to forms of linguistic/textual/discourse analysis.

But if Fowler's *critical* perspective is established in all or most discourse analysis, why does critical discourse analysis need to be distinguished as a separate tradition? One reason is historical. Several early approaches to discourse, such as the work of the Birmingham school linguists who developed analyses of classroom discourse (Sinclair and Coulthard 1975), had mainly descriptive aims. They introduced an elaborate hierarchical framework for coding teachers' and pupils' discourse 'acts', 'moves' and 'transactions' in classroom talk. The intention was to provide an exhaustive structural model of discourse organisation, from the (highest) category, 'the lesson', down to the (lowest) category of the individual speech act. A critical approach to discourse distances itself from descriptivism of this sort. It foregrounds its concern with social constructionism and with the construction of *ideology* in particular. As Theo Van Leeuwen says, 'Critical discourse analysis is, or should be, concerned with . . . discourse as the instrument of the social construction of reality' (1993: 193). Ideological structures are necessarily concerned with the analysis of power relations and social discrimination, for example through demonstrating differential access to discourse networks (see above; Caldas-Coulthard and Coulthard 1996; Fairclough 1989, 2003).

Norman Fairclough gives the clearest account of critical discourse analysis as ideological analysis:

> I view social institutions as containing diverse 'ideological-discursive formations' (IDFs) associated with different groups within the institution. There is usually one IDF which is clearly dominant . . . Institutional subjects are constructed, in accordance with the norms of an IDF, in subject positions whose ideological underpinnings they may be unaware of. A characteristic of a dominant IDF is the capacity to 'naturalise' ideologies, i.e., to win acceptance for them as non-ideological 'common sense'. It is argued that the orderliness of interactions depends in part

upon such naturalised ideologies. To 'denaturalise' them is the objective of a discourse analysis which adopts 'critical' goals. I suggest that
denaturalisation involves showing how social structures determine properties of discourse, and how discourse in turn determines social
structures.

(Fairclough 1995: 27)

The important point about concepts such as 'naturalisation' and 'denaturalisation'
is that they are dynamic processes. They imply a continuing struggle over social
arrangements and acts of imposition and resistance. In fact, the critical perspective is oriented to social change, in two different senses. First, critical discourse
analysis, particularly in Fairclough's work, sets out to understand social changes
in the ideological use of language. We have briefly mentioned Fairclough's arguments about 'technologisation'. Under this heading, he identifies an on-going cultural
'process of redesigning existing discursive practices and training institutional
personnel in the redesigned practices' (Fairclough 1995: 102), brought about partly
through so-called 'social skills training'. Fairclough suggests that social skills
training is marked by the emergence of 'discourse technologists', the policing of
discourse practices, designing context-free discourse techniques and attempts to
standardise them (p. 103). He finds examples in the instituting of 'staff development' and 'staff appraisal' schemes in British universities (and of course elsewhere).
New forms of discourse (e.g., learning terminology that will impress supervisors or
assessors, or learning how to appear efficient, friendly or resourceful) are normalised
(made to appear unexceptional) and policed or monitored, with a system of status-
related and financial rewards and penalties following on from them. Other discursive
shifts that Fairclough has investigated are the conversationalisation of public
discourse and the marketisation of public institutions (again, in particular, universities).

The second aspect of change is the critic's own attempt to resist social changes
held to curtail liberty. Ideological critique is often characterised by some form of
intervention. Notice how Fowler (in the quotation on p. 27 above) mentions 'profit-
ably conceiv[ing] the world in some alternative way'. A critical orientation is not
merely 'deconstructive'; it may aim to be 'reconstructive', reconstructing social
arrangements. Fowler's use of the term 'profitable' is perhaps unfortunate, although
he seems to mean 'more justifiable' or 'more fair'. Fairclough, too, writes that

the problematic of language and power is fundamentally a question of
democracy. Those affected need to take it on board as a political issue,
as feminists have around the issue of language and gender . . . Critical
linguists and discourse analysts have an important auxiliary role to
play here [i.e., secondary to the role of people directly affected] in
providing analyses and, importantly, in providing critical educators with
resources of what I and my colleagues have called 'critical language
awareness'.

(Fairclough 1995: 221; see also Chapter 11)

Critical discourse analysis in this view is a democratic resource to be made available through the education system. Critical discourse analysts need to see themselves as politically engaged, working alongside disenfranchised social groups. This point returns us to issues of method and ethics, of the sort debated by Cameron *et al.* in Chapter 8.

Overview: what discourse analysis can and cannot do

It may be useful to end this overview chapter with a brief consideration of the limitations inherent in the discourse perspective – what discourse analysis can *not* do. Understandably enough, the readings in this book actively construct the discipline of discourse studies as a vibrant one, alert to social divisions and, in some cases, seeking to resist them. Discourse promotes itself as being aware, liberated and liberating, and to us this stance seems generally justified.

Yet there are some basic issues of research methods and interpretation which are not and should not be overlooked in the rush to discourse. Discourse analysis is a committedly *qualitative* orientation to linguistic and social understanding. As hinted earlier, it inherits both the strengths and the weaknesses associated with qualitative research. As weaknesses, there will always be problems in justifying the selection of materials as research data. It is often difficult to say why a particular stretch of conversation of a particular piece of written text has come under the spotlight of discourse analysis, and why certain of its characteristics are attended to and not others. If discourse analysis is able to generalise, it can normally only generalise about process and not about distribution. This is a significant problem for research projects which assert that there are broad social changes in discourse formations within a community, e.g., Fairclough's claims about increasing technologisation. A claim about change over time – and Fairclough's claims are intuitively very convincing – needs to be substantiated with time-sequenced data, linked to some principled method for analysing it, able to demonstrate significant differences. The point is that qualitative, interpretive studies of particular fragments of discourse are not self-sufficient. They need support from other traditions of research, even quantitative surveying. Discourse, therefore, is not a panacea, and is suited to some types of research question and not others.

Discourse data tend not to lend themselves to distributional surveying. If we emphasise the local contexting of language and the shared construction of meaning, then it follows that we cannot confidently identify recurring instances of 'the same' discourse phenomenon (such as a conversational interruption, a racist reference or an intimate form of address). It is certainly true that a lot of quantitative research has been done – and sometimes inappropriately – on discourse data, through gross coding of language forms and expressions that hide significant functional/contextual/inferential differences. But it is also true that discourse analysts often feel the *need* to make distributional claims (e.g., that men interrupt more than women do, that racist discourse is rife in contemporary Britain or that some forms of signalled intimacy redress threats to a person's face) which their data, analysed qualitatively,

may not directly support. One common weakness of discourse analysis is, therefore, that there is a potential mismatch between the analytic method and the
interpretation of data in distributional terms. In-depth, single-case analyses (e.g.,
of a particular conversation or written report) are entirely appropriate in discourse
analytic research, and have full validity, relative to their aims and objectives (usually
to demonstrate meaning-making processes and to build rich interpretations of local
discourse events). But they cannot stand as alternatives to larger-scale projects
based on sampled instances, designed to answer questions about social differences
or social change. Such studies have their own limitations and they risk essentialising and glossing complex local processes. But research is inherently imperfect,
and we would support the line of argument that multiple perspectives and methods
increase the likelihood of reaching good explanations.

Several strands of discourse analysis, as we have seen, find their vigour in
opposing other research trends and assumptions. This is evident in, for example,
discursive psychology's antagonism to quantitative social psychology, and in ethnomethodology and CA's resistance to the 'conventional' sociology of social structure.
In both these cases, discourse theorists argue for more tentativeness, more context-
relatedness, more contingency and more tolerance of ambiguity. It is hard to avoid
the conclusion that the discourse perspective requires us to scale back our ambition
in some ways, again particularly in relation to generalising, when it comes to linguistic and social explanation. The nature of research itself as a discourse practice
needs to be questioned (see Cameron *et al.*, Chapter 8; Gilbert and Mulkay 1984),
but when we question we lose some of the security as well as the hegemony of the
research institutions.

The corresponding power of the discourse analysis perspective is its explanatory and critical depth. Discourse studies offer the possibility of a greater clarity
of vision, specifically of how language permeates human affairs, offering us opportunities but also constraints. Duranti, as a linguistic anthropologist, has written
lucidly about this:

> Having a language is like having access to a very large canvas and to
> hundreds or even thousands of colors. But the canvas and the colors
> come from the past. They are hand-me-downs. As we learn to use them,
> we find out that those around us have strong ideas about what can be
> drawn, in which proportions, in what combinations, and for what
> purposes. As any artist knows, there is an ethics of drawing and coloring
> as well as a market that will react sometimes capriciously, but many
> times quite predictably to any individual attempts to place a mark in
> the history or representation or simply readjust the proportions of certain
> spaces at the margins . . . Just like art-works, our linguistic products
> are constantly evaluated, recycled or discarded.
>
> (Duranti 1997: 334)

Duranti's metaphor captures many of the insights that we have anticipated in this
Introduction, to be filled out and illustrated in the following chapters. But it also

follows that if we can become more aware of the ethics of using language, and of the linguistic market and its practices, we should be better prepared to use language for the purposes we deem valuable. As the 'information revolution' continues to gain new ground, demands will increase on us to acquire new literacies and discourse competences. These competences will include 'technical' literacies, such as the ability to produce and read new media-generated texts (Snyder 1998; Thurlow *et al.* 2004). But they will also include being able to produce reasoned accounts and interpretations of complex discourse events and situations. The ability to reflect critically on and analyse discourse will increasingly become a basic skill for negotiating social life and for imposing a form of interpretive, critical order on the new discursive universe.

Further reading

Apart from the older and more recent sources cited above, many of which include pedagogic texts, there are many recent student-oriented publications on discourse available on the market. They include general reviews of the field (Johnstone 2002; Georgakopoulou and Goutsos 2002; Fairclough 2003; Blommaert 2005), more 'hands-on'/methods-oriented textbooks (Titscher *et al.* 2000; Cameron 2001), and handbooks (Schiffrin *et al.* 2001; Duranti 2004).

References

Bakhtin, M.M. (1981) *The Dialogic Imagination: Four Essays*, edited by M. Holquist. Translated by Vern W. McGee. Austin, TX: University of Texas Press.
—— (1986) *Speech Genres and Other Late Essays*, translated by Vern W. McGee. Austin, TX: University of Texas Press.
Bauman, R. and Scherzer, J. (eds) (1974) *Explorations in the Ethnography of Speaking*, Cambridge: Cambridge University Press.
Bell, A. (1998) 'The discourse structure of news stories', in A. Bell and P. Garrett (eds), *Approaches to Media Discourse*, Oxford: Blackwell. 64–104.
Belsey, C. (1980) *Critical Practice*, London: Methuen.
Benveniste, E. (1971) *Problems in General Linguistics*, Coral Gables, FL: University of Miami Press.
Besnier, N. (1989) 'Information withholding as a manipulative and collusive strategy in Nukulaelae gossip', *Language in Society* 18: 315–41.
Billig, M. (1991) *Ideologies and Beliefs*, London: Sage.
Blommaert, Jan (2005) *Discourse: A Critical Introduction*, Cambridge: Cambridge University Press.
Boden, D. and Zimmerman, D.H. (eds) (1991) *Talk and Social Structure: Studies in Ethnomethodology and Conversation Analysis*, Cambridge: Polity Press.
Brown, G. and Yule, G. (1983) *Discourse Analysis*, Cambridge: Cambridge University Press.
Brown, P. and Levinson, S. (1987) *Politeness: Some Universals in Language Usage*, Cambridge: Cambridge University Press. (Originally published in 1978 as part of E.N. Goody (ed.) *Questions and Politeness*, Cambridge: Cambridge University Press.)

Caldas-Coulthard, R. and Coulthard, M. (eds) (1996) *Texts and Practices: Readings in Critical Discourse Analysis*, London: Routledge.

Cameron, D. (1995) *Verbal Hygiene*, London: Routledge.

—— (2000) *Good to Talk? Living and Working in a Communication Culture*, London: Sage.

—— (2001) *Working with Spoken Discourse*, London: Sage.

Candlin, C.N. (1997) 'General editor's preface', in B.-L. Gunnarsson, P. Linell and B. Nordberg (eds) *The Construction of Professional Discourse*, London: Longman. x–xiv.

Chomsky, N. (1965) *Aspects of the Theory of Syntax*, Cambridge, MA: MIT Press.

Cicourel, A.V. (1973) *Cognitive Sociology: Language and Meaning in Social Interaction*, Harmondsworth: Penguin Education.

Cobley, P. (ed.) (1996) *The Communication Theory Reader*, London: Routledge.

Coupland, N. and Jaworski, A. (eds) (1997) *Sociolinguistics: A Reader and Coursebook*, Basingstoke: Macmillan.

—— and —— (eds) (2007) *The New Sociolinguistics Reader*, Basingstoke: Palgrave Macmillan.

Drew, P. and Heritage, J. (eds) (1992a) *Talk at Work: Interaction in Institutional Settings*, Cambridge: Cambridge University Press.

—— and —— (1992b) 'Analyzing talk at work: An introduction', in P. Drew and J. Heritage (eds) *Talk at Work: Interaction in Institutional Settings*, Cambridge: Cambridge University Press. 3–65.

Duranti, A. (1997) *Linguistic Anthropology*, Cambridge: Cambridge University Press.

—— (2004) *A Companion to Linguistic Anthropology*, Oxford: Blackwell Publishing.

Edwards, D. (1997) *Discourse and Cognition*, London: Sage.

—— and Potter, J. (1992) *Discursive Psychology*, London: Sage.

Fairclough, N. (1989) *Language and Power*, London: Longman.

—— (1992) 'Introduction', in N. Fairclough (ed.) *Critical Language Awareness*, London: Longman.

—— (1995) *Critical Discourse Analysis: The Critical Study of Language*, London: Longman.

—— (2003) *Analysing Discourse: Textual Analysis for Social Research*, London: Routledge.

Fasold, R. (1990) *Sociolinguistics of Language*, Oxford: Blackwell.

Fillmore, C. (1984) 'Remarks on contrastive pragmatics', in J. Fisiak (ed.) *Contrastive Linguistics: Prospects and Problems*, Berlin: Mouton. 119–41.

Foucault, M. (1972) *The Archaeology of Knowledge*, translated by S. Smith. London: Tavistock.

Fowler, R. (1981) *Literature as Social Discourse: The Practice of Linguistic Criticism*, London: Batsford Academic.

Garfinkel, H. (1967) *Studies in Ethnomethodology*, Englewood Cliffs, NJ: Prentice Hall.

—— (1974) 'On the origins of the term "ethnomethodology"', in R. Turner (ed.) *Ethnomethodology*, Harmondsworth: Penguin.

Georgakopoulou, A. and Goutsos, D. (2002) *Discourse: An Introduction*, 2nd edition, Edinburgh: Edinburgh University Press.

Gergen, K.J. (1982) *Toward Transformation in Social Knowledge*, New York: Springer.

—— (1991) *The Saturated Self: Dilemmas of Identity in Contemporary Life*, New York: Basic Books.

Giddens, A. (1991) *Modernity and Self-identity: Self and Society in the Late Modern Age*, Cambridge: Polity Press.

Gilbert, G.N. and Mulkay, M. (1984) *Opening Pandora's Box: A Sociological Analysis of Scientists' Discourse*, Cambridge: Cambridge University Press.

Goffman, E. (1959) *The Presentation of Self in Everyday Life*, New York: Doubleday Anchor.

—— (1967) *Interaction Ritual: Essays on Face-to-Face Behavior*, New York: Doubleday Anchor.

—— (1974) *Frame Analysis: An Essay on the Organization of Experience*, New York: Harper & Row.

—— (1981) 'Footing', in E. Goffman *Forms of Talk*, Philadelphia, PA: University of Pennsylvania Press. 124–59. (First published in *Semiotica* 25 (1979): 1–29.)

—— (1983) 'The interaction order', *American Sociological Review* 48: 1–17.

Graddol, D., Cheshire, J. and Swann, J. (1994) *Describing Language*. 2nd edition, Buckingham: Open University Press.

Greimas, A. (1966) *Semantique Structurale*, Paris: Larousse.

Gumperz, J.J. (1982a) *Discourse Strategies*, Cambridge: Cambridge University Press.

—— (ed.) (1982b) *Language and Social Identity*, Cambridge: Cambridge University Press.

Heller, M. (2003) 'Globalization, the new economy, and the commodification of language and identity', *Journal of Sociolinguistics* 7: 473–92.

Heritage, J. (1984a) 'A change-of-state token and aspects of its sequential placement', in J. Atkinson and J. Heritage (eds) *Structures of Social Action: Studies in Conversation Analysis*, Cambridge: Cambridge University Press. 299–345.

—— (1984b) *Garfinkel and Ethnomethodology*, Oxford: Blackwell.

Hodge, R. and Kress, G. (1991) *Social Semiotics*, Cambridge: Polity.

Hutchby, I. and Wooffitt, R. (1998) *Conversation Analysis*, Cambridge: Polity Press.

Hymes, D. (1972a) 'On communicative competence', in J.B. Pride and J. Holmes (eds) *Sociolinguistics*, Harmondsworth: Penguin. 269–93 (originally published in 1971).

—— (1972b) 'Models of the interaction of language and social life', in J.J. Gumperz and D. Hymes (eds) *Directions in Sociolinguistics*, New York: Holt, Rinehart & Winston and Oxford: Blackwell. 35–71.

Jaworski, A., Coupland, N. and Galasiński, D. (eds) (2004) *Metalanguage: Social and Ideological Perspectives*, Berlin and New York: Mouton de Gruyter.

Johnstone, B. (2002) *Discourse Analysis*, Oxford: Blackwell Publishing.

Kress, G. and Van Leeuwen, T. (1996) *Reading Images: The Grammar of Visual Design*, London: Routledge.

—— and —— (2001) *Multimodal Discourse: The Modes and Media of Contemporary Communication*, London: Arnold.

Labov, W. (1972) 'The transformation of experience in narrative syntax', in W. Labov, *Language in the Inner City*, Philadelphia, PA: University of Pennsylvania Press and Oxford: Blackwell. 354–96.

—— and Fanshel, D. (1977) *Therapeutic Discourse: Psychotherapy as Conversation*, New York: Academic Press.

Lee, D. (1992) *Competing Discourses*, London: Longman.

Leech, G. (1983) *Principles of Pragmatics*, London: Longman.

Lucy, J. (1992) *Language Diversity and Thought: A Reformulation of the Linguistic Relativity Hypothesis*, Cambridge: Cambridge University Press.

Mills, S. (1997) *Discourse*, London: Routledge.

Milroy, J. and Milroy, L. (1999) *Authority in Language: Investigating Language Prescription and Standardisation*, 3rd edition, London: Routledge.

Moerman, M. (1988) *Talking Culture: Ethnography and Conversation Analysis*, Philadelphia, PA: University of Pennsylvania Press.

Ochs, E. (1988) *Culture and Language Development: Language Acquisition and Language Socialization in a Samoan Village*, Cambridge: Cambridge University Press.

—— (1997) 'Narrative', in T.A. Van Dijk (ed.) *Discourse Studies: A Multidisciplinary Introduction. Vol. 1. Discourse as Structure and Process*, London: Sage. 185–207.

Pêcheux, M. (1982) *Language, Semantics and Ideology*, Basingstoke: Macmillan.

Potter, J. (1996) *Representing Reality*, London: Sage.

—— and Wetherell, M. (1987) *Discourse and Social Psychology: Beyond Attitudes and Behaviour*, London: Sage.

Propp, V. (1968) *Morphology of Folk Tale*, Austin, TX: University of Texas Press (first published in Russian, 1928).

Rampton, B. (1995) *Crossing: Language and Ethnicity Among Adolescents*, London: Longman.

—— (2005) *Language in Late Modernity: Interaction in an Urban School*, Cambridge: Cambridge University Press.

Roberts, C., Davies, E. and Jupp, T. (1992) *Language and Discrimination: A Study of Communication in Multi-ethnic Workplaces*, London: Longman.

Sacks, H., Schegloff, E. and Jefferson, G. (1974) 'A simplest systematics for the organization of turn-taking for conversation', *Language* 50: 696–735.

Saville-Troike, M. (2003) *The Ethnography of Communication: An Introduction*, 3rd edition, Oxford: Blackwell Publishing.

Schegloff, E.A., Ochs, E. and Thompson, S.A. (1996) 'Introduction', in E. Ochs, E.A. Schegloff and S.A. Thompson (eds) *Interaction and Grammar*, Cambridge: Cambridge University Press.

Schiffrin, D. (1994) *Approaches to Discourse*, Oxford: Blackwell.

——, Tannen, D. and Hamilton, H.H. (eds) (2001) *The Handbook of Discourse Analysis*, Oxford: Blackwell Publishing.

Searle, J.R. (1969) *Speech Acts: An Essay in the Philosophy of Language*, Cambridge: Cambridge University Press.

—— (1979) 'The classification of illocutionary acts', *Language in Society* 8: 137–51.

Shotter, J. (1993) *Conversational Realities*, London: Sage.

Sinclair, J. McH. and Coulthard, M. (1975) *Towards an Analysis of Discourse: The English Used by Teachers and Pupils*, London: Oxford University Press.

Snyder, I. (ed.) (1998) *Page to Screen: Taking Literacy into the Electronic Era*, London: Routledge.

Sperber, D. and Wilson, D. (1986) *Relevance: Communication & Cognition*, Oxford: Blackwell.

—— and —— (1995) *Relevance: Communication & Cognition*, 2nd edition, Oxford: Blackwell.

—— and —— (1997) 'Remarks on relevance theory and the social sciences', *Multilingua* 16: 145–52.

Stubbs, M. (1983) *Discourse Analysis*, Oxford: Blackwell.

Tannen, D. (1986) *That's Not What I Meant! How Conversational Style Makes or Breaks your Relations with Others*, New York: William Morrow, Ballantine.

Taylor, T. and Cameron, D. (1987) *Analysing Conversation: Rules and Units in the Structure of Talk*, Oxford: Pergamon.

Thomas, J. (1995) *Meaning in Interaction: An Introduction to Pragmatics*, London: Longman.

Thurlow, C., Lengel, L. and Tomic, A. (2004) *Computer Mediated Communication: Social Interaction and the Internet*, London: Sage.

Titscher, S., Meyer, M., Wodak, R. and Vetter, E. (2000) *Methods of Text and Discourse Analysis*, London: Sage.

Toolan, M.J. (1988) *Narrative: A Critical Linguistic Introduction*, London: Routledge.

Turner, R. (1974) *Ethnomethodology*, Harmondsworth: Penguin.

Van Dijk, T.A. (1977) *Text and Context*, London: Longman.

—— (1984) *Prejudice in Discourse*, Amsterdam: Benjamins.

—— (ed.) (1985) *Handbook of Discourse Analysis* (4 volumes), New York: Academic Press.

—— (1988) *News Analysis: Case Studies of International and National News in the Press*, Hillsdale, NJ: Lawrence Erlbaum.

—— (ed.) (1997) *Discourse Studies* (2 volumes), London: Sage.

Van Leeuwen, T. (1993) 'Genre and field in critical discourse analysis', *Discourse & Society* 4: 193–225.

—— (2005) *Introducing Social Semiotics*, London: Routledge.

Vestergaard, T. and Schroeder, K. (1985) *The Language of Advertising*, Oxford: Blackwell.

Watts, Richard J. (2003) *Politeness*, Cambridge: Cambridge University Press.
Watzlawick, P., Beavin-Bavelas, J. and Jackson, D. (1967) *The Pragmatics of Human Communication*, New York: Norton.
Whorf, B.L. (1956) *Language, Thought and Reality: Selected Writings of Benjamin Lee Whorf*, edited by J.B. Carroll, Cambridge, MA: MIT Press.

Journals

The following is a list of journals publishing discourse research.

Discourse & Communication, published by Sage. A new interdisciplinary journal aiming to introduce the qualitative, discourse analytical approach to issues in communication research.

Discourse Processes (subtitled 'a multidisciplinary journal'), published by Ablex. Publishes descriptive linguistic and cognitive as well as interpretive studies of discourse.

Discourse & Society, published by Sage. Specialises in critical discourse analysis.

Discourse Studies, published by Sage. Open to all traditions of discourse analysis.

Human Communication Research, published by and for the International Communication Association. Publishes a wide range of quantitative and some qualitative research on communication.

International Journal of Applied Linguistics, published by Blackwell Publishing. Very broad-based, including applied linguistics, sociolinguistics and some discourse studies.

Journal of Communication, published by the Oxford University Press for International Communication Association. Deals mostly with mass-media communication and other social semiotic approaches to communication.

Journal of Language and Social Psychology, published by Sage. Covers quantitative and experimental research, but is increasingly open to qualitative discourse research on themes relevant to social psychology.

Journal of Multilingual and Multicultural Development, published by Multilingual Matters. Publishes primarily quantitative and qualitative research on inter-cultural communication and language and ethnicity.

Journal of Politeness Research, published by de Gruyter. Specialist journal dealing with linguistic and non-linguistic research on politeness phenomena.

Journal of Pragmatics, published by Elsevier. Focuses mainly on linguistic aspects of pragmatics and discourse, but increasingly open to socially and culturally inclined studies.

Journal of Sociolinguistics, published by Blackwell Publishing. Both editors of this *Reader* are involved editorially, along with Allan Bell. It covers the whole interdisciplinary field of sociolinguistics and discourse studies and is open to innovative approaches.

Language Awareness, published by Multilingual Matters. Promotes varied approaches, including critical and applied approaches to language and discourse.

Language and Communication, published by Pergamon/Elsevier. Another very broad-based journal, publishing theoretical as well as empirical studies.

Language in Society, published by Cambridge University Press. An established sociolinguistics journal, open to discourse analytic research with a strong anthropological/ethnographic bias.

Multilingua, published by Mouton de Gruyter. Originally exploring the interface between language, culture and second language acquisition, now open to all current research in sociolinguistics and discourse analysis.

Narrative Inquiry, published by John Benjamins. Provides an interdisciplinary forum for the study of narratives.

Pragmatics, published by and for the International Pragmatics Association. Wide-ranging, including culturally focused, linguistic and critical approaches to discourse.

Research on Language and Social Interaction, published by Lawrence Erlbaum. Specialises in talk-in-interaction/conversation analytic research.

Semiotica, published by Mouton de Gruyter. Interdisciplinary and orientated towards the analysis of different semiotic systems and multimodality; notable for many review articles of books in all areas of semiotic research.

Text (subtitled 'an interdisciplinary journal for the study of discourse'), published by Mouton de Gruyter. Another broad-based, established journal, open to all traditions of discourse analysis.

Visual Communication, published by Sage. Major journal for visual communication and multimodal discourse research.

PART ONE

Discourse: meaning, function and context

Editors' introduction
to Part One

IN THE GENERAL INTRODUCTION we characterised discourse analysis as
a reaching out beyond the visible or audible forms of language into social context,
and as exploring the interplay between language and social processes. Construing
language as discourse involves orienting to language as a form of social action,
as a functioning form of social action embedded in the totality of social processes.
In this Part of the *Reader* we represent several of the key writers and texts who,
influentially, argued the case for a functional approach to language, initially within
their various disciplines – linguistics (Jakobson), literary criticism (Bakhtin), philosophy (Austin, Grice), linguistic anthropology/sociolinguistics (Gumperz), literature and semiotics (Barthes), and sociology (Schegloff). What is important here is
not so much the disciplinary origins, even though these clearly influence individuals'
ways of theorising and writing. Rather, it is the cumulative perspective that develops
out of their work – pressure towards a notion of discourse (whether so-labelled
or not) and towards new theoretical frameworks for explaining meaning-making
and sense-making as contextual processes. These seven foundational, theoretical
chapters do not make the easiest reading, but it should be helpful to keep referring
back to them from later, more data-based chapters.

Roman Jakobson's text introduces what he saw as the six basic functions
of verbal communication: *referential*, *emotive*, *conative*, *phatic*, *metalingual* and
poetic. Although it focuses specifically on the link between linguistics and poetics,
Jakobson's article clearly demonstrates how, as early as 1960, some European
linguists were committed to a multi-functional view of language. Such a perspective was to become the foundation of Michael Halliday's functional linguistics,
influenced heavily by the functionalism of J.R. Firth, which is itself a contemporary
influence on social semiotic and critical linguistic approaches to discourse. But the
mainstream of descriptive and theoretical linguistics did not follow this line. It
came to be dominated by structural models, culminating in Chomsky's formal and

cognitivist theory of language. We can therefore see modern discourse studies as a re-imposition of some early priorities in functional linguistics, and this is why Jakobson's work remains an important foundational source.

Jakobson challenges the view that using language is a simple exchange of referential information. What he called the conative function attends to relationships between speakers and what communication achieves in this social dimension. The phatic function is realised in aspects of socially organised, ritualised communication; the emotive function relates to the expressive and subjective dimension of talk; the metalinguistic function identifies those ways in which language can be turned in on itself, used reflexively. These concepts recur in the *Reader*. Many of them developed as major traditions of discourse analysis (reflected in the *Reader's* division into Parts). Exploring the poetic function of language, as much of this particular Jakobson reading does, is particularly stimulating for discourse analysis, for example Jakobson's suggestion that 'virtually any poetic message is a quasi-quoted discourse' (p. 53). Mikhail Bakhtin (Chapter 6) takes this idea even further, arguing that our speech is never fully 'our own'; it is also in one sense quotative in recycling the voices of others. The poetic function of language, as Jakobson points out, is not restricted to poetry alone. It surfaces whenever discourse achieves playfulness, self-awareness or creativity, and when we respond to language in these terms. For example, Deborah Tannen (Chapter 31) comments on the pleasure that people derive from sharing a conversational style (in this case, the ethnic style of New Yorkers of Jewish origin) as an emotional and aesthetic experience. The use of particular conversational features (such as fast tempo of speech, frequent asking of questions, reciprocal interruption, and so on) goes well beyond serving the referential function of language. These are recognised and 'safe' elements of the linguistic palette for the co-construction of an exhilarating performance. Likewise, Deborah Cameron (Chapter 29) demonstrates how five young men's informal talk, ranging between gossip about other men and verbal duelling, is full of imaginative and humorous, and sometimes offensive, language. Finally, as we are all aware, everyday, spontaneous narratives not only recount personal experiences and series of events but can be arresting forms of talk (Young, Chapter 28).

The same concern with communicative function dominates J.L. Austin's famous series of lectures, delivered at Harvard University in 1955, about 'How to do things with words' (Chapter 2). In this case, the backdrop is linguistic philosophy and his concern for a 'true' account of what utterances achieve. Austin's method, working with single instances of fabricated utterances, suggests little concern for social context. But his argument is precisely that the function of an utterance (e.g., making a promise or naming a ship) is partly constituted by the social circumstances in which it is uttered. He shows that utterances have to have 'felicitous' or well-suited conditions for their function to be fulfilled, and that utterance meaning lies in the interplay between social circumstances and utterances themselves.

There are some important questions for discourse analysis embedded in this reading. The question, 'Can saying make it so?' is one of them. This is the social constructionist stance (Cameron *et al.*, Chapter 8), developed in detail and with a much heavier theoretical loading in the ethnomethodological tradition (see our general Introduction), and in Critical Discourse Analysis (CDA) (Fairclough, Chapter 9; Van Dijk, Chapter 35). In fact, many major approaches to discourse work from the assumption that what we understand as social reality is, at least in part, produced through language and social interaction (for example, Edwards, Chapter 15, and Schegloff and Sacks, Chapter 16). The exploration of the nature of implied meaning is another central concern of Austin's text, and the distinction between the explicit and implicit functioning of utterances. This perspective again opens up a territory beyond mainstream linguistics, taken up, for example, in John Gumperz's sociolinguistic theory of conversational inferencing (Chapter 4). Another important early observation is Austin's insight that 'function' includes far more than what is achieved '*in* the act of uttering', but also what is achieved *through* utterances. As he writes, 'saying something will often, or even normally, produce certain consequential effects upon the feelings, thoughts or actions of the audience, or of the speaker, or of other persons: and it may be done with design, intention or purpose of producing them' (p. 61). Language is aligned to social action generally, and to communicative goals and strategies, and their social effects.

H.P. Grice's perspective on language and implied meaning, very much in the same philosophical tradition as Austin, was also first developed in a series of lectures at Harvard, this time in 1967. Grice takes many of the emphases we see in Austin's work as his own starting point – that discourse is driven by speakers fulfilling specific goals and purposes, that much of the significant meaning of talk is implicit and needing to be reconstructed by inference, and that talk is essentially a form of collaborative social action. Grice points to the specific importance of the medium of conversation as a resource for making sense of what speakers say. Certain expectations follow from being able to assume, for example, that conversation is a co-operative medium – not in the sense that people are always supportive or compliant but in that they jointly collaborate in the production of meanings and inferences. Talk is a matter of sharing in meaning-making procedures, the starting point for Conversation Analysis (CA) (e.g., Chapters 5, 16, 17, 18 and 36). Austin wanted 'to see talking as a special case or variety of purposive, indeed rational, behavior' (p. 69). His approach to discourse is, therefore, a focusing in on social action and on the conditions under which human communicators can mutually generate meanings and interpret them. Grice's maxims are an attempt to specify some of these conditions. They amount to regular assumptions that we can make about communicative intention which allow us to draw inferences about what people mean. A set of principles guides the way in which conversation takes place (see our general Introduction).

Not surprisingly, many of the chapters in this first Part of the *Reader* are attempts to generalise about 'normal' or 'unexceptional' discourse processes. Jakobson, Austin and Grice are mainly interested in detailing the character of talk between individuals in the most general terms. This reflects the fact that the earliest important contributions to discourse analysis needed to argue against the dominant traditions in linguistics, in linguistic semantics and in the philosophy of language.

They needed to make the case that context is theoretically central to the understanding of language in use. Initially, this took priority over more local studies of discourse in particular settings.

The work we have discussed so far originated, as we have pointed out, in different disciplines, but none of these functional approaches to discourse came to be recognised as an independent tradition of research. A more distinct tradition, which has been (and rightly continues to be) highly influential in all fields of discourse analysis, originated in the US in the 1960s as an off-shoot from sociology. It consolidated around the label *ethnomethodology* (see the general introduction pp. 16–18). Aaron Cicourel offered a definition of ethnomethodology as 'the study of interpretive procedures and surface rules in everyday social practices and scientific activities' (Cicourel 1973: 51). Ethnomethodologists opposed what they saw as the glib and uncritical assumptions made by academics, including social scientists, about how society is structured. They embarked on a radical critique of the *methods* of social and scientific enquiry, and of how specific practices and assumptions are 'naturalised' (made to seem natural or ordinary) and rendered invisible (see Cameron *et al.*, Chapter 8). Through a critique of language and discourse, ethnomethodology tried to show that social facts, and a sense of orderliness in social practices (including research), are generated within those practices themselves. Ethnomethodology is, therefore, the origin of radical social relativism (seeing truth as being relative to local practices, not absolute) and social constructionism (the social or discursive construction of reality), and its influence is still strongly apparent in many strands of discourse analysis, especially in CA and CDA.

John Gumperz explicitly acknowledges his debt to ethnomethodology before outlining his theory of conversational inferencing (Chapter 4), although he argues that in ethnomethodology 'only the pan-cultural aspects of conversational control mechanisms have been dealt with' (p. 79). Gumperz's main interests in discourse and conversation, represented in several major theoretical and empirical collections (see the general Introduction for references), have been specifically linked to cultural diversity and inter-ethnic communication. Chapter 4 gives a clear overview of his theoretical framework and examples of conversational moments when participants make social judgements about people and situations based on small details of linguistic or interactional style, or what he calls 'contextualization cues'. The political imperative in Gumperz's work is that, often, culturally influenced styles of talk, even if only in small details of pronunciation or intonation, can trigger prejudicial stereotypes and inferences about 'personality' or 'social type' or a speaker's 'intention'. In addition to the links between Gumperz's ideas and those of Erving Goffman and Dell Hymes (pointed out in our general Introduction), we should see this strand of discourse analysis as building on ethnomethodology's theorising of interpretive procedures, and building constructively on its critical insights.

Emanuel Schegloff's work is one of the true cornerstones of Conversation Analysis. His paper with Harvey Sacks on the structuring of conversation closings is reprinted as Chapter 18. We have chosen to include Schegloff's theoretical article on 'Talk and social structure' in this first Part of the *Reader* because it argues a controversial but challenging position on the link between language and context. There is wide agreement, in the other articles we have discussed so far, that meaning is located not so much in language itself as in the interaction between language used and the circumstances of use. This is a core claim of discourse analysis and one that Schegloff would not contest. But he is keen to identify the limits to what we can claim about the role of social context in specifying the meaning of talk. His arguments are largely about methods, and specifically about how, as discourse analysts and conversation analysts, we can infer meaning from our knowledge of context. We might have included this reading in Part Two for this reason, the Part on methods in discourse analysis. But Schegloff's arguments are fundamental to how we theorise discourse itself, or what conversation analysts prefer to call 'talk-in-interaction'.

Carrying forward a fundamental sociological line of inquiry, Schegloff does not deny that social structure – in the classical sociological sense of social ordering according to status or professional role or social situation – is relevant to inter-actants. He is arguing that there is a need to *demonstrate* the relevance and 'procedural consequentiality' of any potential social contextual classification to interactants at the moment of interaction. His position is the one we see in ethnomethodology, that social reality is only achieved in specific actors' occasioned (localised) orientations to it. Social reality is only what social actors see as relevant to their actions at any given point.

A contrary position, briefly considered in Part Two of the *Reader* by Cameron *et al.* (Chapter 8), is that this extreme relativism is untenable and altogether too destructive. Also, it is not entirely clear why there needs to be demonstrable evidence – and evidence in the flow of talk itself – of the relevance and consequentiality of the social categories, as Schegloff insists there must be. It is unlikely that inter-actants will often make clear which aspects of social context they are, in fact, 'orienting to' (where orientation will presumably include tacit cognitive processing of the sort usually called 'attending to', 'evaluating' and 'attributing significance to'). Nor is it clear what this evidence would look like. Schegloff's examples are specific patterns of turn-taking in, for instance, legal encounters, but 'evidence of relevance' could presumably include many other markers of selective attention or perceived salience. It is only a committedly empiricist and anti-cognitivist stance that would insist on behavioural (linguistic or non-verbal) marking of relevance. Interestingly enough, Schegloff mentions in a footnote to the Chapter 5 paper (which we have not included) that he and Harvey Sacks had resisted describing the conversational data that they use for their 'Opening up closings' paper, which we reproduce as Chapter 18, as 'contextually specific to American culture'.

In the rough historical time-ordering of Part One of the *Reader*, Mikhail Bakhtin's Chapter 6 on 'The problem of speech genres', written in the 1930s, is clearly out of sequence. We have placed it towards the end of this foundational part of the *Reader* because, in his unique way, Bakhtin manages to be highly contemporary. His work, whose origins and even precise authorship are still mysterious, is probably more widely cited now than at any previous time. The text tends to be repetitive, and we have edited it quite heavily. It is sometimes obscure, partly because of the difficulty in translating his terminology into English from Russian. For example, a key term such as 'utterances' seems to equate to all language use or discourse; 'the national language' sometimes appears to refer to the standard language code of a community, and at other times to any group-based variety of language. Bakhtin's arguments tend to be highly abstract, but they set an agenda for modern perspectives on discourse.

The view of all language as being organised into specific genres is a case in point. Bakhtin presents a highly dynamic view of speech genres, inter-penetrating and 're-accentuating' each other and being continually renewed as they are used. These claims are the basis for an *intertextual* perspective on discourse, seeing discourse as the recontextualising of already-existing forms and meanings, one text echoing and partially replaying the forms, meanings and values of another (what Bakhtin calls 'the organized chain of other utterances'). Bakhtin stresses the active role of the listener and the co-construction of meaning ('the listener becomes the speaker', p. 101), which is now a standard assumption about conversational practice. He is interested in the shifting boundary between the individual and the social structure, anticipating much recent research on selfhood and subjectivity (see Part Five). In a chapter where virtually every sentence is 'a quotable', Bakhtin's text invites us to reconsider what is new and what is actually of long-standing theoretical importance at the interface of language, society, ideology and selfhood.

The final chapter in this Part of the book orients to another rich tradition of work providing inspiration for contemporary discourse analysis. The French semi-otician Roland Barthes originated as a literary critic but, partly through the influence of such linguists as Ferdinand de Saussure and Roman Jakobson, came to focus on the study of *signification* in language and other semiotic systems: film, theatre, visual arts and popular culture more generally. In this sense, Barthes is an important precursor of multimodal discourse analysis (see Chapters 12, 13 and 26).

In Chapter 7, 'Myth Today', which we have left largely unedited here for copyright reasons, Barthes lays foundations for what many social theorists, including discourse analysts, have come to refer to as *ideology*. The concept of ideology refers to people's common assumptions, attitudes and beliefs about social life, which are often treated as stable and immutable, and which shape, maintain and reinforce group relations including patterns of power. Although their origins are purely social, these patterns of thought naturalise and universalise experience through discourse. Barthes specifically locates 'myth' at the metalinguistic level. Signs (e.g., words) are made up of signifiers (meaningful forms) and signifieds (things referred to). Signs are then appropriated into another level of 'second-order' signification, becoming signifiers for other signifieds. The distinction between first- and second-order signification can perhaps be illustrated with reference to another set of Barthes's concepts: *denotation* and *connotation*. Denotation is a level of meaning where a word, an image or another type of sign refers to something relatively concrete, while connotation is the associative or symbolic meaning of the sign – its ideology or its myth. In the chapter we have extracted from Barthes's

Mythologies (published originally in French in 1957), the key and rather famous example that Barthes uses to illustrate myth-formation is a photograph on a magazine cover of an African child-soldier saluting the French flag. The description we have just given is the first-order signification or denotative meaning of the picture. But it is intended, Barthes suggests, to build a sense of equality and loyalty among citizens of the French Empire (second-order signification, connotative meaning, myth, ideology).

Reference

Cicourel, A.V. (1973) *Cognitive Sociology: Language and Meaning in Social Interaction,* Harmondsworth: Penguin Education.

Chapter 1

Roman Jakobson

LINGUISTICS AND POETICS

. . .

L ANGUAGE MUST BE INVESTIGATED in all the variety of its functions. . . . An outline of these functions demands a concise survey of the constitutive factors in any speech event, in any act of verbal communication. The ADDRESSER sends a MESSAGE to the ADDRESSEE. To be operative the message requires a CONTEXT referred to, seizable by the addressee, and either verbal or capable of being verbalized; a CODE fully, or at least partially, common to the addresser and addressee (or in other words, to the encoder and decoder of the message); and, finally, a CONTACT, a physical channel and psychological connection between the addresser and the addressee, enabling both of them to enter and stay in communication. All these factors inalienably involved in verbal communication may be schematized as follows:

```
                         CONTEXT
                         MESSAGE
ADDRESSER ------------------------------------------------- ADDRESSEE
                         CONTACT
                          CODE
```

Each of these six factors determines a different function of language. Although we distinguish six basic aspects of language, we could, however, hardly find verbal messages that would fulfill only one function. The diversity lies not in a monopoly of some one of these several functions but in a different hierarchical order of functions. The verbal structure of a message depends primarily on the predominant

Source: Roman Jakobson, 'Closing statement: linguistics and poetics', in Thomas A. Sebook (ed.) *Style in Language*, Cambridge, Mass: the MIT Press, 1960: 350–77.

function. But even though a set (*Einstellung*) toward the referent, an orientation toward the CONTEXT — briefly the so-called REFERENTIAL, "denotative," "cognitive" function — is the leading task of numerous messages, the accessory participation of the other functions in such messages must be taken into account by the observant linguist.

The so-called EMOTIVE or "expressive" function, focused on the ADDRESSER, aims a direct expression of the speaker's attitude toward what he is speaking about. It tends to produce an impression of a certain emotion whether true or feigned; therefore, the term "emotive" . . . has proved to be preferable to "emotional." The purely emotive stratum of language is presented by the interjections. They differ from the means of referential language both by their sound pattern (peculiar sound sequences or even sounds elsewhere unusual) and by their syntactic role (they are not components but equivalents of sentences). "*Tut! Tut!* said McGinty*"*: the complete utterance of Conan Doyle's character consists of two suction clicks. The emotive function, laid bare in the interjections, flavors to some extent all our utterances, on their phonic, grammatical, and lexical level. If we analyze language from the standpoint of the information it carries, we cannot restrict the notion of information to the cognitive aspect of language. A man, using expressive features to indicate his angry or ironic attitude, conveys ostensible information, and evidently this verbal behavior cannot be likened to such nonsemiotic, nutritive activities as "eating grapefruit" . . . The difference between [big] and the emphatic prolongation of the vowel [bi:g] is a conventional, coded linguistic feature like the difference between the short and long vowel in such Czech pairs as [vi] 'you' and [vi:] 'knows,' but in the latter pair the differential information is phonemic and in the former emotive. As long as we are interested in phonemic invariants, the English /i/ and /i:/ appear to be mere variants of one and the same phoneme, but if we are concerned with emotive units, the relation between the invariant and variants is reversed: length and shortness are invariants implemented by variable phonemes. . . .

Orientation toward the ADDRESSEE, the CONATIVE function, finds its purest grammatical expression in the vocative and imperative, which syntactically, morphologically, and often even phonemically deviate from other nominal and verbal categories. Imperative sentences cardinally differ from declarative sentences: the latter are and the former are not liable to a truth test. When in O'Neill's play *The Fountain*, Nano, "(in a fierce tone of command)," says "Drink!" — the imperative cannot be challenged by the question "is it true or not?" which may be, however, perfectly well asked after such sentences as "one drank," "one will drink," "one would drink." In contradistinction to the imperative sentences, the declarative sentences are convertible into interrogative sentences: "did one drink?" "will one drink?" "would one drink?" "will one drink?" "would one drink?"

The traditional model of language as elucidated particularly by Bühler (1933) was confined to these three functions — emotive, conative, and referential — and the three apexes of this model — the first person of the addresser, the second person of the addressee, and the "third person," properly — someone or something spoken of. Certain additional verbal functions can be easily inferred from this triadic model. Thus the magic, incantatory function is chiefly some kind of conversion of an absent or inanimate "third person" into an addressee of a conative message. For example,

"May this sty dry up, *tfu, tfu, tfu, tfu*" (Lithuanian spell); "Water queen river, daybreak! Send grief beyond the blue sea, to the sea-bottom, like a grey stone never to rise from the sea-bottom, may grief never come to burden the light heart of God's servant, may grief be removed and sink away." (North Russian incantation); "Sun, stand thou still upon Gibeon; and thou, Moon, in the valley of Aj-a-lon. And the sun stood still, and the moon stayed . . ." (Josh. 10.12). We observe, however, three further constitutive factors of verbal communication and three corresponding functions of language.

There are messages primarily serving to establish, to prolong, or to discontinue communication, to check whether the channel works ("Hello, do you hear me?"), to attract the attention of the interlocutor or to confirm his continued attention ("Are you listening?" or in Shakespearean diction, "Lend me your ears!" – and on the other end of the wire "Um-hum!"). This set for CONTACT, or in Malinowski's terms PHATIC function (1953; Chapter 20) may be displayed by a profuse exchange of ritualized formulas, by entire dialogues with the mere purport of prolonging communication. Dorothy Parker caught eloquent examples: "'Well!' the young man said. 'Well!' she said. 'Well, here we are,' he said. 'Here we are,' she said, 'Aren't we?' 'I should say we were,' he said, 'Eeyop! Here we are.' 'Well!' she said. 'Well!' he said, 'well.'" The endeavor to start and sustain communication is typical of talking birds; thus the phatic function of language is the only one they share with human beings. It is also the first verbal function acquired by infants; they are prone to communicate before being able to send or receive informative communication.

A distinction has been made in modern logic between two levels of language, "object language" speaking of objects and "metalanguage" speaking of language. But metalanguage is not only a necessary scientific tool utilized by logicians and linguists; it plays also an important role in our everyday language. Like Molière's Jourdain who used prose without knowing it, we practice metalanguage without realizing the metalingual character of our operations. Whenever the addresser and/or the addressee need to check up whether they use the same code, speech is focused on the CODE: it performs a METALINGUAL (i.e., glossing) function. "I don't follow you – what do you mean?" asks the addressee, or in Shakespearean diction, "What is't thou say'st?" And the addresser in anticipation of such recapturing questions inquires: "Do you know what I mean?" Imagine such an exasperating dialogue: "The sophomore was plucked." "But what is *plucked*?" "*Plucked* means the same as *flunked*." "And *flunked*?" "To be *flunked* is to *fail in an exam*." "And what is *sophomore*?" persists the interrogator innocent of school vocabulary. "A *sophomore* is (or means) a *second-year student*." All these equational sentences convey information merely about the lexical code of English; their function is strictly metalingual. Any process of language learning, in particular child acquisition of the mother tongue, makes wide use of such metalingual operations; and aphasia may often be defined as a loss of ability for metalingual operations.

We have brought up all the six factors involved in verbal communication except the message itself. The set (*Einstellung*) toward the MESSAGE as such, focus on the message for its own sake, is the POETIC function of language. This function cannot be productively studied out of touch with the general problems of language, and, on the other hand, the scrutiny of language requires a thorough consideration of its poetic function. Any attempt to reduce the sphere of poetic function to poetry or to confine poetry to poetic function would be a delusive oversimplification. Poetic function is not the sole function of verbal art but only its dominant, deter-mining function, whereas in all other verbal activities it acts as a subsidiary, accessory constituent. This function, by promoting the palpability of signs, deepens the funda-mental dichotomy of signs and objects. Hence, when dealing with poetic function, linguistics cannot limit itself to the field of poetry.

"Why do you always say *Joan and Margery*, yet never *Margery and Joan*? Do you prefer Joan to her twin sister?" "Not at all, it just sounds smoother." In a sequence of two coordinate names, as far as no rank problems interfere, the precedence of the shorter name suits the speaker, unaccountably for him, as a well-ordered shape of the message.

A girl used to talk about "the horrible Harry." "Why horrible?" "Because I hate him." "But why not *dreadful, terrible, frightful, disgusting?*" "I don't know why, but *horrible* fits him better." Without realizing it, she clung to the poetic device of paronomasia.

The political slogan "I like Ike" /ay layk ayk/, succinctly structured, consists of three monosyllables and counts three diphthongs /ay/, each of them symmetrically followed by one consonantal phoneme, /..l..k..k/. The make-up of the three words presents a variation: no consonantal phonemes in the first word, two around the diphthong in the second, and one final consonant in the third. A similar domin-ant nucleus /ay/ was noticed by Hymes in some of the sonnets of Keats. Both cola of the trisyllabic formula "I like /Ike" rhyme with each other, and the second of the two rhyming words is fully included in the first one (echo rhyme), /layk/ − /ayk/, a paronomastic image of a feeling which totally envelops its object. Both cola alliterate with each other, and the first of the two alliterating words is included in the second: /ay/ − /ayk/, a paronomastic image of the loving subject enveloped by the beloved object. The secondary, poetic function of this electional catchphrase reinforces its impressiveness and efficacy.

As we said, the linguistic study of the poetic function must overstep the limits of poetry, and, on the other hand, the linguistic scrutiny of poetry cannot limit itself to the poetic function. The particularities of diverse poetic genres imply a differently ranked participation of the other verbal functions along with the dominant poetic function. Epic poetry, focused on the third, strongly involves the referential function of language; the lyric, oriented toward the first person, is intimately linked with the emotive function; poetry of the second person is imbued with the conative function and is either supplicatory or exhortative, depending on whether the first person is subordinated to the second one or the second to the first.

Now that our cursory description of the six basic functions of verbal communi-cation is more or less complete, we may complement our scheme of the fundamental factors by a corresponding scheme of the functions:

REFERENTIAL

EMOTIVE   POETIC
     PHATIC   CONATIVE

METALINGUAL

What is the empirical linguistic criterion of the poetic function? In particular, what is the indispensable feature inherent in any piece of poetry? To answer this question we must recall the two basic modes of arrangement used in verbal behavior, *selection* and *combination*. If "child" is the topic of the message, the speaker selects one among the extant, more or less similar, nouns like child, kid, youngster, tot, all of them equivalent in a certain respect, and then, to comment on this topic, he may select one of the semantically cognate verbs – sleeps, dozes, nods, naps. Both chosen words combine in the speech chain. The selection is produced on the base of equivalence, similarity and dissimilarity, synonymity and antonymity, while the combination, the build up of the sequence, is based on contiguity. *The poetic function projects the principle of equivalence from the axis of selection into the axis of combination.* Equivalence is promoted to the constitutive device of the sequence. In poetry one syllable is equalized with any other syllable of the same sequence; word stress is assumed to equal word stress, as unstress equals unstress; prosodic long is matched with long, and short with short; word boundary equals word boundary, no boundary equals no boundary; syntactic pause equals syntactic pause, no pause equals no pause. Syllables are converted into units of measure, and so are morae or stresses.

. . .

In poetry, and to a certain extent in latent manifestations of poetic function, sequences delimited by word boundaries become commensurable whether they are sensed as isochronic or graded. "Joan and Margery" showed us the poetic principle of syllable gradation, the same principle which in the closes of Serbian folk epics has been raised to a compulsory law. Without its two dactylic words the combination "*innocent by*stand*er*" would hardly have become a hackneyed phrase. The symmetry of three disyllabic verbs with an identical initial consonant and identical final vowel added splendor to the laconic victory message of Caesar: "*Veni, vidi, vici.*"

Measure of sequences is a device which, outside of poetic function, finds no application in language. Only in poetry with its regular reiteration of equivalent units is the time of the speech flow experienced, as it is – to cite another semiotic pattern – with musical time. Gerard Manley Hopkins, an outstanding researcher in the science of poetic language, defined verse as "speech wholly or partially repeating the same figure of sound" (1959). Hopkins's subsequent question, "but is all verse poetry?" can be definitely answered as soon as poetic function ceases to be arbitrarily confined to the domain of poetry. Mnemonic lines cited by Hopkins (like "Thirty days hath September"), modern advertising jingles, and versified medieval laws, mentioned by Lotz, or finally Sanscrit scientific treatises in verse which in Indic tradition are strictly distinguished from true poetry (*kāvya*) – all these metrical texts make use of poetic function without, however, assigning to this function the coercing, determining role it carries in poetry. Thus verse actually exceeds the limits of poetry, but at the same time verse always implies poetic function. And apparently no human culture ignores verse-making, whereas there are many cultural patterns without "applied" verse; and even in such cultures which possess both pure and applied verses, the latter appear to be a secondary, unquestionably derived phenomenon. The adaptation of poetic means for some heterogeneous purpose does not conceal their primary essence, just as elements of emotive language, when utilized in poetry, still maintain their emotive tinge. A filibusterer may recite *Hiawatha* because it is long, yet poeticalness still remains the primary intent of this text itself. Self-evidently, the existence of versified, musical, and pictorial commercials does not separate the questions of verse or of musical and pictorial form from the study of poetry, music, and fine arts.

To sum up, the analysis of verse is entirely within the competence of poetics, and the latter may be defined as that part of linguistics which treats the poetic function in its relationship to the other functions of language. Poetics in the wider sense of the word deals with the poetic function not only in poetry, where this function is superimposed upon the other functions of language, but also outside of poetry, when some other function is superimposed upon the poetic function.

. . .

Ambiguity is an intrinsic, inalienable character of any self-focused message, briefly a corollary feature of poetry. Let us repeat with Empson (1955): "The machinations of ambiguity are among the very roots of poetry." Not only the message itself but also its addresser and addressee become ambiguous. Besides the author and the reader, there is the "I" of the lyrical hero or of the fictitious storyteller and the "you" or "thou" of the alleged addressee of dramatic monologues, supplications, and epistles. For instance the poem "Wrestling Jacob" is addressed by its title hero to the Saviour and simultaneously acts as a subjective message of the poet Charles Wesley to his readers. Virtually any poetic message is a quasi-quoted discourse with all those peculiar, intricate problems which "speech within speech" offers to the linguist.

The supremacy of poetic function over referential function does not obliterate the reference but makes it ambiguous. The double-sensed message finds correspondence in a split addresser, in a split addressee, and besides in a split reference, as it is cogently exposed in the preambles to fairy tales of various peoples, for instance, in the usual exordium of the Majorca storytellers: "Aixo era y no era" (It was and it was not). The repetitiveness effected by imparting the equivalence principle to the sequence makes reiterable not only the constituent sequences of the poetic message but the whole message as well. This capacity for reiteration whether immediate or delayed, this reification of a poetic message and its constituents, this conversion of a message into an enduring thing, indeed all this represents an inherent and effective property of poetry.

. . .

In poetry the internal form of a name, that is, the semantic load of its constituents, regains its pertinence. The "Cocktails" may resume their obliterated kinship with plumage. Their colors are vivified in Mac Hammond's lines "The ghost of a Bronx pink lady // With orange blossoms afloat in her hair," and the etymological metaphor attains its realization: "O, Bloody Mary, // The cocktails have crowded not the cocks!" ("At an Old Fashion Bar in Manhattan"). Wallace Stevens's poem "An Ordinary Evening in New Haven" revives the head word of the city name first through a discreet allusion to heaven and then through a direct pun-like confrontation similar to Hopkins's "Heaven-Haven."

The dry eucalyptus *seeks god in the rainy cloud.*
Professor Eucalyptus of New Haven *seeks him in New Haven* . . .
The instinct *for heaven* had its counterpart:
The instinct for earth, *for New Haven*, for his room . . .

The adjective "New" of the city name is laid bare through the concatenation of opposites:

The oldest-newest day is the newest alone.
The oldest-newest night does not creak by . . .

When in 1919 the Moscow Linguistic Circle discussed how to define and delimit the range of *epitheta ornantia*, the poet Majakovskij rebuked us by saying that for him any adjective while in poetry was thereby a poetic epithet, even "great" in the *Great Bear* or "big" and "little" in such names of Moscow streets as *Bol'shaja Presnja* and *Malaja Presnja*. In other words, poeticalness is not a supplementation of discourse with rhetorical adornment but a total re-evaluation of the discourse and of all its components whatsoever.

A missionary blamed his African flock for walking undressed. "And what about yourself?" they pointed to his visage, "are not you, too, somewhere naked?" "Well, but that is my face." "Yet in us," retorted the natives, "everywhere it is face." So in poetry any verbal element is converted into a figure of poetic speech.

My attempt to vindicate the right and duty of linguistics to direct the investigation of verbal art in all its compass and extent can come to a conclusion with the same burden which summarized my report to the 1953 conference at Indiana University: "Linguista sum; linguistici nihil a me alienum puto." If the poet Ransom is right (and he is right) that "poetry is a kind of language," the linguist whose field is any kind of language may and must include poetry in his study. . . .

References

Bühler, K. (1933) "Die Axiomatik der Sprachwissenschaft," *Kant-Studien* 38: 19–90.
Empson, W. (1955) *Seven Types of Ambiguity*, New York: Chatto & Windus, 3rd edition.
Hopkins, G.M. (1959) *The Journals and Papers*, H. House (ed.), London: Oxford University Press.
Malinowski, B. (1953) "The problem of meaning in primitive languages," in C.K. Ogden and I.A. Richards, *The Meaning of Meaning*, 9th edition, New York and London: Routledge & Kegan Paul, 296–336. [See also Chapter 20 of this *Reader*.]

Chapter 2

J.L. Austin

HOW TO DO THINGS WITH WORDS

WHAT I SHALL HAVE to say here is neither difficult nor contentious; the only merit I should like to claim for it is that of being true, at least in parts. The phenomenon to be discussed is very widespread and obvious, and it cannot fail to have been already noticed, at least here and there, by others. Yet I have not found attention paid to it specifically.

It was for too long the assumption of philosophers that the business of a 'statement' can only be to 'describe' some state of affairs, or to 'state some fact', which it must do either truly or falsely. Grammarians, indeed, have regularly pointed out that not all 'sentences' are (used in making) statements:[1] there are, traditionally, besides (grammarians') statements, also questions and exclamations, and sentences expressing commands or wishes or concessions. And doubtless philosophers have not intended to deny this, despite some loose use of 'sentence' for 'statement'. Doubtless, too, both grammarians and philosophers have been aware that it is by no means easy to distinguish even questions, commands, and so on from statements by means of the few and jejune grammatical marks available, such as word order, mood, and the like: though perhaps it has not been usual to dwell on the difficulties which this fact obviously raises. For how do we decide which is which? What are the limits and definitions of each?

But now in recent years, many things which would once have been accepted without question as 'statements' by both philosophers and grammarians have been scrutinized with new care. . . . It has come to be commonly held that many utterances which look like statements are either not intended at all, or only intended in part, to record or impart straightforward information about the facts: for example, 'ethical propositions' are perhaps intended, solely or partly, to evince emotion or to prescribe conduct or to influence it in special ways. . . . We very often also use utterances in ways beyond the scope at least of traditional grammar.

Source: J.L. Austin, *How to do Things with Words*, Oxford: Oxford University Press, 1962.

It has come to be seen that many specially perplexing words embedded in apparently descriptive statements do not serve to indicate some specially odd additional feature in the reality reported, but to indicate (not to report) the circumstances in which the statement is made or reservations to which it is subject or the way in which it is to be taken and the like. To overlook these possibilities in the way once common is called the 'descriptive' fallacy; but perhaps this is not a good name, as 'descriptive' itself is special. Not all true or false statements are descriptions, and for this reason I prefer to use the word 'Constative' . . .

   Utterances can be found . . . such that:

A   they do not 'describe' or 'report' or constate anything at all, are not 'true or false'; and

B   the uttering of the sentence is, or is a part of, the doing of an action, which again would not *normally* be described as, or as 'just', saying something . . .

. . .

Examples:

(a)   'I do (sc. take this woman to be my lawful wedded wife)' – as uttered in the course of the marriage ceremony.

(b)   'I name this ship the *Queen Elizabeth*' – as uttered when smashing the bottle against the stern.

(c)   'I give and bequeath my watch to my brother' – as occurring in a will.

(d)   'I bet you sixpence it will rain tomorrow.'

   In these examples it seems clear that to utter the sentence (in, of course, the appropriate circumstances) is not to *describe* my doing of what I should be said in so uttering to be doing or to state that I am doing it: it is to do it. None of the utterances cited is either true or false: I assert this as obvious and do not argue it. It needs argument no more than that 'damn' is not true or false: it may be that the utterance 'serves to inform you' – but that is quite different. To name the ship *is* to say (in the appropriate circumstances) the words 'I name, etc.'. When I say, before the registrar or altar, 'I do', I am not reporting on a marriage: I am indulging in it.

   What are we to call a sentence or an utterance of this type? I propose to call it a *performative sentence* or a performative utterance, or, for short, 'a performative'. The term 'performative' will be used in a variety of cognate ways and constructions, much as the term 'imperative' is. The name is derived, of course, from 'perform', the usual verb with the noun 'action': it indicates that the issuing of the utterance is the performing of an action – it is not normally thought of as just saying something.

. . .

Are we then to say things like this:

'To marry is to say a few words', or
'Betting is simply saying something'?

Such a doctrine sounds odd or even flippant at first, but with sufficient safeguards it may become not odd at all.

. . .

The uttering of the words is, indeed, usually a, or even *the*, leading incident in the performance of the act (of betting or what not), the performance of which is also the object of the utterance, but it is far from being usually, even if it is ever, the *sole* thing necessary if the act is to be deemed to have been performed. Speaking generally, it is always necessary that the *circumstances* in which the words are uttered should be in some way, or ways, *appropriate*, and it is very commonly necessary that either the speaker himself or other persons should *also* perform certain *other* actions, whether 'physical' or 'mental' actions or even acts of uttering further words. Thus, for naming the ship, it is essential that I should be the person appointed to name her; for (Christian) marrying, it is essential that I should not be already married with a wife living, sane and undivorced, and so on; for a bet to have been made, it is generally necessary for the offer of the bet to have been accepted by a taker (who must have done something, such as to say 'Done'); and it is hardly a gift if I *say* 'I give it you' but never hand it over. . . .

But we may, in objecting, have something totally different, and this time quite mistaken, in mind, especially when we think of some of the more awe-inspiring performatives such as 'I promise to . . .'. Surely the words must be spoken 'seriously' and so as to be taken 'seriously'? This is, though vague, true enough in general – it is an important commonplace in discussing the purport of any utterance whatsoever. I must not be joking, for example, nor writing a poem. . . .

Well we shall next consider what we actually do say about the utterance concerned when one or another of its normal concomitants is *absent*. In no case do we say that the utterance was false but rather that the utterance – or rather the *act*, e.g., the promise – was void, or given in bad faith, or not implemented, or the like. In the particular case of promising, as with many other performatives, it is appropriate that the person uttering the promise should have a certain intention, viz. here to keep his word: and perhaps of all concomitants this looks the most suitable to be that which 'I promise' does describe or record. Do we not actually, when such intention is absent, speak of a 'false' promise? Yet so to speak is *not* to say that the utterance 'I promise that . . .' is false, in the sense that though he states that he does he doesn't, or that though he describes he misdescribes – misreports. For he *does* promise: the promise here is not even *void*, though it is given *in bad faith*. His utterance is perhaps misleading, probably deceitful and doubtless wrong, but it is not a lie or a misstatement. At most we might make out a case for saying that it implies or insinuates a falsehood or a misstatement (to the effect that he does intend to do something): but that is a very different matter. Moreover, we do not speak of a false bet or a false christening; and that we *do* speak of a false promise need commit us no more than the fact that we speak of a false move. 'False' is not necessarily used of statements only.

. . .

Besides the uttering of the words of so-called performative, a good many other things have as a general rule to be right and to go right if we are to be said to have happily brought off our action. What these are we may hope to discover by looking at and classifying types of case in which something *goes wrong* and the act – marrying, betting, bequeathing, christening, or what not – is therefore at least to some extent a failure: the utterance is then, we may say, not indeed false but in general *unhappy*. And for this reason we call the doctrine of *the things that can be and go wrong* on the occasion of such utterances, the doctrine of the *Infelicities*.

Suppose we try first to state schematically – and I do not wish to claim any sort of finality for this scheme – some at least of the things which are necessary for the smooth or 'happy' functioning of a performative (or at least of a highly developed explicit performative, such as we have hitherto been alone concerned with), and then give examples of infelicities and their effects. . . .

A.1 There must exist an accepted conventional procedure having a certain conventional effect, that procedure to include the uttering of certain words by certain persons in certain circumstances, and further,

A.2 the particular persons and circumstances in a given case must be appropriate for the invocation of the particular procedure invoked.

B.1 The procedure must be executed by all participants both correctly and

B.2 completely.

C.1 Where, as often, the procedure is designed for use by persons having certain thoughts or feelings, or for the inauguration of certain consequential conduct on the part of any participant, then a person participating in and so invoking the procedure must in fact have those thoughts or feelings, and the participants must intend so to conduct themselves, and further

C.2 must actually so conduct themselves subsequently.

Now if we sin against any one (or more) of these six rules, our performative utterance will be (in one way or another) unhappy. But, of course, there are considerable differences between these 'ways' of being unhappy – ways which are intended to be brought out by the letter–numerals selected for each heading.

The first big distinction is between all the four rules A and B taken together, as opposed to the two rules C . . . . If we offend against any of the former rules (As or Bs) – that is, if we, say, utter the formula incorrectly, or if, say, we are not in a position to do the act because we are, say, married already, or it is the purser and not the captain who is conducting the ceremony, then the act in question, e.g., marrying, is not successfully performed at all, does not come off, is not achieved. Whereas in the two C cases the act *is* achieved, although to achieve it in such circumstances, as when we are, say, insincere, is an abuse of the procedure. Thus, when I say 'I promise' and have no intention of keeping it, I have promised but. . . . We need names for referring to this general distinction, so we shall call in general those infelicities A.1–B.2 which are such that the act for the performing of which, and in the performing of which, the verbal formula in question is designed, is not achieved, by the name MISFIRES: and on the other hand we may christen those infelicities where the act *is* achieved ABUSES. . . . When the utterance is a misfire, the procedure which we purport to invoke is disallowed or is botched: and our act (marrying, etc.) is void or without effect, etc. We speak of our act as a purported act, or perhaps an attempt – or we use such an expression as 'went through a form of marriage' by contrast with 'married'. On the other hand, in the C cases, we speak of our infelicitous act as 'professed' or 'hollow' rather than 'purported' or 'empty', and as not implemented, or not consummated, rather than as void or without effect. But let me hasten to add that these distinctions are not hard and fast, and more especially that such words as 'purported' and 'professed' will not bear very much stressing. Two final words about being void or without effect. This does not mean, of course, to say that we won't have done anything: lots of things will have been done – we shall most interestingly have committed the act of bigamy – but we shall *not* have done the purported act, viz. marrying. Because despite the name, you do not when bigamous marry twice. . . . Further, 'without effect' does not here mean 'without consequences, results, effects'.

. . .

The performative utterances I have taken as examples are all of them highly developed affairs, of the kind that we shall call *explicit* performatives, by contrast with merely *implicit* performatives. That is to say, they (all) begin with or include some highly significant and unambiguous expression such as 'I bet', 'I promise', 'I bequeath' – an expression very commonly also used in naming the act which, in making such an utterance, I am performing – for example betting, promising, bequeathing, etc. But, of course, it is both obvious and important that we can on occasion use the utterance 'go' to achieve practically the same as we achieve by the utterance 'I order you to go': and we should say cheerfully in either case, describing subsequently what someone did, that he ordered me to go. It may, however, be uncertain in fact, and, so far as the mere utterance is concerned, is always left uncertain when we use so inexplicit a formula as the mere imperative 'go', whether the utterer is ordering (or is purporting to order) me to go or merely advising, entreating, or what not me to go. Similarly 'There is a bull in the field' may or may not be a warning, for I *might* just be describing the scenery, and 'I shall be there' may or may not be a promise. Here we have primitive as distinct from explicit performatives; and there may be nothing in the circumstances by which we can decide whether or not the utterance is performative at all. Anyway, in a given situation it can be open to me to take it as *either* one or the other. It was a performative formula – *perhaps* – but the procedure in question was not sufficiently explicitly invoked. Perhaps I did not *take it as* an order or was not anyway *bound* to take it as an order. The person did not *take it as* a promise: i.e., in the particular circumstance he did not accept the procedure, on the ground that the ritual was incompletely carried out by the original speaker.

. . .

We shall next consider three of the many ways in which a statement implies the truth of certain other statements. One of those that I shall mention has been long known. The others have been discovered quite recently. We shall not put the matter too technically, though this can be done. I refer to the discovery that the ways we can do wrong, speak outrageously, in uttering conjunctions of 'factual' statements, are more numerous than merely by contradiction . . .

1   *Entails*: 'All men blush' entails 'some men blush'. We cannot say 'All men blush but not any men blush', or 'the cat is under the mat and the cat is on top of the mat' or 'the cat is on the mat and the cat is not on the mat', since in each case the first clause entails the contradictory of the second.

2   *Implies*: My saying 'the cat is on the mat' implies that I believe it is . . . We cannot say 'the cat is on the mat but I do not believe it is'. (This is actually not the ordinary use of 'implies': 'implies' is really weaker: as when we say 'He implied that I did not know it' or 'You implied you knew it' (as distinct from believing it.)

3   *Presupposes*: 'All Jack's children are bald' presupposes that Jack has some children. We cannot say 'All Jack's children are bald but Jack has no children', or 'Jack has no children and all his children are bald'.

There is a common feeling of outrage in all these cases. But we must not use some blanket term, 'implies' or 'contradiction', because there are very great differences. There are more ways of killing a cat than drowning it in butter; but this is the sort of thing (as the proverb indicates) we overlook: there are more ways of outraging speech than contradiction merely . . .

The act of 'saying something' in the full normal sense I call, i.e., dub, the performance of a locutionary act, and the study of utterances thus far and in these respects the study of locutions, or of the full units of speech. Our interest in the locutionary act is, of course, principally to make quite plain what it is, in order to distinguish it from other acts with which we are primarily concerned . . .

To perform a locutionary act is in general, we may say, also and *eo ipso* to perform an *illocutionary* act, as I propose to call it. Thus in performing a locutionary act we shall also be performing such an act as:

asking or answering a question;
giving some information or an assurance or a warning;
announcing a verdict or an intention;
pronouncing sentence;
making an appointment or an appeal or a criticism;
making an identification or giving a description;

and the numerous like. (I am not suggesting that this is a clearly defined class by any means.) . . . When we perform a locutionary act, we use speech: but in what way precisely are we using it on this occasion? For there are very numerous functions of or ways in which we use speech and it makes a great difference to our act in some sense – in which way and which *sense* we were on this occasion 'using' it. It makes a great difference whether we were advising, or merely suggesting, or actually ordering, whether we were strictly promising or only announcing a vague intention, and so forth. These issues penetrate a little but not without confusion into grammar, but we constantly do debate them, in such terms as whether certain words (a certain locution) *had the force of* a question, or *ought to have been taken as* an estimate and so on.

I explained the performance of an act in this new and second sense as the performance of an 'illocutionary' act, i.e. performance of an act *in* saying something as opposed to performance of an act *of* saying something; I call the act performed an 'illocution' and shall refer to the doctrine of the different types of function of language here in question as the doctrine of 'illocutionary forces'.

. . .

There is yet a further sense in which to perform a locutionary act, and therein an illocutionary act, may also be to perform an act of another kind. Saying something will often, or even normally, produce certain consequential effects upon the feelings, thoughts, or actions of the audience, or of the speaker, or of other persons: and it may be done with the design, intention or purpose of producing them; and we may then say, thinking of this, that the speaker has performed an act in the nomenclature of which reference is made either (a), only obliquely, or even (b), not at all, to the performance of the locutionary or illocutionary act. We shall call the performance of an act of this kind the performance of a 'perlocutionary' act, and the act performed, where suitable – essentially in cases falling under (a) – a 'perlocution' . . .

Acts of all our three kinds [locutionary, illocutionary and perlocutionary] necessitate, since they are the performing of actions, allowance being made for the ills that all action is heir to. We must systematically be prepared to distinguish between 'the act of doing *x*', i.e., achieving *x*, and 'the act of attempting to do *x*'.

In the case of illocutions we must be ready to draw the necessary distinction, not noticed by ordinary language except in exceptional cases, between:

(a)   the act of attempting or purporting (or affecting or professing or claiming or setting up or setting out) to perform a certain illocutionary act, and
(b)   the act of successfully achieving or consummating or bringing off such an act.

This distinction is, or should be, a commonplace of the theory of our language about 'action' in general. But attention has been drawn earlier to its special importance in connexion with performatives: it is always possible, for example, to try to thank or inform somebody yet in different ways to fail, because he doesn't listen, or takes it as ironical, or wasn't responsible for whatever it was, and so on. This distinction will arise, as over any act, over locutionary acts too; but failures here will not be unhappiness as there, but rather failures to get the words out, to express ourselves clearly, etc.

Since our acts are actions, we must always remember the distinction between producing effects or consequences which are intended or unintended; and (i) when the speaker intends to produce an effect it may nevertheless not occur, and (ii) when he does not intend to produce it or intends not to produce it it may nevertheless occur. To cope with complication (i) we invoke as before the distinction between attempt and achievement; to cope with complication (ii) we invoke the normal linguistic devices of disclaiming (adverbs like 'unintentionally' and so on) which we hold ready for general use in all cases of doing actions.

. . .

The perlocutionary act may be either the achievement of a perlocutionary object (convince, persuade) or the production of a perlocutionary sequel. Thus the act of warning may achieve its perlocutionary object of alerting and also have the perlocutionary sequel of alarming, and an argument against a view may fail to achieve its object but have the perlocutionary sequel of convincing our opponent of its truth ('I only succeeded in convincing him'). What is the perlocutionary object of one illocution may be the sequel of another. For example, warning may produce the sequel of deterring and saying 'Don't', whose object is to deter, may produce the sequel of alerting or even alarming. Some perlocutionary acts are always the producing of a sequel, namely those where there is no illocutionary formula: thus I may surprise you or upset you or humiliate you by a locution, though there is no illocutionary formula 'I surprise you by . . .', 'I upset you by . . .', 'I humiliate you by . . .'

It is characteristic of perlocutionary acts that the response achieved, or the sequel, can be achieved additionally or entirely by non-locutionary means: thus intimidation may be achieved by waving a stick or pointing a gun. Even in the cases of convincing, persuading, getting to obey and getting to believe, we may achieve the response non-verbally; but if there is no illocutionary act, it is doubtful whether this language characteristic of perlocutionary objects should be used. Compare the use of 'got him to' with that of 'got him to obey'. However, this alone is not enough to distinguish illocutionary acts, since we can for example warn or order or appoint or give or protest or apologize by non-verbal means and these are illocutionary acts. Thus we may cock a snook or hurl a tomato by way of protest.

. . .

When we originally contrasted the performative with the constative utterance we said that

1   the performative should be doing something as opposed to just saying something; and
2   the performative is happy or unhappy as opposed to true or false.

Were these distinctions really sound? Our subsequent discussion of doing and saying certainly seems to point to the conclusion that whenever I 'say' anything (except perhaps a mere exclamation like 'damn' or 'ouch') I shall be performing both locutionary and illocutionary acts, and these two kinds of acts seem to be the very things which we tried to use, under the names of 'doing' and 'saying', as a means of distinguishing performatives from constatives. If we are in general always doing both things, how can our distinction survive?

Let us first reconsider the contrast from the side of constative utterances: of these, we were content to refer to 'statements' as the typical or paradigm case. Would it be correct to say that when we state something

1   we are doing something as well as and distinct from just saying something, and
2   our utterance is liable to be happy or unhappy (as well as, if you will, true or false)?

Surely to state is every bit as much to perform an illocutionary act as, say, to want or to pronounce. Of course it is not to perform an act in some specially physically way, other than in so far as it involves, when verbal, the making of movements of vocal organs; but then nor, as we have seen, is to warn, to protest, to promise or to name. 'Stating' seems to meet all the criteria we had for distinguishing the illocutionary act. Consider such an unexceptionable remark as the following:

In saying that it was raining, I was not betting or arguing or warning:
I was simply stating it as a fact.

Here 'stating' is put absolutely on a level with arguing, betting, and warning. . . .
Moreover, although the utterance 'He did not do it' is often issued as a statement, and is then undoubtedly true or false (*this* is if anything is), it does not seem possible to say that it differs from 'I state that he did not do it' in this respect. If someone says 'I state that he did not do it', we investigate the truth of his statement in just the same way as if he had said 'He did not do it' . . .
Moreover, if we think of the alleged contrast, according to which performatives are happy or unhappy and statements true or false, again from the side of supposed constative utterances, notably statements, we find that statements *are* liable to every kind of infelicity to which performatives are liable. Let us look back again and consider whether statements are not liable to precisely the same disabilities as, say, warnings by way of what we called 'infelicities' – that is various disabilities which make an utterance unhappy without, however, making it true or false.
We have already noted that sense in which saying, as equivalent to stating, 'The cat is on the mat' implies that I believe that the cat is on the mat. This is parallel to the sense – is the same sense – as that in which 'I promise to be there' implies that I intend to be there and that I believe I shall be able to be there. So the statement is liable to the *insincerity* form of infelicity; and even to the *breach* form of infelicity in this sense, that saying or stating that the cat is on the mat commits me to saying or stating 'The mat is underneath the cat' just as much as the performative 'I define X as Y' (in the *fiat* sense, say) commits me to using those terms in special ways in future discourse, and we can see how this is connected with such acts as promising. This means that statements can give rise to infelicities of our two C kinds.
Now what about infelicities of the A and B kinds, which rendered the act – warning, undertaking, etc. – null and void? Can a thing that looks like a

statement be null and void just as much as a putative contract? The answer seems to be Yes, importantly. The first cases are A.1 and A.2, where there is no convention (or not an accepted convention) or where the circumstances are not appropriate for its invocation by the speaker. Many infelicities of just this type do infect statements.

We have already noticed the case of a putative statement *presupposing* (as it is called) the existence of that which it refers to; if no such thing exists, 'the statement' is not about anything. Now some say that in these circumstances, if, for example, someone asserts that the present King of France is bald, 'the question whether he is bald does not arise'; but it is better to say that the putative statement is null and void, exactly as when I say that I sell you something but it is not mine or (having been burnt) is not any longer in existence. Contracts often are void because the objects they are about do not exist, which involves a breakdown of reference.

But it is important to notice also that 'statements' too are liable to infelicity of this kind in other ways also parallel to contracts, promises, warnings, etc. Just as we often say, for example, 'You cannot order me', in the sense 'You have not the right to order me', which is equivalent to saying that you are not in the appropriate position to do so: so often there are things you cannot state – have no right to state – are not in a position to state. You *cannot* now state how many people there are in the next room; if you say 'There are fifty people in the next room', I can only regard you as guessing or conjecturing (just as sometimes you are not ordering me, which would be inconceivable, but possibly asking me to rather impolitely, so here you are 'hazarding a guess' rather oddly). Here there is something you might, in other circumstances, be in a position to state; but what about statements about other persons' feelings or about the future? Is a forecast or even a prediction about, say, persons' behaviour really a statement? It is important to take the speech-situation as a whole.

. . .

Once we realize that what we have to study is *not* the sentence but the issuing of an utterance in a speech situation, there can hardly be any longer a possibility of not seeing that stating is performing an act . . .

What then finally is left of the distinction of the performative and constative utterance? Really we may say that what we had in mind here was this:

(a)   With the constative utterance, we abstract from the illocutionary (let alone the perlocutionary) aspects of the speech act, and we concentrate on the locutionary: moreover, we use an oversimplified notion of correspondence with the facts – oversimplified because essentially it brings in the illocutionary aspect. This is the ideal of what would be right to say in all circumstances, for any purpose, to any audience, etc. Perhaps it is sometimes realized.

(b)   With the performative utterance, we attend as much as possible to the illocutionary force of the utterance, and abstract from the dimension of correspondence with facts.

Perhaps neither of these abstractions is so very expedient: perhaps we have here not really two poles, but rather a historical development. Now in certain cases, perhaps with mathematical formulas in physics books as examples of constatives, or with the issuing of simple executive orders or the giving of simple names, say, as examples of performatives, we approximate in real life to finding such things. It was examples of this kind, like 'I apologize', and 'The cat is on the mat', said for no conceivable reason, extreme marginal cases, that gave rise to the idea of two distinct utterances. But the real conclusion must surely be that we need (1) to distinguish between locutionary and illocutionary acts, and (2) specially and critically to establish with respect to each kind of illocutionary act – warnings, estimates, verdicts, statements, and descriptions – what if any is the specific way in which they are intended, first to be in order or not in order, and second, to be 'right' or 'wrong'; what terms of appraisal and disappraisal are used for each and what they mean. This is a wide field and certainly will not lead to a simple distinction of 'true' and 'false'; nor will it lead to a distinction of statements from the rest, for stating is only one among very numerous speech acts of the illocutionary class.

Furthermore, in general the locutionary act as much as the illocutionary is an abstraction only: every genuine speech act is both.

. . .

Note

1   It is, of course, not really correct that a sentence ever *is* a statement: rather, it is *used* in *making a statement*, and the statement itself is a 'logical construction' out of the makings of statements.

Chapter 3

H.P. Grice

LOGIC AND CONVERSATION

. . .

SUPPOSE THAT A AND B are talking about a mutual friend, C, who is now working in a bank. A asks B how C is getting on in his job, and B replies, *Oh quite well, I think; he likes his colleagues, and he hasn't been to prison yet*. At this point, A might well inquire what B was implying, what he was suggesting, or even what he meant by saying that C had not yet been to prison. The answer might be any one of such things as that C is the sort of person likely to yield to the temptation provided by his occupation, that C's colleagues are really very unpleasant and treacherous people, and so forth. It might, of course, be quite unnecessary for A to make such an inquiry of B, the answer to it being, in the context, clear in advance. I think it is clear that whatever B implied, suggested, meant, etc., in this example, is distinct from what B said, which was simply that C had not been to prison yet. I wish to introduce, as terms of art, the verb *implicate* and the related nouns *implicature* (cf. *implying*) and *implicatum* (cf. *what is implied*). The point of this maneuver is to avoid having, on each occasion, to choose between this or that member of the family of verbs for which *implicate* is to do general duty. I shall, for the time being at least, have to assume to a considerable extent an intuitive understanding of the meaning of *say* in such contexts, and an ability to recognize particular verbs as members of the family with which *implicate* is associated. I can, however, make one or two remarks that may help to clarify the more problematic of these assumptions, namely, that connected with the meaning of the word *say*.

In the sense in which I am using the word *say*, I intend what someone has said to be closely related to the conventional meaning of the words (the sentence) he has uttered. Suppose someone to have uttered the sentence *He is in the grip of a*

Source: H.P. Grice, 'Logic and conversation', in Peter Cole and Jerry L. Morgan (eds) *Syntax and Semantics*, Volume 3: *Speech Arts*, New York: Academic Press, 1975, 41–58.

vice. Given a knowledge of the English language, but no knowledge of the circumstances of the utterance, one would know something about what the speaker had said, on the assumption that he was speaking standard English, and speaking literally. One would know that he had said, about some particular male person or animal *x*, that at the time of the utterance (whatever that was), either (1) *x* was unable to rid himself of a certain kind of bad character trait or (2) some part of *x*'s person was caught in a certain kind of tool or instrument (approximate account, of course). But for a full identification of what the speaker had said, one would need to know (a) the identity of *x*, (b) the time of utterance, and (c) the meaning, on the particular occasion of utterance, of the phrase *in the grip of a vice* (a decision between (1) and (2)). This brief indication of my use of *say* leaves it open whether a man who says (today) *Harold Wilson is a great man* and another who says (also today) *The British Prime Minister is a great man* would, if each knew that the two singular terms had the same reference, have said the same thing. But whatever decision is made about this question, the apparatus that I am about to provide will be capable of accounting for any implicatures that might depend on the presence of one rather than another of these singular terms in the sentence uttered. Such implicatures would merely be related to different maxims.

In some cases the conventional meaning of the words used will determine what is implicated, besides helping to determine what is said. If I say (smugly), *He is an Englishman; he is, therefore, brave*, I have certainly committed myself, by virtue of the meaning of my words, to its being the case that his being brave is a consequence of (follows from) his being an Englishman. But while I have <u>said</u> that he is an Englishman, and said that he is brave, I do not want to say that I have <u>SAID</u> (in the favored sense) that it follows from his being an Englishman that he is brave, though I have certainly indicated, and so implicated, that this is so. I do not want to say that my utterance of this sentence would be, STRICTLY SPEAKING, false should the consequence in question fail to hold. So SOME implicatures are conventional, unlike the one with which I introduced this discussion of implicature.

[margin note: SAID = literal? Said = implied?]

I wish to represent a certain subclass of nonconventional implicatures, which I shall call CONVERSATIONAL <u>implicatures,</u> as being essentially connected with certain general features of discourse; so my next step is to try to say what these features are.

The following may provide a first approximation to a general principle. Our talk exchanges do not normally consist of a succession of disconnected remarks, and would not be rational if they did. They are characteristically, to some degree at least, cooperative efforts; and each participant recognizes in them, to some extent, a common purpose or set of purposes, or at least a mutually accepted direction. This purpose or direction may be fixed from the start (e.g., by an initial proposal of a question for discussion), or it may evolve during the exchange; it may be fairly definite, or it may be so indefinite as to leave very considerable latitude to the participants (as in a casual conversation). But at each stage, SOME possible conversational moves would be excluded as conversationally unsuitable. We might then formulate a rough general principle which participants will be expected, other things being equal, to observe, namely: make your conversational contribution such as is required, at the stage at which it occurs, by the accepted purpose or direction of the talk exchange in which you are engaged. One might label this the Cooperative Principle [Grice later refers to this as the CP].

On the assumption that some such general principle as this is acceptable, one may perhaps distinguish four categories under one or another of which will fall certain more specific maxims and sub-maxims, the following of which will, in general, yield results in accordance with the Cooperative Principle. Echoing Kant, I call these categories Quantity, Quality, Relation, and Manner. The category of Quantity relates to the quantity of information to be provided, and under it fall the following maxims:

1   Make your contribution as informative as is required (for the current purposes of the exchange).
2   Do not make your contribution more informative than is required.

(The second maxim is disputable; it might be said that to be overinformative is not a transgression of the CP but merely a waste of time. However, it might be answered that such overinformativeness may be confusing in that it is liable to raise side issues; and there may also be an indirect effect, in that the hearers may be misled as a result of thinking that there is some particular POINT in the provision of the excess of information. However this may be, there is perhaps a different reason for doubt about the admission of this second maxim, namely, that its effect will be secured by a later maxim, which concerns relevance.)

Under the category of Quality falls a supermaxim – 'Try to make your contribution one that is true' – and two more specific maxims:

1   Do not say what you believe to be false.
2   Do not say that for which you lack adequate evidence.

Under the category of Relation I place a single maxim, namely, 'Be relevant.' Though the maxim itself is terse, its formulation conceals a number of problems that exercise me a good deal: questions about what different kinds and focuses of relevance there may be, how these shift in the course of a talk exchange, how to allow for the fact that subjects of conversation are legitimately changed, and so on. I find the treatment of such questions exceedingly difficult, and I hope to revert to them in a later work.

Finally, under the category of Manner, which I understand as relating not (like the previous categories) to what is said but, rather, to HOW what is said is to be said, I include the supermaxim – 'Be perspicuous' – and various maxims such as:

1   Avoid obscurity of expression.
2   Avoid ambiguity.
3   Be brief (avoid unnecessary prolixity).
4   Be orderly.

And one might need others.

It is obvious that the observance of some of these maxims is a matter of less urgency than is the observance of others; a man who has expressed himself with undue prolixity would, in general, be open to milder comment than would a man who has said something he believes to be false. Indeed, it might be felt that the importance of at least the first maxim of Quality is such that it should not be included in a scheme of the kind I am constructing; other maxims come into operation only on the assumption that this maxim of Quality is satisfied. While this may be correct, so far as the generation of implicatures is concerned it seems to play a role not totally different from the other maxims, and it will be convenient, for the present at least, to treat it as a member of the list of maxims.

There are, of course, all sorts of other maxims (aesthetic, social, or moral in character), such as 'Be polite', that are also normally observed by participants in talk exchanges, and these may also generate nonconventional implicatures. The conversational maxims, however, and the conversational implicatures connected with them, are specially connected (I hope) with the particular purposes that talk (and so, talk exchange) is adapted to serve and is primarily employed to serve. I have stated my maxims as if this purpose were a maximally effective exchange of information; this specification is, of course, too narrow, and the scheme needs to be generalized to allow for such general purposes as influencing or directing the actions of others.

As one of my avowed aims is to see talking as a special case or variety of purposive, indeed rational, behavior, it may be worth noting that the specific expectations or presumptions connected with at least some of the foregoing maxims have their analogues in the sphere of transactions that are not talk exchanges. I list briefly one such analog for each conversational category.

1   Quantity. If you are assisting me to mend a car, I expect your contribution to be neither more nor less than is required; if, for example, at a particular stage I need four screws, I expect you to hand me four, rather than two or six.
2   Quality. I expect your contributions to be genuine and not spurious. If I need sugar as an ingredient in the cake you are assisting me to make, I do not expect you to hand me salt; if I need a spoon, I do not expect a trick spoon made of rubber.
3   Relation. I expect a partner's contribution to be appropriate to immediate needs at each stage of the transaction; if I am mixing ingredients for a cake, I do not expect to be handed a good book, or even an oven cloth (though this might be an appropriate contribution at a later stage).
4   Manner. I expect a partner to make it clear what contribution he is making, and to execute his performance with reasonable dispatch.

These analogies are relevant to what I regard as a fundamental question about the CP and its attendant maxims, namely, what the basis is for the assumption which we seem to make, and on which (I hope) it will appear that a great range of implicatures depend, that talkers will in general (other things being equal and in the absence of indications to the contrary) proceed in the manner that these principles prescribe. A dull but, no doubt at a certain level, adequate answer is that it is just a well-recognized empirical fact that people DO behave in these ways; they have learned to do so in childhood and not lost the habit of doing so; and, indeed, it would involve a good deal of effort to make a radical departure from the habit. It is much easier, for example, to tell the truth than to invent lies.

I am, however, enough of a rationalist to want to find a basis that underlies these facts, undeniable though they may be; I would like to be able to think of the standard type of conversational practice not merely as something that all or most do IN FACT follow but as something that it is REASONABLE for us to follow, that we SHOULD NOT abandon. For a time, I was attracted by the idea that observance of the CP and the maxims, in a talk exchange, could be thought of as a quasi-contractual matter, with parallels outside the realm of discourse. If you pass by when I am struggling with my stranded car, I no doubt have some degree of expectation that you will offer help, but once you join me in tinkering under the hood, my expectations become stronger and take more specific forms (in the absence of indications that you are merely an incompetent meddler); and talk exchanges seemed to me to exhibit, characteristically, certain features that jointly distinguish cooperative transactions:

1   The participants have some common immediate aim, like getting a car mended; their ultimate aims may, of course, be independent and even in conflict – each may want to get the car mended in order to drive off, leaving the other stranded. In characteristic talk exchanges, there is a common aim even if, as in an over-the-wall chat, it is a second-order one, namely, that each party should, for the time being, identify himself with the transitory conversational interests of the other.
2   The contributions of the participants should be dovetailed, mutually dependent.
3   There is some sort of understanding (which may be explicit but which is often tacit) that, other things being equal, the transaction should continue in appropriate style unless both parties are agreeable that it should terminate. You do not just shove off or start doing something else.

But while some such quasi-contractual basis as this may apply to some cases, there are too many types of exchange, like quarrelling and letter writing, that it fails to fit comfortably. In any case, one feels that the talker who is irrelevant or obscure has primarily let down not his audience but himself. So I would like to be able to show that observance of the CP and maxims is reasonable (rational) along the following lines: that anyone who cares about goals that are central to conversation/communication (e.g. giving and receiving information, influencing and being influenced by others) must be expected to have an interest, given suitable circumstances, in participation in talk exchanges that will be profitable only on the assumption that they are conducted in general accordance with the CP and the maxims. Whether any such conclusion can be reached, I am uncertain; in any case, I am fairly sure that I cannot reach it until I am a good deal clearer about the nature of relevance and of the circumstances in which it is required.

It is now time to show the connection between the CP and maxims, on the one hand, and conversational implicature on the other.

A participant in a talk exchange may fail to fulfill a maxim in various ways, which include the following:

1   He may quietly and unostentatiously VIOLATE a maxim; if so, in some cases
     he will be liable to mislead.

2   He may OPT OUT from the operation both of the maxim and of the CP; he
     may say, indicate, or allow it to become plain that he is unwilling to coop-
     erate in the way the maxim requires. He may say, for example, *I cannot say
     more; my lips are sealed.*

3   He may be faced by a CLASH: He may be unable, for example, to fulfill the
     first maxim of Quantity (Be as informative as is required) without violating
     the second maxim of Quality (Have adequate evidence for what you say).

4   He may FLOUT a maxim; that is, he may BLATANTLY fail to fulfill it. On the
     assumption that the speaker is able to fulfill the maxim and to do so without
     violating another maxim (because of a clash), is not opting out, and is not,
     in view of the blatancy of his performance, trying to mislead, the hearer is
     faced with a minor problem: How can his saying what he did say be recon-
     ciled with the supposition that he is observing the overall CP? This situation
     is one that characteristically gives rise to a conversational implicature; and
     when a conversational implicature is generated in this way, I shall say that a
     maxim is being EXPLOITED.

I am now in a position to characterize the notion of conversational implicature. A man who, by (in, when) saying (or making as if to say) that *p* has implicated
that *q*, may be said to have conversationally implicated that *q*, PROVIDED THAT (1)
he is to be presumed to be observing the conversational maxims, or at least the
cooperative principle; (2) the supposition that he is aware that, or thinks that, *q* is
required in order to make his saying or making as if to say *p* (or doing so in THOSE
terms) consistent with this presumption; and (3) the speaker thinks (and would
expect the hearer to think that the speaker thinks) that it is within the competence
of the hearer to work out, or grasp intuitively, that the supposition mentioned in
(2) IS required. Apply this to my initial example, to B's remark that C has not yet
been to prison. In a suitable setting A might reason as follows: '(1) B has apparently violated the maxim "Be relevant" and so may be regarded as having flouted
one of the maxims conjoining perspicuity, yet I have no reason to suppose that he
is opting out from the operation of the CP; (2) given the circumstances, I can
regard his irrelevance as only apparent if, and only if, I suppose him to think that
C is potentially dishonest; (3) B knows that I am capable of working out step (2).
So B implicates that C is potentially dishonest.'

The presence of a conversational implicature must be capable of being worked
out; for even if it can in fact be intuitively grasped, unless the intuition is replace-
able by an argument, the implicature (if present at all) will not count as a
CONVERSATIONAL implicature; it will be a CONVENTIONAL implicature. To work
out that a particular conversational implicature is present, the hearer will rely on
the following data:

1   the conventional meaning of the words used, together with the identity of
     any references that may be involved;

2   the CP and its maxims;

3   the context, linguistic or otherwise, of the utterance;
4   other items of background knowledge; and
5   the fact (or supposed fact) that all relevant items falling under the previous headings are available to both participants and both participants know or assume this to be the case.

A general pattern for the working out of a conventional implicature might be given as follows: 'He has said that p; there is no reason to suppose that he is not observing the maxims, or at least the CP; he could not be doing this unless he thought that q; he knows (and knows that I know that he knows) that I can see that the supposition that he thinks that q IS required; he has done nothing to stop me thinking that q; he intends me to think, or is at least willing to allow me to think, that q; and so he has implicated that q.'

I shall now offer a number of examples, which I shall divide into three groups.

Group A

Examples in which no maxim is violated, or at least in which it is not clear that any maxim is violated

A is standing by an obviously immobilized car and is approached by B; the following exchange takes place:

(1)   A: I am out of petrol.
      B: There is a garage round the corner.

(Gloss: B would be infringing the maxim 'Be relevant' unless he thinks, or thinks it possible, that the garage is open, and has petrol to sell; so he implicates that the garage is, or at least may be open, etc.)

In this example, unlike the case of the remark *He hasn't been to prison yet*, the unstated connection between B's remark and A's remark is so obvious that, even if one interprets the supermaxim of Manner, 'Be perspicuous,' as applying not only to the expression of what is said but also to the connection of what is said with adjacent remarks, there seems to be no case for regarding that supermaxim as infringed in this example. The next example is perhaps a little less clear in this respect:

(2)   A: Smith doesn't seem to have a girlfriend these days.
      B: He has been paying a lot of visits to New York lately.

B implicates that Smith has, or may have, a girlfriend in New York. (A gloss is unnecessary in view of that given for the previous example.)

In both examples, the speaker implicates that which he must be assumed to believe in order to preserve the assumption that he is observing the maxim of Relation.

Group B

An example in which a maxim is violated, but its violation is to be explained by the supposition of a clash with another maxim

A is planning with B an itinerary for a holiday in France. Both know that A wants to see his friend C, if to do so would not involve too great a prolongation of his journey:

(3)   A: Where does C live?
      B: Somewhere in the south of France.

(Gloss: There is no reason to suppose that B is opting out; his answer is, as he well knows, less informative than is required to meet A's needs. This infringement of the first maxim of Quantity can be explained only by the supposition that B is aware that to be more informative would be to say something that infringed the maxim of Quality, 'Don't say what you lack adequate evidence for', so B implicates that he does not know in which town C lives.)

Group C

Examples that involve exploitation, that is, a procedure by which a maxim is flouted for the purpose of getting in a conversational implicature by means of something of the nature of a figure of speech

In these examples, though some maxim is violated at the level of what is said, the hearer is entitled to assume that that maxim, or at least the overall Cooperative Principle, is observed at the level of what is implicated.

A FLOUTING OF THE FIRST MAXIM OF QUANTITY

(4)   A is writing a testimonial about a pupil who is a candidate for a philosophy job, and his letter reads as follows: Dear Sir, Mr X's command of English is excellent, and his attendance at tutorials has been regular. Yours, etc.'

(Gloss: A cannot be opting out, since if he wished to be uncooperative, why write at all? He cannot be unable, through ignorance, to say more, since the man is his pupil; moreover, he knows that more information than this is wanted. He must, therefore, be wishing to impart information that he is reluctant to write down. This supposition is tenable only on the assumption that he thinks Mr X is no good at philosophy. This, then, is what he is implicating.)

Extreme examples of a flouting of the first maxim of Quantity are provided by utterances of patent tautologies like *Women are women* and *War is war*. I would wish to maintain that at the level of what is said, in my favored sense, such remarks are totally noninformative and so, at that level, cannot but infringe the first maxim of Quantity in any conversational context. They are, of course, informative at the level of what is implicated, and the hearer's identification of their informative content at this level is dependent on his ability to explain the speaker's selection of this PARTICULAR patent tautology.

. . .

EXAMPLES IN WHICH THE FIRST MAXIM OF QUALITY IS FLOUTED

(5)   *Irony*. X, with whom A has been on close terms until now, has betrayed a secret of A's to a business rival. A and his audience both know this. A says 'X is a fine friend.' (Gloss: It is perfectly obvious to A and his audience that what A has said or has made as if to say is something he does not believe, and the audience knows that A knows that this is obvious to the audience. So, unless A's utterance is entirely pointless, A must be trying to get across some other proposition than the one he purports to be putting forward. This must be some obviously related proposition; the most obviously related proposition is the contradictory of the one he purports to be putting forward.)

(6)   *Metaphor*. Examples like *You are the cream in my coffee* characteristically involve categorical falsity, so the contradictory of what the speaker has made as if to say will, strictly speaking, be a truism; so it cannot be THAT that such a speaker is trying to get across. The most likely supposition is that the speaker is attributing to his audience some feature or features in respect of which the audience resembles (more or less fancifully) the mentioned substance.

It is possible to combine metaphor and irony by imposing on the hearer two stages of interpretation. I say *You are the cream in my coffee*, intending the hearer to reach first the metaphor interpretant 'You are my pride and joy' and then the irony interpretant 'You are my bane.'

(7)   *Meiosis*. Of a man known to have broken up all the furniture one says *He was a little intoxicated*.

(8)   *Hyperbole. Every nice girl loves a sailor*.

Examples in which the second maxim of Quality, 'Do not say that for which you lack adequate evidence', *is flouted* are perhaps not easy to find, but the following seems to be a specimen.

(9)   I say of X's wife, *She is probably deceiving him this evening*. In a suitable context, or with a suitable gesture or tone or voice, it may be clear that I have no adequate reason for supposing this to be the case. My partner, to preserve the assumption that the conversational game is still being played, assumes that I am getting at some related proposition for the acceptance of which I DO have a reasonable basis. The related proposition might well be that she is given to deceiving her husband, or possibly that she is the sort of person who would not stop short of such conduct.

Examples in which an implicature is achieved by real, as distinct from apparent, violation of the maxim of Relation are perhaps rare, but the following seems to be a good candidate.

(10) At a genteel tea party, A says *Mrs X is an old bag*. There is a moment of appalled silence, and then B says *The weather has been quite delightful this summer, hasn't it?* B has blatantly refused to make what HE says relevant to A's preceding remark. He thereby indicates that A's remark should not be discussed and, perhaps more specifically, that A has committed a social gaffe.

· · ·

I have so far considered only cases of what I might call particularized conversational implicature – that is to say, cases in which an implicature is carried by saying that *p* on a particular occasion in virtue of special features of the context, cases in which there is no room for the idea that an implicature of this sort is NORMALLY carried by saying that *p*. But there are cases of generalized conversational implicature. Sometimes one can say that the use of a certain form of words in an utterance would normally (in the ABSENCE of special circumstances) carry such-and-such an implicature or type of implicature. Noncontroversial examples are perhaps hard to find, since it is all too easy to treat a generalized conversational implicature as if it were a conventional implicature. I offer an example that I hope may be fairly noncontroversial.

(11) Anyone who uses a sentence of the form *X is meeting a woman this evening* would normally implicate that the person to be met was someone other than X's wife, mother, sister, or perhaps even close platonic friend. Similarly, if I were to say *X went into a house yesterday and found a tortoise inside the front door*, my hearer would normally be surprised if some time later I revealed that the house was X's own. I could produce similar linguistic phenomena involving the expressions *a garden, a car, a college*, and so on.

· · ·

When someone, by using the form of expression *an X*, implicates that the X does not belong to or is not otherwise closely connected with some identifiable person, the implicature is present because the speaker has failed to be specific in a way in which he might have been expected to be specific, with the consequence that it is likely to be assumed that he is not in a position to be specific. This is a familiar implicature situation and is classifiable as a failure, for one reason or another, to fulfill the first maxim of Quantity. The only difficult question is why it should, in certain cases, be presumed, independently of information about particular contexts of utterance, that specification of the closeness or remoteness of the connection between a particular person or object and a further person who is mentioned or indicated by the utterance should be likely to be of interest. The answer must lie in the following region: transactions between a person and other persons or things closely connected with him are liable to be very different as regards their concomitants and results from the same sort of transactions involving only remotely connected persons or things; the concomitants and results, for instance, of my finding a hole in MY roof are likely to be very different from the concomitants and results of finding a hole in someone else's roof. Information, like money, is often given without the giver's knowing to just what use the recipient will want to put it. If someone to whom a transaction is mentioned gives it further consideration, he is likely to find himself wanting the answers to further questions that the speaker may not be able to identify in advance; if the appropriate specification will be likely to enable the hearer to answer a considerable variety of such questions for himself, then there is a presumption that the speaker should include it in his remark; if not, then there is no such presumption.

Finally, we can now show that, conversational implicature being what it is, it must possess certain features:

1   Since, to assume the presence of a conversational implicature, we have to assume that at least the Cooperative Principle is being observed, and since it is possible to opt out of the observation of this principle, it follows that a generalized conversational implicature can be cancelled in a particular case. It may be explicitly cancelled, by the addition of a clause that states or implies that the speaker has opted out, or it may be contextually cancelled, if the form of utterance that usually carries it is used in a context that makes it clear that the speaker IS opting out.

2   Insofar as the calculation that a particular conversational implicature is present requires, besides contextual and background information, only a knowledge of what has been said (or of the conventional commitment of the utterance), and insofar as the manner of expression plays no role in the calculation, it will not be possible to find another way of saying the same thing, which simply lacks the implicature in question, except where some special feature of the substituted version is itself relevant to the determination of an implicature (in virtue of one of the maxims of Manner). If we call this feature NON-DETACHABILITY, one may expect a generalized conversational implicature that is carried by a familiar, nonspecial locution to have a high degree of non-detachability.

3   To speak approximately, since the calculation of the presence of a conversationsal implicature presupposes an initial knowledge of the conventional force of the expression the utterance of which carries the implicature, a conversational implicatum will be a condition that is not included in the original specification of the expression's conventional force. Though it may not be impossible for what starts life, so to speak, as a conversational implicature to become conventionalized, to suppose that this is so in a given case would require special justification. So, initially at least, conversational implicata are not part of the meaning of the expressions to the employment of which they attach.

4   Since the truth of a conversational implicatum is not required by the truth of what is said (what is said may be true – what is implicated may be false), the implicature is not carried by what is said, but only by the saying of what is said, or by 'putting it that way.'

5   Since, to calculate a conversational implicature is to calculate what has to be supposed in order to preserve the supposition that the Cooperative Principle

is being observed, and since there may be various possible specific explanations, a list of which may be open, the conversational implicatum in such cases will be disjunction of such specific explanations; and if the list of these is open, the implicatum will have just the kind of indeterminacy that many actual implicata do in fact seem to possess.

Chapter 4

John J. Gumperz

SOCIOCULTURAL KNOWLEDGE IN CONVERSATIONAL INFERENCE[1]

'CONVERSATIONAL INFERENCE', as I use the term, is the 'situated' or context-bound process of interpretation, by means of which participants in a conversation assess others' intentions, and on which they base their responses. Conversational inference is ultimately a semantic process, but it is distinguished from linguists' assignment of meaning to utterances or classification of speech acts, as well as from the social scientists' measurement of attitudes. Both conventional linguistic analysis and social science measurement involve the labeling of utterances by other utterances, more often than not after the fact. Conversational inference, by contrast, is part of the very act of conversing. One indirectly or implicitly illustrates one's understanding of what is said through verbal and nonverbal responses, by the way one builds on what one hears to participate in a conversation, rather than through talking about it in abstract terms. It follows that analysis of such processes requires different and perhaps more indirect methods of study which examine meaning as a function of the dynamic pattern of utterances and responses as they occur in conversation.

Recent studies of conversation from a variety of linguistic, psychological, anthropological, and sociological perspectives, have shed light upon a number of issues important to the study of conversational inference. It is generally agreed that grammatical knowledge is only one of several factors in the interpretation process. Aside from physical setting, participants' personal background knowledge, and their attitudes toward each other, sociocultural assumptions concerning role and status relationships, as well as social values associated with various message components, also play an important role. So far, however, treatment of such contextual factors has been primarily descriptive. The procedure has been to identify or list what can potentially affect interpretation. With rare exceptions, there have

Source: John J. Gumperz, 'Sociocultural knowledge in conversational inference', in Muriel Saville-Troike (ed.) *Linguistics and Anthropology*, Georgetown University Round Table on Languages and Linguistics 1977, Washington D.C.: Georgetown University Press, 1977, 191–211.

been no systematic attempts to show how social knowledge is used in situated interpretation. Yet we know that social presuppositions and attitudes change in the
course of interaction, often without a change in extralinguistic context. Therefore,
the social input to conversation is not entirely constant. Assumptions about role
and status relationships vary as the conversation progresses, and these changes are
signalled through speech itself (Gumperz and Cook-Gumperz 1976). The signals
by which this is accomplished can be regarded as a metalanguage or a meta-signalling
system. So far, however, we know very little about this metalanguage. In this paper
I want to suggest at least the outlines of a theory which deals with the question of
how social knowledge is stored in the mind, how it is retrieved from memory, and
how it is integrated with grammatical knowledge in the act of conversing.

. . .

Ethnomethodologists have gone a long way toward producing a theory which
treats conversation as a cooperative endeavor, subject to systematic constraints.
However, a number of important questions still remain to be answered. A social
view of language such as the one ethnomethodologists advocate must be able to
account for interspeaker difference, yet, so far, only the pan-cultural aspects of conversational control mechanisms have been dealt with. A sociolinguist needs to know
how speakers use verbal skills to create contextual conditions that reflect particular
culturally realistic scenes. Furthermore, how is speakers' grammatical and phonological knowledge employed in carrying out these strategies? For example, if regular
speaker change is to take place, participants must be able to scan phrases to predict
when an utterance is about to end. They must be able to distinguish between rhetorical pauses and turn-relinquishing pauses. Although speaker overlap is an integral
part of interaction, conversational cooperation requires that speakers not be interrupted at random. To follow the thematic progression of an argument, moreover,
and to make one's contribution relevant, one must be able to recognize culturally
possible lines of reasoning. To account for all these phenomena, it is necessary to
show how the ethnomethodologists' control mechanisms are integrated into other
aspects of speakers' linguistic knowledge.

To this end, we will look at two examples of actual conversation. . . . We will
analyze two sequences which occurred in public situations. They are representative of a much larger body of data we have collected, both by chance, as in these
examples, and in connection with systematic programs. The first interaction is one
which any native speaker of English would be able to interpret. The second constitutes an interethnic encounter, and we will show how habitual conversational
inferences led to a misinterpretation of intent.

The first incident occurred when I was sitting in an aisle seat on an airplane
bound for Miami, Florida. I noticed two middle-aged women walking towards the
rear of the plane. Suddenly, I heard from behind, 'Tickets, please! Tickets, please!'
At first I was startled and began to wonder why someone would be asking for
tickets so long after the start of the flight. Then one of the women smiled toward
the other and said, 'I TOLD you to leave him at home'. I looked up and saw a
man passing the two women, saying, 'STEP to the rear of the bus, please'.

Americans will have no difficulty identifying this interchange as a joke, and hypothesizing that the three individuals concerned were probably traveling together and were perhaps tourists setting off on a pleasure trip. What we want to investigate is what linguistic knowledge forms the basis for such inferences, and to what extent this knowledge is culturally specific.

The initial utterance, 'Tickets, please', was repeated without pause and was spoken in higher than normal pitch, more than usual loudness, and staccato rhythm. For this reason it sounded like an announcement, or like a stock phrase associated with travel situations. My first inkling that what I heard was a joke came with the woman's statement to her friend, 'I TOLD you to leave him at home'. Although I had no way of knowing if the participants were looking at each other, the fact that the woman's statement was perfectly timed to follow the man's utterance was a cue that she was responding to him, even though her comment was addressed to a third party. Furthermore, the stress on *told* functioned to mark her statement as another stock utterance, contributing to the hypothesis that she and he were engaging in a similar activity. If the statement of the man or the woman had been uttered in normal pitch and conversational intonation, the connection between them might not have been clear. Only after I was able to hypothesize that the participants were joking, could I interpret their utterances. My hypothesis was then confirmed by the man's next statement, 'Step to the rear of the bus, please'. This was also uttered in announcement pitch, loudness, and intonation. In retrospect, we may note that both of the man's utterances were formulaic in nature, and thus culturally specific and context bound. He was exploiting the association between walking down an aisle in a plane and the similar walk performed by a conductor on a train or a bus. In identifying the interaction as a joke, I was drawing on the same situational-association knowledge, as well as on my awareness of the likelihood of joking among travelers bound for Miami.

Thus, suprasegmental and other surface features of speech are crucial to understanding the nature of an interaction. Such features have been extensively discussed in the linguistic literature, but treatments have dealt with the referential meaning of individual sentences. When seen in isolation, sentences can have many intonation and paralinguistic contours, without change in referential meaning. The prevalent view is that these features add expressive overtones to sentences. Moreover, the signs by which listeners recognize these overtones tend to be seen as language independent. If, however, we look at conversational inference rather than referential meaning, we see that paralinguistic and intonation contours play an important role in the identification of interpretative frames.

This identification of specific conversational exchanges as representative of socioculturally familiar activities is the crucial process I call 'contextualization'. It is the process by which we evaluate message meaning and sequencing patterns in relation to aspects of the surface structure of the message, called 'contextualization cues'. The linguistic basis for this matching procedure resides in 'co-occurrence expectations', which are learned in the course of previous interactive experience and form part of our habitual and instinctive linguistic knowledge. Co-occurrence expectations enable us to associate styles of speaking with contextual presuppositions. We regularly rely upon these matching processes in everyday conversation, but they are rarely talked about. In fact, they tend to be noticed only when things go wrong, and even then, the conclusions drawn are more likely to be about the other person's attitudes than about differences in linguistic conventions. Yet, as our next example shows, contextualization expectations are highly culturally specific; that is, they are dependent upon interactants' ethnic or communicative background.

The second incident I am going to relate took place in London, England, on a bus driven by a West Indian driver–conductor. The bus was standing at a stop, and passengers were filing in. The driver announced periodically, 'Exact change, please', as London bus drivers often do. When passengers who had been standing close by either did not have money ready or tried to give him a large bill, the driver repeated, 'Exact change, please'. The second time around, he said 'please' with extra loudness, high pitch, and falling intonation, and he seemed to pause before 'please'. One passenger so addressed, as well as others following him, walked down the bus aisle exchanging angry looks and obviously annoyed, muttering, 'Why do these people have to be so rude and threatening about it?' Was the bus driver really annoyed? Did he intend to be rude, or is the passengers' interpretation a case of cross-cultural misunderstanding?

To understand what happened here and why it happened, it is necessary to go into some more detail about the nature of contextualization cues and their function in conversation. The term 'contextualization cue' refers to any aspect of the surface form of utterances which, when mapped onto message content, can be shown to be functional in the signalling of interpretative frames. In the examples given in this paper, the cues are largely prosodic and paralinguistic, but many other signalling mechanisms can function as contextualization cues, including lexical or phonological choice; use of idiomatic or formulaic expressions such as greetings, openers, interjections, or frozen sequences; or code-switching (Gumperz 1976; Gumperz and Cook-Gumperz 1976). In the present discussion, however, we concentrate on prosody (i.e., intonation and stress) and paralinguistics (pitch register, rhythm, loudness, etc.) since some aspects of these features are always involved in conversation.

. . .

Prosody consists of three basic signalling mechanisms: tone grouping; tonic or nucleus placement within a tone group; and tune, the direction of the tonal change which characterizes the nucleus. Paralinguistic features include, among others, pitch register, loudness, rhythm, and tempo, and apply to the tone group as a whole, rather than to parts thereof.

Among prosodic cues, tone grouping refers to the use of intonation and stress to chunk larger stretches of speech into separable bits of information that are to be processed as single units. Our example:

Exact change please //

could be uttered as a single chunk, as it was the first time the driver said it, or as two chunks:

Exact change / please //

as he said it the second time. To treat *please* as a separate bit of information implies that it is worthy of separate attention. We recognize two types of tone group boundaries: minor tone group, (/) which suggests that the preceding message portion is semantically related to others within a larger whole, and a major tone group, (//) which suggests finality.

The second element of prosody, tonic or nucleus placement, refers to the selection of one or another of the stressed syllables in a tone of group as the nucleus, or the part on which the tonal shift occurs. Nucleus placement is predictable in many types of sentences. Normally, it identifies that portion of the message that is to be regarded as new, as compared to what can be assumed to be shared or given. Note, however, that this is not merely a matter of syntax or lexicon but also a matter of culturally specific practice. If I say

I'm giving my paper //

it is the object, *paper*, which is assumed to carry the new information. In

I'm cancelling my paper //

the verb is normally stressed, since *cancelling*, in our culture, is not a customary activity in relation to paper giving.

The third prosodic mechanism, tune, refers to the fall and rises in tone such as are associated with the intonational contrast between questions and answers. We furthermore distinguish two levels on which the fall or rise can occur: high or low.

please //

please //

A shift to high level generally calls special attention to the segments so marked; a shift to low level often indicates that an item of information is known or expected.

Note that in English, tune is also important in signalling thematic progression. It is used, for example, to show the distinction between dependent and independent clauses.

Because I'm busy / I don't want to be interrupted //

If *busy* were spoken with a fall rather than a rise, this sentence would sound odd.

Paralinguistic cues, finally, are the relative pitch level or loudness of an entire tone group, rather than part of the group as in nucleus placement, and the rhythm or tempo of the utterance. In English, these cues usually signal special discourse functions, such as distinctions in degree of formality; they can also mark quotes, interjections or asides, or indicate, for example, announcing style as in *Tickets, please*.

To be understood at all, all sentences must carry some kind of tone grouping, nucleus placement and tune. When these are in keeping with expectations based on content, no additional meanings are signalled. However, there are also certain optional uses of prosody to highlight unexpected information which function to suggest indirect inferences. For example, isolating an utterance segment as part of a separate tone group, as the bus driver did in my second example, assigns it special importance and invites the listener to infer the reason. Note, however, that in British as well as in American English, tone grouping options are constrained by pragmatic rules. Of the following examples, (1), (2), and (3) are all possible.

1   See that chair over there in the corner. //

2   See that chair / Over there in the corner. //

3   Put that chair over there in the corner, //

4   Put that chair / Over there in the corner. //

Example (4) seems odd, however, since *over there* is semantically a part of the predicate, rather than part of a separate adverbial complement.

Optional nucleus placement on an item which under ordinary conditions would count as given, is unexpected. The hearer's attempt to understand the speaker's motivation constitutes the conversational inference. The woman plane passenger in my first example uses this device in saying 'I told you to leave him at home' and, given our knowledge of similar situations and of the extralinguistic setting, we use this information to identify her utterance as formulaic.

Similarly, the use of high rise or fall when low rise or fall is expected can serve to signal special emphasis. I use the term 'normal information flow' to indicate uses of prosody which are expected and signal no indirect inferences. The term 'contrastiveness', on the other hand, refers to those cases where deviations from expected patterns are exploited conversationally.

Note that while short utterances need not show contrastiveness, longer utterances involving complex, connected discourse employ contrastiveness as an essential part of the signalling process. Only through contrastiveness can we scan utterances to determine the relative importance of various bits of information in longer messages.

. . .

In contrast to prosody, paralinguistic cues are somewhat more optional in English. Nevertheless, they are a regular feature of everyday conversation. In fact, as already suggested, they are our primary means of distinguishing various degrees of formality of talk and degrees of interspeaker involvement, of signalling topic changes, and distinguishing between asides and main parts of the argument. In our first example, the paralinguistic cues enabled us to identify *Tickets, please* as an announcement.

Let us now return to the second example:

Exact change, please.

As previously noted, the West Indian bus driver said this sentence twice, using different contextualization cues in each case. A speaker of British English in repeating this utterance, could optionally (a) place the nucleus on *change* or (b) split the sentence into two tone groups with two nuclei: *change* and *please*. In (a), the normal interpretation would be, '*I said, "change".*' In (b), the separation of *please* would emphasize that word and call attention to the fact that a request has been made. Note that in (b) *please* must carry rising time, to suggest tentativeness and avoid excessive directness, which would seem rude. The bus driver in our example said *please* with falling intonation as well as increased pitch and loudness. Hence, for speakers using British English contextualization conventions, the conclusion of rudeness is natural.

In order to determine whether the interpretation of rudeness corresponds to West Indian contextualization conventions, we want to look at how prosodic and paralinguistic cues normally function in West Indian conversation. Examination of the contextualization conventions employed in our tapes of West Indian Londoners talking to each other, suggests that their use of prosody and paralinguistics is significantly different from that of British English or American English speakers. For example, syntactic constraints on the placement of tone group boundaries differ. West Indians can split a sentence into much smaller tone group units than British English speakers can. Furthermore, their use of rising tone to indicate intersentence connections is much more restricted. Moreover, once a tone group boundary has been established, nucleus placement within such a tone group must be on the last content word of that tone group, regardless of meaning. In contrast to other forms of English, therefore, nucleus placement is syntactically rather than semantically constrained. Finally, pitch and loudness differences serve as a major means of signalling contrastiveness rather than expressiveness. They are regularly used to indicate emphasis without any connotation of excitement or other emotional overtones. To give only one example, in the course of an ordinary, calm discussion, one speaker said,

He was selected/ MAINLY/ because he had a degree//.

The word *mainly* was separated by tone group boundaries and set off from the rest of the sentence by increased pitch and loudness. The context shows that the word *mainly* was used contrastively within a line of reasoning which argued that having practical experience was as important as formal education. Our conclusion is that the West Indian bus driver's *Exact change / please //*was his normal way of emphasizing the word *please*, corresponding to the British English option (b). Therefore, his intention was, if anything, to be polite.

To summarize, then, we conclude that conversational inference processes such as we have discussed involve several distinct elements. On the one hand is the perception of prosodic and paralinguistic cues. On the other is the problem of interpreting them. Interpretation in turn requires, first of all, judgments of expectedness and then a search for an interpretation that makes sense in terms of what we know and what we have perceived. We can never be certain of the ultimate meaning of any message, but by looking at systematic patterns in the relationship of perception of surface cues to interpretation, we can gather strong evidence for the social basis of contextualization conventions.

. . .

Note

1   Work on this paper was supported in part by NIMH grant MN26831–03. Many of the ideas expressed here were developed in discussion with Jenny Cook-Gumperz. I am grateful to Denise Gubbay and other staff members of the National Center for Industrial Language Training, Southall, Middlesex, England, for cooperation in field work and for sharing with me their many insights into problems of interethnic communication. Deborah Tannen assisted in the preparation and organization of the manuscript and provided many helpful suggestions.

References

Gumperz, J. (1976) 'Language communication and public negotiation', in Sanday, P. (ed.) *Anthropology and the Public Interest*, New York: Academic Press.
Gumperz, J. and Cook-Gumperz, J. (1976) Papers on language and context. Working Papers No. 46, Language Behavior Research Laboratory, University of California, Berkeley.

Chapter 5

Emanuel A. Schegloff

TALK AND SOCIAL STRUCTURE[1]

WHETHER STARTING FROM A programmatic address to the structure of face-to-face interaction or from a programmatic concern with the constitutive practices of the mundane world, whether in pursuit of language, culture or action, a range of inquiries in several social science disciplines (most relevantly anthropology, sociology and linguistics) have over the past 25 to 30 years[2] brought special attention to bear on talk-in-interaction. It is not unfair to say that one of the most focused precipitates of this broad interest has been that family of studies grouped under the rubric "conversation analysis." It is, in any case, with such studies of "talk" that I will be concerned in reflecting on "talk and social structure."

Although itself understandable as a sustained exploration of what is entailed in giving an analytic account of "a context" (as in the phrase "in the context of ordinary conversation"), various aspects of inquiry in this tradition of work have prompted an interest in neighboring disciplines in relating features of talk-in-interaction to "contexts" of a more traditional sort – linguistic contexts, cultural contexts, and institutional and social structural contexts. At the same time, investigators working along conversation analytic lines began to deal with talk with properties which were seemingly related to its production by participants oriented to a special "institutional" context; and, wishing to address those distinctive properties rather than ones held in common with other forms of talk (as Sacks had done in some of his earliest work based on group-therapy sessions), these investigators faced the analytic problems posed by such an undertaking.

The interest in the theme "talk and social structure" comes, then, from several directions – the most prominent being technical concerns in the analysis of certain forms of talk on the one hand, and an impulse to effectuate a *rapprochement* with the concerns of classical sociology, and to do so by relating work on talk-in-interaction

Source: Emanuel A. Schegloff, 'Reflections on talk and social structure', in Deirdre Boden and Don H. Zimmerman (eds) *Talk and Social Structure: Studies in Ethnomethodology and Conversation Analysis*, Cambridge: Polity Press in association with Blackwell, 1991, 44–70.

to those social formations which get referred to as "social structures," or generically as "social structure," on the other hand. My reflections will have this latter impulse as their point of departure, but will quickly seek to engage it by formulating and confronting the analytic problems which it poses.

Of course, a term like "social structure" is used in many different ways. In recent years, to cite but a few cases, Peter Blau (1977) has used the term to refer to the distribution of a population on various parameters asserted to be pertinent to interaction, claiming a derivation from Simmel and his notion of intersecting social circles. Many others have in mind a structure of statuses and/or roles, ordinarily thereby building in an inescapable normative component, of just the sort Blau wishes to avoid. Yet others intend by this term a structured distribution of scarce resources and desirables, such as property, wealth, productive capacity, status, knowledge, privilege, power, the capacity to enforce and preserve privilege, etc. Still others, have in mind stably patterned sets of social relations, whether formalized in organizations or more loosely stabilized in networks.

The sense of "social structure" intended in the thematic concern with "talk and social structure" does not range across all these usages. But almost certainly it includes a concern with power and status and its distribution among social formations such as classes, ethnic groups, age grade groups, gender, and professional relations. It is this sense which has animated, for example, the work by West (1979) and Zimmerman and West (1975) on gender and interruption, and West's work (1984) on doctor/patient interaction. And it includes as well a concern with the structured social relations which comprise organizations and occupational practice and the institutional sectors with which they are regularly identified (as, for example, in Atkinson and Drew's treatment of the courts (1979), in the work of Zimmerman and his associates on the police (for instance, Zimmerman 1984; Whalen and Zimmerman 1987), Maynard's work (1984) on the legal system, that of Heritage (1985) on mass-media news, or Boden's (1994) on organization.

. . .

Whatever substantive gains there are to be had from focusing on the relationship between talk and social structure in the traditional sense, this focus is not needed in order to supply conversation analysis with its sociological credentials. The work which is focused on the organization of talk-in-interaction in its own right – work on the organization of turn-taking, or on the organization of sequences, work addressed to the actions being done in turns and the formats through which they are done, work on the organization of repair, and work directed to the many discrete practices of talking and acting through talk which do not converge into domains of organization – this work is itself dealing with social organization and social structures, albeit of a different sort than in the received uses of those terms, and is no less sociological in impulse and relevance (Schegloff 1987).

For some, the fact that conversation analysis (henceforth, CA) concerns itself with the details of talking has meant that it is a form of linguistics. Perhaps so, but certainly not exclusively so. If it is not a distinctive discipline of its own (which it may well turn out to be), CA is at a point where linguistics and sociology (and several other disciplines, anthropology and psychology among them) meet. For the target of its inquiries stands where talk amounts to action, where action projects consequences in a structure and texture of interaction which the talk is itself progressively embodying and realizing, and where the particulars of the talk inform what actions are being done and what sort of social scene is being constituted. Now, from the start, one central preoccupation of sociology and social theory has been with the character of social action and what drives it (reason, passion, interest, utility) – this is familiar enough. Another concern has been with the character of interaction in which action is embedded, for it is observations about some aspects of the character of interaction that motivated such hoary old distinctions as those between *Gemeinschaft* and *Gesellschaft*, between status and contract, and the like. "Action in interaction" is, then, a longstanding theme of social analysis.

CA's enterprise, concerned as it is with (among other things) the detailed analysis of how talk-in-interaction is conducted as an activity in its own right and as the instrument for the full range of social action and practice, is then addressed to one of the classic themes of sociology, although to be sure in a distinctive way. Of the several ways in which CA shows its deep preoccupation with root themes of social science and sociology in particular, these standing conversation analytic preoccupations resonate more with the title of the Atkinson/Heritage collection (1984): they are concerned with "structures of social action" – structures of single actions and of series and sequences of them. Atkinson and Heritage's title is, of course, a thoroughly unveiled allusion to the title of Talcott Parsons's first major work, *The Structure of Social Action* (1937), the work which launched the enterprise of Parsonian action theory. The difference between Parsons's title and the Atkinson/Heritage allusion, "*The Structure* of Social Action" versus "*Structures* of Social Action," may suggest some of the distinctiveness.

Parsons's tack was conceptual and global. For him there was "the structure," and it was arrived at by theoretic stipulation of the necessary components of an analytical unit – the "unit act," components such as "ends," "means," "conditions." This was a thoroughly conceptual enterprise on a thoroughly analytic object. The Atkinson/Heritage "structures of" suggests not only multiplicity of structures, but the empirical nature of the enterprise. The units are concrete activities, and the search for their "components" involves examination and description of empirical instances.

But with all the differences in conception, mode of working, etc., there is a common enterprise here, and it has long been a central one for sociology and the social sciences more generally – to try to get at the character of social action and social interaction. In CA's addressing of this theme and the varied problems and analytic tasks to which it gives rise, it is itself engaged in – "*echt*" sociology, even without the introduction of traditional sociological concerns such as "social structure." But the claim that the problems which have preoccupied conversation analysis are sociological in impulse and import is without prejudice to our engagement with the work which tries to relate talk to more traditional conceptions of social structure. That engagement is already underway.

The reasons for thinking about the relationships of talk and social structure are ready to hand. Both our casual and our studied examination of interaction and talk-in-interaction provide a lively sense of the occasions on which who the parties are relative to one another seems to matter, and matter to *them*. And these include senses of "who they are" that connect directly to what is ordinarily meant by "social structure" – their relative status, the power they differentially can command, the group affiliations they display or can readily have attributed to them such as their racial or ethnic memberships, their gender and age-grade status, their occupational status and its general standing and immediate interactional significance, and the other categories of membership in the society which can matter to the participants and which fall under the traditional sociological rubric "social structure."

The issue I mean to address is not: is there such a thing as gender/class/power/status/organization/etc.? Or: does it affect anything in the world? Rather, the question is: whatever observations we initially make about how such features of social organization as these work and bear on interaction, how do we translate them into defensible, empirically based analyses that help us to get access to previously unnoticed particular details of talk-in-interaction, and appreciate their significance. For the lively sense we may all share of the relevance of social structure along the lines I have mentioned needs to be converted into the hard currency (if you'll pardon the cash nexus) of defensible analysis – analysis which departs from, and can always be referred to and grounded in, the details of actual occurrences of conduct in interaction.

Again, I do not mean to be addressing myself to two apparently neighboring stances, although there may well be implications for them. I am not centrally concerned with those investigators whose primary analytic commitment is to social structure in the received senses of that term, and who mean to incorporate examination of talk into their inquiries because of the role attributable to it in the "production" of social structure. And I do not take up the position (apparently embraced in Goffman 1983) in which the prima-facie relevance of social structure to the organization of interaction is in principle to be disputed (although I do suggest that some received notions may not be sustainable when required to come to terms with the details of actual occurrences). Rather, I mean to formulate and explore the challenges faced by those attracted to the interaction/social structure nexus. A solution must be found to the analytic problems which obstruct the conversion of intuition, casual (however well-informed) observation, or theoretically motivated observation into demonstrable analysis. For without solutions to these problems, we are left with "a sense of how the world works," but without its detailed explication.

My discussion will be organized around three issues: the problem of relevance, the issue of "procedural consequentiality," and a concern for the competing attentional and analytic claims of conversational structures and "social structure" respectively in the analysis of the data of talk-in-interaction.

The problem of relevance

First, *relevance* . . .

The original focus of the work by Sacks which I mean to recall was the way in which persons engaged in talk-in-interaction did their talk, specifically with respect to reference to persons. Sacks noted that members refer to persons by various category terms – as man/woman, protestant/catholic/jew, doctor/patient, white/black/chicano, first baseman/second baseman/shortstop, and the like. He remarked that these category terms come in collections. In presenting them above, they are inscribed in groups: [man/woman], [protestant/catholic/jew]; and so on; and that is the correct way to present them. It is not [man/woman/protestant], [catholic/jew]. This is what is being noted in the observation that the category terms are organized in *collections*.

Some of these collections Sacks called "Pn adequate;" they were adequate to characterize or categorize any member of any population, however specified, whether or not it had been specified (for example, counted, characterized or bounded) in some fashion (Sacks 1972: 32–3). Other collections were not Pn adequate. [Male/female] *is* Pn adequate; [first baseman/second baseman/shortstop . . .] is *not* Pn adequate, because the latter is only usable on populations already specified or characterized as "baseball teams," whereas the former is not subject to such restrictions.

One of Sacks's main points was that there demonstrably are many Pn- adequate category collections. The collection of category terms for gender/sex and age are the most obvious ones, and these two alone serve to allow the posing of the problem of relevance. The point is that since everyone who is an instance of some category in one of those collections is necessarily (for that is the import of Pn adequacy) also an instance of some category in the other, or *an* other, the fact that someone *is* male, or *is* middle aged, or *is* white, or *is* Jewish is, by itself, no warrant for so referring to them, for the warrant of "correctness" would provide for use of any of the other reference forms as well. Some principle of relevance must underlie use of a reference form, and has to be adduced in order to provide for one rather than another of those ways of characterizing or categorizing some member. That is the problem of relevance: not just the descriptive adequacy of the terms used to characterize the objects being referred to, but the relevance that one has to provide if one means to account for the use of some term – the relevance of that term relative to the alternative terms that are demonstrably available.

Now, this problem was developed by Sacks initially in describing how members talk about members. It showed the inadequacy of an account of a conversationalist's reference to another as a "cousin" by reference to the other "actually being a cousin." But, once raised, the point is directly relevant to the enterprise of professional analysts as well. Once we recognize that whoever can be characterized as "male" or as "protestant," or as "president" or whatever, can be characterized or categorized in other ways as well, our scholarly/professional/scientific account cannot 'naively' rely on such characterizations, that is, cannot rely on them with no justification or warrant of their relevance.

Roughly speaking, there are two types of solution to this problem in the methodology of professional analysis. One type of solution can be characterized as the "positivist" stance, in one of the many senses in which that term is currently used. In this view, the way to warrant one, as compared to another, characterization of the participants (for example, in interaction) is the "success" of that way of characterizing them in producing a professionally acceptable account of the data being addressed. "Success" is measured by some "technology" – by statistical significance, a preponderance of historical evidence, and so forth. Sometimes there is an additional requirement that the characterization which produces "successful" analysis be theoretically interpretable; that is, that the selection of descriptive terms for the participants converge with the terms of a professional/scientific theory relevant to the object of description. In this type of solution, which I am calling "positivistic," it does not matter whether or not the terms that are used to characterize the participants in some domain of action, and which have yielded "significant" results, are otherwise demonstrably orientated to or not by the participants being described. That is what makes this solution of the problem "positivist."

The alternative type of solution insists on something else, and that is that professional characterizations of the participants be grounded in aspects of what is going on that are demonstrably relevant to the participants, and at that moment – at the moment that whatever we are trying to provide an account of occurs. Not, then, just that we see them to be characterizeable as "president/assistant," as "chicano/black," as "professor/student," etc. But that for them, at that moment, those are terms relevant for producing and interpreting conduct in the interaction.

This issue should be of concern when we try to bring the kind of traditional sociological analysis that is implied by the term "social structure" to bear on talk-in-interaction. Much of what is meant by "social structure" in the traditional sense directly implicates such characterizations or categorizations of the participants as Sacks was examining. If the sense of social structure we are dealing with is the one that turns on the differential distribution of valued resources in society, whether status or power or money or any of the other "goods" whose distribution can be used to characterize social structure, then that implies a characterization or categorization of the participants on that occasion as one relevantly to be selected from that set of terms. But then the problem presents itself of the relevance of those terms to the participants for what they are doing. Without a show of that warrant, we are back to a "positivistic" stance, even though the animating concerns may be drawn from quite anti-positivistic theoretical sources or commitments.

Now let us be clear about what is and what is not being said here. The point is not that persons are somehow not male or female, upper or lower class, with or without power, professors and/or students. They may be, on some occasion, demonstrably members of one or another of those categories. Nor is the issue that those aspects of the society do not matter, or did not matter on that occasion. We may share a lively sense that indeed they do matter, and that they mattered on that occasion, and mattered for just that aspect of some interaction on which we are focusing. There is still the problem of *showing from the details of the talk or other conduct in the materials* that we are analyzing that those aspects of the scene are what the parties are oriented to. For *that is to show how the parties are embodying for one another the relevancies of the interaction and are thereby producing the social structure.*

The point here is not only methodological but substantive. It is not just to add a methodological apparatus supporting analyses already in hand. It is rather to add to, and potentially to transform, the analysis of the talk and other conduct itself by enriching our account of it with additional detail; and to show that, and how, "social structure" in the traditional sense enters into the production and interpretation of determinate facets of conduct, and is thereby confirmed, reproduced, modulated, neutralized or incrementally transformed in that actual conduct to which it must finally be referred.

This is not, to my mind, an issue of preferring or rejecting some line of analysis, some research program or agenda. It is a problem of analysis to be worked at: how to examine the data so as to be able to show that the parties were, with and for one another, demonstrably orientated to those aspects of who they are, and those aspects of their context, which are respectively implicated in the "social structures" which we may wish to relate to the talk. If we treat this as a problem of analytic craft, we can use it as leverage to enhance the possibility of learning something about how talk-in-interaction is done, for it requires us to return again to the details of the talk to make the demonstration.

Procedural consequentiality

The issue just discussed with respect to the characterization of the participants in some talk-in-interaction also is relevant to a characterization of "the context" in which they talk and interact. "Context" can be as much a part of what traditionally has been meant by "social structure" as attributes of the participants are. So, for example, remarking that some talk is being conducted "in the context of a bureau-cracy," "in a classroom," "on a city street," etc. is part of what is sometimes intended by incorporating the relevance of social structure.

Such characterizations invoke particular aspects of the setting and not others. They involve selections among alternatives, and among subalternatives. For example, one type of formulation of context characterizes it by "place," and this is an alternative to various other sorts of context characterization. But within that context type, various forms of place formulation are available, all of which can be correct (Schegloff 1972). So, although the details of the argument have not been fully and formally worked out for the characterization of context or setting in the way that Sacks worked them out for the characterization of participants, it appears likely that the issue of relevance can be posed in much the same way for context as it has been for person reference.

What I want to do here is add something to this relevance problem for contexts. It concerns what I am calling the "procedural consequentiality" of contexts.

Even if we can show by analysis of the details of the interaction that some char-acterization of the context or the setting in which the talk is going on (such as "in the hospital") is relevant for the parties, that they are oriented to the setting so characterized, there remains another problem, and that is to show how the context or the setting (the local social structure), in that aspect, is procedurally conse-quential to the talk.

How does the fact that the talk is being conducted in some setting (say, "the hospital") issue in any consequences for the shape, form, trajectory, content, or character of the interaction that the parties conduct? And *what is the mechanism by which the context-so-understood has determinate consequences for the talk?*

This is a real problem, it seems to me, because without a specification of such a linkage we can end up with characterizations of context or setting which, however demonstrably relevant to the parties, do little in helping us to analyze, to explain, to understand, to give an account of how the interaction proceeded in the way in which it did, how it came to have the trajectory, the direction, the shape that it ended up having. When a formulation of the context is proposed, it is *ipso facto* taken to be somehow relevant and consequential for what occurs in the context. It is the analyst's responsibility either to deliver analytic specifics of that consequentiality or to abjure that characterization of the context. Otherwise, the analysis exploits a tacit feature of its own discursive format, but evades the corresponding analytic onus. A sense of understanding and grasp is conveyed to, and elicited from, the reader, but is not earned by the elucidation of new observations about the talk.

So, this is an open question, somewhat less formally stated than the other: how shall we find formulations of context or setting that will allow us (a) to connect to the theme that many want to connect to – social structure in the traditional sense, but (b) that will do so in a way that takes into account not only the demonstrable orientation of the participants, but, further, (c) that will allow us to make a direct "procedural" connection between the context so formulated and what actually happens in the talk. Otherwise we have a characterization that "hovers around" the interaction, so to speak, but is not shown actually to inform the production and grasp of the details of its conduct.

As with the issue of "relevance," I am here putting forward not principled objections to the invocation of social structure as context, but jobs to be taken on by those concerned with the intersection of talk and familiar senses of social structure. They challenge us to be alert to possible ways of showing such connections.

. . .

Consider, for example, the case of the courtroom in session (cf. Atkinson and Drew 1979; my remarks here rest on a much looser, vernacular and unstudied sense of the setting). To focus just on the turn-taking organization, it *is* the "courtroom-ness" of courtrooms in session which seems in fact to organize the way in which the talk is distributed among the persons present, among the *categories* of persons present, in the physical setting. So, for example, onlookers (members of the "audience") are not potential next speakers, as the official proceedings go on. And among the others who *are* potential next speakers at various points – the judge, the attorneys, the witness and the like, there are socially organized procedures for determining when they can talk, what they can do in their talk, and the like. It could be argued, then, that to characterize some setting of talk-in-interaction as in a court-in-session characterizes it with a formulation of context which can not only be claimed to connect to the general concern for "social structure" (for it certainly relates to institutional context), but can be shown to be procedurally consequential as well. Insofar as members of the audience sitting behind the bar never get up and talk but rather whisper to one another in asides, whereas the ones in front of the bar talk in defined and regular ways, by the very form of their conduct they show themselves to be oriented to the particular identities that are legally provided by that setting and show themselves to be oriented to "the-court-in-session" as a context.

. . .

Social structure or conversational structure?

The third concern mobilized by the present theme is for the balance between the focus on social structure and the focus on conversational structure in studying talk-in-interaction. These two thematic focuses (we would like to think) are potentially complementary. But are they really? We must figure out how to make them complementary, because they can also be alternatives in a more competitive sense. Each makes its own claims in organizing observation and analysis of the data, and one can pre-empt the other. In particular, the more familiar concerns with social structure can pre-empt new findings about conversational phenomena.

Let me offer some illustrations of this tension, and exemplify them from a recent paper of Zimmerman's, "Talk and its occasion" (1984), whose object of interest is "calls to the police" (an object with which I have also had some experience, cf. Schegloff 1967). The paper's enterprise appears directed specifically to attending both to the concerns of social structure and to the concerns of conversational structure. It offers a full account of this type of talk-in-interaction, and it does so with a sensitivity not only to the social structure involved, but also to the conversational structure of these occurrences. For example, the paper begins with an account of the kind of overall structural organization of the calls, and then focuses on the particular sequence type that makes up most of the calls, namely, an extended request or complaint sequence.

Despite this commitment to both concerns, it seems to me, there is a tendency for the formulated social-structural context to "absorb" and "naturalize" various details of talk. These features of the talk are thereby made unavailable, in practice if not in principle, for notice and analysis as accountable details of the talk. Their character as aspects of the talk produced by reference to some conversational or interactional organization is vulnerable to being slighted, in favor of assimilation to some social-structural, institutional, or vernacularly contextual source. How to balance these competing claims on our attention, when the competition takes this form, will be a matter to which analysts who are concerned with the thematics of talk-and-social structure will have to remain sensitive. . . .

A methodological canon is suggested: establishing relevance and establishing procedural consequentiality should not be "threshold" issues, in the sense that once you have done "enough" to show it, you are finished. Rather they are questions for continuing analysis. And not necessarily in the "loaded" form of "how are they now doing 'calling the police'?", but in "open" form – "what does the form of the talk show about recipient design considerations and about orientation to context (institutional, social-structural, sequential, or whatever)?" Because we "know" that not everything said *in* some context (institutional or other) is relevantly oriented *to* that context.

If the focus of inquiry is the organization of conduct, the details of action, the practices of talk, then every opportunity should be pressed to enhance our understanding of any available detail about those topics. Invoking social structure at the outset can systematically distract from, even blind us to, details of those domains of event in the world.

If the goal of inquiry is the elucidation of *social structure*, one might think that quite a different stance would be warranted, and one would want to give freer play to the effective scope of social structure, and to do so free of the constraints I have been discussing. Though this stance has much to recommend it, it could as well be argued that one does not best serve the understanding of social structure by attributing to it properties which are better understood as the products of other aspects of organized social life, such as interactional structure, or by failing to explicate how social structure is accomplished *in* the conduct. In any case, the understanding of social structure will be enhanced if we explicate how its embodiment in particular contexts on particular occasions permeates the "membrane" (Goffman 1961) surrounding episodes of interaction to register its stamp within them.

. . .

Conclusion

These then are three sorts of issues mobilized, or remobilized, for me when the talk turns to "talk and social structure." However lively our intuitions, in general or with respect to specific details, that it matters that some participants in data we are examining are police, or female, or deciding matters which are specifically constrained by the law or by economic or organizational contingencies, however insistent our sense of the reality and decisive bearing of such features of "social structure" in the traditional sense, the challenge posed is to find a way to show these claims, and show them from the data in three respects:

1   That what is so loomingly relevant for us (as competent members of the society or as professional social scientists) was relevant for the parties to the interaction we are examining, and thereby arguably implicated in their production of the details of that interaction.
2   That what seems inescapably relevant, both to us and to the participants, about the "context" of the interaction is demonstrably consequential for some specifiable aspect of that interaction.
3   That an adequate account for some specifiable features of the interaction cannot be fashioned from the details of the talk and other conduct of the participants as the vehicle by which *they* display the relevance of social-structural context for the character of the talk, but rather that this must be otherwise invoked by the analyst, who furthermore has developed defensible arguments for doing so.

In brief, the issue is how to convert insistent intuition, however correct, into empirically detailed analysis.

This is a heavy burden to impose. Meeting it may well lead to exciting new results. But if it is not to be met in one or more respects, arguments will have to be put forward that the concerns I have discussed are no longer in point, are superseded by other considerations, or must yield to the new sorts of findings that are possible if one holds them in abeyance. Simple invocation of the burden of the sociological past will not suffice.

With respect to social structure, then, as with respect to other notions from social science's past such as "intention," the stance we might well consider is treating them as programmatically relevant for the parties, and hence for us. In principle, some one or more aspects of who the parties are and where/when they are talking may be indispensably relevant for producing and grasping the talk, but these are not decisively knowable a priori. It is not for us to *know* what about context is crucial, but to *discover* it, and to discover *new sorts* of such things. Not, then, to privilege sociology's concerns under the rubric "social structure," but to discover them in the members' worlds, if they are there.

. . .

Notes

1   My thanks to Jennifer Mandelbaum for contributions of tact and clarity in the preparation of this chapter. I am also indebted to Deirdre Boden, Paul Drew, Douglas Maynard and especially Jack Whalen, whose reactions to an earlier draft, or to the reactions of others to the earlier draft, helped in my efforts to arrive at a text which might be understood as I meant it.
2   Editors' note: this article was published in 1991.

References

Atkinson, J.M. and Drew, P. (1979): *Order in Court: The Organisation of Verbal Interaction in Judicial Settings*, London: Macmillan.

Atkinson, J.M. and Heritage, J. (eds) (1984) *Structures of Social Action: Studies in Conversation Analysis*, Cambridge: Cambridge University Press.

Blau, P.M. (1977) *Inequality and Heterogeneity: A Primitive Theory of Social Structure*, New York: Free Press/Macmillan.

Boden, D. (1994) *The Business of Talk: Organizations in Action*, Cambridge: Polity Press.

Goffman, E. (1961) *Encounters*, Indianapolis: Bobbs-Merrill Educational.

—— (1983) 'The interaction order', *American Sociological Review* 48: 1–17.

Heritage, J. (1985) 'Analyzing news interviews: aspects of the production of talk for an "overhearing" audience', in Van Dijk, T. (ed.) *Handbook of Discourse Analysis*, vol. 3: *Discourse and Dialogue*, London: Academic Press, 95–119.

Maynard, D.W. (1984) *Inside Plea Bargaining*, New York: Plenum.

Parsons, T. (1937) *The Structure of Social Action*, New York: McGraw-Hill.

Sacks, H. (1972) 'An initial investigation of the usability of conversational data for doing sociology', in Sudnow, D. (ed.) *Studies in Social Interaction*, New York: Free Press, 31–74.

Schegloff, E. (1967) 'The first five seconds: the order of conversational openings', unpublished Ph.D. dissertation, Department of Sociology, University of California, Berkeley.

—— (1972) 'Notes on a conversational practice: formulating place', in Sudnow, D. (ed.) *Studies in Social Interaction*, New York: Macmillan/Free Press, 75–119.

—— (1987) 'Analyzing single episodes of interaction: an exercise in conversation analysis', *Social Psychological Quarterly* 50: 101–14.

West, C. (1979) 'Against our will: male interruptions of females in cross-sex conversations', *Annals of the New York Academy of Science* 327: 81–97.

——— (1984) *Routine Complications: Troubles in Talk Between Doctors and Patients*, Bloomington, IN: Indiana University Press.

Whalen, M.R. and Zimmerman, D.H. (1987) 'Sequential and institutional contexts in calls for help', *Social Psychology Quarterly* 50: 172–85.

Zimmerman, D.H. (1984) 'Talk and its occasion: the case of calling the police', in Schiffrin, D. (ed.) *Meaning, Form, and Use in Context: Linguistic Applications*, Georgetown University Roundtable on Language and Linguistics, Washington, DC: Georgetown University Press, 210–28.

Zimmerman, D. and West, C. (1975) 'Sex roles, interruptions and silences in conversations', in Thorne, B. and Henley, N. (eds) *Language and Sex: Difference and Dominance*, Rowley, MA: Newbury House, 105–29.

Chapter 6

M.M. Bakhtin

THE PROBLEM OF SPEECH GENRES

ALL THE DIVERSE AREAS of human activity involve the use of language. Quite understandably, the nature and forms of this use are just as diverse as are the areas of human activity. This, of course, in no way disaffirms the national unity of language. Language is realized in the form of individual concrete utterances (oral and written) by participants in the various areas of human activity. These utterances reflect the specific conditions and goals of each such area not only through their content (thematic) and linguistic style, that is, the selection of the lexical, phraseological, and grammatical resources of the language, but above all through their compositional structure. All three of these aspects – thematic content, style, and compositional structure – are inseparably linked to the *whole* of the utterance and are equally determined by the specific nature of the particular sphere of communication. Each separate utterance is individual, of course, but each sphere in which language is used develops its own *relatively stable types* of these utterances. These we may call *speech genres*.

The wealth and diversity of speech genres are boundless because the various possibilities of human activity are inexhaustible, and because each sphere of activity contains an entire repertoire of speech genres that differentiate and grow as the particular sphere develops and becomes more complex. Special emphasis should be placed on the extreme *heterogeneity* of speech genres (oral and written). In fact, the category of speech genres should include short rejoinders of daily dialogue (and these are extremely varied depending on the subject matter, situation, and participants), everyday narration, writing (in all its various forms), the brief standard military command, the elaborate and detailed order, the fairly variegated repertoire of business documents (for the most part standard), and the diverse world of commentary (in the broad sense of the word: social, political). And we must also

Source: M.M. Bakhtin, *Speech Genres and Other Late Essays*, translated by Vern W. McGee, edited by Caryl Emerson and Michael Holquist, Austin: University of Texas Press, 1986.

include here the diverse forms of scientific statements and all literary genres (from the proverb to the multivolume novel). It might seem that speech genres are so heterogeneous that they do not have and cannot have a single common level at which they can be studied. . . . One might think that such functional heterogeneity makes the common features of speech genres excessively abstract and empty. This probably explains why the general problem of speech genres has never really been raised. Literary genres have been studies more than anything else. But from antiquity to the present, they have been studied in terms of their specific literary and artistic features, in terms of the differences that distinguish one from the other (within the realm of literature), and not as specific types of utterances distinct from other types, but sharing with them a common *verbal* (language) nature. The general linguistic problem of the utterance and its types has hardly been considered at all. . . .

A clear idea of the nature of the utterance in general and of the peculiarities of the various types of utterances (primary and secondary), that is, of various speech genres, is necessary, we think, for research in any special area. To ignore the nature of the utterance or to fail to consider the peculiarities of generic subcategories of speech in any area of linguistic study leads to perfunctoriness and excessive abstractness, distorts the historicity of the research, and weakens the link between language and life. After all, language enters life through concrete utterances (which manifest language) and life enters language through concrete utterances as well. The utterance is an exceptionally important node of problems.

Any style is inseparably related to the utterance and to typical forms of utterances, that is, speech genres. Any utterance – oral or written, primary or secondary, and in any sphere of communication – is individual and therefore can reflect the individuality of the speaker (or writer); that is, it possesses individual style. But not all genres are equally conducive to reflecting the individuality of the speaker in the language of the utterance, that is, to an individual style. The most conducive genres are those of artistic literature: here the individual style enters directly into the very task of the utterance, and this is one of its main goals (but even within artistic literature various genres offer different possibilities for expressing individuality in language and various aspects of individuality). The least favorable conditions for reflecting individuality in language obtain in speech genres that require a standard form, for example, many kinds of business documents, military commands, verbal signals in industry, and so on. Here one can reflect only the most superficial, almost biological aspects of individuality (mainly in the oral manifestation of these standard types of utterances). In the vast majority of speech genres (except for literary-artistic ones), the individual style does not enter into the intent of the utterance, does not serve as its only goal, but is, as it were, an epiphenomenon of the utterance, one of its by-products. Various genres can reveal various layers and facets of the individual personality, and individual style can be found in various interrelations with the national language. The very problem of the national and the individual in language is basically the problem of the utterance (after all, only here, in the utterance, is the national language embodied in individual form). The very determination of style in general, and individual style in particular, requires deeper study of both the nature of the utterance and the diversity of speech genres.

. . .

It is especially harmful to separate style from genre when elaborating historical problems. Historical changes in language styles are inseparably linked to changes in speech genres. Literary language is a complex, dynamic system of linguistic styles. The proportions and interrelations of these styles in the system of literary language are constantly changing. Literary language, which also includes nonliterary styles, is an even more complex system, and it is organized on different bases. In order to puzzle out the complex historical dynamics of these systems and move from a simple (and, in the majority of cases, superficial) description of styles, which are always in evidence and alternating with one another, to a historical explanation of these changes, one must develop a special history of speech genres (and not only secondary, but also primary ones) that reflects more directly, clearly, and flexibly all the changes taking place in social life. Utterances and their types, that is, speech genres, are the drive belts from the history of society to the history of language. There is not a single new pheomenon (phonetic, lexical, or grammatical) that can enter the system of language without having traversed the long and complicated path of generic–stylistic testing and modification.

In each epoch, certain speech genres set the tone or the development of literary language. And these speech genres are not only secondary (literary, commentarial, and scientific), but also primary (certain types of oral dialogue – of the salon, of one's own circle, and other types as well, such as familiar, family – everyday, sociopolitical, philosophical, and so on). Any expansion of the literary language that results from drawing on various extraliterary strata of the national language inevitably entails some degree of penetration into all genres of written language (literary, scientific, commentarial, conversational, and so forth) to a greater or lesser degree, and entails new generic devices for the construction of the speech whole, its finalization, the accommodation of the listener or partner, and so forth. This leads to a more or less fundamental restructuring and renewal of speech genres.

. . .

Still current in linguistics are such *fictions* as the "listener" and "understander" (partners of the "speaker"), the "unified speech flow," and so on. These fictions produce a completely distorted idea of the complex and multifaceted process of active speech communication. Courses in general linguistics (even serious ones like Saussure's) frequently present graphic-schematic depictions of the two partners in speech communication – the speaker and the listener (who perceives the speech) – and provide diagrams of the active speech processes of the speaker and the corresponding passive processes of the listener's perception and understanding of the speech. One cannot say that these diagrams are false or that they do not correspond to certain aspects of reality. But when they are put forth as the actual whole of speech communication, they become a scientific fiction. The fact is that when the listener perceives and understands the meaning (the language meaning) of speech, he simultaneously takes an active, responsive attitude toward it. He either agrees or disagrees with it (completely or partially), augments it, applies it, prepares for its execution, and so on. And the listener adopts this responsive attitude for the entire duration of the process of listening and understanding, from the very beginning – sometimes literally from the speaker's first word. Any understanding of live speech, a live utterance, is inherently responsive, although the degree of this activity varies extremely. Any understanding is imbued with response and necessarily elicits it in one form or another: the listener becomes the speaker. . . .

Moreover, any speaker is himself a respondent to a greater or lesser degree. He is not, after all, the first speaker, the one who disturbs the eternal silence of the universe. And he presupposes not only the existence of the language system he is using, but also the existence of preceding utterances – his own and others' – with which his given utterance enters into one kind of relation or another (builds on them, polemicizes with them, or simply presumes that they are already known to the listener). Any utterance is a link in a very complexly organized chain of other utterances.

. . .

The boundaries of each concrete utterance as a unit of speech communication are determined by a *change of speaking subjects*, that is, a change of speakers. Any utterance – from a short (single-word) rejoinder in everyday dialogue to the large novel or scientific treatise – has, so to speak, an absolute beginning and an absolute end: its beginning is preceded by the utterances of others, and its end is followed by the responsive utterances of others (or, although it may be silent, others' active responsive understanding, or, finally, a responsive action based on this understanding). The speaker ends his utterance in order to relinquish the floor to the other or to make room for the other's active responsive understanding. The utterance is not a conventional unit, but a real unit, clearly delimited by the change of speaking subjects, which ends by relinquishing the floor to the other, as if with a silent, *dixi*, perceived by the listeners (as a sign) that the speaker has finished.

This change of speaking subjects, which creates clear-cut boundaries of the utterance, varies in nature and acquires different forms in the heterogeneous spheres of human activity and life, depending on the functions of language and on the conditions and situations of communication. One observes this change of speaking subjects most simply and clearly in actual dialogue where the utterances of the interlocutors or partners in dialogue (which we shall call rejoinders) alternate. Because of its simplicity and clarity, dialogue is a classic form of speech communication. Each rejoinder, regardless of how brief and abrupt, has a specific quality of completion that expresses a particular position of the speaker, to which one may respond or may assume, with respect to it, a responsive position. But at the same time rejoinders are all linked to one another. And the sort of relations that exist among rejoinders of dialogue – relations between question and answer, assertion and objection, assertion and agreement, suggestion and acceptance, order and execution, and so forth – are impossible among units of language (words and sentences), either in the system of language (in the vertical cross section) or within the utterance (on the horizontal plane). These specific relations among rejoinders in a dialogue are only subcategories of specific relations among whole utterances in the process of speech communication. These relations are possible only among utterances of different speech subjects; they presuppose *other* (with respect to the speaker) participants in speech communication. The relations among whole utterances cannot be treated grammatically since, we repeat, such relations are impossible among units of language, and not only in the system of language, but within the utterance as well.

. . .

Complexly structured and specialized works of various scientific and artistic genres, in spite of all the ways in which they differ from rejoinders in dialogue, are by nature the same kind of units of speech communication. They, too, are clearly demarcated by a change of speaking subjects, and these boundaries, while retaining their *external* clarity, acquire here a special internal aspect because the speaking subject – in this case, the *author* of the work – manifests his own individuality in his style, his world-view, and in all aspects of the design of his work. This imprint of individuality marking the work also creates special internal boundaries that distinguish this work from other works connected with it in the overall processes of speech communication in that particular cultural sphere: from the works of predecessors on whom the author relies, from other works of the same school, from the works of opposing schools with which the author is contending, and so on.

The work, like the rejoinder in dialogue, is oriented toward the response of the other (others), toward his active responsive understanding, which can assume various forms: educational influence on the readers, persuasion of them, critical responses, influence on followers and successors, and so on. It can determine others' responsive positions under the complex conditions of speech communication in a particular cultural sphere. The work is a link in the chain of a speech communion. Like the rejoinder in a dialogue, it is related to other work-utterances: both those to which it responds and those that respond to it. At the same time, like the rejoinder in a dialogue, it is separated from them by the absolute boundaries created by a change of speaking subjects.

. . .

The speaker's speech will is manifested primarily in the *choice of a particular speech genre*. This choice is determined by the specific nature of the given sphere of speech communication, semantic (thematic) considerations, the concrete situation of the speech communication, the personal composition of its participants, and so on. And when the speaker's speech plan with all its individuality and subjectivity is applied and adapted to a chosen genre, it is shaped and developed within a certain generic form. Such genres exist above all in the great and multifarious sphere of everyday oral communication, including the most familiar and the most intimate.

We speak only in definite speech genres, that is, all our utterances have definite and relatively stable typical *forms of construction of the whole*. Our repertoire of oral (and written) speech genres is rich. We use them confidently and skillfully *in practice,* and it is quite possible for us not even to suspect their existence *in theory.* Like Molière's Monsieur Jourdain who, when speaking in prose, had no idea that was what he was doing; we speak in diverse genres without suspecting that they exist. Even in the most free, the most unconstrained conversation, we cast our speech in definite generic forms, sometimes rigid and trite ones, sometimes more flexible, plastic, and creative ones (everyday communication also has creative genres at its disposal). We are given these speech genres in almost the same way that we are given our native language, which we master fluently long before we begin to study grammar. We know our native language – its lexical composition and grammatical structure – not from dictionaries and grammars but from concrete utterances that we hear and that we ourselves reproduce in live speech communication with people around us. We assimilate forms of language only in forms of utterances and in conjunction with these forms. The forms of language and the typical forms of utterances, that is, speech genres, enter our experience and our consciousness together, and in close connection with one another. To learn to speak means to learn to construct utterances (because we speak in utterances and not in individual sentences, and, of course, not in individual words). Speech genres organize our speech in almost the same way as grammatical (syntactical) forms do.

. . .

The generic forms in which we cast our speech, of course, differ essentially from language forms. The latter are stable and compulsory (normative) for the speaker, while generic forms are much more flexible, plastic, and free. Speech genres are very diverse in this respect. A large number of genres that are widespread in everyday life are so standard that the speaker's individual speech will is manifested only in its choice of a particular genre, and, perhaps, in its expressive intonation. Such, for example, are the various everyday genres of greetings, farewells, congratulations, all kinds of wishes, information about health, business, and so forth. These genres are so diverse because they differ depending on the situation, social position, and personal interrelations of the participants in the communication. These genres have high, strictly official, respectful forms as well as familiar ones. And there are forms with varying degrees of familiarity, as well as intimate forms (which differ from familiar ones). These genres also require a certain tone; their structure includes a certain expressive intonation. These genres, particularly the high and official ones, are compulsory and extremely stable. The speech will is usually limited here to a choice of a particular genre. And only slight nuances of expressive intonation (one can take a drier or more respectful tone, a colder or warmer one; one can introduce the intonation of joy, and so forth) can express the speaker's individuality (his emotional speech intent). But even here it is to re-accentuate genres. This is typical of speech communication: thus, for example, the generic form of greeting can move from the official sphere into the sphere of familiar communication, that is, it can be used with parodic-ironic re-accentuation. To a similar end, one can deliberately mix genres from various spheres.

In addition to these standard genres, of course, freer and more creative genres of oral speech communication have existed and still exist: genres of salon conversations about everyday, social, aesthetic, and other subjects, genres of table conversation, intimate conversations among friends, intimate conversations within the family, and so on. (No list of oral speech genres yet exists, or even a principle on which such a list might be based.) The majority of these genres are subject to free creative reformulation (like artistic genres, and some, perhaps, to a greater degree). But to use a genre freely and creatively is not the same as to create a genre from the beginning; genres must be fully mastered in order to be manipulated freely.

. . .

Any utterance is a link in the chain of speech communion. It is the active position of the speaker in one referentially semantic sphere or another. Therefore, each utterance is characterized primarily by a particular referentially semantic content. The choice of linguistic means and speech genre is determined primarily by the referentially semantic assignments (plan) of the speech subject (or author). This is the first aspect of the utterance that determines its compositional and stylistic features.

The second aspect of the utterance that determines its composition and style is the *expressive* aspect, that is, the speaker's subjective emotional evaluation of the referentially semantic content of his utterance. The expressive aspect has varying significance and varying degrees of force in various spheres of speech communication, but it exists everywhere. There can be no such thing as an absolutely neutral utterance. The speaker's evaluative attitude toward the subject of his speech (regardless of what his subject may be) also determines the choice of lexical, grammatical, and compositional means of the utterance. The individual style of the utterance is determined primarily by its expressive aspect. This is generally recognized in the area of stylistics. Certain investigators even reduce style directly to the emotionally evaluative aspect of speech.

. . .

When selecting words, we proceed from the planned whole of our utterance, and this whole that we have planned and created is always expressive. The utterance is what radiates its expression (rather, our expression) to the word we have selected, which is to say, invests the word with the expression of the whole. And we select the word because of its meaning, which is not in itself expressive but which can accommodate or not accommodate our expressive goals in combination with other words, that is, in combination with the whole of our utterance. The neutral meaning of the word applied to a particular actual reality under particular real conditions of speech communication creates a spark of expression. And, after all, this is precisely what takes place in the process of creating an utterance. . . .

A speech genre is not a form of language, but a typical form of utterance; as such the genre also includes a certain typical kind of expression that inheres in it. In the genre, the word acquires a particular typical expression. Genres correspond to typical situations of speech communication, typical themes, and, consequently, also to particular contacts between the *meanings* of words and actual concrete reality under certain typical circumstances. Hence also the possibility of typical expressions that seem to adhere to words. This typical expression (and the typical intonation that corresponds to it) does not have that force of compulsoriness that language forms have. . . . Speech genres in general submit fairly easily to re-accentuation, the sad can be made jocular and gay, but as a result something new is achieved (for example, the genre of comical epitaphs).

. . .

The words of a language belong to nobody, but still we hear those words only in particular individual utterances, we read them in particular individual works, and in such cases the words already have not only a typical, but also (depending on the genre) a more or less clearly reflected individual expression, which is determined by the unrepeatable individual context of the utterance.

Neutral dictionary meanings of the words of a language ensure their common features and guarantee that all speakers of a given language will understand one another, but the use of words in live speech communication is always individual and contextual in nature. Therefore, one can say that any word exists for the speaker in three aspects: as a neutral word of a language, belonging to nobody; as an *others'* word, which belongs to another person and is filled with echoes of the other's utterance; and, finally, as *my* word, for, since I am dealing with it in a particular situation, with a particular speech plan, it is already imbued with my expression. In both of the latter aspects, the word is expressive, but, we repeat, this expression does not inhere in the word itself. It originates at the point of contact between the word and actual reality, under the conditions of that real situation articulated by the individual utterance. In this case the word appears as an expression of some evaluative position of an individual person (authority, writer, scientist, father, mother, friend, teacher, and so forth), as an abbreviation of the utterance.

In each epoch, in each social circle, in each small world of family, friends, acquaintances, and comrades in which a human being grows and lives, there are always authoritative utterances that set the tone — artistic, scientific, and journalistic works on which one relies, to which one refers, which are cited, imitated, and followed. In each epoch, in all areas of life and activity, there are particular traditions that are expressed and retained in verbal vestments: in written works, in utterances, in sayings, and so forth. There are always some verbally expressed leading ideas of the "masters of thought" of a given epoch, some basic tasks, slogans, and so forth.

. . .

This is why the unique speech experience of each individual is shaped and developed in continuous and constant interaction with others' individual utterances. This experience can be characterized to some degree as the process of *assimilation* — more or less creative — of others' words (and not the words of a language). Our speech, that is, all our utterances (including creative works), is filled with others' words, varying degrees of otherness or varying degrees of "our-own-ness," varying degrees of awareness and detachment. These words of others carry with them their own expression, their own evaluative tone, which we assimilate, rework, and re-accentuate.

. . .

Utterances are not indifferent to one another, and are not self-sufficient; they are aware of and mutually reflect one another. These mutual reflections determine their character. Each utterance is filled with echoes and reverberations of other utterances to which it is related by the communality of the sphere of speech communication. Every utterance must be regarded primarily as a *response* to preceding utterances of the given sphere (we understand the word "response" here in the broadest sense). Each utterance refutes, affirms, supplements, and relies on the others, presupposes them to be known, and somehow takes them into account. After all, as regards a given question, in a given matter, and so forth, the utterance occupies a particular *definite* position in a given sphere of communication. It is impossible to determine its position without correlating it with other positions. Therefore, each utterance is filled with various kinds of responsive reactions to other utterances of the given sphere of speech communication. These reactions take various forms: others' utterances can be introduced directly into the utterance, or one may introduce words or sentences, which then act as representatives of the whole utterance. Both whole utterances and individual words can retain their alien expression, but they can also be re-accentuated (ironically, indignantly, reverently, and so forth). Others' utterances can be repeated with varying degrees of reinterpretation. They can be referred to as though the interlocutor were already well aware of them; they can be silently presupposed; or one's responsive reaction to them can be reflected only in the expression of one's own speech – in the selection of language means and intonations that are determined not by the topic of one's own speech but by the others' utterances concerning the same topic. . . . The utterance is filled with *dialogic overtones*, and they must be taken into account in order to understand fully the style of the utterance. After all, our thought itself – philosophical, scientific, and artistic – is born and shaped in the process of interaction and struggle with others' thought, and this cannot but be reflected in the forms that verbally express our thought as well.

. . .

Any utterance, when it is studied in greater depth under the concrete conditions of speech communication, reveals to us many half-concealed or completely concealed words of others with varying degrees of foreignness. Therefore, the utterance appears to be furrowed with distant and barely audible echoes of changes of speech subjects and dialogic overtones, greatly weakened utterance boundaries that are completely permeable to the author's expression. The utterance proves to be a very complex and multiplanar phenomenon if considered not in isolation and with respect to its author (the speaker) only, but as a link in the chain of speech communication and with respect to other, related utterances (these relations are usually disclosed not on the verbal – compositional and stylistic – plane, but only on the referentially semantic plane).

. . .

The topic of the speaker's speech, regardless of what this topic may be, does not become the object of speech for the first time in any given utterance; a given speaker is not the first to speak about it. The object, as it were, has already been articulated, disputed, elucidated, and evaluated in various ways. Various viewpoints, world-views, and trends cross, converge, and diverge in it. The speaker is not the biblical Adam, dealing only with virgin and still unnamed objects, giving them names for the first time. . . . . The utterance is addressed not only to its own object, but also to others' speech about it. But still, even the slightest allusion to another's utterance gives the speech a dialogical turn that cannot be produced by any purely referential theme with its own object. The attitude toward another's word is in principle distinct from the attitude toward a referential object, but the former always accompanies the latter. We repeat, an utterance is a link in the chain of speech communication, and it cannot be broken off from the preceding links that determine it both from within and from without, giving rise within it to unmediated responsive reactions and dialogic reverberations. . . .

We have already said that the role of these others, for whom my thought becomes actual thought for the first time (and thus also for my own self as well) is not that of passive listeners, but of active participants in speech communication. From the very beginning, the speaker expects a response from them, an active responsive understanding. The entire utterance is constructed, as it were, in anticipation of encountering this response.

An essential (constitutive) marker of the utterance is its quality of being directed to someone, its *addressivity*. As distinct from the signifying units of a language – words and sentences – that are impersonal, belonging to nobody and addressed to nobody, the utterance has both an author (and, consequently, expression, which we have already discussed) and an addressee. This addressee can be an immediate participant-interlocutor in an everyday dialogue, a differentiated collective of specialists in some particular area of cultural communication, a more or less differentiated public, ethnic group, contemporaries, like-minded people, opponents and enemies, a subordinate, a superior, someone who is lower, higher, familiar, foreign, and so forth. And it can also be an indefinite, unconcretized *other* (with various kinds of monological utterances of an emotional type). All these varieties and conceptions of the addressee are determined by that area of human activity and everyday life to which the given utterance is related. Both the composition and, particularly, the style of the utterance depend on those to whom the utterance is addressed, how the speaker (or writer) senses and imagines his addressees, and the force of their effect on the utterance. Each speech genre in each area of speech communication has its own typical conception of the addressee, and this defines it as a genre.

. . .

Chapter 7

Roland Barthes

MYTH TODAY

WHAT IS A MYTH, TODAY? I shall give at the outset a first, very simple answer, which is perfectly consistent with etymology: *myth is a type of speech*.[1]

Myth is a type of speech

Of course, it is not *any* type: language needs special conditions in order to become myth: we shall see them in a minute. But what must be firmly established at the start is that myth is a system of communication, that it is a message. This allows one to perceive that myth cannot possibly be an object, a concept, or an idea; it is a mode of signification, a form. Later, we shall have to assign to this form historical limits, conditions of use, and reintroduce society into it: we must nevertheless first describe it as a form.

It can be seen that to purport to discriminate among mythical objects according to their substance would be entirely illusory: since myth is a type of speech, everything can be a myth provided it is conveyed by a discourse. Myth is not defined by the object of its message, but by the way in which it utters this message: there are formal limits to myth, there are no 'substantial' ones. Everything, then, can be a myth? Yes, I believe this, for the universe is infinitely fertile in suggestions. Every object in the world can pass from a closed, silent existence to an oral state, open to appropriation by society, for there is no law, whether natural or not, which forbids talking about things. A tree is a tree. Yes, of course. But a tree as expressed by Minou Drouet is no longer quite a tree, it is a tree which is decorated, adapted

Source: Roland Barthes, *Mythologies*, selected and translated from the French by Annette Lavers, London: Jonathan Cape, 1972, 105–59. (Originally published in 1957.)

to a certain type of consumption, laden with literary self-indulgence, revolt, images, in short with a type of social *usage* which is added to pure matter.

Naturally, everything is not expressed at the same time: some objects become the prey of mythical speech for a while, then they disappear, others take their place and attain the status of myth. Are there objects which are *inevitably* a source of suggestiveness, as Baudelaire suggested about Woman? Certainly not: one can conceive of very ancient myths, but there are no eternal ones; for it is human history which converts reality into speech, and it alone rules the life and the death of mythical language. Ancient or not, mythology can only have an historical foundation, for myth is a type of speech chosen by history: it cannot possibly evolve from the 'nature' of things.

Speech of this kind is a message. It is therefore by no means confined to oral speech. It can consist of modes of writing or of representations; not only written discourse, but also photography, cinema, reporting, sport, shows, publicity, all these can serve as a support to mythical speech. Myth can be defined neither by its object nor by its material, for any material can arbitrarily be endowed with meaning: the arrow which is brought in order to signify a challenge is also a kind of speech. True, as far as perception is concerned, writing and pictures, for instance, do not call upon the same type of consciousness; and even with pictures, one can use many kinds of reading: a diagram lends itself to signification more than a drawing, a copy more than an original, and a caricature more than a portrait. But this is the point: we are no longer dealing here with a theoretical mode of representation: we are dealing with *this* particular image, which is given for *this* particular signification. Mythical speech is made of a material which has *already* been worked on so as to make it suitable for communication: it is because all the materials of myth (whether pictorial or written) presuppose a signifying consciousness, that one can reason about them while discounting their substance. This substance is not unimportant: pictures, to be sure, are more imperative than writing, they impose meaning at one stroke, without analysing or diluting it. But this is no longer a constitutive difference. Pictures become a kind of writing as soon as they are meaningful: like writing, they call for a *lexis*.

We shall therefore take *language*, *discourse*, *speech*, etc., to mean any significant unit or synthesis, whether verbal or visual: a photograph will be a kind of speech for us in the same way as a newspaper article; even objects will become speech, if they mean something. This generic way of conceiving language is in fact justified by the very history of writing: long before the invention of our alphabet, objects like the Inca *quipu*, or drawings, as in pictographs, have been accepted as speech. This does not mean that one must treat mythical speech like language; myth in fact belongs to the province of a general science, coextensive with linguistics, which is *semiology*.

Myth as a semiological system

For mythology, since it is the study of a type of speech, is but one fragment of this vast science of signs which Saussure postulated some forty years ago under the name of *semiology*. Semiology has not yet come into being. But since Saussure himself, and sometimes independently of him, a whole section of contemporary research has constantly been referred to the problem of meaning: psycho-analysis, structuralism, eidetic psychology, some new types of literary criticism of which Bachelard has given the first examples, are no longer concerned with facts except inasmuch as they are endowed with significance. Now to postulate a signification is to have recourse to semiology. I do not mean that semiology could account for all these aspects of research equally well: they have different contents. But they have a common status: they are all sciences dealing with values. They are not content with meeting the facts: they define and explore them as tokens for something else.

Semiology is a science of forms, since it studies significations apart from their content. I should like to say one word about the necessity and the limits of such a formal science. The necessity is that which applies in the case of any exact language. Zhdanov made fun of Alexandrov the philosopher, who spoke of '*the spherical structure of our planet.*' '*It was thought until now*', Zhdanov said, '*that form alone could be spherical.*' Zhdanov was right: one cannot speak about structures in terms of forms, and vice versa. It may well be that on the plane of 'life', there is but a totality where structures and forms cannot be separated. But science has no use for the ineffable: it must speak about 'life' if it wants to transform it. Against a certain quixotism of synthesis, quite platonic incidentally, all criticism must consent to the *ascesis*, to the artifice of analysis; and in analysis, it must match method and language. Less terrorized by the spectre of 'formalism', historical criticism might have been less sterile; it would have understood that the specific study of forms does not in any way contradict the necessary principles of totality and History. On the contrary: the more a system is specifically defined in its forms, the more amenable it is to historical criticism. To parody a well-known saying, I shall say that a little formalism turns one away from History, but that a lot brings one back to it. Is there a better example of total criticism than the description of saintliness, at once formal and historical, semiological and ideological, in Sartre's *Saint-Genet*? The danger, on the contrary, is to consider forms as ambiguous objects, half-form and half-substance, to endow form with a substance of form, as was done, for instance, by Zhdanovian realism. Semiology, once its limits are settled, is not a metaphysical trap: it is a science among others, necessary but not sufficient. The important thing is to see that the unity of an explanation cannot be based on the amputation of one or other of its approaches, but, as Engels said, on the dialectical co-ordination of the particular sciences it makes use of. This is the case with mythology: it is a part both of semiology inasmuch as it is a formal science, and of ideology inasmuch as it is an historical science: it studies ideas-in-form.[2]

Let me therefore restate that any semiology postulates a relation between two terms, a signifier and a signified. This relation concerns objects which belong to different categories, and this is why it is not one of equality but one of equivalence. We must here be on our guard for despite common parlance which simply says that the signifier *expresses* the signified, we are dealing, in any semiological system, not with two, but with three different terms. For what we grasp is not at all one term after the other, but the correlation which unites them: there are, therefore, the signifier, the signified and the sign, which is the associative total of the first two terms. Take a bunch of roses: I use it to *signify* my passion. Do we have here, then, only a signifier and a signified, the roses and my passion? Not even that: to put it accurately, there are here only 'passionified' roses. But on the plane of analysis, we do have three terms; for these roses weighted with passion perfectly and correctly allow themselves to be decomposed into roses and passion: the former and the latter existed before uniting and forming this third object, which is the sign. It is as true to say that on the plane of experience I cannot dissociate the roses from the message they carry, as to say that on the plane of analysis I cannot confuse the roses as signifier and the roses as sign: the signifier is empty, the sign is full, it is a meaning. Or take a black pebble: I can make it signify in several ways, it is a mere signifier; but if I weigh it with a definite signified (a death sentence, for instance, in an anonymous vote), it will become a sign. Naturally, there are between the signifier, the signified and the sign, functional implications (such as that of the part to the whole) which are so close that to analyse them may seem futile; but we shall see in a moment that this distinction has a capital importance for the study of myth as semiological schema.

Naturally these three terms are purely formal, and different contents can be given to them. Here are a few examples: for Saussure, who worked on a particular but methodologically exemplary semiological system – the language or *langue* – the signified is the concept, the signifier is the acoustic image (which is mental) and the relation between concept and image is the sign (the word, for instance), which is a concrete entity.[3] For Freud, as is well known, the human psyche is a stratification of tokens or representatives. One term (I refrain from giving it any precedence) is constituted by the manifest meaning of behaviour, another, by its latent or real meaning (it is, for instance, the substratum of the dream); as for the third term, it is here also a correlation of the first two: it is the dream itself in its totality, the parapraxis (a mistake in speech or behaviour) or the neurosis, conceived as compromises, as economies effected thanks to the joining of a form (the first term) and an intentional function (the second term). We can see here how necessary it is to distinguish the sign from the signifier: a dream, to Freud, is no more its manifest datum than its latent content: it is the functional union of these two terms. In Sartrean criticism, finally (I shall keep to these three well-known examples), the signified is constituted by the original crisis in the subject (the separation from his mother for Baudelaire, the naming of the theft for Genet); Literature as discourse forms the signifier; and the relation between crisis and discourse defines the work, which is a signification. Of course, this tri-dimensional pattern, however constant in its form, is actualized in different ways: one cannot therefore say too often that semiology can have its unity only at the level of forms, not contents; its field is limited, it knows only one operation: reading, or deciphering.

In myth, we find again the tri-dimensional pattern which I have just described: the signifier, the signified and the sign. But myth is a peculiar system, in that it is constructed from a semiological chain which existed before it: it is *a second-order semiological system*. That which is a sign (namely the associative total of a concept and an image) in the first system, becomes a mere signifier in the second. We must here recall that the materials of mythical speech (the language itself, photography, painting, posters, rituals, objects, etc.), however different at the start, are reduced to a pure signifying function as soon as they are caught by myth. Myth sees in them only the same raw material; their unity is that they all come down to the status of a mere language. Whether it deals with alphabetical or pictorial writing, myth wants to see in them only a sum of signs, a global sign, the final term of a first semiological chain. And it is precisely this final term which will become the first term of the greater system which it builds and of which it is only a part. Everything happens as if myth shifted the formal system of the first significations sideways. As this lateral shift is essential for the analysis of myth, I shall represent it in the following way, it being understood, of course, that the spatialization of the pattern is here only, a metaphor:

It can be seen that in myth there are two semiological systems, one of which is staggered in relation to the other: a linguistic system, the language (or the modes of representation which are assimilated to it), which I shall call the *language object*, because it is the language which myth gets hold of in order to build its own system; and myth itself, which I shall call *metalanguage*, because it is a second language, *in which* one speaks about the first. When he reflects on a metalanguage, the semiologist no longer needs to ask himself questions about the composition of the language object, he no longer has to take into account the details of the linguistic schema; he will only need to know its total term, or global sign, and only inasmuch as this term lends itself to myth. This is why the semiologist is entitled to treat in the same way writing and pictures: what he retains from them is the fact that they are both *signs*, that they both reach the threshold of myth endowed with the same signifying function, that they constitute, one just as much as the other, a language-object.

It is now time to give one or two examples of mythical speech. I shall borrow the first from an observation by Valéry.[4] I am a pupil in the second form in a French *lycée*. I open my Latin grammar, and I read a sentence, borrowed from Aesop or Phaedrus: *quia ego nominor leo*. I stop and think. There is something ambiguous about this statement: on the one hand, the words in it do have a simple meaning: *because my name is lion*. And on the other hand, the sentence is evidently there in order to signify something else to me. Inasmuch as it is addressed to me, a pupil in the second form, it tells me clearly: I am a grammatical example meant to illustrate the rule about the agreement of the predicate. I am even forced to realize that the sentence in no way signifies its meaning to me, that it tries very little to tell me something about the lion and what sort of name he has; its true and fundamental signification is to impose itself on me as the presence of a certain agreement of the predicate. I conclude that I am faced with a particular, greater, semiological system, since it is co-extensive with the language: there, is, indeed, a signifier, but this signifier is itself formed by a sum of signs, it is in itself a first semiological system (*my name is lion*). Thereafter, the formal pattern is correctly unfolded: there is a signified (*I am a grammatical example*) and there is a global signification, which is none other than the correlation of the signifier and the signified; for neither the naming of the lion nor the grammatical example are given separately.

And here is now another example: I am at the barber's, and a copy of *Paris-Match* is offered to me. On the cover, a young Negro in a French uniform is saluting, with his eyes uplifted, probably fixed on a fold of the tricolour. All this is the *meaning* of the picture. But, whether naively or not, I see very well what it signifies to me: that France is a great Empire, that all her sons, without any colour discrimination, faithfully serve under her flag, and that there is no better answer to the detractors of an alleged colonialism than the zeal shown by this Negro in serving his so-called oppressors. I am therefore again faced with a greater semiological system: there is a signifier, itself already formed with a previous system (*a black soldier is giving the French salute*); there is a signified (it is here a purposeful mixture of Frenchness and militariness); finally, there is a presence of the signified through the signifier.

Before tackling the analysis of each term of the mythical system, one must agree on terminology. We now know that the signifier can be looked at, in myth, from two points of view: as the final term of the linguistic system, or as the first term of the mythical system. We therefore need two names. On the plane of language, that is, as the final term of the first system, I shall call the signifier: *meaning* (*my name is lion, a Negro is giving the French salute*); on the plane of myth, I shall call it: *form*. In the case of the signified, no ambiguity is possible: we shall retain the name *concept*. The third term is the correlation of the first two: in the linguistic system, it is the *sign*; but it is not possible to use this word again without ambiguity, since in myth (and this is the chief peculiarity of the latter), the signifier is already formed by the signs of the language. I shall call the third term of myth the *signification*. This word is here all the better justified since myth has in fact a double function: it points out and it notifies, it makes us understand something and it imposes it on us.

The form and the concept

The signifier of myth presents itself in an ambiguous way: it is at the same time meaning and form, full on one side and empty on the other. As meaning, the signifier already postulates a reading, I grasp it through my eyes, it has a sensory reality (unlike the linguistic signifier, which is purely mental), there is a richness in it: the naming of the lion, the Negro's salute are credible wholes, they have at their disposal a sufficient rationality. As a total of linguistic signs, the meaning of the myth has its own value, it belongs to a history, that of the lion or that of the Negro: in the meaning, a signification is already built, and could very well be self-sufficient if myth did not take hold of it and did not turn it suddenly into an empty, parasitical form. The meaning is *already* complete, it postulates a kind of knowledge, a past, a memory, a comparative order of facts, ideas, decisions.

When it becomes form, the meaning leaves its contingency behind; it empties itself, it becomes impoverished, history evaporates, only the letter remains. There is here a paradoxical permutation in the reading operations, an abnormal regression from meaning to form, from the linguistic sign to the mythical signifier. If one encloses *quia ego nominor leo* in a purely linguistic system, the clause finds again there a fullness, a richness, a history: I am an animal, a lion, I live in a certain country, I have just been hunting, they would have me share my prey with a heifer, a cow and a goat; but being the stronger, I award myself all the shares for various reasons, the last of which is quite simply that *my name is lion*. But as the form of the myth, the clause hardly retains anything of this long story. The meaning contained a whole system of values: a history, a geography, a morality, a zoology, a Literature. The form has put all this richness at a distance: its newly acquired penury calls for a signification to fill it. The story of the lion must recede a great deal in order to make room for the grammatical example, one must put the biography of the Negro in parentheses if one wants to free the picture, and prepare it to receive its signified.

But the essential point in all this is that the form does not suppress the meaning, it only impoverishes it, it puts it at a distance; it holds it at one's disposal. One believes that the meaning is going to die, but it is a death with reprieve; the meaning loses its value, but keeps its life, from which the form of the myth will draw its nourishment. The meaning will be for the form like an instantaneous reserve of history, a tamed richness, which it is possible to call and dismiss in a sort of rapid alternation: the form must constantly be able to be rooted again in the meaning and to get there what nature it needs for its nutriment; above all, it must be able to hide there. It is this constant game of hide-and-seek between the meaning and the form which defines myth. The form of myth is not a symbol: the Negro who salutes is not the symbol of the French Empire: he has too much presence, he appears as a rich, fully experienced, spontaneous, innocent, *indisputable* image. But at the same time this presence is tamed, put at a distance, made almost transparent; it recedes a little, it becomes the accomplice of a concept which comes to it fully armed, French imperiality: once made use of, it becomes artificial.

Let us now look at the signified: this history which drains out of the form will be wholly absorbed by the concept. As for the latter, it is determined, it is at once historical and intentional; it is the motivation which causes the myth to be uttered. Grammatical exemplarity, French imperiality, are the very drives behind the myth. The concept reconstitutes a chain of causes and effects, motives and intentions. Unlike the form, the concept is in no way abstract: it is filled with a situation. Through the concept, it is a whole new history which is implanted in the myth. Into the naming of the lion, first drained of its contingency, the grammatical example will attract my whole existence: Time, which caused me to be born at a certain period when Latin grammar is taught; History, which sets me apart, through a whole mechanism of social segregation, from the children who do not learn Latin; pedagogic tradition, which caused this example to be chosen from Aesop or Phaedrus; my own linguistic habits, which see the agreement of the predicate as a fact worthy of notice and illustration. The same goes for the Negro-giving-the-salute: as form, its meaning is shallow, isolated, impoverished; as the concept of French imperiality, here it is again tied to the totality of the world: to the general History of France, to its colonial adventures, to its present difficulties. Truth to tell, what is invested in the concept is less reality than a certain knowledge of reality; in passing from the meaning to the form, the image loses some knowledge: the better to receive the knowledge in the concept. In actual fact, the knowledge contained in a mythical concept is confused, made of yielding, shapeless associations. One must firmly stress this open character of the concept; it is not at all an abstract, purified essence; it is a formless, unstable, nebulous condensation, whose unity and coherence are above all due to its function.

In this sense, we can say that the fundamental character of the mythical concept is to be *appropriated*: grammatical exemplarity very precisely concerns a given form of pupils, French imperiality must appeal to such and such group of readers and not another. The concept closely corresponds to a function, it is defined as a tendency. This cannot fail to recall the signified in another semiological system, Freudianism. In Freud, the second term of the system is the latent meaning (the content) of the dream, of the parapraxis, of the neurosis. Now Freud does remark that the second-order meaning of behaviour is its real meaning, that which is appropriate to a complete situation, including its deeper level; it is, just like the mythical concept, the very intention of behaviour.

A signified can have several signifiers: this is indeed the case in linguistics and psycho-analysis. It is also the case in the mythical concept: it has at its disposal an unlimited mass of signifiers: I can find a thousand Latin sentences to actualize for me the agreement of the predicate, I can find a thousand images which signify to me French imperiality. This means that *quantitively*, the concept is much poorer than the signifier, it often does nothing but re-present itself. Poverty and richness are in reverse proportion in the form and the concept: to the qualitative poverty of the form, which is the repository of a rarefied meaning, there corresponds the richness of the concept which is open to the whole of History; and to the quantitative abundance of the forms there corresponds a small number of concepts. This repetition of the concept through different forms is precious to the mythologist, it allows him to decipher the myth: it is the insistence of a kind of behaviour which reveals its intention. This confirms that there is no regular ratio between the volume of the signified and that of the signifier. In language, this ratio is proportionate, it hardly exceeds the word, or at least the concrete unit. In myth, on the contrary, the concept can spread over a very large expanse of signifier. For instance, a whole book may be the signifier of a single concept; and conversely, a minute form (a word, a gesture, even incidental, so long as it is noticed) can serve as signifier to a concept filled with a very rich history. Although unusual in language, this disproportion between signifier and signified is not specific to myth: in Freud, for instance, the parapraxis is a signifier whose thinness is out of proportion to the real meaning which it betrays.

As I said, there is no fixity in mythical concepts: they can come into being, alter, disintegrate, disappear completely. And it is precisely because they are historical that history can very easily suppress them. This instability forces the mythologist to use a terminology adapted to it, and about which I should now like to say a word, because it often is a cause for irony: I mean neologism. The concept is a constituting element of myth: if I want to decipher myths, I must somehow be able to name concepts. The dictionary supplies me with a few: Goodness, Kindness, Wholeness, Humaneness, etc. But by definition, since it is the dictionary which gives them to me, these particular concepts are not historical. Now what I need most often is ephemeral concepts, in connection with limited contingencies: neologism is then inevitable. China is one thing, the idea which a French petit-bourgeois could have of it not so long ago is another: for this peculiar mixture of bells, rickshaws and opium-dens, no other word possible but *Sininess*.[5] Unlovely?

One should at least get some consolation from the fact that conceptual neologisms are never arbitrary: they are built according to a highly sensible proportional rule.

The signification

In semiology, the third term is nothing but the association of the first two, as we saw. It is the only one which is allowed to be seen in a full and satisfactory way, the only one which is consumed in actual fact. I have called it: the signification. We can see that the signification is the myth itself, just as the Saussurean sign is the word (or more accurately the concrete unit). But before listing the characters of the signification, one must reflect a little on the way in which it is prepared, that is, on the modes of correlation of the mythical concept and the mythical form.

First we must note that in myth, the first two terms are perfectly manifest (unlike what happens in other semiological systems): one of them is not 'hidden' behind the other, they are both given *here* (and not one here and the other there). However paradoxical it may seem, *myth hides nothing*: its function is to distort, not to make disappear. There is no latency of the concept in relation to the form: there is no need of an unconscious in order to explain myth. Of course, one is dealing with two different types of manifestation: form has a literal, immediate presence; moreover, it is extended. This stems – this cannot be repeated too often – from the nature of the mythical signifier, which is already linguistic: since it is constituted by a meaning which is already outlined, it can appear only through a given substance (whereas in language, the signifier remains mental). In the case of oral myth, this extension is linear (*for my name is lion*); in that of visual myth, it is multi-dimensional (in the centre, the Negro's uniform, at the top, the blackness of his face, on the left, the military salute, etc.). The elements of the form therefore are related as to place and proximity: the mode of presence of the form is spatial. The concept, on the contrary, appears in global fashion, it is a kind of nebula, the condensation, more or less hazy, of a certain knowledge. Its elements are linked by associative relations: it is supported not by an extension but by a depth (although this metaphor is perhaps still too spatial): its mode of presence is memorial.

The relation which unites the concept of the myth to its meaning is essentially a relation of *deformation*. We find here again a certain formal analogy with a complex semiological system such as that of the various types of psycho-analysis. Just as for Freud the manifest meaning of behaviour is distorted by its latent meaning, in myth the meaning is distorted by the concept. Of course, this distortion is possible only because the form of the myth is already constituted by a linguistic meaning. In a simple system like the language, the signified cannot distort anything at all because the signifier, being empty, arbitrary, offers no resistance to it. But here, everything is different: the signifier has, so to speak, two aspects: one full, which is the meaning (the history of the lion, of the Negro soldier), one empty, which is the form (*for my name is lion*; *Negro-French-soldier-saluting-the-tricolour*). What the concept distorts is of course what is full, the meaning: the lion and the Negro are deprived of their history, changed into gestures. What Latin exemplarity distorts is the naming of the lion, in all its contingency; and what French imperiality obscures is also a primary language, a factual discourse which was telling me about the salute of a Negro in uniform. But this distortion is not an obliteration: the lion and the Negro remain here, the concept needs them; they are half-amputated, they are deprived of memory, not of existence: they are at once stubborn, silently rooted there, and garrulous, a speech wholly at the service of the concept. The concept, literally, deforms, but does not abolish the meaning; a word can perfectly render this contradiction: it alienates it.

What must always be remembered is that myth is a double system; there occurs in it a sort of ubiquity: its point of departure is constituted by the arrival of a meaning. To keep a spatial metaphor, the approximative character of which I have already stressed, I shall say that the signification of the myth is constituted by a sort of constantly moving turnstile which presents alternately the meaning of the signifier and its form, a language object and a metalanguage, a purely signifying and a purely imagining consciousness. This alternation is, so to speak, gathered up in the concept, which uses it like an ambiguous signifier, at once intellective and imaginary, arbitrary and natural.

I do not wish to prejudge the moral implications of such a mechanism, but I shall not exceed the limits of an objective analysis if I point out that the ubiquity of the signifier in myth exactly reproduces the physique of the *alibi* (which is, as one realizes, a spatial term): in the alibi too, there is a place which is full and one which is empty, linked by a relation of negative identity ('I am not where you think I am; I am where you think I am not'). But the ordinary alibi (for the police, for instance) has an end; reality stops the turnstile revolving at a certain point. Myth is a *value*, truth is no guarantee for it; nothing prevents it from being a perpetual alibi: it is enough that its signifier has two sides for it always to have an 'elsewhere' at its disposal. The meaning is always there to *present* the form; the form is always there to *outdistance* the meaning. And there never is any contradiction, conflict, or split between the meaning and the form: they are never at the same place. In the same way, if I am in a car and I look at the scenery through the window, I can at will focus on the scenery or on the window-pane. At one moment I grasp the presence of the glass and the distance of the landscape; at another, on the contrary, the transparence of the glass and the depth of the landscape; but the result of this alternation is constant: the glass is at once present and empty to me, and the landscape unreal and full. The same thing occurs in the mythical signifier: its form is empty but present, its meaning absent but full. To wonder at this contradiction I must voluntarily interrupt this turnstile of form and meaning, I must focus on each separately, and apply to myth a static method of deciphering, in short, I must go against its own dynamics: to sum up, I must pass from the state of reader to that of mythologist.

And it is again this duplicity of the signifier which determines the characters of the signification. We now know that myth is a type of speech defined by its intention (*I am a grammatical example*) much more than by its literal sense (*my name is lion*); and that in spite of this, its intention is somehow frozen, purified, eternalized, *made absent* by this literal sense (*The French Empire? It's just a fact: look at this good Negro who salutes like one of our own boys*). This constituent ambiguity of mythical speech has two consequences for the signification, which henceforth appears both like a notification and like a statement of fact.

Myth has an imperative, buttonholing character: stemming from an historical concept, directly springing from contingency (a Latin class, a threatened Empire), it is I whom it has come to seek. It is turned towards me, I am subjected to its intentional force, it summons me to receive its expansive ambiguity. If, for instance, I take a walk in Spain, in the Basque country,[6] I may well notice in the houses an architectural unity, a common style, which leads me to acknowledge the Basque house as a definite ethnic product. However, I do not feel personally concerned, nor, so to speak, attacked by this unitary style: I see only too well that it was here before me, without me. It is a complex product which has its determinations at the level of a very wide history: it does not call out to me, it does not provoke me into naming it, except if I think of inserting it into a vast picture of rural habitat. But if I am in the Paris region and I catch a glimpse, at the end of the rue Gambetta or the rue Jean-Jaurès, of a natty white chalet with red tiles, dark brown half-timbering, an asymmetrical roof and a wattle-and-daub front, I feel as if I were personally receiving an imperious injunction to name this object a Basque chalet: or even better, to see it as the very essence of *basquity*. This is because the concept appears to me in all its appropriative nature: it comes and seeks me out in order to oblige me to acknowledge the body of intentions which have motivated it and arranged it there as the signal of an individual history, as a confidence and a complicity: it is a real call, which the owners of the chalet send out to me. And this call, in order to be more imperious, has agreed to all manner of impoverishments: all that justified the Basque house on the plane of technology – the barn, the outside stairs, the dove-cote, etc. – has been dropped; there remains only a brief order, not to be disputed. And the adhomination is so frank that I feel this chalet has just been created on the spot, *for me*, like a magical object springing up in my present life without any trace of the history which has caused it.

For this interpellant speech is at the same time a frozen speech: at the moment of reaching me, it suspends itself, turns away and assumes the look of a generality: it stiffens, it makes itself look neutral and innocent. The appropriation of the concept is suddenly driven away once more by the literalness of the meaning. This is a kind of *arrest*, in both the physical and the legal sense of the term: French imperiality condemns the saluting Negro to be nothing more than an instrumental signifier, the Negro suddenly hails me in the name of French imperiality; but at the same moment the Negro's salute thickens, becomes vitrified, freezes into an eternal reference meant to *establish* French imperiality. On the surface of language something has stopped moving: the use of the signification is here, hiding behind the fact, and conferring on it a notifying look; but at the same time, the fact paralyses the intention, gives it something like a malaise producing immobility: in order to make it innocent, it freezes it. This is because myth is speech *stolen and restored*. Only, speech which is restored is no longer quite that which was stolen: when it was brought back, it was not put exactly in its place. It is this brief act of larceny, this moment taken for a surreptitious faking, which gives mythical speech its benumbed look.

One last element of the signification remains to be examined: its motivation. We know that in a language, the sign is arbitrary: nothing compels the acoustic image *tree* 'naturally' to mean the concept *tree*: the sign, here, is unmotivated. Yet this arbitrariness has limits, which come from the associative relations of the word: the language can produce a whole fragment of the sign by analogy with other signs (for instance one says *aimable* in French, and not *amable*, by analogy with *aime*). The mythical signification, on the other hand, is never arbitrary; it is always in part motivated, and unavoidably contains some analogy. For Latin exemplarity to meet the naming of the lion, there must be an analogy, which is the agreement of the predicate; for French imperiality to get hold of the saluting Negro, there must be identity between the Negro's salute and that of the French soldier. Motivation is necessary to the very duplicity of myth: myth plays on the analogy between meaning and form, there is no myth without motivated form.[7] In order to grasp the power of motivation in myth, it is enough to reflect for a moment on an extreme case. I have here before me a collection of objects so lacking in order that I can find no *meaning* in it; it would seem that here, deprived of any previous meaning, the form could not root its analogy in anything, and that myth is impossible. But what the form can always give one to read is disorder itself: it can give a signification to the absurd, make the absurd itself a myth. This is what happens when commonsense mythifies surrealism, for instance. Even the absence of motivation does not embarrass myth; for this absence will itself be sufficiently objectified to become legible: and finally, the absence of motivation will become a second-order motivation, and myth will be re-established.

Motivation is unavoidable. It is none the less very fragmentary. To start with, it is not 'natural': it is history which supplies its analogies to the form. Then, the analogy between the meaning and the concept is never anything but partial: the form drops many analogous features and keeps only a few: it keeps the sloping roof, the visible beams in the Basque chalet, it abandons the stairs, the barn, the weathered look, etc. One must even go further: a *complete* image would exclude myth, or at least would compel it to seize only its very completeness. This is just what happens in the case of bad painting, which is wholly based on the myth of what is 'filled out' and 'finished' (it is the opposite and symmetrical case of the myth of the absurd: here, the form mythifies an 'absence', there, a surplus). But in general myth prefers to work with poor, incomplete images, where the meaning is already relieved of its fat, and ready for a signification, such as caricatures, pastiches, symbols, etc. Finally, the motivation is chosen among other possible ones: I can very well give to French imperiality many other signifiers beside a Negro's salute: a French general pins a decoration on a one-armed Senegalese, a nun hands a cup of tea to a bed-ridden Arab, a white school-master teaches attentive piccaninnies: the press undertakes every day to demonstrate that the store of mythical signifiers is inexhaustible.

The nature of the mythical signification can in fact be well conveyed by one particular simile: it is neither more nor less arbitrary than the ideograph. Myth is a pure ideographic system, where the forms are still motivated by the concept which they represent while not yet, by a long way, covering the sum of its possibilities for representation. And just as, historically, ideographs have gradually left the concept and have become associated with the sound, thus growing less and less motivated, the worn out state of a myth can be recognized by the arbitrariness of its signification: the whole of Molière is seen in a doctor's ruff.

Reading and deciphering myth

How is a myth received? We must here once more come back to the duplicity of its signifier, which is at once meaning and form. I can produce three different types of reading by focusing on the one, or the other, or both at the same time.[8]

1   If I focus on an empty signifier, I let the concept fill the form of the myth without ambiguity, and I find myself before a simple system, where the signification becomes literal again: the Negro who salutes is an *example* of French imperiality, he is a *symbol* for it. This type of focusing is, for instance, that of the producer of myths, of the journalist who starts with a concept and seeks a form for it.[9]

2   If I focus on a full signifier, in which I clearly distinguish the meaning and the form, and consequently the distortion which the one imposes on the other, I undo the signification of the myth, and I receive the latter as an imposture: the saluting Negro becomes the *alibi* of French imperiality. This type of focusing is that of the mythologist: he deciphers the myth, he understands a distortion.

3   Finally, if I focus on the mythical signifier as on an inextricable whole made of meaning and form, I receive an ambiguous signification: I respond to the constituting mechanism of myth, to its own dynamics, I become a reader of myths. The saluting Negro is no longer an example or a symbol, still less an alibi: he is the very *presence* of French imperiality.

The first two types of focusing are static, analytical; they destroy the myth, either by making its intention obvious, or by unmasking it: the former is cynical, the latter demystifying. The third type of focusing is dynamic, it consumes the myth according to the very ends built into its structure: the reader lives the myth as a story at once true and unreal.

If one wishes to connect a mythical schema to a general history, to explain how it corresponds to the interests of a definite society, in short, to pass from semiology to ideology, it is obviously at the level of the third type of focusing that one must place oneself: it is the reader of myths himself who must reveal their essential function. How does he receive this particular myth *today*? If he receives it in an innocent fashion, what is the point of proposing it to him? And if he reads it using his powers of reflection, like the mythologist, does it matter which alibi is presented? If the reader does not see French imperiality in the saluting Negro, it was not worth weighing the latter with it; and if he sees it, the myth is nothing more than a political proposition, honestly expressed. In one word, either the intention of the myth is too obscure to be efficacious, or it is too clear to be believed. In either case, where is the ambiguity?

This is but a false dilemma. Myth hides nothing and flaunts nothing: it distorts; myth is neither a lie nor a confession: it is an inflexion. Placed before the dilemma which I mentioned a moment ago, myth finds a third way out. Threatened with disappearance if it yields to either of the first two types of focusing, it gets out of this tight spot thanks to a compromise – it *is* this compromise. Entrusted with 'glossing over' an intentional concept, myth encounters nothing but betrayal in language, for language can only obliterate the concept if it hides it, or unmask it if it formulates it. The elaboration of a second-order semiological system will enable myth to escape this dilemma: driven to having either to unveil or to liquidate the concept, it will *naturalize* it.

We reach here the very principle of myth: it transforms history into nature. We now understand why, *in the eyes of the myth-consumer*, the intention, the adhomination of the concept can remain manifest without however appearing to have an interest in the matter: what causes mythical speech to be uttered is perfectly explicit, but it is immediately frozen into something natural; it is not read as a motive, but as a reason. If I read the Negro-saluting as symbol pure and simple of imperiality, I must renounce the reality of the picture, it discredits itself in my eyes when it becomes an instrument. Conversely, if I decipher the Negro's salute as an alibi of coloniality, I shatter the myth even more surely by the obviousness of its motivation. But for the myth-reader, the outcome is quite different: everything happens as if the picture *naturally* conjured up the concept, as if the signifier *gave a foundation* to be signified: the myth exists from the precise moment when French imperiality achieves the natural state: myth is speech justified *in excess*.

Notes

1   Innumerable other meanings of the word 'myth' can be cited against this. But I have tried to define things, not words.

2   The development of publicity, of a national press, of radio, of illustrated news, not to speak of the survival of a myriad rites of communication which rule social appearances makes the development of a semiological science more urgent than ever. In a single day, how many really non-signifying fields do we cross? Very few, sometimes none. Here I am, before the sea; it is true that it bears no message. But on the beach, what material for semiology! Flags, slogans, signals, sign-boards, clothes, suntan even, which are so many messages to me.

3   The notion of *word* is one of the most controversial in linguistics. I keep it here for the sake of simplicity.

4   *Tel Quel*, II, p. 191.

5   Or perhaps *Sinity*? Just as if Latin/latinity = Basque/x, x = Basquity.

6   I say 'in Spain' because, in France, petit-bourgeois advancement has caused a whole 'mythical' architecture of the Basque chalet to flourish.

7   From the point of view of view of ethics, what is disturbing in myth is precisely that its form is motivated. For if there is a 'health' of language, it is the arbitrariness of the sign which is its grounding. What is sickening in myth is its resort to a false nature, its superabundance of significant forms, as in these objects which decorate their usefulness with a natural appearance. The will to weigh the signification with the full guarantee of nature causes a kind of nausea: myth is too rich, and what is in excess is precisely its motivation. This nausea is like the one I feel before the arts which refuse to choose between *physis* and *anti-physis*, using the first as an ideal and the second as an economy. Ethically, there is a kind of baseness in hedging one's bets.

8   The freedom in choosing what one focuses on is a problem which does not belong to the province of semiology: it depends on the concrete situation of the subject.

9   We receive the naming of the lion as a pure *example* of Latin grammar because we are, *as grown-ups*, in a creative position in relation to it. I shall come back later to the value of the context in this mythical schema.

Discussion points
for Part One

1   Give short definitions of the following concepts, and comment on how each of them relates to the general concept of *discourse*: *speech*, *writing*, *language*, *a language*, *talk*, *communication*, *social action*, *social practice*.

2   List some of the 'poetic' features of everyday conversation between friends. What aesthetic dimensions are in play? What are the routines or sub-genres of everyday conversation that involve a 'metalinguistic' (or reflexive or self-aware) dimension?

3   Look back at our reconstructed dialogue (Extract 1, p. 8) in the general Introduction. Focus on each single utterance. Which speech act labels seem most appropriate to describe the illocutionary force or function of each utterance?

4   In the same extract, describe how each utterance is sequentially related to the utterance that precedes it and follows it. Explain how one particular utterance is 'procedurally consequential' for what follows it.

5   Review H.P. Grice's four conversational maxims of quantity, quality, relation and manner (in Chapter 3). Consider the following utterance to be a speaker's answer to an invitation you've just made, to go along to a mutual friend's house for a drink: *um I'm not − I sort of think I ought to be getting back ... you know there's a lot happening today*. Analyse the utterance in terms of how it keeps to or breaks each conversational maxim.

6   Consider this claim from Mikhail Bakhtin: 'Any utterance ... reveals to us many half-concealed ... words of others, with varying degrees of foreignness' (Chapter 6, p. 106). Try to apply it to the discourse of our Editors' introduction to this book. In what ways does our text (and probably most academic writing) 'half-conceal the words of others'? Who are these 'others'? How do we recognise their 'words'? How are they 'concealed'?

Methods and resources for analysing discourse

Editors' introduction
to Part Two

I N PREPARING THIS BOOK we at first resisted the suggestion of including a section of methods for the study of discourse. Discourse analysis, we wanted to argue, is not simply a method. Its basic assumptions about the local and emergent construction of meaning and value would be obscured if we incorporated readings (and some do exist) that offered set rules and procedures for discourse analysts to follow. It is important to hold on to this objection. At the same time, studying language as discourse *does* mean adopting a certain perspective on the asking and answering of study questions, on treating language and other types of texts as 'data', on representing language and semiotic material, and on interacting with people treated as 'social actors'. The concept of discourse brings with it an agenda of theoretical issues that are related to how research is and can be done, and these are the themes we want to pick up in this Part of the book.

First we should make it clear that there are some senses of the term discourse which are too abstract to make any detailed, direct, empirical procedure for studying discourses feasible. In relation, for example, to Norman Fairclough's sense of discourse (Chapter 9), it is not conceivable that any one 'discourse' will offer itself directly for inspection or analysis. This very definition of discourse (similar to Foucault's sense – see the Introduction to Part Six) requires it to be an elusive and veiled phenomenon. Similarly, if we consider Fairclough's sense of the term 'discourse community', we cannot expect to identify a neatly bounded community of speakers or communicators, in the classic sociolinguistic sense of William Labov's research (1972). But even according to Fairclough's theoretical approach, discourses *are* systematically linked to data – to texts, which are potential sites for empirical investigation. This means that, as in most approaches to discourse, we do need to engage in empirical linguistic study of some sort, and to establish principles according to which empirical investigation may proceed.

The chapter by Deborah Cameron, Elizabeth Frazer, Penelope Harvey, Ben Rampton and Kay Richardson (Chapter 8) is a wide-ranging and stimulating discussion not only of some practical aspects of linguistic research but also of its theoretical grounding. Cameron *et al*. begin with clear outlines of three general orientations in social research: *positivism, relativism* and *realism*. Their arguments lead them to dismiss the positivist orientation absolutely. They say that 'the limits of positivism are severe and restrictive' (p. 141) for the study of language use, even though it is widely seen by others as *the* scientific approach. As Cameron and colleagues suggest, studying the local contextualisation of meaning is incompatible with a formal, measurement-based, distributional, empiricist, scientistic orientation to 'language behaviour'. Discourse theory, itself, rules out certain research methods.

Cameron and colleagues then consider relativist research approaches, and specifically the radical ethnomethodological arguments we met in Part One of the *Reader* about the interactional construction of social reality. Their line is that language research, such as their own, which addresses various sorts of social inequality cannot avoid the 'reality' of social structures, having an existence outside of language and interaction. They are, therefore, committed to what one might call a 'mild', or 'less-than-radical' social relativism, and they take this forward into their discussion of relationships between researchers and the people they research – which is the main thrust of the chapter. Cameron *et al*. then sketch out three idealised patterns of relationship – *ethical, advocacy* and *empowerment* relationships – arguing that the third is the morally and theoretically required option. It should be valuable to bear these ideal types in mind when reading the particular studies of discourse reported in later parts of the *Reader*. At that point, the empowerment stance will probably appear to be not only idealised but unattainable in its full form. We might ask whether the phenomenon called 'academic research' is, in fact, able to encompass the ideal of 'researching on, for and with' researched populations, as part of a process of empowering them. Cameron and colleagues acknowledge this in their own discussion, but this does not prevent the chapter being a compelling discussion of the moral and socio-political framing of research, and of how discourse analysis should position itself as a research practice.

In Chapter 9, Norman Fairclough makes a case for critical language awareness, which he anchors in Critical Discourse Analysis (for some reason, the convention is to use upper-case in this phrase) and in people's critical awareness of discourse. In some ways, Fairclough's concern here is similar to that of Cameron *et al*. in Chapter 8 in that he proposes an applied view of CDA to empower social actors in the way they manage their lives. The late-capitalist, postmodern way of life is dominated by a knowledge-based or information-based economy. It leads to the ever-increasing semioticisation of social and economic life, requiring individuals to be aware of the various discourses surrounding and regulating their lives. Such discourses, which are constituted by and are constitutive of systems of knowledge and experience from specific perspectives, are imposed on societies by politicians, institutions and various 'experts' in a wide range of largely mediatised genres of communication. But, as Fairclough demonstrates, these powerful discourses can be evaluated, appropriated and subverted, much in the way that

Bakhtin suggested (Chapter 6). But it is only through explicit language education that the resource of critical language/discourse awareness can be made fully available to people.

Fairclough suggests that some of the key areas where discourse and contemporary social life intersect – and where awareness-raising is particularly necessary – are social differences and social identities, the commodification of discourse, democracy, and new global capitalism. For example, social differences generate a multiplicity of voices. In an increasingly complex social world these voices become less 'pure' (more hybrid and more heterogeneous). Social meanings overlap and conflict with each other (intertextuality). From this complexity and mixing, new discourses, genres and styles can emerge, unsettling older conventions and identities. New social arrangements emerge, nowadays based as much on lifestyles as on traditional social structures according to social class or race. Identity becomes more 'managed' and aspirational. Language and discourse become increasingly commodified, as evidenced by the proliferation of old and new media. Styles and genres of speech become 'packaged up' as service-based industries expand (e.g., for the purposes of tele-sales). Images take on monetary value (e.g., in 'themed' restaurants, parks and resorts). Democracy is premised on the idea of dialogue, negotiation and argument, and global capitalism creates opportunities for people to access new discourses and systems of knowledge. But it also constitutes a threat to individual, national and other local forms of governance. Therefore, critical discourse awareness is needed to resist new forms of exploitation, but also to make use of heightened reflexivity and opportunities for change in postmodern society.

The ideas of discursive hybridity, pointing to the absence of fixed boundaries between styles and genres of language, and people's fusing of multiple styles and registers when they communicate, once again have strong echoes of Bakhtin (Chapter 6). Like Bakhtin, Fairclough conceives of texts as ad-mixtures of pre-existing genres and texts, which, in turn, are informed by (in his sense) different discourses. Fairclough builds this into his programme of CDA, which

> aims to provide a framework for systematically linking properties of discoursal interactions and texts with features of their social and cultural circumstances. The network of social practices is described from a specifically discoursal perspective as an 'order of discourse' consisting of discourses and genres in particular relationships with each other, but with an orientation to shifts in boundaries within and between orders of discourse as part of social and cultural change.
>
> (p. 154)

Chapter 9 is a useful illustration of how Fairclough incorporates social theory into CDA, bringing discourse analysis to bear on themes such as social change, globalisation and social exclusion. (Cameron's Chapter 30 usefully extends some of these perspectives.)

These grand themes do, however, need to connect to 'on-the-ground' analysis of text. Discourse analysis needs to be a to-ing and fro-ing between more abstract/

theoretical and more concrete/textual phenomena, an alternation between what are often called micro and macro levels of analysis. At the micro level we have texts and data which, first, need to be 'captured', held in some way to become available for analysis. For interactional data this will usually involve electronic audio recording or audio-visual recording. We have not included a chapter that reviews and advises on such techniques, but Duranti (1997) is a particularly helpful source. Further detail on methods in sociolinguistics, which overlap with those used in many studies of spoken discourse (e.g., interviewing procedures, sampling of spontaneous uses of language, issues of 'naturalness', and methods in observational research) can be found in Coupland and Jaworski (1997, Chapters 8–11).

One specific facet of discourse-analytic research on language texts, again with theoretical implications, is the practice of transcribing spoken interaction into a written form. Conversation analysts and discourse analysts have developed sophisticated means of representing speech in writing, many going well beyond orthographic conventions (the familiar writing system we are using here). We include two readings on transcription in this Part of the *Reader*, one detailing what has become close to a standard form of transcript notation in conversation analysis and many discourse studies – the one originally developed by Gail Jefferson in her research on conversation (see Chapter 10). The other reading is a reflexive discussion by Elinor Ochs of how any transcribing practice must reflect the interests and priorities of the researchers who are using it (Chapter 11). Ochs also presents a system – a modified version of the Jefferson conventions – appropriate to her own research on child language development.

In many ways, Jefferson's transcript conventions are an attempt to construct, from scratch, a new set of resources for representing those aspects of speech production and delivery that, in linguistics, have been called paralinguistic (e.g., voice quality) and prosodic features (e.g., rate of speaking, pitch movement and stress – these last two usually referred to as intonation features). Linguistic studies of prosody have not produced a simple, uniform notational system for representing such features. In discourse studies we often find rather ad hoc conventions being used. Non-vocal features, such as gaze direction, are sometimes represented, difficult though this is to achieve. Gaze refers to where a speaker's eyes are focused at any one point – in fact, this is difficult to determine even with the use of video-recordings, let alone to represent in a transcript.

Outside of Jefferson's system there is no regular way, for example, of representing laughter, even though it is a crucial and hardly rare aspect of the affective functioning of talk. Some of Jefferson's conventions are inherited from phonetics, and in particular from the International Phonetic Association (IPA)'s transcript notation, but with variation too. For example, the IPA uses a single dot to represent vowel-lengthening, while most CA and DA researchers use a colon. The general principle behind Jefferson's transcript is to use commonplace, orthographic English spelling as far as possible to show phonetic and prosodic/paralinguistic characteristics. The broader ambition is to capture, in a reasonably readable format, all or most of the features of spoken delivery that speakers and listeners are likely to attend to and respond to.

The Jefferson conventions have, as we said above, gained widespread accept-ance in Conversation Analysis and beyond, so it is important to become familiar with them. It is, nevertheless, true that the system raises several theoretical and descriptive dilemmas, for example in its ways of representing vowel qualities, where it stops well short of the IPA level of phonetic detail. Several particular problems come to mind. In the examples given in Chapter 10, it is difficult to justify repre-senting 'just' as 'ju::ss', when other stop consonants (/p/, /t/, /k/, etc.) that are also likely to have been de-emphasised in speech are not deleted from the transcript. Again, placing the length-marking colons after the 'e' in 're::ally' rather than after the 'a' seems arbitrary, unless the claim is that it is the first part of the diph-thongal vowel in that word which is the prolonged segment (and many accents have monophthongs in this position anyway). It is not clear why vowel reduction – of 'your' to 'yih' – should be represented and not other reduced vowels, which are commonplace in most varieties of spoken English. Which dialects are represented in the transcripts, and how do we know which of their features would be salient? Why show some elided segments with inverted comma (e.g., 's'pose') and not others? The underlining convention to show emphasis shows very little sensitivity to syllable structure (see Jefferson's implied suggestion that a single consonant, e.g., in 'way', can bear emphasis; the 'w' consonant may be prolonged, but emphasis would inevitably be carried through the whole syllable). In these and potentially many other ways, the system is wayward in its representation of phonetic processes in speaking, so we should think of it as, at best, a semi-formal device. It is undeni-ably a useful and common one.

Ochs's discussion of transcription as theory provides a very valuable reflection on transcribing in general and on Jefferson's conventions in particular. Ochs starts with the basic question of what we mean by calling linguistic and other sorts of text 'data' for discourse analysis, and how transcripts cannot avoid being *selective* representations of them. Orthography is itself one form of selectivity. The form of a transcript encourages readers to use it in different ways. It reflects cultural biases, and both theoretical and practical biases in the research. Ochs's chapter is, in fact, a mix of theoretical discussion and practical hints, including a detailed list of possible conventions, more detailed and in many ways better rationalised than Jefferson's in its coverage of non-verbal features. It is very useful as a general resource for analytic projects involving transcription, although Ochs's general stance is that there is, and can be, no perfect transcription – only a transcription that meets particular needs and is systematically linked to one's goals and theoretical assumptions about linguistic meaning, social meaning and social context.

In every instance of empirically grounded work on discourse, researchers have to make decisions about how best to transcribe their data to suit their own prior-ities. At the same time, it is important to make transcripts clear enough and informative enough for readers who are unacquainted with the original recordings. In future it is likely to become the norm for spoken discourse data to be made available as audio or audio-visual files for 'readers' to access more directly, but that day hasn't quite arrived. Even when it does, there will continue to be a need to represent data through transcription, in order to focus analytically upon the details of texts of different sorts. As you work through different chapters of the *Reader* you will find considerable variation in the use of transcription conventions. This is not inherently a problem, if we see transcriptions as aids to analysis and interpretation, rather than being 'correct' or 'incorrect' in themselves.

The next two chapters, by Theo Van Leeuwen (Chapter 12) and David Graddol (Chapter 13), demonstrate the quite new concept of *multimodality*, or multimodal discourse analysis (see also Fairclough, Chapter 9). This is a more or less explicit extension of several traditions we have already discussed – Barthes' semiotics, Bakhtin's *heteroglossia* or *multiple voicing*, CDA and linguistic anthropology. The key development is to widen discourse analysis to deal with many different communicative modes or modalities such as voice/sound (Chapter 12), and visual/typographical features of a written text (Chapter 13). Both chapters show how the multimodal characteristics of texts mediate relationships between text producers and users (readers, listeners or viewers, see also Chapter 26). Although strictly speaking these are not 'methodological' chapters, we include them here to exemplify methods used in multimodal discourse analysis and as points of departure for future explorations and studies in multimodality.

Chapter 12 describes some analytic tools for analysing (non-linguistic) sound, such as film sound-effects and music, with regard to the positioning of listeners vis-à-vis 'soundscapes'. For example, a sound or a group of sounds can be central to the listener's appreciation and involvement and will demand his/her reaction. In this case, to use a visual metaphor, the sound is the 'figure' (the focal point of attention). Sounds can, alternatively, constitute part of the listener's experience but more remotely, as a familiar part of the context. Now the sound is the background or the 'ground' against which some other 'figure' becomes more prominent. Sound may be part of the listener's physical environment but not part of his/her social world ('field'). By foregrounding some sounds and backgrounding others, texts *perspectivise* sounds in hierarchical relations of relative salience. By manipulating the relative loudness and prominence of sounds, texts create different degrees of *social distance* between what they represent and the listener, from the closeness and intimacy of a soft noise or a whispered voice to the increased formality of a louder, higher and tenser sound/voice.

In Chapter 13 Graddol starts by identifying a number of intersecting social discourses (or areas of knowledge) represented in a relatively short text – a wine label. They include compulsory information on the alcoholic strength, volume and type of the wine, a health warning (on wine labels in the US), and optional information such as lifestyle issues. These include what food dishes the wine would best accompany, the origin and history of the wine, conditions of production, and so on. In fact, the main function of the optional discourses may be not so much 'informative' but commercial, advertising the product in ways that might not be otherwise permitted by law. For example, the word 'excellent' may refer to the wine's suitability as accompaniment to certain dishes, more than to the overall quality of the product itself. This tension between the informative, promotional and health-warning discourses is represented in the visual design of the bottle and, particularly, in the typographical design and layout of its front and back labels. As Graddol says, the promotional text in a wine label may use a traditional serif font, connoting values of tradition, culture and human agency, while the health warning is printed in a modern, sans serif font, connoting rationality, factuality and modernism.

References

Coupland, N. and Jaworski, A. (eds) (1997) *Sociolinguistics: A Reader and Coursebook*, Basingstoke: Macmillan.

Duranti, A. (1997) *Linguistic Anthropology*, Cambridge: Cambridge University Press.

Labov, W. (1972) *Sociolinguistic Patterns*, Philadelphia, PA: University of Pennsylvania Press and Oxford: Blackwell.

Chapter 8

Deborah Cameron, Elizabeth Frazer, Penelope Harvey, Ben Rampton and Kay Richardson

POWER/KNOWLEDGE: THE POLITICS OF SOCIAL SCIENCE

A S MANY COMMENTATORS HAVE pointed out – perhaps the fullest and most insistent statement can be found in the various works of Michel Foucault [see Chapter 33] – social science is not and has never been a neutral enquiry into human behaviour and institutions. It is strongly implicated in the project of social control, whether by the state or by other agencies that ultimately serve the interests of a dominant group.

As a very obvious illustration, we may notice what an enormous proportion of all social research is conducted on populations of relatively powerless people. It is factory workers, criminals and juvenile delinquents as opposed to their bosses or victims who fill the pages of social science texts. Doubtless this is partly because members of powerful elites often refuse to submit to the probing of researchers – their time is valuable, their privacy jealously guarded. But it is also because a lot of social research is directly inspired by the need to understand and sometimes even to contain 'social problems' – the threats (such as crime or industrial disruption) that powerless groups are felt to pose to powerful ones.

Foucault observes, putting a new spin on the familiar saying 'knowledge is power', that the citizens of modern democracies are controlled less by naked violence or the economic power of the boss and the landlord than by the pronouncements of expert discourse, organised in what he calls 'regimes of truth' – sets of understandings which legitimate particular social attitudes and practices. Evidently, programmes of social scientific research on such subjects as 'criminality' or 'sexual deviance' or 'teenage motherhood' have contributed to 'regimes of truth'. In studying and presenting the 'facts' about these phenomena, they have both helped to construct particular people ('criminals', 'deviants', 'teenage mothers') as targets for social control and influenced the form the control itself will take.

Source: Deborah Cameron, Elizabeth Frazer, Penelope Harvey, M.B.H. Rampton and Kay Richardson, *Researching Language: Issues of Power and Method*, London: Routledge, 1992.

We could consider, for example, the medico-legal discourses interpreting but also, crucially, regulating the behaviour of women. Recently, some acts of aggression by women have been explained as a consequence of hormonal disturbance ('pre-menstrual syndrome'); conversely, some instances of women drinking while pregnant have been explained (and indeed punished) as acts of conscious negligence (since they may lead to problems for the newborn, most seriously 'foetal alcohol syndrome'). There are two things to note here. One is that although the categories 'pre-menstrual syndrome' and 'foetal alcohol syndrome' are presented as objective and value-free scientific discoveries, it is clear that these new pieces of knowledge function as forms of social control over women. The other is that although they may seem to contradict one another (since one makes women less responsible for damage they cause while the other makes them more responsible than in the past) they nevertheless complement each other at a higher level of analysis: they fit and reinforce the logic of that broader control discourse feminists call 'sexism'.

This interplay of power and knowledge (Foucaultians write 'power/knowledge') and the historical link between social science and social control pose obvious dilemmas for the radical social scientist. We have to recognise that we are inevitably part of a tradition of knowledge, one which we may criticise, certainly, but which we cannot entirely escape. Even the most iconoclastic scholar is always in dialogue with those who went before. Our own disciplines, anthropology, sociology and linguistics, have problematic histories. Scholars of language and society may be less powerful than lawyers and doctors, but we have certainly contributed to 'regimes of truth' and regulatory practices which are hard to defend.

. . .

It would be quite irresponsible to deny the real effects of research in our disciplines or to play down the contribution they have made to maintaining and legitimating unequal social arrangements. And in this light, our hopes of 'empowering' the subjects of linguistic research might start to look at best naïve. Perhaps it would be better to stop doing social science research altogether?

The questions of how 'empowering' social research can hope to be, and whether in the end certain kinds of research should be undertaken at all are certainly serious ones. . . . For us, though, the starting point was that we had done research in situations of inequality, and we felt a need to reappraise critically the ways we had gone about it, making explicit issues of method that were not necessarily foregrounded at the time.

Linguistic interaction is social interaction, and therefore the study of language use is fundamental to our understanding of how oppressive social relations are created and reproduced. If, as we believed, the politics of language is real politics, it is at least worth considering whether knowledge about it could be framed in a way that research subjects themselves would find relevant and useful.

Theoretical issues: the status of academic knowledge

Our early discussions of how research on language might empower its subjects raised general theoretical questions in two main areas: one was the status of academic knowledge itself and the other concerned the relation between researcher and researched in the making of knowledge. . . .

We will go on to distinguish a number of approaches or 'isms', which differ in their conceptions of reality, the object of knowledge, and therefore in their opinions about how it can be described and explained. Initially we will distinguish two broad categories among scientists and social scientists: those who subscribe to *positivism* and those who do not. Among the non-positivists we will further distinguish between *relativist* and *realist* approaches.

It must be acknowledged that positivism, relativism and realism are complex positions whose definition is contested rather than fixed. Our presentation of them will simplify the picture by describing a sort of 'ideal-typical' position rather than the nuances of any specific theorist's actual position. . . .

Positivism

Positivism entails a commitment to study of the frequency, distribution and patterning of observable phenomena, and the description, in law-like general terms, of the relationship between those phenomena. . . . Positivism is strongly averse to postulating the reality of entities, forces or mechanisms that human observers cannot see. Such things are myths, mere theoretical inventions which enable us to predict and explain observable events but cannot be seen as the stuff of reality itself. At the same time, positivism is strongly committed to the obviousness and unproblematic status of what we *can* observe: observations procured in a scientific manner have the status of value-free facts.

This distinction between fact and value is important. Though confident that there are methods which can provide a clear view of reality, positivism is very much aware of the potential for observation to be value laden, especially in the social as opposed to natural sciences. Indeed, for many it is a mark of 'pseudoscientific' theories like Marxism and psychoanalysis that their adherents will see what they want, or what the theory dictates they should; such theories are shot through with political bias. Nor can you set up a controlled experiment to test Marx's hypothesis that the class in society which owns the means of production will also have control of political and cultural institutions by virtue of their economic dominance. It might well be true that there are no known counterexamples to Marx's statement, but we still cannot say that the statement itself holds up. It would be difficult to set out to falsify this statement, as positivism requires, because so many variables are involved and there seems to be no way of isolating and manipulating the relevant one. Because it does not provide us with hypotheses that can be in principle falsified, Marxism for strict positivists is a pseudoscience rather than a science.

. . .

Challenges to positivism

Positivism is the 'hegemonic' position, the one scientists have generally been taught to regard not as a scientific method but as *the* scientific method. That is why we have grouped alternative positions as 'challenges to positivism': however different

they may be from one another, they are obliged to define themselves first and fore-
most in opposition to positivism, the dominant 'common sense' of modern science.
As this section makes clear, though, the two main challenges we identify – relativism
and realism – are by no means 'the same thing'.

Relativism

Relativism does not recognise the observer's paradox (see p. 139) as a problem
because relativism does not recognise the fact/value distinction. Reality for a relativist is not a fixed entity independent of our perceptions of it. Our perceptions
in turn depend on (are relative to) the concepts and theories we are working with
whenever we observe. We invariably have some preconceived notion of what is
there to be seen, and it affects what we actually see. Thus someone training as
a doctor, say, has to learn to see in a different way: the 'reality' she sees in a chest
X-ray is different from what she saw before she did her training, and different again
from what a traditional healer from a non-allopathic perspective would see. The
history of ideas and the sociology of knowledge provide many examples of scientific
theories having close links with the oral and cultural values of their time and place.

Dale Spender (1980) cites a good example of how language plays a part in
linking scientific theories with social assumptions. Psychologists investigating
people's visual perception discovered two ways of responding to a figure on a ground:
abstracting it from its context (the ground) or relating it to its context. These
responses were labelled 'field independence' and 'field dependence' respectively.
They were also associated with the behaviour of male subjects ('field independence')
and female subjects ('field dependence'). Spender's point is that it is not a coincidence that the male-associated strategy was given a label implying a more positive
evaluation – 'independence' is conceived as both a positive and a male characteristic. The female tendency could have been called 'context awareness' and the male
tendency 'context unawareness'. That this alternative did not occur to the scientist
has nothing to do with the nature of his findings about visual perception, and everything to do with his social preconceptions (i.e. he took it for granted that the positive
term must be accorded to what men do).

Relativism in the social sciences particularly addresses the role of language in
shaping an actor's social reality, as opposed to merely reflecting or expressing some
pre-existent, non-linguistic order. The 'Sapir-Whorf hypothesis of linguistic relativity' has inspired a great deal of discussion on the language dependence of social
reality. As Sapir argued:

> The fact of the matter is that the 'real world' is to a large extent uncon-
> sciously built up on the language habits of the group. No two languages
> are ever sufficiently similar to be considered as representing the same
> social reality. The worlds in which different societies live are different
> worlds, not the same world with different labels attached.
>
> (Sapir 1949: 162)

Subsequently, many social theorists and philosophers in the phenomenological tradition have stressed that social order exists *only* as a product of human activity. For

some, this can even mean that there is no social reality, no facts, other than the actor's subjective experience.

Ethnomethodology [see Chapter 5] is a development of this tradition which illustrates both the strengths and the weaknesses of relativism. Ethnomethodology takes very seriously indeed the actor's subjective experience of a situation, to the point of denying any other reality. In particular, it is hostile to the Marxist notion of historical forces determining actors' lives, and to the structuralist postu-lation of social structures which coerce people into social roles and hierarchical relations. In this view, a social researcher is just like anyone else, an actor experi-encing a situation: all research can really ever amount to is the reporting of one's experience. Clearly, this is an extreme anti-positivist position.

The problem here, though, is that in their zeal to emphasise the actor's own role in constructing a social world, ethnomethodologists have left us with a picture which implies that social actors could in principle construct the world exactly as they pleased. More precisely, they have given no account of why we cannot do this.

What makes this problematic? Very crudely, you might say it is a variant of not being able to see the wood for the trees. Indeed, since they deny the exist-ence of higher-level social structures or social forces that the individual actor is unaware of, ethnomethodologists must be sceptical of the idea that the trees in any sense add up to a wood. For them there is no 'big picture' into which the study of some particular phenomenon like a tree must be fitted.

We can put the point a bit more technically. Ethnomethodology is one of those approaches that emphasise the 'micro' level of social organisation – a single inter-action between two people, say – over the 'macro' level of institutions and classes, and so forth. In contrast to positivists, who conceive of explanation as stating general statistical regularities, ethnomethodologists give explanatory weight to the subject's account of herself. This means that if a woman says something like 'being a woman has made no difference to my life', the ethnomethodologist has no theoretical warrant for invoking the macro-category of gender. Here the ethnomethodologist is reacting against the Marxist idea of 'false consciousness', which implies that people are entirely deluded about the circumstances of their lives and that nothing a subject says should be taken at face value. Ethnomethodologists find this too deterministic (as well as condescending). For them, the way things are is the way subjects say they are.

For us, though we do not necessarily embrace the idea of false consciousness, this absolute faith in the subject's own account poses very serious problems. We do want to pay attention to actors' own understandings, but do we want to give them the last word in every case? We would prefer to say that whatever they say, people are not completely free to do what they want to do, be what they want to be. For we would want to claim that on the contrary, social actors are schooled and corrected, they come under pressure to take up certain roles and occupa-tions, they are born into relations of class, race, gender, generation, they occupy specific cultural positions, negotiate particular value systems, conceptual frame-works and social institutions, have more or less wealth and opportunity . . . and so on, *ad infinitum*. As Berger and Luckmann say (1967), social reality may be a human product but it faces humans like a coercive force. It is a grave weakness of ethnomethodology, and more generally of relativism, that it offers no convincing account of that fact.

This critical view of relativism brings us closer to a 'realist' position, arguing that there is indeed a social reality for actors and researchers to study and understand.

Realism

Realism, like relativism, accepts the theory ladenness of observation [see Chapter 11] but not the theory-dependent nature of reality itself. Realism posits a reality existing outside and independent of the observer, but also stresses that this reality may be impossible to observe or to describe definitively.

Realism parts company with positivism on the question of reality being only what we can observe. Neither the social order nor gravity can be observed, and therefore in positivist terms neither is 'real' (strictly speaking, only the observable effects of a gravitational field are real; the gravitational field for positivists is an artificial theoretical construct). Realism, as its name suggests, is committed to the notion that things like gravity *are* real, though at any time an observer might describe them incorrectly and so give a misleading or mistaken account of their real character. It follows, too, that for realism explanation is more than just stating regularities or predicting outcomes (the positivist model). When a realist describes the workings of gravity she believes she is giving an account of how the world works and not just stating what would be likely to happen if you conducted a particular operation in the world.

In the philosophical project of deciding what counts as 'real' – atoms and molecules, tables and chairs, rainbows, societies, classes and genders – there is still everything to play for. The area is full of ambiguities: for example, does the Sapir-Whorf hypothesis imply that reality itself is linguistically determined or that actors' experience of it, their 'mental reality', is? Commentators have expressed differing opinions on this. And does a 'mental reality' count as 'real'? These are hard questions, and philosophers have not resolved them.

What is hard to dispute, though, is the proposition that whatever the ultimate status of 'social reality', it is, partly at least, a *human* product. The continuing existence of such phenomena as social rules, behavioural rituals, institutions, e.g., marriage and government, is dependent on human action. Human action maintains these phenomena, and they are therefore susceptible to change and transformation by human beings.

The study of social reality

The challenges to positivism we have just considered have implications for the study of social reality. For if the experience of social actors is language and culture dependent, and if we grant that there are many languages and cultures, a number of problems for social science present themselves at once.

To begin with, and whether or not she believes it has an independent objective reality, the social researcher cannot take it for granted that she knows or recognises exactly what a social phenomenon or event is when she sees it. A woman turning over the earth in a flower bed with a spade might immediately be understood by an observer to be 'digging the garden'. In fact, though, the digger's own understandings and intentions would be an important part of the reality – she might not be gardening, but preparing to bury the budgie. Even if she were gardening, the observer who simply recorded this might miss some very important aspects of the scene: the gardener might be letting off steam after a row with her children, relaxing after a hard day at the office or worshipping the Goddess Earth by cultivating her. These meanings are properly a part of the reality being observed; the question 'what is going on here' cannot be answered without reference to the agent's own understanding of what she is doing.

If there are problems discovering exactly what is going on in one's own backyard, so to speak, if the objective and non-interactive observation assumed by positivism as the ideal is impossible or useless even so close to home, the problems for social scientists who study cultures and social groups not their own are even more acute. There are two main problems: the existence of differing and shifting conceptual frameworks, and the difficulty of translating from one to another. Can the researcher situate herself within the conceptual framework of the researched and thereby understand what is going on? And can she give an account of this 'otherness' for an audience of readers who can relate to her (original) conceptual framework but not the framework of her subjects? We might be alive to the dangers of ethnocentrism, but in the end, can anything be done about it?

Some influential philosophers have replied in the negative, arguing that there are no universally valid standards by which to judge the rightness or wrongness of belief systems; conceptual frameworks cannot validly be compared. This is a strongly relativist position. It has also been strongly opposed by those who argue that there is in fact a fundamental level of shared human experience and concepts. We are all sentient, rational beings who inhabit a world of solid objects: we must all have an understanding of the continued existence of objects in time and space, of cause and effect, and so on. Given such a 'bridgehead' between different human societies it is not so hard to see how we come to understand that someone else can have a different idea from ours of what causes rain, for instance. In other words, it is at least arguable that even radically unfamiliar conceptual frameworks can come to make sense to the observer.

But whether or not one holds an extreme relativist position, this debate highlights the problem that social reality is not just transparent to the observer. The social scientist must validate her understandings and interpretations with the community of researchers of which she is part (thus again raising the issue of theory-dependence in social scientific observation), but also and crucially she must validate her observations with the actors being observed. Asking what people are doing and why, as social scientists must, makes interaction with them inescapable.

You cannot validate a particular observation simply by repeating it. However many questionnaires you give out or interviews you conduct, it is impossible to be sure that all respondents who gave the 'same' answer meant the same thing by it, and that their responses are a direct representation of the truth. Furthermore, since persons are social actors the researcher cannot treat descriptions of their behaviour as chains of cause and effect, in the way one might describe the motion of billiard balls. To be sure, there are regularities to be discovered in the social world, but they are there because of people's habits, intentions, understandings and learning. Social scientists have to be concerned with what produces regularities as well as with the regularities themselves; and once again, this implies interaction with the researched.

. . .

The relations between researcher and researched: ethics, advocacy and empowerment

. . .

In this section we will distinguish three positions researchers may take up *vis-à-vis* their subjects: ethics, advocacy and empowerment. We will argue that ethics and advocacy are linked to positivist assumptions, while the more radical project of empowerment comes out of relativist and realist understandings.

Ethics

The potentially exploitative and damaging effects of being researched on have long been recognised by social scientists. We touched earlier on one important source of potential damage, the way social science is used within regimes of truth, or directly for social control. Even when you do not work for a government agency, and whatever your own political views, it is always necessary to think long and hard about the uses to which findings might be put, or the effects they might have contrary to the interests of subjects. If a researcher observes, for example, that the average attainment of some group of schoolchildren is less than might be anticipated, that can colour the expectations of teachers and contribute to the repetition of underachievement by the same group in future. That might be very far from what the researcher intended, but an ethically aware social scientist will see the possible dangers and perhaps try to forestall them.

A second worry is that the researcher might exploit subjects during the research process. One controversy here concerns the acceptability of covert research, in which subjects cannot give full informed consent because the researcher is deliberately misleading them as to the nature and purpose of the research, or perhaps concealing the fact that research is going on at all. For instance, a great deal of research in social psychology relies on subjects thinking the experimenter is looking for one thing when she is really looking for something else. Some sociological studies have involved the researcher 'passing' as a community member; and some sociolinguists have used the technique of getting subjects to recount traumatic experiences because the surge of powerful emotions stops them from being self-conscious about their pronunciation, circumventing the observer's paradox. In cases like these one wonders how far the end justifies the means. Even when the deception is on the face of it innocuous, it raises ethical problems because it is a deception.

. . .

Apart from preventing the abuse of subjects, an ethical researcher will be advised to ensure that their privacy is protected (e.g. by the use of pseudonyms when the findings are published) and where appropriate to compensate them for inconvenience or discomfort (whether in cash, as commonly happens in psychology, or in gifts, as from anthropologists to a community, or in services rendered, as with many sociolinguistic studies).

In ethical research, then, there is a wholly proper concern to minimise damage and offset inconvenience to the researched, and to acknowledge their contribution (even where they are unpaid, they will probably be thanked in the researcher's book or article). But the underlying model is one of 'research *on*' social subjects. Human subjects deserve special ethical consideration, but they no more set the researcher's agenda than the bottle of sulphuric acid sets the chemist's agenda. This position follows, of course, from the positivist emphasis on distance to avoid inter-ference or bias. However, it is also open to positivistically inclined researchers to go beyond this idea of ethics and make themselves more directly accountable to the researched. They may move, in other words, to an *advocacy* position.

Advocacy

What we are calling the 'advocacy position' is characerised by a commitment on the part of the researcher not just to do research *on* subjects but research *on and for* subjects. Such a commitment formalises what is actually a rather common devel-opment in field situations, where a researcher is asked to use her skills or her authority as an 'expert' to defend subjects' interests, getting involved in their campaigns for healthcare or education, cultural autonomy or political and land rights, and speaking on their behalf.

. . .

Labov (1982) suggests two principles. One is the principle of 'error correc-tion': if we as researchers know that people hold erroneous views on something, we have a responsibility to attempt to correct those views. (This, incidentally, is a clear example of 'commitment' and 'objectivity' serving the exact same ends; Labov believes in or is committed to putting truth in place of error.) The second principle is that of 'the debt incurred'. When a community has enabled linguists to gain important knowledge, the linguist incurs a debt which must be repaid by using the said knowledge on the community's behalf when they need it. This is clearly an advocacy position.

Labov further stresses that the advocate serves the community, and that polit-ical direction is the community's responsibility. As an outsider, Labov accepts — and counsels others to accept — an auxiliary role. 'They [linguists] don't claim for themselves the right to speak for the community or make the decision on what forms of language should be used' (Labov 1982: 27).

. . . The important point we want to make is that while Labov's position is in some ways extremely radical, it is so *within a positivist framework*. That framework sets limits on Labov's advocacy, and without underestimating the usefulness and sincerity of what he says and what he has done, we have to add that in our view the limits of positivism are severe and restrictive.

Labov's positivism is clearly visible in his uneasy juxtaposition of 'objectivity' and 'commitment'. Obviously he is worried that a researcher's advocacy might undermine the validity of her findings (the 'bias' or 'pseudoscience' problem). He gets around the problem by claiming that [in the specific case of the Ann Arbor 'Black English' trial], the one reinforced or enhanced the other. It was the work of African American linguists, many motivated at least partly by social and political considerations, that resolved the disagreements, anomalies, distortions and errors of previous work on 'Black English'. The field became better, more objective and more scientific as a result of these linguists' commitment.

This is a powerful and effective argument if one is inclined to place emphasis on notions of factual truth, error, bias, etc. – in other words, it is a positivistic argument. For a non-positivist it concedes too much – the absolute fact/value distinction for example, and the notion that there is one true account that we will ultimately be able to agree on. . . .

Empowerment

So far we have spoken of 'empowerment' and 'empowering research' as if the meaning of those expressions were self-evident. It will surprise no one if we now admit that they are not transparent or straightforward terms. As soon as we have dealt with the positivist objection that 'empowering research' is biased and invalid, we are likely to face more sophisticated questions from more radical quarters, in particular, 'what do you mean by power and what is empowerment?', followed swiftly by 'and how do you know who needs or wants to be "empowered"?' . . .

Our own position on power draws on both Foucaultian and non-Foucaultian understandings. We do treat power metaphorically as a property which some people in some contexts can have more of than others – that is, we cannot follow Foucault all the way in his rejection of the 'economic' metaphor. On the other hand we follow him in understanding it as a multiple relation (not something that has a single source, as in Marxism or Maoism); in emphasising its connection with knowledge and 'regimes of truth'; and in recognising the links between power and resistance.

Our decision to retain some notion of people or groups being more or less powerful exposes us to a further challenge, however. A sceptic might well ask how the would-be empowering researcher recognises who has more and who has less power: are we implying that the powerful and the powerless are recognisable to researchers as the poor and the wealthy are recognisable to economists? Obviously, if we were Marxists or Maoists who took economic ownership or gun-holding as straight forward indicators of power we could answer 'yes' to the sceptic's question. Since we find these views simplistic we are obliged to answer more thoughtfully. For if the 'real' centre of power is impossible to locate and we cannot identify who has power and who has not, how can we talk blithely about 'empowering research' as if it were easy to see where power lies and to alter its distribution?

We think this question lends weight to our argument that people's own definitions and experiences have to be considered. But consulting those involved, though it tells us something about how they perceive the question of power, does not automatically solve the problem: once again, we encounter the issue we discussed in relation to ethnomethodology, whether the actor's subjective account is the ultimate or only truth. Is, say, the happy slave's account of her experience the final account of it? To that we have to respond that the spectre of moral relativism is a frightening one. We would not want to be in a position where we could not assert, for instance, that slavery is wrong, or that extremes of wealth and poverty are unjust and undesirable.

The sceptic who thinks our notion of power simplistic, and challenges us to identify these 'powerless' people whom we propose to empower, has perhaps over-simplified the notion of empowerment. We must return here to the principle that power is not monolithic – the population does not divide neatly into two groups, the powerful and the powerless – from which it follows that 'empowering' cannot be a simple matter of transferring power from one group to the other, or giving people power when before they had none. Precisely because power operates across so many social divisions, any individual must have a complex and multiple identity: the person becomes an intricate mosaic of differing power potentials in different social relations. And we should not forget a further complication, that those who are dominated in particular social relations can and do develop powerful oppositional discourses of resistance – feminism, Black power, gay pride, for example – to which, again, people respond in complex ways. Importantly, though, the extent to which oppositional discourses and groupings are organised or alter-native meanings generated varies: some groups are more cohesive and more effective in resistance than others. . . .

Empowering research

. . .

We have characterised 'ethical research' as *research on* and 'advocacy research' as *research on and for*. We understand 'empowering research' as *research on, for and with*. One of the things we take that additional 'with' to imply is the use of inter-active or dialogic research methods, as opposed to the distancing or objectifying strategies positivists are constrained to use. It is the centrality of interaction 'with' the researched that enables research to be empowering in our sense; though we understand this as a necessary rather than a sufficient condition.

We should also point out that we do not think of empowerment as an absolute requirement on all research projects. There are instances where one would not wish to empower research subjects: though arguably there is political value in researching on powerful groups, such an enterprise might well be one instance where 'research on' would be the more appropriate model. But if we are going to raise the possibility of 'research on, for and with' as an appropriate goal in some contexts, we must also acknowledge that the standards and constraints of positivist 'research on' – objectivity, disinterestedness, non-interaction – will not be appro-priate in those contexts. This raises the question: what alternative standards would be appropriate?

Whatever standards we propose at this stage can only be provisional: much more discussion is needed. . . .

The three main issues we will take up in this provisional way are (a) the use of interactive methods; (b) the importance of subjects' own agendas; and (c) the question of 'feedback' and sharing knowledge. On each of these points we will begin with a programmatic statement and then pose various questions in relation to it.

(a)   'Persons are not objects and should not be treated as objects.'

The point of this statement is not one that needs to be laboured, since we believe most researchers would find it wholly uncontentious that persons are not objects, and are entitled to respectful treatment. What is more contentious is how strictly we define 'treating persons as objects', and whether if we make the definition a strict one we can avoid objectification and still do good ('valid') research.

We have raised the question of whether 'ethical research' permits methods (e.g., concealment of the researcher's purpose) that might be regarded as objectifying. Indeed, we have asked whether non-interactive methods are by definition objectifying, and thus inappropriate for empowering research. If empowering research is research done 'with' subjects as well as 'on' them it must seek their active co-operation, which requires disclosure of the researcher's goals, assumptions and procedures.

On the question of whether this kind of openness undermines the quality or validity of the research, it will already be clear what we are suggesting. We have devoted a great deal of space in this chapter to the argument that interaction *enhances* our understanding of what we observe, while the claims made for non-interaction as a guarantee of objectivity and validity are philosophically naïve.

The question before us, then, is how we can make our research methods more open, interactive and dialogic. This is not a simple matter, particularly in situations of inequality.

(b)   'Subjects have their own agendas and research should try to address them.'

One of the ways in which researchers are powerful is that they set the agenda for any given project: what it will be about, what activities it will involve, and so on. But from our insistence that 'persons are not objects' it obviously follows that researched persons may have agendas of their own, things they would like the researcher to address. If we are researching 'with' them as well as 'on and for' them, do we have a responsibility to acknowledge their agendas and deal with them in addition to our own?

This might involve only fairly minor adjustments to research procedures: making it clear, for instance, that asking questions and introducing topics is not the sole prerogative of the researcher. While traditional handbooks for positivist research warn against addressing questions subjects might ask, interactive methods oblige the researcher not only to listen but also, if called upon, to respond. But making space for subjects' agendas might mean rather more than this. It might mean allowing the researched to select focus for joint work, or serving as a resource or facilitator for research they undertake themselves. . . .

Activities that are 'added on' in order to meet subjects' needs may turn out to generate new insights into the activities the researcher defined: in other words, 'our' agenda and 'theirs' may sometimes intertwine.

(c)   'If knowledge is worth having, it is worth sharing.'
This is perhaps the most complicated of the issues we are raising here. Is it, or should it be, part of the researcher's brief to 'empower' people in an educational sense, by giving them access to expert knowledge, including the knowledge a research project itself has generated?

First, let us backtrack: what is this 'expert knowledge'? For, to a very substantial degree, social researchers' knowledge is and must be constructed out of subjects' own knowledge; if this is made explicit (as arguably it should be) the effect might be to demystify 'expert knowledge' as a category. Such a blurring of the boundary between what 'we' know and what 'they' know, brought about by making explicit the processes whereby knowledge acquires its authority and prestige, might itself be empowering. But it does complicate the picture of 'sharing knowledge', suggesting that there are different sorts of knowledge to be shared and different ways of sharing.

. . .

Most research, even when it is precisely concerned with finding out what subjects think, does not provide opportunities for reinterpretation [allowing informants to gain new perspective on what they know or believe]. Indeed, for the positivist researcher such intervention would be anathema, since a cardinal rule is to leave your subjects' beliefs as far as possible undistributed. Needless to say, we are not greatly upset if our practice separates us from positivist researchers. But it might also seem to separate us from the many researchers who, sincerely and properly concerned about the imbalance of power between themselves and their subjects, follow the apparently very different practice of 'letting subjects speak for themselves'. There is a convention in some contemporary research of reproducing subjects' own words on the page unmediated by authorial comment, in order to give the subject a voice of her own and validate her opinions. This *non*-intervention might also be claimed as an empowering move.

In assessing these two strategies, intervention versus 'giving a voice', one might want to distinguish between what is empowering in the context of *representing* subjects (that is, in a text such as an article, a book or a film) and what is empowering in the context of *interacting* with them. In the former context we see that there may be value in non-intervention (though see Bhavnani (1988), who criticises some instances for perpetuating stereotypes and reproducing disinformation). But in the latter context we have our doubts whether subjects are most empowered by a principled refusal to intervene in their discourse. Discourse after all is a historical construct: whether or not intervention changes someone's opinions, it is arguable that they gain by knowing where those opinions have 'come from' and how they might be challenged or more powerfully formulated. Clearly, it is a principle we use when we teach: not only do we engage with students' views, we engage with them *critically*. The question we are raising, then, is whether there is some merit in extending that practice from the context of the classroom to the context of research.

Even if we decide to answer this question in the affirmative, other questions remain as to how knowledge can be shared, and what the effects might be. There is also the question of how to integrate educational or knowledge-sharing aims into the broader scope of a researched project. . . .

References

Berger, P. and Luckmann, T. (1967) *The Social Construction of Reality*, Harmondsworth: Penguin.

Bhavnani, K. (1988) 'Empowerment and social research: some comments', *Text* 81 (2): 41–50.

Labov, W. (1982) 'Objectivity and commitment in linguistic science: the case of the Black English trial in Ann Arbor', *Language in Society* 11: 165–201.

Sapir, E. (1949) *Selected Writings in Language, Culture and Personality*, Mandelbaum, D. (ed.) Berkeley, CA: University of California Press.

Spender, D. (1980) *Man Made Language*, London: Routledge & Kegan Paul.

Chapter 9

Norman Fairclough

GLOBAL CAPITALISM AND CRITICAL AWARENESS OF LANGUAGE

. . .

I **WANT TO ARGUE THAT** as the shape of the new global social order becomes clearer, so too does the need for a critical awareness of language as part of people's resources for living in new ways in new circumstances. Our educational practices have some way to go before they begin to match up to our educational needs. At the same time, although I continue using the expression 'critical language awareness' (CLA) because it is relatively well-known, it has also become clearer that what is at issue is a critical awareness of discourse which includes other forms of semiosis as well as language: visual images in particular are an increasingly important feature of contemporary discourse (Kress and Van Leeuwen 1996; see also Chapters 12, 13, 26 in this *Reader*).

An example: the discourse of 'flexibility'

I shall begin with an example which points to a number of features of social life in contemporary ('late modern') society which demand a critical awareness of discourse. Most accounts of change in contemporary social life give a more or less central place to change in the economic system: the change from 'Fordism' to 'flexible accumulation', as Harvey (1990) puts it. Fordism is the 'mass production' form of capitalism (named after the car magnate Henry Ford) which dominated the earlier part of this century. Flexible accumulation is a more complex concept but it basically means greater flexibility at various levels – in production (the production process can be quickly shifted to produce small batches of different products), in

Source: Norman Fairclough, 'Global capitalism and critical awareness of language', *Language Awareness*, 8 (2), 1999: 71–83.

the workforce (part-time and short-term working, extensive reskilling of workers), in the circulation of finance, and so forth. Harvey points out that some academic analysts see 'flexibility' as no more than a new discourse which is ideologically motivated – if working people can be persuaded that 'flexibility' is an unavoidable feature of contemporary economies, they are more likely to be 'flexible' about their jobs disappearing, the need to retrain, deteriorating pay and conditions of work, and so forth. Harvey disagrees. Flexibility is a real feature of contemporary economies for which there is ample scientific evidence – though that does not mean that 'flexible accumulation' has totally displaced 'Fordism', the reality is rather a mix of old and new regimes. Nor does it mean that the discourse of flexibility is irrelevant to the reality of flexible accumulation. Far from it: *the discourse is an irreducible part of the reality*. The change from Fordism to flexible accumulation is inconceivable without the change in economic discourse. Why? Because the emerging global economy is the site of a struggle between the old and the new, and the discourse of flexibility is a vital symbolic weapon in that struggle. It is as Bourdieu (1998) has put it a 'strong discourse', that is a discourse which is backed by the strength of all the economic and social forces (the banks, the multinational companies, politicians, and so on) who are trying to make flexibility – the new global capitalism – even more of a reality than it already is. Neoliberal discourse contributes its own particular, symbolic, form of strength to the strength of these social forces.

Let me briefly clarify my example. My focus is on the metaphor of 'flexibility' which is at the centre of the economic discourse of 'flexible accumulation' for which Harvey (1990: 47–97) gives an analytical account – including, for example, its construction of the labour market in terms of 'core' and 'periphery' employees. Elements of this discourse, and especially the metaphor of flexibility itself, are widely distributed within many types of non-economic discourse (examples shortly). The discourse of flexible accumulation enters complex and shifting configurations with other discourses within a field I am calling 'neoliberal discourse' – for instance with a management discourse which centres on the 'mission statement' which Swales and Rogers (1995) have described.

One accessible place to find the discourse of flexibility used within this struggle over global economy is in the books written by management 'gurus' which seem to dominate airport and railway station bookshops (for example Peters 1994). But it is a discourse that turns up in many other contexts. One of them is politics – New Labour's 'Third Way', for instance, can be summed up as follows: economic flexibility (on the model of the World Bank and the IMF) is inevitable, but government must strive to include those it socially excludes. Here is Blair in his first major speech after becoming Prime Minister:

> We must never forget that a strong, competitive, flexible economy is the prerequisite for creating jobs and opportunities. But equally we must never forget that it is not enough. The economy can grow while leaving behind a workless class whose members become so detached that they are no longer full citizens.

> (Blair 1997)

But the discourse of flexibility also penetrates into everyday language. Here for instance is an extract from an ethnographic interview with 'Stephen' from Cleveland in North-East England who does 'fiddly jobs', i.e. works illegally in the black economy while claiming social benefits. He is talking about the work he does:

> It's a matter of us being cheaper. It's definitely easier than having a lot of lads taken on permanently. It would cost them more to put them on the books or pay them off. It's just the flexibility. You're just there for when the jobs come up, and he [the 'hirer and firer'] will come and get you when you're needed. You need to be on the dole to be able to do that. Otherwise you'd be sitting there for half the year with no work and no money at all.
>
> (Quoted in MacDonald 1994: 515)

We might pessimistically think of everyday language as colonised by this discourse of the powerful, and that is no doubt partly true, but here is 'Stephen' appropriating the discourse in constructing his own perfectly coherent rationale for his (illegal) way of living. One aspect of economic flexibility from his perspective is that companies need the flexibility of workers doing fiddly jobs.

Like other prominent discourses, the discourse of flexibility draws some comment and critique – a critical awareness of language is not wholly something which has to be brought to people from outside, it arises within the normal ways people reflect on their lives as part of their lives. But this ordinary form of critique has its limits. People need to know about discourses like this – for instance, what insights it gives us into the way economies work or could work, and what other insights it cuts us off from; whose discourse it is, and what they gain from its use; what other discourses there are around, and how this one has become so dominant. People practically need to know such things, because not knowing them makes it harder for them to manage in various parts of their lives: as trade unionists – whether resisting shifts to part-time and short-time work is fighting the inevitable; as managers what strengths and limitations the metaphor of flexibility has for their organisations; as citizens – whether there is a 'Third Way'; as parents what sort of world to prepare their children for. But such knowledge about discourse has to come from outside, from theory and research, via education.

I want to proceed by discussing, with a focus on discourse, several key features of late modern society which this example touches on, and which I think help make the case for critical awareness of discourse. Actually the earlier ones arise more easily from the example of the discourse of flexibility than the later ones. I discuss these features of late modernity under the following headings: the relationship between discourse, knowledge and social change in our 'information' or 'knowledge-based' society; what Smith (1990) has called the 'textually mediated' nature of contemporary social life; the relationship between discourse and social difference; the commodification of discourse; discourse and democracy. I shall then draw these together by tying the case for CLA to the nature of the new global capitalism, and conclude the paper with discussions of how CLA is anchored in 'critical discourse analysis' (and, through that, in critical social science generally), critical discourse awareness and critical pedagogy.

Discourse, knowledge and social change

The example points to a relationship between change in economic discourse, new economic knowledge, and change in economic practices. As I stated earlier, it is a matter of discourse, not just language – knowledges are increasingly constituted in multisemiotic ways in contemporary society (Kress and Van Leeuwen 1996; New London Group 1996). Information- or knowledge-based late modern societies are characterised, as Giddens has put it, by enhanced reflexivity – we are constantly reshaping our social practices on the basis of knowledge about those practices. This is true in the domain of work but also, for instance, in how people conduct their personal relationships – the media are full of expert advice. On one level, reflexivity is an inherent property of all social practices – any social practice includes the constructions of that practice produced by its practitioners as part of the practice. What is different about late modernity is the ways in which 'expert systems' (such as the sciences and social sciences) are systematically integrated into reflexive processes (Giddens 1991). These expert systems can be thought of as evaluating existing knowledges in the practical domain in focus (for example the economy) and producing new knowledges. Since knowledges are constituted as discourses, particular ways of using language, this means that they are in the business of evaluating and changing discourses. Evaluating discourses means setting them against shifting understandings of what material possibilities there are in the practical domain concerned (for example the economy), which are, in turn, instantiated within new discourses. In such practical contexts, discourses are evaluated not in terms of some impossible 'absolute truth', but in terms of 'epistemic gain' – whether they yield knowledges which allow people to improve the way in which they manage their lives.

The business of evaluating and changing knowledges and discourses is something which an increasing number of people are involved in as part of the work they do. It is a major concern of educational institutions to teach them how to do this, and part of the current preoccupation with 'learning to learn', and other thematisations of 'learning' in contemporary education and business – 'the learning society', businesses as 'learning organisations', 'lifelong learning' – see, for example, the Dearing Report on universities *Higher Education in the Learning Society* (National Committee of Inquiry into Higher Education 1997). What I want to argue is that the resources for learning and for working in a knowledge-based economy include a critical awareness of discourse – an awareness of how discourse figures within social practices, an awareness that any knowledge of a domain of social life is constituted as one discourse from among a number of co-existing or conceivable discourses, that different discourses are associated with different perspectives on the domain concerned and different interests, an awareness of how discourses can work ideologically in social relations of power, and so forth. It is on the basis of such understandings of how discourse works within social practices that people can come to question and look beyond existing discourses, or existing relations of dominance and marginalisation between discourses, and so advance knowledge. If on the other hand language and other semiotic modalities are viewed as simply transparent media for reflecting what is, the development of knowledge is likely to be impeded.

Textually mediated social life

The presence of the discourse of flexibility in Stephen's talk is an illustration of the textual mediation of social life: in contemporary societies, the discourses/ knowledges generated by expert systems enter our everyday lives and shape the way we live them. Contemporary societies are knowledge-based not only in their economies but even, for instance, in the ways in which people conduct their personal relationships. Expert knowledges/discourses come to us via texts of various sorts which mediate our social lives – books, magazines, radio and television programmes, and so forth. These processes of textual mediation bind together people who are scattered across societies into social systems – one of Smith's examples is how textually mediated constructions of femininity lock women scattered across social space into the economic system of commodity production and consumption, in that femininity is constructed in terms of the purchase and use of commodities such as clothes (Smith 1990). Moreover, the distances in space and time across which these processes of textual mediation operate are increasing. Modernity can be seen as a process of 'time/space compression', the overcoming of spatial and temporal distance, and late modernity is marked by a twist in that process which is widely referred to as 'globalisation' (Harvey 1990; Giddens 1991). The vehicles for this spatio-temporally extended textual mediation are the new media – radio, television, and information technology.

As everyday lives become more pervasively textually mediated, people's lives are increasingly shaped by representations which are produced elsewhere. Representations of the world they live in, the activities they are involved in, their relationships with each other, and even who they are and how they (should) see themselves. The politics of representation becomes increasingly important – whose representations are these, who gains what from them, what social relations do they draw people into, what are their ideological effects, and what alternative representations are there? The example of Stephen's talk is a case in point. His representation of his own life in the black economy draws upon the discourse of flexibility. We might question whether his construction of his own life and identity has been ideologically invested, drawn into the social relations between the powerful groups who control economies and back neoliberalism and the rest of us. However, the picture is more complex and more hopeful. As I suggested earlier, his talk does not simply reproduce the discourse of flexibility, it works it in a particular – and ironic – way into a rationale for his own way of living based on a perfectly coherent, if non-standard, view of the new capitalism – part of the flexibility that companies need is the flexibility of illegal black labour. The example shows that people are not simply colonised by such discourses, they also appropriate them and work them in particular ways. Textually mediated social life cuts both ways – it opens up unprecedented resources for people to shape their lives in new ways drawing upon knowledges, perspectives and discourses which are generated all over the world. But in so doing it opens up new areas of their lives to the play of power. There is a colonisation–appropriation dialectic at work. Whether on balance people gain or lose depends on where they are positioned in social life – the fact that new possibilities are opened up does not mean people are unconditionally free to take them. But my main point is this: if people are to live in this complex world rather than just be carried along by it, they need resources to examine their placing within this dialectic between the global and the local – and those resources include a critical awareness of language and discourse which can only come through language education.

Discourse, social difference and social identity

Discourses are partial and positioned, and social difference is manifest in the diversity of discourses within particular social practices. Neoliberal economic discourse, for instance, is only one of many economic discourses and, as I have indicated earlier, it corresponds to a specific perspective and set of interests. Critical awareness in this case is a matter of seeing the diversity of discourses and their positioned nature.

But there are other aspects of social difference. Late modern societies are increasingly socially diverse societies, not only in that migration has led to greater ethnic and cultural diversity, but also because various lines of difference which were until recently relatively covered over have become more salient differences of gender and sexual orientation, for example. Differences are partly semiotic in nature – different languages, different social dialects, different communicative styles, different voices, different discourses. The predominant ethos, for instance, in European societies is that differences which have in the past been suppressed should now be recognised. But since people need to work together across difference, differences have to be negotiated. Working across differences is a process in our individual lives, within the groups we belong to, as well as between groups. Working across differences entails semiotic hybridity – the emergence of new combinations of languages, social dialects, voices, genres and discourses. Hybridity, heterogeneity, intertextuality are salient features of contemporary discourse also because the boundaries between domains and practices are in many cases fluid and open in a context of rapid and intense social change – the negotiation of social difference includes, for instance, the negotiation of differences between educators, advertisers and business managers, and between students and consumers of commodities, within educational institutions which are increasingly forced into operating in market ways. But negotiating differences is simultaneously negotiating identities – working out how I or we relate to others is simultaneously working out who I am or who we are. The radical disarticulations and rearticulations of contemporary social life radically unsettle social identities, and the search for and construction of identities is a constant process and a major preoccupation, but it should be framed in terms of the problem of learning to live with difference (New London Group 1996). Once again, people need from education a range of resources for living within socially and culturally diverse societies and avoiding their dangers, including chauvinism and racism. A critical awareness of discourse is part of what is needed.

Commodification of discourse

There is still a link, if a more tenuous one, between my next theme and the example of the discourse of flexibility. I referred earlier to the books of management gurus which fill airport bookstalls and are filled with neoliberal economic discourse. These books are about big business, but they are also big business themselves. They are generally rather successful commodities, as one can see from the impressive sales figures which are often emblazoned on their covers. The stuff these commodities are made of is, of course, paper, ink and so forth, but it is also language and other sorts of semiotic stuff. They are worked up into commodities, carefully designed to sell. Semiotic stuff is a feature of a great many commodities these days – the nature of commodities has been changing, with a shift in emphasis broadly from goods that are more physical than cultural (like cars) to goods that are more cultural than physical (like books, or television programmes, or advertisements). Many goods now are services, like what you pay for in a smart restaurant which is not just the food but the ambiance, which includes the appearance, behaviour and talk of the staff – language is part of the service, part of the goods. As commodities become semioticised, discourse becomes commodified (Lyotard 1986–7) – it becomes open to processes of economic calculation, it comes to be designed for success on markets. For instance, service industries are full of forms of ostensibly ordinary talk which are designed to seem ordinary, to mobilise all the selling power of ordinariness in a society which values it even in institutional and organisational contexts.

The commodification of discourse could be seen as part of a more general application of instrumental or 'means-end' rationality to discourse which also takes the form of government and other organisations making discourse more bureaucratic. I have referred to this elsewhere as 'technologisation of discourse' (Fairclough 1996) – instrumental rationality applied in the shaping and reshaping of discursive practices (such as interviews) within more general processes of engineering institutional cultures to enhance their 'performativity' (Lyotard 1984). Technologisation of discourse produces general formulas for change which tend to ignore differences of context, so that one effect of such cultural technologisation is normalisation, homogenisation and the reduction of difference – for instance the imposition of a standardised audit culture and the discourse that goes with it (the discourse of 'quality control') throughout the public domain, including education. This process rests upon a critical awareness of discourse, but it also calls for a critical awareness of discourse amongst those who are on the receiving end of it, people who work in commercial, governmental and public service organisations in a variety of capacities.

Discourse and democracy

The discourse of flexibility is predominant within the political systems of, for instance, Great Britain and the USA – all of the major parties use it and take it for granted. It is part of a widely observed narrowing down of the political spectrum – parties are becoming increasingly similar in their policies, and the differences between them are increasingly differences of style. One aspect of this process is what Marcuse identified 30 years ago as 'the closing down of the universe of discourse' (Marcuse 1964) – the predominance of a single economic-political discourse across the political spectrum.

We might see the narrowing of political discourse as a symptom of the political system becoming cut off from the sources of political diversity and change in social life. This has been widely debated in recent years as a crisis of the 'public sphere' (Habermas 1989; Calhoun 1992), troubles to do with the apparent absence of effective spaces and practices where people as citizens can deliberate over issues of common social and political concern, and their deliberations can shape the policy decisions that are made. The broadcast media are full of dialogue on such issues, but it is a dialogue that is deeply flawed in terms of its public sphere credentials – in terms of who has access to it, in terms of what gets onto its agendas, in terms of who controls its flow, and in terms of it being designed to maximise audience and entertain. The task of reconstructing the public sphere is at the heart of the defence and enhancement of democracy. It is already being undertaken within social movements which are active outside the official political system. But it is also a task for educational institutions including schools and universities, whose standing as public spheres has been undermined by recent institutional changes (Giroux 1997). One way forward here is suggested by Billig (1991): that we conceive of teaching people to think as teaching people to argue, and put our energies into making educational institutions as open as possible as spaces for argument. Negotiating across difference is again a central concern for the contemporary public sphere – political dialogue in socioculturally diverse societies has to be oriented to alliances around particular sets of issues. In this case, a critical awareness of discourse is essential for the work of experimentation and design which is necessary to find effective forms of dialogue which facilitate open argumentation and forms of action in common which do not suppress difference (Fairclough 1998).

Critical awareness of discourse and the new global capitalism

I began from the example of neoliberal economic discourse. The choice of example was not incidental, because it is the new global capitalism which this discourse simultaneously represents and constitutes that makes critical awareness of discourse an increasingly necessary resource for people. The new global capitalism opens up new possibilities for people yet at the same time creates new problems. A critical awareness of discourse is necessary for both – on the one hand, for opening up new knowledges in the knowledge-based economy, and for exploring new possibilities for social relationships and identities in socially diverse communities; on the other hand, for resisting the incursions of the interests and rationalities of economic, governmental and other organisational systems into everyday life – such as the commodification of the language of everyday life, the colonising incursions of textually mediated representations and the threat of global capitalism to democracy, for example, in the ways it manipulates national governments. Late modernity is characterised by increasing reflexivity including language reflexivity, and people need to be equipped both for the increasing knowledge-based design of discursive practices within economic and governmental systems, and for critique and redesign of these designed and often globalised practices as workers, consumers, citizens, members of social and lifestyle groups (for example as women, Blacks, trade unionists, environmental activists, and so forth).

Critique: social science, discourse analysis, discourse awareness

The need for critical awareness of discourse in contemporary society should make it a central part of language education in schools, colleges and universities. I come to some educational issues later. Such a critical discourse awareness programme would rest upon and recontextualise (Bernstein 1990) critical research on discourse, which in turn is based in critical traditions in social science. While these are obviously not the focus of this paper, readers may find useful a brief sketch of one view of critical discourse analysis and critical social science, starting with the latter.

Social life can be seen as constituted by networks of social practices, each of which consists of various elements including discourse (as well as material activities, institutional rituals, social relations, beliefs and values) articulated together in a dialectical relationship, such that each element internalises all others without being reducible to them – each element has its own distinctive logic and generative power (Collier 1994; Chouliaraki and Fairclough 1999; Harvey 1996). A critical social science explicates both structural relations between and within social practices within such networks, and the dialectical tension between structure and event which makes structures both preconditions for events and (transformed) outcomes of them (Chouliaraki and Fairclough 1999; Bourdieu and Wacquant 1992). One view of critique is the concept of 'explanatory critique' associated with 'critical realism' (Bhaskar 1986; Collier 1994): critique involves four stages – identification of a problem, identification of what it is in the network of social practices that gives rise to the problem, consideration of whether and how the problem is functional in sustaining the system (for example whether it works ideologically), and identification of real possibilities within the domain of social life in question for overcoming the problem. What constitutes a problem can only be established through dialogue between those involved – often not an easy process, or one that yields clear answers.

Critical research on discourse has been carried out under the names of 'critical discourse analysis' and 'critical linguistics' (Fairclough and Wodak 1997). Critical discourse analysis aims to provide a framework for systematically linking properties of discoursal interactions and texts with features of their social and cultural circumstances. The network of social practices is described from a specifically discoursal perspective as an 'order of discourse' consisting of discourses and genres in particular relationships with each other, but with an orientation to shifts in boundaries within and between orders of discourse as part of social and cultural change. Particular discursive events and longer-term series of events tied to specific social conjunctures are described in terms of the potentially innovative ways in which they draw upon the orders of discourse which condition them – it is that relationship to orders of discourse that mediates the connection between detailed semiotic/linguistic features of texts and interactions, and social and cultural structures and processes. Problems of two sorts are in focus: needs-based problems – discursive practices which in some way go against people's needs (for example, forms of doctor–patient communication which do not allow patients to recount what they see as all the relevant aspects of their health problems); and problems with representations (for example constructions of social groups such as women or cultural minorities which have detrimental social consequences for them).

Critical discourse awareness programmes will be concerned to recontextualise this body of research in ways which transform it, perhaps quite radically, into a practically useful form for educational purposes, including a metalanguage.

Critical discourse awareness and education

Recent educational reforms have sharply raised the question of what education is for, and for whom. The dominant view of education – evident, for instance, in the recent Dearing Report *Higher Education in the Learning Society* (National Committee of Inquiry into Higher Education 1997) – sees it as a vocationally-oriented transmission of given knowledge and skills. What is perhaps most distinctive about this view of education is its focus upon the teaching and learning of 'key skills' which are seen as transferable from one sphere of life to another, and as the basis for future success including successful 'lifelong learning'. Given that one of these key skills is 'communication' (the others identified in the Dearing Report are numeracy, information technology and learning to learn), this view of education rests upon a view of discourse – discourse as 'communication skills'.

What is wrong with seeing discourse as communication skills? Let me focus on three problems. First, it is assumed that a communication skill, once learnt, can be freely transferred from one context to another. I think there is an interesting connection between this assumption and the tendencies I have identified as textually mediated social life and the technologisation of discourse – discursive practices are indeed transferred across contexts in late modern social life. But what this first assumption misses is what I have referred to as the colonisation–appropriation dialectic (which is also a global–local dialectic) – even where such transfers take place, it does not mean that we find the same discursive practice in all contexts, for even the most globally dispersed discursive practice is always locally recontextualised, transformed and appropriated. It is inviting disaster to assume that if you have learnt to interview candidates for admission to university, you know how to interview personalities on a television chat show. Second, it is assumed that there is a simple relationship between what is actually said (or more generally done) in the course of some social practice, and skills, internalised models of how to say/do it – that discourse is a mere instantiation of such models (Fairclough 1988). On the contrary, discourse is a complex matching of models with immediate needs in which what emerges may be radically different from any model, ambivalent between models, or a baffling mixture of models, and where flair and creativity may have more impact than skill. Thirdly, and most seriously, it is assumed that there is a given and accepted way of using language to do certain things, as if discourse was a simple matter of technique, whereas any way of using language which gets to be given and accepted does so through applications of power which violently exclude other ways, and any way of using language within any social practice is socially contestable and likely to be contested. From this point of view, any reduction of discourse to skills is complicit with efforts on the part of those who have power to impose social practices they favour by getting people to see them as mere techniques.

In critiquing the view of discourse as communication skills, I am also critiquing the view of education as a transmission of knowledge and skills. For viewing discourse as skills is just one aspect of viewing knowledge and skills in general as determinate, uncontested, and given externally to the learner; and it is only on such assumptions about what is to be taught and learnt that the process can be viewed as 'transmission'. We can broaden out the argument against discourse as skills into a different view of knowledge and skills in education: they are always provisional and indeterminate, contested and, moreover, at issue in social relationships, within which all teachers and learners are positioned. In a critical view of education, knowledge and 'skills' are indeed taught and learnt, but they are also questioned – a central concern is what counts as knowledge or skill (and therefore what does not), for whom, why, and with what beneficial or problematic consequences. In the Dearing Report, higher education promotes knowledge, skills and understanding; my comments here take understanding to mean a questioning of knowledge and skills, and problematise the foregrounding of 'key skills' in the Report.

Perhaps it has always been the case that education has been relatively critical for some, though usually for a small elite. In the new work order (Gee *et al.* 1996), there is a need for a small elite of symbolic-analytic workers for whom the new system may demand a critical education (including a critical awareness of discourse). The danger is a new form of educational stratification which separates them from those likely to become other categories of workers (routine production workers, and workers in service industries) or to join the 'socially excluded' (including unemployed). That would be in line with the contemporary tendency of the purposes of education to narrow down towards serving the needs of the economy. The alternative is some vision of education for life within which a critical awareness of discourse is necessary for all.

References

Bernstein, B. (1990) *The Structuring of Pedagogic Discourse*, London: Routledge.
Bhaskar, R. (1986) *Scientific Reasoning and Human Emancipation*, London: Verso.
Billig, M. (1991) *Ideology and Opinion*, London: Sage.
Blair, Tony (1997) Speech at the Aylesbury Housing Estate, Southwark, 2 June.
Bourdieu, P. (1998) 'L'essence du neo-liberalisme', *Le Monde Diplomatique*, March.
—— and Wacquant, L. (1992) *An Invitation to Reflexive Sociology*, Cambridge: Polity Press.
Calhoun, C. (1992) *Habermas and the Public Sphere*, Cambridge, MA: MIT Press.
Chouliaraki, L. and Fairclough, N. (1999) *Discourse in Late Modernity*, Edinburgh: Edinburgh University Press.

Collier, A. (1994) *Critical Realism*, London: Verso.

Fairclough, N. (1988) 'Register, power and sociosemantic change', in D. Birch and M. O'Toole (eds) *The Functions of Style*, London: Pinter Publications.

—— (1996) 'Technologisation of discourse', in C. Caldas-Coulthard and M. Coulthard (eds) *Texts and Practices: Readings in Critical Discourse Analysis*, London: Routledge.

—— (1998) 'Democracy and the public sphere in critical research on discourse', paper given at conference on Discourse, Politics and Identity in Europe, Vienna, April.

—— and Wodak, R. (1997) 'Critical discourse analysis', in T. Van Dijk (ed.) *Discourse as Social Interaction*, London: Sage.

Gee, J., Hull, G. and Lankshear, C. (1996) *The New Work Order: Behind the Language of the New Capitalism*, London: Allen & Unwin.

Giddens, A. (1991) *Modernity and Self-identity*, Cambridge: Polity Press.

Giroux, H. (1997) *Pedagogy and the Politics of Hope*, Boulder, CO: Westview Press.

Habermas, J. (1989) *Structural Transformation of the Public Sphere*, Cambridge, MA: MIT Press.

Harvey, D. (1990) *The Condition of Postmodernity*, Oxford: Blackwell.

—— (1996) *Justice, Nature and the Geography of Difference*, Oxford: Blackwell.

Kress, G. and Van Leeuwen, T. (1996) *Reading Images: The Grammar of Visual Design*, London: Routledge.

Lyotard, J.-F. (1984) *The Postmodern Condition*, Manchester: University of Manchester Press.

—— (1986/7) 'Rules and paradoxes and the svelte appendix', *Cultural Critique* 5: 209–19.

MacDonald, R. (1994) 'Fiddly jobs, undeclared working and the something for nothing society', *Work, Employment and Society* 8 (4): 507–30.

Marcuse, H. (1964) *One-dimensional Man*, London: Abacus.

National Committee of Inquiry into Higher Education (1997) *Higher Education in the Learning Society (The Dearing Report)*, London: HMSO.

New London Group (1996) 'A pedagogy of multiliteracies: designing social futures', *Harvard Educational Review* 66 (1): 60–92.

Peters, T. (1994) *The Tom Peters Seminar*, London: Vintage Books.

Smith, D. (1990) *Texts, Facts and Femininity*, London: Routledge.

Swales, J. and Rogers, P. (1995) 'Discourse and the projection of corporate culture: The Mission Statement', *Discourse & Society* 6 (2): 223–42.

Chapter 10

J. Maxwell Atkinson and John Heritage

JEFFERSON'S TRANSCRIPT NOTATION

T HE TRANSCRIPT NOTATION often used in conversation analytic research, has been developed by Gail Jefferson. It is a system that continues to evolve in response to current research interests. Sometimes it has been necessary to incorporate symbols for representing various non-vocal activities, such as gaze, gestures, and applause.

Previous experience suggests that it is useful to group symbols with reference to the phenomena they represent.

Simultaneous utterances

Utterances starting simultaneously are linked together with either double or single left-hand brackets:

       Tom: I used to smoke a lot when I was young
  [[Bob: [[I used to smoke Camels

Overlapping utterances

When overlapping utterances do not start simultaneously, the point at which an ongoing utterance is joined by another is marked with a single left-hand bracket, linking an ongoing with an overlapping utterance at the point where overlap begins:

      Tom: I used to smoke ⌐a lot
  [Bob: ⌐He thinks he's real tough

Source: J. Maxwell Atkinson and John Heritage (eds) *Structures of Social Action: Studies in Conversation Analysis*, Cambridge: Cambridge University Press, 1984, ix–xvi.

The point where overlapping utterances stop overlapping is marked with a single right-hand bracket:

>]　Tom:　　I used to smoke ⌈a lot⌉ more than this
> 　　Bob:　　　　　　　　　[I see]

Contiguous utterances

When there is no interval between adjacent utterances, the second being latched immediately to the first (without overlapping it), the utterances are linked together with equal signs:

> =　Tom:　　I used to smoke a lot=
> 　　Bob:　　　=He thinks he's real tough

The equal signs are also used to link different parts of a single speaker's utterance when those parts constitute a continuous flow of speech that has been carried over to another line, by transcript design, to accommodate an intervening interruption:

> Tom:　　I used to smoke ⌈a lot more than this=
> Bob:　　　　　　　　　[You used to smoke
> Tom:　　=but I never inhaled the smoke

Sometimes more than one speaker latches directly onto a just-completed utterance, and a case of this sort is marked with a combination of equal signs and double left-hand brackets:

> 　　　　Tom:　　I used to smoke a lot=
> =[[　Bob:　　=[[He thinks he's tough
> 　　　　Ann:　　　　So did I

When overlapping utterances end simultaneously and are latched onto by a subsequent utterance, the link is marked by a single right-handed bracket and equal signs:

> 　　　Tom:　　I used to smoke ⌈a lot⌉=
>]=　Bob:　　　　　　　　　[I see]=
> 　　　Ann:　　=So did I

Intervals within and between utterances

When intervals in the stream of talk occur, they are timed in tenths of a second and inserted within parentheses, either within an utterance:

> (0.0)　Lil:　　When I was (0.6) oh nine or ten

or between utterances:

    Hal: step right up
           (1.3)
    Hal: I said step right up
           (0.8)
    Joe: Are you talking to me

A short untimed pause within an utterance is indicated by a dash:

    — Dee: Umm — my mother will be right in

Unlimited intervals heard between utterances are described within double parentheses and inserted where they occur:

    ((pause))   Rex: Are you ready to order
                       ((pause))
                Pam: Yes thank you we are

Characteristics of speech delivery

In these transcripts, punctuation is used to mark not conventional grammatical units but, rather, attempts to capture characteristics of speech delivery. For example, a colon indicates an extension of the sound or syllable it follows:

    co:lon   Ron: What ha:ppened to you

and more colons prolong the stretch:

    co :: lons   Mae: I ju::ss can't come
                 Tim: I'm so:::sorry re:::ally I am

The other punctuation marks are used as follows:

. A period indicates a stopping fall in tone, not necessarily the end of a sentence.
, A comma indicates a continuing intonation, not necessarily between clauses of sentences.
? A question mark indicates a rising inflection, not necessarily a question.
⸮ A combined question mark/comma indicates a rising intonation weaker than that indicated by a question mark.
! An exclamation point indicates an animated tone, not necessarily an exclamation.
— A single dash indicates a halting, abrupt cutoff, or, when multiple dashes hyphenate the syllables of a word or connect strings of words, the stream of talk so marked has a stammering quality.

Marked rising and falling shifts in intonation are indicated by upward and downward pointing arrows immediately prior to the rise or fall:

   ↓↑   Thatcher: I am however (0.2) very ↓fortunate (0.4) in having
                          (0.6) ↑mar:vlous dep↓uty

Emphasis is indicated by underlining:

   Ann: It happens to be <u>mine</u>

Capital letters are used to indicate an utterance, or part thereof, that is spoken much louder than the surrounding talk:

   Announcer: an the winner: ↓iz:s (1.4) RACHEL ROBERTS for
             Y↑ANKS

A degree sign is used to indicate a passage of talk which is quieter than the surrounding talk:

   °°   M: ·hhhh (.)°U<u>m</u> ::°'Ow is yih <u>m</u>other by: th'<u>wa</u>:y.h

Audible aspirations (hhh) and inhalations (·hhh) are inserted in the speech where they occur:

   hhh   Pam: An thi(hh)s is for you hhh
   ·hhh   Don: ·hhhh O(hh) tha(h)nk you rea(hh)lly

A 'gh' placed within a word indicates gutturalness:

   gh   J: Ohgh(h)h hhuh <u>huh</u> <u>huh</u> ·huh

A subscribed dot is used as a "hardener." In this capacity it can indicate, for example, an especially dentalized "t":

   dọt   J: Was it ↑ la:s' nigḥṭ.

Double parentheses are used to enclose a description of some phenomenon with which the transcriptionist does not want to wrestle.

These can be vocalizations that are not, for example, spelled gracefully or recognizably:

   (( ))   Tom: I used to ((cough)) smoke a lot
           Bob: ((sniff)) He thinks he's tough
           Ann: ((snorts))

or other details of the conversational scene:

> Jan: This is just delicious
> ((telephone rings))
> Kim: I'll get it

or various characterizations of the talk:

> Ron: ((in falsetto)) I can do it now
> Max: ((whispered)) He'll never do it

When part of an utterance is delivered at a pace quicker than the surrounding talk, it is indicated by being enclosed between "less than" signs:

> ><   Steel: the Gua:rdian <u>new</u>spaper <u>loo</u>ked through >the mani-
> festoes< la:<u>st</u> ↑week

Transcriptionist doubt

In addition to the timings of intervals and inserted aspirations and inhalations, items enclosed within single parentheses are in doubt, as in:

> (   ) Ted: I ('spose I'm not)
> (Ben):   We all (t–   )

Here "spose I'm not," the identity of the second speaker, and "t–" represent different varieties of transcriptionist doubt.

Sometimes multiple possibilities are indicated:

> Ted: I (spoke to Mark)
>   ('spose I'm not)
>
> Ben: We all try to figure a (tough angle) for it
>   (stuffing girl)

When single parentheses are empty, no hearing could be achieved for the string of talk or item in question:

> Todd: My (   ) catching
> (   ): In the highest (   )

Here the middle of Todd's utterance, the speaker of the subsequent utterance, and the end of the subsequent utterance could not be recovered.

Gaze direction

The gaze of the speaker is marked above an utterance, and that of the addressee below it. A line indicates that the party marked is gazing toward the other. The absence of a line indicates lack of gaze. Dots mark the transition movement from nongaze to gaze, and the point where the gaze reaches the other is marked with an X:

```
Beth:   . . . .    ┌ X_____
            Terry ─┘ Jerry's fa ┌ scinated with elephants
Don:              . . . . . └ X_____
```

Here Beth moves her gaze toward Don while saying "Terry"; Don's gaze shifts toward and reaches hers just after she starts to say "fascinated."

If gaze arrives within a pause each tenth of a second within the pause is marked with a dash:

```
Ann:                          . . . ┌X_____
            Well (--- -) We coulda used ┘a liddle, marijuana.=
Beth:               └x_____
```

Here Beth's gaze reaches Ann three-tenths of a second after she has said "Well-" and one-tenth of a second before she continues with "We coulda used . . . "

Commas are used to indicate the dropping of gaze:

```
Ann:    _____
            Karen has this new hou:se. en it's got all this
Beth:   _____ , , ,
```

Here Beth's gaze starts to drop away as Ann begins to say "new."

Movements like head nodding are marked at points in the talk where they occur:

```
Ann:    _____
            Karen has this new hou:se. en it's got all this
Beth:   _____ , , ,              ((Nod))
```

Here Beth, who is no longer gazing at Ann, nods as the latter says "got."

Asterisks are used in a more ad hoc fashion to indicate particular phenomena discussed in the text. In the following fragment, for example, Goodwin uses them to indicate the position where Beth puts food in her mouth:

```
Ann:    _____
            =like─(0.2) ssilvery: :g─go : ld wwa:ll ┌ paper.
Beth:               ******* [. .] └x_____
```

Applause

Strings of *X*'s are used to indicate applause, with lower- and uppercase letters marking quiet and loud applause respectively:

        Audience: xxXXXXXXXXXXXXXxxx

Here applause amplitude increases and then decreases.
        An isolated single clap is indicated by dashes on each side of the x:

        Audience: −x−

Spasmodic or hesitant clapping is indicated by a chain punctuated by dashes:

        Audience: −x−x−x

A line broken by numbers in parentheses indicates the duration of applause from the point of onset (or prior object) to the nearest tenth of a second. The number of *X*'s does *not* indicate applause duration except where it overlaps with talk, as in the second of the following examples:

        Speaker: I beg >to supp↓ort the m↓otion<=
                   ┝─────── (8.0) ───────┥
        Audience: =xx−xxXXXXXXXXXXXXXxxxx−x
        Speaker: THIS ↓WEEK SO >THAT YOU CAN STILL MAKE
        Audience: [xx−XXXXXXXXXXXXXXXXXXXXX]=
        Speaker: =[[YER MINDS UP<
        Audience: =[[XXXXXXXXXXXXXXXXX ((edited cut))

Other transcript symbols

The left-hand margin of the transcript is sometimes used to point to a feature of interest to the analyst at the time the fragment is introduced in the text. Lines in the transcript where the phenomenon of interest occurs are frequently indicated by arrows in the left-hand margin. For example, if the analyst had been involved in a discussion of continuations and introduced the following fragment:

          Don: I like that blue one very much
    →   Sam: And I'll bet your wife would like it
          Don: If I had the money I'd get one for her
    →   Sam: And one for your mother too I'll bet

the arrows in the margin would call attention to Sam's utterances as instances of continuations.
        Horizontal ellipses indicate that an utterance is being reported only in part, with additional speech coming before, in the middle of, or after the reported fragment,

depending on the location of the ellipses. Thus, in the following example, the parts of Don's utterance between "said" and "y'know" are omitted:

Don: But I said . . . y' know

Vertical ellipses indicate that intervening turns at talking have been omitted from the fragment:

Bob: Well I always say give it your all

.

.

.

Bob: And I always say give it everything

Codes that identify fragments being quoted designate parts of the chapter authors' own tape collections.

Chapter 11

Elinor Ochs

TRANSCRIPTION AS THEORY

Naturalistic speech as a database

. . .

A PERVASIVE SENTIMENT among those who draw from performance
data is that the data they utilize are more accurate than intuition data: their
data constitute the real world – what *is* as opposed to what *ought* to be. There are
many issues that could be entertained concerning this orientation. Here I would
like to address the problem of what in fact are the performance data for such
researchers: even here the internal issues are manifold. There is the issue of data
collection: the means of observing and recording, the conditions (setting, time,
etc.) under which the data are collected, and so on. The influence of the observer
on *the* observed is, of course, a classic concern within the philosophy of science
(Borger and Cioffi 1970; Popper 1959).

The utilization of mechanical means of recording may appear to eliminate some
of these problems. An audiotape recorder registers a wide range of sounds and a
video-tape recorder registers visual behavior falling within its scope. (We are
ignoring for now the problem of camera placement; use of zoom versus wide-angle
lens, and so on.) A stand taken in this chapter is that the problems of selective
observation are not eliminated with the use of recording equipment. They are
simply *delayed* until the moment at which the researcher sits down to transcribe
the material from the audio- or videotape. At this point, many of the classic
problems just emerge.

A major intention of this chapter is to consider with some care the transcription process. We consider this process (a) because for nearly all studies based on

Source: Elinor Ochs, 'Transcription as theory', in Elinor Ochs and Bambi B. Schiefflen (eds) *Developmental Pragmatics*, New York: Academic Press, 1979, 43–72.

performance, *the transcriptions are the researcher's data*; (b) because *transcription is a selective process reflecting theoretical goals and definitions*; *and* (c) because, with the exception of conversational analysis (Sacks, Schegloff and Jefferson 1974), *the process of transcription has not been foregrounded in empirical studies of verbal behavior.* The focus of this discussion will be on the nature of transcription for child language behavior. . . .

One of the important features of a transcript is that it should not have too much information. A transcript that is too detailed is difficult to follow and assess. A more useful transcript is a more selective one. Selectivity, then, is to be encouraged. But selectivity should not be random and implicit. Rather, the transcriber should be conscious of the filtering process. The basis for the selective transcription should be clear. It should reflect what is known about children's communicative behavior. For example, it should draw on existing studies of children's cognitive, linguistic, and social development. Furthermore, the transcript should reflect the particular interests – the hypotheses to be examined – of the researcher.

One of the consequences of ignoring transcription procedure is that researchers rarely produce a transcript that does reflect their research goals and the state of the field. Furthermore, developmental psycholinguists are unable to read from one another's transcripts the underlying theoretical assumptions.

Yet, these skills are critical in understanding and assessing the generalizations reached in a particular study. As already noted, the transcriptions are the researcher's data. What is on a transcript will influence and constrain what generalizations emerge. For example, the use of standard orthography rather than phonetic representation of sounds will influence the researcher's understanding of the child's verbal behavior. One area of behavior that is 'masked' by the use of standard orthography is sound play (Keenan 1974). The use of standard orthography forces a literal interpretation on utterances that otherwise may be simply objects of phonological manipulation. The use of standard orthography is based on the assumption that utterances are pieces of information, and this, in turn, assumes that language is used to express ideas. In sound play, the shape rather than the content of utterances is foregrounded and the function of language is playful and phatic (in the case of sound-play dialogue) rather than informative: where the researcher uses standard orthography, not all instances of sound play can be easily seen. This assumes importance when a case of sound play is reported in the literature, as in my own situation. It is difficult to assess whether its rare appearance in the literature reflects the nature of children's verbal behavior or the nature of psycholinguistic transcription procedures.

. . .

Page layout

A first item to attend to in organizing and appraising a transcript is the way in which the data are physically displayed on each page. As members of a culture, we, the transcribers, bring into the transcription process a biased spatial organization. We display our data with the cultural expectation that certain items will be noticed before *others* and that certain items will be seen as part of particular units and categories (e.g., utterances, turns at talk).

Top-to-bottom biases

Across many cultures, there is a convention whereby written language is decoded from the top to the bottom of each inscription. The reading of conversational transcripts takes no exception to this norm, and, generally, the history of a discourse is unfolded in a downward direction. Utterances that appear below other utterances are treated as occurring later in time.

As our eyes move from top to bottom of a page of transcription, we interpret each utterance in light of the verbal and nonverbal behavior that has been previously displayed. In examining adult-adult conversation, overwhelmingly we treat utterances as *contingent* on the behavioral history of episode. For example, unless marked by a topic shifter (Sacks and Schegloff 1974), the contents of a speaker's turn are usually treated as in some way *relevant* to the immediately prior to turn. The expectation of the reader matches the expectation of adult speakers [see Grice, Chapter 3], and by and large inferences based on contingency are correct. These expectations and assumptions are reflected in the format in which adult conversations are typically displayed. Speaker's turns are placed below one another, as in dramatic script (from *Love's Labor's Lost,* I. xxi):

> ARMADO: Boy, what sign is it when a man of great spirit grows melan-
> choly?
> MOTH: A great sign, sir, that he will look sad.

Here, for example, Moth's utterance is interpreted with respect to Armado's previous utterance. The reader makes such links as his eyes move line by line down the page. If the reader misses a reading or has not understood an utterance, he frequently looks back to the immediately preceding line (above). Practices such as linking back (above) and linking forward (below) again reflect expectations of turn-by-turn relevance.

When we examine the verbal and nonverbal behavior of young children, important differences emerge with respect to adult communicative norms. In particular, the expectation that a speaker usually makes utterances contingent on prior talk does not match that for adult speakers. This is particularly the case in interactive situations involving a child and one or more conversational partners. Young children frequently "tune out" the utterances of their partner, because they are otherwise absorbed or because their attention span has been exhausted, or because they are bored, confused, or uncooperative.

We cannot necessarily count on an immediately prior utterance, particularly that of another speaker, to disambiguate a child's verbal act. We also cannot count on the child to signal noncontingency in a conventional manner. This means that we cannot even be certain that an utterance of a child that follows an immediately prior question is necessarily a response to that question. . . .

The connection between this discussion and the transcription process is that the format of a transcript influences the interpretation process carried out by the reader (researcher). Certain formats encourage the reader to link adjacent utterances and turns, whereas others encourage the reader to treat verbal acts more independently. For example, the standard "script" format described earlier tends to impose a contingent relation between immediately adjacent utterances of different speakers. Such an imposition is appropriate to the extent that it matches the conventional behavior of the speakers themselves. Such a transcript is thus far more appropriate to adult western speech than to the speech of language-acquiring children.

. . .

Left-to-right biases

The European culture of literacy socializes its members to encode ideas not only from top to bottom, but from left to right of the writing surface. For a page of transcription, this directionality means that within each line utterances to the left of other utterances have been produced earlier. Similarly, words to the left of other words on the same line have been uttered earlier. Leftness is linked with priority and also with inception of a statement or entire discourse.

Very close to its association with priority and inception is the link between leftness and prominence in written expression. This is clearest within the sentence in English, where subjects or topics normally appear to the left of their predicates in the declarative modality. Topics constitute the major arguments of a proposition, and subjects control verb agreement and a number of other syntactic processes.

These associations may influence the overall organization of a transcription in at least two ways. Most studies of child language involve the child interacting with just one other individual, usually an adult. In this situation, the transcriber who has opted for parallel placement of speaker turns has to decide which speaker is to be assigned to the leftmost speaker column and which to the right.

A brief review of the adult-child interaction literature indicates that, with some exception, the overwhelming tendency is for researchers to place the adult's speaker column to the left of the child's speaker column. I would like to point out here that this tendency may not be arbitrary. Rather, it may reflect perceived notions of dominance and control. That is, the researcher may be quite subtly influenced by an adult's status as caretaker or competent speaker in letting this figure assume the predominant location on the page of transcription.

The placement of the adult in the leftmost position may not only reflect but actually *reinforce* the idea of the adult as a controlling figure. How could this reinforcement come about? Recall that leftness is associated not only with prominence (e.g., placement of subject in English standard active declarative sentences), but with *temporal priority* in English-language transcripts. Each line of transcription starts at the left margin and moves towards the right. The decoding of each line as well is affected by this directionality. If the reader wants to look back at prior talk, then the eyes are orientated to the left. If the reader wants to locate the starting point of an utterance, the eyes move left until they locate the initiation of talk following a pause, interruption or final interactional boundary.

These expectations concerning where talk initiates could very well affect judge-ments concerning the initiation of a *sequence* of talk. A tendency for the western reader may be to turn to the left to locate such initiation points in a verbal inter-action. In particular, readers may turn to talk in the leftmost speaker column as a "natural" location for opening up an interactional sequence. Looking to the right-hand column of talk, is, in this sense, a less "natural" move in the pursuit of an interactional opening.

This means that whichever speaker is assigned to the leftmost column has a better than average probability of being an initiator of a sequence of talk. In tran-scripts in which the adult is assigned to this speaker column, the adult becomes the more probable occupant of the initiator role.

. . .

Placement of nonverbal and verbal behavior

In studies of child-language development, there is an overwhelming preference for foregrounding verbal over nonverbal behavior. This is due to at least three sources:

The first and most obvious is the *goal* of the research at hand. The researcher is, after all, concerned primarily with language. Nonverbal context is usually considered to the extent that it directly relates to the utterance produced.

A second source is the *method of recording* child behavior. Child-language studies have relied upon three basic means of obtaining data: diary method, audiotape recording plus notetaking and video-tape recording. While the use of video-tape allows a relatively detailed view of nonverbal behavior and environment, it is still a relatively restricted mode of documentation within developmental psycho-linguistics. . . .

A third source of verbal foregrounding stems from using *analyses of adult communicative behavior as models*. In nearly all linguistic, sociological, and psycho-logical treatments of adult–adult speech behavior, nonverbal considerations in the immediate situation are minimized or ignored. Where nonverbal behavior is attended to, such behavior tends to be treated as a set of variables that co-occur with language but do not necessarily constitute part of the idea conveyed. By and large, the message content is considered to be conveyed through language.

One of the major advances within child language in the past decade has been the understanding of the communicative import of nonverbal behavior among young children. There are now numerous documents of the communicative skills of chil-dren before language emerges. These studies show that nonverbal behavior may be an *alternative* rather than an accompaniment to verbal behavior. Children are able to employ gesture, body orientation and eye gaze to perform a variety of commun-icative acts (e.g., pointing out the existence of some object, requesting some future action from the intended addressee, offering, demonstrating, etc.). The emergence of language is understood as a move away from a primary reliance on nonverbal means towards greater reliance on verbal means to convey an intention. In the course of this process, verbal means are employed conjointly with nonverbal means and *together* they convey the child's intentions.

· · ·

A practical fact to be reckoned with is that it takes more space to represent nonverbal behavior than to represent verbal behavior. This might be minimized by a well-developed system of notation for nonverbal features. However, there are just so many features that one would want to symbolize in code-like fashion. In the typical transcript, utterances would be surrounded by notes on nonverbal context, and the researcher would be faced with sorting out the forest from the trees in many of the analyses to be carried out.

An above or below representation of nonverbal and verbal behavior becomes increasingly unfeasible the greater the amount of nonverbal information there is to report. We should consider, before going on, the extent to which we need to deal with quantities of nonverbal data. One could argue, for example, that only in the very early stages of communication development is the detailed recording of nonverbal context critical to assessing intentionality. In looking over a great many transcripts, I see that while reliance on the immediate context lessens over developmental time, it is still the case that children continue to rely heavily on the immediate setting well into the multiworld stage. This generalization holds more for certain physical and social conditions than for others. For example, where a child is talking in bed at night or in the semi-darkness of early morning, nonverbal considerations are minimized. Where a child is carrying out some activity other than talking, for example, eating, playing, in a daylight setting, nonverbal considerations take on a greater importance. Not only setting but also co-participants seem to affect the extent to which here and now is communicatively significant for the child. Whereas an adult may lead the child into discussions of past and future events, child–child interaction is rooted in the here and now. . . .

To understand the role of eye gaze, gesture, action and setting in peer interaction, consider the following scene, involving Toby and David Keenan at age three years and five months. While earlier months of recording involved the children interacting in their bedroom in near darkness between 6 a.m. and 7 a.m., at this time of the year, the morning light was considerably brighter. The children made greater use of stuffed animals and blankets and played in a number of locations within the room. The piece of recording which we are examining shows Toby and David sitting face to face on Toby's bed. David is sucking his thumb, holding a toy rabbit and security blanket. Toby holds a monkey wrapped inside his security blanket. Prior to the moment at hand, Toby had announced that his blanket was a *steamroller* and David had agreed. Both Toby and David are looking down at Toby's blanket. At this moment, David begins to hum, where upon Toby interrupts, saying *yeah Im gonna make car/*.

In the course of his utterance, Toby performs a series of actions. In the course of *Im gonna make* he moves his blanket and monkey to his right side. (His blanket unfolds in the process.) Between *make* and *car* there is a slight pause (a 'beat'), and in this pause, Toby begins pushing his blanket into a ball, completing the process as he utters the word *car*. Following this sequence of actions, Toby says *heres here thats handle/.* In the course of this utterance, yet another series of actions is performed. Immediately following *heres,* Toby picks up a section of the blanket, holding it in the air for one 'beat' between *thats* and *handle.* While uttering *handle,* he pushes the section down to the bed. Immediately he says *and thats people,* picking up another section of the blanket in the space of a beat between *thats* and *people.* Following the uttering of *people,* Toby drops that section of the blanket. Actions and utterances of similar character follow.

This description indicates the amount of nonverbal data that needs to be recorded to assess the nature of reference and other speech acts carried out by the child. For example, without indicating accompanying nonverbal behavior, we would not know if *steamroller* and *car* named the same referent, and we would not know the referents for the deictic terms *heres, here,* and *thats.* The detailed recording of accompanying movements and eye gaze is, then, not superfluous to an analysis of communicative competence.

This description as well indicates the difficulties of integrating verbal and nonverbal behavior. It indicates the amount of nonverbal data that needs to be reported for a small number of utterances. (In the preceding description, four utterances are examined.) While the situation is reported in "prose style", it indicates the difficulties in following exactly what is happening across both nonverbal and verbal modalities when both are reported in the same descriptive space.

The situation just examined illustrates yet a further feature of nonverbal and verbal behavior that is not captured in any of the transcripts written for or by developmental psycholinguists. This feature is that of *interoccurrence.* Verbal behavior may occur one or more times in the course of some other action carried out by a participant. Alternatively, nonverbal actions may be carried out one or several times in the course of any one single utterance. . . . Careful observation shows that typically utterances and actions do not start at the same point in time. An utterance usually precedes or follows the initiation of some nonverbal act. For example, in the situation reported above, the action of picking up a section of the blanket overlaps but *precedes* the utterance of *here thats handle.* Alternatively, the same action occurs in the *middle* of the subsequent utterance *and thats people.*

The initiation points of utterances and actions provide clues concerning the organization of a communicative act. For example, in the utterances treated above, the relation of verbal and nonverbal behavior differs. In the first case (*here thats handle*), verbal behavior makes reference to and predicates something about an object that is already a focus of attention. The verbal act identified an object previously indicated through nonverbal means. In the second case (*and thats people*), reference is expressed initially through verbal means and only subsequently through nonverbal means. Here nonverbal means clarify what object is being referred to by the lexical item *that.* In these two utterances, then, nonverbal and verbal behavior may carry out different types of communicative work. . . .

Ideally, we want our transcript to meet practical as well as theoretical considerations. We want our transcript to express the relation between non-verbal and verbal behavior as accurately as possible: we want it to encode not only prior and subsequent behaviors, but co-occurrent and interoccurrent behaviors as well. We do not want a transcript that discourages the reader from integrating verbal and nonverbal acts. On the other hand, we want a readable transcript, one that displays clearly and systematically utterances and contexts.

One possible solution to these demands is to display verbal and nonverbal data in separate locations but to use *superscripts* to locate where verbal and nonverbal acts occur. In so doing, utterances and nonverbal information would be distinguishable, yet, through superscripting, would be integrated. Where children are young, where the setting is light (daytime), where actions are varied and frequent, nonverbal information should be given prominence. In these situations, nonverbal behavior should be reported to the *left* of a participant's verbal behavior. Both nonverbal and verbal behavior of a participant are placed within that participant's behavior column.

Table 11.1 illustrates the use of superscripting with a re-reporting of the situation outlined earlier. Certain symbols will be used to describe nonverbal actions and frames, as well as matters of timing. These symbols are explained in the following section.

Transcription symbols for verbal and nonverbal behavior

The orthographic representation of utterances will vary according to the goals of the research undertaken. Scollon's work (1976) indicates that utterances at the single-word stage should be transcribed phonetically. As the child's pronunciation approaches adult norms, use of phonetic representation should be less critical. However, there are situations in which the speech of older participants is best represented phonetically. These include instances of sound play (Keenan 1974) and

Table 11.1 Numbered actions are explained in the nonverbal column

David		Toby	
Nonverbal	Verbal	Nonverbal	Verbal
[1]sucks thumb ⇓ Toby's blanket	(1.2)[1] mm//mm	[2]moves blanket & monkey towards rt., >	//yeah][2] Im gonna make, (³.) car[4]
		[3]blanket, blanket reaches rest loc.	
		[4]pushes blanket into ball	heres/
		[5]picks up part of blanket	[5]here thats? (⁶.)
		[6]holds part, ⇓ part	[7]handle≠
		[7]pushes part down	
		[8]picks up another part, holds it	and thats, (⁸.)
		[9]releases part	people≠[9]

Table 11.2 Verbal transcription

What to Mark	How to Mark	Why
1 Utterance boundary	/ placed at end of utterance example: *don't make ears funny / he cry / like that /*	Utterance = basic unit in assessing and measuring communicative development.
2 No gap (latching)	= placed between utterances with no time gap example: *look ≠ look ≠ look ≠ look*	Utterances should have a single intonation contour and single breath group, but there are cases in which more than one intonational contour appears in single breath unit. Each contour may correspond to an informational unit. To mark contours linked in this way (no gap), we use "latch marks" (=).
3 Pause length	(.3) placed before utterance; utterances separated by significant pauses should be placed on separate lines example: *and / lettuce / man's eating lettuce /* (5) *one day / was little rabbit / called Lucy /* (.) indicates very slight pause example: *gonna (.) throwit (.) fields /*	a partly defines utterance boundary b partly define "turn" (turn = utterance bounded by significant pause or by utterance of other participant) c number of utterances per turn may be measure of control d may signal end of topic sequence or propositional sequence e may signal leavetaking of floor, elicit feedback from next speaker f may signal distress (cognitive, linguistic, disagreement)
4 Overlap	// placed at beginning of overlap,] placed at end of overlapped utterances overlapped utterances go on same line example: A *steamroller's stuck //now] /* B *oh dear] dear /*	a like pause length, indicates sensitivity to turn and utterance units; may show child or caretaker sensitivity to informational units b frequency and placement of overlap may be variable in caretaker speech c may be important in assessing cultural differences in language socialization

Table 11.2 continued

What to Mark	How to Mark	Why
5 Self-interruption	– placed at point of interruption example: *want some – all of it /*	a may reflect trouble spots in interaction (see 3); trouble can be cognitive, sociological, etc., e.g., can't get reference established, can't get attention of addressee b extent to which speaker can reformulate utterance indicates ability to (1) self-correct, (2) paraphrase

6 Intonation prosodic quality	, marks low rise
	? marks high rise
	. marks low fall (only use in adult speech)
	! marks exclamatory utterance
	place, ?.! at end of utterance
	capital letters mark increased volume:
	example:
	   YOU SILLY /
	_____ marks stress
	example:
	   I want that one /.
	: : : marks lengthened syllable (each : = one "beat")
	example:
	   hello:: /
	(( )) marks other voice qualities, e.g.,
	((LF)) laugh
	((WH)) whisper
	((CR)) cry
	((WM)) whimper
	((WN)) whine
	((GR)) grunt
		a may mark new information
		b may mark hearer selection (e.g., self or other, human versus toy, etc.)
		c may mark communicative act
		d may mark utterance boundary
		e : : : may be tied to marking of aspect

7 Audible breathing	-h marks in-breath h marks out-breath (h) marks laughter	a may indicate utterance boundary b hesitation marker
8 Metatranscription marks	( ) unclear reading, no hearing achieved (cow) tentative reading X / repetition of prior utterance, e.g., *no / X / X /*	

Table 11.3 Nonverbal transcription

What to Mark	How to Mark	Why
1. Changes in gross motor activity	Bloom *et al.* (unpublished manuscript 1974) suggest using present progressive tense to describe action simultaneous with utterance. Use simple present tense to describe action prior or subsequent to utterance. Put action prior to utterance on line above, simultaneous action on same line, and subsequent action on line below utterance (in nonverbal column). If using videotape, mark precise overlap of action and utterance with a superscripted number above point in utterance. example: *[want¹cow /¹grabs cow* If superscripts are used, use only present tense to describe action, as simultaneity is otherwise marked.	a aids in determining reference and predication b aids in interpretation of communicative act (self-description, refusal, etc.) c aids in interpretation of interactional sequence (nonverbal means of accomplishing 1st or 2nd part of a sequential pair d provides information linking utterance to change of state or change of object. e indicates child's understanding of or ability to express tense of aspect.

2 Eye gaze	⇑ looks up (+target: +name)
	⇓ looks down (+target: +name)
	example:
	  ⇑M (use initial for person)
	  ⇓ car
	  > towards right
	  < towards left
	  ∇ facing camera
	  △ back of head to camera
		a indicates intended addressee, referent
		b indicates extent to which child attending
		c indicates extent to which speech is planned

Table 11.3 continued

What to Mark	How to Mark	Why
	example: >⇊ M (looks down towards right of monitor screen at mother)	
3 Gestures	PT pointing R reaching HD holding up TG tugging OF offer	a primary means of reference b indicates communicative act (e.g., summons, offer, description)
4 Body orientation	⊂ marks direction of pelvis (bird's eye view) example: A (A and B are facing ∩ each other; A's body ∪ is facing camera, B's B back is to camera)	a provides social "frame" for talk and action b indicates extent to which participants engaged in focused interaction

instances of unintelligible speech. Furthermore, strictly standard orthography should be avoided. Rather, a modified orthography such as that adopted by Sacks *et al.* (1974) [see Chapter 10] should be employed. A modified orthography captures roughly the way in which a lexical item is pronounced versus the way in which it is written. For example, modified orthography includes such items as *gonna, wanna, whazat, yah see?, lemme see it*, and the like.

The conventions will be presented in the form of detailed tables (see Tables 11.2 and 11.3). In these tables, three types of information will be provided. First, the tables will present each behavioral property to be represented in the transcript. Second, the convention for representing each of the properties will be displayed, along with an illustration of its use. Third, the tables will briefly point out the motivation for marking this property, its significance in an assessment of communicative competence.

Do our data have a future?

The discussion of transcription and theory presented here is to be taken as a first venture into a vast wilderness of research concerns. Many issues have not been addressed. Furthermore, certain transcription conventions invite modification by others with expertise in the field. . . .

A greater awareness of transcription form can move the field in productive directions. Not only will we able to read much more off our own transcripts, we will be better equipped to read the transcriptions of others. This, in turn, should better equip us to evaluate particular interpretations of data (i.e., transcribed behavior).

Our data may have a future if we give them the attention they deserve.

References

Bloom, L., Lightbrown, P.M. and Hood, L. (1974) 'Conventions for transcription of child language recordings', unpublished manuscript, Teachers College, Columbia University.

Borger, R. and Cioffi, F. (1970) *Explanation in the Behavioural Sciences: Confrontations*, Cambridge: Cambridge University Press.

Keenan, E. Ochs (1974) 'Conversational competence in children', *Journal of Child Language* 1: 163–85.

Popper, K. (1959) *The Logic of Scientific Discovery*, New York: Science Editions, Inc.

Sacks, H., Schegloff, E. and Jefferson, G. (1974) 'A simplest systematics for the organization of turn-taking in conversation', *Language* 50: 696–735.

Scollon, R. (1976) *Conversations with a One Year Old*, Honolulu: University of Hawaii Press.

Chapter 12

Theo Van Leeuwen

SOUND IN PERSPECTIVE

Perspective and social distance

EVERY SEMIOTIC MODE can create relations between what is being presented or represented and the receiver, the reader or viewer or listener of the message. Images do it through two slightly different and complementary ways of spatial positioning, *size of frame* and *perspective*.

Sizes of frame such as the close shot, the medium shot, the long shot and so on create a certain *distance* between the viewer and the people, places and things represented in the picture. The relations expressed by these distances derive from our everyday experience, from the distances we keep from different kinds of people, places and things in everyday life. Edward Hall (for example, 1966: 110–20) has described this in relation to our interactions with people, but the same applies to interactions with places and things. According to Hall, we carry with us an invisible set of boundaries beyond which we allow only certain people to come. The zone of 'personal distance', the distance at which you can touch the other person, is for those who are close to us – if others enter it this will be experienced as an act of aggression. 'Social distance' is for more businesslike and formal interactions. At this distance we keep people 'at arm's length'. 'Public distance' is for larger and more formal group interactions. It is the distance we keep from people 'who are and are to remain strangers'. To all these distances correspond different fields of vision. At personal distance only head and shoulders are in sharp vision, and as it happens this corresponds to the close shot, as usually defined in the world of film and television. At social distance we see a little less than the whole figure, which roughly corresponds to the medium shot, and at public distance we see the whole figure with space around him or her, which corresponds to the long

Source: Theo Van Leeuwen, *Speech, Music, Sound*, Basingstoke: Macmillan, 1999.

shot. In this way close shots position viewers in a relation of *imaginary* intimacy with what is represented, while medium shots create more formal kinds of imaginary relations, and long shots portray people as though they fall outside the viewer's social orbit, either because they are strangers or because they are much lower or higher in social status. In reality this may not be the case. The people we see in long shot may be people like us. But that is not the point. The point is that viewers are addressed *as though* these people are not part of their world.

Perspective creates horizontal and vertical angles. Vertical angles can make us literally and figuratively 'look up at' or 'down on' what is represented in a picture – or make us see it from the position of an equal, at eye-level. The vertical angle is therefore connected to imaginary *power* relations, be it the power of the viewer over what is represented, or the power of what is represented over the viewer. The glamorous role models in advertisements, for instance, tend to be shown from below, so that we look up at them, while the products are shown from above, so that they seem within reach of our hands, and under our control. Horizontal angles can be frontal, confronting us directly and unavoidably with what is represented, *involving* us with what is represented, or profile, making us see it from the side-lines, as it were, in a more detached way – and there are of course many in-between possibilities.

These concepts can be used to ask what *attitudes* a given image expresses towards what it represents. Who or what is positioned close to or far away from us, and why? Who or what are we made to look up to or down on, and why? Who or what are we brought face to face with, and who or what do we see in the more detached side-on way? The answers to these questions are usually found in the context. In a Dutch junior high school geography textbook two pictures appeared side by side as part of a double page headlined 'The Third World in Our Street'. The picture on the left showed three women with headscarves, in long shot, on the other side of the street, and turned away from the viewer. In other words, these women were portrayed as strangers, as people outside the social orbit of 'us', Dutch high school students. The picture on the right showed a young couple, a white girl and a black boy, sitting at an outdoor café table, the girl's hand on the boy's arm. They were shown in a much closer shot and from a more frontal angle. A different imaginary relation was suggested here. The couple was portrayed, if not quite as 'our' friends, sitting at the same table, then at least as 'people like us', frequenting the same café. This school book therefore addresses Dutch high school students as though they are all white and *autochtoon* ('native') as the Dutch say, even though in reality many of them are not white and/or *allochtoon* ('non-native').

Perspective and the picture frame were invented in the Renaissance, when it became important to make pictures mobile by detaching them from their environment (for example, the walls of the church), and to encode specific, individual points of view in them. That the Renaissance also invented *musical* perspective is less well known. In 1597 the Venetian composer Giovanni Gabrieli (1557–1612) wrote a piece called *Sonata pian'e forte*. The piece was not, as might be thought, written for a keyboard instrument, but for two groups of instruments, the one consisting of a viola and three trombones, the other consisting of a cornet and another three trombones. When they played together, the music was loud (*forte*),

Figure 12.1 Annotated score of Edvard Grieg's 'Arietta'
(*Lyrical Pieces*, Op. 12, No. 1)

when either of the two sections played alone it was soft (*piano*). This was quite an invention. Even today many types of modern popular music do not use dynamics as a means of expression, and many digital keyboard instruments do not allow for it. Particular genres of music may have a characteristic overall loudness level, or perhaps use different levels for different types of song, but they do not make much use of dynamics within songs, as a means of expression. In the polyphonic music of Gabrieli's time, too, the instruments all played at the same level throughout. It was not until some 100 years after Gabrieli wrote his 'Sonata' that Bartolomeo Cristofori developed the first keyboard instrument that allowed dynamic variation, the *gravicembalo col piano e forte*, better known as the piano, and another 50 years before dynamic marks became common in classical music scores. For my piano teacher the composer's marks were not enough. As his annotations in Figure 12.1 show, he taught me to carefully hierarchize the three voices of Grieg's 'Arietta', with the melody loudest (*p-mf*), the sustained bass notes second loudest (*p*), and the undulating broken chords very soft (*ppp*). I will return to the significance of this later in the chapter.

Sound and image are distinctly different media. There is, for instance, no equivalent of the 'frontal' and 'side on' angle in sound. Sound is a wrap-around medium. But there are also similarities. Both can create relations between the subject they represent and the receiver they address, and in both this is related to distance, in two ways. The first is the way of *perspective*, which hierarchizes elements of what is represented by placing some in the foreground, some in the middle ground and some in the background, either literally, as in a landscape, or figuratively, as on the cover of a book, which may have letters in the foreground and a photograph in the background, or as in the soundtrack of a film, which may have dialogue in the foreground and music in the background. The second is the way of *social distance*, which creates relations of different degrees of formality between what is represented and the viewer or listener, such as intimacy (the very close shot, the whispered voice), informality (the close or medium close shot, the relaxed, casual voice), formality (the medium long or long shot, the louder, higher and tenser voice which 'projects' the message).

Perspective and the soundscape

Sound dubbing technicians in radio and film divide the soundtrack into three zones – close, middle and far distance. Murray Schafer (1977: 157) quotes the radio engineer A.E. Beeby:

> The three-stage plan divides the whole sound scene (called 'Scenic') into three main parts. These are 'the 'Immediate', the 'Support' and the 'Background'. The chief thing to bear in mind is that the 'Immediate' effect is to be listened to, while the 'Support' and the 'Background' effects are merely to be heard . . . The 'Support' effect refers to sounds taking place in the immediate vicinity which have a direct bearing on the subject in hand, leaving the 'Background' effect to its normal job of setting the scene. Take for example the recording of a commentary at a fun-fair. The 'Immediate' effect would be the commentator's voice. Directly behind this would come the 'Support' effects of whichever item of fairground amusement he happened to be referring to, backed, to a slightly lesser degree, by the 'Background' effect of music and crowd noises.

Walter Murch, key sound technician on most of George Lucas' and Francis Ford Coppola's films, expresses the same idea (Weis and Belton 1985: 357):

> The thing is to think of the sound in layers, to break it down in your mind into different planes. The character lives near the freeway, so you've got this generalized swash of traffic sound, but then occasionally a plane flies over: these are the long, atmospheric sounds. On top of these you then start to list the more specific elements: the door closes, the gunshots, the bats that live in the attic – who knows? Isolated moments. Once you've done that, once you can separate out the backgrounds from the foregrounds, and the foregrounds from the mid-grounds, then you go out and record . . . Since each of the layers is separate, you can still control them, and you can emphasize certain elements, and de-emphasize others the way an orchestrator might emphasize the strings versus the trombones, or the tympani versus the woodwinds.

The terms differ. Beeby has 'Immediate', 'Support' and 'Background', Murch 'fore-ground', 'mid-ground' and 'background'. Murray Schafer (1977: 157) uses yet another set of terms and definitions. He defines 'Figure' as 'the focus of interest', the sound 'signal', 'Ground' as the setting or context, the 'keynote sound', and 'Field' as 'the place where the observation takes place, the soundscape'. The ideas, however, are essentially the same. The 'three-stage plan' means dividing the sounds which are heard simultaneously into three groups and then *hierarchizing* these groups, treating some as more important than others. *What* is made important in this way will vary, but it will always be treated as a 'signal', as something the listener must attend to and/or react to and/or act upon, while background sounds are 'heard but not listened to', disattended, treated as something listeners do not need to react to or act upon. We will adopt Schafer's terms, but with the proviso that they do not only apply to places in the literal sense, but also to symbolic places or positions, for instance in music, and that sometimes there might be just two layers, a foreground and a background, instead of three.

Schafer also distinguishes between *hifi* and *lofi* soundscapes. Hifi soundscapes allow discrete sounds to be heard from a great distance because of the low ambient noise level. Think of a very quiet library, where you can hear someone pick up a pen or turn a page from twenty-five metres away. In lofi soundscapes, on the other hand, individual sounds get blurred, obscured in a tangle, a wall of sound which may be as close to the listener as the other side of the street. In such soundscapes perspective is lost and amplification becomes necessary if one wants to be heard. They have become so common in the contemporary urban environment that acoustic engineers deliberately create walls of 'masking noise', even in libraries, because they believe people find discrete noises distracting, or even disturbing:

> If a masking noise is uninterrupted and not too loud, and if it has no information content, it will become an acceptable background noise and will suppress other objectionable intruding noises, making them sound psychologically quieter.
>
> (Doelle 1972: 6)

As already mentioned, any sound may be Figure, Ground or Field. Even sounds which are clearly intended to stand out, such as bells, alarms and sirens, may become Ground, for instance in the big city. It all depends on the position of the listener. In my workroom the tapping of the keys of my computer keyboard and the hum of my computer are Figure, a car starting up outside and the sometimes raucous voices of the men drinking beer outside the pub across the road are Ground, while the 'swash of traffic noise' in the High Street, a little further away, is Field. If a car alarm went off outside it would simply mix in with the Ground and not form a 'signal' for me.

Anne Skelly, a student participating in my sound seminar at Macquarie University, drew my attention to the use of perspective in BBC sound effects collections. A track of a two-horse brake on a hard road, from the collection *Vanishing Sounds in Britain* had the rumble of the wheels and the creaking of the springs as Figure, the gallop of the horses as Ground, and rural sounds such as cows, roosters and church bells as Field. It thereby positioned the listener in that world of vanishing sounds as a kind of country squire, rather than, say, as a farmhand. In other words, what is Figure, what Ground and what Field, depends either on the listener's relation to the represented world (my real position as a writer working at home), or on the way such a relation has been *created* for the listener in sound mixes, musical compositions and so on (my imaginary position as a country squire in the world of yesteryear). I may then enjoy my vicarious ride in the horse-drawn carriage or distance myself from it, dismissing it as typical of the BBC's glorification of England's past, but in either case I will know that the track has been designed to make me identify with the country squire, even if I subsequently do something with it which it was not designed for.

In all this we should also remember that sound is dynamic: it can move us *towards* or *away from* a certain position, it can *change* our relation to what we hear. A Dutch television documentary showed a Christ statue on top of a hill, to the accompaniment of choral church music. The camera then tilted down to the busy expressway at the foot of the hill, and the roar of the expressway faded in to drown the music. This distanced the audience from the religious sentiments evoked earlier.

Here are two further examples. The first is a track from a French 'ambient sounds' recording by Eloisa Mathieu, *Ambient Sounds at Costa-Rica: Afternoon at the La Selva Biological Station*. Three distinct groups of sound can be heard, The Field is the sound of cicadas, hence a continuous 'broadband' sound, a kind of drone. The Ground is formed by a variety of birdcalls, hence by more discrete, individual sounds which nevertheless continue without noticeable gaps throughout the track. The Figure is the cry of a single howler monkey, more intermittent, and only entering after a while. The sleeve notes state that sound mixer Jean Roche 'had the task of mixing the recordings, to recreate atmospheres unique to each habitat'. But perhaps Roche has done more than that. Perhaps he also adapted the scene to a fit a design schema more typical of the modern city than of the tropical forest. To anyone who has heard the deafening noise of cicadas on a summer afternoon it is immediately clear that the level of the cicadas on this track is far too low relative to the other sounds. They are turned into a background, a Field, like the 'masking noise' in the library, or the traffic on the High Street nearby my work room. It is also clear that the aural point of view created by the mix is physically impossible. No one could simultaneously be so close to so many different birds that the sound of each and every one of them would dominate that of the cicadas to the extent it does on this track – and then be closer still to the howler monkey. This is not a recreation of the sounds of the forest. It recreates the three zones of the social world of the modern city dweller – the zone of the significant others whose utterances we must react to or act on (the monkey, closest to our own species uttering specific and rather dramatic howls), the wider support group or community; whose members are still individually recognizable but less closely known, and whose actions we perceive as predictable and repetitive (the birds – or the men in the pub across the road), and the mass of strangers, who all blur together in one indistinct whole (the cicadas – or the cars on the high street nearby).

In other words, we have here a typical 'schema' which can be realized in different types of sound environments and soundtracks. But there are schemas and then there are the things you can do with the schemas. In Hollywood films action and dialogue are usually in the foreground and the music which creates the mood and the emotional temperature of the scene in the background – a typical schema in which emotion must be 'held back' and remain subservient to the action. As the film composer Leonid Sabaneev put it:

> In general, music should understand that in the cinema it should nearly always remain in the background: it is, so to speak, a tonal figuration,

the 'left hand' of the melody on the screen, and it is a bad business when this left hand begins to creep into the foreground and obscure the melody.

(quoted in Gorbman 1987: 76)

But in a climactic scene from Jane Campion's *The Piano* (1993) the pattern is reversed. It is the scene in which Stewart (Sam Neill) chops off Ada's (Holly Hunter) finger with an axe. In this scene the *music* is Figure, more specifically; the musical theme which, throughout the film, has been associated with Ada's inner emotions of loss and longing – emotions which, as a mute, she cannot express in words. The sounds of the gushing rain and of Stewart's violent actions and screaming, on the other hand, recede into the background, as if her inner world has, for her, and hence also for us, the audience, more reality and more relevance than the outside events, however cruel and oppressive they may be (cf. Van Leeuwen, 1998 for a more elaborate analysis).

This is just one example of the way dynamics can hierarchize speech, music and other sounds, whether on film soundtracks or in the environment (think of the muzak and public announcements in railway stations, airports, supermarkets and so on), and whether in conventional or less conventional ways. In John Cage's piece *4′ 33″* ('a piece in three movements during which no sounds are intentionally produced') the pianist sits at the piano for 4 minutes and 33 seconds without playing. All he or she has to do is to indicate the three movements by means of arm movements, and then to close the lid of the piano at the end of the piece. Thus the background (sniffs, coughs, the rustle of clothes, the traffic outside the concert hall) becomes foreground, and the audience must consciously attend to what they normally disattend: 'My favourite piece', Cage said, 'is the one we hear all the time if we are quiet' (Cage 1968: 59).

Groups of people speaking (or chanting, or singing) simultaneously may also be perspectivally hierarchized. In Dutch Protestant churches, as no doubt in many other churches, the Lord's Prayer is spoken by the whole congregation in unison. But the minister's amplified voice projects the words carefully and stands out clearly against the unamplified voices of the members of the congregation, who mostly mumble. In many advertising jingles and pop songs the voice of the male solo singer is foregrounded while the female 'back-up' vocalists are re-recorded at a lower level, so that they will act as accompaniment, background, support.

In music, as in painting or photography, perspective can be used to depict landscapes. A beautiful example is Charles Ives' 'Housatonic at Stockbridge', part 3 of his *Three Places in New England*. The Housatonic is a river and Stockbridge is a town – Ives himself described the scene on which the music is based:

A Sunday morning walk that Mrs Ives and I took near Stockbridge the summer after we were married. We walked in the meadows along the river and heard the distant singing from the church across the river. The mist had not entirely left the river bed and the colours, the running water, the banks and the trees were something one would always remember.

(quoted in Mellers 1964: 45)

When the music begins, we hear the strings play very soft, misty chords and patterns that drift along irregularly and seemingly haphazardly, with a piano adding twinkles of light. After a while we hear a distant melody, a hymn melody, played on horn and lower strings. Gradually this melody gets louder, but the sounds of nature, instead of being overwhelmed by it, pushed into the background, also become louder and the two kinds of sound begin to clash, in a conflict between the unpredictable and ever-shifting rhythms of nature and the world of order and communal values expressed by the hymn – a conflict also expressed in many other American cultural products, for instance in Westerns.

But musical perspective can also be used in less pictorial ways, to represent, indeed, to enact and celebrate, key aspects of the social structure of modern life. When I practised Grieg's 'Arietta' according to the instructions of my teacher, I learnt an important lesson about the use of perspective in Western music: the melody must be Figure and the accompaniment Ground. The melody thus acts as the individual, asserting him or herself, and standing out from the background as an individual, while the accompanying voices act as the 'community' around the individual, serving and supporting him or her in more or less predictable and repetitive ways – through patterns whose modulations follow the lead of the melody. As Tagg (1990: 108) has pointed out, this is by no means a general feature of music:

> Few of us really comprehend the interaction and symbolism of the various voices in Renaissance polyphony or medieval motets. Even fewer of us comprehend Afro-Sudanic polyrhythms or the Tunisian nouba. This is because we use the dualism of melody-accompaniment as a common basis for constructing musical meaning, whether the creator's name be Haydn or AC/DC. The melody-accompaniment dualism has parallels in other European modes of thought; with the figure/ground of visual arts, the hero/story of novel writing, the particular/general of natural sciences, etc. These foreground/background relationships seem to make clear distinctions between the individual and the rest of social and natural reality.

Tagg has also interpreted the typical perspective of 'hard' rock 'n' roll along these lines. The modern urban environment, he says, is a lofi soundscape characterized by broadband noises such as car engines, air conditioning and refrigerator hums and so on. This kind of sound is rare in nature – only some insects (for instance cicadas!) produce it. Another one of its characteristics is the absence of reverberation and distance perception. In an empty street you would hear the sound of a car reverberate for a long time. But our streets are not empty, and by the time the softer sound of a car's reverberation could be heard it would already be drowned by the louder sounds of many other cars: 'by drowning discrete reverb in this way, the overall impression of acoustic space is that it is crowded and close' (Tagg 1990: 111). Rock 'n' roll accompaniment is similarly characterized by broadband sound and reverb, so much so that the sound as a whole becomes 'crowded' and 'homogenized', with 'the long sounds filling up all the holes to create a wall of sound'.

The singers or solo instruments must then scream and shout to be heard across the din (ibid.: 112).

The perspective of more recent dance music is quite different. 'Drum 'n' bass' tracks such as, for instance, Dual Fusion's 'AnythingGoes', Art of Noise's 'Something Always Happens', or Love Corporation's 'Give Me Some Love', reverse the traditional pattern of European music. They have the melody (the individual) in the background and the accompaniment (the group) in the foreground. The complex and shifting rhythms of the drums and the bass constitute the Figure, the drums with the breakbeat, a clean, clear and close rustle of snare drum taps, sticks on closed hihats and so on, the bass at a more steady tempo, with short, deep and dampened notes. Both drums and bass in fact sound as though they are not played in an actual space at all, but inside the head or the body, with all the sound absorbed inside. The Ground is usually some kind of keyboard sound, an organ playing sustained chords that alternate rather than progress, or a piano playing repetitive patterns which shift from one phase into another every once in a while. The Field, finally, is made up of intermittent snippets, natural and 'techno' sound effects, voices, fragments sampled from the history of black music – all very soft, very distant, completely backgrounded by the prominent rhythms in the foreground. When the track begins we usually hear the Ground and/or the Field only – the Figure does not enter until after a while. In other words, the intro gives us the *context* – the immediate context, as represented by the keyboard playing repetitive patterns and/or chords (chords are simultaneously sounding sounds, the 'community of sounds'); and the wider cultural context, consisting of faint echoes from the real world (the ocean, all sorts of human grunts and groans) and/or from the musical traditions of the recent and not so recent past (jazz solo phrases, snippets of song and so on). The drum and bass, the rhythm we can *dance* on, becomes the foreground, the text. *Action*, tuning into the world, becoming part of it, moving the body in tune with it, following a rhythm which seems to come from within and yet joins us to others, as rhythms always do – that is what is foregrounded here, not a melody, not a musical statement sung or played by some individual soloist, some lone star admired from afar and imaginarily identified with by individual fans who must keep their bodies still in chairs.

We can now summarize:

1   The semiotic system of aural perspective divides simultaneous sounds into groups, and places these groups at different distances from the listener, so as to make the listener *relate* to them in different ways.

2   The sound may either be divided into three groups (positioned as Figure, Ground and Field) or two groups (positioned as Figure and Ground or as Figure and Field). When there is no perspective, there is only a Figure. The significance of these positions can be glossed as follows:

Figure
If a sound or group of sounds is positioned as Figure, it is thereby treated as the most important sound, the sound which the listener must identify with, and/or react to and/or act upon.

Ground

If a sound or group of sounds is positioned as Ground, it is thereby treated as still part of the listener's social world, but only in a minor and less involved way. We are to treat it as we treat the familiar faces we see every day and the familiar places we move through every day, in other words, as a context we take for granted and only notice when it is not there any longer.

Field

If a sound or group of sounds is positioned as Field, it is thereby treated as existing, not in the listener's social, but in his or her physical world. We are to treat it as we would treat the people that crowd the streets through which we walk, or the trees that populate the forest past which we drive.

3   The meanings of Figure, Ground and Field, as described above, are made more specific by the context in which they occur, as the examples in this section have hopefully illustrated.

4   The system of perspective can be *played with* in different ways, for instance by *not* placing one sound in the foreground and the other in the background, as in 'Housatonic at Stockbridge', or by reversing conventional patterns, as in the case of *The Piano* and 'drum 'n' bass' music.

5   Perspective is *realized* by the relative loudness of the simultaneous sounds, regardless of whether this results from the levels of the sounds themselves, from the relative distance of the people or objects that produce them, or from the way a soundtrack is mixed.

6   Perspective has been a key system in the semiotics of sound, as historically evidenced by the increasing importance of dynamics in European music, and more recently by the increasing importance of the role of the sound mixer, first in radio and film, and now also and especially in many forms of popular music, where the mixer is considered as much of an artist as the musician, and may even perform live.

Sound and social distance

When we are close to people (literally and figuratively) we speak more softly than when we have a more formal relation with them or speak to them in the context of a more formal occasion. As distance grows, the voice not only becomes louder, but also higher and sharper. The same applies to musical instruments – think of the difference between the blaring trumpets of a military brass band and the muted intimacy of Miles Davis' trumpet.

In the beginning of this chapter we made a link between 'social distance', as mapped out by Edward Hall, and 'size of frame'. Hall relates social distance also to the voice (1964, 1966: 184–5). At 'very close' range (3 in. to 6 in.), he says, the voice will be a soft whisper, and the message 'top secret', for the ears of one (very special) person only. At 'close' range (8 in. to 12 in.) it will be an audible whisper, still sounding 'very confidential', still meant to be heard by one person only. At 'near' range (12 in. to 20 in.) the voice will be soft indoors and 'full' outdoors, carrying an effect of confidentiality, At 'close neutral' range (20 in. to 36 in.) we speak in a soft voice at low volume, about 'personal subject matter', while at 'far neutral' range (4.5 ft to 5 ft) we speak in a 'full voice', about 'non-personal matters'. At 'public distance' (5.5 ft to 8 ft) the voice is 'full with slight overloudness', conveying 'public information for others to hear'. When we speak 'across the room' (8 ft to 20 ft) our voices will be loud, and we will no longer be talking to one or two people, but to a whole group. When, finally, we 'stretch the limits of distance' (20 to 24 ft indoors, and up to 100 ft outdoors) we are probably hailing people from a distance or shouting farewells. Hall stresses that these distances are culturally specific. At 'far neutral' range, for instance, 'the American voice is under that of the Arab, the Spaniard, the South Asian Indian and the Russian, and somewhat above that of the English upper class, the South East Asian and the Japanese' (1964: 44).

So long as there is no selective amplification by means of microphones or mixing, the scale running from the intimate whisper of the lover to the hysterical scream of the demagogue remains interlocked with the scale running from soft to loud. The only difference between the system of 'perspective' and the system of 'social distance' is that social distance applies to single sounds, while perspective applies to simultaneous sounds and has relative rather than absolute levels. But the technology of amplification and recording has uncoupled the two, and allowed them to become independent semiotic variables. As a result a soft breathy whisper can now stand out clearly against loud drums or brass sections, and is no longer only for the ears of one very special person, but audible by thousands. Conversely, the screams of rock singers can be played at a comfortable level, to be heard by one person only, as he or she walks along with headphones on. Social distance is un-coupled from real distance, and from voice level, and now conveyed primarily by *voice quality*, on a scale running from the voiceless whisper, via the very soft and low voice in which we can hear the breath and other signs of the speaker's close presence, to the high, tense voice, and, ultimately, the rasping scream. The same scales could be constructed for musical instruments and non-musical sounds such as engines – compare the put-put of a boat to the screaming racing car or jet. The close miking of voices and instruments, finally, can further enhance closeness, while adding reverb can enhance a sense of space and distance.

In music this led to new styles of singing which soon made earlier music-hall and vaudeville styles seem quaint and antiquated. The 'crooning' style of Bing Crosby pioneered this, suggesting the 'intimate, personal relationship with fans that worked best for domestic listeners' (Frith 1988: 19). The word 'suggest' is crucial – amplification allows singers to address us *as though* they have a personal relation-ship with us, even though they are in reality as distant from us as can be. The close relationship is imaginary. The opposite is also possible, bringing the public world into the private world, for instance by listening to the rasping voices of 'hard rock' singers in the intimacy of our living rooms. These voices are not only hard and loud but also high, on average an octave above the normal, speaking level of the singers. As Tagg (1990: 112) has described it, they shout and scream to be heard over the noise of the city, in which:

> shouting to a friend on the other side of the street becomes impossible because there is a wall of sound between the two of you. The rock singer must therefore raise the volume, pitch and sharpness/roughness of timbre of his or her voice to be heard, just as the instrumental soloists must 'cut' and 'bang' their way through the ambient sound of the environment.

In Skylab's drum 'n' bass track 'The Trip', a voice sings in whispers, almost next to our ear, while we hear the much louder drums *at the same level*, and equally closely miked. It is a physically impossible aural vantage point. Perhaps the drums, with their exceptionally close presence and lack of reverb, must be heard as being 'in our head' rather than out there in space, and the female singer as whispering words in our ears – 'I start to dream', 'Close your eyes': on much of the track there is no other sound, as if the rest of the world has ceased to exist.

Not only singers and instrumentalists, also speakers began to exploit this new tool for engineering imaginary social relations. Politicians became aware of it in the 1930s, when Roosevelt initiated his 'fireside chats', in which he replaced oratory with 'calm, measured statements' and addressed his audience 'as though he were actually sitting on the front porch or in the parlour with them' (Barnouw 1968: 8). In the same period the BBC talks department encouraged radio speakers to speak more casually and adopt a low-key, conversational manner (Cardiff 1981), and Goebbels urged German radio announcers to use local dialects and speak more informally and colloquially, to 'sound like the listener's best friend', as he put it (quoted in Leitner 1980). By today's standards the commentators and radio speakers of that period were still barking at their audiences, but the idea had taken hold, even if its full fruition had to wait till the breakthrough of television, in the early 1960s.

Radio and television speakers change their voice (and microphone distance) according to the genre of the broadcast or the type of station for which they work (Van Leeuwen 1982, 1984, 1992). Newsreading, for instance, is a relatively formal genre and as a result most newsreaders' voices become higher and tenser when they read the news. The disc jockeys of some commercial radio stations seek to 'energize' the listeners through the way they speak. According to the breakfast announcer of a Top 40 station in Sydney, Australia:

> You've got to sound 'up', but there's a thin line between that and sounding a bit mindless, spewing out those words, you know, spilling them out and screaming . . . Your sound has got to be a 'hey let's get it happening' sort of approach, like 'we're here having a good time'.
> (quoted in Van Leeuwen 1992: 238)

The announcers of a Sydney 'easy listening' station, on the other hand, aimed at a 'relaxed', 'muted' and 'gentle' sound, and used closely miked, soft, low and breathy voices. The same contrasts can be observed between the voices in commercials –

think of the difference between the excited pitch of the hard-sell second-hand car salesman and the seductive breathy whisper of the voice in a perfume ad.

We can now summarize:

1 The sound of the voice is an important factor in the system of social distance, alongside other factors such as potential for touch and field of vision. In the age of amplification and recording it becomes an independent semiotic system, the system of (aural) social distance, able to create imaginary social relations between what is presented or represented by a sound and the listener. These distances form a continuum, but the significance of the key points on the scale can be described as follows:

Intimate distance
The relation between the sound and the listener is one of real or imaginary *intimacy* – what is presented or represented by the sound is regarded as one would regard someone with whom one is intimate, in speech, intimate distance is realized by whispering or maximally soft voices.

Personal distance
The relation between the sound and the listener is a real or imaginary *personal* relation – what is presented or represented by the sound is regarded as one would regard a friend with whom one can discuss highly personal matters. In speech it is realized by a soft, relaxed voice at low pitch and volume.

Informal distance
The relation between the sound and the listener is a real or imaginary *informal* relation – what is presented or represented by the sound is regarded as one would regard someone with whom one has a businesslike but nevertheless informal encounter. In speech it is realized by a full voice at somewhat higher pitch and volume.

Formal distance
The relation between the sound and the listener is a real or imaginary *formal* relation – what is presented or represented by the sound is regarded as one would regard people to whom one speaks in a formal or public context. In speech it is realized by an overloud, higher and tenser, 'projected' voice.

Public distance
The relation between the sound and the listener 'stretches the limits' and is regarded as one would regard someone who can only just be reached when one shouts at the top of one's voice – hence it is realized by the maximally loud sound.

2 These relations can also extend to places and things. We can, for instance, have an intimate relationship with the tools we use everyday (a handbag, a computer, a car) and a more formal relationship with the machine in the office we pass every day but never touch. Water can sound close enough to touch (softly lapping water, the rustle of a small stream), or far away (the surf, the roar of a waterfall). The saxophone of Archie Shepp can address us in a hoarse whisper, or sound like a foghorn in the mist.

3   The microphone and the mixing panel have turned perspective and social distance into independent variables, allowing the close and the distant, the personal and the impersonal, the formal and the informal, the private and the public, to be mixed in various ways and to various degrees.

4   Recording techniques can aid the perception of social distance. Close miking enhances a sense of close presence to the source of the sound, and adding reverb enhances a sense of space and distance.

Immersion

The opposite of perspective is immersion, wrap-around sound. Low frequency sounds (bass) are especially important here. They carry further (think of the foghorn) and fill spaces more completely. They are also harder to tie to a particular spot and seem to come from everywhere at once.

Evergreen forests produce this kind of perspective and so do medieval churches. The amplification of the low frequencies and the long reverberation time of these places submerge the listener in sound. Perspective and hierarchization disappear. The individual no longer feels separate from the crowd, but becomes fully integrated and immersed in the environment:

> The sound in Norman and Gothic churches, surrounding the audience, strengthens the link between the individual and the community: The loss of high frequencies and the resulting impossibility of localising the sound makes the believer part of a world of sound. He does not face the sound in enjoyment – he is wrapped up by it.
>
> (Blaukopf 1960: 180)

Interestingly, this is also the condition of the lofi urban environment which we discussed earlier – provided you give up trying to be heard above the noise and allow yourself to swim with the stream, as happens, perhaps, in the modern dance club:

> Low frequency sounds seek blend and diffusion rather than clarity and focus. The listener is not an audience which concentrates but is at the centre of the sound, massaged by it, flooded by it. Such listening conditions are those of a classless society, a society seeking unification and integrity.
>
> (Schafer 1977: 118)

Today this can also be achieved individually. The ear, with speakers in every corner, can become a cocoon of booming bass sounds, literally vibrating the listener, and the walkman can achieve what Jane Campion achieved in the scene from *The Piano* I discussed earlier, the foregrounding of the inner emotions and the backgrounding of the sounds of the world around us. In Nada Yoga the same kind of effect is strived for, making the body vibrate with the sound of the mantra, and removing yourself from your immediate environment, in an attempt to find inner integrity.

Just as visual perspective has been challenged since the beginning of the twentieth century, first by new forms of modern art such as cubism and the collage, later by mass media forms such as magazine layout and television graphics, so aural perspective, too, has been challenged, by avant-garde composers like Xenakis, but, above all, by new forms and technologies of listening which aim at immersion and participation, rather than at concentrated listening and imaginary identification.

References

Barnouw, E. (1968) *The Golden Web – A History of Broadcasting in the United States 1933–1953*, New York: Oxford University Press.

Blaukopf, K. (1960) 'Problems of architectural acoustics in musical sociology', *Gravesane Blätter* V (19–20): 180–7.

Cage, J. (1968) *Silence*, London: Calder & Boyars.

Cardiff, D. (1981) 'The serious and the popular: aspects of the evolution of style in the radio talk 1928-1939', *Media, Culture and Society* 2 (1): 29–47.

Doelle, L. (1972) *Environmental Acoustics*, New York: McGraw Hill.

Frith, S. (1988) *Music for Pleasure*, Cambridge: Polity.

Gorbman, C. (1987) *Unheard Melodies – Narrative Film Music*, London: BFI.

Hall, E.T. (1964) 'Silent assumptions in social communication', in D.McK. Rioch and E.A. Weinstein (eds) *Disorders of Communication, Research Publications, Association for Research in Nervous and Mental Diseases* 42: 41–55.

—— (1966) *The Hidden Dimension*, New York: Doubleday.

Leitner, G. (1980) 'BBC English and Deutsche Rundfunksprache: a comparative and historical analysis of the language on the radio', *International Journal of the Sociology of Language* 26: 75–100.

Mellers, W. (1964) *Music in a New Found Land – Themes and Developments in the History of American Music*, London: Faber & Faber.

Schafer, R.M. (1977) *The Tuning of the World*, Toronto: McClelland & Stewart.

Tagg, P. (1990) 'Music in mass media studies. Reading sounds for example', in K. Roe and U. Carlsson (eds) *Popular Music Research*, Nordicom-Sweden (2): 103–15.

Van Leeuwen, T. (1982) 'Professional speech: accentual and junctural style in radio announcing', unpublished MA (Hons) Thesis, Macquarie University, Sydney.

—— (1984) 'Impartial speech – observations on the intonation of radio newsreaders', *Australian Journal of Cultural Studies* 2 (1): 84–99.

—— (1992) 'Rhythm and social context', in P. Tench (ed.) *Studies in Systemic Phonology*, London: Frances Pinter.

Weis, E. and Belton, J. (eds) (1985) *Film Sound – Theory and Practice*, New York: Columbia University Press.

Chapter 13

David Graddol

THE SEMIOTIC CONSTRUCTION
OF A WINE LABEL

THE WORD 'TEXT' carries with it, for many people, connotations of substantial content and seriousness of communicative purpose but the majority of texts which circulate in late modern times do not easily fit this description. For example, the packaging and labelling on food sold in supermarkets gives rise to a multitude of ephemeral texts which are in many ways typical of a consumer society. One might expect that the transient function of packaging would mean that limited resources would be expended on its design but, as all consumers are aware, this is not usually the case. A great deal of care goes into the creation of packaging and it routinely deploys a variety of semiotic resources – verbal, visual and sometimes tactile and olfactory.

One reason for this is that packaging serves several purposes, such as protecting the merchandise during distribution and storage, encouraging a shopper to buy the product, and informing the consumer of its content and potential use. It must accomplish all of these functions within a variety of constraints including legal (the law governs what must and may be said on labels), economic (such as the cost of packaging in relation to the cost of the goods, or a supermarket's requirements for display and merchandising), practical (such as the size and shape of the goods) and cultural (including the need to draw on discourses of consumer desire and to take account of social patterns of consumption). What might be perceived as its main function (that of persuading purchasers to buy) must be accomplished within a time constraint – the packaging must hail the potential purchaser from the shelves, draw attention to its presence among competitors' products, and communicate desirability both at a distance and on closer inspection.

The sophistication of packaging design thus reflects a complexity in communicative function. This point is well illustrated by the labels that can be found on

Source: David Graddol, 'The semiotic construction of a wine label', in Sharon Goodman and David Graddol (eds) *Redesigning English: New Texts, New Identities*, London and New York: Routledge, in association with The Open University, UK, 1996, 73–81.

Figure 13.1 The back label from a Californian wine as locally sold

the back of bottles of wine, such as that illustrated in Figure 13.1, taken from a Californian wine sold in California. I will examine the design of such labels more closely, showing how they address a multiple readership in complex and, at times, contradictory ways reflecting many of the ambiguities and contradictions associated with the consumer subject in industrialized societies.

The multimodal nature of the label

The label shown in Figure 13.1 communicates its complex message by means of a variety of codes and devices in addition to the verbal channel. These semiotic modalities include:

- a code of numbers: 100%, 750 ml; numerical value of the bar code;
- the bar code;
- nibbles around the label indicating the batch and time of bottling (not shown);
- graphic design features such as rules;
- words, which are organized in space;
- typography a visual coding of language.

The label is thus a multimodal text. As a consequence the meanings conveyed by the label are potentially complex: different messages may be conveyed through each mode, and these may reinforce each other or give rise to tensions and even contradictions – not necessarily in the basic information conveyed but in the way the reader is addressed.

The complexity of audience address

Before it reaches the supermarket shelves, the bottle will be handled by many intermediaries such as shippers, wholesalers, buyers for the supermarket, store managers and shelf fillers. At each stage the labelling must present the product in a way that ensures the best treatment so that it eventually achieves a prominent place in the store. In the supermarket it must speak to purchasers, persuading them that the product is attractive and worth the price being asked. There is thus no sole occasion on which the label serves its communicative function nor only one kind of person who will read it.

The different semiotic resources of the text are employed to address this multiple audience in a way that recognizes the different social and economic relations the text producer wishes to construct with each. For example, the bar code addresses the retailer, or rather the machines and computer systems used for stock control and pricing; the bar code also impinges on the relation between retailer and customer, since it records details of the particular transaction (location, time, quantity) in order to build profiles of consumer activity for marketing purposes. Bar codes are thus difficult things to integrate into a label design. If they are too prominent they may highlight the retailer's convenience and interest more than that of the consumer, drawing attention to the goods as revenue potential rather than as a satisfier of consumer need or desire. Unfortunately, in order to be read by automated check-out tills (and thus minimize staff costs) such bar codes need to be of a minimum size and standard placement. Practical label design must thus compromise between the two potentially competing requirements. In Figure 13.1 the bar code is located in the lower portion of the label, marked off from the main text by a rule.

It is not clear who is intended to read the batch information that is communicated by nibbles on the label edge. It addresses, however, some of the legal and institutional relations that govern the exchange of goods between manufacturer, distributor, retailer, customer and consumer. It is a part of the text that is not ordinarily read, but may become a focus of interest if these economic, legal and social relations are called into question – such as in the case of damaged or contaminated goods. The fact that this code is not transparent to the consumer, of course, is a part of that social relation.

The contradictory nature of the consumer-subject

The most prominent part of the text of the label is clearly addressed to the consumer. But food buying is a complex social as well as economic activity which is highly structured according to region, ethnicity, social class and gender. A retailer's market research, for example, may show that wine in their supermarkets is bought mainly by women but drunk largely by men, or that higher price wines are bought mainly for meals to which guests are invited.

This means that the label will, at the very least, have to address the consumer-purchaser, the consumer-host and the consumer-guest. And how does such a wine label speak to guests at the dinner table, and what does it say about the host's taste, judgement, wealth and hospitality? This will depend to large measure on the cultural practices with which the consumption of wine is associated. What, for example, is the significance of serving wine at the dinner table (in different countries, among different social and ethnic groups)? What little rituals of opening and serving are associated with it? In Britain, a supermarket brand name on the label may, for example, reassure the consumer-purchaser that a particular wine is of reliable quality and good value, but the consumer-guest may regard it as more suitable for family consumption than for a special occasion.

Heteroglossia in the text

There is a further contradiction in the way the consumer is addressed which arises from the legislation governing label design.

The text in Figure 13.1, for example, contains two paragraphs: the upper one addresses the consumer as one with desires, appetites and choices. The lower text, however, addresses the reader as a consumer who has certain rights and to whom the manufacturer has certain duties of care. The result is that consumers are simultaneously told that this wine will enhance their life, and that it will damage it. This particular contradiction arises from the law governing wine labelling in California, but the words and descriptions that can be placed on wine labels are, in most countries, highly regulated. By regulating the ways in which the reader can be addressed by the text they regulate also the kinds of social relation that can be established with a reader. There is thus a contradiction which arises from the competing 'interests' established by consumer law and the manufacturer/retailer and which results in different voices being represented in the text.

The contradictions are clearly signalled by the language genres in which the two fragments are written. The persuasive text is highly evaluative, using words like *civilized* and *gracious*. It incorporates the reader in this evaluation by the use of the first person: 'wine has been with *us*', '*our* culture'. The Surgeon General's warning, in contrast, draws on language genres of information giving and objective authority. It uses modal constructions such as *should not*, terms from a formal scientific register, *alcoholic beverages*, employs a discourse of medical cause and effect, *because of the risk of birth defects*, uses impersonal address in the third person, *women should not*, or in the second person, *impairs your ability*, and includes enumerated paragraphs.

These two text fragments thus not only give contradictory messages at the surface level ('drink and enjoy' versus 'drink and die'), they also position the reader in quite different ways and attempt to construct different ideas about what it is to be a consumer. In the remainder of this reading I want to examine this heteroglossia more closely, showing how the tension between promotion and regulation affects other parts of the text and how the perception of contradiction is minimized by visual design.

The legal restrictions

There is certain information which must by law be given on labels carried by the wine sold in the European Union (EU), such as the alcoholic strength, volume, country of origin and category of wine. There are also various kinds of optional information, such as recommendations to the consumer about:

- dishes with which the wine might be served;
- manner of serving; appropriate handling of the wine;
- proper storage of the wine;
- the history of the particular wine or of the bottler;
- the natural and technical conditions under which the wine was made.

If information is neither required nor optional, then it cannot be given on the label. The purpose of the legislation is to ensure that consumers know exactly what they are getting and are not misled about the quality of the wine. For example, EU law states that compulsory information, including the country of origin and category of wine, shall be given in one or more official languages of the community so that the consumer can easily understand it. EU law establishes different classes of wine, of which 'Table Wine' is one of the lowest, but in many cases this can be stated in the national language of origin. Hence a phrase such as *vin de table* is acceptable on a bottle of French wine sold in Britain and *vino da tavola* would be accepted on a bottle of Italian wine. By printing the classification in the national language, the label designers may feel that the perceived quality of the wine will be indirectly enhanced. But only standard, familiar non-English phrases can be used on wine sold in Britain. If the wine is the produce of more than one country, this description must be in English, because the regulators fear that the majority of British consumers would fail to understand if it were given in French or Italian. Indeed, it may give a false impression of quality if consumers recognized the language as being the national language of a traditional wine-producing country, but did not actually understand what it meant.

Such 'language display' in advertising is more usually associated with the English language worldwide: the perceived value of many consumer products is enhanced by being associated with a piece of English language text. In Europe, however, the use of English in connection with wine does not usually enhance the perceived quality of the product, since England is not a traditional wine-producing country.

The regulatory structure which governs label design has a wider effect on the discourse of back labels. Since quality and desirability cannot be stated explicitly, labels typically communicate indirectly through conventional discourses which have grown up around the marketing and consumption of wine in different countries. The label on a red wine bottle from France may state that the wine is an excellent accompaniment to red meat and cheese. A label from an Italian wine might add that it will be ideal with pasta or pizza. These descriptions are not directly informative: they are the conventional terms in which good red wine is described. More importantly, they allow a word like 'excellent' (which cannot be used to describe the wine itself) to be used in connection with the wine's suitability to accompany conventional foods.

There has also arisen a code of specificity about wine in which the more specific the details of the wine's origins, content and use, the better the wine is deemed to be. In part this has arisen from the *appellation* system used in France to identify the quality of wines, but it has led to a generic discourse which now extends to wine from many other countries. For example, one variety of Italian wine sold in Britain carries the following text on its back label:

UVA DI TROIA

This wine is the result of Australian Winemaking Consultant Kym Milne MW joining forces with Italian Winemaker Augusto Càntele to produce a premium red wine from an indigenous Italian variety in the southern Italian region of Puglia.

Uva di Troia is an ancient grape variety which still exists in small quantities in Puglia. Following fermentation on skins to extract flavour, the wine was matured for 12 months in new and one year old French oak barriques.

This elegant, medium bodied wine exhibits fruit flavours of ripe plums, balanced with toasty oak and complex, 'roasted' flavours.

This text gives highly specific information which indicates that the wine is to be regarded as being of a higher quality than is suggested by the strict legal category of *vino da tavola*, which the front label bears. The Californian label in Figure 13.1, on the other hand, is extremely unspecific: it finds little to say about this wine in particular but extols the virtue of wine in general. The implication is that this is really an ordinary table wine without particular character.

The importance of visual design

The strict regulation of what must and can be said on wine labels may be one reason why visual design is so important. There are fewer legal restrictions on appearance than on words. In fact, European regulations have very little to say about visual design other than that lettering must be clear and legible, with minimum heights specified for key information, and that key information should be visible within one 'field of view' (i.e. either all on the front or all on the back).

This limited prescription does nevertheless explain one major feature of the visual design. Since basic information, such as the name, must be displayed clearly on the front label so that it is visible on a supermarket shelf, this means that *all* the key information is usually placed on the front label and the optional information located on the back.

Between the front label and the back label there is the bottle itself, containing the main contents, which has a colour and shape which conventionally indicates the style of wine. The bottle as a whole, then, can be regarded as a single text with an internal structure of front, body and back. It is interesting to note how this structure emerges from particular constraints of liquid container design, super-market design, consumer behaviour and legislation and yet also conforms to a common generic text structure. For example, the Text Encoding Initiative (TEI) which provides an international standard for the mark up of texts in electronic form, assumes that the basic structure of all texts can be described by the categories of <front>, <body> and <back>. The text created by a wine bottle thus shares the structure of a book or a newspaper. The front label shows the title and other 'headline' information about the wine. The bottle provides the main contents, and the back label includes textual apparatus not dissimilar to the index at the back of a book, providing detailed data about contents and use.

Visual design is used extensively to resolve some of the contradictions which arise from regulations which govern the verbal. For example, the contradiction between upper and lower text fragments in Figure 13.1 means that the label speaks with at least two distinct voices but the priority between these voices is clearly signalled by the placing of the promotional text at the start of the reading path. The Surgeon General's warning is marked off by a horizontal rule and relegated 'below stairs' with the other 'housekeeping' text fragments such as the bar code.

The status of the two parts of the text, promotional and warning, is also clearly signalled typographically. The persuasive, upper text is in a serif typeface called Centaur. The Surgeon General's warning is set in a sans serif face called Helvetica. Few readers will recognize the typefaces employed, but they will intuitively make very different associations with each. In order to understand how the text works at this typographic level it is necessary to understand something of the historical development of the two typefaces.

Typographic design

The first printed books showed remarkable sophistication in typographic design. There are only 26 letters in the English alphabet, but the first founts of type produced to print English in the fifteenth century contained over 400 different character shapes or *sorts*. This was because early printers tried as far as possible to reproduce the look of hand-copied books, which had by then reached a level of artistry and illustration that was extremely hard to match mechanically. Gradually, as printing technology became more mechanized and books cheaper, competition from handmade books declined. But improved printing technology led, ironically, to a decline in the subtlety of page design and typography. The range of sorts used by printers reduced by over a quarter and hand-finishing became increasingly rare. (Modern desk-top publishing has further reduced the range of characters used – to below 200 in many cases. It also has made more popular the spelling *font* which is used elsewhere in this chapter because of its association with newer printing technology.) In addition, there existed for many centuries a limited number of printed text types (such as books and handbills), and these tended to be set indiscriminately in whatever fount a local printer happened to have to hand. There was, in other words, little systematic distinction in the way that typefaces were employed.

However, a new typographic design order emerged in the nineteenth century, largely as a result of the increasing requirements of a consumer society for a variety of printed matter which advertised, instructed, warned and decoratively packaged the new goods of the industrial age. There was also a need in the commercial sector for specialized information giving, such as railway timetables and corporate accounts, requiring new forms of text layout and typographic distinction. The range of communicative functions of texts also became greatly extended in comparison to previous generations – from advertising hoardings which needed to persuade at a distance, to annually updated voting registers required to service an increasingly democratic society. This variety of function demanded new forms of type design. New typesetting technologies (such as the Linotype and Monotype machines) and a range of new typefaces were created in the later part of the nineteenth century to satisfy such needs.

However, it was not enough merely to invent new forms of typeface: also required were new conventions for their deployment. The limited range of standard 'jobbing' founts formerly used by printers were superseded by a wide range of founts, available in different styles (such as 'roman', 'italic' and 'bold'), each with different historical associations and conventional functions. One key distinction in modern typography is now between the traditional faces modelled on classical Roman incised lettering (which carried decorative lines known as serifs) and the simpler, more geometric sans serifs which first appeared in the industrial age. Figures 13.2 and 13.3 illustrate some of the key differences. This distinction is used to good effect in the label shown in Figure 13.1.

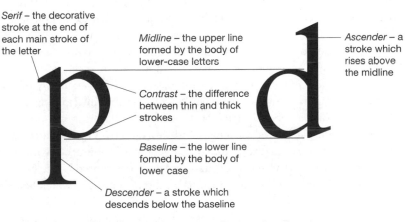

Figure 13.2 Centaur is a serif typeface modelled on handwriting

Figure 13.3 Helvetica is a sans serif based on a simpler, more geometric design

Wine label typography

The typography of the label in Figure 13.1 can now be seen to be an integral part of its overall design, clearly distinguishing the two competing voices and giving them different priorities and cultural associations. Centaur, in which the upper, promotional text is set, was designed by the American typographer Bruce Rogers (1870–1957) just before World War One and released by Monotype in 1929. Centaur self-consciously attempted to create a face with 'humanist' character, based closely on handwritten models (in fact it was modelled on an early Italian typeface designed by Jenson in the fifteenth century). The genre of typeface (early, Renaissance, handwritten) as well as the particular design (twentieth-century American) helps the promotional text convey values of human agency, of culture and history appropriate for a Californian wine.

Helvetica, in which the Surgeon General's warning is set, was created in Switzerland in 1957 but its design origins lie in German realist faces of the final years of the nineteenth century. Indeed, one typographer has described Helvetica and similar faces as 'cultural souvenirs of the bleakest days of the industrial revolution' (Bringhurst 1992: 189). Helvetica, however, is better seen as the outcome of a moment in twentieth-century culture which sought to produce a utilitarian typeface for objective information texts. Jakob Erbar, the Bauhaus designer of one of the first sans serifs designed for text (as opposed to display type) acknowledged that his 'aim was to design a printing type which would be free of all individual characteristics, possess thoroughly legible letter forms, and be a purely typographic creation' (cited in Tracy 1986: 93). Helvetica is a typical information face, used for such things as captions, headings, motorway signs. The health warning is thus set in an impersonal 'no nonsense' twentieth-century, rationalist face which has become associated with hygiene, factuality and modernism.

In addition to the typeface there is an important political economy of space at work in the typographic design. The upper text is 'bicameral' (mixing upper and lower case) which means that the space occupied by the lettering is modulated and given rhythm by the pattern of ascenders and descenders. Furthermore, the text is slightly letter spaced, permitting it to expand generously and occupy more room. In contrast, the lower text is set in capitals and in a condensed type. Not only is there a certain meanness but also a uniformity in the use of space which helps signal impersonality.

The typographic design is thus consonant with the language genre used in each text fragment. Typography and words combine to position a reader in similar ways.

Conclusion

I have tried to show how the genre of the back label is historically located in terms of regulatory structures, in terms of the conventional promotional discourses which have arisen within a consumer society, in terms of the cultural history of graphic design, and in the more diffuse forms of intertextual resources which promotional discourse about wine draws on. I have tried also to show the importance of visual design in the construction of labels, in addressing the different audiences and meeting contradictory needs, and in disciplining the heteroglossia which necessarily arises in such texts.

Labelling is no different from other, more conventional texts, in the way it attempts to position readers within particular social and economic relationships and in the way it speaks with several, at times contradictory, voices. Visual communication is still poorly understood, despite the fact that visual design is becoming a more prominent feature of texts in mass circulation. Packaging has been given less scholarly attention, perhaps, than its impact on people's everyday lives warrants.

References

Bringhurst, R. (1992) *The Elements of Typographic Style*, Point Roberts, WA: Hartley & Marks.
Tracy, W. (1986) *Letters of Credit: A View of Type Design*, London: Gordon Fraser.

Discussion points
for Part Two

1   In relation to Cameron and colleagues' description of three stances towards academic research (ethics, advocacy and empowerment) in Chapter 8, what are the typical stances adopted towards informants by Conversation Analysis and Critical Discourse Analysis? (Refer to Chapters 5, 17 or 18 as examples of the CA approach, and to Chapters 9 or 35 as examples of CDA.)

2   Try to identify the differences between a general form of discourse analysis and an approach that deserves to be called CDA. What does 'critical' mean in this context? If it implies some personal, political stance on the issues being researched, can we expect there to be any agreement on analysis? Is there any possibility for discourse analysis to be objective?

3   Compare the two uses of the word 'flexible' by Tony Blair and Stephen in Chapter 11 (p. 148). Both quotes may be said to constitute different discourses, different ways of speaking about the same concept. Search the internet for terms such as 'graffiti' (e.g., newspaper articles condemning graffiti as acts of vandalism, sites which sell posters of graffiti art, fashion photographs with graffiti as background). What sorts of ideologies, assumptions, 'expert' opinions, regimes of truth, etc. (see Chapter 8) stand behind such differently constructed discourses. Conduct more, similar searches for different discourses of 'globalisation', 'tourism', 'liberation', 'voice', 'face', 'black' and so on. Add any other terms you think would reveal interesting ideological profiles.

4   As a group activity, listen to a good-quality, short recording of a piece of spontaneous conversation – perhaps 20 seconds long. Individually, make an orthographic transcription of the talk. Compare transcribed versions. Are they all the same? How has it been possible for different people to produce (what probably are) very similar transcripts? Where do the 'rules' for transcribing speech in this standard, orthographic way come from? What does an orthographic transcription show, and what does it not show? Now try to re-transcribe the same sequence using Gail Jefferson's conventions. Once again, compare the different versions. We would expect there to be much more variation now. Assess why different versions have tried to show different features. What have the transcribers been trying to capture. How successful have they been? Is there such a thing as a 'perfect' transcription?

5   Listen to a soundtrack of a feature film with the picture turned off. Concentrate on the dialogue, musical score and sound effects in different

scenes and identify which of the sounds constitute 'figure', 'ground' and 'field' as defined in Chapter 12.

6   Stand in front of a classmate and try saying the same sentence, e.g. *I'd like you to come with me*, or *Don't look at me like that* in different tones of voice: whispering, in a soft relaxed voice, in a full voice, in a loud voice, and shouting. Try varying your pitch between low and high. How do differences in loudness and pitch affect the meaning of your utterances in terms of interpersonal distance between you and your addressee, as well as their illocutionary force?

7   What are the meanings implied in the visual design (typography, layout, colour) of the cover of this book? What (for you) are the connotative or ideological meanings carried by the use of names on the cover, and by how the names are aligned? In your view, does the choice and arrangement of colours have any 'second-order' meaning? On the covers of academic books generally, how are meanings such as 'serious', 'important' or 'accessible' implied by visual design?

Sequence and structure

Editors' introduction
to Part Three

W E H A V E S E E N that sequence and structure are the focal concerns of Conversation Analysis (CA). Many other approaches to discourse emphasise how texts and (in the more material sense of the term) discourses are organised as patterned entities. To some extent this reflects the long-standing concerns of linguistics with matters of composition and structure. But there are also some more important reasons for attending to discourse structure, some of which we have already encountered. If, as Bakhtin suggests, we need to see language-in-use as organised into various speech genres, and, more generally, if discourses (in Fairclough's definition) are organised as sets of ideological meanings and values, then discovering patterns in discourse is a primary objective. We could argue that patterns in discourse relate to structures or 'orders' of society and ideology. In CA terms, the sorts of structuring that interactants submit to conversationally and reproduce in their talk already form a core dimension of 'social structure'. This was Schegloff's argument in Chapter 5, and it connects to what Giddens (1991) has called the process of 'structuration'. Therefore, as we have said before, there is a direct link between conversational production of the interaction order and production of the social order. Here we see one of the main ways in which discourse analysis is able to use micro-level (linguistic, textual, intertextual) commentary to help explain macro-level (societal, cultural, ideological) processes. (Papers collected in Coupland *et al.* 1999 treat this question in more depth; it is briefly discussed by Cameron *et al.*, Chapter 8.)

   In Labov and Waletzky's (1967) structural analysis of the stories told by street-gang youngsters, summarised in William Labov's single-authored paper (Chapter 14), we are introduced to some core concepts for the analysis of *narrative* which have been used productively in many other social settings. For example, Allan Bell's (1991) analysis of newspaper 'stories' builds directly on Labov's narrative categories. Labov's structural analysis is, in itself, very valuable. But it is worth emphasising the title of Labov's text – the 'transformation of experience in narrative'. Labov shows how discourse structuring in the genre of narrative not only recounts but refashions experience. This is most apparent in the 'evaluation' component of narrative – the means by which a narrator explains the purpose and 'so what' of a story. Stories, for example among young street-gang members, function to establish social status for the narrator-protagonist, in both dimensions of context – the story context and the story-telling context. This is why we find features in narratives that Labov calls 'intensifiers'. These include non-verbal gestures, expressive pronunciation and repetition. Similarly, 'comparators' compare events that did occur with those that did not; 'correlatives' combine events into single accounts; 'explicatives' explain complications inherent in the narrative for listeners. These are sets of syntactic and pragmatic devices that Labov considers in the source article (not included in the excerpted text). They are some of the means by which experience, in the telling of it, is transformed when it is animated and performed.

By way of contrast, we have included Derek Edwards's article (Chapter 15). Edwards suggests that to take Labov's schema and to impose it on any narrative has a limiting effect on the analysis. For him, such a rigid schema is not capable of accounting for the rhetorical and interactional intricacy of narratives. First, the scene-setting 'orientation' may, in fact, provide relevant information about the recounted events. There is a high degree of idealisation in categories such as 'complicating action' and 'evaluation'. Then, 'evaluation' may be a more pervasive feature running through entire narrative episodes rather than in a limited number of selected clauses. Also, with 'abstract' and 'orientation' being optional elements in Labov's model, most of the representational and categorial work is left to just one element: 'complicating action'. Edwards is pointing to the limitations of bringing any preformed category system to bear on narrative (or any other genre of) discourse, even though he would admit that Labov's template does capture a useful generalisation about typical narrative structure.

Consistent with the tenets of CA and discursive psychology (a version of CA developed in the psychology literature), Edwards prefers to analyse narratives (as well as other forms of discourse) by examining their interactional and *emergent* structure. In order to make sense of the story teller's unfolding account of the events and their own position-taking in relation to these events and other participants, Edwards focuses on the step-by-step rhetorical design. Where does a story begin? Which social categories are constructed and used? Are there competing stories or accounts? Which ones does the teller align with? The general CA question is: What is being accomplished in the on-going business of talk? The sequencing of events in narrative is not a universal structure but something a speaker achieves when (re-)presenting events and legitimating some account of events that is relevant for the current activity. In narrative activity people take stances and authenticate versions of events, and themselves as speakers (see also Young, Chapter 28).

Harvey Sacks's essay, Chapter 16, introduces the methodology of membership category analysis (MCA) which has its roots in CA and ethnomethodology. It is concerned with the sequential organisation of talk, the way category descriptions are used in conversation especially with regard to their sequential relevance. Sacks illustrates his point with the following two-sentence mini-story: 'The baby cried. The mommy picked it up'. Through a rather elaborate analysis of this short example, Sacks demonstrates how the organisation of social knowledge relies upon conventional categories and our understanding of how they inter-relate in order to 'make sense'. He explains why, other things being equal, most people would understand the story as the 'mommy' picking up *her* 'baby', *in response to* the previous activity of the baby crying. The explanation lies partly in the iconic properties of talk. In this case this includes the assumption that actions in two consecutive utterances, without any temporal markers, will be understood to be ordered in the same sequence as the utterances themselves – the 'picking up' is understood to come after the 'crying'. Sacks, introduces the term 'membership categorization device' to refer to the meanings that categories achieve in talk. We understand that 'the mommy' picks up 'the baby' because we commonsensically associate the categories of 'baby' and 'mommy'. The relevant (but implied) membership categorisation device is 'the family', forming a 'team' relationship between the categories mentioned. Additionally, the notion of 'category-bound activities' ties the activity of 'crying' to the category 'baby' – crying is what we commonsensically expect babies to do. It is in this way, Sacks argues, people's capacity for practical sense-making is based on their capacity to recognise such categorisations and devices.

In Chapter 17, Anita Pomerantz deals with one of the central areas of interest in CA – so-called 'preference structure'. In this case, Pomerantz's conversation data show speakers' patterns or preferences in how they express agreements and disagreements with something just said. The starting point of the chapter is that assessments are routinely produced as part of interaction, and that through assessments, participants claim knowledge of the topic at hand. Discursive actions (or conversational turns) following assessments, as well as other types of utterances – agreements or disagreements – may be *preferred* or *dispreferred*. They may be either what conversationalists normally expect will follow next (preferred actions) or what they will find unusual or somewhat discordant (dispreferred actions). Although agreements tend to be generally preferred actions, disagreements can sometimes also be preferred following some particular forms of assessment, such as self-deprecation (e.g., *I'm really not good at science*). The chapter makes a clear connection between normal conversational sequence and the form/function of utterances. Pomerantz offers a useful inventory of modifications of agreements (e.g., 'upgrades', 'downgrades' where a next-speaker emphasises or plays down an earlier assessment), and of disagreements (e.g., 'delays', holding off from agreeing). She illustrates them with a number of different structures and strategies from naturally occurring talk. Apart from its descriptive insight, this sort of research has given strong foundations to further work in pragmatics and the ethnography of communication, especially in the area of speech act realisation and politeness, most notably compliments and compliment responses (see Brown and Levinson, Chapter 22; Holmes, Chapter 23).

'Opening up closings' by Emanuel Schegloff and Harvey Sacks (Chapter 18) is one of the truly classic papers in CA. We can read it for its richly detailed insights into the structural patterns that speakers deploy when they close conversations.

But it is probably more important to read it as an agenda-setting statement for the discipline of CA, and as an outline of its principles and methodological priorities. To this extent it follows on directly from the Sacks chapter and confirms many of its central points. Schegloff and Sacks are very explicit, early in the chapter, about the 'technical' nature of CA, and this term resurfaces at several points. They refer to CA as striving to be 'a naturalistic observational discipline' able to 'deal with the details of social action(s) rigorously, empirically and formally' (p. 262). We can make sense of these claims when we see the emphasis CA places on 'actual data' and when we remember the interpretive restrictions that Schegloff argued (in Chapter 5, which is in fact a later development of ideas that are expressed in this chapter) should apply in how analysts use contextual information. There is certainly a sort of 'formalism' in CA. Its transcribing conventions (see Chapter 10) suggest a particular form of rigour in the representation of data. At the same time, terms such as 'formal' and 'empirical' run counter to the general priorities that linguists and philosophers have brought to the study of discourse – as evidenced in Part One of the *Reader*. For them, discourse deals in function more than form. It reaches out to understandings of social context to build its analyses, rather than ruling some aspects of social context out-of-bounds. This is why there are enduring tensions between CA and discourse analysis, despite their many shared ambitions and insights (see Hutchby's chapter, Chapter 36). There is an irony in sociologists (in the name of CA) striving for naturalism and empiricism in their dealings with discourse, while linguists are very largely striving to shake off the formalism and empiricism of early versions of linguistics. (These issues are debated in more detail in Coupland and Jaworski 1997.)

In Deborah Schiffrin's work we see how CA's passion for analysing structure can usefully be developed into close analysis of individual discourse particles – in the case Schiffrin considers in Chapter 19, the particle *oh*. It is through discourse analysis that many linguistic features excluded from most traditional accounts of sentence structure and meaning come to prominence. As Schiffrin says, it is difficult to attribute much semantic or grammatical meaning to *oh*, yet it makes an important regular contribution to discourse structure – particularly through marking how listeners receive new and newly salient information from speakers, and how this changes their knowledge states. The initial motivation for a speaker to use the particle *oh* is therefore primarily a cognitive one. To put it another way, *oh* is the linguistic reflex of cognitive realignment. We may well be able to detect a speaker's (or our own) cognitive realignment to information without a discourse marker being present in the text. But the fact of marking these realignments, in all of the many sub-contexts Schiffrin illustrates, does conversational work in the relational or inter-personal dimension too. *Oh* can mark that a speaker is occupying a 'listener' role, or perhaps the role of a 'supportive listener'. It can signal that a consensus of understanding has been achieved, at a particular moment in talk. Alternatively, it can signal disjunction and a listener's surprise at not sharing a point of view or a knowledge state.

So the general view of discourse functioning that Schiffrin's analysis gives us is the same multi-functional one we saw in many of the introductory chapters in

Part One. Talk realises and fulfils multiple communicative goals and functions simultaneously – ideational (or information-related), relational (or interpersonal) and identity-related. It performs these functions simultaneously and in a multi-layered fashion. In Schiffrin's study of *oh* we can see how a tiny discourse particle helps to manage the informational/ideational structure of talk, while also functioning at the level of negotiating social roles and relationships.

References

Bell, A. (1991) *The Language of News Media*, Oxford: Blackwell.

Coupland, N. and Jaworski, A. (1997) 'Relevance, accommodation and conversation: modelling the social dimension of communication', *Multilingua* 16: 233–58.

Coupland, N., Sarangi, S. and Candlin, C. (eds) (1999) *Sociolinguistics and Social Theory*, London: Longman.

Giddens, A. (1991) *Modernity and Self-identity: Self and Identity in the Late Modern Age*, Cambridge: Polity Press.

Labov, W. and Waletzky, J. (1967) 'Narrative analysis: oral versions of personal experience', in J. Helm (ed.) *Essays on the Verbal and Visual Arts: Proceedings of the 1966 Annual Spring Meeting of the American Ethnological Society*, Seattle, WA: University of Washington Press. 12–44. (reprinted in *Journal of Narrative and Life History* 7/1-4 Special issue: *Oral Versions of Personal Experience: Three Decades of Narrative Analysis*, M.G.W. Bamberg (ed.), 3–38).

Chapter 14

William Labov

THE TRANSFORMATION OF EXPERIENCE IN NARRATIVE

. . .

IN A PREVIOUS STUDY we have presented a general framework for the analysis of narrative which shows how verbal skills are used to evaluate experience (Labov and Waletzky 1967). In this chapter we examine the narratives we obtained in our study of south-central Harlem from preadolescents (9 to 13 years old), adolescents (14 to 19), and adults to see what linguistic techniques are used to evaluate experience within the black English [BE] vernacular culture . . .

It will be helpful for the reader to be acquainted with the general character and impact of narratives in black vernacular style. We will cite here in full three fight narratives from leaders of vernacular peer groups in south-central Harlem who are widely recognized for their verbal skills and refer to these throughout the discussion to illustrate the structural feature of narrative. The first is by Boot.[1]

Extract 1
(Something Calvin did that was really wild?)
> Yeah.
a   It was on a Sunday
b   and we didn't have nothin' to do after I – after we came from church.
c   Then we ain't had nothin' to do.
d   So I say, "Calvin, let's go get our – out our dirty clothes on and play in the dirt."
e   And so Calvin say, "Let's have a rock – a rock war."
f   And I say, "All right."

Source: William Labov, *Language in the Inner City: Studies in the Black English Vernacular*, Philadelphia, PA: University of Pennsylvania Press and Oxford: Blackwell.

g   So Calvin had a rock.
h   And we as – you know, here go a wall
i   and a far away here go a wall.
j   Calvin th'ew a rock.
k   I was lookin' and – uh –
l   And Calvin th'ew a rock.
m   It oh – it almost hit me
n   And so I looked down to get another rock;
o   Say "Ssh!"
p   An' it pass me.
q   I say, "Calvin, I'm bust your head for that!"
r   Calvin stuck his head out.
s   I th'ew the rock
t   An' the rock went up,
u   I mean – went up –
v   came down
w   an' say [slap!]
x   an' smacked him in the head
y   an' his head busted.

The second narrative is by Larry H., a core member of the Jets gang. This is one of three fight stories told by Larry which match in verbal skill his outstanding performance in argument, ritual insults, and other speech events of the black vernacular culture.

Extract 2
a   An' then, three weeks ago I had a fight with this
     other dude outside
b   He got mad
     'cause I wouldn't give him a cigarette.
c   Ain't that a bitch?
     (Oh yeah?)
d   Yeah, you know, I was sittin' on the corner an' shit,
     smokin' my cigarette, you know
e   I was high, an' shit.
f   He walked over to me,
g   "Can I have a cigarette?"
h   He was a little taller than me,
     but not that much.
i   I said, "I ain't got no more, man,"
j   'cause, you know, all I had was one left.
k   An' I ain't gon' give up my last cigarette unless I got some more.
l   So I said, "I don't have no more, man."
m   So he, you know, dug on the pack,
     'cause the pack was in my pocket.
n   So he said, "Eh man, I can't get a cigarette, man?
o   I mean – I mean we supposed to be brothers, an' shit,"

p   So I say, "Yeah, well, you know, man, all I got is one, you dig it?"

q   An' I won't give up my las' one to nobody.

r   So you know, the dude, he looks at me,

s   An' he – I 'on' know –
     he jus' thought he gon' rough that motherfucker up.

t   He said, "I can't get a cigarette."

u   I said, "Tha's what I said, my man".

v   You know, so he said, "What you supposed to be *bad*, an' shit?

w   What, you think you *bad* an' shit?"

x   So I said, "Look here, my man,

y   I don't think I'm bad, you understand?

z   But I mean, you know, if I had it,
     you could git it

aa   I like to see you with it, you dig it?

bb   But the sad part about it,

cc   You got to do without it.

dd   That's all, my man."

ee   So the dude, he 'on' to pushin' me, man.
     (Oh he pushed you?)

ff   An' why he do that?

gg   *Everytime somebody fuck with me,*
     why they do it?

hh   I put that cigarette down,

ii   An' boy, let me tell you,
     I beat the shit outa that motherfucker.

jj   I tried to *kill* 'im – over one cigarette"

kk   I tried to *kill* 'im. Square business!

ll   After I got through stompin' him in the face, man,

mm   You know, all of a sudden I went crazy!

nn   I jus' went crazy.

oo   An' I jus' wouldn't stop hittin the motherfucker.

pp   Dig it, I couldn't stop hittin' 'im, man,
     till the teacher pulled me off o' him.

qq   An' guess what? After all that I gave the dude the cigarette,
     after all that.

rr   Ain't that a bitch?
     (How come you gave 'im a cigarette?)

ss   I 'on' know.

tt   I jus' gave it to him.

uu   An' he smoked it, too!

Among the young adults we interviewed in our preliminary exploration of south-central Harlem, John L. struck us immediately as a gifted story teller; the following is one of many narratives that have been highly regarded by many listeners.

Extract 3

(What was the most important fight that you remember, one that sticks in your mind . . .)

a   Well, one (I think) was with a girl.

b   Like I was a kid, you know,

c   And she was the baddest girl, *the baddest girl in the neighborhood.*

d   If you didn't bring her candy to school,
she would punch you in the mouth;

e   And you had to kiss her
when she'd tell you.

f   This girl was only about 12 years old, man,

g   but she was a killer.

h   She didn't take no junk;

i   She whupped all her brothers.

j   And I came to school one day

k   and I didn't have no money.

l   My ma wouldn't give me no money.

m   And I played hookies one day,

n   (She) put something on me.[2]

o   I played hookies, man,

p   so I said, you know, I'm not gonna play hookies no more
'cause I don't wanna get a whupping

q   So I go to school

r   and this girl says, "Where's the candy?"

s   I said, "I don't have it."

t   She says, powww!

u   So I says to myself, "There's gonna be times
my mother won't give me money
because (we're) a poor family

v   And I can't take this all, you know, every time she
don't give me any money."

w   So I say, "Well, I just gotta fight this girl.

x   She gonna hafta whup me.

y   I hope she don't whup me."

z   And I hit the girl: powwww!

aa   and I put something on it.

bb   I win the fight.

cc   That was one of the most important.

This discussion will first review briefly the general definition of narrative and its overall structure. . . . The main body of narratives cited are from our work in south-central Harlem, but references will be made to materials drawn from other urban and rural areas, from both white and black subjects.

Definition of narrative

We define narrative as one method of recapitulating past experience by matching a verbal sequence of clauses to the sequence of events which (it is inferred) actually occurred. For example, a pre-adolescent narrative:

> **Extract 4**
> a   This boy punched me
> b   and I punched him
> c   and the teacher came in
> d   and stopped the fight.

An adult narrative:

> **Extract 5**
> a   Well this person had a little too much to drink
> b   and he attacked me
> c   and the friend came in
> d   and she stopped it.

In each case we have four independent clauses which match the order of the inferred events. It is important to note that other means of recapitulating these experiences are available which do not follow the same sequence; syntactic embedding can be used:

> **Extract 6**
> a   A friend of mine came in just
>   in time to stop
>   this person who had a little too much to drink
>   from attacking me.

Or else the past perfect can be used to reverse the order:

> **Extract 7**
> a   The teacher stopped the fight.
> b   She had just come in.
> c   I had punched this boy.
> d   He had punched me.

Narrative, then, is only one way of recapitulating this past experience: the clauses are characteristically ordered in temporal sequence; if narrative clauses are reversed, the inferred temporal sequence of the original semantic interpretation is altered: *I punched this boy/and he punched me* instead of *This boy punched me/and I punched him*.

With this conception of narrative, we can define a *minimal narrative* as a sequence of two clauses which are *temporally ordered*: that is, a change in their order will result in a change in the temporal sequence of the original semantic interpretation.

In alternative terminology, there is temporal juncture between the two clauses, and a minimal narrative is defined as one containing a single temporal juncture.

The skeleton of a narrative then consists of a series of temporally ordered clauses which we may call *narrative clauses*. A narrative such as 4 or 5 consists entirely of narrative clauses. Here is a minimal narrative which contains only two:

Extract 8

a   I know a boy named Harry.
b   Another boy threw a bottle at him right in the head
c   and he had to get seven stitches.

This narrative contains three clauses, but only two are narrative clauses. The first has no temporal juncture, and might be placed after *b* or after *c* without disturbing temporal order. It is equally true at the end and at the beginning that the narrator knows a boy named Harry. Clause *a* may be called a *free clause* since it is not confined by any temporal juncture. . . .

It is only independent clauses which can function as narrative clauses – and as we will see below, only particular kinds of independent clauses. In the representation of narratives in this section, we will list each clause on a separate line, but letter only the independent clauses. . . .

The overall structure of narrative

Some narratives, like 4, contain only narrative clauses; they are complete in the sense that they have a beginning, a middle, and an end. But there are other elements of narrative structure found in more fully developed types. Briefly, a fully-formed narrative may show the following:

Extract 9

1   Abstract.
2   Orientation.
3   Complicating action.
4   Evaluation.
5   Result or resolution.
6   Coda.

Of course there are complex chainings and embeddings of these elements, but here we are dealing with the simpler forms. Complicating action has been characterized above, and the result may be regarded for the moment as the termination of that series of events. We will consider briefly the nature and function of the abstract, orientation, coda, and evaluation.

The abstract

It is not uncommon for narrators to begin with one or two clauses summarizing the whole story.

Extract 10

(Were you ever in a situation where you thought you were in serious danger of being killed?)

    I talked a man out of – Old Doc Simon I talked him out of pulling the trigger.

When this story is heard, it can be seen that the abstract does encapsulate the point of the story. In 11 there is a sequence of two such abstracts.

Extract 11

(Were you ever in a situation where you were in serious danger of being killed?)

a   My brother put a knife in my head.
    (How'd that happen?)
b   Like kids, you get into a fight
c   and I twisted his arm up behind him.
d   This was just a few days after my father died . . .

Here the speaker gives one abstract and follows it with another after the interviewer's question. Then without further prompting, he begins the narrative proper. The narrative might just as well have begun with the free clause *d; b* and *c* in this sense are not absolutely required, since they cover the same ground as the narrative as a whole. Larry's narrative (see Extract 2) is the third of a series of three, and there is no question just before the narrative itself, but there is a well-formed abstract:

a   An' then, three weeks ago I had a fight with this other dude outside.
b   He got mad
    'cause I wouldn't give him a cigarette.
c   Ain't that a bitch?

Larry does not give the abstract in *place* of the story; he has no intention of stopping there, but goes on to give the full account.

    What then is the function of the abstract? It is not an advertisement or a warning: the narrator does not wait for the listener to say, "I've heard about that," or "Don't tell me that now." If the abstract covers the same ground as the story, what does it add? We will consider this problem further in discussing the evaluation section below.

Orientation

At the outset, it is necessary to identify in some way the time, place, persons, and their activity or the situation. This can be done in the course of the first several narrative clauses, but more commonly there is an orientation section composed of free clauses. In Boot's narrative (Extract 1), clause *a* sets the time (*Sunday*); clause *b* the persons (*we*), the situation (*nothin' to do*) and further specification of the time (*after we come from church*); the first narrative clause follows. In Larry's narrative (Extract 2), some information is already available in the abstract (the time – *three weeks ago*; the place – *outside of school*); and the persons – *this other dude and Larry*). The orientation section then begins with a detailed picture of the situation – *Larry sittin' on the corner, high.*

Many of John L.'s narratives begin with an elaborate portrait of the main character – in this case, clauses *a–i* are all devoted to *the baddest girl in the neighborhood*, and the first narrative clause brings John L. and the girl face to face in the schoolyard.

The orientation section has some interesting syntactic properties; it is quite common to find a great many past progressive clauses in the orientation section – sketching the kind of thing that was going on before the first event of the narrative occurred or during the entire episode. But the most interesting thing about orientation is its *placement*. It is theoretically possible for all free orientation clauses to be placed at the beginning of the narrative, but in practice, we find much of this material is placed at strategic points later on, for reasons to be examined below.

The coda

There are also free clauses to be found at the ends of narratives; for example, John L.'s narrative ends:

cc.   That was one of the most important

This clause forms the *coda*. It is one of the many options open to the narrator for signalling that the narrative is finished. We find many similar forms.

Extract 12
And that was that.

Extract 13
And that – that was it, you know.

Codas may also contain general observations or show the effects of the events of the narrator. At the end of one fight narrative, we have

Extract 14
I was given the rest of the day off.
And ever since then I haven't seen the guy
'cause I quit.
I quit, you know.
No more problems.

Some codas which strike us as particularly skillful are strangely disconnected from the main narrative. One New Jersey woman told a story about how, as a little girl, she thought she was drowning, until a man came along and stood her on her feet – the water was only four-feet deep.

Extract 15

And you know that man who picked me out of the water?
He's a detective in Union City
And I see him every now and again.

These codas (14, 15) have the property of bridging the gap between the moment of time at the end of the narrative proper and the present. They bring the narrator and the listener back to the point at which they entered the narrative. There are many ways of doing this: in 15, the other main actor is brought up to the present: in 14, the narrator. But there is a more general function of codas which subsumes both the examples of 14, 15 and the simpler forms of 12, 13. Codas close off the sequence of complicating actions and indicate that none of the events that followed were important to the narrative. A chain of actions may be thought of as successive answers to the question "Then what happened?"; "And then what happened?" After a coda such as *That was that*, the question "Then what happened?" is properly answered, "Nothing; I just told you what happened." It is even more obvious after the more complex codas of 14 and 15; the time reference of the discourse has been reshifted to the present, so that "what happened then?" can only be interpreted as a question about the present; the answer is "Nothing; here I am." Thus the "Disjunctive" codas of 14 and 15 forestall further questions about the narrative itself: the narrative events are pushed away and sealed off.[3]

Evaluation

Beginnings, middles, and ends of narratives have been analyzed in many accounts of folklore or narrative. But there is one important aspect of narrative which has not been discussed – perhaps the most important element in addition to the basic narrative clause. That is what we term the *evaluation* of the narrative: the means used by the narrator to indicate the point of the narrative, its *raison d'être*: why it was told, and what the narrator is getting at. There are many ways to tell the same story, to make very different points, or to make no point at all. Pointless stories are met (in English) with the withering rejoinder, "So what?" Every good narrator is continually warding off this question; when his narrative is over, it should be unthinkable for a bystander to say, "So what?" Instead, the appropriate remark would be, "He did?" or similar means of registering the reportable character of the events of the narrative.

The difference between evaluated and unevaluated narrative appears most clearly when we examine narrative of vicarious experience. In our first series of interviews with preadolescents in south-central Harlem, we asked for accounts of favorite television programs; the most popular at the time was "The Man from U.N.C.L.E."

Extract 16

a   This kid – Napoleon got shot
b   and he had to go on a mission,
c   And so this kid, he went with Solo.

d   So they went
e   And this guy – they went through the window,
f   and they caught him.
g   And then he beat up them other people.
h   And they went
i   and then he said
     that this old lady was his mother
j   and then he – and at the end he say
     that he was the guy's friend.

This is typical of many such narratives of vicarious experience that we collected. We begin in the middle of things without any orientation section; pronominal reference in many ways ambiguous and obscure throughout. But the meaningless and disorientated effect of 16 has deeper roots. None of the remarkable events that occur *is evaluated*. We may compare 16 with a narrative of personal experience told by Norris W., eleven years old:

Extract 17
a   When I was in fourth grade –
     no, it was in third grade –
b   This boy he stole my glove.
c   He took my glove
d   and said that his father found it downtown on the ground
     (And you fight him?)
e   I told him that it was impossible for him to find downtown
     'cause all those people were walking by
     and just the father was the only one that found it?
f   So he got all (mad).
g   Then I fought him.
h   I knocked him all out in the street.
i   So he say he give.
j   and I kept on hitting him.
k   Then he started crying
l   and ran home to his father.
m   And the father told him
n   that he ain't find no glove.

This narrative is diametrically opposed to 16 in its degree of evaluation. Every line and almost every element of the syntax contributes to the point, and that point is self-aggrandizement. Each element of the narrative is designed to make Norris look good and "this boy" look bad. Norris knew that this boy stole his glove – had the nerve to just walk off with it and then make up a big story to claim that it was his. Norris didn't lose his cool and started swinging; first he destroyed this boy's fabrication by logic, so that everyone could see how phony the kid was. Then this boy lost his head and got mad and started fighting. Norris beat him up, and was so outraged at the phony way he had acted that he didn't stop when the kid surrendered – he "went crazy" and kept on hitting him. Then this punk started crying, and ran home to his father like a baby. Then his father – his *very own father* told him that his story wasn't true.

Norris's story follows the characteristic two-part structure of fight narratives in the BE vernacular; each part shows a different side of his ideal character. In the account of the verbal exchange that led up to the fight, Norris is cool, logical, good with his mouth, and strong in insisting on his own right. In the second part, dealing with the action, he appears as the most dangerous kind of fighter, who "just goes crazy" and "doesn't know what he did." On the other hand, his opponent is shown as dishonest, clumsy in argument, unable to control his temper, a punk, a lame, and a coward. Though Norris does not display the same degree of verbal skill that Larry shows in Extract 2, there is an exact point-by-point match in the structure and evaluative features of the two narratives. No one listening to Norris's story within the framework of the vernacular value system will say "So what?" The narrative makes its point and effectively bars this question.

If we were to look for an evaluation section in 17 concentrating upon clause ordering as in Labov and Waletzky (1967), we would have to point to *d–e*, in which the action is suspended while elaborate arguments are developed. This is indeed the major point of the argument, as shown again in the dramatic coda *m–n*. But it would be a mistake to limit the evaluation of 17 to *d–e*, since evaluative devices are distributed throughout the narrative. We must therefore modify the scheme of Labov and Waletzky (1967) by indicating E as the focus of waves of evaluation that penetrate the narrative as in Figure 14.1.

A complete narrative begins with an orientation, proceeds to the complicating action, is suspended at the focus of evaluation before the resolution, concludes with the resolution, and returns the listener to the present time with the coda. The evaluation of the narrative forms a secondary structure which is concentrated in the evaluation section but may be found in various forms throughout the narrative. . . .

We can also look at narrative as a series of answers to underlying questions:

a   Abstract: what was this about?
b   Orientation: who, when, what, where?
c   Complicating action: then what happened?
d   Evaluation: so what?
e   Result: what finally happened?

Only *c*, the complicating action, is essential if we are to recognize a narrative, as pointed out above. The abstract, the orientation, the resolution, and the evaluation answer questions which relate to the function of effective narrative: the first three to clarify referential functions, the last to answer the functional question *d* – why the story was told in the first place. But the reference of the abstract is broader than the orientation and complicating action: it includes these and the evaluation so that the abstract not only states what the narrative is about, but why it was told. The coda is not given in answer to any of these five questions, and it is accordingly found less frequently than any other element of the narrative. The coda *puts off* a question – it signals that questions *c* and *d* are no longer relevant.

. . .

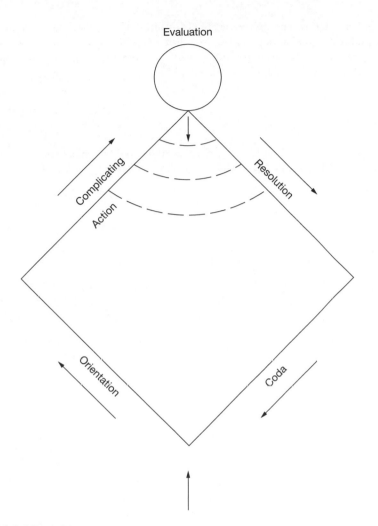

Figure 14.1 Narrative structure

Notes

1   Remarks in parentheses are by the interviewer. The initial questions asked by the interviewer are also given to help clarify the evaluative focus of the narrative.

2   To *put something on someone* means to 'hit him hard'. See also aa, *I put something on it* 'I hit hard'.

3   The coda can thus be seen as one means of solving the problem of indicating the end of a "turn" at speaking. As Harvey Sacks has pointed out, a sentence is an optimal unit for the utterance, in that the listener's syntactic competence is employed in a double sense – to let him know when the sentence is complete and also when it is his turn to talk. Narratives require other means for the narrator to signal the fact that he is beginning a long series of sentences which will form one "turn" and to mark the end of that sequence. Many of the devices we have been discussing here are best understood in terms of how the speaker and the listener let each other know whose turn it is to talk. Traditional folk tales and fairy tales have fixed formulas which do this at the

beginning and the end, but these are not available for personal narratives. It can also be said that a good coda provides more than a mechanical solution for the sequencing problem: it leaves the listener with a feeling of satisfaction and completeness that matters have been rounded off and accounted for.

Reference

Labov, W. and Waletzky, J. (1967) 'Narrative analysis' in *Essays on the Verbal and Visual Arts*, Helm, J. (ed.), Seattle, WA: University of Washington Press, 12–44.

Chapter 15

Derek Edwards

NARRATIVE ANALYSIS

. . .

THERE ARE THREE KINDS of objects at which any analysis of narratives might be aimed: (1) the nature of the *events* narrated; (2) people's perception or *understanding* of events; and (3) the *discourse* of such understandings and events. We can think of these as three crudely separated kinds of analysis.

Type 1: pictures of events
Type 2: pictures of mind
Type 3: discursive actions

Of course, these are ways of approaching any discourse, not just narrative.

Type 1 corresponds to the basic aims of ethnography and oral histories, in which stories and descriptions are collected as a route (however compromised) to the things that are their topic – to matters and events beyond the talk. It is also part of common-sense practices, in ordinary talk, texts, courtrooms, classrooms, and scientific publications, that discourse about events is produced as, and taken to be, a way of telling and finding out about those events, with due caution for lies and errors. Type 2 takes one step back from events themselves, and takes a psychological interest in the speaker. It treats people's discourse as how they 'see' things (again, through a glass however darkly), whether as representatives of groups or cultures, or as individuals. This corresponds to much of cognitive and narrative psychology and cognitive anthropology.

Type 3 focuses on discourse itself, as a performative domain of social action. Both the nature of events (type 1), and the nature of people's perspectives on events

Source: Derek Edwards, *Discourse and Cognition*, London: Sage, 1997.

(type 2), are considered to be *at stake* here (worked up, managed, topicalized, implied, and so on), rather than simply available, in the discourse. Type 3 is broadly characteristic of discursive psychology, and of conversation analysis, rhetorical analysis, sociology of scientific knowledge (SSK), and some varieties of narratology. Type 3 essentially reverses the order of the three. Discourse is, analytically, what we have got, what we start with. Whereas we might assume, common-sensically, that events come first, followed by (distorted) understandings of them, followed by (distorted) verbal expressions of those understandings, type 3 inverts that, and treats both understandings and events themselves as participants' concerns – the stuff the talk works up and deals with.

With these three types in mind we may turn to some ways of defining and analysing narrative, starting with Jerome Bruner's.

> Narrative requires . . . four crucial grammatical constituents if it is to be effectively carried out. It requires, first, a means for emphasizing human '*agentivity*' – action directed toward goals controlled by agents. It requires, secondly, that a sequential order be established and maintained – that events and states be '*linearized*' in a standard way. Narrative, thirdly, also requires a sensitivity to what is canonical and what violates canonicality in human interaction. Finally, narrative requires something approximating a narrator's *perspective*: it cannot, in the jargon of narratology, be 'voiceless'.
>
> (Bruner 1990: 77, emphasis added)

Bruner's broad definition is a useful place to start, in that it is specifically oriented to narrative *psychology*, and because it includes elements of various other descriptive schemes and definitions, such as Kenneth Burke's (1945). Burke suggested a scheme which he called 'dramatism', which deals with matters such as motives, persuasion, stories, and so on, by defining five elements that make up a well-formed story: 'What was done (act), when or where it was done (scene), who did it (agent), how he [*sic*] did it (agency), and why (purpose)' (1945: xv). Bruner (1990) glosses these five elements as: Action, Scene, Actor, Instrument, and Goal. Into these elements is then inserted Trouble, in the form of some kind of imbalance or conflict between the five elements, and this is what gives rise to the subsequent actions, events, and resolutions that make up a coherent, bounded narrative.

A related set of criteria is provided by Kenneth Gergen (1994: 189–90). Well-formed narratives have (1) a valued endpoint, goal, or 'point'; (2) an ordering of events, not necessarily told in the order in which they occur (flashbacks, insertions, etc., are possible); (3) stable identities for the main characters, which may develop; (4) causal links and explained outcomes; (5) demarcation signs – in conversations especially, marking where stories start and end. Gergen's list is clearly similar to Bruner's and to Burke's, and there are others which also draw on general narratology, but none of them are identical. Why not? Are the differences minor and terminological, or are they matters that the authors might insist on? How might the differences be resolved, or, alternatively, by what criteria should we prefer one definition to another? It is not simply a matter of pointing to actual instances of

stories and showing that one definition fits better than another, because each definition specifies, somewhat circularly, what would count as a good ('well-formed')
example.

Definitions of this kind can be understood as analysts' efforts at nailing down
common-sense categories: efforts at defining what a story or narrative is, as distinct
from, say, a sermon, lecture, scientific explanation, or any other discourse category.
The participants themselves display sensitivity to what *that* story should contain,
and one imagines that Bruner's, Burke's, and Gergen's lists accord with those kinds
of participants' sensibilities, although that would be a matter for research rather
than stipulation.

. . .

The more detailed definitions of narrative become, then the more specific they
are to particular genres (for example, Propp 1928/1968) or events, and the less
generally applicable they are as analytic schemes. On the other hand, the looser
their definition, the more they dissolve into the tropes, concerns, and devices of
discourse in general. The problem of too broad a definition, of seeing virtually all
discourse as narrative, is that it starts to lose explanatory power. As Kenneth Gergen
suggests, definitions of narrative can only be definitions of specific cultural forms:
'rather than seek a definitive account [of narrative structure] . . . there is a virtual
infinity of possible story forms, but due to the exigencies of social co ordination,
certain modalities are favored over others in various historical periods' (1994: 195).

Narratology deals with the internal structures of narratives, with distinctions
between narratives of different kinds, and also with distinctions between narratives
and other kinds of discourse. Hayden White (1973) takes from literary theory four
basic categories, *tragedy*, *comedy*, *romance*, and *satire*, and suggests that these are
appropriate labels for a wide range of literary, historical, and everyday narratives.
The four categories have been taken up and applied in a variety of psychologically
oriented treatments of personal narratives, including Gergen and Gergen (1988),
Murray (1989), and Schafer (1976). Kevin Murray provides a concise summary,
which I condense a little further here:

> . . . 'comedy' involves the victory of youth and desire over age and
> death . . . 'Romance' concerns the restoration of the honoured past
> through a series of events that involve a struggle . . . between a hero and
> forces of evil . . . In 'tragedy' the individual fails to conquer evil and is
> excluded from the social unit. The nobility of this failure is contrasted
> with the satire of 'irony', which deals in the discovery that comedy,
> romance, and tragedy are mere schemes of mortals to control experi-
> ence: individuals are not so pure, nor is the social order so healthy.
>
> (1989: 181–2)

It is easy to see how these categories might be applied to actual instances. But even
literary works, let alone ordinary talk, have to be *fitted* to the four types, giving
rise to various sub-types, overlaps, and mixtures. The problem for narrative analysis

is that of *idealization* – the adoption of an analytic category scheme in advance of examining specific instances, perhaps even a scheme whose original domain of application was different (in this case, literary genres), and seeing how something such as stories collected in interviews can be fitted to them.

In order to illustrate the problems of applying category schemes, let us briefly consider a particularly influential one that is widely used in narrative analysis: that of William Labov (1972; Labov and Waletzky 1967; see Chapter 14). Labov's categories of the structure and functions of oral narratives are shown in Extract 15.1, which is an example provided by Catherine Kohler Riessman (1993: 59) in a book on the methodology of narrative analysis. Riessman presents the example positively, as one to which Labov's categories can be usefully applied (Riessman uses the scheme in her own research), rather than as one of the 'many narratives [that] do not lend themselves to Labov's framework' (1993: 59).

Labov's categories are signalled by the letter codes assigned to each numbered line. The codes, as glossed by Riessman, are as follows: 'to provide an Abstract for what follows (A), Orient the listener (O), carry the Complicating Action (CA), Evaluate its meaning (E), and Resolve the action (R)' (1993: 59; note that Labov's scheme also specifies an optional sixth item, a 'Coda' that brings us back to the present). Extract 15.1 is taken from a husband's talk about incidents leading up to a divorce. . . .

Extract 15.1 (Applying Labov's categories)

30	and (.) finally, ah, it's, this is actually a crucial incident	A
31	because I <u>finally</u> got up and (.)	CA
32	and (.) went into the other room	CA
33	(.) she was in the laundry room with the door closed and	O
34	(.) knocked on the door and said	CA
35	'When are you going to be done with this?'	CA
36	'cause we, we were going to talk.	O
37	And she kind of held up her hand like this and went 'no'.	CA
38	And I got absolutely bullshit	E
39	I put my <u>fist</u> through the door ((*Interviewer*: uh-huh))	R
40	which is not the kind of stuff that I, that I do, you know	E
41	I'm <u>not</u> a real physically violent person at <u>all</u>.	E

(Riessman 1993: 59, untimed pauses)

Some of the problems of *applying* Labov's categories *as an analytic scheme*, and by extension other related pre-defined analytic codes and categories, can be seen in this example. The thing to do is to try assigning alternative categories, and see how plausible, or strained, that becomes. Of course, this leaves aside the appropriateness of having subdivided the talk into precisely those twelve discrete 'clauses' (the twelve lines) in the first place. Line 30 is coded as an 'Abstract', although 'a crucial incident' might reasonably be judged an Evaluation rather than a summary of events. Less obviously, try considering line 31 as an Evaluation. The expression 'because I finally got up', including the emphasis on 'finally', surely reinforces the notion of a 'crucial incident' having just taken place, together with a sense of the narrator's judgment (evaluation) of that incident – enough to 'finally' make him get up. Again, it is not clear why 'And I got absolutely bullshit' (line 38) is not a next occurrence or Complicating Action (CA) rather than an Evaluation (E), unless all emotion descriptions are automatically considered Evaluations. Part of the problem here is that the single category 'Complicating Action' (CA) seems to contain the bulk of what one might common-sensically assume is the basic story-line, the sequence of events, which means that, as an analytic scheme for stories, much of the content must remain largely unanalysed.

The category 'Orientation', in Labov's scheme, supposedly informs the listener of the circumstances of the action, a kind of contextual scene-setting – time, place, situation, participants. But surely this under-specifies what is going on in lines 33 and 36. The narrative sense of 'she was in the laundry room with the door closed' is not merely circumstantial; she was not doing the laundry. Rather, it helps define the nature of the wife's actions at that juncture, making a secretive and illicit phone call (she was 'talking to her lover on the phone', Riessman 1993: 59), just as 'we were going to talk' establishes, in contrast to that, the less objectionable activity she was (according to him) supposed to be doing at that time with her husband. . . . What matters with these utterances is not that we categorize them under Orientation, or Complicating Action, or Evaluation, or whatever, and then deal with those categories, but, rather, that we grasp what they are doing, as specific, precisely worded, occasioned formulations.

Without labouring the point, similar kinds of reassignments and complications are possible for the rest of the narrative in Extract 15.1. 'Evaluation' is likely to be a pervasively relevant concern in story-telling, rather than something exclusively coded in a specific item or slot, while the inclusion of an Abstract and Orientation are in any case considered optional in oral narratives (Labov 1972), again leaving 'Complicating Action' with a very heavy and rather uninformative analytic burden. 'Orientation' includes the kinds of story details that can occur anywhere in a narrative, and perform significant business (see Drew 1978, and Schegloff, 1972, on 'formulating place'). In other words, when we come to dealing with specific story details, we are immediately dealing with the contingencies of discourse per se, of descriptions, reports, accounts, and so on, rather than something specific about narrative. It is by collecting stories through interviews, taking them out of the inter-actional (and rhetorical) contexts of their production, and formulating check-list categories of their structural components that we obtain a rather idealized notion of how they work.

The identification of general story schemas across a wide range of stories is clearly an important analytic goal. But despite being derived from and for empirical analysis, Labov's categories are idealized as well as empirical. That is, they define the kinds of things a story *ought* to contain, theoretically, in order to count as a story. They become less useful when used as a set of pre-coded analytic slots into which we should try to place an actual story's contents. The temptation for analysts using the scheme is to start with the categories and see how the things people say can be fitted into them, and, having coded everything as one category or another, to call that the analysis, and then compare it to other findings. In that role, as a coding scheme, these kinds of structural categories impose rather than reveal, obscuring the particularity of specific details, and how that particularity is crucial for the occasioned, action-performative workings of discourse (cf. discussions in Langellier 1989: 248; Linde 1993: 66).

Competing stories

. . . Stories may be rhetorically designed to manage their own credibility, and to counter alternatives. . . . The point I want to emphasize here, which both Bruner and (more emphatically) Gergen also appreciate, is the rhetorical, interaction-oriented nature not only of those kinds of formulations, but of narratives generally.

A basic issue in telling a story of events in your life is where to begin: 'Where one chooses to begin and end a narrative can profoundly alter its shape and meaning' (Riessman 1993: 18). Where to start a story is a major, and rhetorically potent, way of managing causality and accountability. It is an issue not only for personal narratives, but for accounts of all kinds, including histories of nation states, and stories of immigration and ethnicity: who actually belongs where? Starting when? Whose country *is* it? From Britain to Bosnia to New Zealand (Wetherell and Potter 1992), and the so-called 'Indian' natives of North America (Cronon 1992), alternative narratives compete in terms of precisely when and where they start.

Then there is what to include: which words/categories to use? To whom, for whom, for what, and at what juncture is the story told? What alternatives are being countered or aligned with? What current interactional business is being managed? It is not just a matter of possessing a narrative mind, whose mental operations turn events into best-sense personal stories. Telling stories is discursive action doing discursive business. This certainly emerges when studying research interviews, but those essentially work *against* interactional considerations, because they tend to substitute, for the ordinary occasions on which stories might be told, got-up occasions for set-piece performances-for-interview. It is better to collect samples of natural talk, where possible, if we want to see how talk performs interactional work other than informing researchers who are interested in narratives, in family relations, in violence, or social attitudes, or whatever.

As an example of 'where to start', consider Extract 15.2, which occurs near the beginning of Jeff's and Mary's first session with their relationship counsellor. Jeff, it may be noted (for brevity's sake), places his wife's recent affair with another man as the origin of their current marital difficulties. But it is Mary who takes the first opportunity to outline their troubles.

Extract 15.2

```
1   Counsellor:  (. . .) P'haps (.) uh in in in your words
2                or (.) either of your words you better (0.8)
3                st↑art from the beginning as to why:, you
4                went to Relate in the first place, (0.6)
5                and then the difference between the⌈:n and now.
6   Jeff:                                          ⌊Shall I
7                (        ) start now or (      )?=
```

8   *Mary*:   =Uh? (.)

9   *Jeff*:   °'n you jus (.) keep on going.°

10   (.)

11 *Mary*:   Yeh. (.) U:m (3.0) <u>we</u>ll. What happened,

12   Jeff started doing some exa:ms (.) which (.)

13   la:sted abou:t (0.2) four <u>years</u>.= And be<u>fore</u> that,

14   (0.8) >this is when we were living in the

15   hospital,< (.) we was always doing <u>some</u> exa:ms,

16   (1.0) <u>sin</u>ce we've me:t, (0.5) at <u>some</u> point, (.)

17   which has lasted some time.

18   (0.8)

19   Anyway Jeff was doing u:m (.) a degree:, (.) that

20   (0.3) la:sted must've bee:n about (0.5) we were

21   just coming to the e:nd. (0.7) Just last summer.

22   (1.0)

23   A:nd <u>dur</u>ing that time I felt that, (0.8) u:m (1.0)

24   he didn't pay any att<u>en</u>tion to me: that (0.4) um

25   (0.2) ↑alth↑<u>ough</u> we had a s- we still had a fairly

26   good rel<u>a</u>tionship, .hh I didn't feel there was

27   anything wro:ng, .h but (.) <u>a</u>t the time, (.)

28   I ↑didn't really think anything too <u>much</u> abou:t

29   (0.2) these pr↑oblems. (0.6) but (.) it must have

30   all like come to a <u>head</u>. (0.8) Then I felt like

31   he was neg<u>lec</u>ting me:, he didn't wanna know,

32   <u>I</u> was working too har:d, .hh u:m, (0.8) and then

33   I had the two children I felt I was being left on

34   my ow:n, (0.8) uhh (.) an' the:n (.) I started

35   going round with my friends quite a bit, (1.6)

36   u:m, (0.4) ↑<u>just</u> to get out of the <u>hou</u>se.

37   (0.4)

38   For some rel↑ief.

39   (1.0)

40   And then: I <u>met</u> °somebody e:lse,° (0.8) an:d u:m

41   (1.4) <u>had</u> (0.6) an aff<u>air</u>, (.) uh (.) and then I

Rather than starting with her recent affair, Mary starts several years back (lines 12–17) with events that (according to her) led up to it, and therefore somewhat account for it. According to Mary, Jeff's continual and long-term exam preparations led to her feeling neglected (lines 30–1), even though she herself was 'working too har:d' (line 32) and had the children to look after. Mary's own hard work stands as a counter to any suggestion (which Jeff actually develops later) that he was doing all the work for the family while she went off and indulged herself. The affair itself is offered by Mary as an understandable event-in-sequence, a sequence culpably implicating Jeff, and an unlooked-for consequence of her going out with friends, '↑just to get out of the <u>hou</u>se. (0.4) For some rel↑ief' (lines 34–8).

The rhetorical design of Mary's story (which continues beyond the extract provided) is clear, even without a full interactional analysis of her various accounts, and of Jeff's, which I shall not provide here. In starting her story with events prior to the affair, and in formulating those events in specific ways, Mary manages to provide an accountable basis for her actions, while at the same time attending to likely (and no doubt familiar, and in any case forthcoming) counter-versions from Jeff. Any notion of an irresponsible *neglect* of her family (a notion which Jeff later develops) is countered, ahead of its production in counselling, by an account of *his prior* neglect of her. Any notion that their problems are those of a *happy marriage* spoiled by a wife's sexual adventures (another of Jeff's themes) are countered by the prior problems she outlines. And, should Jeff try to claim that everything was *basically* fine between them prior to the affair (which he does), Mary attends to that ('we still had a fairly good re<u>la</u>tionship, .hh I didn't feel there was anything wro:ng', lines 25–7), while recounting the underlying, partly unnoticed (and there- fore uncomplained-of, should he point that out) pattern of neglect. There is an interaction-oriented exquisiteness in the detail and subtlety of these kinds of stories (and more that I have not picked out here) that is easily missed on a first reading, and missable altogether where stories of this kind are collected and analysed struc- turally, and in isolation, or as reflections of events or cognitions.

Narrative truth and authenticity

In the social and human sciences, in anthropological, ethnographic, psychological, and other research domains, narrative analysis is generally a matter of collecting interviews about particular kinds of life experiences (for example Linde 1993, recorded interviews on choice of profession), and fitting them to various analytical categories and schemas.

> The purpose is to see how respondents in interviews impose order on the flow of experience to make sense of events and actions in their lives. The methodological approach examines the informant's story and analyses how it is put together, the linguistic and cultural resources it draws on, and how it persuades a listener of authenticity.
>
> (Riessman 1993: 2)

These notions of 'persuasion' and 'authenticity' reflect a recurrent theme in narra- tive theory, which is the interpersonal functions of story-telling. Despite that theme, interactional orientations tend to be underplayed *in actual analyses* of narratives, by virtue of the focus on structural story schemas, data from interviews and written literature, and in the location of narrative studies within the theoretical domains of self, identity, and personal growth.

As Riessman (1993) notes, in the 'life story method' (for example, Bruner 1990; Josselson and Lieblich 1993; Murray 1989; Plummer 1995) the usual thing is to mix analysis and data, and blur the distinction. Rather than focusing analysis on transcribed materials and their interactional settings, the analyst uses quotations from informants' talk as illustrations of analysts' summaries, gists, generalizations, and glosses. This glosses-and-quotes treatment of discourse materials is reminiscent of essays on works of literature, though sometimes transcripts are also used (Linde 1993; Young 1987; see Chapter 28). Generally, the analyst's 'authorial voice and interpretative commentary knit the disparate elements together and determine how readers are to understand [the informant's] experience. . . . Illustrative quotes from the interview provide evidence for the investigator's interpretation of the plot twists' (Riessman 1993: 30).

One advantage of interviewing-for-narratives is that it allows participants to develop long turns and tell things 'in their own way', in contrast to the more question–answer kinds of format used in other interview research, where personal narratives and 'anecdotal' replies may even be systematically prevented from developing. More structured research methods (questionnaires, experiments, structured interviews, etc.) may treat personal stories as some kind of noise or nuisance, to be discouraged by the use of standard questions, fixed topics, a fixed range of possible responses, and/or analytic methods that break up and lose whatever conversational or narrative flow might still have been captured on audiotape. Nevertheless, narrative interviewing is still interviewing, and 'in their own way' tends to be treated as definitive of how respondents 'see' things, rather than an instance of interaction-oriented talk.

'Authenticity' in life story interview studies is generally taken not as a participants' concerted accomplishment, something discursively constructed, but, rather, as some kind of built-in feature bequeathed by the methodology of collecting personal stories (in contrast to more impersonal methodologies). Non-authenticity in such settings may be treated as a kind of forgivable *abberation*, behind which may nevertheless lie a deeper, and recoverable, psychological truth: 'When talking about their lives, people lie sometimes, forget a lot, exaggerate, become confused, and get things wrong. Yet they *are* revealing truths. These truths don't reveal the past "as it actually was", aspiring to a standard of objectivity. They give us instead the truths of our experiences' (Personal Narratives Group 1989: 261, original emphasis).

This is a 'type 2' treatment of discourse, approaching it as a kind of window on participants' perspectives. Again, it is essential to separate the notion I am promoting here of discourse's action-orientation from any notion that this is a cynical and mistrusting way to deal with people. It is neither to trust nor to mistrust, but to analyse. It is to treat *all* talk as performative, as action-oriented, as doing something, such that issues of sincerity, truth, honest confession, lies, errors, confabulations, and so on, are matters that talk itself must manage, and *does* manage, in analysable ways. The management of authenticity, as a participants' concern or accomplishment, is explored in a wide variety of discourse studies. These include Edwards and Potter (1992), Lynch and Bogen (1996), and Wooffitt (1992) on factual authenticity and the credibility of reports; Widdicombe (1993) and Widdicombe and Wooffitt (1995) on persons as authentic members, holders of, or spokespersons for a particular social identity; and Whalen and Zimmerman (1990) on how those two things (personal identity and the authenticity of reports) may be managed simultaneously.

For example, Sue Widdicombe and Robin Wooffitt (1995) are concerned with the discourse of social identity. In their materials, 'authenticity' is at stake with regard to membership (and therefore speakers' rights to talk *as* members) of a youth sub-culture whose appearance, tastes, and other preferences might be taken as signs of mere conformity to a standard group image. Respondents deal with that issue by telling fragments of life stories that build authentic membership in terms of self-expression or personal choice. Like Mary does with regard to Jeff (Extract 15.2 above) . . . one way they do it is to place decisive details *further back* in the 'taleworld' of events than the rhetorical alternative would require. In Extract 15.3, 'MR1' is a 'goth' talking to an interviewer, 'I'. The important notion here, in the context of analysing personal narratives, is how the notion of a 'true self' is discursively managed, rather than being something that is simply available in this kind of talk, lying behind and generating it.

Extract 15.3

```
 1   MR1:   yeah 'cos I started wearing make up, and I
 2          didn't even know about other people wearing it
 3          1 st- I star- I just started wearing it and
 4          putting on these black clothes and things like
 5          that an' then ⎡ I went
 6   I:                  ⎣ ahha
 7   MR1    I went into town one week because like I was
 8          considered really freaky by everybody
 9          because .hh all these people who lived on this
10          estate hadn't ever seen anybody like me before (.)
11          I went into town one evening an' walked by this
12          pub an' saw loads of people with hair, spiked up
13          an' things like that an' er a lot more way out than
14          me even though I was considered the biggest freak
15          of the area- they were a lot more way out than me-
                   (from Widdicombe and Wooffitt (1995: 148))
```

Widdicombe and Wooffitt focus on how, in snatches of 'autobiography', respondent 'MR1' manages his authenticity, both as an independent agent, and also as a member of a sub-cultural group. His narrated change of appearance, in the way it is described as personal and spontaneous, and in its sequential placing prior to his knowledge of other people looking similar (lines 1–4), follows a pattern of narrative accountability found across a range of other interviews. MR1's story rhetorically counters any 'negative inferences regarding the reasons for that change . . . that speakers were copying or influenced by others, or conforming to a particular image' (1995: 149). The narrative in lines 7 to 15 (which runs on after line 15) is produced as a specific episode within a larger pattern of events, in which the speaker had already started, spontaneously, to adopt the persona that would eventually make him identifiable as a member of a group.

Widdicombe and Wooffitt's analysis brings out the way in which autobiographical stories are intrinsically, and in detail, interaction-oriented and rhetorical. Personal stories attend to motive and accountability, to alternative readings, alternative identities. Bruner suggests that young children learn to narrate events within the context of family relations, disputes, and the negotiation of identities, where 'narrative becomes an instrument for telling not only what happened but also why it justified the action recounted . . . narrating becomes not only an expository act but a rhetorical one' (1990: 86–7). This should not be thought of as something restricted to people with especially delicate identities to manage. It is an issue also even for the most literary and interactionally marooned of written autobiographies (Freeman 1993), although the interaction-oriented nature of autobiographical discourse emerges most clearly in spoken interaction, and through applying the kinds of discursive and conversation analytic methods used by Widdicombe and Wooffitt.

References

Bruner, J.S. (1990) *Acts of Meaning*, Cambridge, MA: Harvard University Press.

Burke, K. (1945) *A Grammar of Motives*, New York: Prentice Hall.

Cronon, W. (1992) 'A place for stories: nature, history, and narrative', *Journal of American History* 78 (4): 1347–76.

Drew, P. (1978) 'Accusations: the occasioned use of members' knowledge of "religious geography" in describing events', *Sociology* 12: 1–22.

Edwards, D. and Potter, J. (1992) *Discursive Psychology*, London: Sage.

Freeman, M. (1993) *Rewriting the Self: History, Memory, Narrative*, London: Routledge.

Gergen, K.J. (1994) *Realities and Relationships*, Cambridge, MA: Harvard University Press.

—— and Gergen, M.M. (1988) 'Narrative and self as relationship', in L. Berkowitz (ed.) *Advances in Experimental Social Psychology*, New York: Academic Press.

Josselson, R. and Lieblich, A. (eds) (1993) *The Narrative Study of Lives*, volume 1, London: Sage.

Labov, W. (1972) *Language of the Inner City*, Philadelphia, PA: Philadelphia University Press.

—— and Waletzky, J. (1967) 'Narrative analysis: oral versions of personal experience', in J. Helm (ed.) *Essays on the Verbal and Visual Arts*, Seattle, WA: University of Washington Press.

Langellier, K.M. (1989) 'Personal narratives: perspectives on theory and research', *Text and Performance Quarterly* 9 (4): 243–76.

Linde, C. (1993) *Life Stories: The Creation of Coherence*, Oxford: Oxford University Press.

Lynch, M. and Bogen, D. (1996) *The Spectacle of History: Speech, Text, and Memory at the Iran–Contra Hearings*, Durham, NC: Duke University Press.

Murray, K.D. (1989) 'The construction of identity in the narratives of romance and comedy', in J. Shotter and K.J. Gergen (eds) *Texts of Identity*, London: Sage.

Personal Narratives Group (eds) (1989) *Interpreting Women's Lives: Feminist Theory and Personal Narratives*, Indianapolis, IN: Indiana University Press.

Plummer, K. (1995) 'Life story research', in J.A. Smith, R. Harré and L. Van Langenhove (eds) *Rethinking Methods in Psychology*, London: Sage.

Propp, V.J. (1928/1968) *Morphology of te Folktale*, Austin, TX: University of Texas Press.

Riessman, C.K. (1993) *Narrative Analysis*, London: Sage.

Schafer, R. (1976) *A New Language for Psychoanalysis*, New Haven, CT: Yale University Press.

Schegloff, E.A. (1972) 'Notes on a conversational practice: formulating place', in D. Sudnow (ed.) *Studies in Social Interaction*, Glencoe, IL: Free Press.

Wetherell, M. and Potter, J. (1992) *Mapping the Language of Racism: Discourse and the Legitimation of Exploitation*, Hemel Hempstead: Harvester Wheatsheaf.

Whalen, M.R. and Zimmerman, D.H. (1990) 'Describing trouble: practical epistemology in citizen calls to the police', *Language and Society* 19: 465–92.

White, H. (1973) *Metahistory: The Historical Imagination in Nineteenth Century Europe*, Baltimore, MD: Johns Hopkins University Press.

Widdicombe, S. (1993) 'Autobiography and change: rhetoric and authenticity of "gothic" style', in E. Burman and I. Parker (eds) *Discourse Analytic Research: Repertoires and Readings of Texts in Action*, Hemel Hempstead: Harvester Wheatsheaf.

—— and Wooffitt, R. (1995) *The Language of Youth Subcultures: Social Identity in Action*, Hemel Hempstead: Harvester Wheatsheaf.

Wooffitt, R.C. (1992) *Telling Tales of the Unexpected: The Organization of Factual Discourse*, Hemel Hempstead: Harvester Wheatsheaf.

Young, K.G. (1987) *Taleworlds and Storyrealms: The Phenomenology of Narrative*, Dordrecht: Martinus Nijhoff.

Chapter 16

Harvey Sacks

'THE BABY CRIED. THE MOMMY PICKED IT UP'

. . .

T HE INITIAL DATA is the first two sentences from a 'story' offered by a two year and nine months old girl to the author of the book *Children Tell Stories*. It goes: 'The baby cried. The mommy picked it up.' I shall first make several observations about these two sentences. . . .

When I hear, 'The baby cried. The mommy picked it up,' one thing I hear is that the mommy who picks the baby up is the mommy of the baby. That is a first observation. (You will, of course, notice that the second sentence lacks a genitive. It does not read, 'Its mommy picked it up,' or variants thereof.)

Now it is not only that *I* hear that the mommy is the mommy of the baby, but I feel rather confident that, at least many of the natives among you hear that also. That is a second observation.

Is it some kind of magic?

One of my tasks is going to be to construct an apparatus which will provide for the foregoing facts to have occurred; an apparatus, that is, which will show how it is that we come to hear the fragment as we do.

Some more: I take it we hear two sentences. Call the first S1, and the second S2; the first reports an occurrence, O1, and the second reports an occurrence, O2. Now, I take it we hear that as S2 follows S1, so O2 followed O1. That is a third observation. And also: We hear that O2, occurs because of O1; that is, the, explanation for O2 occurring is that O1 did. That is a fourth observation.

I want the apparatus to show how we come to hear those facts also.

If, I asked you to explain the group of observations which I have made, observations which you could have made just as well — and let me note, they are *not*

Source: Harvey Sacks, *Lectures on Conversation*, Volume 1. Edited by Gail Jefferson, Oxford: Blackwell, 1992, 243–51. (Based on a lecture draft dated 20 February 1966.)

proposed as sociological findings, but rather do they pose some of the problems which sociology shall have to resolve – you might well say something like the following: We hear that it is the mommy of the baby who picks the baby up, because she's the one who ought to pick it up, and (you might eventually add) if she's the one who ought to pick it up, and it was picked up by somebody who could be her, then it was her, or was probably her.

You might go on: While it is quite clear that not any two consecutive sentences, nor even any consecutive sentences that report occurrences are heard, and properly heard, as reporting that the occurrences have occurred in the order which the sentences have, if the occurrences ought to occur in that order, and if there is no information to the contrary (such as a phrase at the beginning, of the second, like 'before that, however') then the order of the sentences indicates the order of the occurrences. And these two sentences do present the order of the occurrences they report in the proper order for such occurrences. If the baby cried it ought to have cried before the mother picked it up, and not after. Hearing it that way the second is explained by the first; hearing them as simultaneous or with the second preceding the first, some further explanation is needed and none being present we may suppose that it is not needed.

Now let me make a fifth observation: All of the foregoing can be done by many or perhaps any of us without knowing what baby or what mommy it is that might be being talked of.

With this fifth observation it may now be noticed that what we've essentially been saying so far is that the pair of sentences seem to satisfy what a Member might require of some pair of sentences for them to be recognizable as 'a possible description.' They 'sound like a description' and some form of words can, apparently, sound like a description. To recognize that some form of words is a possible description does not require that one must first inspect the circumstances it may be characterizing.

That 'possible descriptions' are recognizable as such, is quite an important fact, for Members, and for sociologists.

The, reader ought to be able to think out some of its import for Members; for example, the economies it affords them. It is the latter clause, 'and for sociologists,' that I wish to now attend.

Were it not so both that Members have an activity they do, 'describing,' and that at least, some cases of that activity produced, for them, forms of words recognizable as at least possible descriptions without having to do an inspection of the circumstances they might characterize, then it might well be that sociology would necessarily be the last of the sciences to be doable. For, unless sociologists could study such things as these 'recognizable descriptions,' we might only be able to investigate such activities of Members as in one or another way turned on 'their knowledge of the world' when sociologists could employ some established, presumptively correct scientific characterizations of the phenomena Members were presumably dealing with, knowing about.

If, however, Members have a phenomenon, 'possible descriptions' which are recognizable per se, then the sociologist need not in the first instance know how it is that babies and mommies do behave to examine the composition of such possible descriptions as Members produce and recognize. Sociology and anthropology need not await developments in botany or genetics or analyses of the light spectra to gain a secure position from which Members' knowledge, and the activities for which it is relevant, might be investigated.

What the sociologist ought to seek to build is an apparatus which will provide for how it is that any activities, which Members do in such a way as to be recognizable as such to Members, are done, and done recognizably. Such an apparatus may be called 'a culture.' It will of course generate and provide for the recognizability of more than just 'possible descriptions'.

My reason for having gone through the observations I have so far made was to give you some sense, right off, of the fine power of a culture. It does not merely fill brains in roughly the same way, it fills them so that they are alike in fine detail. The sentences we are considering are after all rather minor, and yet the operation of the culture, whatever it will look like, is such that you all, or many of you, hear just what I said you heard, and many of us are quite unacquainted with each other. I am, then, dealing with something real and something finely powerful.

We may begin to work at the construction of the apparatus. I'm going to introduce several of the terms we need. The first term is 'membership categorization device' (or just 'categorization device'). By this term I shall intend: Any collection of membership categories, containing at least a category, which may be applied to some population containing at least a Member, so as to provide, by the use of some rules of applications, for the pairing of at least a population Member and a categorization device member. A device is then a collection plus rules of application.

An instance of a categorization device is the one called 'sex:' its collection is the two categories (male, female). It is important to observe that a collection consists of categories 'that go together:' For now, that may merely be seen as a constraint of the following sort; I could say that some set of categories were a collection, and be wrong. I shall present some rules of application very shortly.

Before doing that, however, let me observe that 'baby' and 'mommy' can be seen to be categories from one collection: The collection whose device is called 'family' and which consists of such categories as (baby, mommy, daddy, etc.) where by 'etcetera' we mean that there are others, but not any others, not, for example, 'shortstop'.

Let me introduce a few rules of application. It may be observed that if a Member uses a single category from any membership categorization device then they can be recognized to be doing *adequate reference* to a person. We may put the observation in a negative form: It is not necessary that some multiple of categories from categorization devices be employed for recognition, that a person is being referred to, to be made; a single category will do. (We do not by this mean that more cannot be used, only that for reference to persons to be recognized more need not be used.) With that observation we can formulate a 'reference satisfactoriness' rule, which we call the 'economy rule.' It holds: A single category from any membership categorization device can be referentially adequate.

A second rule I call the 'consistency rule,' It holds: If some population of persons is being categorized and if a category from some device's collection has been used to categorize a first Member of the population, then that category or other categories of the same collection *may* be used to categorize further Members of the population. The former rule was a 'reference satisfactoriness' rule; this latter one is a 'relevance' rule.

The economy rule having provided for the adequate reference of 'baby,' the consistency rule tells us that if the first person has been categorized as 'baby' then further persons may be referred to by other categories of a collection of which it is a Member, and thus that such other categories as 'mommy' and 'daddy' are relevant given the use of 'baby.'

While in its currently weak form and alone, the consistency rule may exclude no category of any device, even in this weak form (the 'may' form – we shall eventually introduce a 'must' form) a corollary of it will prove to be useful. The corollary is a hearer's maxim. It holds: If two or more categories are used to categorize two or more Members to some population, and those categories can be heard as categories from the same collection, hear them that way. Let us call the foregoing 'the consistency rule corollary.' It has the following sort of usefulness. Various membership categorization device categories can be said to be ambiguous. That is, the same categorial word is a term occurring in several distinct devices, and can in each have quite a different reference; they may or may not be combinably usable about a single person. So, for example, 'baby' occurs in the device 'family' and also in the device 'stage of life' whose categories are such as (baby, child, . . . adult). A hearer who can use the consistency rule corollary will regularly not even notice that there might be an ambiguity in the use of some category among a group which it can be used to hear as produced via the consistency rule.

It is of course clear that the two categories 'baby' are sometimes combinably referential and sometimes not. A woman may refer to someone as 'my baby' with no suggestion that she is using the category that occurs in the stage of life device; her baby may well be a full-fledged adult. In the case at hand that problem does not occur, and we shall be able to provide the bases for its not occurring, i.e., the bases for the legitimacy of hearing the single term 'baby' as referring to a person located by reference both to the device 'family' and to the device 'stage of life.'

With this, let us modify the observations of [the first full paragraph on this page, above] as follows: The consistency rule tells us that if a first person has been categorized as 'baby' the further persons may be referred to by categories from either the device 'family' or from the device 'stage of life.' However, if a hearer has a second category which can be heard as consistent with one locus of a first then the first is to be heard as *at least* consistent with the second.

Given the foregoing we may proceed to show how the combined reference of 'baby' is heard for our two sentences, and also how 'the mommy' is heard as 'the mommy of the baby.' We shall deal with the latter task first, and we assume from now on that the consistency rule corollary has yielded at least that 'baby' and 'mommy' are heard as from the device 'family.' We assume that without prejudice to the further fact that 'baby' is also heard as 'baby' from the device 'stage of life.'

The device 'family' is one of a series which you may think of by a prototypical name, 'team.' One central property of such devices is that they are, what I am going to call, 'duplicatively organized.' I mean with that term to point out the following:

When such a device is used on a population what is done is to take its categories, treat the set of categories as defining a unit, and place Members of the population into cases of the unit. If a population so treated is counted, one counts not numbers of daddies, numbers of mommies and numbers of babies, but numbers of families – numbers of 'whole families,' numbers of 'families without fathers,' etc.

A population so treated is partitioned into cases of the unit, cases for which what properly holds is that the various persons partitioned into any case are 'co-incumbents' of that case.

To these ways of dealing with populations categorized by way of devices that are duplicatively organized there are correlative 'hearer's maxims.' One that is relevant to our current task holds: If some population has been categorized by use of categories from some device whose collection has the 'duplicative organization' property, and a Member is presented with a categorized population which *can be heard* as co-incumbents of a case of that device's unit, then hear it that way. (We shall consider the italicized phrase shortly.) Now let it be noticed that this rule is of far more general scope than we may seem to need, and in focussing on a property like 'duplicative organization' it permits a determination of an expectation (of sociologists) as to how some categorized population will be heard independently of a determination of how it is heard. It is then formal and predictive, as well of course as quite general.

Now, by the phrase 'can be heard' we mean to rule out predictions of the following sort. Some duplicatively organized devices have proper numbers of incumbents for certain categories of any unit. (At any given time a nation-state may have but one president, a family but one father, a baseball team but one shortstop on the field, etc.) If more incumbents of a category are proposed as present in the population than a unit's case can properly take then the 'can be heard' constraint is not satisfied, and a prediction would not be made.

The foregoing analysis shows us then how it is that we come to hear, given the fact that the device 'family' is duplicatively organized, and the 'can be heard' constraint being satisfied, 'the mommy' to be 'the mommy of the baby.' It does of course much more than that. It permits us to predict, and to understand how we can predict, that a statement such as: 'The first baseman looked around. The third baseman scratched himself . . .' will be heard as saying 'the first baseman of the team on which the third baseman is also a player . . .' and the converse.

Or, putting the claim more precisely, it shows us how, in part. In part, because for the materials at hand it happens that there are other means for providing that the same hearing be made, means which can operate in combination with the foregoing – otherwise sufficient ones – to further assure the hearings we have observed. . . . Let us now undertake our second task, to show how 'the baby' is heard in its combined form, i.e., as the category with that name from both the 'stage of life' device, and from the 'family' device.

Let me introduce a term which I am going to call 'category-bound activities.' While I shall not now give an intendedly careful definition of the term, what I shall do is to indicate what I mean to notice with it and then in a while offer a procedure for determining for some of its proposed cases that they are indeed cases of it. By the term I intend to notice that many activities are taken by Members to be done by some particular or several particular categories of Members where the categories are categories from membership categorization devices.

Let me notice then, as is obvious to you, that 'cry' is bound to 'baby;' that is, to the category 'baby' which is a member of the collection from the 'stage of life' device. Again, the fact that Members know that this is so only serves, for the sociologist, to pose some problem. What we want is to construct some means by reference to which a class, which proposedly contains at least the activity-category 'cry' and presumably others, may have the inclusion of its candidate-members assessed. We will not be claiming that the procedure is definitive as to exclusion of a candidate-member, but we will claim that it is definitive as to inclusion of a candidate-member.

It may be observed that the members of the 'stage of life' collection are 'positioned' (baby . . . adolescent . . . adult . . .), an observation which, for now, we shall leave unexamined. I want to describe a procedure for praising or degrading Members, the operation of which consists of the use of the fact that some activities are 'category-bound.' If there are such procedures, that will provide one strong sense of the notion 'category-bound activities' and also will provide for any given candidate activity a means of warrantably deciding that it is a member of the class of category-bound activities.

For some positioned-category devices it can be said as between any two categories of such a device that A is either higher or lower than B, and if A is higher than B, and B is higher than C, then A is higher than C.

We have some activity which is a candidate-member of the class 'category-bound activities' and which is proposedly bound to some category C. Then, a member of either A or B who does that activity may be seen to be degrading himself, and may be said to be 'acting like a C.' Alternatively if some candidate-activity is proposedly bound to A, a member of C who does it is subject to being said to be acting like an A where that assertion constitutes 'praising.'

If we, using the 'stage of life' categories, subject 'crying' to such a test we do find that its candidacy as a member of the class 'category-bound activities' is warrantable. In the case of 'crying' the results are even stronger. For, it appears, if a 'baby' is subject to some circumstances which would for such a one warrant crying, and he does not, then his 'not crying' is observable, and may be used to propose that he is acting like a big boy where that assertion is taken to be 'praise.'

The foregoing procedure can obviously enough be used for other devices and other candidate-activities. Other procedures may also be used; for example, one way to decide that an activity is category-bound is to see whether, the fact of membership being unknown, it can be 'hinted at' by naming the activity as something one does.

S: So, you can't watch television. Is there anything you can stay
      interested in?
C: No, not really.
S: What interests did you have before?
C: I was a hair stylist at one time. I did some fashions now and then.
      Things like that.
S: Then why aren't you working?

C: Because I don't want to, I guess. Maybe that's why.

S: But do you find that you just can't get yourself going?

C: No. Well, as far as the job goes?

S: Yes.

C: Well, I'll tell you. I'm afraid. I'm afraid to go out and look for a job. That's what I'm afraid of. But more, I think I'm afraid of myself because I don't know. I'm just terribly mixed up.

S: You haven't had any troubles with anyone close to you?

C: Close to me. Well, I've been married three times and I'm– Close, you mean, as far as arguments or something like that?

S: Yes.

C: No, nobody real close. I'm just a very lonely person. I guess I'm very–

S: There's nobody who loves you.

C: Well, I feel that somebody must some place, but I don't know where or who.

S: Have you been having some sexual problems?

C: All my life.

S: Uh huh. Yeah.

C: Naturally. You probably suspect – as far as the hair stylist and – either go one way or the other. There is a straight or homosexual, something like that. I'm telling you, my whole life is just completely mixed up and turned over and it's just smashed and smashed and I'm not kidding.

Having constructed a procedure which can warrant the candidacy of some activity as a member of the class category-bound activities, and which warrants the membership of 'cry' and provides for its being bound to 'baby,' i.e., that category 'baby' which is a member of the 'stage of life' collection, we move on to see how it is that 'the baby' in our sentence is heard in the combined reference we have proposed.

We need, first, another hearer's maxim: If a category-bound activity is asserted to have been done by a member of some category where, if that category is ambiguous (i.e., is a member of at least two different devices) but where at least for one of those devices the asserted activity is category-bound to the given category, then hear that *at least* the category from the device to which it is bound is being asserted to hold.

The foregoing maxim will then provide for hearing 'The baby cried' as referring to at least 'baby' from the 'stage of life' device. The results obtained from the use of the consistency rule corollary being independent of that, are combinable with it. The consistency rule corollary gave us at least that 'the baby' was the category from the device 'family.' The combination gives us both.

If our analysis seems altogether too complicated for the rather simple facts we have been examining, then we invite the reader to consider that our machinery has intendedly been 'overbuilt.' That is to say it may turn out that the elaborateness of our analysis, or its apparent elaborateness, will disappear when one begins to consider the amount of work that the very same machinery can perform.

Chapter 17

Anita Pomerantz

PREFERENCE IN CONVERSATION: AGREEING AND DISAGREEING WITH ASSESSMENTS

ONE SYSTEMATIC ENVIRONMENT in which assessments are proffered is in turns just subsequent to coparticipants' initial assessments. Just as the proffering of an initial assessment is the first speaker's claim of access to the assessed referent, the proffering of a second is the second speaker's claim of access to that referent.[1] The description of assessment pairs as serial claims of access, however, leaves unexplicated the procedures used to coordinate the assessments: the initial one with an anticipated next and a subsequent one with the just prior. This analysis now turns to some of the features of the coordination of second assessments with their priors.[2] Second assessments have been described as subsequent assessments that refer to the same referents as in the prior assessments. This feature may be restated as a speaker's procedural rule: A recipient of an initial assessment turns his or her attention to that which was just assessed and proffers his or her own assessment of this referent. Though speakers do coordinate their second assessments with the prior ones by assessing the same referents, there are finer ways in which they coordinate their talk. Consider the following sequence of assessments:

(10) (JS. II.28)

    J: T's- tsuh beautiful day out isn't it?
    L: Yeh it's jus' gorgeous . . .

J's initial assessment is an expression of approval, incorporating the positive descriptor "beautiful." In proffering a praise assessment, he invites the recipient to coparticipate in praising the referent, that is, to agree with him by proffering a subsequent praise assessment. In a next turn to an assessment that invites

Source: Anita Pomerantz, 'Agreeing and disagreeing with assessments: some features of preferred/dispreferred turn shapes', in J. Maxwell Atkinson and John Heritage (eds) *Structures of Social Action*, Cambridge: Cambridge University Press, 1984, 57–101.

agreement, a recipient may, and often does, elect to agree with the prior. In datum (10) above, L's second assessment is a second praise assessment; it is a second expression of approval, incorporating the positive descriptor "gorgeous." The initial assessment invites a subsequent agreement; the second assessment is proffered as an agreement.

While a recipient may elect to agree with a prior assessment that invites agreement, the recipient may alternatively elect to disagree. The following excerpt illustrates this option:

> (22) (NB: IV: 11.-1)
>
> A₁ A: <u>God</u> izn it <u>dreary</u>.
>
>   (0.6)
>
>   A: ⌈ Y'know I don't think-
>
> A₂ B: ⌊ ·hh- It's <u>warm</u> though,

A's initial assessment is a complaint about the weather, incorporating the negative descriptor "dreary." In proffering the complaint, A invites the recipient, B, to coparticipate in complaining about the weather — to agree with her by proffering a subsequent complaint assessment.[3]

B's second assessment is proffered as a partial disagreement with A's prior complaint. The inclusion of "though" does the work of claiming to agree with the prior while marking, and accompanying, a shift in assessed parameters which partially contrasts with the prior. It contrasts insofar as it is not proffered as a subsequent complaint assessment.[4]

It was proposed earlier that the proffering of an initial assessment to a recipient who may expectably claim access to the referent assessed provides the relevance of the recipient's second assessment. It was also suggested that this proposal, as it stands, leaves unexplicated the ways in which the parts of the assessment pairs are coordinated one with the other. A refinement of the earlier proposal is now in order.

In proffering an initial assessment, a speaker formulates the assessment so as to accomplish an action or multiple actions, for example, praise, complain, compliment, insult, brag, self-deprecate. In the next turn to the initial proffering, an action by the recipient is relevant: to agree or disagree with the prior. Agreement/disagreement names alternative actions that become relevant upon the profferings of initial assessments. Such agreements and disagreements are performed, by and large, with second assessments.

The proffering of an initial assessment, though it provides for the relevance of a recipient's agreement *or* disagreement, may be so structured that it invites one next action over its alternative. A next action that is oriented to as invited will be called a *preferred next action*; its alternative, a *dispreferred next action*.

Agreement is a preferred next action across a large diversity of initial assessments.[5] Agreement is not *invariably* — across all initial assessments — a preferred next action. What is the preferred next action is structured, in part, by the action performed with the initial assessment. For example, subsequent to a self-deprecation, the usual preference for agreement is nonoperative: An agreement with a prior self-deprecation is dispreferred. . . .

An import of the preference status of actions is that it bears on how those actions are performed. Isolatable turn-and-sequence shapes provide for different kinds of actualizations of the actions being performed with and through them. Two types of shapes are of interest for this study: One type is a design that maximizes the occurrences of the actions being performed with them, utilizes minimization of gap between its initiation and prior turn's completion, and contains components that are explicitly stated instances of the action being performed. The other type minimizes the occurrences of the actions performed with them, in part utilizing the organization of delays and nonexplicitly stated action components, such as actions other than a conditionally relevant next. The respective turn shapes will be called *preferred-action turn shape* and *dispreferred-action turn shape*.

. . .

Agreements (agreement preferred)

For a recipient to agree with a prior assessment, he or she should show that *his or her* assessment of the referent just assessed by the prior speaker stands in agreement with the prior speaker's assessment. Different types of agreements are produced with second assessments.

One type of agreement is the *upgrade*. An upgraded agreement is an assessment of the referent assessed in the prior that incorporates upgraded evaluation terms relative to the prior.[6] Two common techniques for upgrading evaluations are:

(1)   A stronger evaluative term than the prior, given graded sets of descriptors, is selected:

>   (10) (JS. II.28)
>   J: T's- tsuh beautiful day out isn't it?
>   →   L: Yeh it's just gorgeous . . .
>
>   (13) (M.Y.)
>   A: That (heh) s(heh) sounded (hhh)
>   g(hh)uh!
>   →   B: That sound' —— that sounded <u>lovely</u> . . .
>
>   (18) (MC: 1)
>   A: Isn't he cute
>   →   B: O::h he: :s a: :DORable

(2)   An intensifier modifying the prior evaluative descriptor is included:

>   (23) (CH: 4.-14)
>   M: You must admit it was fun the night we
>   we ⌊nt down
>   →   J: ⌈It was great fun . . .

(24) (SBL: 2.1.8.-5)

    B: She seems like a nice little ⎡lady

→   A: ⎣Awfully nice

       little person.

(7) (JS: I: 11)

    E: Hal couldn' get over what a good <u>buy</u> that

       was, ⎡(Jon),

→   J: ⎣Yeah That's a r- e (rerry good buy).

. . .

Another type of agreement is *same* evaluation. In this type, a recipient asserts the same evaluation as the prior speaker's evaluation. To assert the same evaluation, a recipient may repeat the prior evaluative terms, marking it as a second in a like series with, for example, "too":

(19) (JK: 3)

    C: . . . She was a nice lady—I liked her

→   G: I liked her too

(26) (J & J)

    A: Yeah I like it (   )

→   B: I like it too . . .

or include proterms indicating same as prior:

(27) (GTS: 4: 6)

    R: Ohh man, that was bitchin.

→   J: That was.

(28) (GTS: 4: 15)

    K: . . . He's terrific!

→   J: He is.

(29) (SBL: 2.1.8.-5)

    B: I think <u>everyone</u> enjoyed just sitting around
       talking.

→   A: I do <u>too</u>.

. . .

A third type of agreement is the *downgrade*. A downgraded agreement is an assessment of the same referent as had been assessed in the prior with scaled-down or weakened evaluation terms relative to the prior.

(31) (GJ:1)

      A: She's a fox!
→   L: Yeh, she's a pretty girl.

(15) (NB: VII: 2)

      E: ẹ-that <u>Pa</u>:t <u>i</u>sn'she a do: :ll?
→   M: [¡Yeh isn't she pretty,

(14) (SBL: 2.2.4.-3)

      A: Oh it was just beautiful.
→   B: Well <u>thank</u> you uh I thought it was quite nice.

(32) (KC: 4: 10)

      F: That's beautiful
→   K: Is'n it pretty

Downgraded agreements frequently engender disagreement sequences. One response that conversants make when disagreed with is to reassert the positions that they have previously taken. In response to downgraded assessments, participants often reassert stronger assessments.

(31) (GJ: 1)

      A: She's a fox.
      L: Yeh, she's a pretty girl.
→   A: Oh, she's gorgeous!

(15) (NB: VII: 2)

      E: ẹ-that <u>Pa</u>: t <u>i</u>sn'she a do: :ll?
      M: [¡Yeh isn't she pretty,
         (.)
→   E: <u>Oh</u>: she's a beautiful girl.

(33) (AP: 1)

      G: That's fantastic
→   B: Isn't that good
      G: That's marvelous

(14) (SBL: 2.2.4.-3)

      B: An I thought thet uh (1.0) uhm Gene's (1.0)
          singing was ——
      A: Oh, was lo vely.
      B: [pretty much like himse lf
→   A: [Yes, uh huh,
        it's- Oh it was wonderful

. . .

Disagreements (agreement preferred)

When conversants feel that they are being asked to agree with co-conversants' assessments, they may nonetheless find themselves in the position of disagreeing with them. A substantial number of such disagreements are produced with stated disagreement components delayed or withheld from early positioning within turns and sequences. When a conversant hears a coparticipant's assessment being completed and his or her own agreement/disagreement is relevant and due, he or she may produce delays, such as "no talk," requests for clarification, partial repeats, and other repair initiators, turn prefaces, and so on. Incorporating delay devices constitutes a typical turn shape for disagreements when agreements are invited.

One type of delay device is "no immediately forthcoming talk." Upon the completion of an assessment that invites agreement or confirmation, a conversant, in the course of producing a disagreement, may initially respond with silence. In the fragments below, gaps are notated with ($\rightarrow$), disagreement turns with (D).

(22) (NB: IV: 11.-1)

      A: God izn it <u>dreary</u>.

($\rightarrow$)   (0.6)

      A: [Y'know I don't think-

(D) B: ['hh It's <u>warm</u> though,

(36) (SBL: 2.1.7.-14)

      A: (   ) cause those things take working at,

($\rightarrow$)   (2.0)

(D) B: (hhhhh) well, they [<u>do</u>, but

      A: [They aren't accidents,

      B: No, they take working at, But on the other hand, some people are born with uhm (1.0) well a sense of humor, I think is something yer <u>born</u> with Bea.

      A: Yes. Or it's c- I have the- eh yes, I think a lotta people <u>are</u>, but then I think it can be de<u>ve</u>loped, <u>too</u>.

($\rightarrow$)   (1.0)

(D) B: Yeah,   but [there's

      A: [Any-

      A: Any of those attributes can be developed.

(37) (TG: 3)

      A: . . . You sound very far a<u>w</u>ay.

($\rightarrow$)   (0.7)

      B: I <u>do</u>?

      A: Ymeahm.

(D) B: mNo <u>I</u>'m no:t,

Another class of delay devices includes repair initiators. In the course of producing a disagreement, a recipient may request clarification with "what?" "Hm?" questioning repeats, and the like. In the following excerpts, clarification requests are marked with (*), disagreements/disconfirmations with (D).

(38) (MC: 1: 30)
        L: Maybe it's just ez well Wilbur,
(*)   W: Hm?
        L: Maybe it's just ez <u>well</u> you don't know.
           (2.0)
(D) W: Well ./ uh-I say it's sus<u>pi</u>cious it could be
           something <u>good</u> <u>too</u>.

(39) (TG: 1)
        B: Why <u>wh</u>hat'sa <u>m</u>attuh with y-Yih sou ⌜nd=
        A: ⌞Nothing.
        B: = <u>HA:</u>PPY, hh
(*)   A: I sound ha:p ⌜py?
        B: ⌞Ye:uh.
           (0.3)
(D) A: No:,

(37) (TG: 3)
        A: . . . You sound very far a<u>way</u>. (0.7)
(*)   B: I <u>do</u>?
        A: Meahm.
(D) B: mNo? <u>I</u>'m no:t,

Disagreement components may also be delayed within turns. Conversants start the turns in which they will disagree in some systematic ways. One way consists of prefacing the disagreement with "uh's," "well's" and the like, thus displaying reluctancy or discomfort.[7] Another way is to preface the disagreement by agreeing with the prior speaker's position. Agreement prefaces are of particular interest because agreements and disagreements are, of course, contrastive components. When they are included within a same turn, the agreement component is conjoined with the disagreement component with a contrast conjunction like "but." An apparent puzzle regarding the agreement-plus-disagreement turn shape is *why* recipients agree with assessments when they will shortly disagree with them.

. . .

Although both agreement and disagreement components are present in the agreement-plus-disagreement turn organization, such turn shapes are used for disagreeing rather than agreeing. That is, disagreement, and not agreement, is centrally sequentially implicative in next turn.

. . .

Self-deprecating assessments

When a speaker produces a self-deprecating assessment, the recipient's agreement or disagreement is relevant in the next turn. An agreement with a prior speaker's self-critical assessment amounts to the second speaker's criticism of his or her coparticipant.

Criticisms of one's coparticipants are a class of actions that often are performed in dispreferred-action turn/sequence shapes. . . .

A substantial number of coparticipant criticisms are performed by speakers' delaying or withholding the criticisms from early positioning within turns and sequences.

In the following datum, D is asked to assess A's newly acquired print. (+) indicates favorable assessment, (−) indicates critical assessment.

```
(51) (JS: I.-1)
         A:  D'yuh li:ke it?
  (+)    D:  ˙hhh Yes I do like it=
  (→)    D:  =although I rreally: :=
         C:  =Dju make it?
         A:  No We bought it, It's a ˙hh a Mary Kerrida print.
         D:  O:h (I k-)=
         A:  =Dz that make any sense to you?
         C:  Mm mh. I don' even know who she is.
         A:  She's that's, the Sister Kerrida, ⌐who,
         D:                                    ⌊˙hhh
         D:  Oh ⌐that's the one you to:ld ⌐me you bou:ght.=
         C:     ⌊Oh-                      |
         A:                               ⌊Ye:h
         D:  ⌐Ya:h.
         A:  ⌊Right
             (1.0)
         A:  It's worth, something,
             (1.0)
         A:  There's only a hundred of 'm
             (0.5)
         D:  Hmm
         E:  Which picture is that.
         A:  The one thet says Life.
             (1.5)
         A:  (                    ).
  (−)    D:  ˙hhh Well I don't- I'm not a great fan of this
             type of a:rt. There are certain- ones I see
             thet I like, But I like the w- =
         E:  =Is there ano ⌐thuh way of spelling Life?
  (−)    D:               ⌊-more realistic-
         A:  hhmh!
```

```
      E:   That's all ⌐ I wd loo(hh)k fo(h),
      D:           ⌊ hh!
(−)   D:   Yih d-know why I don't go fer this type of uh::
           art, Becuz it- it strikes me ez being the
           magazine adverti:sement ty:pe. Which some uh-uh
           some a' them are really great. But tuhm I-my,
           taste in art is for the more uh:: ub it-t-treh-
           it tends tuh be realistic.
```

A speaker's coparticipant criticism may be potential through a number of turns in which no stated criticism is produced. That is, a speaker may withhold a criticism in one sequential environment and come to state it in another.

. . .

When coparticipant criticisms are proffered, the criticism turns frequently have weak-type criticism components. This feature may be seen most clearly with criticisms that are delivered with contrastive prefaces:

(26)   (J & J)
       ((B is assessing a coparticipant's change of hair color))
       B: I like it too but uhh hahheh It blows my mind

(51)   (JS: I.-1)
       E: ˙hhh Yes I do like it=although I really:::
                   .
                   .
                   .
                   .
                   .
       E: ˙hhh Well I don't- I'm not a great fan of this type of a:rt . . .

With this type of construction, the prefacing favorable assessment is typically a moderately positive term (e.g. "like") and the prefaced unfavorable assessment is generally formed as an exception.

The contrastive-preface turn shape for coparticipant criticisms (favorable assessment plus critical assessment) is structurally similar to the turn shape for disagreements (agreement plus disagreement). In each case the contrastive prefacing component is a weak or token instance of the preferred action; the prefaced component is a weak instance of the sequentially implicative dispreferred action.

Subsequent to self-deprecations, the alternative actions of agreeing or disagreeing are nonequivalent. When conversants overtly agree, they of course endorse the prior criticisms as their own. Participants may be critical, and recognized as such, even when they do not overtly agree with the criticisms. If criticizing a co-conversant is viewed as impolite, hurtful, or wrong (as a dispreferred action), a conversant may hesitate, hedge, or even minimally disagree rather than agree with the criticism. When conversants disagree with prior self-deprecations, they show support of their co-conversants. If supporting co-conversants is viewed as natural, right, and/or desirable (as a preferred action), conversants would state their disagreements with prior self-deprecations overtly.

. . .

When disagreements are performed, disagreement components generally occupy the entire self-deprecation response units. That is, there are routinely no contrastive components before or after the disagreements as part of the units. . . .

Partial repeats. Disagreements may include partial repeats that challenge and/or disagree with their priors.[8] They are often followed in the same turn or in a subsequent turn by other disagreement components. In the following fragments, responses to self-deprecations include partial repeats (PR) followed by stated disagreements (D):

    (56) (AP: fn)

            L: You're not bored (huh)?

(PR) S: Bored?=

(D)   S: =No. We're fascinated.

    (57) (SBL: 1.6.-1)

            B: . . . I'm tryina get slim.

(PR) A: Ye: ah? ⌈ You get slim, my <u>hea</u>vens.

            B: ⌊ heh heh heh heh hh hh

(D)   A: You don't need to get any slimmah,

    (58) (JG: II.2.14a)

            C: . . . c(h)ept in my old age I'm: slowin down

                Considera ⌈ bly.˙ ˙hhhhhh

(PR) D: ⌊ He:ll <u>Old</u> age.   ⌉=

(D)   D: =⌈ What'r you thirdy fi:v ⌈ ve?

            C: ⌊ hheh – heh-heh-heh-heh ⌋ e-h ⌋ hYhe(h)e(h)e(h)es

            D: hh-hh hhh-hhh!

            C: ˙t ˙hhhhhhhh ⌈ hhh

(D)   D: ⌊ But a <u>y</u>oung thirdy fi:ve.

    (59) (JG: 4.6.-6)

            C: I have no dates.   I don't go:

                there ⌈ is no sense in hanging onto the clothes.

            J: ⌊ (Are you-) ((high pitch))

(PR) J: What do ya mean you don't have any

                da:tes ((low pitch))

            C: Well: I just don't go out anymore that's all

(D)   J: Oh: that's ridiculous

Negations. Disagreements may include negations like "no," "hm-mh," "not." A "no" may occur as a first component in an answer to a self-deprecating question:

(60) (JG: 2)

    R: Did she get my card.
    C: Yeah she gotcher card.
    R: Did she t'ink it was terrible
→ C: No she thought it was very adohrable.

(61) (SBL: 2.1.8.-8)

    B: I was wondering if I'd ruined <u>yer</u>- weekend
             ⌈ by uh
    A: ⌊ No. No. Hm-mh. No. I just loved to have- . . .

(56) (AP: fn)

    ((L, the hostess, is showing slides.))
    L: You're not bored (huh)?
    S: Bored?=
→ S: =No. We're fascinated

or as a first component in a response to a self-deprecating assertion:

(55) (SBL: 2.2.3.-15)

    A: . . . I feel like uh her and I play alike hehh
→ B: No. You play beautifully.

(20) (MC: 1.-45)

    L: . . . En I thought tuh myself- ((with a gravelly yodel))
          -gee whi:z when do I get smart. I'm so dumb I don't
          even know it. hhh! — heh!
→ W: Y-no, y-you're yer not du:mb, my God you- you hit it
          right on the head, . . .

A disagreement may be an assertion that contains the prior deprecating term negated with a "not":

(30) (MC: 1.-45)

    L: . . . I'm so dumb I don' t even know it. hhh! — heh!
→ W: y-no, y-you're not du:mb, . . .

(31) (JK: l)

    G: . . . but it's not bad for an old lady.
→ C: You're not old, Grandma . . .

Compliments. Disagreements with prior self-deprecations very frequently include evaluative terms. Such terms are contrastively classed relative to the prior self-deprecatory formulations; they are favorable, complimentary evaluative terms:

(55) (SBL: 2.2.3.-15)

    A: I mean I feel good when I'm playing with her because
          I feel like uh her and I play a<u>like</u> hehh

→   B: No. You play beautifully.

(63) (SBL: 2.2.3.-40)

    B: And I never was a grea(h)t Bri(h)dge play(h)er
          Clai(h)re,

→   A: Well I think you've always been real good,

(64) (MC)

    C: . . . 'ere Momma She talks better than I do

→   B: Aw you talk fine

(60) (JG: 2)

    R: Did she get my card.
    C: Yeah she gotcher card.
    R: Did she t'ink it was terrible

→   C: No she thought it was very adohrable.

(21) (NB: IV: 1.6)

    A: . . . ˙hhh Oh well it's <u>me</u> too Portia, hh yihknow
          I'm no bottle a' milk,
          (0.6)

→   P: Oh:: well <u>yer</u> easy tuh get along with, but <u>I</u>
          know he's that way.

(61) (SBL: 2.1.8.-8)

    B: I was wondering if I'd ruined <u>yer-week</u>end
              by uh
              [
    A: <u>No</u>.

→   A: No. Hm-mh. No. I just loved to have- . . .

(56) (AP: fn)

    L: You're not bored (huh)?
    S: Bored? No. we're fascinated.

(65) (EB: 1)

    S: . . . I hope by next semester it'll be a bi(h)t
          b(h)edd(h)er heh heh heh heh ˙hh
          ˙hh heh (prob'ly not)
             [
    B: (   ) You're doing very great no:w

. . .

Agreements with prior self-deprecations may be performed with stated agreement components. When they are, they are accomplished, prevalently, with weak agreement types.

One kind of agreement that occurs in response to self-deprecations is formed by the recipient proffering a second self-deprecation, formulating it as second in an agreement sequence. The deprecating attribute that the prior speaker claimed may also be claimed by the recipient:

(74) (EB: 1:2)

        B: Not only that he gets everything done.
           (pause)
        B: Everybody else- not everybody else,
           <u>I</u> have my desk full of trash.
→   S: Me too . . .

or may be upgraded by the recipient:

(75) (SBL: 2.2.3.-20)

        A: And I shoulda went <u>back</u> tuh diamonds.
→   B: I think we were _[<u>all</u> so confused,
        A: So-
→   B: I know I wasn't <u>bidding</u> right, I wasn't —
           eh playing right, I wa'nt doing <u>anything</u> right.

With responses such as "Me too" and "I think we were *all* so confused" recipients implicitly agree with the prior self-deprecations by proposing themselves as "also" instances. The agreements are weak in that, though they agree, they simultaneously undermine the prior self-deprecations by proposing that the prior deprecating attributes are more generally shared . . . and/or are less negative than prior speakers had proposed.

Notes

1   When persons partake in social activities, they routinely offer assessments. Assessments are produced as products of participation; with an assessment, a speaker claims knowledge of that which he or she is assessing.

       He or she may acknowledge a prior assessment:

(JS:II:61)

        E: Oh I I: loved _[it.
→   L: Yeah.
        L: Ih w'z- en' we have never <u>seen</u> it.

(SBL:2.1.7.–1)

        B: Well her niece is _[here, and she's a <u>lovely</u>=
        A;   Yeah
        B: =person.
→   A: Uh huh

He or she may produce an assessment as a recipient of news just delivered:

(JG:R:1)

    F: ·hh how iz our fri::end

    N: Oh: he'z much better i'm 'fraid --

            hh <u>h</u> <u>h</u> <u>h</u>

→ F: [Well uh that's <u>marvelous</u>

(Coliseum call 71)

    S: Is there something going on down north there (   )

    D: Yeah the Coliseum blew up.

    S: It did?

    D: Yeah, it's killed a bunch of people and I don't

          know how many's injured. It's a hell of a mess.

→ S: Oh, that's too bad.

(SBL:I:11.–2)

    B: <u>Say</u> didju see anything in the paper <u>last</u> night

         or hear anything on the local radio, hh Ruth

         Henderson and I drove down, to, Ventura

         yesterday.

    A: Mm hm,

    B: And on the way home we saw the -- most gosh awful

         <u>wreck</u>.

       .

       .

       .

       .

       .

    B: <u>Boy</u>, it was a <u>bad</u> one, though.

→ A: Well that's too ba:d.

He or she may proffer a qualified assessment of the referent assessed in the prior, marking the assessment as based on other than direct access:

(NB:PT:3:r:ca)

    L: Jeeziz <u>Chris</u>'shu sh'd <u>see</u> that house E(h)mma

         <u>yih</u> av no idea h <u>hh</u>mhh

→ E: [I <u>bet</u> it's a drea:m ....

(JG:II.1.–4)

    D: . . . oh I gotta n- <u>I</u> don'know th' las' time I

         talked t'yuh=I'm out here et Taft High School

         now, —— In the uh West Valley not too far frm

         home=I'm the boys' Dean out there, so I gotta

         new jo:b 'n=

    C: = Yeah?

    D: So it's a pretty good setup yihknow,

→ C: W'l my god it sounds marvelous Don.

For a fuller discussion, see Pomerantz (1975), chap 2.

2   How second assessments are coordinated with initial assessments are intricately bound up with how initials are coordinated with anticipatable nexts. In this chapter,

however, features of initial assessments remain, by and large, unexplicated. References to some aspects of initial assessments are included only insofar as the analysis to date requires.

3   Whereas it is being argued that the initial complaint assessment invites agreement or a subsequent complaint assessment, it also should be mentioned that negative assessments, as a class, often are converted by one party or the other in a subsequent turn into positive assessments.

4   The sequential work that "though" does, that is, accompanying disagreements containing parameter shifts, may be seen in the following assessment series as well:

(F.N.)
    A_1 A: Good shot
    A_2 B: Not very solid though
          A: You get any more solid you'll be terrific

A's initial assessment is a praise assessment, incorporating the positive descriptor "good." The second assessment is proffered as a *qualification* of the prior: With the "though," B claims to accept the prior while proffering a critical assessment ("not very solid"). The second may be formed as a qualification of the initial assessment inasmuch as there is a shift in the parameter being assessed: The second specifies the solidness (or lack of which) as a feature of the shot to assess, moreover, to assess critically, that is, in contrast with the prior assessment.

    In the assessment pair

(NB: IV:11.–1)
    A_1 A: <u>God</u> izn it <u>dreary</u>.
         .

         .

    A_2 P: ·hh- it's <u>warm</u> though

P's assessment is proffered as a qualification in that it contrastively assesses a shifted parameter; A critically assesses the weather appearance, B non-critically assesses the weather temperature.

5   The prevalence of agreements that are organized as *preferred* actions is, clearly, not confined to assessment sequences.

6   The upgraded-agreement type being described is an upgraded assessment with no referent shift relative to the prior. In the corpus, one apparent exception is a second assessment that contains an upgraded evaluation and a rather subtle referent shift:

(JS:II:137)
    A_1 A: They look nice to<u>ge</u>ther.
    A_2 B: Yes they're lovely.

In the second assessment, the evaluation term "lovely" is upgraded relative to the prior term "nice." The referent however is slightly altered relative to the prior. In A_1, "how they look together" is assessed. In A_2, the objects ("they") are assessed with an appearance assessment.

    The modification in referent in A_2 relative to the prior can be seen to anticipate that speaker's partial disagreement with the prior speaker's assessment:

(JS:II:137)
    A: They look nice to<u>ge</u>ther.
    B: Yes they're lovely. But I particularly like

the blue en gray, ⌈ en white,
A: ⌊ Yeah
B: What's so nice about this is you get <u>two</u>
       nice pieces.

A's initial assessment is of the objects "together" – B's subsequent assessment separates them, formulating them as "*two* nice pieces."

7   Some illustrations of turns containing pre-disagreement prefaces are provided:

(MC:1.–30)
       L: Maybe it's just ez <u>well</u> you don't know.
             (2.0)
→   W: Well, uh-I say it's sus<u>pi</u>cious it could be
             something <u>good</u> ⌈ too
       L: ⌊ Mmhm mmhm
             (1.0)
→   L: Well — I can't think it would be too good, ...

(SBL:1.1.10.–4)
       B: Oh, how sad.
       B: And that went wrong.
             (1.0)
→   A: Well, uh --
       B: That surgery, I mean.
       A: I don't-

(MC:1.–27)
       L: Maybe, en maybe by instinct, she took over
             from there, not really realizing, the extent
             of it?
→   W: Uh:: hh
       L: You think that's possible with her?
             (1.5)
→   W: Uh well/ I'll tell you,

(SBL:2.1.7.–14)
       A: . . . cause those things take working at,
             (2.0)
       B: (hhhhh) well, they do, but-

8   For a discussion of forms and functions of some repeat types, see Jefferson (1972).

Reference

Jefferson, G. (1972) 'Side sequences', in D. Sudnow, *Studies in Social Interaction*, New York: Free Press. 294–338.

Chapter 18

Emanuel A. Schegloff and Harvey Sacks

OPENING UP CLOSINGS

OUR AIM IN THIS PAPER is to report in a preliminary fashion on analyses we have been developing of closings of conversation. Although it may be apparent to intuition that the unit 'a single conversation' does not simply end, but is brought to a close, our initial task is to develop a technical basis for a closing problem. This we try to derive from a consideration of some features of the most basic sequential organization of conversation we know of – the organization of speaker turns. . . .

This project is part of a program of work undertaken several years ago [this paper was first delivered to the American Sociological Association in 1969] to explore the possibility of achieving a naturalistic observational discipline that could deal with the details of social action(s) rigorously, empirically, and formally. For a variety of reasons that need not be spelled out here, our attention has focused on conversational materials; suffice it to say that this is not because of a special interest in language, or any theoretical primacy we accord conversation. Nonetheless, the character of our materials as conversational has attracted our attention to the study of conversation as an activity in its own right, and thereby to the ways in which any actions accomplished in conversation require reference to the properties and organization of conversation for their understanding and analysis, both by participants and by professional investigators. This last phrase requires emphasis and explication.

We have proceeded under the assumption (an assumption borne out by our research) that insofar as the materials we worked with exhibited orderliness, they did so not only for us, indeed not in the first place for us, but for the coparticipants who had produced them. If the materials (records of natural conversations) were orderly, they were so because they had been methodically produced by members of the society for one another, and it was a feature of the conversations that we treated as data that they were produced so as to allow the display by the

Source: Emanuel A. Schegloff and Harvey Sacks, 'Opening up closings', *Semiotica*, 7: 289–327.

coparticipants to each other of their orderliness, and to allow the participants to display to each other their analysis, appreciation, and use of that orderliness. Accordingly, our analysis has sought to explicate the ways in which the materials are produced by members in orderly ways that exhibit their orderliness, have their orderliness appreciated and used, and have that appreciation displayed and treated as the basis for subsequent action.

In the ensuing discussion, therefore, it should be clearly understood that the 'closing problem' we are discussing is proposed as a problem for conversational-ists; we are not interested in it as a problem for analysts except insofar as, and in the ways, it is a problem for participants. (By 'problem' we do not intend puzzle, in the sense that participants need to ponder the matter of how to close a conver-sation. We mean that closings are to be seen as achievements, as solutions to certain problems of conversational organization.) . . .

The materials with which we have worked are audiotapes and transcripts of naturally occurring interactions (i.e., ones not produced by research intervention such as experiment or interview) with differing numbers of participants and differ-ent combinations or participant attributes. There is a danger attending this way of characterizing our materials, namely, that we be heard as proposing the assured relevance of numbers, attributes of participants, etc., to the way the data are produced, interpreted, or analyzed by investigators or by the participants them-selves. Such a view carries considerable plausibility, but for precisely that reason it should be treated with extreme caution, and be introduced only where warrant can be offered for the relevance of such characterizations of the data from the data themselves.

. . .

It seems useful to begin by formulating the problem of closing technically in terms of the more fundamental order of organization, that of turns. Two basic features of conversation are proposed to be: (1) at least, and no more than, one party speaks at a time in a single conversation; and (2) speaker change recurs. The achievement of these features singly, and especially the achievement of their co-occurrence, is accomplished by co-conversationalists through the use of a 'machinery' for ordering speaker turns sequentially in conversation. The turn-taking machinery includes as one component a set of procedures for organizing the selec-tion of 'next speakers', and, as another, a set of procedures for locating the occasions on which transition to a next speaker may or should occur. The turn-taking machinery operates utterance by utterance. That is to say . . . it is within any current utterance that possible next speaker selection is accomplished, and upon possible completion of any current utterance that such selection takes effect and transition to a next speaker becomes relevant. We shall speak of this as the 'tran-sition relevance' of possible utterance completion. . . . Whereas these basic features . . . deal with a conversation's ongoing orderliness, they make no provision for the closing of conversation. A machinery that includes the transition relevance of possible utterance completion recurrently for any utterance in the conversation generates an indefinitely extendable string of turns to talk. Then, an initial problem concerning closings may be formulated: HOW TO ORGANIZE THE SIMULTANEOUS

ARRIVAL OF THE CO-CONVERSATIONALISTS AT A POINT WHERE ONE SPEAKER'S COMPLETION WILL NOT OCCASION ANOTHER SPEAKER'S TALK, AND THAT WILL NOT BE HEARD AS SOME SPEAKER'S SILENCE. The last qualification is necessary to differentiate closings from other places in conversation where one speaker's completion is not followed by a possible next speaker's talk, but where, given the continuing relevance of the basic features and the turn-taking machinery, what is heard is not termination but attributable silence, a pause in the last speaker's utterance, etc. It should suggest why simply to stop talking is not a solution to the closing problem: any first prospective speaker to do so would be hearable as 'being silent' in terms of the turn-taking machinery, rather than as having suspended its relevance. . . .

How is the transition relevance of possible utterance completion lifted? A proximate solution involves the use of a 'terminal exchange' composed of conventional parts, e.g., an exchange of 'good-byes'. . . . We note first that the terminal exchange is a case of a class of utterance sequences which we have been studying for some years, namely, the utterance pair, or, as we shall refer to it, the adjacency pair. . . . Briefly, adjacency pairs consist of sequences which properly have the following features: (1) two utterance length, (2) adjacent positioning of component utterances, (3) different speakers producing each utterance. The component utterances of such sequences have an achieved relatedness beyond that which may otherwise obtain between adjacent utterances. That relatedness is partially the product of the operation of a typology in the speakers' production of the sequences. The typology operates in two ways: it partitions utterance types into 'first pair parts' (i.e., first parts of pairs) and second pair parts; and it affiliates a first pair part and a second pair part to form a 'pair type'. 'Question-answer', 'greeting-greeting,' 'offer-acceptance/refusal' are instances of pair types. . . . Adjacency pair sequences, then, exhibit the further features (4) relative ordering of parts (i.e. first pair parts precede second pair parts) and (5) discriminative relations (i.e., the pair type of which a first pair part is a member is relevant to the selection among second pair parts). . . .

In the case of that type of organization which we are calling 'overall structural organization', it may be noted that at least initial sequences (e.g., greeting exchanges), and ending sequences (i.e., terminal exchanges) employ adjacency pair formats. It is the recurrent, institutionalized use of adjacency pairs for such types of organization problems that suggests that these problems have, in part, a common character, and that adjacency pair organization . . . is specially fitted to the solution of problems of that character. . . .

But it may be wondered, why are two utterances required for either opening or closing? . . . What two utterances produced by different speakers can do that one utterance cannot do it: by an adjacently positioned second, a speaker can show that he understood what a prior aimed at, and that he is willing to go along with that. Also, by virtue of the occurrence of an adjacently produced second, the doer of a first can see that what he intended was indeed understood, and that it was or was not accepted. . . .

We are then proposing: If WHERE transition relevance is to be lifted is a systematic problem, an adjacency pair solution can work because: by providing that transition relevance is to be lifted after the second pair part's occurrence, the occurrence of the second pair part can then reveal an appreciation of, and agreement to, the intention of closing NOW which a first part of a terminal exchange reveals its speaker to propose. Given the institutionalization of that solution, a range of ways of assuring that it be employed have been developed, which make drastic difference between one party saying "good-bye" and not leaving a slot for the other to reply, and one party saying "good-bye" and leaving a slot for the other to reply. The former becomes a distinct sort of activity, expressing anger, brusqueness, and the like, and available to such a use by contrast with the latter. It is this consequentiality of alternatives that is the hallmark of an institutionalized solution. . . .

In referring to the components of terminal exchanges, we have so far employed "good-bye" as an exclusive instance. But, it plainly is not exclusively used. Such other components as "ok", "see you", "thank you", "you're welcome", and the like are also used. Since the latter items are used in other ways as well, the mere fact of their use does not mark them as unequivocal parts of terminal exchanges. . . .

The adjacency pair is one kind of 'local', i.e., utterance, organization. It does NOT appear that FIRST parts of terminal exchanges are placed by reference to that order of organization. While they, of course, occur after some utterance, they are not placed by reference to a location that might be formulated as 'next' after some 'last' utterance or class of utterances. Rather, their placement seems to be organized by reference to a properly initiated closing SECTION.

The [relevant] aspect of overall conversational organization concerns the organization of topic talk. . . . If we may refer to what gets talked about in a conversation as 'mentionables', then we can note that there are considerations relevant for conversationalists in ordering and distributing their talk about mentionables in a single conversation. There is, for example, a position in a single conversation for 'first topic'. We intend to mark by this term not the simple serial fact that some topic gets talked about temporally prior to others, for some temporally prior topics such as, for example, ones prefaced by "First, I just want to say . . .", or topics that are minor developments by the receiver of the conversational opening of "how are you" inquiries, are not heard or treated as 'first topic' is to accord it to a certain special status in the conversation. Thus, for example, to make a topic 'first topic' may provide for its analyzability (by coparticipants) as 'the reason for' the conversation, that being, furthermore, a preservable and reportable feature of the conversation. In addition, making a topic 'first topic' may accord it a special importance on the part of its initiator . . . .

These features of 'first topics' may pose a problem for conversationalists who may not wish to have special importance accorded some 'mentionable', and who may not want it preserved as 'the reason for the conversation'. It is by reference to such problems affiliated with the use of first topic position that we may appreciate such exchanges at the beginnings of conversations in which news IS later reported, as:

A: What's up.
B: Not much. What's up with you?
A: Nothing.

Conversationalists, then, can have mentionables they do not want to put in first topic position, and there are ways of talking past first topic position without putting them in.

A further feature of the organization of topic talk seems to involve 'fitting' as a preferred procedure. That is, it appears that a preferred way of getting mention-ables mentioned is to employ the resources of the local organization of utterances in the course of the conversation. That involves holding off the mention of a mentionable until it can 'occur naturally', that is, until it can be fitted to another conversationalist's prior utterance. . . .

There is, however, no guarantee that the course of the conversation will provide the occasion for any particular mentionable to 'come up naturally'.

This being the case, it would appear that an important virtue for a closing structure designed for this kind of topical structure would involve the provision for placement of hitherto unmentioned mentionables. The terminal exchange by itself makes no such provision. By exploiting the close organization resource of adjacency pairs, it provides for an immediate (i.e., next turn) closing of the conver-sation. That this close-ordering technique for terminating not exclude the possibility of inserting unmentioned mentionables can be achieved by placement restrictions on the first part of terminal exchanges, for example, by requiring 'advance note' or some form of foreshadowing.

. . .

The first proper way of initiating a closing section that we will discuss is one kind of (what we will call) 'pre-closing'. The kind of pre-closing we have in mind takes one of the following forms, "We-ell . . .", "O.K . . .", "So-oo", etc. (with downward intonation contours), these forms constituting the entire utterance. These pre-closings should properly be called 'POSSIBLE pre-closing', because providing the relevance of the initiation of a closing section is only one of the uses they have. One feature of their operation is that they occupy the floor for a speaker's turn without using it to produce either a topically coherent utterance or the initi-ation of a new topic. With them a speaker takes a turn whose business seems to be to 'pass,' i.e., to indicate that he has not now anything more or new to say, and also to give a 'free' turn to the next, who, because such an utterance can be treated as having broken with any prior topic, can without violating topical coher-ence take the occasion to introduce a new topic. . . . When this opportunity is exploited . . . then the local organization otherwise operative in conversation, including the fitting of topical talk, allows the same possibilities which obtain in any topical talk. The opening . . . may thus result in much more ensuing talk than the initial mentionable that is inserted. . . . The extendability of conversation to great lengths past a possible preclosing is not a sign of the latter's defects with respect to initiating closings, but of its virtues in providing opportunities for further topic talk that is fitted to the topical structure of conversation.

. . . The other possibility is that coconversationalists decline an opportunity to insert unmentioned mentionables. In that circumstance, the pre-closing may be answered with an acknowledgement, a return 'pass' yielding a sequence such as:

A: O.K.
B: O.K.

thereby setting up the relevance of further collaborating on a closing section. When the possible pre-closing is responded to in this manner, it may constitute the first part of the closing section.

. . .

Clearly, utterances such as "*O.K.*", "*We-ell*", etc. (where those forms are the whole of the utterance), occur in conversation in capacities other than that of 'pre-closing'. It is only on some occasions of use that these utterances are treated as pre-closings. . . .

[They] operate as possible pre-closings when placed at the analyzable (once again, TO PARTICIPANTS) end of a topic.

. . . Not all topics have an analyzable end. One procedure whereby talk moves off a topic might be called 'topic shading', in that it involves no specific attention to ending a topic at all, but rather the fitting of differently focused but related talk to some last utterance in a topic's development. But co-conversationalists may specifically attend to accomplishing a topic boundary, and there are various mechanisms for doing so; these may yield 'analyzable ends,' their analyzability to participants being displayed in the effective collaboration required to achieve them.

For example, there is a technique for 'closing down a topic' that seems to be a formal technique for a class of topic types, in the sense that for topics that are of the types that are members of the class, the technique operates without regard to what the particular topic is. . . . We have in mind such exchanges as:

A: Okay?
B: Alright

Such an exchange can serve, if completed, to accomplish a collaboration on the shutting down of a topic, and may thus mark the next slot in the conversational sequence as one in which, if an utterance of the form "We-ell", "O.K.", etc. should occur, it may be heard as a possible pre-closing.

Another 'topic-bounding' technique involves one party's offering of a proverbial or aphoristic formulation of conventional wisdom which can be heard as the 'moral' or 'lesson' of the topic being thereby possibly closed. Such formulations are 'agreeable with'. When such a formulation is offered by one party and agreed to by another, a topic may be seen (by them) to have been brought to a close. Again, an immediately following "We-ell" or "O.K." may be analyzed by its placement as doing the alternative tasks a possible pre-closing can do.

Dorrinne: Uh-you know, it's just like bringin the- blood up.
Theresa: Yeah well, THINGS UH ALWAYS WORK OUT FOR THE
// BEST
Dorrinne: Oh certainly. Alright //Tess.

(1) *Theresa:*   Oh huh,
    Theresa: Okay,
    Dorrinne: G'bye.
    Theresa: Goodnight,

(2) *Johnson:*   . . . and uh, uh we're gonna see if we can't uh tie in
                    our plans a little better.
    Baldwin: Okay // fine.
    Johnson: ALRIGHT?
    Baldwin: RIGHT.
    Johnson: Okay boy,
    Baldwin: Okay
    Johnson: Bye // bye
    Baldwin: G'night

. . .

What the preceding discussion suggests is that a closing section is initiated, i.e., turns out to have begun, when none of the parties to a conversation care or choose to continue it. Now that is a WARRANT for closing the conversation, and we may now be in a position to appreciate that the issue of placement, for the initiation of closing sections as for terminal exchanges, is the issue of warranting the placement of such items as will initiate the closing at some 'here and now' in the conversation. The kind of possible pre-closing we have been discussing – "O.K.", "We-ell", etc. – is a way of establishing one kind of warrant for undertaking to close a conversation. Its effectiveness can be seen in the feature noted above, that if the floor offering is declined, if the "O.K." is answered by another, then together these two utterances can constitute not a possible, but an actual first exchange of the closing section. The pre-closing ceases to be 'pre-' if accepted, for the acceptance establishes the warrant for undertaking a closing of the conversation at some 'here'.

We may now examine other kinds of pre-closings and the kinds of warrants they may invoke for initiating the beginning of a closing section. The floor-offering-exchange device [above] is one that can be initiated by any party to a conversation. In contrast to this, there are some . . . devices whose use is restricted to particular parties. We can offer some observations about telephone contacts, where the formulation of the parties can be specified in terms of the specific conversation, i.e., caller – called. What we find is that there are, so to speak, 'caller's techniques' and 'called's techniques' for inviting the initiation of closing sections. . . .

One feature that many of them have in common [is] that they employ as their warrant for initiating the closing the interests of the other party. It is in the specification of those interests that the techniques become assigned to one or another party. Thus, the following invitation to a closing is caller-specific and makes reference to the interests of the other.

A discussion about a possible luncheon has been proceeding:

A: Uhm livers 'n an gizzards 'n stuff like that makes it real yummy.
   Makes it too rich for *me* but: makes it yummy.
A: *Well* I'll letchu go. I don't wanna tie up your phone.

And, on the other hand, there are such called-specific techniques, also making reference to the other's interests, as

A: This is costing you a lot of money.

There are, of course, devices usable by either party which do not make reference to the other's interests, most familiarly, "I gotta go".

. . .

The 'routine' questions employed at the beginnings of conversations, e.g., "what are you doing?", "where are you going?", "how are you feeling?", etc., can elicit those kinds of materials that will have a use at the ending of the conversation in warranting its closing, e.g., "Well, I'll let you get back to your books", "why don't you lie down and take a nap?", etc. By contrast with our earlier discussion of such possible pre-closings as "O.K." or "We-ell", which may be said to accomplish or embody a warrant for closing, these may be said to announce it. That they do so may be related to the possible places in which they may be used.

. . .

It is the import of some of the preceding discussion that there are slots in conversation 'ripe' for the initiation of closing, such that utterances inserted there may be inspected for their closing relevance. To cite an example, "why don't you lie down and take a nap" properly placed will be heard as an initiation of a closing section, not as a question to be answered with a "Because . . ." (although, of course, a coparticipant can seek to decline the closing offering by treating it as a question). To cite actual data:

B has called to invite C, but has been told C is going out to dinner:

B: Yeah. Well get on your clothes and get out and collect some of that
   free food and we'll make it some other time Judy then.
C: Okay then Jack
B: Bye bye
C: Bye bye

While B's initial utterance in this excerpt might be grammatically characterized as an imperative or a command, and C's "Okay" as a submission or accession to it, in no sense but a technical syntactic one would those be anything but whimsical characterizations. While B's utterance has certain imperative aspects in its language form, those are not ones that count; his utterance is a closing initiation; and

C's utterance agrees not to a command to get dressed (nor would she be inconsistent if she failed to get dressed after the conversation), but to an invitation to close the conversation. The point is that no analysis – grammatical, semantic, pragmatic, etc. – of these utterances taken singly and out of sequence, will yield their import in use, will show what coparticipants might make of them and do about them. That B's utterance here accomplishes a form of closing initiation, and C's accepts the closing form and not what seems to be proposed in it, turns on the placement of these utterances in the conversation. Investigations which fail to attend to such considerations are bound to be misled. [Schegloff and Sacks go on to discuss 'pre-topic closing offerings', utterances like "Did I wake you up?", which offer listeners a means of moving into a closing section.]

. . .

Once properly initiated, a closing section may contain nothing but a terminal exchange and accomplish a proper closing thereby. Thus, a proper closing can be accomplished by:

A: *O*.K.
B: O.K.
A: Bye Bye
B: Bye

Closing sections may, however, include much more. There is a collection of possible component parts for closing sections which we cannot describe in the space available here. Among others, closings may include 'making arrangements', with varieties such as giving directions, arranging later meetings, invitations, and the like; reinvocation of certain sorts of materials talked of earlier in the conversation, in particular, reinvocations of earlier-made arrangements (e.g., "See you Wednesday") and reinvocations of the reason for initiating the conversation (e.g., "Well, I just wanted to find out how Bob was"), not to repeat here the earlier discussion of materials from earlier parts of the conversation to do possible pre-closings; and components that seem to give a 'signature' of sorts to the type of conversation, using the closing section as a place where recognition of the type of conversation can be displayed (e.g., "Thank you"). Collections of these and other components can be combined to yield extended closing sections, of which the following is but a modest example:

B: Well that's why I *said* "I'm not gonna say anything, I'm not making
    any *comments* // about anybody"
C: Hmh
C: Ehyeah
B: Yeah
C: Yeah
B: *Al*righty. Well *I'll* give you a call before we decide to come down.
    O.K.?
C: O.K.

B: *Al*righty
C: O.K.
B: We'll see you then
C: O.K.
B: *Bye* bye
C: Bye

However extensive the collection of components that are introduced, the two crucial components (FOR THE ACHIEVEMENT OF PROPER CLOSING; other components may be important for other reasons, but not for closing *per se*) are the terminal exchange which achieves the collaborative termination of the transition rule, and the proper initiation of the closing section which warrants the undertaking of the routine whose termination in the terminal exchange properly closes the conversation.

. . .

To capture the phenomenon of closings, one cannot treat it as the natural history of some particular conversation; one cannot treat it as a routine to be run through, inevitable in its course once initiated. Rather, it must be viewed, as much conversation as a whole, as a set of prospective possibilities opening up at various points in the conversation's course; there are possibilities throughout a closing, including the moments after a 'final' good-bye, for reopening the conversation. Getting to a termination, therefore, involves work at various points in the course of the conversation and of the closing section; it requires accomplishing. For the analyst, it requires a description of the prospects and possibilities available at the various points, how they work, what the resources are, etc., from which the participants produce what turns out to be the finally accomplished closing.

. . .

Symbols used in transcriptions

/	—	indicates upward intonation
//	—	indicates point at which following line interrupts
(n.0)	—	indicates pause of n.0 seconds
( )	—	indicates something said but not transcribable
(word)	—	indicates probable, but not certain, transcription
but	—	indicates accent
emPLOYee	—	indicates heavy accent
DO	—	indicates very heavy accent
: : : :	—	indicates stretching of sound immediately preceding, in proportion to number of colons inserted
becau-	—	indicates broken word

Chapter 19

Deborah Schiffrin

OH AS A MARKER OF INFORMATION MANAGEMENT

U NDERSTANDING DISCOURSE MARKERS requires separating the contribution made by the marker itself from the contribution made by characteristics of the discourse slot in which the marker occurs. We must pose the following questions. Does an item used as a marker have semantic meaning and/or grammatical status which contributes to its discourse function? And how does such meaning interact with a sequential context of the marker to influence production and interpretation?

I examine [a] discourse marker in this chapter – *oh* – whose uses are not clearly based on semantic meaning or grammatical status. . . . *Oh* is traditionally viewed as an exclamation or interjection. When used alone, without the syntactic support of a sentence, *oh* is said to indicate emotional states, e.g. surprise, fear, or pain (*Oxford English Dictionary* 1971, Fries 1952). (1) and (2) illustrate *oh* as exclamation:

   (1) *Jack:*   Was that a serious picture?
      Freda: **Oh**:! Gosh yes!
   (2) *Jack:*   Like I'd say, 'What d'y'mean you don't like classical music?'
      Freda: '**Oh**! I can't stand it! It's draggy.'

Oh can also initiate utterances, either followed by a brief pause:

   (3) *Freda:*   **Oh**, well they came when they were a year.

or with no pause preceding the rest of the tone unit:

   (4) *Jack:*   Does he like opera? **Oh** maybe he's too young.

Source: Deborah Schiffrin, *Discourse Markers*, Cambridge: Cambridge University Press, 1987.

We will see, regardless of its syntactic status or intonational contour, that *oh* occurs as speakers shift their orientation to information. (A very similar view of *oh* is Heritage (1984: 299), who views *oh* as a particle 'used to propose that its producer has undergone some kind of change in his or her locally current state of knowledge, information, orientation or awareness'.) We will see that speakers shift orientation during a conversation not only as they respond affectively to what is said (e.g., as they exclaim with surprise as in 1 and 2), but as they replace one information unit with another, as they recognize old information which has become conversationally relevant, and as they receive new information to integrate into an already present knowledge base. All of these are **information management tasks** in which *oh* has a role: *oh* pulls from the flow of information in discourse a temporary focus of attention which is the target of self and/or other management.

. . .

Oh in repairs

Repair is a speech activity during which speakers locate and replace a prior information unit. Because they focus on prior information, repairs achieve information transitions anaphorically – forcing speakers to adjust their orientation to what has been said before they respond to it in upcoming talk.

Almost anything that anyone says is a candidate for repair either by the speaker him/herself or by a listener. Once an utterance actually is subjected to repair, however, the method by which it is repaired is more restricted than its initial selection: although both repair initiation and completion can be performed by a listener (other-initiation, other-completion), speakers are more likely to participate in their own repairs either by initiating (self-initiation) or completing (self-completion) the repair. (Schegloff, Jefferson and Sacks 1977 speak of this tendency as the preference for self-repair.)

Oh in repair initiation

Oh prefaces self-initiated and other-initiated repairs. Example 5 shows *oh* at self-initiated repairs. In (5), Freda is answering a question about whether she believes in extra-sensory perception (ESP) by describing her husband Jack's abilities to predict future political events.

> (5) I mean . . . he can almost foresee: . . . eh : : for instance with
>   Nixon . . . . . . He said . . . now he's not in a medical field my
>   husband. He said coagulating his blood, . . . uh thinning his –
>   Nixon's blood . . . will not be good for him, if he should be oper-
>   ated on. **Oh** maybe it's just knowledge. I don't know if that's ESP
>   or not in that c– in this case.

Freda recategorizes a particular description from an instance of ESP to an instance of knowledge: this self-repair is initiated with *oh*. Another self-repair from *coagulating* to *thinning* is marked with *uh*. Two other self-repairs, the addition of background information following *he said*, and replacement of *that c—* by *this case*, are not marked.

. . .

Not all self-initiated repairs are actual replacements of one unit of information with another: in some, speakers search for information to fill a temporary gap in recall. In (6), for example, Jack interrupts a story to provide background information about his age at the time of the reported experience – which he cannot then remember precisely. *Oh* fills the slot between his self-interruption and his first attempt at specifying his age.

> (6) There was a whole bunch of oth– I was about– **oh**: younger than
>   Robert. I was about uh . . . maybe Joe's age. Sixteen.

Note that *uh* seems to serve the same general function as *oh* in this example: both are place-holders for Jack as he searches for information. But *oh* initiates the repair (it is preceded by a self-interruption), whereas *uh* continues the repair.

Example (7) illustrates other-initiated repairs. (Differentiating other-initiated repairs from disagreements often requires interpretation of speaker intent, especially when the same phrases are used, e.g., *what do you mean X?*. Because it is not always possible (from either an analyst's or participant's viewpoint) to know whether it is one's information output that is being corrected (repair), or one's knowledge of information that is being assessed (disagreement), I am including any replacement by one speaker of what another has said as other-repair. Note that this ambiguity may be one reason why other-repairs are marked forms of repair.) In (7), I am explaining what I mean by 'ethnic group'.

> (7) *Debby:*   By ethnic group I meant nationality. Okay like um Irish
>   or:– I guess there aren't ⎡too many Irish Jews but ⎤ =
>   *Jack:*   ⎣I see! Yeh yeh. **Oh** yes = ⎦
>   *Debby:*   = Italian:
>   *Jack:*   = there is!

Jack's *I see* acknowledges my description of ethnic group. His *Oh yes there is!* is an other-initiated repair to my assertion about Irish Jews.

. . .

Oh in repair completion

Repairs are completed when the repairable is replaced by a new item; additional completion can be provided through confirmation of the replacement. When the replacement is issued by the same speaker who had issued the repairable, we can speak of self completion; when the repairable is replaced by another speaker, of other completion. *Oh* prefaces both self and other-completions. . . . Example (7) showed combinations of other-initiated and other-completed repairs. . . .

   Oh also occurs when one party completes a repair initiated by the other – when other-initiated repairs are self-completed, and when self-initiated repairs are other-completed. In 8, for example, Zelda and Henry are answering my questions about who they visit.

> (8) *Henry:*   Ah: who can [answer that,] the kids. We have nobody =
>   *Zelda:*   [Our kids.   ]
>   *Henry:*   = else.   **Oh** yeh we– my sister =
>   *Zelda:*   Yeh, you have a sister.
>   *Zelda:*   = we see in the summertime a lot.

Henry forgets to mention his sister: thus, Zelda other-initiates a repair to this effect. Henry then self-completes the repair by replacing his earlier answer with one which includes his sister as someone whom he visits.

. . .

   In sum, that self and other participate in both initiation and completion of repair shows a speaker/hearer division of responsibility for information management. Self initiation and completion of repair show speakers' sensitivity to their own **production** of discourse: by locating and replacing an item from an outgoing utterance, speakers display their productive efforts. Other-initiation and completion of repair show hearers' sensitivity to their **reception** of discourse: by locating and replacing an item from an incoming utterance, hearers display their pursual of understanding and their effort to interpret what is being said as it is being received. Thus, jointly managed repairs are evidence of a participation framework in which both producer and recipient of talk replace information units and publicly redistribute knowledge about them.

   [We omit a detailed section where Schiffrin considers *oh* in repairs achieved through clarification sequences]

Oh in question/answer/acknowledgement sequences

Another speech activity which explicitly manages and distributes information is the three-part sequence of question, answer, and acknowledgement. Question/answer pairs complete a proposition, which may then be verbally acknowledged by the questioner – the individual who first opened the proposition for completion. The conditions under which *oh* prefaces questions, answers, and acknowledgements are sensitive to the different information management tasks accomplished in these turns.

Question/answer pairs

Question/answer pairs are adjacency pairs, i.e., sequentially constrained pairs in which the occurrence of a first-pair-part creates a slot for the occurrence of a second-pair-part (a conditional relevance), such that the non-occurrence of that second-pair-part is heard as officially absent [see Chapter 18]. One reason why questions constrain the next conversational slot is semantic: WH-questions are incomplete propositions; yes–no questions are propositions whose polarity is unspecified (e.g., Carlson 1983). Completion of the proposition is up to the recipient of the question, who either fills in the WH-information or fixes the polarity. This semantic completion allows a speaker/hearer re-orientation toward an information unit, i.e., redistribution of knowledge about a proposition.

OH WITH QUESTIONS

Question/answer pairs are rarely couplets which are totally disconnected from their containing discourse. In fact, some questions are quite explicitly connected to immediately prior utterances: for example, requests for clarification are often formulated as syntactic questions. Other questions are used to request elaboration of what has just been said. Example (9) shows that like requests for clarification, requests for elaboration may also be prefaced by *oh*.

> (9) *Val:*   Is it safe?
>   *Freda:* Uh: we found a safe way! But it's the long way!
>   *Val:*   **Oh** it's a special way?

Elaboration requests are similar to clarification requests because they, too, focus on prior information. There are two differences, however. First, clarification requests indicate a reception problem which will be resolved through upcoming clarification; elaboration requests acknowledge receipt of information which has been sufficiently interpreted to allow the receiver to prompt its further development. Second, compliance with a clarification request is the amendment of **old** information; compliance with an elaboration request is provision of **new** information.

Despite these differences, both clarification and elaboration requests can be prefaced by *oh* because both display speakers' receipt of information (partial or complete) at the same time that they solicit further information. The only other questions prefaced by *oh* are those which are suddenly remembered by a speaker as previously intended. Prior to (10), for example, I had been checking my interview schedule, when I saw a question that I had not yet asked.

> (10) *Debby:*   **Oh** listen, I forgot to ask you what your father did when
>   you were growing up.

Like requests for clarification and elaboration, the suddenly remembered question in (10) displays the questioner's receipt of information – although here, the just-received information may not be presented by an interlocutor, but may be recalled by the speaker him/herself. In short, questions through which speakers only solicit information are not prefaced by *oh*; it is only questions which are evoked by the reception of information which may be prefaced by *oh*.

Answers to questions are prefaced with *oh* when a question forces an answerer to reorientate him/herself to information — that is, when the question makes clear that information presumed to be shared is not so, or that a similar orientation toward information was wrongly assumed. At the same time, answers with *oh* make explicit to the questioner the violation of a prior expectation about information.

Such re-orientations may be caused by a mismatch between the information that the questioner assumed to be shared: the questioner may have assumed too much or too little to be shared, or the questioner may have made a wrong assumption. Consider (11). I have told Irene that I am a student at a local university.

> (11) *Irene:*   How can I get an appointment t'go down there t'bring my son on a tour?
>
> *Debby:*   **Oh** I didn't even know they gave tours! I'm not the one t'ask about it.

Irene's son is interested in attending the university, and she assumes that I would know (as a student) that the university gives tours to prospective students. But since I had no knowledge of the tours, Irene's question had assumed more shared information than was warranted: my *oh* shows both my receipt of this new information and alerts Irene to her misguided expectation as to what information we had shared.

. . .

Oh with acknowledgement of answers

Question/answer pairs are often followed by the questioner's response to the informational content of the answer which had been elicited. Such responses may vary from evaluations of the answer (endorsements, challenges) to re-solicitations of the answer (as accomplished through requests for clarification). (That certain registers, such as teacher talk, use a three-part question/answer/evaluation format is well known. See e.g., Mehan 1979.) Another possible response is acknowledgement of the answer, i.e., the questioner's display of receipt of the answer.

Consider, however, that exactly **what** is acknowledged varies depending upon whether the questioner finds that the answer to his/her question contains anticipated information. . . .

In (12), for example, Irene's answer does not conform to the expectations encoded through my question:

> (12) *Debby:*   So what, you have *three* kids?
>
> *Irene:*   I have *four*. ⎡Three boys⎤ and a girl.
>
> *Debby:*   ⎣*Four* kids. ⎦   **Oh** I didn't know that.

Note that I am not distinguishing old from new information: both anticipated and unanticipated answers provide **new** information. But new information which has been anticipated creates less of a reorientation than does new information which has not been anticipated. . . .

Oh and the status of information

Thus far we have focused on speech activities whose goal is the management of information and whose exchange structure helps accomplish that goal. We have seen that *oh* marks different tasks involved in this management: the production and reception of information, the replacement and redistribution of information, the receipt of solicited, but unanticipated, information. *Oh* is more likely to be used when locally provided information does not correspond to a speaker's prior expectations: in repairs, questions, answers, and acknowledgements, *oh* marks a shift in speaker's orientation to information.

Use of *oh* is hardly confined to speech activities whose exchange structure is focused on information management. In this section, I examine *oh* first, as a marker of recognition of familiar information – more specifically, old information which has become newly relevant – and second, as a marker of new information receipt.

Oh as recognition display

Recognition of familiar information is often conversationally triggered. In the following examples, one speaker prompts another into recall, which is then explicitly marked not only with *oh*, but with confirmation of the correctness of the prompt, and/or provision of information testifying to the speaker's prior knowledge.

In (13), I prompt Zelda and Henry through use of *do you know X?*

> (13) *Debby:*   No this–d'you–d'you know um: I was talkin' to the
> Kramers, down, 4500.
> *Zelda:*   **Oh** yeh, Freda?
> *Debby:*   ⌈Yeh.⌉
> *Henry:*   ⌊**Oh** ⌋ yeh. Jack?

Both Zelda and Henry mark their recognition with *oh* and with elaboration of the topic which I have evoked (the Kramers' first names). . . . Recognition of familiar information may also result from the speaker's own cognitive search for a particular piece of known information. In (14), for example, Zelda and Henry are telling me about their favorite restuarants; Henry has just said that they have been eating out more than ever.

> (14) *Zelda:*   And uh– **Oh**! We– when we go to the kids, we always
> eat out.
> We eat at the F1– Blue Fountain.

It sounds as if Zelda is about to add another restaurant to her list of favorites (because of her initial *and*). But she switches to a reason for the frequency with which they have been dining out (*when we go to the kids, we always eat out*), and then mentions another restaurant (*Blue Fountain*). The reason seems to be a sudden recall, and it is the reason that is marked by *oh*.

. . .

Oh as information receipt

Oh also marks a speaker's receipt of new information. In (15), for example, Zelda doesn't know prior to Irene's telling her that Irene's husband Ken had been fixing their back door. Note how Irene prompts Zelda's realization by introducing the news discourse topic with *y'know*. . . .

> (15) *Irene:* You know who was bangin' out there for twenty minutes.
> Ken. He didn't know where I was. =
> *Zelda:* **Oh**
> *Irene:* [= He was fixin' the back ⌉ door.
> *Zelda:* [**Oh** I didn't hear him! ⌋

Speakers also introduce new discourse topics by tying them to information they assume their hearers will find familiar. Henry and Zelda know that my parents own a house near their summer home. In (16), they are trying to find a location with which I am familiar in order to locate their summer home for me.

> (16) *Debby:* Where are you? Which– ⌈which street?⌉
> *Henry:* ⌊We're on ⌋ Arkansas.
> Right from– across from the bank.
> *Zelda:* D'y'know where the Montclair is? And the Sea View?
> D'you ever ride down the:– ⌈uh ⌉   The =
> *Debby:* ⌊The ⌋ motels? There?
> *Zelda:* = motels. On the boardwalk. ⌈D'you go bike riding? ⌉
> *Henry:* ⌊Do you know where Abe's ⌋
> is? ⌋ Right across the =
> *Debby:* Yeh I know where Abe's is. ⌋
> *Henry:* = street.
> *Debby:* **Oh** it's that way.

When I finally do acknowledge a familiar location (*where Abe's is*), Henry locates his home in relation to that place. I then acknowledge receipt of this new piece of information.

. . .

Oh and shifts in subjective orientation

Speaker orientation to information is not just a matter of recognition and receipt of the informational content of ongoing discourse. Orientation also involves the **evaluation** of information: speakers respond affectively and subjectively to what is said, what they are thinking of, and what happens around them. Just as speakers display shifts in objective orientation, so too, do they display shifts in subjective orientation. And not surprisingly, *oh* can be used when speakers display shifts in expressive orientation.

One such subjective orientation is **intensity**: a speaker is so committed to the truth of a proposition that future estimates of his or her character hinge on that truth (Labov 1984). In (17), for example, I have unintentionally provoked a disagreement between Freda and Jack about something for which they both display strong feelings: girls' high schools. Note Freda's repetition, meta-talk, and contrastive stress on *do* — all expressions of intensity commonly used in argument (Schiffrin 1982: Chapter 8).

(17a) *Debby:*   Well I think there's a lot of competition between girls.
                 In an *all* girls school. More than well– more
                 academically ⎡anyway.⎤
      Freda: ⎣**Oh** ⎦ yes. **Oh** yes. They're better
                 students I *do* believe that.

Later in the argument, Freda responds to Jack's accusation that the girls' high school which she and I both attended is no longer academically respected. Her defense intensifies when Jack adds to his accusation the demise of the local boys' high school.

(17b) *Jack:*   In fact it had lost its popularity, didn't it.
                Girls' High. ⎡   ⎤ And Central High.
      Freda: ⎣No.⎦   **Oh** no.

She later solicits endorsement of her position from me. Note her use of *oh yes* upon receipt of my endorsement, and, as preface to her response to Jack's question – a response which intensifies her position about the academic quality of Girls' High still further.

(17c) *Freda:*   You went there more recently
                 than ⎡I. ⎤
      Debby: ⎣Yeh.⎦ ⎡Um . . . it's–⎤
      Jack: ⎣Doesn't   ⎦
                 hold the: . . like it *used* to.
      Debby: It still has a reputation. ⎡   ⎤ In some ways.
      Freda: ⎣**Oh** yes.⎦
      Jack: But, like it did?
      Freda: **Oh** yes. Girls' High is still rated. Y'know Girls' High is
                 rated higher than Central. I just read recently that Girls'
                 High is *still* rated the highest.

Thus, in (17), *oh* accompanies Freda's increasingly intensive orientation toward her position. The cumulative interactional effect of these progressive shifts in Freda's own commitment in her position is increased distance from Jack's position.

. . .

Why *oh*?

We have seen that *oh* marks different tasks of information management in discourse. These productive and receptive tasks, however, are hardly dependent on *oh*: speakers are certainly able to replace, recognize, receive, and re-evaluate information without verbalization through *oh*. Why, then, does *oh* occur?

Since the overall role of *oh* is in information state transitions, let us begin with this component of talk. One of the basic goals of talk is the exchange of information. This goal can be realized because speakers and hearers redistribute knowledge about entities, events, states, situations, and so on – whatever real world knowledge is being represented through talk. Furthermore, because discourse involves the **exchange** of information, knowledge and meta-knowledge are constantly in flux, as are degrees of certainty about, and salience of, information. Another way of saying this is that information states are constantly evolving over the course of a conversation: what speakers and hearers can reasonably expect one another to know, what they can expect about the other's knowledge of what they know, how certain they can expect one another to be about that knowledge, and how salient they can expect the other to find that knowledge are all constantly changing. In short, information states are dynamic processes which change as each one of their contributing factors changes.

Oh has a role in information state transitions because *oh* marks a focus of speaker's attention which then also becomes a candidate for hearer's attention. This creation of a joint focus of attention not only allows transitions in information state, but it marks information as more salient with a possible increase in speaker/hearer certainty as to shared knowledge and meta-knowledge. So it is by verbally marking a cognitive task, and opening an individual processing task to a hearer, that *oh* initiates an information state transition.

But suggesting that *oh* has a pragmatic effect – the creation of a joint focus – does not really answer the question of **why** *oh* has this pragmatic effect. To try to answer this question, let us consider in more detail how *oh* is situated in social interaction.

First, *oh* makes evident a very general and pervasive property of participation frameworks: the division of conversational labor between speaker and hearer. Back-channel *oh*, for example, ratifies the current participation structure of the conversation: speaker remains speaker, and hearer remains hearer. Thus, *oh* as back-channel not only marks information receipt, and marks an individual as an occupant of a specific participation status (active recipient), but it also ratifies the current division of turn-taking responsibilities in the exchange structure.

Second, *oh* displays individuals in specific participation statuses and frameworks. Because *oh* displays one's own ongoing management of information, its user is temporarily displayed as an individual active in the role of utterance reception. Recall that *oh* is used not only as a back-channel response, but to incorporate requested clarifications and unanticipated answers into talk. These uses display a hearer as an active recipient of information who acknowledges and integrates information as it is provided. This functional capacity is complementary to the speaker's capacity as animator (Goffman 1981: 144): both display individuals as occupants of mechanically defined nodes in a system of information transmission.

Oh displays still another aspect of participation frameworks: speaker/hearer alignment toward each other. We have seen that individuals evaluate each other's orientations: what one defines as an appropriate level of commitment to a proposition, another may define as inappropriate. Different speaker/hearer alignments can be characterized in part by whether individuals share subjective orientations toward a proposition. For example, we might characterize an argument as an alignment in which Speaker A is committed to the truth of a proposition to which B is not similarly committed, and Speaker B is committed to the truth of another proposition to which A is not similarly committed. When *oh* marks a speaker's realization of the other's unshared commitment, then, it may serve as a signal of a potentially argumentative stance. Thus, it is because *oh* makes accessible speaker/hearer assumptions about each others' subjective orientations toward information, that it can display speaker/hearer alignments toward each other.

And, finally, consider that conversation requires a delicate balance between the satisfaction of one's own needs and the satisfaction of others' needs. Included is not only an individual cognitive need – individuals need time (no matter how short) to transform the content that they have in mind into talk – but a reciprocal social need: individuals need to receive appreciation for self and show deference to others (Goffman 1967; Chapter 21; Lakoff 1973; Tannen 1984). *Oh* may help service individuals' cognitive needs by providing time to focus on informational tasks – while still displaying one's interactional presence in deference to the satisfaction of social needs.

In sum, although *oh* is a marker of information management tasks which are essentially cognitive, the fact that it verbalizes speakers' handling of those tasks has interactional consequences. Thus, use of *oh* may very well be cognitively motivated. But once an expression makes cognitive work accessible to another during the course of a conversation, it is open for pragmatic interpretation and effect – and such interpretations may become conventionally associated with the markers of that work. Intended interactional effects and meanings may thus account for the use of *oh* as readily as the initial cognitive motivation. Such conventionalized effects may further explain why speakers verbally mark information management tasks with *oh*.

References

Carlson, L. (1983) *Dialogue Games*, Dordrecht: Reidel.
Fries, C. (1952) *The Structure of English*, London: Longman.
Goffman, E. (1967) 'The nature of deference and demeanor' in *Interaction Ritual*, New York: Anchor Books, 49–95.

—— (1981) 'Footing', in *Forms of talk*, 124–57, Philadelphia, PA: University of Pennsylvania Press. (Originally published 1979 in *Semiotica* 25: 1–29.)

Heritage, J. (1984) 'A change-of-state token and aspects of its sequential placement', in Atkinson, J.M. and Heritage, J. (eds) *Structures of Social Action: Studies in Conversation Analysis*, Cambridge: Cambridge University Press, 299–345.

Labov, W. (1984) 'Intensity', in Schiffrin, D. (ed.) *Meaning, Form and Use in Context: Linguistic Applications,* Georgetown University Round Table on Languages and Linguistics 1984, Washington, DC: Georgetown University Press, 43–70.

Lakoff, R. (1973) 'The logic of politeness, or minding your p's and q's', *Papers from the 9th Regional Meeting, Chicago Linguistic Society,* Chicago, IL: Linguistics Department, University of Chicago, 292–305.

Mehan, H. (1979) *Learning Lessons: Social Organization in the Classroom*, Cambridge, MA: Harvard University Press.

Oxford English Dictionary (1971), Oxford: Oxford University Press.

Schegloff, E., Jefferson, G. and Sacks, H. (1977) 'The preference for self-correction in the organization of repair in conversation', *Language* 53: 361–82.

Schiffrin, D. (1982) 'Discourse markers: semantic resources for the construction of conversation', Ph.D. dissertation, University of Pennsylvania.

Tannen, D. (1984) *Conversational Style: Analyzing Talk Among Friends*, Norwood, NJ: Ablex.

Discussion points
for Part Three

1   Try to apply William Labov's categories of narrative structure to the following
    text. It's a personal narrative told to a researcher by an adolescent male (see
    Garrett *et al.* 2003). A few small details have been changed, to protect the
    speaker's anonymity. In this extract (.) denotes a short pause. Underlined
    syllables are heavily stressed. (( )) encloses speech that isn't fully audible. The
    final question mark denotes rising intonation not a grammatical (interroga-
    tive) question.

    ah (.) ((anyway)) (.) there was <u>one</u> time when (.) you know I was
    in <u>Boys'</u> Brigade an (.) went to ad<u>ven</u>ture camp (.) you know I
    was the only only <u>col</u>oured person there like an (.) you know we
    sort of <u>all</u> have had a <u>laugh</u> they were <u>none</u> of them were <u>ra</u>cist
    or nothing (.) and you <u>know</u> (.) few couple of days we all had a
    <u>laugh</u> on the <u>as</u>sault courses and stuff an (.) you know (.) they
    all they all took the <u>mick</u> out of everyone you know we had this
    little <u>book</u> (.) and everyone took the <u>mick</u> out of you (.) an (.)
    you know it was like <u>ev</u>eryone (.) an (.) there was <u>one</u> time when
    (.) we were all playing pool on the pool table (.) and I saw you
    know I saw the <u>latch</u> on the thing so I thought oh I know (.) if
    I put my <u>hand</u> down this pool table hole you know and I can (.)
    tief a few <u>games</u> like (.) you know keep the <u>latch</u> up (.) an (.)
    <u>puts</u> my hand down you know (.) ten minutes later I realise I
    couldn't get it back <u>out</u> (.) (laughing) so I thought oh <u>no</u> (.)
    I got my <u>hand</u> stuck down a <u>pool</u> table (.) you know so (.) they
    had to go and find the <u>care</u>taker an he was he was like about
    <u>three</u> <u>hours</u> eventually until they found the caretaker you know I
    had to <u>stand</u> in this <u>one</u> place w- <u>one</u> hand stuck in the pool table
    you know (.) and <u>one</u> hand trying to eat my <u>tea</u> and my <u>food</u> and
    stuff (.) an (.) you know (.) come across and he said <u>oh</u> (.) he
    said how are we gonna get your <u>hand</u> out then? (.) an he goes oh
    (.) there's only <u>one</u> thing we can do like you know (.) I said what's
    that he said we'll have to saw the whole <u>pool</u> table in half (.)
    I said how you going to do that? w- he said (.) you know (.) go
    to the <u>thing</u> (.) goes out to the <u>gar</u>den shed like in the back and
    brings out this <u>mass</u>ive <u>chain</u>saw (.) you know he's <u>saw</u>ing the
    <u>whole</u> <u>pool</u> table in half n my hand comes <u>out</u> eventually (.) and
    they all take the <u>mick</u> out of you at the <u>end</u> (.) you know and they

all comes up to me and they goes <u>oh</u> (.) and we have (referring to himself) <u>Ain</u>slee you know getting his <u>hand</u> stuck down a pool table (.) and he turned round and says <u>oh</u> it's the first time the <u>black's</u> ever <u>pott</u>ed him<u>self</u>?

2   In the above text, what are the features that strike you as the best indications that what the speaker is doing is 'telling a story'? Are there utterances/phrases in the text that have special force or meaning by virtue of occurring in particular parts or phases of the narrative?

3   How does this speaker use 'voices' in his narrative? Which utterances are 'voiced' or quoted? What is the value or function of quotation of this sort in narrative discourse?

4   Think of how you respond to compliments, such as *That's a nice sweater* or (about a recent argument) *I think you handled that brilliantly*. What is the most likely set of responses you'd make to these and other compliments? What do you think is the 'preferred' response to each of the above examples, for example in terms of forms of 'agreement' and 'disagreement' with the judgements made in the compliments? Are there some sorts of compliments that have different 'preference structures' attached to them?

5   Identify the discourse markers that the story-teller uses in the above extract. Start with *ah* and *anyway*, and consider his repeated use of *you know*. What functions do the various discourse markers perform, in relation to the organisation of (a) ideational or informational meanings, (b) identity meanings and (c) relational or interpersonal meanings?

Reference

Garrett, Peter, Coupland, Nikolas and Williams, Angie (2003) *Investigating Language Attitudes: Social Meanings of Dialect, Ethnicity and Performance*, Cardiff: University of Wales Press.

Negotiating social relationships

Editors' introduction
to Part Four

THE OPENING CHAPTER in this Part is a classic text by the anthropologist Bronislaw Malinowski, first published in 1923. The original date of publication is important for two reasons. First, it indicates Malinowski's pioneering theoretical work, establishing the basic theme of this Part of the *Reader* – how language achieves closeness and intimacy between people, what he referred to as 'phatic communion'. Second, it explains the rather dated rhetoric of the paper, which, like most other of Malinowski's writings, is based on his research in the Pacific. Certainly, references by a white, middle-class anthropologist to 'savage tribes' or to 'the primitive mind . . . among savages or our own uneducated classes' are by today's standards the voice of colonial power and of ethic and class prejudice. But regardless of these historical limitations, Malinowski's placing of language (and more specifically *talk*) at the centre of social relations is highly significant. Phatic communion, 'a type of speech in which ties of union are created by a mere exchange of words' (p. 29), is a prototypical manifestation of sociability through discourse.

One of the important aspects of phatic communion which drew analysts' interest was its ritualistic character. It was mainly John Laver's (1974, 1981) work that first refined the ideas put forward by Malinowski, and Laver pointed out that phatic communion is ritualised usage in at least two senses. First, phatic communion, like much of everyday conversation (Cheepen 1988), is highly predictable. Like other ritualistic behaviour, phatic communion proceeds according to well-established patterns or scripts. Anyone who has been to more than one drinks party can attest that 'all' conversations we had there were 'exactly the same'. But there is a good reason for this apparent repetitiveness of phatic communion, and that brings us to the second understanding of its ritualistic aspect. In line with a cultural anthropological approach to communication (e.g., Leach 1976), the term 'ritual' refers to the wide range of activities in which people engage during transitional or *liminal*

(Turner 1969) moments in social time and space. These are ceremonies such as baptisms, weddings, funerals, initiation rites and birthdays, especially birthdays marking 'significant' ages, e.g., 18, 21, and all the 'round-number' birthdays at decade boundaries. In other words, all our *rites of passage*, big or small, are marked by rituals. Verbal and non-verbal ritualistic activities help social actors in these situations to overcome the unusually significant face-threat associated with the uncertainty of the situation (moving from one state to another) and often being the centre of attention. Having a script to follow makes such occasions (e.g., weddings) bearable and manageable by giving all the participants clear and pre-defined roles to play and things to say.

However, social rituals are enacted more often than this. Meeting new people, starting and closing conversations, or just having a chat while taking time off work in an office are, according to Laver, all marginal phases of interaction which resemble other rites of passage. They place social actors in liminal spaces. Phatic communion, then, offers us mini-scripts to pass through these moments in a non-threatening and socially acceptable way. Malinowski's original definition of phatic communion, and Laver's elaboration of it, centre on its use to deflect the potentially hostile effects of silence in situations where talk is conventionally anticipated. This, again, requires a brief comment. On the one hand, such an approach relegates phatic communion to the realm of trivial and unimportant talk. It may make the partici-pants in a speech event comfortable, but in itself the talk is seemingly dismissed as a 'filler' for silence: we might call it 'small talk', 'gossip' or 'chit-chat'. Nikolas Coupland *et al.* (1992) and Justine Coupland (1999) re-examine this relative neg-ativity in academic and everyday metalanguage about phatic communion. They show that 'phaticity' is an important and intricate discursive practice, co-constructed by all participants in delicate negotiations of face and social distance. Besides, silence need not always be a signal of interpersonal unease or communicative problems (Jaworski 2000).

This discussion of the sociable nature of talk and treating everyday encounters as mini performances or rituals was developed with great insight by the Amer-ican sociologist, Erving Goffman, whose chapter 'On face-work' is reproduced as Chapter 21. We have already mentioned Goffman in our general Introduction, and his influence on discourse analytic research of sociability (and social interaction generally) is so great that we would have liked to devote far more space to his writing. Goffman takes us further towards a local perspective on communication. His analyses were grounded in his own informal observation of North American social and interactional styles of interaction. The sub-title of the book from which we have excerpted Chapter 21 is 'Essays on face-to-face behavior' (first published in 1967), and we have selected a famous essay dealing with the ritu-alised nature of talk and with the intriguing concept of 'face'. The concept of face should be understood in the sense in which we use it in the expression 'saving face'. It refers to our public image or persona. It has become a major theme in discourse studies, most notably developed in Brown and Levinson's research on 'politeness' (see Chapters 22 and 23). Goffman uses the concept of face to analyse how a person's standing and integrity are 'managed' in everyday interaction, how people are attentive to their own and others' faces, and how they deal with moments that threaten esteem and credibility.

The metaphor that dominates Goffman's analyses is that of the theatre, and when he uses the terms 'actor' (often in preference to 'speaker' or 'listener') and 'performance' (often instead of 'talk' or 'behaviour') he is deliberately invoking the theatrical senses of these terms. The idea of 'poise' (self-control), the concept of face itself, suggest stage masks that people carefully select and wear to conjure up specific images and effects. Goffman strips away the levels of control and self-management that produce conventionalised social behaviour in public. He helps us recognise these traits and practices – in ourselves and others – but perhaps he also leaves us feeling rather like voyeurs of social processes. Goffman picks up what is most ordinary in social interaction and, brilliantly, identifies the goals, strategies and conceits that are interwoven into everyday face-to-face communication.

Not surprisingly, very many aspects of Goffman's work have left a deep imprint on the methods and assumptions of discourse analysis. We can list some of them:

- the view of language in use as social action, and, as we have just mentioned, seeing people as social actors;
- the assumption that discourse does not merely happen but is achieved, as part of strategic performances;
- the role of discourse in the construction and management of individuals and 'selfhood';
- studying how individual people's language is co-ordinated with other people's, so that social interaction is a delicately collaborative achievement;
- discourse as, in many regards, pre-structured, predictable and ritualistic;
- the orderliness of talk (e.g., 'the little ceremonies of greeting and farewell' (p. 309)) being explicable in terms of speakers' concerns for protecting and extending their relationships (see Schegloff and Sacks, Chapter 18);
- building a sociological 'map' of social norms and customs through analysis of local patterns of talk ('the traffic rules of social interaction' (p. 301).

Goffman's writings are clearly contributions to sociological analysis. His writing is peppered with phrases such as 'in our society' and comments on potentially different practices and norms for interaction in different cultural groups. Most obviously he is a sociologist mapping out the sociology of human relationships. Goffman does not give us examples of specific utterances, and his analyses are therefore largely built around general categories of utterance (e.g., 'employing courtesies', 'making a belittling demand' or 'providing explanations') or of non-verbal behaviour ('avoidance' or 'leave-taking'). But these categories, the building blocks of Goffman's interactional analysis which he sometimes calls 'moves', are of course speech-act types of the sort Austin (Chapter 2) and Grice (Chapter 3) were discussing in slightly more formal terms. They are functional and pragmatic units of the sort that Watzlawick et al. (1967) saw as the architecture of relational communication. Despite their widely differing origins, we again see a confluence of ideas and interests in these foundational texts – in studying the discursive basis of everyday communication.

A combination of Goffman's work on face and interaction and Grice's perspective on conversational co-operativity left Penelope Brown and Stephen C. Levinson two main legacies in formulating their Politeness Theory (Chapter 22). Grice (Chapter 3) in fact mentions politeness as a specific dimension of talk where it is possible to formulate general conversational maxims, and this is largely what Brown and Levinson have done. They built a model of the normal expectations communicators make about how to 'save face'. The extract we reproduce here comes from their original work (first published as an extended paper in 1978, and later reprinted in book form in 1987), and it gives an outline of the theory. Due to limited space we cannot reproduce their elaborate taxonomy of politeness strategies, which Brown and Levinson illustrate in their original text with numerous examples, mainly from English, Tamil and Tzeltal. But we have provided a short Appendix, summarising these strategies (pp. 322–323).

As we have said, politeness theory has Goffman's notion of face at its heart. Face, for Brown and Levinson, has two aspects: a want to be liked and appreciated by others, *positive face*, and a want to be left free of imposition, *negative face*. Both positive and negative faces can be damaged or threatened in contact with others, when a *face-threatening act* (FTA) of some sort is performed. Thus, individuals adopt various politeness strategies to mitigate or avoid the face-threat associated with such speech acts as criticisms and accusations (threatening to positive face), or requests and orders (threatening to negative face). Mitigation strategies in discourse then take the form of either *indirectness* (in the sense of violating Grice's co-operative principle), or they can be *direct with a mitigating comment* before an FTA is performed. A rather crass example of this second case is when a criticism is preceded by a compliment. A less crass instance is when we criticise someone by saying 'I'm sorry to say this but . . .'. Another instance is when an accusation is accompanied by the speaker giving an account or a justification, as in 'Everybody knows you shouldn't act like that'.

Politeness theory has become an enormously influential paradigm in discourse analysis. It has spawned a large body of literature on politeness strategies and face in different contexts and in different social and cultural groups. It has offered a comprehensive system for describing and explaining the communicative behaviour of individuals across a wide range of speech events. Janet Holmes's Chapter 23 is an example of a study that documents the differences in politeness strategies among men and women. In the book on gender and politeness from which this chapter is extracted, Holmes defines politeness as a way of making one's interlocutor feel good. In her detailed, qualitative and quantitative examination of ethnographically collected data (coming predominantly from middle-class, white New Zealand English speakers), Holmes demonstrates consistently how, other things being equal, women use strategies typically associated with showing greater concern for the other, and do this more than men do. This finding seems to be corroborated by a number of other studies of gender and language in other communities.

Questions of interpretation are extremely important here. We obviously need to ask ourselves whether we interpret certain strategies used predominantly by women as 'polite' *because* they are used by women. Holmes suggests that some instances of stereotypical male talk (e.g., verbal aggression) which appear to be offensive and impolite, may actually signal in-group rapport and camaraderie, not unlike Brown and Levinson's positive politeness. In other words, men and women may, at times, be *equally* polite in their own terms, but achieve this in dramatically different ways, not always acceptable to the other group.

Such a view could then be challenged from positions assuming unequal power relations between the sexes. It could be argued that if women do politeness by showing less aggression than men, it is because they are in a less powerful social position that doesn't allow them to use conventionalised aggression as much as (powerful) men do. However, in her review of male–female differences in speech, Milroy (1992) suggests that this view of politeness is a stereotype. For example, she argues that men in powerful jobs (say, top executives of large companies) are likely to follow the stereotypically female patterns of politeness (e.g., hedging their requests or using indirectness) precisely because they are powerful. 'You wouldn't have time to type this letter for me?' may be a sufficiently explicit and 'more effective' request from a male boss to a female secretary than 'Type this letter'. In the Part Five of the *Reader*, Deborah Cameron (Chapter 29) goes even further in questioning the explanations of 'typical' linguistic behaviour in men and women. She argues that they, too, often conform to our stereotypes of what is 'normal', predictable and accepted behaviour by men and women.

The next two chapters, by Deborah Tannen and Cynthia Wallat (Chapter 24) and Nikolas Coupland and Virpi Ylänne (Chapter 25), are concerned with a different aspect of interpersonal communication: discourse *framing*. Drawing on linguistic, sociological and cognitive work, Tannen and Wallat start with a helpful summary of related concepts such as 'frame', 'footing' and 'knowledge schema'. They apply these terms to an analysis of a paediatric consultation, in which the doctor shifts *register* (style of speaking), signalling how the speech event is restructured from moment to moment. Style shifts mark changes in the type of activity she is engaged in (medical examination of the child, giving explanations to the mother, giving explanations to students, recording diagnosis), and changes in the 'participation framework' (speaking to the child, or mother, or student). This chapter shows also how frames are established interactively, as part of a negotiative process and through conversational work. The doctor alternates between the interactive frames of 'examination' and 'consultation' on the one hand, and 'social encounter' on the other. In this way she shows sensitivity to the mother, for whom unmitigated, matter-of-fact talk about her child's impairment could be emotionally difficult to cope with. Thus, to ease the mother's emotional burden, the doctor 'blunts the effect of the information she imparts by using circumlocutions and repetitions; pausing and hesitating; and minimizing the significant danger of the arteriovenous malformation by using the word 'only' ('only danger'), by using the conditional tense ('that would be the danger'), 'and by stressing what sounds positive, that they're not going to get worse' (pp. 341–2). These framing devices, not unlike Gumperz's contextualization cues (see Chapter 4) perform the dual role of signalling what kind of frame is being established in interaction at the moment of speaking, and forming part of the message communicated within this frame, too.

Coupland and Ylänne problematise the notion of small talk by examining patterns of 'weather talk' in travel agencies encounters between agents and clients. They apply Goffman's idea of interactional frames, i.e., patterns of expectations of what goes on in a specific communicative episode, to demonstrate the multiplicity and multifunctionality of this activity. Thus, weather talk may be exploited as the archetypal form of phatic communion (Malinowski, Chapter 20). It can involve highly procedural, transitional or 'in passing' talk, orienting to the environment external to the local context of interaction. But they also show that weather talk also creates interpersonal closeness in discussions of shared experience, leading to intimate and self-disclosive talk. But also, as part of the travel agent's script for selling a holiday, the weather is framed as a commodity, part of the marketised discourse that abounds in travel contexts.

This Part of the *Reader* ends with an example of a study of relational issues in a medium other than language – visual communication. Gunther Kress and Theo Van Leeuwen's study of the meaning of visual images as a semiotic system is a multidisciplinary project which draws on history of art, semiotics and linguistics. The authors argue that language is only one of the representational and communicative systems and can no longer be considered as central to human communication. For them, the *semiotic landscape* (the world of meaning) in which we live has undergone a transformation and is now dominated by *multimodality*, or diversity of media (see our Introduction to Part Two). Visual images present us with an interpretive challenge. We can see them and (in most cases) be sure what they 'show', but the processes of visual representation are far more subtle than being able to say what a picture 'shows'. In their analysis of the structural relationships of elements within visual images and their compositional arrangements, Kress and Van Leeuwen give us the basis for an understanding of how these images are constructed; a key to *visual literacy*.

In the chapter we have extracted here, Kress and Van Leeuwen illustrate the types of interpersonal relationship that can be established between the (human) subject of an image and its viewer. They examine three dimensions of interpersonal relations that are typically associated with discursive patterns of communication: distance, rapport and power, and they link them to three formal aspects of image making: closeness of the shot, frontal/oblique angle, and high/low angle. Kress and Van Leeuwen propose that these relationships are patterned in the following way. Close shot = intimate/personal; medium shot = social; long shot = impersonal. Frontal angle = involvement; oblique angle = detachment. High angle = viewer power; eye-level angle = equality; low angle = represented participant power. Compare Van Leeuwen's analysis of perspective and interpersonal distance in his analysis of sound (Chapter 12).

References

Cheepen, C. (1988) *The Predictability of Everyday Conversation*, London: Pinter.

Coupland, J. (2000) 'Introduction', in J. Coupland (ed.) *Small Talk*, London: Longman. 1–25.

Coupland, J., Coupland, N. and Robinson, J.D. (1992) '"How are you?": Negotiating phatic communion', *Language in Society* 21: 207–30.

Jaworski, A. (2000) 'Silence and small talk', in J. Coupland (ed.) *Small Talk*, London: Longman. 110–32.

Laver, J. (1974) 'Communicative functions of phatic communion', in A. Kendon, R.M. Harris and M. Ritche Key (eds) *Organization of Behavior in Face-to-face Interaction*, The Hague: Mouton, 215–38.

—— (1981) 'Linguistic routines and politeness in greeting and parting', in F. Coulmas (ed.) *Conversational Routine: Explorations in Standardized Communication Situations and Prepatterned Speech*, The Hague: Mouton. 289–304.

Leach, E.R. (1976) *Culture and Communication: The Logic by which Symbols are Connected. An Introduction to the Use of Structuralist Analysis in Social Anthropology*, Cambridge: Cambridge University Press.

Milroy, L. (1992) 'New perspectives in the analysis of sex differentiation in language', in K. Bolton and H. Kwok (eds) *Sociolinguistics Today: International Perspectives*, London: Routledge. 163–79.

Turner, V. (1969) *The Ritual Process: Structure and Anti-structure*, Chicago, IL: Aldine.

Watzlawick, P., Beavin-Bavelas, J. and Jackson, D. (1967) *The Pragmatics of Human Communication*, New York: Norton.

Chapter 20

Bronislaw Malinowski

ON PHATIC COMMUNION

. . .

THE CASE OF LANGUAGE used in free, aimless, social intercourse requires special consideration. When a number of people sit together at a village fire, after all the daily tasks are over, or when they chat, resting from work, or when they accompany some mere manual work by gossip quite unconnected with what they are doing – it is clear that here we have to do with another mode of using language, with another type of speech function. Language here is not dependent upon what happens at that moment, it seems to be even deprived of any context of situation. The meaning of any utterance cannot be connected with the speaker's or hearer's behaviour, with the purpose of what they are doing.

A mere phrase of politeness, in use as much among savage tribes as in a European drawing-room, fulfils a function to which the meaning of its words is almost completely irrelevant. Inquiries about health, comments on weather, affirmations of some supremely obvious state of things – all such are exchanged, not in order to inform, not in this case to connect people in action, certainly not in order to express any thought. It would be even incorrect, I think, to say that such words serve the purpose of establishing a common sentiment, for this is usually absent from such current phrases of intercourse; and where it purports to exist, as in expressions of sympathy, it is avowedly spurious on one side. What is the *raison d'être*, therefore, of such phrases as 'How do you do?' 'Ah, here you are,' 'Where do you come from?' 'Nice day to-day' – all of which serve in one society or another as formulae of greeting or approach?

I think that, in discussing the function of speech in mere sociabilities we come to one of the bedrock aspects of man's nature in society. There is in all human

Source: Bronislaw Malinowski, 'The problem of meaning in primitive languages' in C.K. Ogden and I.A. Richards (eds) *The Meaning of Meaning*, London: Routledge & Kegan Paul, 1923, 296–336.

beings the well-known tendency to congregate, to be together, to enjoy each other's company. Many instincts and innate trends, such as fear or pugnacity, all the types of social sentiments such as ambition, vanity, passion for power and wealth, are dependent upon and associated with the fundamental tendency which makes the mere presence of others a necessity for man.

Now speech is the intimate correlate of this tendency, for, to a natural man, another man's silence is not a reassuring factor, but, on the contrary, something alarming and dangerous. The stranger who cannot speak the language is to all savage tribesmen a natural enemy. To the primitive mind, whether among savages or our own uneducated classes, taciturnity means not only unfriendliness but directly a bad character. This no doubt varies greatly with the national character but remains true as a general rule. The breaking of silence, the communion of words is the first act to establish links of fellowship, which is consummated only by the breaking of bread and the communion of food. The modern English expression, 'Nice day to-day' or the Melanesian phrase, 'Whence comest thou?' are needed to get over the strange and unpleasant tension which men feel when facing each other in silence.

After the first formula, there comes a flow of language, purposeless expressions of preference or aversion, accounts of irrelevant happenings, comments on what is perfectly obvious. Such gossip, as found in primitive societies, differs only a little from our own. Always the same emphasis of affirmation and consent, mixed perhaps with an incidental disagreement which creates the bonds of antipathy. Or personal accounts of the speaker's views and life history, to which the hearer listens under some restraint and with slightly veiled impatience, waiting till his own turn arrives to speak. For in this use of speech the bonds created between hearer and speaker are not quite symmetrical, the man linguistically active receiving the greater share of social pleasure and self-enhancement. But though the hearing given to such utterances is as a rule not as intense as the speaker's own share, it is quite essential for his pleasure, and the reciprocity is established by the change of roles.

There can be no doubt that we have here a new type of linguistic use – *phatic communion* I am tempted to call it, actuated by the demon of terminological invention – a type of speech in which ties of union are created by a mere exchange of words. Let us look at it from the special point of view with which we are here concerned; let us ask what light it throws on the function or nature of language. Are words in phatic communion used primarily to convey meaning, the meaning which is symbolically theirs? Certainly not! They fulfil a social function and that is their principal aim, but they are neither the result of intellectual reflection, nor do they necessarily arouse reflection in the listener. Once again we may say that language does not function here as a means of transmission of thought.

But can we regard it as a mode of action? And in what relation does it stand to our crucial conception of context of situation? It is obvious that the outer situation does not enter directly into the technique of speaking. But what can be considered as *situation* when a number of people aimlessly gossip together? It consists in just this atmosphere of sociability and in the fact of the personal communion of these people. But this is in fact achieved by speech, and the situation in all such cases is created by the exchange of words, by the specific feelings which form convivial gregariousness, by the give and take of utterances which make up ordinary gossip. The whole situation consists in what happens linguistically. Each utterance is an act serving the direct aim of binding hearer to speaker by a tie of some social sentiment or other. Once more language appears to us in this function not as an instrument of reflection but as a mode of action.

I should like to add at once that though the examples discussed were taken from savage life, we could find among ourselves exact parallels to every type of linguistic use so far discussed. The binding tissue of words which unites the crew of a ship in bad weather, the verbal concomitants of a company of soldiers in action, the technical language running parallel to some practical work or sporting pursuit – all these resemble essentially the primitive uses of speech by man in action and our discussion could have been equally well conducted on a modern example. I have chosen the above from a savage community, because I wanted to emphasize that such and no other is the nature of *primitive* speech.

Again in pure sociabilities and gossip we use language exactly as savages do and our talk becomes the 'phatic communion' analysed above, which serves to establish bonds of personal union between people brought together by the mere need of companionship and does not serve any purpose of communicating ideas. . . . Indeed there need not or perhaps even there must not be anything to communicate. As long as there are words to exchange, phatic communion brings savage and civilized alike into the pleasant atmosphere of polite, social intercourse.

It is only in certain very special uses among a civilized community and only in its highest uses that language is employed to frame and express thoughts. In poetic and literary production, language is made to embody human feelings and passions, to render in a subtle and convincing manner certain inner states and processes of mind. In works of science and philosophy, highly developed types of speech are used to control ideas and to make them common property of civilized mankind.

Even in this function, however, it is not correct to regard language as a mere residuum of reflective thought. And the conception of speech as serving to translate the inner processes of the speaker to the hearer is one-sided and gives us, even with regard to the most highly developed and specialized uses of speech, only a partial and certainly not the most relevant view.

To restate the main position arrived at in this section we can say that language in its primitive function and original form has an essentially pragmatic character; that it is a mode of behaviour, an indispensable element of concerted human action. And negatively: that to regard it as a means for the embodiment or expression of thought is to take a one-sided view of one of its most derivate and specialized functions.

. . .

Chapter 21

Erving Goffman

ON FACE-WORK: AN ANALYSIS OF RITUAL ELEMENTS IN SOCIAL INTERACTION

EVERY PERSON LIVES IN A WORLD of social encounters, involving him either in face-to-face or mediated contact with other participants. In each of these contacts, he tends to act out what is sometimes called a line – that is, a pattern of verbal and nonverbal acts by which he expresses his view of the situation and through this his evaluation of the participants, especially himself. Regardless of whether a person intends to take a line, he will find that he has done so in effect. The other participants will assume that he has more or less willfully taken a stand, so that if he is to deal with their response to him he must take into consideration the impression they have possibly formed of him.

The term face may be defined as the positive social value a person effectively claims for himself by the line others assume he has taken during a particular contact. Face is an image of self delineated in terms of approved social attributes – albeit an image that others may share, as when a person makes a good showing for his profession or religion by making a good showing for himself.

A person tends to experience an immediate emotional response to the face which a contact with others allows him; he cathects his face; his "feelings" become attached to it. If the encounter sustains an image of him that he has long taken for granted, he probably will have few feelings about the matter. If events establish a face for him that is better than he might have expected, he is likely to "feel good"; if his ordinary expectations are not fulfilled, one expects that he will "feel bad" or "feel hurt." In general, a person's attachment to a particular face, coupled with the ease with which disconfirming information can be conveyed by himself and others, provides one reason why he finds that participation in any contact with others is a commitment. A person will also have feelings about the face sustained for the other participants, and while these feelings may differ in quantity and direction from

Source: Erving Goffman, *Interaction Ritual: Essays on Face-to-Face Behavior*, Garolen City, NY: Anchor/ Doubleday, 1967.

those he has for his own face, they constitute an involvement in the face of others that is as immediate and spontaneous as the involvement he has in his own face. One's own face and the face of others are constructs of the same order; it is the rules of the group and the definition of the situation which determine how much feeling one is to have for face and how this feeling is to be distributed among the faces involved.

1) A person may be said to *have*, or *be in*, or *maintain* face when the line he effectively takes presents an image of him that is internally consistent, that is supported by judgements and evidence conveyed by other participants, and that is confirmed by evidence conveyed through impersonal agencies in the situation. At such times the person's face clearly is something that is not lodged in or on his body, but rather something that is diffusely located in the flow of events in the encounter and becomes manifest only when these events are read and interpreted for the appraisals expressed in them.

. . .

2) A person may be said to *be in wrong face* when information is brought forth in some way about his social worth which cannot be integrated, even with effort, into the line that is being sustained for him. A person may be said to *be out of face* when[3] he participates in a contact with others without having ready a line of the kind participants in such situations are expected to take. The intent of many pranks is to lead a person into showing a wrong face or no face, but there will also be serious occasions, of course, when he will find himself expressively out of touch with the situation.

When a person senses that he is in face, he typically responds with feelings of confidence and assurance. Firm in the line he is taking, he feels that he can hold his head up and openly present himself to others. He feels some security and some relief — as he also can when the others feel he is in wrong face but successfully hide these feelings from him.

. . .

Following common usage, I shall employ the term *poise* to refer to the capacity to suppress and conceal any tendency to become shamefaced during encounters with others.

In our Anglo-American society, as in some others, the phrase "to lose face" seems to mean to be in wrong face, to be out of face, or to be shamefaced. The phrase "to save one's face" appears to refer to the process by which the person sustains an impression for others that he has not lost face. Following Chinese usage, one can say that "to give face" is to arrange for another to take a better line than he might otherwise have been able to take, the other thereby gets face given him, this being one way in which he can gain face.

As an aspect of the social code of any social circle, one may expect to find an understanding as to how far a person should go to save his face. Once he takes on a self-image expressed through face he will be expected to live up to it. In different ways in different societies he will be required to show self-respect, abjuring certain actions because they are above or beneath him, while forcing himself to perform others even though they cost him dearly. By entering a situation in which he is given a face to maintain, a person takes on the responsibility of standing guard over the flow of events as they pass before him. He must ensure that a particular *expressive order* is sustained – an order that regulates the flow of events, large or small, so that anything that appears to be expressed by them will be consistent with his face. . . .

Just as the member of any group is expected to have self-respect, so also he is expected to sustain a standard of considerateness; he is expected to go to certain lengths to save the feelings and the face of others present, and he is expected to do this willingly and spontaneously because of emotional identification with the others and with their feelings. In consequence, he is [disinclined to witness the defacement of others.] The person who can witness another's humiliation and unfeelingly retain a cool countenance himself is said in our society to be "heart-less," just as he who can unfeelingly participate in his own defacement is thought to be "shameless."

The combined effect of the rule of self-respect and the rule of considerateness is that the person tends to conduct himself during an encounter so as to maintain both his own face and the face of the other participants. This means that the line taken by each participant is usually allowed to prevail, and each participant is allowed to carry off the role he appears to have chosen for himself. A state where everyone temporarily accepts everyone else's line is established. This kind of mutual acceptance seems to be a basic structural feature of interaction, especially the inter-action of face-to-face talk. It is typically a "working" acceptance, not a "real" one, since it tends to be based not on agreement of candidly expressed heart-felt evaluations, but upon a willingness to give temporary lip service to judgements with which the participants do not really agree.

The mutual acceptance of lines has an important conservative effect upon encounters. Once the person initially presents a line, he and the others tend to build their later responses upon it, and in a sense become stuck with it. Should the person radically alter his line, or should it become discredited, then confusion results, for the participants will have prepared and committed themselves for actions that are now unsuitable.

Ordinarily, maintenance of face is a condition of interaction, not its objective. Usual objectives, such as gaining face for oneself, giving free expression to one's true beliefs, introducing depreciating information about the others, or solving prob-lems and performing tasks, are typically pursued in such a way as to be consistent with the maintenance of face. To study face-saving is to study the traffic rules of social interaction; one learns about the code the person adheres to in his move-ment across the paths and designs of others, but not where he is going, or why he wants to get there. One does not even learn why he *is* ready to follow the code, for a large number of different motives can equally lead him to do so. He may want to save his own face because of his emotional attachment to the image of self which it expresses, because of his pride or honor, because of the power his presumed status allows him to exert over the other participants, and so on. He may want to save the others' face because of his emotional attachment to an image of them, or because he feels that his coparticipants have a moral right to this protection, or because he wants to avoid the hostility that may be directed toward him if they lose their face. He may feel that an assumption has been made that he is the sort of person who shows compassion and sympathy toward others, so that to retain his own face, he may feel obliged to be considerate of the line taken by the other participants.

By *face-work* I mean to designate the actions taken by a person to make whatever he is doing consistent with face. Face-work serves to counteract "incidents" – that is, events whose effective symbolic implications threaten face. Thus poise is one important type of face-work, for through poise the person controls his embarrassment and hence the embarrassment that he and others might have over his embarrassment. Whether or not the full consequences of face-saving actions are known to the person who employs them, they often become habitual and standardized practices; they are like traditional plays in a game or traditional steps in a dance. Each person, subculture, and society seems to have its own characteristic repertoire of face-saving practices. It is to this repertoire that people partly refer when they ask what a person or culture is "really" like. And yet the particular set of practices stressed by particular persons or groups seems to be drawn from a single logically coherent framework of possible practices. It is as if face, by its very nature, can be saved only in a certain number of ways, and as if each social grouping must make its selections from this single matrix of possibilities.

The members of every social circle may be expected to have some knowledge of face-work and some experience in its use. In our society, this kind of capacity is sometimes called tact, *savoir-faire*, diplomacy, or social skill. Variation in social skill pertains more to the efficacy of face-work than to the frequency of its application, for almost all acts involving others are modified, prescriptively or proscriptively, by considerations of face.

If a person is to employ his repertoire of face-saving practices, obviously he must first become aware of the interpretations that others may have placed upon his acts and the interpretations that he ought perhaps to place upon theirs. In other words, he must exercise perceptiveness. . . .

I have already said that the person will have two points of view – a defensive orientation toward saving his own face and a protective orientation toward saving the others' face. Some practices will be primarily defensive and others primarily protective, although in general one may expect these two perspectives to be taken at the same time. In trying to save the face of others, the person must choose a tack that will not lead to loss of his own; in trying to save his own face, he must consider the loss of face that his action may entail for others.

. . .

The basic kinds of face-work

The avoidance process

The surest way for a person to prevent threats to his face is to avoid contacts in which these threats are likely to occur. In all societies one can observe this in the avoidance relationship and in the tendency for certain delicate transactions to be conducted by go-betweens. Similarly, in many societies, members know the value of voluntarily making a gracious withdrawal before an anticipated threat to face has had a chance to occur.

Once the person does chance an encounter, other kinds of avoidance practices come into play. As defensive measures, he keeps off topics and away from activities that would lead to the expression of information that is inconsistent with the line he is maintaining. At opportune moments he will change the topic of conversation or the direction of activity. He will often present initially a front of diffidence and composure, suppressing any show of feeling until he has found out what kind of line the others will be ready to support for him. Any claims regarding self may be made with belittling modesty, with strong qualifications, or with a note of unseriousness; by hedging in these ways he will have prepared a self for himself that will not be discredited by exposure, personal failure, or the unanticipated acts of others. And if he does not hedge his claims about self, he will at least attempt to be realistic about them, knowing that otherwise events may discredit him and make him lose face.

Certain protective maneuvers are as common as these defensive ones. The person shows respect and politeness, making sure to extend to others any ceremonial treatment that might be their due. He employs discretion; he leaves unstated facts that might implicitly or explicitly contradict and embarrass the positive claims made by others. He employs circumlocutions and deception, phrasing his replies with careful ambiguity so that the others' face is preserved even if their welfare is not. He employs courtesies, making slight modifications of his demands on or appraisals of the others so that they will be able to define the situation as one in which their self-respect is not threatened. In making a belittling demand upon the others, or in imputing uncomplimentary attributes to them, he may employ a joking manner, allowing them to take the line that they are good sports, able to relax from their ordinary standards of pride and honor. And before engaging in a potentially offensive act, he may provide explanations as to why the others ought not to be affronted by it. For example, if he knows that it will be necessary to withdraw from the encounter before it has terminated, he may tell the others in advance that it is necessary for him to leave, so that they will have faces that are prepared for it. But neutralizing the potentially offensive act need not be done verbally; he may wait for a propitious moment or natural break — for example, in conversation, a momentary lull when no one speaker can be affronted — and then leave, in this way using the context instead of his words as a guarantee of inoffensiveness.

When a person fails to prevent an incident, he can still attempt to maintain the fiction that no threat to face has occurred. The most blatant example of this is found where the person acts as if an event that contains a threatening expression has not occurred at all. He may apply this studied nonobservance to his own acts — as when he does not by outward sign admit that his stomach is rumbling — or to the acts of others, as when he does not "see" that another has stumbled. Social life in mental hospitals owes much to this process; patients employ it in regard to their own peculiarities, and visitors employ it, often with tenuous desperation, in regard to patients. In general, tactful blindness of this kind is applied only to events that, if perceived at all, could be perceived and interpreted only as threats to face.

A more important, less spectacular kind of tactful overlooking is practiced when a person openly acknowledges an incident as an event that has occurred, but not as an event that contains a threatening expression. If he is not the one who is responsible for the incident, then his blindness will have to be supported by his forbearance; if he is the doer of the threatening deed, then his blindness will have to be supported by his willingness to seek a way of dealing with the matter, which leaves him dangerously dependent upon the cooperative forbearance of the others.

Another kind of avoidance occurs when a person loses control of his expressions during an encounter. At such times he may try not so much to overlook the incident as to hide or conceal his activity in some way, thus making it possible for the others to avoid some of the difficulties created by a participant who has not maintained face. Correspondingly, when a person is caught out of face because he had not expected to be thrust into interaction, or because strong feelings have disrupted his expressive mask, the others may protectively turn away from him or his activity for a moment, to give him time to assemble himself.

The corrective process

When the participants in an undertaking or encounter fail to prevent the occurrence of an event that is expressively incompatible with the judgements of social worth that are being maintained, and when the event is of the kind that is difficult to overlook, then the participants are likely to give it accredited status as an incident – to ratify it as a threat that deserves direct official attention – and to proceed to try to correct for its effects. At this point one or more participants find themselves in an established state of ritual disequilibrium or disgrace, and an attempt must be made to re-establish a satisfactory ritual state for them. I use the term *ritual* because I am dealing with acts through whose symbolic component the actor shows how worthy he is of respect or how worthy he feels others are of it. The imagery of equilibrium is apt here because the length and intensity of the corrective effort is nicely adapted to the persistence and intensity of the threat. One's face, then, is a sacred thing, and the expressive order required to sustain it is therefore a ritual one.

The sequence of acts set in motion by an acknowledged threat to face, and terminating in the re-establishment of ritual equilibrium, I shall call an *interchange*. Defining a message or move as everything conveyed by an actor during a turn at taking action, one can say that an interchange will involve two or more moves and two or more participants. Obvious examples in our society may be found in the sequence of "Excuse me" and "Certainly," and in the exchange of presents or visits. The interchange seems to be a basic concrete unit of social activity and provides one natural empirical way to study interaction of all kinds. Face-saving practices can be usefully classified according to their position in the natural sequence of moves that comprise this unit. Aside from the event which introduces the need for a corrective interchange, four classic moves seem to be involved.

There is, first, the *challenge*, by which participants take on the responsibility of calling attention to the misconduct; by implication they suggest that the threatened claims are to stand firm and that the threatening event itself will have to be brought back into line.

The second move consists of the *offering*, whereby a participant, typically the offender, is given a chance to correct for the offense and re-establish the expressive order. Some classic ways of making this move are available. On the one hand, an attempt can be made to show that what admittedly appeared to be a threatening expression is really a meaningless event, or an unintentional act, or a joke not meant to be taken seriously, or an unavoidable, "understandable" product of extenuating circumstances. On the other hand, the meaning of the event may be granted and effort concentrated on the creator of it. Information may be provided to show that the creator was under the influence of something and not himself, or that he was under the command of somebody else and not acting for himself. When a person claims that an act was meant in jest, he may go on and claim that the self that seemed to lie behind the act was also projected as a joke. When a person suddenly finds that he has demonstrably failed in capacities that the others assumed him to have and to claim for himself — such as the capacity to spell, to perform minor tasks, to talk without malapropisms, and so on — he may quickly add, in a serious or unserious way, that he claims these incapacities as part of his self. The meaning of the threatening incident thus stands, but it can now be incorporated smoothly into the flow of expressive events.

Challenge
Offer
Accept
Gratitude

. . .

After the challenge and the offering have been made, the third move can occur: the persons to whom the offering is made can *accept* it as a satisfactory means of re-establishing the expressive order and the faces supported by this order. Only then can the offender cease the major part of his ritual offering.

In the terminal move of the interchange, the forgiven person conveys a sign of *gratitude* to those who have given him the indulgence of forgiveness.

The phases of the corrective process — challenge, offering, acceptance, and thanks — provide a model for interpersonal ritual behavior, but a model that may be departed from in significant ways. For example, the offended parties may give the offender a chance to initiate the offering on his own before a challenge is made and before they ratify the offense as an incident. This is a common courtesy, extended on the assumption that the recipient will introduce a self-challenge. Further, when the offended persons accept the corrective offering, the offender may suspect that this has been grudgingly done from tact, and so he may volunteer additional corrective offerings, not allowing the matter to rest until he has received a second or third acceptance of his repeated apology. Or the offended persons may tactfully take over the role of the offender and volunteer excuses for him that will, perforce, be acceptable to the offended persons.

An important departure from the standard corrective cycle occurs when a challenged offender patently refuses to heed the warning and continues with his offending behavior, instead of setting the activity to rights. This move shifts the play back to the challengers. If they countenance the refusal to meet their demands, then it will be plain that their challenge was a bluff and that the bluff has been called. This is an untenable position; a face for themselves cannot be derived from it, and they are left to bluster. To avoid this fate, some classic moves are open to them. For instance, they can resort to tactless, violent retaliation, destroying either themselves or the person who had refused to heed their warning. Or they can withdraw from the undertaking in a visible huff – righteously indignant, outraged, but confident of ultimate vindication. Both tacks provide a way of denying the offender his status as an interactant, and hence denying the reality of the offensive judgment he has made. Both strategies are ways of salvaging face, but for all concerned the costs are usually high. It is partly to forestall such scenes that an offender is usually quick to offer apologies; he does not want the affronted persons to trap themselves into the obligation to resort to desperate measures.

It is plain that emotions play a part in these cycles of response, as when anguish is expressed because of what one has done to another's face, or anger because of what has been done to one's own. I want to stress that these emotions function as moves, and fit so precisely into the logic of the ritual game that it would seem difficult to understand them without it. In fact, spontaneously expressed feelings are likely to fit into the formal pattern of the ritual interchange more elegantly than consciously designed ones.

Making points – the aggressive use of face-work

Every face-saving practice which is allowed to neutralize a particular threat opens up the possibility that the threat will be willfully introduced for what can be safely gained by it. If a person knows that his modesty will be answered by others' praise of him, he can fish for compliments. If his own appraisal of self will be checked against incidental events, then he can arrange for favorable incidental events to appear. If others are prepared to overlook an affront to them and act forbearantly, or to accept apologies, then he can rely on this as a basis for safely offending them. He can attempt by sudden withdrawal to force the others into a ritually unsatisfactory state, leaving them to flounder in an interchange that cannot readily be completed. Finally, at some expense to himself, he can arrange for the others to hurt his feelings, thus forcing them to feel guilt, remorse, and sustained ritual disequilibrium.

When a person treats face-work not as something he need be prepared to perform, but rather as something that others can be counted on to perform or to accept, then an encounter or an undertaking becomes less a scene of mutual considerateness than an arena in which a contest or match is held. The purpose of the game is to preserve everyone's line from an inexcusable contradiction, while scoring as many points as possible against one's adversaries and making as many gains as possible for oneself. An audience to the struggle is almost a necessity. The general method is for the person to introduce favorable facts about himself and unfavorable facts about the others in such a way that the only reply the others will be able to think up will be one that terminates the interchange in a grumble, a meager excuse, a face-saving I-can-take-a-joke laugh, or an empty stereotyped comeback of the "Oh yeah?" or "That's what you think" variety. The losers in such cases will have to cut their losses, tacitly grant the loss of a point, and attempt to do better in the next interchange. Points made by allusion to social class status are

sometimes called snubs; those made by allusions to moral respectability are sometimes called digs; in either case one deals with a capacity at what is sometimes
called "bitchiness."

. . .

Cooperation in face-work

When a face has been threatened, face-work must be done, but whether this is
initiated and primarily carried through by the person whose face is threatened, or
by the offender, or by a mere witness, is often of secondary importance. Lack of
effort on the part of one person induces compensatory effort from others; a contribution by one person relieves the others of the task. In fact, there are many minor
incidents in which the offender and the offended simultaneously attempt to initiate
an apology. Resolution of the situation to everyone's apparent satisfaction is the
first requirement; correct apportionment of blame is typically a secondary consideration. Hence terms such as tact and *savoir-faire* fail to distinguish whether it is
the person's own face that his diplomacy saves or the face of the others. Similarly,
terms such as *gaffe* and *faux pas* fail to specify whether it is the actor's own face he
has threatened or the face of other participants. . . . Tact in regard to face-work
often relies for its operation on a tacit agreement to do business through the language
of hint – the language of innuendo, ambiguities, well-placed pauses, carefully
worded jokes, and so on. The rule regarding this official kind of communication is
that the sender ought not to act as if he had officially conveyed the message he has
hinted at, while the recipients have the right and the obligation to act as if they
have not officially received the message contained in the hint. Hinted communication, then, is deniable communication; it need not be faced up to. It provides a
means by which the person can be warned that his current line or the current situation is leading to loss of face, without this warning itself becoming an incident.

   Another form of tacit cooperation, and one that seems to be much used in
many societies, is reciprocal self-denial. Often the person does not have a clear
idea of what would be a just or acceptable apportionment of judgements during
the occasions, and so he voluntarily deprives or depreciates himself while indulging
and complimenting the others, in both cases carrying the judgements safely past
what is likely to be just. The favorable judgements about himself he allows to come
from the others; the unfavorable judgements of himself are his own contributions.
This "after you, Alphonse" technique works, of course, because in depriving himself
he can reliably anticipate that the others will compliment or indulge him. Whatever
allocation of favors is eventually established, all participants are first given a chance
to show that they are not bound or constrained by their own desires and expectations, that they have a properly modest view of themselves, and that they can be
counted upon to support the ritual code. Negative bargaining, through which each
participant tries to make the terms of the trade more favorable to the other side,
is another instance; as a form of exchange perhaps it is more widespread than the
economist's kind.

A person's performance of face-work, extended by his tacit agreement to help others perform theirs, represents his willingness to abide by the ground rules of social interaction. Here is the hallmark of his socialization as an interactant. If he and the others were not socialized in this way, interaction in most societies and most situations would be a much more hazardous thing for feelings and faces. The person would find it impractical to be orientated to symbolically conveyed appraisals of social worth, or to be possessed of feelings – that is, it would be impractical for him to be a ritually delicate object. And as I shall suggest, if the person were not a ritually delicate object, occasions of talk could not be organized in the way they usually are. It is no wonder that trouble is caused by a person who cannot be relied upon to play the face-saving game.

The ritual roles of the self

So far I have implicitly been using a double definition of self: the self as an image pieced together from the expressive implications of the full flow of events in an undertaking; and the self as a kind of player in a ritual game who copes honorably or dishonorably, diplomatically or undiplomatically, with the judgemental contingencies of the situation. . . .

Once the two roles of the self have been separated, one can look to the ritual code implicit in face-work to learn how the two roles are related. When a person is responsible for introducing a threat to another's face, he apparently has a right, within limits, to wriggle out of the difficulty by means of self-abasement. When performed voluntarily these indignities do not seem to profane his own image. It is as if he had the right of insulation and could castigate himself qua actor without injuring himself qua object of ultimate worth. By token of the same insulation he can belittle himself and modestly underplay his positive qualities, with the understanding that no one will take his statements as a fair representation of his sacred self. On the other hand, if he is forced against his will to treat himself in these ways, his face, his pride, and his honor will be seriously threatened. Thus, in terms of the ritual code, the person seems to have a special license to accept mistreatment at his own hands that he does not have the right to accept from others. Perhaps this is a safe arrangement because he is not likely to carry this license too far, whereas the others, were they given this privilege, might be more likely to abuse it.

Further, within limits the person has a right to forgive other participants for affronts to his sacred image. He can forbearantly overlook minor slurs upon his face, and in regard to somewhat greater injuries he is the one person who is in a position to accept apologies on behalf of his sacred self. This is a relatively safe prerogative for the person to have in regard to himself, for it is one that is exercised in the interests of the others or of the undertaking. Interestingly enough, when the person commits a *gaffe* against himself, it is not he who has the license to forgive the event; only the others have that prerogative, and it is a safe prerogative for them to have because they can exercise it only in his interests or in the interests of the undertaking. One finds, then, a system of checks and balances by which each participant tends to be given the right to handle only those matters which he will have little motivation for mishandling. In short, the rights and oblig-ations of an interactant are designed to prevent him from abusing his role as an object of sacred value.

. . .

Face and social relationships

When a person begins a mediated or immediate encounter, he already stands in some kind of social relationship to the others concerned, and expects to stand in a given relationship to them after the particular encounter ends. This, of course, is one of the ways in which social contacts are geared into the wider society. Much of the activity occurring during an encounter can be understood as an effort on everyone's part to get through the occasion and all the unanticipated and uninten-tional events that can cast participants in an undesirable light, without disrupting the relationships of the participants. And if relationships are in the process of change, the object will be to bring the encounter to a satisfactory close without altering the expected course of development. This perspective nicely accounts, for example, for the little ceremonies of greeting and farewell which occur when people begin a conversational encounter or depart from one. Greetings provide a way of show-ing that a relationship is still what it was at the termination of the previous coparticipation, and, typically, that this relationship involves sufficient suppression of hostility for the participants temporarily to drop their guards and talk. Farewells sum up the effect of the encounter upon the relationship and show what the partici-pants may expect of one another when they next meet. The enthusiasm of greetings compensates for the weakening of the relationship caused by the absence just termi-nated, while the enthusiasm of farewells compensates the relationship for the harm that is about to be done to it by separation. Greetings, of course, serve to clarify and fix the roles that the participants will take during the occasion of talk and to commit participants to these roles, while farewells provide a way of unambigu-ously terminating the encounter. Greetings and farewells may also be used to state, and apologize for, extenuating circumstances – in the case of greetings for circum-stances that have kept the participants from interacting until now, and in the case of farewells for circumstances that prevent the participants from continuing their display of solidarity. These apologies allow the impression to be maintained that the participants are more warmly related socially than may be the case. This posi-tive stress, in turn, assures that they will act more ready to enter into contacts than they perhaps really feel inclined to do, thus guaranteeing that diffuse channels for potential communication will be kept open in the society.

It seems to be a characteristic obligation of many social relationships that each of the members guarantees to support a given face for the other members in given situations. To prevent disruption of these relationships, it is therefore necessary for each member to avoid destroying the others' face. . . . Furthermore, in many relationships, the members come to share a face, so that in the presence of third parties an improper act on the part of one member becomes a source of acute embarrassment to the other members. A social relationship, then, can be seen as a way in which the person is more than ordinarily forced to trust his self-image and face to the tact and good conduct of others.

The nature of the ritual order

. . .

Throughout this paper it has been implied that underneath their differences in culture, people everywhere are the same. If persons have a universal human nature, they themselves are not to be looked to for an explanation of it. One must look rather to the fact that societies everywhere, if they are to be societies, must mobilize their members as self-regulating participants in social encounters. One way of mobilizing the individual for this purpose is through ritual; he is taught to be perceptive, to have feelings attached to self and a self expressed through face, to have pride, honor, and dignity, to have considerateness, to have tact and a certain amount of poise. These are some of the elements of behavior which must be built into the person if practical use is to be made of him as an interactant, and it is these elements that are referred to in part when one speaks of universal human nature.

Universal human nature is not a very human thing. By acquiring it, the person becomes a kind of construct, built up not from inner psychic propensities but from moral rules that are impressed upon him from without. These rules, when followed, determine the evaluation he will make of himself and of his fellow-participants in the encounter, the distribution of his feelings, and the kinds of practices he will employ to maintain a specified and obligatory kind of ritual equilibrium. The general capacity to be bound by moral rules may well belong to the individual, but the particular set of rules which transforms him into a human being derives from requirements established in the ritual organization of social encounters. And if a particular person or group or society seems to have a unique character all its own, it is because its standard set of human-nature elements is pitched and combined in a particular way. Instead of much pride, there may be little. Instead of abiding by the rules, there may be much effort to break them safely. But if an encounter or undertaking is to be sustained as a viable system of interaction organized on ritual principles, then these variations must be held within certain bounds and nicely counterbalanced by corresponding modifications in some of the other rules and understandings. Similarly, the human nature of a particular set of persons may be specially designed for the special kind of undertakings in which they participate, but still each of these persons must have within him something of the balance of characteristics required of a usable participant in any ritually organized system of social activity.

Chapter 22

Penelope Brown and Stephen C. Levinson

POLITENESS: SOME UNIVERSALS IN LANGUAGE USAGE

Assumptions: properties of interactants

W E MAKE THE FOLLOWING assumptions: that all competent adult members of a society have (and know each other to have):

1   'Face', the public self-image that every member wants to claim for himself, consisting in two related aspects:
    (a) negative face: the basic claim to territories, personal preserves, rights to non-distraction – i.e., to freedom of action and freedom from imposition
    (b) positive face: the positive consistent self-image or 'personality' (crucially including the desire that this self-image be appreciated and approved of) claimed by interactants.
2   Certain rational capacities, in particular consistent modes of reasoning from ends to the means that will achieve those ends.

Face

Our notion of 'face' is derived from that of Goffman (1967; [see Chapter 21]) and from the English folk term, which ties face up with notions of being embarrassed or humiliated, or 'losing face'. Thus face is something that is emotionally invested, and that can be lost, maintained, or enhanced, and must be constantly attended to in interaction. In general, people cooperate (and assume each other's cooperation) in maintaining face in interaction, such cooperation being based on the mutual vulnerability of face. That is, normally everyone's face depends on everyone else's being maintained, and since people can be expected to defend their faces if

Source: Penelope Brown and Stephen C. Levinson, *Politeness: Some Universals in Language Usage*, Cambridge: Cambridge University Press, 1987.

threatened, and in defending their own to threaten others' faces, it is in general in every participant's best interest to maintain each other's face, that is to act in ways that assure the other participants that the agent is heedful of the assumptions concerning face given under (1) above. . . .

Furthermore, while the content of face will differ in different cultures (what the exact limits are to personal territories, and what the publicly relevant content of personality consists in), we are assuming that the mutual knowledge of members' public self-image or face, and the social necessity to orient oneself to it in inter-action, are universal.

Face as wants

. . . We treat the aspects of face as basic wants, which every member knows every other member desires, and which in general it is in the interests of every member to partially satisfy. In other words, we take in Weberian terms the more strongly rational *zweckrational* model of individual action, because the *wertrational* model (which would treat face respect as an unquestionable value or norm) fails to account for the fact that face respect is not an unequivocal right. In particular, a mere bow to face acts like a diplomatic declaration of good intentions; it is not in general required that an actor fully satisfy another's face wants. Second, face can be, and routinely is, ignored, not just in cases of social breakdown (affrontery) but also in cases of urgent cooperation, or in the interests of efficiency.

Therefore, the components of face given above may be restated as follows. We define:

> **negative face**: the want of every 'competent adult member' that his actions be unimpeded by others;
> **positive face**: the want of every member that his wants be desirable to at least some others.

Negative face, with its derivative politeness of non-imposition, is familiar as the formal politeness that the notion 'politeness' immediately conjures up. But posi-tive face, and its derivative forms of positive politeness, are less obvious. The reduction of a person's public self-image or personality to a want that one's wants be desirable to at least some others can be justified in this way. The most salient aspect of a person's personality in interaction is what that personality requires of other interactants – in particular, it includes the desire to be ratified, understood, approved of, liked or admired. The next step is to represent this desire as the want to have one's goals thought of as desirable. In the special sense of 'wanting' that we develop, we can then arrive at positive face as here defined. To give this some intuitive flesh, consider an example. Mrs B is a fervent gardener. Much of her time and effort are expended on her roses. She is proud of her roses, and she likes others to admire them. She is gratified when visitors say 'What lovely roses; I wish ours looked like that! How do you do it?', implying that they want just what she has wanted and achieved.

. . .

Rationality

We here define 'rationality' as the application of a specific mode of reasoning . . . which guarantees inferences from ends or goals to means that will satisfy those ends. Just as standard logics have a consequence relation that will take us from one proposition to another while preserving truth, a system of practical reasoning must allow one to pass from ends to means and further means while preserving the 'satis-factoriness' of those means. . . .

Intrinsic FTAs

Given these assumptions of the universality of face and rationality, it is intuitively the case that certain kinds of acts intrinsically threaten face, namely those acts that by their nature run contrary to the face wants of the addressee and/or of the speaker. By 'act' we have in mind what is intended to be done by a verbal or non-verbal communication, just as one or more 'speech acts' can be assigned to an utterance.

First distinction: kinds of face threatened

We may make a first distinction between acts that threaten negative face and those that threaten positive face.

Those acts that primarily threaten the addressee's (H's) negative-face want, by indicating (potentially) that the speaker (S) does not intend to avoid impeding H's freedom of action, include:

1   Those acts that predicate some future act A of H, and in so doing put some pressure on H to do (or refrain from doing) the act A:
    (a) orders and requests (S indicates that he wants H to do, or refrain from doing, some act A)
    (b) suggestions, advice (S indicates that he thinks H ought to (perhaps) do some act A)
    (c) remindings (S indicates that H should remember to do some A)
    (d) threats, warnings, dares (S indicates that he – or someone, or something – will instigate sanctions against H unless he does A)
2   Those acts that predicate some positive future act of S toward H, and in so doing put some pressure on H to accept or reject them, and possibly to incur a debt:
    (a) offers (S indicates that he wants H to commit himself to whether or not he wants S to do some act for H, with H thereby incurring a possible debt)
    (b) promises (S commits himself to a future act for H's benefit)
3   Those acts that predicate some desire of S toward H or H's goods, giving H reason to think that he may have to take action to protect the object of S's desire, or give it to S:

   (a) compliments, expressions of envy or admiration (S indicates that he likes or would like something of H's)

   (b) expression of strong (negative) emotions toward H – e.g., hatred, anger, lust (S indicates possible motivation for harming H or H's goods)

     Those acts that threaten the positive-face want, by indicating (potentially) that the speaker does not care about the addressee's feelings, wants, etc. – that in some important respect he doesn't want H's wants – include:

1   Those that show that S has a negative evaluation of some aspect of H's positive face:

   (a) expressions of disapproval, criticism, contempt or ridicule, complaints and reprimands, accusations, insults (S indicates that he doesn't like/want one or more of H's wants, acts, personal characteristics, goods, beliefs or values)

   (b) contradictions or disagreements, challenges (S indicates that he thinks H is wrong or misguided or unreasonable about some issue, such wrongness being associated with disapproval)

2   Those that show that S doesn't care about (or is indifferent to) H's positive face:

   (a) expressions of violent (out-of-control) emotions (S gives H possible reason to fear him or be embarrassed by him)

   (b) irreverence, mention of taboo topics, including those that are inappropriate in the context (S indicates that he doesn't value H's values and doesn't fear H's fears)

   (c) bringing of bad news about H, or good news (boasting) about S (S indicates that he is willing to cause distress to H, and/or doesn't care about H's feelings)

   (d) raising of dangerously emotional or divisive topics, e.g., politics, race, religion, women's liberation (S raises the possibility or likelihood of face-threatening acts (such as the above) occurring; i.e., S creates a dangerous-to-face atmosphere)

   (e) blatant non-cooperation in an activity – e.g., disruptively interrupting H's talk, making non-sequiturs or showing non-attention (S indicates that he doesn't care about H's negative- or positive-face wants)

   (f) use of address terms and other status-marked identifications in initial encounters (S may misidentify H in an offensive or embarrassing way, intentionally or accidentally)

Note that there is an overlap in this classification of FTAs, because some FTAs intrinsically threaten both negative and positive face (e.g., complaints, interruptions, threats, strong expressions of emotion, requests for personal information).

Second distinction: threats to H's face versus threats to S's

Second, we may distinguish between acts that primarily threaten *H's* face (as in the above list) and those that threaten primarily *S's* face. To the extent that S and H are cooperating to maintain face, the latter FTAs also potentially threaten H's face. FTAs that are threatening to S include:

1   Those that offend S's negative face:
    (a) expressing thanks (S accepts a debt, humbles his own face)
    (b) acceptance of H's thanks or H's apology (S may feel constrained to mini-mize H's debt or transgression, as in 'It was nothing, don't mention it.')
    (c) excuses (S indicates that he thinks he had good reason to do, or fail to do, an act which H has just criticized; this may constitute in turn a crit-icism of H, or at least cause a confrontation between H's view of things and S's view)
    (d) acceptance of offers (S is constrained to accept a debt, and to encroach upon H's negative face)
    (e) responses to H's *faux pas* (if S visibly notices a prior *faux pas*, he may cause embarrassment to H; if he pretends not to, he may be discomfited himself)
    (f) unwilling promises and offers (S commits himself to some future action although he doesn't want to; therefore, if his unwillingness shows, he may also offend H's positive face)
2   Those that directly damage S's positive face:
    (a) apologies (S indicates that he regrets doing a prior FTA, thereby damaging his own face to some degree – especially if the apology is at the same time a confession with H learning about the transgression through it, and the FTA thus conveys bad news)
    (b) acceptance of a compliment (S may feel constrained to denigrate the object of H's prior compliment, thus damaging his own face; or he may feel constrained to compliment H in turn)
    (c) breakdown of physical control over body, bodily leakage, stumbling or falling down, etc.
    (d) self-humiliation, shuffling or cowering, acting stupid, self-contradicting
    (e) confessions, admissions of guilt or responsibility – e.g., for having done or not done an act, or for ignorance of something that S is expected to know
    (f) emotion leakage, non-control of laughter or tears

These two ways of classifying FTAs (by whether S's face or H's face is mainly threat-ened, or by whether it is mainly positive face or negative face that is at stake) give rise to a four-way grid which offers the possibility of cross-classifying at least some of the above FTAs. However, such a cross-classification has a complex relation to the ways in which FTAs are handled.

Strategies for doing FTAs

In the context of the mutual vulnerability of face, any rational agent will seek to avoid these face-threatening acts, or will employ certain strategies to minimize the threat. In other words, he will take into consideration the relative weightings of

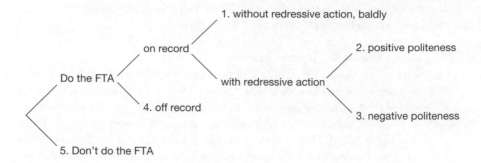

Figure 22.1 Possible strategies for doing FTAs

(at least) three wants: (a) the want to communicate the content of the FTA *x*, (b) the want to be efficient or urgent, and (c) the want to maintain H's face to any degree. Unless (b) is greater than (c), S will want to minimize the threat of his FTA.

The possible sets of strategies may be schematized exhaustively as in Figure 22.1 in this schema, we have in mind the following definitions.

An actor goes **on record** in doing an act A if it is clear to participants what communicative intention led the actor to do A (i.e., there is just one unambiguously attributable intention with which witnesses would concur). For instance, if I say 'I (hereby) promise to come tomorrow' and if participants would concur that, in saying that, I did unambiguously express the intention of committing myself to that future act, then in our terminology I went 'on record' as promising to do so.

In contrast, if an actor goes **off record** in doing A, then there is more than one unambiguously attributable intention so that the actor cannot be held to have committed himself to one particular intent. So, for instance, if I say 'Damn, I'm out of cash, I forgot to go to the bank today', I may be intending to get you to lend me some cash, but I cannot be held to have committed myself to that intent (as you would discover were you to challenge me with 'This is the seventeenth time you've asked me to lend you money'). Linguistic realizations of off-record strategies include metaphor and irony, rhetorical questions, understatement, tautologies, all kinds of hints as to what a speaker wants or means to communicate, without doing so directly, so that the meaning is to some degree negotiable.

Doing an act **baldly**, **without redress**, involves doing it in the most direct, clear, unambiguous and concise way possible (for example, for a request, saying 'Do X!'). This we shall identify roughly with following the specifications of Grice's maxims of cooperation [Chapter 3]. Normally, an FTA will be done in this way only if the speaker does not fear retribution from the addressee, for example in circumstances where (a) S and H both tacitly agree that the relevance of face demands may be suspended in the interests of urgency or efficiency; (b) where the danger to H's face is *very* small, as in offers, requests, suggestions that are clearly in H's interest and do not require great sacrifices of S (e.g., 'Come in' or 'Do sit down'); and (c) where S is vastly superior in power H, or can enlist audience support to destroy H's face without losing his own.

By **redressive action** we mean action that 'gives face' to the addressee, that is, that attempts to counteract the potential face damage of the FTA by doing it in such a way, or with such modifications or additions, that indicate clearly that no such face threat is intended or desired, and that S in general recognizes H's face wants and himself wants them to be achieved. Such redressive action takes one of two forms, depending on which aspect of face (negative or positive) is being stressed.

Positive politeness is orientated toward the positive face of H, the positive self-image that he claims for himself. Positive politeness is approach-based; it 'anoints' the face of the addressee by indicating that in some respects, S wants H's wants (e.g., by treating him as a member of an in-group, a friend, a person whose wants and personality traits are known and liked). The potential face threat of an act is minimized in this case by the assurance that in general S wants at least some of H's wants; for example, that S considers H to be in important respects, 'the same' as he, with in-group rights and duties and expectations of reciprocity, or by the implication that S likes H so that the FTA doesn't mean a negative evaluation in general of H's face.

Negative politeness, on the other hand, is orientated mainly toward partially satisfying (redressing) H's negative face, his basic want to maintain claims of territory and self-determination. Negative politeness, thus, is essentially avoidance based, and realizations of negative-politeness strategies consist in assurances that the speaker recognizes and respects the addressee's negative-face wants and will not (or will only minimally) interfere with the addressee's freedom of action. Hence negative politeness is characterized by self-effacement, formality and restraint, with attention to very restricted aspects of H's self-image, centring on his want to be unimpeded. Face-threatening acts are redressed with apologies for interfering or transgressing, with linguistic and non-linguistic deference, with hedges on the illocutionary force of the act, with impersonalizing mechanisms (such as passives) that distance S and H from the act, and with other softening mechanisms that give the addressee an 'out', a face-saving line of escape, permitting him to feel that his response is not coerced.

There is a natural tension in negative politeness, however, between (a) the desire to go on record as a prerequisite to being seen to pay face, and (b) the desire to go off record to avoid imposing. A compromise is reached in **conventionalized indirectness**, for whatever the indirect mechanism used to do an FTA, once fully conventionalized as a way of doing that FTA it is no longer off record. Thus many indirect requests, for example, are fully conventionalized in English so that they are on record (e.g., 'Can you pass the salt?' would be read as a request by all participants; there is no longer a viable alternative interpretation of the utterance except in very special circumstances). And between any two (or more) individuals, any utterance may become conventionalized and therefore on record, as is the case with passwords and codes.

A purely conventional 'out' works as redressive action in negative politeness because it pays a token bow to the negative-face wants of the addressee. That is, the fact that the speaker bothers to phrase his FTA in a conventionally indirect way shows that he is aware of and honours the negative-face wants of H.

Factors influencing the choice of strategies

. . . In this section we argue that any rational agent will tend to choose the same genus of strategy under the same conditions – that is, make the same moves as any other would make under the circumstances. This is by virtue of the fact that the particular strategies intrinsically afford certain payoffs or advantages, and the relevant circumstances are those in which one of these payoffs would be more advantageous than any other.

We consider these in turn – first the intrinsic payoffs and then the relevant circumstances – and then relate the two.

The payoffs: *a priori* considerations

Here we present a fairly complete list of the payoffs associated with each of the strategies, derived on *a priori* grounds.

By going *on record*, a speaker can potentially get any of the following advantages: he can enlist public pressure against the addressee or in support of himself; he can get credit for honesty, for indicating that he trusts the addressee; he can get credit for outspokenness, avoiding the danger of being seen to be a manipulator; he can avoid the danger of being misunderstood; and he can have the opportunity to pay back in face whatever he potentially takes away by the FTA.

By going *off record*, on the other hand, a speaker can profit in the following ways: he can get credit for being tactful, non-coercive; he can run less risk of his act entering the 'gossip biography' that others keep of him; and he can avoid responsibility for the potentially face-damaging interpretation. Furthermore, he can give (non-overtly) the addressee an opportunity to be seen to care for S (and thus he can test H's feelings towards him). In this latter case, if H chooses to pick up and respond to the potentially threatening interpretation of the act, he can give a 'gift' to the original speaker. Thus, if I say 'It's hot in here' and you say 'Oh, I'll open the window then!', you may get credit for being generous and cooperative, and I avoid the potential threat of ordering you around.

For going on record with *positive politeness*, a speaker can minimize the face-threatening aspects of an act by assuring the addressee that S considers himself to be 'of the same kind', that he likes him and wants his wants. Thus a criticism, with the assertion of mutual friendship, may lose much of its sting – indeed, in the assumption of a friendly context it often becomes a game and possibly even a compliment (as between opposite-sexed teenagers). Another possible payoff is that S can avoid or minimize the debt implications of FTAs such as requests and offers, either by referring (indirectly) to the reciprocity and on-going relationship between the addressee and himself (as in the reference to a pseudo prior agreement with *then* in 'How about a cookie, then') or by including the addressee and himself equally as participants in or as benefitors from the request or offer (for example, with an inclusive 'we', as in 'Let's get on with dinner' from the husband glued to the TV).

For going on record with *negative politeness*, a speaker can benefit in the following ways: he can pay respect, deference, to the addressee in return for the FTA, and can thereby avoid incurring (or can thereby lessen) a future debt; he can maintain

social distance, and avoid the threat (or the potential face loss) of advancing familiarity towards the addressee; he can give a real 'out' to the addressee (for example,
with a request or an offer, by making it clear that he doesn't really expect H to
say 'Yes' unless he wants to, thereby minimizing the mutual face loss incurred if
H has to say 'No'); and he can give conventional 'outs' to the addressee as opposed
to real 'outs', that is, pretend to offer an escape route without really doing so,
thereby indicating that he has the other person's face wants in mind.

Finally, the payoff for the fifth strategic choice, 'Don't do the FTA', is simply
that S avoids offending H at all with this particular FTA. Of course S also fails
to achieve his desired communication, and as there are naturally no interesting
linguistic reflexes of this last-ditch strategy, we will ignore it in our discussion
henceforth.

For our purpose, these payoffs may be simplified to the following summary:
On-record payoffs:

(a)   clarity, perspicuousness
(b)   demonstrable non-manipulativeness

Bald-on-record (non-redressed) payoff:

efficiency (S can claim that other things are more important than face,
or that the act is not an FTA at all)

Plus-redress payoff: S has the opportunity to give face

(a)   positive politeness – to satisfy H's positive face, in some respect
(b)   negative politeness – to satisfy H's negative face, to some degree

Off-record payoffs:

(a)   S can satisfy negative face to a degree greater than that afforded by the negative-
politeness strategy
(b)   S can avoid the inescapable accountability, the responsibility for his action,
that on-record strategies entail.

. . .

The circumstances: sociological variables

In this section we argue that the assessment of the seriousness of an FTA (that is,
the calculations that members actually seem to make) involves the following factors
in many and perhaps all cultures:

1   The 'social distance' (D) of S and H (a symmetric relation).
2   The relative 'power' (P) of S and H (an asymmetric relation).
3   The absolute ranking (R) of impositions in the particular culture.

An immediate clarification is in order. We are interested in D, P, and R only to the extent that the actors think it is mutual knowledge between them that these variables have some particular values. Thus these are not intended as *sociologists'* ratings of *actual* power, distance, etc., but only as *actors'* assumptions of such ratings, assumed to be mutually assumed, at least within certain limits.

Our argument here has an empirical basis, and we make the argument in as strong a form as our ethnographic data will allow.

COMPUTING THE WEIGHTINESS OF AN FTA

For each FTA, the seriousness or weightiness of a particular FTA *x* is compounded of both risk to S's face and risk to H's face, in a proportion relative to the nature of the FTA. Thus apologies and confessions are essentially threats to S's face (as we have seen), and advice and orders are basically threats to H's face, while requests and offers are likely to threaten the face of both participants. However, the way in which the seriousness of a particular FTA is weighed seems to be neutral as to whether it is S's or H's face that is threatened, or in what proportion. So let us say that the weightiness of an FTA is calculated thus:

$$W_x = D(S,H) + P(H,S) + R_x$$

where W_x is the numerical value that measures the weightiness of the FTA *x*, $D(S,H)$ is the value that measures the social distance between S and H, $P(H,S)$ is a measure of the power that H has over S, and R_x is a value that measures the degree to which the FTA *x* is rated an imposition in that culture. We assume that each of these values can be measured on a scale of 1 to *n*, where *n* is some small number. Our formula assumes that the function that assigns a value to W_x on the basis of the three social parameters does so on a simple summative basis. Such an assumption seems to work surprisingly well, but we allow that in fact some more complex composition of values may be involved. In any case, the function must capture the fact that all three dimensions P, D, and R contribute to the seriousness of an FTA, and thus to a determination of the level of politeness with which, other things being equal, an FTA will be communicated.

First, we must clarify our intent. By D and P we intend very general pan-cultural social dimensions which nevertheless probably have 'emic' correlates. We are not here interested in what factors are compounded to estimate these complex parameters; such factors are certainly culture-specific. For instance, $P(H,S)$ may be assessed as being great because H is eloquent and influential, or is a prince, a witch, a thug, or a priest; $D(S,H)$ as great because H speaks another dialect or language, or lives in the next valley, or is not a kinsman. More specifically, we can describe these factors as follows.

D is a symmetric social dimension of similarity/difference within which S and H stand for the purposes of this act. In many cases (but not all), it is based on an assessment of the frequency of interaction and the kinds of material or non-material goods (including face) exchanged between S and H (or parties representing S or H, or for whom S and H are representatives). An important part of the assessment of D will usually be measures of social distance based on stable social attributes.

The reflex of social closeness is, generally, the reciprocal giving and receiving of positive face.

P is an asymmetric social dimension of relative power, roughly in Weber's sense. That is, P(H,S) is the degree to which H can impose his own plans and his own self-evaluation (face) at the expense of S's plans and self-evaluation. In general there are two sources of P, either of which may be authorized or unauthorized – material control (over economic distribution and physical force) and metaphysical control (over the actions of others, by virtue of metaphysical forces subscribed to by those others). In most cases an individual's power is drawn from both these sources, or is thought to overlap them. The reflex of a great P differential is perhaps archetypally 'deference', as discussed below.

R is a culturally and situationally defined ranking of impositions by the degree to which they are considered to interfere with an agent's wants of self-determination or of approval (his negative- and positive-face wants). In general there are probably two such scales or ranks that are emically identifiable for negative-face FTAs: a ranking of impositions in proportion to the expenditure (a) of services (including the provision of time) and (b) of goods (including non-material goods like information, as well as the expression of regard and other face payments). These intra-culturally defined costings of impositions on an individual's preserve are in general constant only in their rank order from one situation to another. However, even the rank order is subject to a set of operations that shuffles the impositions according to whether actors have specific rights or obligations to perform the act, whether they have specific reasons (ritual or physical) for not performing them, and whether actors are known to actually *enjoy* being imposed upon in some way.

So an outline of the rankings of negative-face impositions for a particular domain of FTAs in a particular culture involves a complex description like the following:

1   (a) rank order of impositions requiring services
     (b) rank order of impositions requiring goods

2   Functions on (1):
     (a) the lessening of certain impositions on a given actor determined by the obligation (legally, morally, by virtue of employment, etc.) to do the act A; and also by the enjoyment that the actor gets out of performing the required act
     (b) the increasing of certain impositions determined by reasons why the actor *shouldn't* do them, and reasons why the actor *couldn't* (easily) do them

For FTAs against positive face, the ranking involves an assessment of the amount of 'pain' given to H's face, based on the discrepancy between H's own desired self-image and that presented (blatantly or tacitly) in the FTA. There will be cultural rankings of aspects of positive face (for example, 'success', 'niceness', 'beauty', 'generosity'), which can be re-ranked in particular circumstances, just as can negative-face rankings. And there are personal (idiosyncratic) functions on these rankings; some people object to certain kinds of FTAs more than others. A person who is skilled at assessing such rankings, and the circumstances in which they vary, is considered to be graced with 'tact', 'charm', or 'poise'.

We associate with each of these variables D, P, and R, a value from 1 to *n* assigned by an actor in particular circumstances. No special substantial claim is intended; the valuation simply represents the way in which (for instance) as S's power over H increases, the weightiness of the FTA diminishes. One interesting side effect of this numerical representation is that it can describe these intuitive facts: the threshold value of risk which triggers the choice of another strategy is a constant, independent of the way in which the value is composed and assessed. Thus one goes off record where an imposition is small but relative S–H distance and H's power are great, and also where H is an intimate equal of S's but the imposition is very great.

. . .

Editors' appendix: list of politeness strategies

Positive politeness strategies:

Notice, attend to H (his/her interests, wants, needs, goods)
Exaggerate (interest, approval, sympathy with H)
Intensify interest to H
Use in-group identity markers
Seek agreement
Avoid disagreement
Presuppose/raise/assert common ground
Joke
Assert or presuppose S's knowledge of and concern for H's wants
Offer, promise
Be optimistic
Include both S and H in the activity
Give (or ask for) reasons
Assume or assert reciprocity
Give gifts to H (goods, sympathy, understanding, cooperation)

Negative politeness strategies:

Be direct/conventionally indirect
Question, hedge
Be pessimistic
Minimise the size of imposition on H
Give deference
Apologise
Impersonalise S and H: avoid pronouns 'I' and 'you'
State the FTA as a general rule
Nominalise
Go on record as incurring a debt, or as not indebting H

Off-record strategies:

Those violating Grice's conversational maxims, see Chapter 3.

VIOLATE MAXIM OF RELEVANCE

Give hints/clues
Give association clues
Presuppose

VIOLATE MAXIM OF QUALITY

Understate
Overstate
Use tautologies
Use contradictions
Be ironic
Use metaphors
Use rhetorical questions

VIOLATE MAXIM OF MANNER

Be ambiguous
Be vague
Over-generalise
Displace H
Be incomplete, use ellipsis

Reference

Goffman, E. (1967) *Interaction Ritual*, New York: Anchor Books. [See also Chapter 21 of this *Reader*.]

Chapter 23

Janet Holmes

WOMEN, MEN AND POLITENESS: AGREEABLE AND DISAGREEABLE RESPONSES

Example 1

Two thirteen year-olds discussing a schoolteacher.

David: He's a real dickhead he just bawls you out without listening at
        all

Oliver: yeah what an ass-hole/ I can't stand him he's always raving
        raving on

THE DISCUSSION OF INTERACTIVE FEATURES such as inter-
ruption and minimal responses makes it very clear that the crucial aspects of
these features from the point of view of politeness is their function in relation to
the on-going discourse (Holmes 1995). Do they disrupt or support the talk of
others? Do they threaten to take over the floor or do they encourage the current
speaker to continue?

Extending the analysis further in this direction, it is obvious that the content
of responses to the talk of others is another aspect of politeness behaviour. Agreeing
with others, confirming their opinions and assertions, as illustrated by Oliver in
Example 1 and Sal and Pat in Example 2 is supportive and positively polite behaviour (Brown and Levinson 1987: 112; [Chapter 22]).

Example 2

Two young women watching TV together.

Sal: in that *Our House* um . . . she's the mother of teenage kids
      ⌈and she
Pat: ⌊oh yeah that's an awful program isn't it
Sal: mmmm
Pat: it's got that dick who's in the Cocoon film

Source: Janet Holmes, *Women, Men and Politeness*, London: Longman, 1995.

Sal: oh god he's insufferable!
Pat: and he's so fucking wise ⌈and so so FUCKING American
Sal: ⌊yeah
Sal: and everybody else is always WRONG
Pat: yes and he's always right . . .

(Pilkington 1992: 45)

This example illustrates that . . . overlapping and simultaneous talk can be supportive in effect. It also illustrates another pattern, namely, the tendency for women to agree with each other where possible. There is a great deal of evidence that in informal and casual interaction women tend to adopt the strategy of seeking agreement to a greater extent than men do, both in single-sex and mixed-sex contexts . . . Coates (1989: 118), for example, comments on the ways in which the women in the discussions she taped work together and collaborate with each other 'to produce shared meanings'. Participants build on each other's contributions, complete each other's utterances, and affirm each other's opinions giving an overall impression of talk as a very cooperative enterprise. Eckert (1990: 122) reports similar patterns among a group of adolescent girls, commenting that 'not one topic is allowed to conclude without an expression of consensus'. (It is interesting to note that this is also a pattern which is typical of more formal Maori interaction, suggesting that cross-cultural contrasts may mirror the gender contrasts observable in middle-class western society.)

A small but very interesting New Zealand study provides further evidence of this pattern. Jane Pilkington (1992) recorded the interactions between a group of women and a group of men working on different nights in a bakery. Her data for the women shows the same supportive and cooperative patterns in New Zealand women's speech as those described by Coates (1989) in the speech of the British women she recorded. The women developed each other's contributions, collaborating 'to produce a text by adding to what the previous speaker has just said', and they provided each other with a great deal of positive encouraging feedback. Facilitative tags were frequent as they encouraged others to comment and contribute. The women completed each other's utterances and agreed frequently. The impression is one of verbal cooperation and conversational sharing.

Example 3

Two young women working together in bakery.
Sal: perhaps next time I see Brian I'll PUMP him for
          ⌈information/ Brian tells me
May: ⌊   the goss
Sal: ⌈I know it's about six years old but
May: ⌊   [*laugh*] but
          I'd forgotten it

(Pilkington 1992: 46)

The men's interactions were very different. There were very few explicitly agreeing responses. Where a woman would have been likely to agree or at least respond, there were often long pauses between speakers. Indeed, Pilkington describes the male talk as typically combative, a kind of verbal sparring, a point which will be discussed further below. This study, then, though small, provides support for the view of New Zealand women as more positively polite than New Zealand men.

Both Gilbert and Stubbe examined the kinds of responses produced by New Zealand school pupils in the discussions they analysed. In the groups of fifteen year-olds (Gilbert 1990), the girls in the single-sex group used more agreeing positive responses than pupils in any other group (74 per cent), while the boys in the single-sex group used the fewest (54 per cent). In mixed-sex groups there were no gender differences in the overall proportion of positive responses; 63 per cent of both girls' and boys' responses were positive. Here is further evidence that the norms of interaction for each group are rather different, and again when girls and boys interact with each other, there is evidence of accommodation since these differences are reduced.

Maria Stubbe (1991) examined the relative numbers of agreeing and disagreeing responses produced by the eleven and twelve year-old children in the pairs she recorded. She found no significant differences in the proportions of agreeing responses produced by girls or boys in single-sex and mixed-sex pairs. There was an overwhelming preference for agreement in all pairs, so that agreeing responses outnumber disagreeing responses by 2:1. With these younger speakers, then, the differences between male and female pairs, in terms of the proportion of agreeing responses, disappeared.

The really interesting pattern that this analysis revealed, however, was in the types of disagreement responses preferred by the girls and boys. Overall, the boys tended to use more 'bald' disagreements than the girls, especially in discussion with another boy.

Example 4

Two eleven year-olds discussing a problem.
Ray: I think I'd tell my friend
Rees: no that's stupid

The girls, by contrast, tended to modify or qualify their disagreeing responses, so that they were not so confrontational. Such responses allowed for, and indeed encouraged, further discussion of the point of difference between the speakers.

Example 5

Two eleven year-olds discussing a problem.
Pam: I think she should go with her mum
Hanna: but she'd really rather stay um/with her father though
        wouldn't she

The pattern that Stubbe identified is summarised in Figure 23.1.

It has been suggested that in many contexts being polite means maximising areas of agreement and minimising disagreement (e.g., Brown and Levinson 1987; Leech 1983). Yet clearly people do not always agree, and it is interesting to note that when this happens, women and men tend to approach the problem posed for

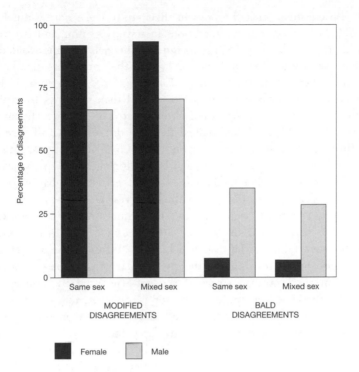

Figure 23.1 Modified and bald disagreements and gender

Source: Stubbe (1991: 88)

politeness differently. What polite options are there if one does not agree with the views expressed by a conversational partner? One can change the topic, or keep silent, but both these involve a high risk of offence if they are not skilfully managed (see West and García 1988). Softening the disagreeing response is perhaps the most obvious strategy for a twelve year-old. The girls in Stubbe's study adopted this polite disagreement strategy almost twice as often as the boys.

The boys were much more willing to contradict overtly others or 'baldly' disagree with their conversational partners – a response that is certainly regarded in many contexts as very face threatening (Brown and Levinson 1987 [Chapter 22]). In fact the boys were six times more likely than the girls to respond with a bald disagreement. This again suggests that there may be different norms for females and males, or different levels of tolerance of overt disagreement.

These results are consistent with those of others. Jenkins and Cheshire (1990: 284) conclude their analysis of the interactions between young teenagers with a comment which aptly sums up the research in this area in a number of different countries. They say that

> on the whole, the girls were careful, sensitive listeners who knew when to speak and what kind of comment it is appropriate to make . . . the conversational style of the girls, overall, can be described as cooperative, generous and designed to allow the participation of everybody on equal terms.

They also comment that the boys in their study were not so much competitive as unskilled in cooperative interaction. In a study of nine and twelve year-old Dutch children, van Alphen (1987) reported that the girls' groups avoided disagreement, while the boys, when they did not ignore the comments of others, tended explicitly to challenge or dispute them. Tannen (1990) notes in a study of 'best friends' talk' that the girls were more concerned than the boys to avoid explicit disagreement. Goodwin (1980) noted similar patterns among African-American school-age children in the United States: the girls did not generally use bald challenges or threats, while these were frequent in the boys' interactions. And Sheldon's research (1990; 1992a; 1992b) suggests girls develop such skill at an early age. She describes the 'verbal conflict mediation skills' of preschool girls who effectively used mitigating strategies to disagree without aggressive confrontation.

Similar patterns have been reported for adults (Maltz and Borker 1982). Women tend to soften their disagreeing utterances more often than men. In the United States, for example, Marjorie Swacker (1979) found that women used more modified disagreements than men in the question sessions at the end of conference papers. And in an Australian study of the patterns used by language learners, Munro (1987) reported that the women used more 'softened' disagreements than the men. Men, on the other hand, seemed more willing than women to disagree baldly. This was also apparent in the study discussed above of the different ways in which women and men used elicitations in New Zealand seminars. The men were twice as likely as the women to use antagonistic elicitations. In a detailed analysis of the interactions of a group of female and male business managers, Susan Schick Case (1988: 52) reported that 'the masculine style was an assertively aggressive one that proposed, opposed, competed'. And in her study of the interactions between New Zealand males working in a bakery, Jane Pilkington found that the men tended to challenge and disagree with each other more explicitly and overtly than the women.

Example 6
Young men working together in bakery.
Ben: . . . and ah they're very smart
Dan: well then how come they keep getting caught all the time?
Sam: maybe that's why they ⌈(. . . . . .)
Ben: ⌊they don't Dan / you've got to be
really clever to pull one you know

(Pilkington 1992: 52)

The men provided conflicting accounts of the same event, argued about a range of topics such as whether apples were kept in cases or crates, and criticised each other constantly for apparently minor differences of approach to things. Their strategies for amusing each other were often to ridicule the previous speaker's utterance, to put them down or to insult them, as illustrated in Example 7.

Example 7
Young men working in bakery discussing what apples are packed in.
Ray: crate!

Sam: case!

Ray: what

Sam: they come in cases Ray not crates

Ray: oh same thing if you must be picky over every one thing

Sam: just shut your fucking head Ray!

Ray: don't tell me to fuck off fuck (. . . .)

Sam: I'll come over and shut yo

Jim: *(Laughingly using a thick sounding voice)* yeah I'll have a crate of apples thanks

Ray: no fuck off Jim

Jim: a dozen . . .

Dan: *(amused)* shitpicker!

(Pilkington 1992: 53)

Listening to these interactions, it is very clear that the talk of the young men contrasts quite starkly with the cooperative, agreeing, mutually supportive talk of the women (illustrated in Example 3) in exactly the same context – working in the bakery – on a different night.

Women and men appear once again to be operating according to different rules of interaction. For the women, being negatively polite involves avoiding disagreement. Being positively polite is being friendly, and this involves confirming, agreeing and encouraging the contributions of others. But these politeness strategies are not typical of the interchanges described above between males. These young New Zealand men, like the young boys in the classroom discussion groups, are quite prepared to disagree baldly and to challenge the statements of others overtly. Indeed for this group, insults and abuse appear to be strategies for expressing solidarity and mateship, or ways of maintaining and reinforcing social relationships.

This kind of verbal sparring is reported by others who have examined all-male interaction (e.g. Dundes *et al.* 1972; Labov 1972). Labov (1972) described the ritual insults which occurred in the speech of New York adolescent gang members. In New Zealand, an analysis of the exchanges in a rugby changing room before a match demonstrated that the verbal interaction consisted almost entirely of insults – predominantly of a sexually humiliating kind (Kuiper 1991). People of both genders may use swear words to indicate their group membership (see, for example Hughes 1992), but Kuiper's study identifies insults which appear to serve as coercive devices to maintain solidarity and discipline between team members.

It appears, then, that at least in some contexts, female and male interactive norms contrast quite dramatically. The overall impression from the various studies discussed here is that male interaction is typically more competitive, aggressive and argumentative than female. For females, being negatively polite involves avoiding, minimising or mitigating disagreements; being positively polite involves agreeing with others, encouraging them to talk, expressing support verbally and ensuring they get a fair share of the talking time. For males, different norms appear to prevail. They can disagree baldly, challenge others' statements, interrupt and compete for the floor without intending to cause offence. In some contexts, aggressive and competitive verbal behaviour appears to be experienced as thoroughly enjoyable, and mutual insults may even serve as expressions of positive politeness and solidarity.

. . .

Transcription conventions

I have generally transcribed utterances as simply as possible. Normal punctuation is used for examples which were noted down, but not recorded on tape or video. For recorded examples, no punctuation is imposed on the transcription, but I have used the following conventions to record features relevant to the particular examples.

Pause length is indicated by slashes: / indicates a short pause and // a slightly longer pause.

Emphatic stress is indicated by capitals: e.g. CRAZY.

Turns: the relationship between speakers' turns is indicated visually: e.g. minimal feedback is placed at the point it occurs. Nell's *mm* occurs in the pause between Max's words *them* and *she's*.

> Max: I mean I have no idea what story Pat had told them //
> Nell: mm
> Max: she's got a vivid imagination

Simultaneous speech is indicated with brackets:

> Nell: mm/tricky/   did ⌈you ask her   ⌉
> Max: ⌊I didn't know   ⌋ what to say

Unclear speech is indicated as follows: (. . . . . .).

References

Brown, P. and Levinson, S. (1987) *Politeness: Some Universals in Language Usage*, Cambridge: Cambridge University Press.

Coates, J. (1989) 'Gossip revisited: language in all-female groups', in Coates, J. and Cameron, D. (eds) *Women in their Speech Communities*, London: Longman, 94–121.

Dundes, A., Leach, J.W. and Özkök, B. (1972) 'The strategy of Turkish boys' verbal dueling rhymes', in Gumperz, J.J. and Hymes, D. (eds) *Directions in Sociolinguistics*, New York: Holt Rinehart and Winston, 130–60.

Eckert, P. (1990) 'Cooperative competition in adolescent "girl talk"', *Discourse Processes* 13: 91–122.

Gilbert, J. (1990) 'Secondary school students talking about science: language functions, gender and interactions in small group discussions', MA thesis, Wellington: Victoria University.

Goodwin, M.H. (1980) 'Directive-response speech sequences in girls' and boys' task activities', in McConnell-Ginet, S., Borker, R. and Furman, N. (eds) *Women and Language
in Literature and Society*, New York: Praeger, 157–73.

Holmes, J. (1995) *Women, Men and Politeness*, London: Longman.

Hughes, S.E. (1992) 'Expletives of lower working-class women', *Language in Society* 21 (2):
291–303.

Jenkins, N. and Cheshire, J. (1990) 'Gender issues in the GCSE oral English examination:
part 1', *Language and Education* 4: 261–92.

Kuiper, K. (1991) 'Sporting formulae in New Zealand English; two models of male solidarity', in Cheshire, J. (ed.) *English Around the World: Sociolinguistic Perspectives*,
Cambridge: Cambridge University Press, 200–9.

Labov, W. (1972) 'Rules for ritual insults', in Kochman, T. (ed.), *Rappin' and Stylin' Out*,
Chicago, IL: University of Illinois Press, 265–314. [Reprinted in Coupland, N. and
Jaworski, A. (eds) (1997) *Sociolinguistic: A Reader and Coursebook*, London: Macmillan,
473–86.]

Leech, G.N. (1983) *Principles of Pragmatics*, London: Longman.

Maltz, D.N. and Borker, R.A. (1982) 'A cultural approach to male–female miscommunication', in Gumperz, J.J. (ed.) *Language and Social Identity*, Cambridge: Cambridge
University Press, 196–216.

Munro, F. (1987) 'Female and male participation in small-group interaction in the ESOL
classroom', unpublished term's project, graduate diploma in TESOL, Sydney: Sydney
College of Advanced Education.

Pilkington, J. (1992) '"Don't try to make out that I'm nice!": the different strategies women
and men use when gossiping', *Wellington Working Papers in Linguistics* 5: 37–60.

Schick Case, S. (1988) 'Cultural differences, not deficiencies: an analysis of managerial
women's language', in Rose, S. and Larwood, L. (eds) *Women's Careers: Pathways and
Pitfalls*, New York: Praeger, 41–63.

Sheldon, A. (1990) 'Pickle fights: gendered talk in preschool disputes', *Discourse Processes* 13:
5–31.

—— (1992a) 'Conflict talk: sociolinguistic challenges to self-assertion and how young girls
meet them', *Merrill-Palmer Quarterly* 38 (1): 95–117.

—— (1992b) 'Preschool girls' discourse competence: managing conflict', in Hall, K.,
Bucholtz, M. and Moonwomon, B. (eds) *Locating Power*, Proceedings of the Second
Berkeley Women and Language Conference, 4–5 April 1992, vol. 2, Berkeley, CA:
Berkeley Women and Language Group, University of California, 528–39.

Stubbe, M. (1991) 'Talking at cross-purposes: the effect of gender on New Zealand primary
schoolchildren's interaction strategies in pair discussions', MA thesis, Wellington:
Victoria University.

Swacker, M. (1979) 'Women's verbal behaviour at learned and professional conferences',
in Dubois, B.-L. and Crouch, I. (eds) *The Sociology of the Languages of American Women*,
San Antonio, TX: Trinity University, 155–60.

Tannen, D. (1990) 'Gender differences in topical coherence: creating involvement in best
friends' talk', *Discourse Processes* 13: 73–90.

van Alphen, I. (1987) 'Learning from your peers: the acquisition of gender-specific speech
styles', in Dédé Brouwer and Dorian De Haan (eds), *Women's Language, Socialisation
and Self-image*, Dordrecht: Foris, 58–75.

West, C. and García, A. (1988) 'Conversational shift work: a study of topical transitions
between women and men', *Social Problems* 35 (5): 551–75.

Chapter 24

Deborah Tannen and Cynthia Wallat

INTERACTIVE FRAMES AND KNOWLEDGE SCHEMAS IN INTERACTION: EXAMPLES FROM A MEDICAL EXAMINATION/ INTERVIEW[1]

Introduction

GOFFMAN (1981a) INTRODUCED the term "footing" as "another way of talking about a change in our frame for events," "a change in the alignment we take up to ourselves and the others present as expressed in the way we manage the production or reception of an utterance" (p. 128). He describes the ability to shift footing within an interaction as "the capacity of a dexterous speaker to jump back and forth, keeping different circles in play" (p. 156). Goffman asserts that "linguistics provides us with the cues and markers through which such footings become manifest, helping us to find our way to a structural basis for analyzing them" (p. 157). Using linguistic "cues and markers" as a "structural basis for analyzing" talk in a pediatric interaction, we show that a mismatch of knowledge schemas can trigger frame switches which constitute a significant burden on the pediatrician when she conducts her examination of a child in the mother's presence. Combining the perspectives of a social psychologist (Wallat) and a linguist (Tannen), we thus examine the specifics of talk in interaction in a particular setting to provide a basis for understanding talk in terms of shifting frames.

Like many of our colleagues, we make use of video-tape to analyze interaction which is evanescent in nature. In his description of the theoretical and methodological complexity of making informed use of filmed records in social psychological research, Kendon (1979) cautions that micro-analytic analysis must be based on a theoretical perspective involving "context analysis." He sees context analysis as a conceptual framework which presumes that participants are not isolated senders and receivers of messages. When people are in each other's presence, all their verbal and nonverbal behaviors are potential sources of communication, and their

Source: Deborah Tannen and Cynthia Wallat, 'Interactive frames and knowledge schemas in interaction: examples from a medical examination/interview', *Social Psychology Quarterly*, 50 (2): 205–16, 1987.

actions and meanings can be understood only in relation to the immediate context, including what preceded and may follow it. Thus, interaction can be understood only in context: a specific context. We have chosen the pediatric setting as an exemplary context of interaction. Understanding how communication works in this context provides a model which can be applied in other contexts as well.

In examining talk in a pediatric setting, we are interested in the duality of what emerges in interaction: the stability of what occurs as a consequence of the social context, and the variability of particular interactions which results from the emergent nature of discourse. On one hand, meanings emerge which are not given in advance; on the other, meanings which are shaped by the doctor's or patient's prior assumptions (as we will argue, their knowledge schemas) may be resistant to change by the interlocutor's talk.

As Cicourel (1975) cautioned over a decade ago, when social scientists create a database for addressing the issues involved in integrating structure and process in the study of participants in medical settings, their textual material should "reflect the complexities of the different modalities and emergent contextual knowledge inherent in social interaction" (p. 34). One important way that Cicourel, and after him Richard Frankel (1989), sought to observe such complexities has been to compare discourse produced in spoken and written modalities. We have adopted this practice and have also developed a method of analyzing video-tapes of participants in more than one setting.

. . .

Frames and schemas

The term "frame," and related terms such as "script," "schema," "prototype," "speech activity," "template," and "module," have been variously used in linguistics, artificial intelligence, anthropology and psychology. Tannen (1979) reviews this literature and suggests that all these concepts reflect the notion of structures of expectation. Yet that early treatment of a variety of concepts of frames and schemas in the disciplines of linguistics, cognitive psychology and artificial intelligence said little about the type of frames that Goffman (1974) so exhaustively analyzed, as he himself observed (Goffman 1981b). The present paper broadens the discussion of frames to encompass and integrate the anthropological/sociological sense of the term.

The various uses of "frame" and related terms fall into two categories. One is interactive "frames of interpretation" which characterize the work of anthropologists and sociologists. We refer to these "frames," following Bateson (1972), who introduced the term, as well as most of those who have built on his work, including scholars in the fields of anthropology (Frake 1977), sociology (Goffman 1974) and linguistic anthropology (Gumperz 1982; Hymes 1974). The other category is knowledge structures, which we refer to as "schemas," but which have been variously labeled in work in artificial intelligence (Minsky 1975; Schank and Abelson 1977), cognitive psychology (Rumelhart 1975), and linguistic semantics (Chafe 1977; Fillmore 1975; 1976).

Interactive frames

The interactive notion of frame refers to a definition of what is going on in interaction, without which no utterance (or movement or gesture) could be interpreted.
To use Bateson's classic example, a monkey needs to know whether a bite from
another monkey is intended within the frame of play or the frame of fighting.
People are continually confronted with the same interpretative task. In order to
comprehend any utterance, a listener (and a speaker) must know within which
frame it is intended: for example, is this joking? Is it fighting? Something intended
as a joke but interpreted as an insult (it could of course be both) can trigger a fight.

Goffman (1974) sketched the theoretical foundations of frame analysis in the
work of William James, Alfred Schutz and Harold Garfinkel to investigate the
socially constructed nature of reality. Building on their work, as well as that of
linguistic philosophers John Austin and Ludwig Wittgenstein, Goffman developed
a complex system of terms and concepts to illustrate how people use multiple
frameworks to make sense of events even as they construct those events. Exploring
in more detail the linguistic basis of such frameworks, Goffman (1981a) introduced
the term "footing" to describe how, at the same time that participants frame events,
they negotiate the interpersonal relationships, or "alignments," that constitute those
events.

The interactive notion of frame, then, refers to a sense of what activity is
being engaged in, how speakers mean what they say. As Ortega y Gasset (1959:
3), a student of Heidegger, puts it, "Before understanding any concrete statement,
it is necessary to perceive clearly 'what it is all about' in this statement and 'what
game is being played.'"[2] Since this sense is gleaned from the way participants
behave in interaction, frames emerge in and are constituted by verbal and nonverbal
interaction.

Knowledge schemas

We use the term "knowledge schema" to refer to participants' expectations about
people, objects, events and settings in the world, as distinguished from alignments
being negotiated in a particular interaction. Linguistic semanticists have been interested in this phenomenon, as they have observed that even the literal meaning of
an utterance can be understood only by reference to a pattern of prior knowledge.
This is fundamental to the writing of Heidegger (for example, 1962: 199), as in
his often quoted argument (p. 196) that the word "hammer" can have no meaning
to someone who has never seen a hammer used. To borrow an example from
Fillmore (1976), the difference between the phrases "on land" and "on the ground"
can be understood only by reference to an expected sequence of actions associated
with travel on water and in the air, respectively. Moreover, the only way anyone
can understand any discourse is by filling in unstated information which is known
from prior experience in the world. This became clear to researchers in artificial
intelligence as soon as they tried to get computers to understand even the simplest
discourse – hence, for example, the need for Schank and Abelson's (1977) restaurant script to account for the use of the definite article "the" in a minimal discourse
such as, "John went into a restaurant; he asked the waitress for a menu."

Researchers in the area of medical sociology and anthropology such as Kleinman (1980) and Mishler (1984) have observed the problem of doctors' and patients' divergent knowledge schemas, although they may not have used this terminology. Cicourel (1983), for example, describes the effects of differing "structures of belief" in a gynecological case. The contribution of our analysis is to show the distinction and interaction between knowledge schemas and interactive frames.

At an earlier stage of this study, we referred to an interactive notion of frame as "dynamic" and the knowledge structure notion of schema as "static," but we now realize that all types of structures of expectations are dynamic, as Bartlett (1932), whose work underlies much of present-day schema theory, pointed out, and as others (for example, Frake 1977) have emphasized. That is, expectations about objects, people, settings, ways to interact, and anything else in the world are continually checked against experience and revised.

The interaction of frames and schemas

We demonstrate here a particular relationship between interactive frames and knowledge schemas by which a mismatch in schemas triggers a shifting of frames. Before proceeding to demonstrate this by reference to detailed analysis of pediatric interaction, we will illustrate briefly with reference to an example of a trivial, fleeting and mundane interchange that was part of a telephone conversation.

One author (Tannen) was talking to a friend on the telephone, when he suddenly yelled, "YOU STOP THAT!" She knew from the way he uttered this command that it was addressed to a dog and not her. She remarked on the fact that when he addressed the dog, he spoke in something approximating a southern accent. The friend explained that this was because the dog had learned to respond to commands in that accent, and, to give another example, he illustrated the way he plays with the dog: "I say, 'GO GIT THAT BALL!'" Hearing this, the dog began running about the room looking for something to fetch. The dog recognized the frame "play" in the tone of the command; he could not, however, understand the words that identified an outer frame, "*referring* to playing with the dog," and mistook the reference for a literal invitation to play.

This example illustrates, as well, that people (and dogs) identify frames in interaction by association with linguistic and paralinguistic cues – the way words are uttered – in addition to what they say. That is, the way the speaker uttered "You stop that!" was associated with the frame "disciplining a pet" rather than "chatting with a friend." Tannen drew on her familiarity with the use of linguistic cues to signal frames when she identified her friend's interjection "You stop that!" as addressed to a dog, not her. But she also drew on the knowledge that her friend was taking care of someone's dog. This was part of her knowledge schema about her friend. Had her schema included the information that he had a small child and was allergic to dogs, she might have interpreted the same linguistic cues as signaling the related frame, "disciplining a misbehaving child." Furthermore, her expectations about how any speaker might express orders or emotions, i.e. frame such expressions, were brought to bear in this instance in conjunction with her expectations about how this particular friend is likely to speak to her, to a dog and to a child; that is, a schema for this friend's personal style. Thus frames and schemas interacted in her comprehension of the specific utterance.

The remainder of this paper illustrates frames and schemas in a video-taped interaction in a medical setting: the examination of a child by a pediatrician in the presence of the mother. It demonstrates that an understanding of interactive frames accounts for conflicting demands on the pediatrician. In addition to communicative demands arising from multiple interactive frames, much of the talk in the pediatric encounter can be understood as resulting from differing knowledge schemas of the mother and the pediatrician. This will be illustrated with reference to their schemas for health and cerebral palsy. Finally, it is the mismatch in knowledge structure schemas that prompts the mother to ask questions which require the doctor to switch frames.

Background of the study

The video-tapes on which our analysis is based were obtained from the Child Development Center of the Georgetown University Medical School, following our presentation of a proposal to the Center's Interdisciplinary Research Committee. The video-tapes had been made as raw material for a demonstration tape giving an overview of the Center's services, and therefore documented all the encounters involving a single family and Center staff, which took place over three weeks.

The primary goal of the Center is to provide interdisciplinary training to future professionals in serving developmentally disabled children and their families. Staff members work in interdisciplinary teams which include an audiologist, speech pathologist, pediatrician, social worker, nutritionist, dentist, nurses and an occupational, an educational and a physical therapist. Each professional meets with the child and, in some cases, other family members; then all meet to pool the results of their evaluations, which are presented to the parents in a group meeting.

The parents of Jody, the 8-year-old cerebral palsied child in this study, were referred to the Center by the parents of another child. Their chief concern was Jody's public school placement in a class for mentally retarded children. Their objective, which was met, was to have a Center representative meet with the supervisor of special education in their district and have Jody placed in a class for the orthopedically rather than mentally handicapped.

In addition to the spastic cerebral palsy (paralysis resulting from damage to the brain before or during birth), Jody was diagnosed as having a seizure disorder; a potentially lethal arteriovenous malformation in her brain (this was subsequently, and happily, rediagnosed as a less dangerous malformation involving veins only, rather than both arteries and veins); facial hemangiomas (red spots composed of blood-filled capillaries); and slight scoliosis (curvature of the spine).

We began our analysis by focusing on the pediatrician's examination/interview, which took place with the mother present. As part of our analysis, we met, separately, with the doctor and the mother, first talking with them and then reviewing segments of the tape. The mother expressed the opinion that this doctor "was great," in explicit contrast with others who "cut you off and make you feel stupid" and deliver devastating information (for example, "she'd be a vegetable") in an offhand manner.

Interactive frames in the pediatric examination

The goal of this paper is to show that examining Jody in her mother's presence constituted a significant burden on the pediatrician, which can be attributed to a conflict in framing resulting from mismatched schemas. To demonstrate this inter-action between frames and schemas, we will first show what framing is and how it works, beginning with the crucial linguistic component of register.

Linguistic registers

A key element in framing is the use of identifiable linguistic registers. Register, as Ferguson (1985) defines it, is simply "variation conditioned by use:" conventional-ized lexical, syntactic and prosodic choices deemed appropriate for the setting and audience. . . .

In addressing the child, the pediatrician uses "motherese": a teasing register characterized by exaggerated shifts in pitch, marked prosody (long pauses followed by bursts of vocalization), and drawn out vowel sounds, accompanied by smiling. For example, while examining Jody's ears with an ophthalmoscope (ear light), the pediatrician pretends to be looking for various creatures, and Jody responds with delighted laughter:

> Doctor: Let me look in your ear. Do you have a monkey in your ear?
> Child: [laughing] No::::.
> Doctor: No:::? . . . Let's see. . . . I . . see . . . . . . a birdie!
> Child: ⌜ [laughing] No:::.
> Doctor: ⌊ [smiling] No.

In stark contrast to this intonationally exaggerated register, the pediatrician uses a markedly flat intonation to give a running account of the findings of her examina-tion, addressed to no present party, but designed for the benefit of pediatric residents who might later view the video-tape in the teaching facility. We call this "reporting register." For example, looking in Jody's throat, the doctor says, with only slight stumbling:

> Doctor: Her canals are are fine, they're open, um her tympanic mem-
>   brane was thin, and light,

Finally, in addressing the mother, the pediatrician uses conventional conversational register, as for example:

> Doctor: As you know, the important thing is that she does have diffi-
>   culty with the use of her muscles.

Register shifting

Throughout the examination the doctor moves among these registers. Sometimes she shifts from one to another in very short spaces of time, as in the following example in which she moves smoothly from teasing the child while examining her throat, to reporting her findings, to explaining to the mother what she is looking for and how this relates to the mother's expressed concern with the child's breathing at night.

> [Teasing register]
>
> Doctor: Let's see. Can you open up like this, Jody. Look.
>   [Doctor opens her own mouth]
> Child: Aaaaaaaaaaaaaah.
> Doctor: ⌈ Good. That's good.
> Child: ⌊ Aaaaaaaaaaaah
>
> [Reporting register]
>
> Doctor: /Seeing/ for the palate, she ⌈ has a high arched palate →
> Child: ⌊ Aaaaaaaaaaaaaaaaaaaaaaaaaah
> Doctor: but there's no cleft,
>   [maneuvers to grasp child's jaw]
>
> [Conversational register]
>
>   . . . what we'd want to look for is to see how she . . . moves
>   her palate. . . . Which may be some of the difficulty with
>   breathing that we're talking about.

The pediatrician's shifts from one register to another are sometimes abrupt (for example, when she turns to the child and begins teasing) and sometimes gradual (for example, her reporting register in "high arched palate" begins to fade into conversational register with "but there's no cleft," and come to rest firmly in conversational register with "what we'd want to look for . . ."). In the following example, she shifts from entertaining Jody to reporting findings and back to managing Jody in a teasing tone:

> [Teasing register]
>
> Doctor: That's my light.
> Child: /This goes up there./
> Doctor: It goes up there. That's right.
>
> [Reporting register]
>
>   Now while we're examining her head we're feeling for lymph
>   nodes in her neck . . . or for any masses . . . okay . . . also you
>   palpate the midline for thyroid, for goiter . . . if there's any.

[Teasing register]

> Now let us look in your mouth. Okay? With my light. Can you
> open up real big? . . . Oh, bigger. . . . Oh bigger. . . . Bigger.

Frame shifting

Although register shifting is one way of accomplishing frame shifts, it is not
the only way. Frames are more complex than register. Whereas each audience is
associated with an identifiable register, the pediatrician shifts footings with each
audience. In other words, she not only talks differently to the mother, the child
and the future video audience, but she also deals with each of these audiences in
different ways, depending upon the frame in which she is operating.

The three most important frames in this interaction are the social encounter,
examination of the child and a related outer frame of its videotaping, and consultation with the mother. Each of the three frames entails addressing each of the
three audiences in different ways. For example, the social encounter requires that
the doctor entertain the child, establish rapport with the mother and ignore the
video camera and crew. The examination frame requires that she ignore the mother,
make sure the video crew is ready and then ignore them, examine the child, and
explain what she is doing for the future video audience of pediatric residents.
The consultation frame requires that she talk to the mother and ignore the crew
and the child – or, rather, keep the child "on hold," to use Goffman's term, while
she answers the mother's questions. These frames are balanced nonverbally as well
as verbally. Thus the pediatrician keeps one arm outstretched to rest her hand on
the child while she turns away to talk to the mother, palpably keeping the child
"on hold."

Juggling frames

Often these frames must be served simultaneously, such as when the pediatrician
entertains the child and examines her at the same time, as seen in the example
where she looks in her ear and teases Jody that she is looking for a monkey. The
pediatrician's reporting register reveals what she was actually looking at (Jody's ear
canals and tympanic membrane). But balancing frames is an extra cognitive burden,
as seen when the doctor accidentally mixes the vocabulary of her diagnostic report
into her teasing while examining Jody's stomach:

[Teasing register]

Doctor: Okay. All right. Now let me /?/ let me see what I
         can find in there. Is there peanut butter and jelly?
         Wait a minute.⌐
Child: ⌐No⌐
Doctor: ⌐No peanut butter and jelly in there?
Child: No.

[Conversational register]

Doctor: Bend your legs up a little bit. . . . That's right.

[Teasing register]

Okay? Okay. Any peanut butter and jelly in here?⌐
Child: └No⌐
Doctor: └No.
No. There's nothing in there. Is your spleen palpable over
there?⌐
Child: └No.

The pediatrician says the last line, "Is your spleen palpable over there?" in the same
teasing register she was using for peanut butter and jelly, and Jody responds with
the same delighted giggling "No" with which she responded to the teasing questions about peanut butter and jelly. The power of the paralinguistic cues with which
the doctor signals the frame "teasing" is greater than that of the words spoken,
which in this case leak out of the examination frame into the teasing register.

In other words, for the pediatrician, each interactive frame, that is, each identifiable activity that she is engaged in within the interaction, entails her establishing
a distinct footing with respect to the other participants.

The interactive production of frames

Our analysis focuses on the pediatrician's speech because our goal is to show that
the mismatch of schemas triggers the frame switches which make this interaction
burdensome for her. Similar analyses could be performed for any participant in any
interaction. Furthermore, all participants in any interaction collaborate in the negotiation of all frames operative within that interaction. Thus, the mother and child
collaborate in the negotiation of frames which are seen in the pediatrician's speech
and behavior.

For example, consider the examination frame as evidence in the pediatrician's
running report of her procedures and findings for the benefit of the video audience. Although the mother interrupts with questions at many points in the
examination, she does not do so when the pediatrician is reporting her findings
in what we have called reporting register.[3] Her silence contributes to the maintenance of this frame. Furthermore, on the three of seventeen occasions of reporting
register when the mother does offer a contribution, she does so in keeping with
the physician's style: Her utterances have a comparable clipped style.

The homonymy of behaviors

Activities which appear the same on the surface can have very different meanings
and consequences for the participants if they are understood as associated with
different frames. For example, the pediatrician examines various parts of the child's
body in accordance with what she describes at the start as a "standard pediatric
evaluation." At times she asks the mother for information relevant to the child's

condition, still adhering to the sequence of foci of attention prescribed by the pediatric evaluation. At one point, the mother asks about a skin condition behind the child's right ear, causing the doctor to examine that part of Jody's body. What on the surface appears to be the same activity – examining the child – is really very different. In the first case the doctor is adhering to a preset sequence of procedures in the examination, and in the second she is interrupting that sequence to focus on something else, following which she will have to recover her place in the standard sequence.

Conflicting frames

Each frame entails ways of behaving that potentially conflict with the demands of other frames. For example, consulting with the mother entails not only interrupting the examination sequence but also taking extra time to answer her questions, and this means that the child will get more restless and more difficult to manage as the examination proceeds. Reporting findings to the video audience may upset the mother, necessitating more explanation in the consultation frame. Perhaps that is the reason the pediatrician frequently explains to the mother what she is doing and finding and why.

Another example will illustrate that the demands associated with the consultation frame can conflict with those of the examination frame, and that these frames and associated demands are seen in linguistic evidence, in this case by contrasting the pediatrician's discourse to the mother in the examination setting with her report to the staff of the Child Development Center about the same problem. Having recently learned that Jody has an arteriovenous malformation in her brain, the mother asks the doctor during the examination how dangerous this condition is. The doctor responds in a way that balances the demands of several frames:

> Mother: I often worry about the danger involved too. →
> Doctor: └Yes.
> Cause she's well I mean like right now, . . . uh . . . in her present condition. →
> Doctor: └mhm
> Mother: I've often wondered about how dangerous they they are to her right now.
> Doctor: We:ll . . . um . . . the only danger would be from bleeding. . . . Fróm them. If there was any rupture, or anything like that. Which CAN happen. . . . um . . . that would be the danger.
> Mother: └mhm
> Doctor: . . . Fór that. But they're . . . . . . mm . . . nót going to be something that will get worse as time goes on.
> Mother: Oh I see.
> Doctor: But they're just thére. Okay?

The mother's question invoked the consultation frame, requiring the doctor to give the mother the information based on her medical knowledge, plus take into account the effect on the mother of the information that the child's life is in danger. However, the considerable time that would normally be required for such a task is limited because of the conflicting demands of the examination frame: the child is "on hold" for the exam to proceed. (Notice that it is admirable sensitivity of this doctor that makes her aware of the needs of both frames. According to this mother, many doctors have informed her in matter-of-fact tones of potentially devastating information about her child's condition, without showing any sign of awareness that such information will have emotional impact on the parent. In our terms, such doctors acknowledge only one frame – examination – in order to avoid the demands of conflicting frames – consultation and social encounter. Observing the burden on this pediatrician, who successfully balances the demands of multiple frames, makes it easy to understand why others might avoid this.)

The pediatrician blunts the effect of the information she imparts by using circumlocutions and repetitions; pausing and hesitating; and minimizing the significant danger of the arteriovenous malformation by using the word "only" ("only danger"), by using the conditional tense ("that would be the danger"), and by stressing what sounds positive, that they're not going to get worse. She further creates a reassuring effect by smiling, nodding and using a soothing tone of voice. In reviewing the video-tape with us several years after the taping, the pediatrician was surprised to see that she had expressed the prognosis in this way, and furthermore that the mother seemed to be reassured by what was in fact distressing information. The reason she did so, we suggest, is that she was responding to the immediate and conflicting demands of the two frames she was operating in: consulting with the mother in the context of the examination.

Evidence that this doctor indeed felt great concern for the seriousness of the child's condition is seen in her report to the staff regarding the same issue:

> Doctor: . . . uh: I'm not sure how much counseling has been dóne, . . . wíth these parents, . . . around . . . the issue . . . of the a-v malformation. Mother asked me questions, . . . about the operability, inoperability of it, . . . u:m . . . which I was not able to answer. She was told it was inoperable, and I had to say well yes some of them are and some of them aren't. . . . And I think that this is a . . . a . . . an important point. Because I don't know whether . . . the possibility of sudden death, intracranial hemorrhage, if any of this has ever been discússed with these parents.

Here the pediatrician speaks faster, with fluency and without hesitation or circumlocution. Her tone of voice conveys a sense of urgency and grave concern. Whereas the construction used with the mother, "only danger," seemed to minimize the danger, the listing construction used with the staff ("sudden death, intracranial hemorrhage"), which actually refers to a single possible event, gives the impression that even more dangers are present than those listed.

Thus the demands on the pediatrician associated with consultation with the mother; those associated with examining the child and reporting her findings to the video audience; and those associated with managing the interaction as a social encounter are potentially in conflict and result in competing demands on the doctor's cognitive and social capacities.

Knowledge schemas in the pediatric interaction

Just as ways of talking (that is, of expressing and establishing footing) at any point in interaction reflect the operation of multiple frames, similarly, what individuals choose to say in an interaction grows out of multiple knowledge schemas regarding the issues under discussion, the participants, the setting, and so on. We have seen that conflicts can arise when participants are orientated toward different interactive frames, or have different expectations associated with frames. Topics that the mother introduces in the consultation frame sometimes interfere with the doctor's conducting the examination, and time the doctor spends examining Jody in areas in which she has had no problems does not help the mother in terms of what prompted her to take Jody to the Child Development Center: a concern that she was regressing rather than improving in skills. Similarly, when participants have different schemas, the result can be confusion and talking at cross-purposes, and, frequently, the triggering of switches in interactive frames. We will demonstrate this with examples from the pediatrician's and mother's discussions of a number of issues related to the child's health and her cerebral palsy.

Mismatched schemas

Before examining Jody, the pediatrician conducts a medical interview in which she fills out a form by asking the mother a series of questions about Jody's health history and current health condition. After receiving negative answers to a series of questions concerning such potential conditions as bowel problems, bronchitis, pneumonia and ear infections, the pediatrician summarizes her perception of the information the mother has just given her. However, the mother does not concur with this paraphrase:

> Doctor: Okay. And so her general overall health has been good.
> Mother: . . . . . . [sighs] Not really. . . . uh: . . . back . . . uh . . .
> after she had her last seizure, . . . uh . . . uh . . . it was
> pretty cold during this . . . that time . . . a:nd uh . . . it
> seemed that she just didn't have much energy,⌐
> Doctor: └mm
> Mother: . . . and she uh . . . her uh . . . . . . motor abilities at the
> time didn't seem . . . very good. . . . She kept bumping into
> walls, . . . and falling, and . . . uh

The mother's schema for health is a comprehensive one, including the child's total physical well-being. The child's motor abilities have not been good; therefore her health has not been good. In contrast, the pediatrician does not consider motor abilities to be included in a schema of health. Moreover, the pediatrician has a schema for cerebral palsy (cp): she knows what a child with cp can be expected to do or not do, i.e. what is "normal" for a child with cp. In contrast, as emerged

in discussion during a staff meeting, the mother has little experience with other cp
children, so she can only compare Jody's condition and development to those of
non-cp children.

Throughout our tapes of interaction between Jody's mother and the pediatrician, questions are asked and much talk is generated because of unreconciled
differences between the mother's and doctor's knowledge schemas regarding health
and cerebral palsy, resulting from the doctor's experience and training and the
mother's differing experience and personal involvement.

Mismatches based on the cp schema account for numerous interruptions of the
examination frame by the mother invoking the consultation frame. For example,
as briefly mentioned earlier, the mother interrupts the doctor's examination to ask
about a skin eruption behind the child's ear. The mother goes on to ask whether
there is a connection between the cerebral palsy and the skin condition because
both afflict Jody's right side. The doctor explains that there is no connection. The
mother's schema for cp does not include the knowledge that it would not cause
drying and breaking of skin. Rather, for her, the skin condition and the cp become
linked in a "right-sided weakness" schema.

Similar knowledge schema mismatches account for extensive demands on the
pediatrician to switch from the examination to the consultation frame. When Jody
sleeps, her breathing sounds noisy, as if she were gasping for air. The mother is
very concerned that the child might not be getting enough oxygen. When the doctor
finishes examining the child's throat and moves on to examine her ears, the mother
takes the opportunity to interrupt and state her concern. The doctor halts the examination, turns to the mother and switches to the consultation frame, explaining that
the muscle weakness entailed in cp also affects the muscles used in breathing; therefore Jody's breathing sounds "coarse" or "floppy." However, this does not mean
that she is having trouble breathing.

    Doctor: Jody? . . . I want to look in your ears. . . . Jody?
    Mother: This problem that she hás, . . . is not . . . interfering
               with her breathing, is it?
    Child: /Hello/ [spoken into ophthalmoscope]
    Doctor: No.
    Mother: It just appears that way?
    Doctor: Yes. It's very . . . it's . . . really . . . it's like flóppy you
               know that that's why it sounds the way it is.
    Mother: She worries me at night.
    Doctor: Yes
    Mother: Because uh . . . when she's asleep I keep checking on hér
               so she doesn't⌐
    Doctor: As you know the important⌐
    Mother: I keep
               thinking she's not breathing properly.
               [spoken while chuckling]
    Doctor: As you know, the impórtant thing is that she dóes have
               difficulty with the use of her muscles.⌐
    Mother: mhm

Doctor: So she has difficulty with the use of muscles, . . . as far
as the muscles of her chest, that are used with breathing.
Y'know as well as the drooling, the muscles with swallowing,
and all that ⌈ so all her muscles
Mother: ⌊ Is there some exercise
/to strengthen or help that/.

The mother's schemas for health and cerebral palsy do not give her the expectation that the child's breathing should sound noisy. Rather, for her, noisy breathing is "wheezing," which fits into a schema for ill health: noisy breathing is associated with difficulty breathing. In fact, the parents, in the initial medical interview at the Child Development Center, characterize Jody as having difficulty breathing, and this is entered into the written record of the interview.

These schemas are not easily altered. The pediatrician's assurance that Jody is not having trouble breathing goes on for some time, yet the mother brings it up again when the doctor is listening to Jody's chest through a stethoscope. Again the doctor shifts from the examination frame to the consultation frame to reassure her at length that the child is not having trouble breathing, that these sounds are "normal" for a child with cerebral palsy.

Doctor: Now I want you to listen, Jody. We're going to listen to you
breathe. Can you? Look at me. Can you go like this? [inhales]
Good. Oh you know how to do all this. You've been to a lot
of doctors. [Jody inhales] Good. Good. Once . . . good. Okay.
Once more. Oh you have a lot of extra noise on this side.
Go ahead. Do it once more. ⌈Once more.
Mother: ⌊That's the particular noise she
makes when she sleeps. [chuckle]
Doctor: Once more. Yeah I hear all that. One more. One more.
[laughs] Once more. Okay. That's good. She has very coarse
breath sounds um . . . and you can hear a lot of the noises
you hear when she breathes you can hear when you listen.
But there's nothing that's⌉
Mother: ⌊That's the kind of noise I hear
when she's sleeping at night.
Doctor: ⌈Yes,⌋
Yes. There's nothing really as far as a pneumonia is concerned
or as far as any um anything here. There's no wheezing um
which would suggest a tightness or a constriction of the thing.
There's no wheezing at all. What it is is mainly very coarse
due to the . . . the wide open kind of flopping.

Nonetheless, during the session in which the staff report their findings to the parents, when the pediatrician makes her report, the mother again voices her concern that the child is having trouble breathing and refers to the sound of Jody's breathing as "wheezing." At this point the doctor adamantly reasserts that there is no wheezing. What for the mother is a general descriptive term for the sound of noisy breathing is for the doctor a technical term denoting a condition by which the throat passages are constricted.

An understanding of the mother's schemas accounts for the resilience of her concern about the child's breathing, despite the doctor's repeated and lengthy reassurances. Our point here is that the mismatch in schemas — that is, the mother's association of noisy breathing with difficulty breathing and the doctor's dissociation of these two conditions and her emphasis on the medical definition of "wheezing" (irrelevant to the mother) — creates a mismatch in expectations about what counts as adequate reassurance. This mismatch causes the mother to ask questions which require the doctor to shift frames from examination to consultation.

Summary and conclusion

We have used the term "frame" to refer to the anthropological/sociological notion of a frame, as developed by Bateson and Goffman, and as Gumperz (1982) uses the term "speech activity." It refers to participants' sense of what is being done, and reflects Goffman's notion of footing: the alignment participants take up to themselves and others in the situation. We use the term "schema" to refer to patterns of knowledge such as those discussed in cognitive psychology and artificial intelligence. These are patterns of expectations and assumptions about the world, its inhabitants and objects.

We have shown how frames and schemas together account for interaction in a pediatric interview/examination, and how linguistic cues, or ways of talking, evidence and signal the shifting frames and schemas. An understanding of frames accounts for the exceedingly complex, indeed burdensome nature of the pediatrician's task in examining a child in the mother's presence. An understanding of schemas accounts for many of the doctor's lengthy explanations, as well as the mother's apparent discomfort and hedging when her schemas lead her to contradict those of the doctor. Moreover, and most significantly, it is the mismatch of schemas that frequently occasions the mother's recurrent questions which, in their turn, require the doctor to interrupt the examination frame and switch to a consultation frame.

The usefulness of such an analysis for those concerned with medical interaction is significant. On a global level, this approach begins to answer the call by physicians (for example, Brody 1980 and Lipp 1980) for deeper understanding of the use of language in order to improve services in their profession. On a local level, the pediatrician, on hearing our analysis, was pleased to see a theoretical basis for what she had instinctively sensed. Indeed, she had developed the method in her private practice of having parents observe examinations, paper in hand, from behind a one-way mirror, rather than examining children in the parents' presence.

The significance of the study, however, goes beyond the disciplinary limits of medical settings. There is every reason to believe that frames and schemas operate in similar ways in all face-to-face interaction, although the particular frames and schemas will necessarily differ in different settings. We may also expect, and must further investigate, individual and social differences both in frames and schemas and in the linguistic as well as nonverbal cues and markers by which they are identified and created.

Transcription conventions

[		Brackets linking two lines show overlap: Two voices heard at once
]		Reversed-flap brackets shows latching No pause between lines
/ /		/words/ in slashes reflect uncertain transcription
/?/		indicates inaudible words
?		indicates rising intonation, not grammatical question
.		indicates falling intonation, not grammatical sentence
:		following vowels indicates elongation of sound
. .		Two dots indicate brief pause, less than half second
. . .		Three dots indicate pause of at least half second; more dots indicate longer pauses
→		Arrow at left highlights key line in example Arrow at right means talk continues without interruption→ on succeeding lines of text
′		Accent mark indicates primary stress
CAPS		indicate emphatic stress

Notes

1   This chapter . . . is a final synthesis of a long-term project analyzing videotapes made at Georgetown University's Child Development Center. We are grateful to the Center administrators and staff who gave us permission to use the tapes, and to the pediatrician, the mother, and the parent coordinator for permission to use the tapes and for taking the time to view and discuss them with us. We thank Dell Hymes for his observations on how our work blends social psychological and sociolinguistic concerns. Tannen is grateful to Lambros Comitas and the Department of Philosophy and the Social Sciences of Teachers College Columbia University for providing affiliation during her sabbatical leave which made possible the revision of the manuscript. We thank Douglas Maynard for incisive editorial suggestions. . . .

2   Thanks to A.L. Becker for the reference to Ortega y Gasset. For a discussion on framing based on numerous examples from everyday life, see chapter 5, "Framing and Reframing," in Tannen (1986).

3   The notion of "reporting register" accounts for a similar phenomenon described by Cicourel (1975) in an analysis of a medical interview.

References

Bartlett, F.C. (1932) *Remembering*, Cambridge: Cambridge University Press.

Bateson, G. (1972) *Steps to an Ecology of Mind*, New York: Ballantine.

Brody, D.S. (1980) 'Feedback from patients as a means of teaching non-technological aspects of medical care', *Journal of Medical Education* 55: 34–41.

Chafe, W. (1977) 'Creativity in verbalization and its implications for the nature of stored knowledge', in Freedle, R. (ed.) *Discourse Production and Comprehension*, Norwood, NJ: Ablex, 41–55.

Cicourel, A.V. (1975) 'Discourse and text: cognitive and linguistic processes in studies of social structure', *Versus* 12: 33–84.

—— (1983) 'Language and the structure of belief in medical communication', in Fisher, S. and Dundas Todd, A. (eds) *The Social Organization of Doctor–Patient Communication*, Washington, DC: Center for Applied Linguistics, 221–39.

Ferguson, C.A. (1985) Editor's introduction. Special language registers, Special issue of *Discourse Processes* 8: 391–4.

Fillmore, C.J. (1976) 'The need for a frame semantics within linguistics', *Statistical Methods in Linguistics*, 5–29, Stockholm: Skriptor.

Frake, C.O. (1977) 'Plying frames can be dangerous: some reflections on methodology in cognitive anthropology', *The Quarterly Newsletter of the Institute for Comparative Human Cognition* 1: 1–7.

Frankel, R.M. (1989) '"I was wondering – could Raid affect the brain permanently d'y'-know?": Some observations on the intersection of speaking and writing in calls to a poison control center', *Western Journal of Speech Communication* 53: 195–226.

Goffman, E. (1974) *Frame Analysis*, New York, Harper & Row.

—— (1981a) *Forms of Talk*, Philadelphia, PA: University of Pennsylvania Press.

—— (1981b) 'Reply to review of frame analysis by Norma Denzin', *Contemporary Sociology* 10: 60–8.

Gumperz, J.J. (1982) *Discourse Strategies*, Cambridge: Cambridge University Press.

Heidegger, M. (1962) *Being and Time*, New York: Harper & Row.

Hymes, D. (1974) 'Ways of speaking', in Bauman, R. and Sherzer, J. (eds) *Explorations in the Ethnography of Speaking*, Cambridge: Cambridge University Press, 433–510.

Kendon, A. (1979) 'Some theoretical and methodological aspects of the use of film in the study of social interaction', in Ginsburg, G.P. (ed.) *Emerging Strategies in Social Psychological Research*, New York: Wiley, 67–94.

Kleinman, A. (1980) *Patients and Healers in the Context of Culture: An Exploration of the Borderland Between Anthropology, Medicine and Psychiatry*, Berkeley, CA: University of California Press.

Lipp, M.R. (1980) *The Bitter Pill: Doctors, Patients and Failed Expectations*, New York: Harper & Row.

Minsky, M. (1975) 'A framework for representing knowledge', in Winston, P.H. (ed.) *The Psychology of Computer Vision*, New York: McGraw Hill, 211–77.

Mishler, E. (1984) *The Discourse of Medicine: Dialectics of Medical Interviews*, Norwood, NJ: Ablex.

Ortega y Gasset, J. (1959) 'The difficulty of reading', *Diogenes* 28: 1–17.

Rumelhart, D.E. (1975) 'Notes on a schema for stories', in Bobrow, D.G. and Collins, A. (eds) *Representation and Understanding*, New York: Academic Press, 211–36.

Schank, R.C. and Abelson, R.P. (1977) *Scripts, Plans, Goals, and Understanding: An Inquiry into Human Knowledge Structures*, Hillsdale, NJ: Erlbaum.

Tannen, D. (1979) 'What's in a frame? Surface evidence for underlying expectations', in Freedle, R. (ed.) *New Directions in Discourse Processing*, Norwood, NJ: Ablex.

Tannen, D. (1986) *That's Not What I Meant!: How Conversational Style Makes or Breaks your Relations with Others*, New York: William Morrow.

Chapter 25

Nikolas Coupland and Virpi Ylänne

RELATIONAL FRAMES IN WEATHER TALK

TALK ABOUT THE WEATHER has, since Malinowski (see Chapter 20), been taken as a paradigmatic case of phatic communion. The weather appears to offer conversationalists a topic of talk, and a way of relating to each other, that falls within the usually accepted bounds of small talk. The weather, it might be argued, is a neutral topic, accessible to all participants, non-person-focussed and uncontroversial. The weather seems well suited to filling out those moments in social interaction when people are 'avoiding other problems' (Robinson 1985), merely maintaining a conversational flow, attending to non-transactional purposes and doing 'timeout talk' (Coupland 2000). Malinowski is in fact quite specific about the weather as a phatic resource:

> Inquiries about health, comments on weather, affirmations of some supremely obvious state of things – all such are exchanged, not in order to inform, not in this case to connect people in action, certainly not in order to express any thought.
>
> (1923: 313; see also Chapter 20: 296)

> The breaking of silence, the communion of words is the first act to establish links of fellowship. . . . The modern English expression *Nice day today* . . . [is] needed to get over the strange and unpleasant tension which men [*sic*] feel when facing each other in silence.
>
> (1923: 314; see also Chapter 20: 297)

Our intention in this chapter is to elaborate on these 'classical' readings of weather talk and recontextualise them. We want, firstly, to ask what precisely is it about the weather that imbues it with the supposed attribute of 'neutrality', and to show how weather talk in fact functions relationally in naturally occurring talk. Our data

Source: Written specifically for this collection.

are extracts of audio-recorded interaction from two corpora of travel agency talk. At one level, travel agency talk is representative of the broader category of service encounters, where posted servers interact with clients who have, primarily, transactional goals. We try to gain some perspective on how 'the weather' in fact features in small talk and on how it is deployed in specific instances. But because our data are specific to travel agencies, we have the opportunity to explore other, less obviously phatic, framings of the topic of 'weather' (including 'climate', 'environment', etc.), where people construct different meanings and values around this theme in their talk. After all, travel agencies and the tourist trade invest heavily in economic formulations of weather and the weather can be very far from an incidental, neutral concern. Observing how weather features in different discursive frames (cf. Goffman 1974; Tannen 1993; Tannen and Wallat, this volume) should help us to identify how the small talk frame for weather is constituted, and what its boundaries are.

Our source data are two sets of audio-recorded data – uncontrolled samples of naturally occurring interaction in travel agencies in Cardiff, the capital city of Wales (see Coupland 1988, Ylänne-McEwen 2004). Both corpora were gathered with the permission of travel agency staff and clients and transcribed orthographically, but using some of the familiar additional conventions developed for conversation analysis by Gail Jefferson (see Chapter 10). First names at the head of each extract are fictionalised names of the assistants principally involved. Clients are identified by fictionalised titles and last names (this general pattern of naming was conventional in the settings we were investigating). Some contextual information is given at the head of each extract. Single brackets enclose utterances that are hard to hear in the recordings; double brackets enclose our own comments on nonverbal or contextual features of the interaction. Our analysis is based on the transcripts in conjunction with the original audio-recordings, plus our own field notes (each of us was a present but non-participant observer of the original speech events).

The first extracts, below, illustrate how participants in the data occasionally talk about the weather as an element of their timeout and classically 'phatic' talk. This function of phatic weather talk is in fact rare in the two corpora, constituting a total of seven instances which make reference to local weather conditions on the day of the interaction or on previous days from a total of 195 recorded interactions.

The weather in passing

One account for the weather's suitability as a topic for small talk is that the weather is 'merely' an environmental concern, a backdrop to situated and focused social action. It is a matter of passing concern, which we experience in states of transition between activities – such as eating breakfast and being at work. If small talk occurs on the street, speakers may be quite literally in passage, moving in different directions between homes and places of work or leisure. Speakers may comment 'in passing' about the weather, which is pertinent to their transitional states at the moment of their chance encounters. People on radically different trajectories will predictably comment on a briefly shared environment, the weather, as it is temporarily experienced by them together.

The weather is itself in transition. Its quality of unpredictability (especially in Britain) ensures that there will very often be a change-of-state to comment upon – cf. Malinowski's 'Nice day today', 'Warmer than yesterday', and so on. But it is a predictable unpredictability, since we have rather fixed normative expectations for the weather relative to the seasons – 'for the time of year'. The surface motivation for talking about the weather is likely to be that the weather has changed, or that it has broken our expectations. It is in fact interesting to speculate that many forms of small talk will be based in commentaries on local change – updating on recent happenings, movements and experiences. Weather talk can therefore play off the intersection of various dimensions of change and movement – people moving through space and between activities, temporarily interconnecting with shifting atmospheric conditions.

Extract 1

From the closing sequence of a 10 minute encounter in which the client has come to confirm her holiday booking. Recorded in mid January.

```
 1   Emma: what'll happen now in about ten days to two weeks time (.)
 2        you'll get a confirmation from (.) ourselves and Thomsons and
 3        on that it'll give you the date that we have to receive the  balance
                                                                      [
 4   Mrs Davies:                                                      yes that's
 5        right
(22.0) ((Mrs Davies puts documents in handbag and gets ready to go))
 6   Mrs Davies: looks lovely out there (but) it's not ((slight giggle))
                                                      [
 7   Emma:                                            is it cold?
 8   Mrs Davies: (2 sylls) the wind is terrible I can't understand (what's=
                                         [   ]
 9   Emma:                               oh
10   Mrs Davies: =happening)
11   Emma: mind you good day to have your washing out providing it'll=
                                                    [   ]
12   Mrs Davies:                                    ((slight laugh))
13   Emma: =stay on the line
14   Mrs Davies: well it wouldn't (.) pegs would fly away
               [   ]
15   Emma:     ((slight laugh))
16   Mrs Davies: oh! ((sigh)) that's it then (3.0) many thanks for all attentions=
17   Emma: =that's okay no problem at all (.) that's what I'm here for and if
18        you've got any queries or anything over the next couple of weeks
19        just give me a ring
20   Mrs Davies: (4 sylls) I'll probably be in again later I'm trying to book
21        something for my daughter
22   Emma: yeah! no problem at all
23   Mrs Davies: (right ho) thank you!
24   Emma: thanks Mrs Davies! bye bye!
```

Extract 1 captures something of this experience, as Mrs Davies prepares to leave the travel agency on a blustery day. After putting away the documents she has been referring to in the process of booking her holiday with Emma, the assistant, she says that it *looks lovely out there*. She is referring to and physically orienting to the external environment she is about to experience. Of course this is a rather literalist reading of how weather talk comes into play in this extract. A further quality of this moment is its highly marked transitional nature *within* the speech encounter. The utterance *looks lovely out there* breaks the 22 second silence following Emma's explanation of how the booking Mrs Davies has made will be confirmed, and the client's agreement marker. In terms of Schegloff and Sacks's classical analysis of conversational closings (Chapter 18), the putting away of the papers is itself a possible pre-closing move, and weather talk begins the verbal closing and leaving sequence. The weather as topic occupies lines 6–15 of the extract, and it is followed in line 16 by the client's sigh (*oh!*), retrospecting on the encounter (*that's it then*), thanking (*many thanks for all attentions*), and other linked and patterned turns which achieve closing. At line 6, then, the transactional frame has been broken by non-verbal actions (putting papers away, postural orientation to the street) and by weather talk itself, but also by a key-shift to laughter (first audible in line 6; the weather sequence is also closed by slight laughter at line 15).

In Extract 1, weather talk is therefore done 'in passing' in the more general sense of occurring at a moment of discursive transition, and it is in fact a rhetorical device for marking and achieving transition – here, orientation to leave-taking. This general pattern is strongly represented in the data, as shown in Extracts 2 and 3.

Extract 2

The client and the assistant are looking through various holiday options for a late deal holiday in July. The transcript begins near the beginning of the encounter, as the client sits down. The client has asked about late deals and Melanie is taking out brochures. Recorded in early June.

```
 1   Mrs Hill: it's warm in this office isn't it? ooh!
                                        [
 2   Melanie:                          very warm yes (it's extreme) ((typing on
 3       computer terminal)) X27 (1.0) I'll try and get my er little fan fixed
 4       soon ((Melanie confirms dates, departure airport and duration . . .))
 5   Mrs Hill: so I could afford to wait really erm
 6   Melanie: well I don't know if Airtours have gone down from the fee you
 7       had in mind it may not be worth you waiting
 8   Mrs Hill: mm (12.0)
 9   Mrs Hill: I can't (imagine) how you can work in this ((slight laugh)) it's like
10       a sauna in here (.) it's really close
11   Melanie: I don't suppose I notice it cos I've been here all day it was colder
12       (.) earlier on
13   Mrs Hill: I think what it is is cos it's erm (.) it's rained (4 sylls) it's got
14       (sort of like) a really close atmosphere outside (over there)
                                        [ ]
15   Melanie:                          mm
16   Mrs Hill: (that's why it's so much cooler)
17   Melanie: second of July it'll search for me . . .
```

Extract 3

The client is booking a day trip by coach. Three minutes into the encounter, Elizabeth, the assistant, is telephoning the coach company. It is a rainy and windy day in late May.

1   *Elizabeth*: ((on the phone)) no could we have pick up point at Westgate
2   Street on this one please?
(40.0) ((Elizabeth on the phone waiting for a response))
3   *Mrs Hughes*: we sat out the garden yesterday no tights and er just a blouse=
                                                                         [
4   *Elizabeth*:   I know it's
5   amazing isn't it!
6   *Mrs Hughes*: =look at today I was shocked when I got out of bed
7   *Elizabeth*: that's right (.) no two days are alike are they?
8   *Mrs Hughes*: no well hope it's better than this <u>next</u> week
9   *Elizabeth*: ((on the phone)) hello? (1.0) seats number (2.0) that's fine
10   thank you Sally bye (.) ((to client)) seats nineteen and twenty
11 *Mrs Hughes*: oh right

In each of these sequences, talk about the weather features at moments where the verbal enactment of travel agency business is temporarily suspended. These occur when silent bureaucratic activity progresses the main transactional business (such as entering data onto a computer), or where a pause in proceedings is enforced by the assistant having to wait or search for information. In Extract 2 Mrs Hill's comment beginning *it's warm* (line 1) is made while the assistant looks for brochures. The client reformulates her observation about temperature, beginning at line 9 after a 12 second silence, and the sequence ends at line 17 when Melanie's computer accepts her search request. In Extract 3 Mrs Hughes embarks on her comments about warm weather at line 3 after a lengthy pause and the sequence ends at line 9 when Elizabeth has to respond to a tour operator on the telephone.

As well as being moments of transition in terms of discourse structure, these are liminal moments (cf. Goffman 1971; Rampton 1999), periods of relative indeterminacy when the normative constraints of travel agency discourse are not fully operative. As Rampton argues, liminal moments are opportunities for social actors to re-evaluate and potentially reconstruct their participation in communicative events. For this reason they tend to involve, in various ways, reflexivity. Weather talk is no exception, and the comments offered about 'the weather' in each of Extracts 1–3 are better described as comments about how environmental conditions impact on speakers themselves and their activities. In Extract 1, Mrs Davies anticipates a degree of discomfort when she leaves and goes out into the wind; in Extract 2, participants comment how the heat is making the office uncomfortable, and in Extract 3 that the weather is shockingly different from the previous day. Weather talk introduces evaluative comments about the circumstances of interaction and about participants' affective responses to them. It breaks away from the achievement of transactional/instrumental goals and focuses reflexively on details of how the transaction has been contextualised and how it is being experienced.

The weather as shared experience

In transactional discourse speakers perform in their institutional roles – here as client and assistant. In interstitial weather talk, they perform as individuals and as 'co-experiencers of the weather' (cf. Ylänne-McEwen's 2004 analysis of role-shifting as a pervasive characteristic of travel agency discourse). The weather is, after all, likely to affect co-present talk participants simultaneously and more or less equally. To this extent it is an appropriate resource for relational talk, talk which may achieve a degree of solidarity by emphasising shared feelings (positive politeness in Brown and Levinson's terms, see Chapter 22).

But more specifically, speakers feel entitled to assume (at least within the UK context) that weather/environment conditions will draw similar, convergent responses from their listeners. Listeners will agree that a sunny day is 'nice', rain is 'horrid' or 'nasty', winter cold is 'bitter' and heat waves 'unbearable' (cf. Coupland and Coupland 1997). More dynamically and discursively, it is striking how speakers design their comments about the weather to elicit evaluative consensus. For example, in Extracts 2 and 3 the principal weather-evaluating utterance is structured as 'it's ADJECTIVE isn't it?' (Extract 2 lines 1 and 10, Extract 3 lines 5–6). The tag question with falling tone seeks confirmation of an uncontroversial claim, and each of the cited instances draws confirmation from the next speaker in the following turn. Mrs Davies in Extract 1 does not use the tagged format when she comments that *the wind is terrible* (line 8), and she does not get Emma's agreement in the next turn. But Emma, the assistant, does engage in similarly evaluative comments to Mrs Davies's. Her *mind you* (line 11) is not establishing a contrary claim about the wind, only posing a more positive formulation of its implications for Mrs Davies – 'looking on the bright side' of a minor trouble (see Coupland *et al.* 1991), but here in a formulaic and phatic manner. Matched laughter across speaker turns (lines 6 to 15) bolsters the degree of consensus achieved.

Sharing in weather talk, again as illustrated in the three extracts, can go well beyond consensual evaluation, towards intimacy. Through talking evaluatively about the weather, speakers can introduce details of their personal lives and feelings, and explore those of their addressees. The weather exchange in Extract 1 incorporates Mrs Davies's oblique self-presentation as being somehow disoriented (*I can't understand ((what's happening))*) and a brief portrayal of the drama of Mrs Davies's washing day. Extract 3 involves mention of personal decisions about whether to wear trousers and wearing *no tights and er just a blouse*.

Weather mattering

As in Malinowski's analysis, talk about the weather can certainly be ritualised and prefigured, and it may be that speakers actually have little investment in their comments about it, even when they voice strong affect. In the Extracts we have considered so far, it is easy to believe that Mrs Davies, for example, may not actually find the wind as terrible as she claims, and that Mrs Hughes and Elizabeth may be overstating their 'shock' and 'amazement' at a cold day in late May. We might ask how relevant climatic conditions (heat, cold, rain, etc.) truly are to most people's daily experiences. Are people perhaps being rather systematically dis-ingenuous in their weather evaluations, sacrificing veracity in the service of relational effect? (Brown and Levinson list exaggeration as one micro-strategy of positive politeness.) Perhaps weather states are generally of little consequence to us in the cocooned modern environments that many of us inhabit, despite our convention-ally strongly valenced adjectives to describe it. One hallmark of urban modernity is to have engineered spaces and devices for rendering the weather largely irrele-vant to our routines – clothing, umbrellas, public transport, shopping malls, super-stores, as well as some more extravagant instances, such as sports stadiums and pleasure domes with roofs. Isn't our exaggerated evaluation of weather states just 'hot air'?

The contrary case can be made, however, for weather *mattering*, and impacting on people's lifestyle choices and possibilities. Broadcast and print media are ardent propagators of the weather. This is probably because the weather is linked in many ways to our increasingly leisure-oriented lives, and to our bodily self-presentations in work and leisure. In Extract 4 the primary transactional function is for a client, Mrs Taylor, to collect her tickets. Much of the talk is filled out around issues of weather and clothing.

Extract 4

The client is collecting tickets for her Scandinavian holiday. It is raining heavily outside.
The client comes in and approaches the assistant's desk. Recorded in late May.

1   *Mrs Taylor*: oh dear oh dear what a day!
2   *Bethan*: awful isn't it!
                        [
3   *Mrs Taylor*:   that's right my name's Veronica Taylor and I've come to
4   collect tickets
                           [
5   *Bethan*:   all right (2.0) let's have a look
((Bethan goes to fetch tickets)) (65.0)
6   *Bethan*: it's here in the (3 sylls) ((slight laugh))
7   *Mrs Taylor*: yes
8   *Bethan*: looking forward to it?
9   *Mrs Taylor*: oh gosh yes I'm trying to think what to pack (.) when you have
10   this sort of weather it puts you off ((laughs))
11 *Bethan*: it's terrible isn't it I think you need one suitcase for the summer
12   clothes and then one suitcase for the winter clothes
13 *Mrs Taylor*: ((smiling)) oh dear
14 *Bethan*: ((quietly)) that's probably the best ((louder)) what you need to do
15   is er to sign the bottom of that
((4.5 minutes later; Bethan is writing the ticket))
16 *Mrs Taylor*: it's very difficult to know what to take though because as I say er
17   everywhere seems to have had <u>a</u>typical weather (.) I've had friends
18   who've just come back from <u>Tur</u>key and they were cold and the
19   Turkish people there were saying we've <u>never</u> had this sort of=
                                            [   ]
20 *Bethan*:   (it's funny though)

21   *Mrs Taylor*: =cold in in you know May and em so I haven't (dear oh dear)
              [   ]
22   *Bethan*:   ((slight laugh)) oh yeah
23   *Bethan*: don't really know what to do for the best
                                    [
24   *Mrs Taylor*:   yeah (.) take layers
25   *Bethan*: mm
26   *Mrs Taylor*: two thin jumpers so that one jumper can go on top of the other
27   one ((laughs))
28   *Bethan*: and the plastic mac and er (.) it'll probably be boiling when you=
                        [   ]   [
29   *Mrs Taylor*:   oh yes   that's=
30   *Bethan*: =get over there
31   *Mrs Taylor*: =right that's why I've got my plastic mac here
32   *Bethan*: right there we go
33   *Mrs Taylor*: good=
34   *Bethan*: =all done

The first spoken exchange involves the client commenting on 'bad weather' and the assistant's endorsement of the evaluation. We can call *what a day!* (line 1) a *conventional weather focuser*. A speaker uses it to signal a strong affective evaluation of the weather (supported here by the *oh dears*, encoding a negative appraisal) which is fleshed out semantically by the listener's appreciation of the respect in which the weather is extreme – hot, cold, foggy, or, in this case, wet. The exchange establishes a degree of solidarity between participants – they orient together to the weather and express a shared evaluation of it. The exchange obviously also opens the encounter (Laver's 'initiatory function' – see Laver 1981), gives participants access to each other's identities and stances (Laver's 'exploratory function'), and forestalls the potential threat of non-talk (Laver's 'propitiatory function'). Even in this service encounter setting, speakers are able to embark on talk by constructing a frame in which institutional roles are less salient than personal roles, or at least apparently so. This frame shifts in the following two turns (lines 3–5) where the institutional roles of client and assistant become operative. Specifically, Mrs Taylor announces her name and her goal for the encounter in institutionally relevant terms: she mentions collecting tickets, which is a familiar stage in the institutional procedure of booking a holiday. At this point, arguably, talk ceases to be 'small'.

As happens in many of the encounters in the data, however, Bethan's question at line 8 reinstates the more personally oriented frame. Both participants can assume that an assistant (in her institutional role) does not need to know whether a client (in her complementary institutional role) is looking forward to the holiday in question. The assistant has no professional interest in this, because the transaction, in a legalistic sense, has already been completed. By implication, Bethan's question is very probably heard outside of the institutional frame. The personal details that Mrs Taylor offers in response, and her reinstating of the weather topic at lines 9–10, are consistent with the frame-shift Bethan has triggered. Clothes, suitcases and packing preferences for variable weather seem to be themes more amenable to personal than professional judgement. Better evidence than our own judgement of thematic appropriateness is the sequential arrangement of talk at this point. The speakers produce multiple endorsements and elaborations of each other's comments in the interaction up to line 14 and again some minutes later, from line 16 up to the encounter's closing sequence (lines 32–4). The utterances *oh gosh yes* (line 9), *it's terrible isn't it* (line 11) and *that's probably the best* (line 14) all have retrospective reference and express agreement and mutual support. The smile (at line 13) and the repeated laughter (marked at lines 10, 22, and 27) again index support and shared experience, as forms of positive politeness. All of this talk clearly relates to travel, which is Bethan's professional domain, but Bethan's alignment to the topics in this sequence is that of a layperson. Participants manu-facture a social consensus in working out a shared response to a weather issue. They move towards intimacy in the detail of their accounts (e.g. in talk about how many jumpers [sweaters] to take, and about their inability to decide, and perhaps via an element of reflexive parody in mentioning the stereotypical tourist's *plastic mac* [raincoat]).

This weather talk, like the opening exchange of the encounter, deserves in one sense to be labelled small talk, in contrast to the (few elements of) transactionally focused talk in this encounter. The assistant has repositioned (de-professionalised) herself by constructing the personal frame. Talk about the weather and packing suitcases for travel is almost infinitely extensible, unlike the bounded and struc-tured non-verbal and verbal stages of the transaction itself (the institutional procedure of giving, receipting and collecting tickets). Of course, the weather exchanges are *not irr*elevant to the transactional dimension of the encounter, because Bethan's 'personal' style may well help sell the next holiday. Business reputedly thrives on 'niceness' and it is ultimately impossible to separate 'customer relations' from the instrumental goals of selling. But our point about 'mattering' here is that, in the personal frame, the weather seems to be occasioning dilemmas and decisions which do genuinely engage these speakers. So this is not desemanticised, phatic weather talk in the Malinowski sense. It is better described as 'relational travel talk', orienting to travellers' concerns about being 'suitably dressed' for the multiple climates that modern travel places around them. Knowing *what to do for the best* (line 23) here includes selecting clothes for climates, clothes from different usage categories (*the summer clothes* and *the winter clothes* – lines 11–12). This talk identi-fies what we might think of as a semi-technical competence associated with modern travel, proposing solutions to a recurrent difficulty of leisure travel. These exchanges represent leisure/travel as a 'challenge' and a 'task' – the lexicon of work more than of enjoyment.

Weather as a commodity

There is one pervasive manner in which weather talk in our data operates outside the domain of small talk. This is when the weather is represented as a saleable commodity, when clients and assistants attach commercial value to the weather as part of the holiday packages they are selling and buying. Extracts 5 and 6 illustrate the marketised discourse of weather that abounds in travel agencies.

Extract 5

The clients have come to enquire about the price of a flydrive holiday to Florida. The
extract starts two minutes into the conversation. Recorded in mid May.

 1   *Cathy*: the cheapest one we've got was two forty nine today
      ((Clients and Cathy talk about prices on Ceefax)) (4.0)
 2   *Cathy*: any particular date in June?
 3   *Mr Lane*: (no)
      ((Cathy typing))
 4   *Cathy*: two weeks?
 5   *Mr Lane*: er is it possible to extend it (would it be) possible to extend it
 6   to three?
 7   *Cathy*: (I'll find out now for you)
      (20.0) ((Cathy typing))
 8   *Mr Lane*: is it so cheap at the moment because of the exchange rate?
 9   *Cathy*: er yeah because it's really out of season at the moment as well
10   *Mr Lane*: it's <u>out</u> of season
11   *Cathy*: well it's not peak season (.) so they tend to reduce their
12   *Mr Lane*: what's the weather like then?
13   *Cathy*: it's very warm it's actually er (.) May and June are probably the
14   nicest time to go because it doesn't get humid you know I mean July
15   August is very very humid very humid out there
(5.0) ((Cathy typing))
16   *Mr Lane*: so (winter is the best time do) you reckon?
17   *Cathy*: er no I was out there in the summer I went out there August
(3.0)
18   *Mr Lane*: that's the trouble isn't it all the exotic locations for us are in the
19   wrong time of year (probably)
                                      [
20   *Cathy*:   yeah ((laughs))
21   *Mr Lane*: if you're ready to go on holiday everybody else is in the winter
                                      [   ]
22   *Cathy*:   that's right yeah
(17.0)
23   *Cathy*: the cheapest one shown up on our screen is two hundred and seventy
24   nine pound it's on the sixth of June (.) that's a flydrive but it's Orlando

Extract 6

The client and the assistant have been discussing various holiday destinations. Sue is
commenting on the merits of Majorca as a destination. Recorded in September.

 1   *Mrs Evans*: . . . the er beaches are very nice and it's not too commercialised
 2   *Sue*: no not if you go up the north
 3   *Mrs Evans*: yes
 4   *Sue*:   and they're much nicer beaches than Ibiza
                                      [
 5   *Mrs Evans*:   and what kind of what kind of temperatures w–

6   will we find in May?
                    [
7   *Sue:*   be quite nice in May very nice it'll be about
                            [ ]   [
8   *Mrs Evans:*   um   sunbathing?
9   *Sue:* oh gosh yes it'll be in the 70s in the in May be very nice
                                                [
10   *Mrs Evans:*   yes it's one reason
11   we don't want to leave it s too much later cos it'd be too hot for
12   the=
                        [
13   *Sue:*   cos it'd be too hot then be nice in=
14   *Mrs Evans:* =children
15   *Sue:* =May though warm enough to you perhaps you need a cardigan at
16   night but it'd be warm enough during the day to sunbathe
17   *Mrs Evans:* and er what about the other Greek islands rather than you
18   mentioned Corfu

There is systematic inter-linkage of the concepts of weather, time/season, value and demand in the speakers' evaluation of holiday destinations in these Extracts, with costs explicitly mentioned in Extract 5 (lines 1, 8 and 23–4). Low price and 'good weather' are the fundamental positives here, with convenience (of time and place) also referred to. The negotiations involve establishing the best available trade-offs between cost and weather. In these three extracts, 'good weather' in the resorts is represented, for example, by *very warm*, *in the 70s*, *warm enough*, and 'bad weather' by *very humid*, *too hot* and *too hot for the children*. Clients are buying weather they consider 'nice' in relation to cost and convenience.

There are some distinctive lexico-grammatical patterns in the marketised representation of weather. The concept of *out of season* (Extract 5, lines 10 and 11) formalises the relationship of weather to money – the period when costs fall because of low convenience or less desirable weather. In fact, it is only in this marketised domain that the topic of 'the weather' is regularly lexicalised in the phrase *the weather* (Extract 5, line 12), along with *temperatures* (Extract 6, line 5), as opposed to the conventional form with the dummy pronoun 'it' – 'it's hot', etc. The frequent relativising of temperature assessments ('warm enough', 'too hot', etc.) indicates their commodification. The weather, and especially temperature, is being rather literally valued as a key attribute of the available product. There are common expressions such as those with *got* which express prospective purchasers' control and ownership of the weather. One example (outside the extracts we use here) is when an assistant advises avoiding a particular time of year on the grounds that *you haven't got the weather then*, meaning that the weather will not be warm enough for the holiday to be entirely desirable. Clients sometimes say that they have open preferences for holiday destinations, except in respect of the weather, for example when a client says *I don't mind where I go as long as it's sunny*.

With the guidance of travel agency assistants, clients are manipulating the variables of money, weather and convenience to construct and control the future experiences of their package holidays, much as they select a grade of hotel or a resort with specific facilities. In fact, weather is redefined as a tourist facility, indexed through bar-charts in travel brochures showing hours of sunshine per day by month in different resorts.

Overview: Frames for weather talk

Weather talk in the travel agency data emerges as a functionally diverse and variably contextualised phenomenon, certainly not uniformly contained within the notion of phatic communion. Most obviously, we need to segregate Malinowski's phatic interpretation of weather talk from the commercially and transactionally relevant instances we discussed in the previous section. In some modes of travel agency talk the weather is a fully commercialised theme. Clients buy and assistants sell weather as a core commodity of packaged holiday. The discourses of commodified leisure audible in travel agency talk are part of a broad and powerful cultural value-set. Climate, and particularly the sun, still defines much of the appeal and marketability of the Mediterranean and other similar resorts. Ways of speaking evaluatively and comparatively about the weather (as we saw in Extracts 5 and 6) are central to this particular cultural ideology of leisure. Weather in this frame is anything but 'small'; indeed it is big business.

Our comments on Extract 4 suggested that there is also an 'intermediate' frame for weather talk which, while linked to the tourist trade and commercialised travel, is focused more interpersonally than transactionally. In that Extract we saw a client and an assistant engaging in sharing personal experiences about how to 'cope' with the weather in their decisions about clothes and packing. In this frame, weather achieves significance in relation to lifestyle choices. The Malinowskian account of small talk seems to be only partly relevant to instances like this one. The client and assistant certainly show no sense of commenting here on 'some supremely obvious state of things', as Malinowski suggested for phatic talk. On the contrary, they show high involvement and mutual support for each other's complaints and suggestions, even though there do appear to be conventional (and probably gender-linked) ways of speaking for achieving support. Just as leisure can itself no longer be thought of as the necessarily marked mode of social existence, relative to work as the unmarked category, we should be wary of assuming that talk involved in planning and responding to leisure travel is somehow insignificant. Malinowski's dictums have always carried the inappropriate implication that relational talk is peripheral and incidental, and of course the designation 'small talk' risks perpetuating this stance.

The first extracts we commented on come closest to illustrating Malinowski's phatic communion in the travel agency data, although we have emphasised the positive relational and procedural functions of weather talk here too. We argued that it is indeed appropriate to view many instances of weather talk in service encounters as being done 'in passing', outside the transactional movement of the speech events. But we would again resist equating 'non-transactional' with 'peripheral'. Weather talk has a clear structuring potential in these interactions. It provides a means for speakers to signal, for example, an orientation to concluding interaction, and partly through reinstating the relevance of the environment outside of the physical location where talk is currently set. To say that weather talk 'fills' spaces where transactional talk has been suspended is therefore to underestimate its role in the management of the encounter more generally.

Finally, we have noted how weather talk can achieve relational intimacy, and of course this is central to Malinowski's sense of the term 'communion'. But the weather does not offer intimacy merely through the fact of talking together on a 'neutral' topic. We showed how, in the first three extracts, speakers make evaluations of the weather which they can expect to be consensually shared by addressees, because they are part of a conventional evaluative discourse in the speech community. This consensus is achieved in the sequencing of conversational turns in the data. More than this, comments about the weather seem, on the basis of the data, able to function as a bridge into intimate and self-disclosive talk, even in this relatively public and transactionally-defined speaking situation. Through moving in and out of weather talk, speakers can reconstitute the normative expectations or frames on which their interactions are based. Weather talk, therefore, also has a metacommunicative potential.

References

Coupland, Justine (2000) (ed.) *Small Talk*, Harlow: Pearson Education.

Coupland, Nikolas (1988) *Dialect in Use*, Cardiff: University of Wales Press.

—— and Coupland, Justine (1997) 'Bodies, beaches and burn-times: "environmentalism" and its discursive competitors', *Discourse & Society* 8 (1): 7–25.

——, —— and Giles, Howard (1991) *Language, Society and the Elderly. Discourse, Identity and Ageing*, Oxford: Blackwell.

Goffman, Erving (1971) *Relations in Public: Microstudies of the Public Order*, London, Allen Lane: Penguin.

—— (1974) *Frame Analysis*, Harmondsworth: Penguin.

Laver, John (1981) 'Linguistic routines and politeness in greeting and parting', in Florian Coulmas (ed.) *Conversational Routine: Explorations in Standardized Communication Situations and Prepatterned Speech*, The Hague: Mouton. 289–304.

Malinowski, Bronislaw (1923) 'The problem of meaning in primitive languages', in C.K. Ogden and I.A. Richards (eds) *The Meaning of Meaning*, London: Routledge & Kegan Paul. 296–336. (See also Chapter 20 of this *Reader*.)

Rampton, Ben (1999) 'Sociolinguistics and cultural studies: new ethnicities, liminality and interaction', *Social Semiotics* 9 (3): 355–74.

Robinson, W. Peter (1985) 'Social psychology and discourse', in Teun A. Van Dijk (ed.) *Handbook of Discourse Analysis, Vol. 1*, London: Academic Press. 107–44.

Ylänne-McEwen, Virpi (2004) 'Shifting alignment and negotiating sociality in travel agency discourse', *Discourse Studies* 6 (4): 519–38.

Chapter 26

Gunther Kress and
Theo Van Leeuwen

VISUAL INTERACTION

. . .

IMAGES INVOLVE two kinds of participants, *represented participants* (the people, the places and things depicted in images), and *interactive participants* (the people who communicate with each other *through* images, the producers and viewers of images), and three kinds of relations: (1) relations between represented participants; (2) relations between interactive and represented participants (the interactive participants' attitudes towards the represented participants); and (3) relations between interactive participants (the things interactive participants do to or for each other through images).

Interactive participants are therefore real people who produce and make sense of images in the context of social institutions which, to different degrees and in different ways, regulate what may be 'said' with images, and how it should be said, and how images should be interpreted. In some cases the interaction is direct and immediate. Producer and viewer know each other and are involved in face-to-face interaction, as when we make photographs of each other to keep in wallets or pin on pinboards, or draw maps to give each other directions, or diagrams to explain ideas to each other. But in many cases there is no immediate and direct involvement. The producer is absent for the viewer, and the viewer is absent for the producer. Think of photographs in magazines. Who is the producer? The photographer who took the shot? The assistant who processed and printed it? The agency who selected and distributed it? The picture editor who chose it? The layout artist who cropped it and determined its size and position on the page? Most viewers will not only never meet all these contributors to the production process face to face, but also have only a hazy, and perhaps distorted and glamourized idea of the production processes

Source: Gunther Kress and Theo Van Leeuwen, *Reading Images: The Grammar of Visual Design*, London: Routledge, 1996.

behind the image. All they have is the picture itself, as it appears in the magazine. And producers, similarly, can never really know their vast and absent audiences, and must, instead, create a mental image of 'the' viewers and 'the' way viewers make sense of their pictures. In everyday face-to-face communication it is easy enough to distinguish interactive participants from represented participants: there is always an image-producer and a viewer (who, depending on the situation, may swap roles with the producer, add to the scribbled floorplan or diagram, for instance), and then there are the represented participants (for instance, the people on the quick sketch of the dinner table arrangement, or the landmarks on the hand-drawn map), and these may, of course, include the producer and/or the viewer themselves. Producer and viewer are physically present. The participants they represent need not be. But when there is a disjunction between the context of production and the context of reception, the producer is not physically present, and the viewer is alone with the image and cannot reciprocate – an illuminating exception is the case of the 'defacement' of billboard advertisements, when graffiti artists 'respond' to the initial 'turn' or statement of the image.

Something similar occurs in writing. Writers, too, are not usually physically present when their words are read, and must address their readers in the guise of represented participants, even when they write in the first person. Readers, too, are alone with the written word, and cannot usually become writers in turn. Literary theorists (e.g. Booth 1961; Chatman 1978) have addressed this problem by distinguishing between 'real' and 'implied' authors, and between 'real' and 'implied' readers. The 'implied author' is a disembodied voice, or even 'a set of implicit norms rather than a speaker or a voice' (Rimmon-Kenan 1983: 87): 'he, or better, *it* has no voice, no direct means of communicating, but instructs us silently, through the design of the whole, with all the voices, by all the means it has chosen to let us learn' (Chatman 1978: 148). The 'implied reader', 'preferred reading position', etc., similarly, is 'an image of a certain competence brought to the text and a structuring of such competence within the text' (Rimmon-Kenan 1983: 118): the text selects a 'model reader' through its 'choice of a specific linguistic code, a certain literary style' and by presupposing 'a specific encyclopedic competence' on the part of the reader (Eco 1979: 7). This we can know. Of this we have evidence in the text itself. Real authors and real readers we cannot ultimately know. This bracketing out of real authors and real readers carries the risk of forgetting that texts, literary and artistic texts as much as mass-media texts, are produced in the context of real social institutions, in order to play a very real role in social life – in order to do certain things to or for their readers, and in order to communicate attitudes towards aspects of social life and towards people who participate in them, whether authors and readers are consciously aware of this or not. Producers, if they want to see their work disseminated, must work within more or less rigidly defined conventions, and adhere to the more or less rigidly defined values and beliefs of the social institution within which their work is produced and circulated. Readers will at least recognize these communicative intentions and these values and attitudes for what they are, even if they do not ultimately accept them as their own values and beliefs. They can 'recognize the substance of what is meant while refusing the speaker's interpretations and assessments' (Scannell 1994: 11).

364 GUNTHER KRESS AND THEO VAN LEEUWEN

However important and real this disjunction between the context of production and the context of reception, the two do have elements in common: the image itself, and a knowledge of the communicative resources that allow its articulation and understanding, a knowledge of the way social interactions and social relations can be encoded in images. It is often said that the knowledge of the producer and the knowledge of the viewer differ in a fundamental respect: the former is active, allowing the 'sending' as well as the 'receiving' of 'messages'; the latter is passive, allowing only the 'receiving' of 'messages'. Producers are able to 'write' as well as 'read', viewers are only able to 'read'. Up to a point this is true, at least in the sense that the production of images is still a specialized activity, so that producers 'write' more fluently and eloquently, and more frequently, than viewers. But we hope our attempts to make that knowledge explicit will show that the interactive meanings are visually encoded in ways that rest on competencies shared by producers and viewers. The articulation and understanding of social meanings in images derives from the visual articulation of social meanings in face-to-face interaction, the spatial positions allocated to different kinds of social actors in interaction (whether they are seated or standing, side by side or facing each other frontally, etc.). In this sense the interactive dimension of images is the 'writing' of what is usually called 'non-verbal communication', a 'language' shared by producers and viewers alike.

The disjunction between the context of production and the context of reception has yet another effect: it causes social relations to be *represented rather than enacted*. Because the producers are absent from the place where the actual communicative transaction is completed, from the locus of reception, they cannot say 'I' other than through a substitute 'I'. Even when the viewer receives an image of the 'real author' or a contributor to the production process, the presenter in a television programme, the painter in a self-portrait, the owner of the company (or the worker in the centuries-old distillery) in an advertisement, that image is only an image, a double of the 'real author', a representation, detached from his or her actual body. And the 'real authors' may also speak in the guise of someone else, of a 'character', as when, instead of the owner of a company, it is Uncle Sam, or a larger than life walking and talking teddy bear, who addresses us in an advertisement. This dimension of representation is another one which has been studied extensively in literary theory (e.g., Genette 1972). The relation between producer and viewer, too, is represented rather than enacted. In face-to-face communication we must respond to a friendly smile with a friendly smile, to an arrogant stare with a deferential lowering of the eyes, and such obligations cannot easily be avoided without appearing impolite, unfriendly or impudent. When images confront us with friendly smiles or arrogant stares, we are not obliged to respond, even though we do recognize how we are addressed. The relation is only represented. We are *imaginarily* rather than really put in the position of the friend, the customer, the lay person who must defer to the expert. And whether or not we identify with that position will depend on other factors — on our real relation to the producer or the institution he or she represents, and on our real relation to the others who form part of the context of reception. All the same, whether or not we identify with the way we are addressed, we do understand how we are addressed, because we do understand the way images represent social interactions and social relations. It is the business of this chapter to try and make those understandings explicit.

The image act and the gaze

In Figure 26.1 on the left we see photographs from which the Australian Antarctic explorer Sir Douglas Mawson looks directly at the viewer. The schematic drawing of a 'generalized' explorer is on the right, and this explorer does not look at the viewer. The photos and the drawing serve different communicative functions: the photos (especially the close-up) seek above all to bring about an imaginary relation between the represented explorer and the children for whom the book is written, a relation perhaps of admiration for, and identification with, a national hero. And this means also that the image-producer (the institution of educational publishing) addresses the children in the voice of the national hero and makes that national hero an 'educational' voice. The drawing, on the other hand, seeks, first of all, to be read as a piece of objective, factual information, and in this way aims to set into motion the actual process of learning.

There is then, a fundamental difference between pictures from which represented participants look directly at the viewer's eyes, and pictures in which this is not the case. When represented participants look at the viewer, vectors, formed by participants' eyelines, connect the participants with the viewer. Contact is

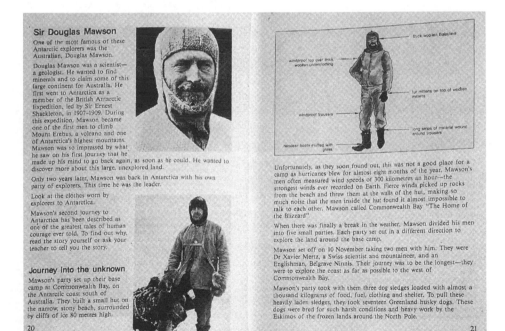

Figure 26.1 Antarctic explorer

Source: Oakley 1985

Figure 26.2 Recruitment poster

Source: Alfred Leete 1914, Imperial War Museum

established, even if it is only on an imaginary level. In addition there may be a further vector, formed by a gesture in the same direction, as in Figure 26.2.

This visual configuration has two related functions. In the first place it creates a visual form of direct address. It acknowledges the viewers explicitly, addressing them with a visual 'you'. In the second place it constitutes an 'image act'. The producer uses the image to do something to the viewer. It is for this reason that we have called this kind of image a 'demand', following Halliday (1985): the participant's gaze (and the gesture, if present) demands something from the viewer, demands that the viewer enter into some kind of imaginary relation with him or her. Exactly what kind of relation is then signified by other means, for instance by the facial expression of the represented participants. They may smile, in which case the viewer is asked to enter into a relation of social affinity with them; they may stare at the viewer with cold disdain, in which case the viewer is asked to relate to them, perhaps, as an inferior relates to a superior; they may seductively pout at the viewer, in which case the viewer is asked to desire them. The same applies to gestures. A hand can point at the viewer, in a visual 'Hey, you there, I mean you', or invite the viewer to come closer, or hold the viewer at bay with a defensive gesture, as if to say: stay away from me. In each case the image wants something from the viewers – wants them to do something (come closer, stay at a distance) or to form a pseudo-social bond of a particular kind with the represented participant. And in doing this, images define to some extent who the viewer is (e.g., male, inferior to the represented participant, etc.), and in that way exclude other viewers.

. . .

According to Belting (1990) 'the suggestion of reciprocity between the viewer and the person depicted in the image' had a devotional purpose. By the thirteenth century, monks in their cells 'had before their eyes images of the Virgin and her crucified son, so that while reading, praying and sleeping, they could look upon them and *be looked upon* with the eyes of compassion' (p. 57, our italics).

. . .

Other pictures address us indirectly. Here the viewer is not object, but subject of the look, and the represented participant is the object of the viewer's dispassionate scrutiny. No contact is made. The viewer's role is that of an invisible onlooker. All images which do not contain human or quasi-human participants looking directly at the viewer are of this kind. For this reason, again following Halliday (1985), we have called this kind of image an 'offer' – it 'offers' the represented participants to the viewer as items of information, objects of contemplation, impersonally, as though they were specimens in a display case.

It is always interesting to study which kinds of represented participants are, in a given context, depicted as demanding an imaginary social response of some kind from the viewer, and which are not. In the Australian primary school social studies textbook *Our Society and Others*, for instance, immigrant families smile at the viewer. However, the human participants in pictures from these immigrants' countries of origin do not look at the viewer, not even in close-up portraits, as, for instance, in the portrait of an Italian grandmother who stayed behind. In the chapter on Aborigines, by contrast, hardly any of the Aboriginal participants look at the viewer. The Aboriginal poet Oodgeroo Noonuccal, referred to in the book as Kath Walker, and depicted in close-up in the last illustration of that chapter, is the only exception (see Figure 26.3 on p. 372). Her expression, her make-up, her hair style and dress hardly distinguish her from non-Aboriginal women of her age. At most her skin is somewhat darker, but even that is not very pronounced in the black-and-white shot. Other Aboriginal people in the chapter are much more clearly depicted as 'other', and even if they do, occasionally, look directly at the viewer, they do so from a long distance, which greatly diminishes the impact of their look, or are figures in the background, looking blankly and more or less accidentally in the direction of the camera. Aboriginal people, in this primary school textbook, are depicted as objects of contemplation, not as subjects for the pupil to enter into an imaginary social relation with. Immigrants, by contrast, at least once they are in Australia, are portrayed as people with whom the pupils should engage more directly, and in a friendly way, as equals.

The choice between 'offer' and 'demand', which must be made whenever people are depicted, is not only used to suggest different relations with different 'others', to make viewers engage with some and remain detached from others; it can also characterize pictorial genres. In some contexts, for instance television newsreading and the posed magazine photograph, the 'demand' picture is preferred: these contexts require a sense of connection between the viewers and the authority figures, celebrities and role models they depict. In other contexts, for example feature film and television drama and scientific illustration, the 'offer' is preferred: here a real or imaginary barrier is erected between the represented participants and the viewers, a sense of disengagement, in which the viewer must have the illusion that the represented participants do not know they are being looked at, and in which the represented participants must pretend that they are not being watched. And what in one context is accepted convention may in another be a startling mistake or an innovative experiment. Film theorists (e.g., Allen 1977; Wollen 1982) have hailed the look at the camera as a daring, Brechtian, 'self-reflexive' style figure, but in television newsreading the look at the camera is commonplace and, we would think, not exactly 'self-reflexive' – at least for the presenters: an interviewee who looks at the camera in a television news programme breaks the rules in an unacceptable way. Not everyone may address the viewer directly. Some may only be looked *at*, others may themselves be the bearers of the look. There is an issue of communicative power or 'entitlement' (Sacks 1992) involved in this, not only in pictures, but also in everyday face-to-face communication, for instance in interactions between men and women:

> As he answers the girl's last statement he begins talking and reaches the point where normally he would look away, but instead he is still staring at her. This makes her uncomfortable, because she is forced either to lock eyes with him, or to look away from him while *he* is talking. If he continues to talk and stare while she deflects her eyes, it puts her into the 'shy' category, which she resents. If she boldly locks eyes with him, he has forced her into a 'lover's gaze', which she also resents.
>
> (Morris 1977: 76)

Diagrams, maps and charts are most often found in contexts that offer the kind of knowledge which, in our culture, is most highly valued – objective, dispassionate knowledge, ostensibly free of emotive involvement and subjectivity. Hence the 'demand' is rare in these visual genres. But there are contexts in which the two forms of address are combined. School textbooks, for instance, may construct a progression from 'demand' to 'offer' pictures, and this not only in the course of a chapter, as in the chapter on Antarctic exploration, but also in the course of a whole book or series of books, and indeed, in the course of education as a whole: illustrations that serve to involve students emotively in the subject matter gradually drop out as higher levels of education are reached. In senior highschool textbooks we find 'demand' pictures at most in the cartoons which, in almost apologetic fashion, seek to alleviate the seriousness of the text from time to time, as in a cartoon in a geography textbook (Bindon and Williams 1988) where a girl looks despondently at the viewer, with the words 'What does hypothesis mean?' in a dialogue balloon emanating from her mouth. In the context of education, the 'demand' picture plays an ambivalent role. On the one hand, it is not a highly valued form, but a form deemed suitable only for beginners, a form one grows out of as one climbs the educational ladder; on the other hand, it plays an indispensable role in educational strategy: objective knowledge must, apparently, be built upon a foundation of emotive involvement, of identification with celebratory mythologies, for instance. This foundation must then, gradually, be repressed, for if it is not repressed, the knowledge built on it cannot be seen to be objective. Outside the sphere of education, the value of the 'demand' picture will depend on the assumed educational level of the reader. When, for instance, the mass media (or automatic teller machines) begin to use 'demand' pictures, those educated in the linguistic and visual genres of objective knowledge and impersonal address may feel patronized, 'addressed below their class'. Those not so educated (or those who contest the value of such an education) would have felt that communication had become more effective (and more fun) than was the case in the era of more formal and impersonal public communication.

The meanings conveyed by 'demands' and 'offers' can be related to the grammatical system of person. As we have seen, 'demand' pictures address the viewer directly, realizing a visual 'you'. But this is not matched by a visual 'I'. The 'I' is absent in pictures, or rather, objectified, hiding behind a he/she/they. The 'demand' picture therefore recalls more the language of, for instance, advertisements and instructions, where 'you's' abound but 'I's' are rare, than say, of the language of personal letters where 'I's' and 'you's' are likely to be equally common. 'Real producers' cannot refer to themselves directly. They must speak impersonally, as in bureaucratic and scientific language, where 'I's' are also repressed. The public, on the other hand, is addressed directly. And yet, as we have seen, the distinction between 'offers' and 'demands' derives historically from attempts of Renaissance painters to find ways of saying 'I', in the self-portraits which expressed their new found self-confidence and status of independent artists rather than humble craftsmen.

. . .

Size of frame and social distance

There is a second dimension to the interactive meanings of images, related to the 'size of frame', to the choice between close-up, medium shot and long shot, and so on. Just as image-producers, in depicting human or quasi-human participants, must choose to make them look at the viewer or not, so they must also, and at the same time, choose to depict them as close to or far away from the viewer – and this applies to the depiction of objects also. And like the choice between the 'offer' and the 'demand', the choice of distance can suggest different relations between represented participants and viewers. In handbooks about film and television production size of frame is invariably defined in relation to the human body. Even though distance is, strictly speaking, a continuum, the 'language of film and television' has imposed a set of distinct cut-off points on this continuum, in the same way as languages impose cut-off points on the continuum of vowels we can produce. Thus the close shot (or 'close-up') shows head and shoulders of the subject, and the very close shot ('extreme close-up', 'big close-up') anything less than that. The medium close shot cuts off the subject approximately at the waist, the medium shot approximately at the knees. The medium long shot shows the full figure. In the long shot the human figure occupies about half the height of the frame, and the very long shot is anything 'wider' than that. Stylistic variants are possible, but they are always seen and talked about in terms of this system, as when film and television people talk of 'tight close shots' or 'tight framing', or about the amount of 'headroom' in a picture (i.e., space between the top of the head and the upper frame line).

In everyday interaction, social relations determine the distance (literally and figuratively) we keep from one another. Edward Hall (e.g., 1966: 110–20) has shown that we carry with us a set of invisible boundaries beyond which we allow only certain kinds of people to come. The location of these invisible boundaries is determined by configurations of sensory potentialities – by whether or not a certain distance allows us to smell or touch the other person, for instance, and by how much of the other person we can see with our peripheral (60°) vision. 'Close personal distance' is the distance at which 'one can hold or grasp the other person' and therefore also the distance between people who have an intimate relation with each other. Non-intimates cannot come this close, and if they do so, it will be experienced as an act of aggression. 'Far personal distance' is the distance that 'extends from a point that is just outside easy touching distance by one person to a point where two people can touch fingers if they both extend their arms', the distance at which 'subjects of personal interests and involvements are discussed'. 'Close social distance' begins just outside this range and is the distance at which 'impersonal business occurs'. 'Far social distance' is 'the distance to which people move when somebody says "Stand away so I can look at you"' – 'business and social interaction conducted at this distance a more formal and impersonal character than in the close phase'. 'Public distance', finally, is anything further than that, 'the distance between people who are and are to remain strangers'. These judgements apply, of course, within a particular culture, and Hall cites many examples of the misunderstandings which can arise from intercultural differences in the interpretation of distance.

With these differences correspond different fields of vision. At intimate distance, says Hall (1964), we see the face or head only. At close personal distance we take in the head and the shoulders. At far personal distance we see the other person from the waist up. At close social distance we see the whole figure. At far social distance we see the whole figures 'with space around it'. And at public distance we can see the torso of at least four or five people. It is clear that these fields of vision correspond closely to the traditional definitions of size of frame in film and television, in other words, that the visual system of size of frame derives from the 'proxemics', as Hall calls it, of everyday face-to-face interaction. Hall is aware of this and in fact acknowledges the influence of the work of Grosser, a portrait painter, on his ideas. According to Grosser (quoted in Hall 1966: 71–2), at a distance of more than 13 feet, people are seen 'as having little connection with ourselves', and hence 'the painter can look at his model as if he were a tree in a landscape or an apple in a still life'. Four to eight feet, on the other hand, is the 'portrait distance':

> the painter is near enough so that his eyes have no trouble in under-
> standing the sitter's solid forms, yet he is far enough away so that
> the foreshortening of the forms presents no real problem. Here at the
> normal distance of social intimacy and easy conversation, the sitter's

soul begins to appear. . . . Nearer than three feet, within touching
distance, the soul is far too much in evidence for any sort of disinter-
ested observation.

The distances people keep, then, depend on their social relation – whether this is
the more permanent kind of social relation on which Hall mainly concentrates (the
distinction between intimates, friends, acquaintances, strangers, etc.) or the kind
of social relation that lasts for the duration of a social interaction and is determined
by the context (someone in the audience of a speech given by an acquaintance or
relative would nevertheless stay at public distance, the distance of the 'stranger').
But these distances also, and at the same time, determine how much of the other
person is in our field of vision – just as does the framing of a person in a portrait
or film shot.

Like the 'demand' picture, the close-up came to the fore in the Renaissance.
Ringbom (1965) argues that it has its origin in devotional pictures, where it served
to provide 'the "near-ness" so dear to the God-seeking devout' (p. 48). In Italian
and Dutch paintings of the early sixteenth century it acquired a 'dramatic' function, allowing 'the subtlest of emotional relationships with a minimum of dramatic
scenery' (*ibid.*).

The people we see in images are for the most part strangers. It is true that we
see some of them (politicians, film and television stars, sports heroes, etc.) a good
deal more than others, but this kind of familiarity does not of itself determine
whether they will be shown in close shot or medium shot or long shot. The relation between the human participants represented in images and the viewer is
once again an imaginary relation. People are portrayed *as though* they are friends,
or *as though* they are strangers. Images allow us to imaginarily come as close to
public figures as if they were our friends and neighbours – or to look at people
like ourselves as strangers, 'others'. In the primary school social studies textbook
from which we have quoted several examples, three Aboriginal boys are shown in
long shot, occupying only about a quarter of the height of the 'portrait' format
frame. The caption reads 'These people live at Redfern, a suburb of Sydney.' They
are shown impersonally, as strangers with whom we do not need to become
acquaintances, as 'trees in a landscape'. Although they do look at the viewer, they
do so from such a distance that it barely affects us. Indeed, they are so small that
we can hardly distinguish their facial features. 'Their soul does not yet begin to
appear', to coin Grosser's words. The caption, significantly, gives them no name;
in fact, where the more friendly 'boys' could have been, the quite formal 'people'
has been used.

The portrait of the Aboriginal poet Oodgeroo Noonuccal (Figure 26.3) is a
right close shot. *She* is depicted in a personal way. If this was all we could see of
her reality, we would be close enough to touch her. As mentioned, the section
in which the photo occurs concludes a chapter on Aborigines in which no other
Aborigine smiles at the viewer in this way. One of her poems is quoted: 'Dark
and white upon common ground/ In club and office and social round/ Yours the
feel of a friendly land/ The grip of the hand' (Oakley *et al.* 1985: 164). But
Noonuccal's message is not borne out by the way 'dark and white' are portrayed
in the chapter.

Figure 26.3 Oodgeroo Noonuccal
Source: Oakley 1985

Patterns of distance can become conventional in visual genres. In current affairs television, for example, 'voices' of different status are habitually framed differently: the camera 'moves in for bigger close-ups of subjects who are revealing their feelings, whereas the set-up for the "expert" is usually the same as that for the interviewer – the breast pocket shot'. Both kinds of 'statused participants' tend to be 'nominated' (their names appear on the screen in superimposed captions) and 'have their contributions framed and summed up' (Brunsdon and Morley 1978: 65). In other words, distance is used to signify respect for authorities of various kinds, on television as in face-to-face interaction.

In diagrams the human figure is almost always shown in medium long or long shot – objectively, 'as if he were a tree in a landscape'. The pictures in Figure 26.4 illustrated a front-page newspaper story about a murder case in Sydney. The diagrams show exactly what happened, from an objectifying and impersonal distance (and from a high angle). The close-up photos accompany testimonies by former patients of the victim, but are represented as also 'friends' of us readers of the *Sydney Morning Herald*, and therefore as people whose relation with the victim we should identify with. The personal and the impersonal, the emotive and the detached, are combined.

. . .

Involvement and the horizontal angle

When we prolong the converging parallels formed by the walls of the houses in Figure 26.5 they come together in two vanishing points. Both points are located

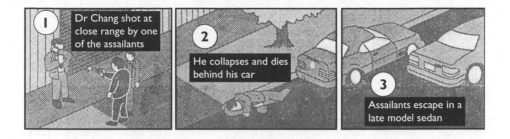

HIS PATIENTS

Victor was not only my doctor but my friend. I just can't believe that anyone would want to harm him.

Fiona Coote, 21. Heart transplant in 1984 at age 14. Another at 16.

The sense of reassurance Dr Chang was able to give his patients was astonishing.

Jim Cameren, 60, former Liberal Speaker of Legislative Assembly. Heart transplant 1986.

Australia has lost one of its greatest. He treated you like a very close friend. There was very little he wouldn't do for you.

Geoffrey Monk, 46. Heart surgery 1978, Heart transplant 1984.

Figure 26.4 The murder of Dr Chang

Source: *Sydney Morning Herald*, 5 July 1991

Figure 26.5 Aborigines

Source: Oakley 1985

outside the vertical boundaries of the image, as shown in Figure 26.6. These vanishing points allow us to reconstruct what we can see even without the aid of geometrical projection: the scene has been photographed from an oblique angle. The photographer has not situated her/himself in front of the Aborigines, but has photographed them from the side.

Figure 26.7 shows how the position from which the photo was taken can be reconstructed by dropping lines from the vanishing points in such a way that they meet to form a 90° angle on the line drawn through the closest corner of the cottages. Figure 26.8 shows the scene from above. The line (ab) represents the frontal plane of the subject of the photograph: the line formed by the front of the cottages, which, as it happens, is also the line along which the Aborigines are lined up. The line (cd) represents the frontal plane of the photographer (and hence of the viewer). Had these two lines been parallel to one another, the horizontal angle would have been frontal, in other words, the photographer would have been positioned in front of the Aborigines and their cottages, facing them. Instead, the two lines diverge: the angle is oblique. The photographer has not aligned her/himself with the subject, not faced the Aborigines, but viewed them 'from the sidelines'.

Horizontal angle, then, is a function of the relation between the frontal plane of the image-producer and the frontal plane of the represented participants. The two can either be parallel, aligned with one another, or form an angle, diverge from one another. The image can have either a frontal or an oblique point of view. It should be noted that this is not strictly an either/or distinction. There are degrees of obliqueness, and we will, in fact, speak of a frontal angle so long as the vanishing point(s) still fall(s) within the vertical boundaries of the image (they may fall outside the horizontal boundaries).

Figure 26.8 has a frontal angle. As shown in Figure 26.9, there is only one major vanishing point, and it lies inside the vertical boundaries of the image. Figure 26.10 shows how the frontal plane of the photographer (line ab) and the frontal plane of the represented participants (line cd) run parallel – that is, *if one only considers one set of represented participants*, the teachers, the blackboard and the reading chart. The frontal plane of the Aboriginal children (line ef) makes an angle of 90° with the frontal plane of the teachers and with the frontal plane of the photographer. The Aboriginal children have been photographed from a very oblique angle.

The difference between the oblique and the frontal angle is the difference between detachment and involvement. The horizontal angle encodes whether or not the image-producer (and hence, willy-nilly, the viewer) is 'involved' with the represented participants or not. The frontal angle says, as it were: 'what you see here is part of our world, something we are involved with.' The oblique angle says: 'what you see here is *not* part of our world, it is *their* world, something *we* are not involved with.' The producers of these two photographs have, perhaps unconsciously, aligned themselves with the white teachers and their teaching tools, but *not* with the Aborigines. The teachers are shown as 'part of our world', the Aborigines as 'other'. And as viewers we have no choice but to see these represented participants as they have been depicted. We are addressed as viewers for whom 'involvement' takes these particular values. In reality, they might not – we might be Aboriginal viewers, for example. It is one thing for the viewer to be

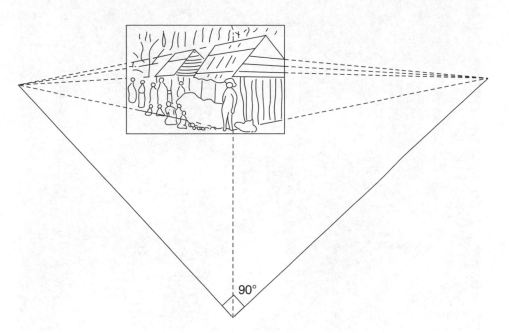

Figure 26.6 Schematic drawing: vanishing points of 'Aborigines' (Figure 26.5)

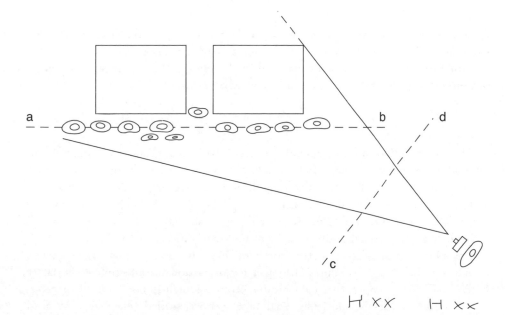

Figure 26.7 Schematic drawing: top view of 'Aborigines' (Figure 26.5)

Figure 26.8 Aboriginal children at school
Source: Oakley 1985

limited by what the photograph shows (and to understand what this means, for example exclusion, in the case of an Aboriginal viewer); it is another thing to actually identify with the viewpoint encoded in the photo. We can accept or reject, but either way we first need to understand what is meant.

. . .

In the depiction of humans (and animals) 'involvement' and 'detachment' can interact with 'demand' and 'offer' in complex ways. The body of a represented participant may be angled away from the plane of the viewer, while his or her head and/or gaze may be turned towards it (see e.g., Figure 26.12 on p. 381) – or vice versa. The result is a double message: 'although I am not a part of your world, I nevertheless make contact with you, from my own, different world'; or 'although this person is part of our world, someone like you and me, we nevertheless offer his or her image to you as an object for dispassionate reflection.' The latter is the case, for example, in an illustration from a Dutch junior highschool geography textbook (Bols *et al*. 1986: 21). In a section entitled 'De Derde Wereld in onze straat' ('The Third World in our street'), two pictures are shown side by side. On the left we see three older women, their headscarves an emblem of their status as immigrants. They are photographed from an oblique angle, hence as 'not part of our world' and in long shot, hence as 'others', 'strangers'. On the right

Figure 26.9 Schematic drawing: vanishing point of 'Aboriginal children at school' (Figure 26.8)

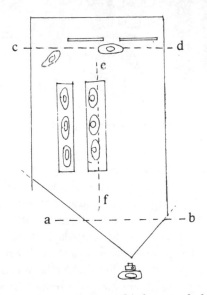

Figure 26.10 Schematic drawing: top view of 'Aboriginal children at school' (Figure 26.8)

we see, left in the foreground, a blonde girl, clearly meant to be taken as Dutch, with a black friend, who has his arm around her. The angle is a good deal more frontal than that of the shot of the three women, and the shot is a close-up: she is shown as like 'us', Dutch highschool students, and from 'close personal' distance. But she does not make contact with the viewers. She does not invite the viewers to identify with her, and with her relationship to a black man. Instead, the viewer is invited to contemplate her relationship detachedly, to ponder the fact that some people like 'us' have relationships with black people, but not, it is implicitly suggested, 'we' viewers ourselves. She is a phenomenon to be observed, not a person addressing the viewer.

Figure 26.11 Photograph of author's parents, 1968

Equally complex and ambivalent is the back view. One of the authors, at age 21, photographed his parents in a snow-covered park, just outside Brussels (Figure 26.11), and, perhaps more importantly, it was this picture he chose to pin on the pinboard of his student room in Amsterdam, rather than one of the other, more frontal pictures he had taken on the same day. At the time, his feelings for his parents were complex. Deep attachment was mixed with only half-understood desire to distance himself from the world in which he was brought up. Perhaps the picture crystallized these confused emotions for him. On the one hand, it showed his parents turning their back on him, walking away from him (a reversal, of course, of the actual situation); on the other hand, it showed this gesture of 'turning one's back', in a sense, 'frontally', in a maximally 'confronting' way. But to expose one's back to someone is also to make oneself vulnerable, and this implies a measure of trust, despite the abandonment which the gesture also signifies. Perhaps the picture reminded him of a passage from a Dutch novel he liked at the time:

> Through the window he sees them walk away. 'How much I love that man', he thinks, and how impossible he has made it for me to express that. . . . His mother has linked arms with him. With hesitant steps she walks beside him on the frozen pavement. He keeps looking at them until they turn the corner, near the tall feathered poplars.
>
> (Wolkers 1965: 61)

How is 'involvement' realized in language? Perhaps the system of possessive pronouns comes closest to realizing the kinds of meanings we have discussed here. But the two systems, the visual system of horizontal angle and the linguistic system of possessive pronouns, differ in many ways. Involvement, as we have seen, is always plural, a matter of 'mine' and 'his/her/its'; a matter of distinguishing between what belongs to 'us' and what to 'them'. And while in language one cannot easily have *degrees* of 'ourness' and 'theirness', in images such gradation is an intrinsic part of the system of involvement. Finally, there is no 'yours' in the system of horizontal angle. The visual 'you-relation' is, as we have seen, realized by the system of 'offer' and 'demand'. Perspective puts a barrier between the viewer and the represented participants, even in the case of a frontal angle: the viewer looks *at* the represented participants and has an attitude towards them, but does not imaginarily engage with them.

Power and vertical angle

Textbooks of film appreciation never fail to mention camera height as an important means of expression in cinematography. A high angle, it is said, makes the subject look small and insignificant, a low angle makes it look imposing and awesome: 'Low angles generally give an impression of superiority, exaltation and triumph . . . high angles tend to diminish the individual, to flatten him morally by reducing him to ground level, to render him as caught in an insurmountable determinism' (Martin 1968: 37–8). But this leaves the viewer out of the picture. We would rather say it in a somewhat different way: if a represented participant is seen from a high angle, then the relation between the interactive participants (the producer of the image, and hence also the viewer) and the represented participants is depicted as one in which the interactive participant has power over the represented participant – the represented participant is seen from the point of view of power. If the represented participant is seen from a low angle, then the relation between the interactive and represented participants is depicted as one in which the represented participant has power over the interactive participant. If, finally, the picture is at eye level, then the point of view is one of equality and there is no power difference involved.

This is, again, a matter of degree. A represented participant can tower high above us or look down on us ever so slightly. In many of the illustrations in school textbooks we look down rather steeply on people – workers in the hall; children in a school yard. In such books the social world lies at the feet of the viewer, so to speak: knowledge is power. The models in magazine advertisements and features, and newsworthy people and celebrities in magazine articles, on the other hand, generally look down on the viewer: these models are depicted as exercising symbolic power over us. It is different, again, with pictures of the products advertised in the advertisements: these are usually photographed from a high angle, depicted as within reach, and at the command of the viewer.

How is power realized in language? Here we need, again, to remember the difference between face-to-face communication and mediated communication. In the classroom, for example, power will manifest itself first of all in the relation between teacher and pupil. This, as Cate Poynton has shown (1985), is in the main realized through the *difference* between the linguistic forms that may be used by the teachers and the linguistic forms that may be used by the pupils; in other words, through a lack of reciprocity between the choices available to each party in the interaction. The teacher may use first names in addressing the pupils; the pupils may not use first names in addressing teachers. The teacher may use imperatives to 'demand goods-and-services'; the pupils would have to use polite forms, for instance, questions. This lack of reciprocity has its effect on every level of language: phonology, grammar, vocabulary, discourse, and on ideational, interpersonal, as well as textual meanings. If there is, in face-to-face communication, any question of power relation between represented participants and the pupils, then this results from the power relation between the teacher and the pupils.

. . .

Two portraits and two children's drawings

Rembrandt's famous *Self-portrait with Saskia* dates from 1634 (Figure 26.12). John Berger (1972: 111) calls it 'an advertisement of the sitter's good fortune, prestige and wealth', and he adds, 'like all such advertisements it is heartless'. Yet, from the point of view of the interactive meanings we have discussed in this chapter, the painting is perhaps a little more complex than Berger's remarks suggest. On the one hand, it is a 'demand' picture – Rembrandt and Saskia smile at the viewer, Rembrandt perhaps a little more effusively and invitingly than Saskia: he even raises his glass in a gesture directed at the viewer. On the other hand, he has shown himself and Saskia from behind, and from what Hall would call 'close social' distance, with Saskia a little further away from the viewer than Rembrandt – her head is considerably smaller than Rembrandt's even though she is sitting on his lap and should therefore, strictly speaking, be closer to the viewer than Rembrandt (the angle at which her head is turned to acknowledge the viewer also seems unnatural). Is Rembrandt distancing himself (and Saskia even more) from the viewer, excluding the viewer from involvement and intimacy with his new-found (and Saskia's already established) social status, thus contradicting the invitation? Perhaps, but the portrait is also a self-portrait. Rembrandt, the miller's son, now married into a wealthy and respectable family and living in grand style, also distances *himself* from his new self (and to some extent from Saskia), as if he cannot feel fully involved and intimate with his new environment. As a self-portrait the picture may be self-congratulatory and smug, 'heartless', but it also betrays a degree of alienation, positioning the represented Rembrandt in a complex and contradictory social class position, between the world of his origins, which is also the point of view of the picture, and the world of Saskia into which he has moved. This, we think, makes it a little less smug, and a little more touching than Berger gave it credit for.

Figure 26.13 shows a later self-portrait, painted in 1661. By this time, Saskia has died and Rembrandt has gone bankrupt. He now lives with his former housekeeper, Hendrickje, in a more downmarket neighbourhood, and in much reduced

Figure 26.12
Self-portrait with Saskia
(Rembrandt, 1634)

Source: Pinakotek, Dresden

Figure 26.13
Self-portrait (Rembrandt,
1661)

Source: Kunsthistorisches
Museum, Vienna

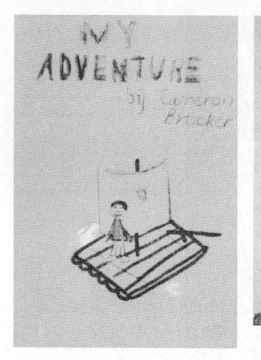

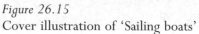

Figure 26.14
Cover illustration of 'My adventure'

Figure 26.15
Cover illustration of 'Sailing boats'

circumstances. In this portrait he is able to come to face to face with himself, to confront himself (and the viewer) squarely and intimately with himself 'He is an old man now. All has gone, except a sense of the question of existence, of existence as a question' (Berger 1972: 112).

The picture on the cover of 'My Adventure', the story by an eight-year-old boy (Figure 26.14) constitutes a 'demand': the little boy is looking at us; and smiling. He seeks our recognition. He wants to be acknowledged. On the other hand, the angle is oblique, and high, and the boy is shown from a great distance. Not only does the writer of this story show himself in the role of being shipwrecked, he also shows himself as 'other' (the oblique angle), as someone over whom the viewer has power (the high angle) and as socially distant, a 'stranger' (the long shot). In other words, he uses the interactive resources of the subjective image (quite precociously, we feel) to show himself as small, insignificant and alienated, yet demanding recognition from the viewer. At the same time the act of drawing himself like this affords him, as the producer of the image, some power over that image of himself, an outlet for his feelings. In support of this interpretation it can be noted that the boy does not exactly play a heroic role in the story. After creating the raft, and just as the raft 'started to be good fun', everything goes wrong for him: he loses his money and never finds it again, the raft collapses and is lost irretrievably, and the hero has to walk all the way home, wet and cold. It is an unhappy ending for a hero unable to control the unpleasant events that happen to him.

Figure 26.15 is the front cover of a 'story' on sailing boats by a child from the same class as the author of 'My Adventure'. Its subject is similar: people on a boat. But the systems of 'image act', 'social distance' and 'attitude' take on very different values. The characters do not look at us: the picture is an 'offer'. The angle is frontal and eye level, and the two figures in the boat are neither particularly distant, nor particularly close. There is no setting, no texture, no colour, no light and shade. The sailing boat is drawn with geometrical accuracy. But for the two figures, simply drawn, and more or less identical, except for their size (a father and son?), this could be a technical drawing. As such it suits the objective, generic, title, 'Sailing Boats', just as the cover illustration of 'My Adventure' suits that story's subjective, specific title. In most of the illustrations inside the essay, no human figures are seen, as though the child already understands that the 'learning' of technical matters should be preceded by a 'human element' to attract non-initiates to the subject.

Clearly, children actively experiment both with the interactive resources of language and with the interactive resources of visual communication. They are active sign-makers. And the different ways in which these two children represent boats show two different subjectivities at work.

References

Allen, J. (1977) 'Self-reflexivity in documentary', *Cinetracts* 2: 37–44.

Belting, H. (1990) *The Image and its Public in the Middle Ages*, New Rochelle, NY: Aristide D. Caratzay.

Berger, J. (1972) *Ways of Seeing*, Harmondsworth: Penguin.

Bindon, H. and Williams, H. (1988) *Geography Research Project: A Senior Student's Handbook*, Melbourne: Edward Arnold.

Bols, P., Houppermans, M., Krijger, C., Lentjes, W., Savelkouls, T., Terlingen, M. and Teune, P. (1986) *Werk aan de Wereld*, Ben Bosch: Malmberg.

Booth, W.C. (1961) *The Rhetoric of Fiction*, Chicago, IL: Chicago University Press.

Brunsden, C. and Morley, D. (1978) *Everyday Television: Nationwide*, London: BFI.

Chatman, S. (1978) *Story and Discourse*, Ithaca, NY: Cornell University Press.

Eco, U. (1979) *The Role of the Reader*, Bloomington, IN: Indiana University Press.

Genette, G. (1972) *Narrative Discourse*, Oxford: Blackwell.

Hall, E. (1964) 'Silent assumptions in social communication', *Disorders of Communication* 42: 41–55.

——— (1966) *The Hidden Dimension*, New York: Doubleday.

Halliday, M.A.K. (1985) *An Introduction to Functional Grammar*, London: Edward Arnold.

Martin, M. (1968) *Le Langage cinématographique*, Paris: Éditions du Cerf.

Morris, D. (1977) *Manwatching*, London: Cape.

Oakley, M. *et al.* (1985) *Our Society and Others*, Sydney: McGraw-Hill.

Poynton, C. (1985) *Language and Gender: Making the Difference*, Geelong: Deakin University Press.

Rimmon-Kenan, S. (1983) *Narrative Fiction: Contemporary Poetics*, London: Methuen.

Ringbom, S. (1965) *Icon to Narrative: The Rise of the Dramatic Close-Up in Fifteenth-Century Painting*, Abo: Abo Akademie.

Sacks, H. (1992) *Lectures on Conversation*, Oxford: Blackwell.

Scannell, P. (1994) 'Communicative intentionality in broadcasting', unpublished paper.

Wolkers, J. (1965) *Een Roos van Vlees*, Amsterdam: Meulenhoff.

Wollen, P. (1982) 'Godard and counter-cinema: *Vent d'est*', in Nichols, B. (ed) *Movies and Methods*, vol. 2, Berkeley and Los Angeles, CA: University of California Press.

Discussion points for Part Four

1   Think of the range of situations where you would expect to find people engaging in 'small talk'. Do these situations have anything in common? What topics and modes of talk constitute small talk? (In other words, how do we recognise small talk when we hear it?) Is there a contrasting notion of 'full' or 'hard' talk? What is that like, formally and functionally and contextually?

2   To what extent does Brown and Levinson's concept of 'politeness' match the everyday use of the same term? What sorts of politeness, in the more technical sense of this concept, fall outside the usual meaning of 'being polite'? How would the everyday sense of 'being rude' be handled by Brown and Levinson's framework?

3   Erving Goffman once wrote that everyday communication is not a matter of stage performance, but that it's not easy to say in what ways it is *not* stage performance. Can we distinguish between discourse genres which are full 'performances' and others which are less fully so? What are the main discourse characteristics of 'full performance', for example when a performer (such as a stand-up comedian or a news reader) performs for an audience? What participation frameworks are usually in place? Think of situations when ordinary people (non-professionals) come close to performing their talk in something like the same way. Where do the similarities and differences lie?

4   Review Brown and Levinson's check-list of politeness strategies (summarised on pages 322–3). Which of the listed strategies strike you are being used more by some social groups than others – younger versus older people, males versus females, and so on? Whether your beliefs are correct or not, how is it that we are able to make judgements of this sort? Where do our understandings about discourse in social life come from? Do you think that your beliefs about how language is used might be just as important as the facts?

5   Make a note of up to ten consecutive mentions of the weather in your presence. These may be conversations in which you are or are not designated as a ratified speaker. They may be from TV or radio programmes, etc. Record, as accurately as possible, who says what to whom, in what circumstances and for what apparent purpose? Using the terminology from Chapters 24 and 25, identify different *frames* for discussing the weather in the encounters that you have observed. You may replace the weather with any other topic of your choice (e.g. health, money, politics, football, etc.).

6   Try out Kress and Van Leeuwen's predictions about types of implied relation-
     ship, power and intimacy between yourself as viewer and a range of visual
     images, such as images of people in magazine product advertisements.
     Can you spot any general patterns in how, for example, women tend to be
     posed and shot in glamour advertisements, versus how they are posed and
     shot in ads for domestic products? What makes us find a visual image
     'intimate', and are there different types of intimacy that can be constructed
     semiotically?

Identity and subjectivity

Editors' introduction
to Part Five

A S WE SAW IN DISCUSSING Harvey Sacks's idea of membership categorisation devices (Introduction to Part Three), the discursive world is
populated by familiar categories of people. We tend to accept many people-
categories as natural ones, even though, from a different point of view, we are
endorsing distinctions and identities that people may well not feel they actually
inhabit. Social identity, and the process of social identification, has become a key
theme in discourse analysis where the ambition is often to scrutinise the use of
identity categories and to challenge the 'natural' assumptions that follow.

We begin this Part of the *Reader* with a theoretically and politically powerful
text by Stuart Hall, concerned with ideological and discursive constructions of
black people in Britain. It was written during a long period of Conservative Party
government ('Thatcher's Britain'). Hall retrospects on his own TV programmes,
provocatively titled *The Whites of Their Eyes*, in relation to dominant media modes
of representing black ethnic identity in Britain. He identifies familiar tropes and
personas through which black identity has been represented, such as 'the slave-
figure', 'the native' and 'the clown', and critiques 'the white eye through which
they are seen' (p. 402). Hall's point is not that these are uniformly 'negative'
representations. In fact, he stresses their ambivalence and how, over time, they
resurface in new forms, with their racist qualities hidden under new TV formats
and contexts.

It is this last point – the fact that we need to look closely at the local contextualisation of identity – that establishes the need for a discourse analysis perspective.
Many other sorts of research – such as simple, quantitative surveys of media content
– can give us overviews of how often and in what general ways social and ethnic
groups are represented in mass media. Results from such research are important, but they need to be complemented by closer, text-based analysis. What
often emerges from close analysis is precisely Hall's point about ambivalence,

particularly in relation to identity. Identity is, after all, a subtle and multi-layered phenomenon, to the extent that, individually, we are usually reticent to accept (or, to use a more consumerist metaphor 'buy into') identity categories with reference to ourselves. We often experience identity as complex, and the term 'identity hybridity' has come into common usage in academic research. It refers to a sense of people being not fully contained by singular social categories of race, gender, age, place, and so on. It stands in opposition to what are often called 'essentialist' readings of identity – reducing identity simplistically to lists of who people 'essentially' are.

A good deal of sociological writing on selfhood echoes these sentiments. Not only should we recognise a multiplicity of personal and social identities, but we have to see identities being worked through discursive processes. For example, Anthony Giddens refers to 'the reflexive project of the self' (1990, 1991; see also discussion in Coupland et al. 1993). He conceptualises identity as a process, not as a state, and as a series of choices one continually makes about one's self and one's lifestyle rather than a set of personal attributes, and as emerging from one's relationships with others. Although Giddens does not offer an empirically oriented programme for the analysis of how these processes are actually mediated in discourse, he puts discourse at the centre of his theory of selfhood by adopting a discursive metaphor of identities construed as 'biographical narratives':

> The reflexive project of the self, which consists in the sustaining of coherent, yet continuously revised, biographical narratives, takes place in the context of multiple choice as filtered through abstract systems. In modern social life, the notion of lifestyle takes on a particular significance. The more tradition loses its hold, and the more daily life is reconstituted in terms of the dialectical interplay of the local and the global, the more individuals are forced to negotiate lifestyle choices among a diversity of options.
>
> (Giddens 1991: 5)

However, as Giddens points out, the new conditions of life that have contributed to this 'dynamisation' of selfhood have generated restlessness and anxiety. Traditional systems of belief based on faith have given way to secularisation and the emergence of a multitude of competing ideologies (of which religious faith is only one). The versions of self that people can choose for themselves come from an increasing pool of options which are often unfamiliar to them, bringing new risks and conflicting interests. Consumerist discourse and the discourse of lifestyle choice, propagated by advertising for example, stands in conflict with the discourse/lifestyle of prudence that dominates discussions of welfare system reforms. Giddens refers to these problems as 'tribulations of the self', and discusses them in terms of four pairs of oppositions: unification versus fragmentation, powerlessness versus appropriation, authority versus uncertainty, personalised versus commodified experience.

These dilemmas are on-going in contemporary life and can only be resolved temporarily by engaging a particular type of ideology, relationship or activity, through which an individual can show his or her stance or allegiance towards a particular way of living. The sites for such position-taking are to be found in inter-action between the self and the contexts in which the person operates, whether we think of other human agents, mediated communication, or more abstract notions such as ideologies. In all these processes, discourse constitutes not only identities, but also social relations and categories, and other aspects of people's social lives (cf. Shotter 1993; Coupland *et al.* 1993). The social contructionist approach to identity (e.g., Gergen 1985; Potter and Wetherell 1987; Potter 1996) is echoed quite explicitly in all the other chapters in this Part of the *Reader*. Katherine Young's chapter on 'Narrative embodiments' makes a link between identity viewed as the physical, embodied self and a discursive enactment of this identity through narrative. Her case study deals with a patient in a medical consultation. This is a situation in which the self is typically displaced from the body; an anxiety-provoking experience that may be likened to Giddens's notion of fragmentation, resulting from having to cope with the relatively unfamiliar realm of medicine. The patient, a seventy-year-old man, a professor of Jewish history and literature, is first asked by the doctor about different parts of his body. Then, he is asked to take off his clothes, and he undergoes a thorough medical examination. Both the interview and the physical examination fragment the patient's self even further by attending to 'only one part of his body' at a time.

In the course of the interview and the examination, the patient tells several narratives which re-construct his displaced self. He manages to establish a link between the realm of medicine and the *storyrealm* by recounting his experiences from the Second World War, as a prisoner of Auschwitz, a refugee, a patient of American army doctors, and so on. Although he is careful to maintain a thematic link with the frame of the medical consultation, the *taleworld* which he creates lies outside of the medical frame and allows him to be seen as a legitimate actor and a full-fledged individual. The narratives become enclaves in which the patient's self finds refuge while being fragmented and displaced by the discourse of medicine.

The first of Deborah Cameron's two chapters in this Part focuses on the discur-sive construction of heterosexual male identity in an informal conversation among five American college students. In terms not unlike Giddens's 'reflexive project of the self', Cameron views gender identity as social performances (cf. Austin, Chapter 2; Goffman, see above and the Introduction to Part Four). She draws on Judith Butler's ideas (see Chapter 34) about gender being a 'repeated stylization of the body' (p. 420), which has a conventionalising but not essentialising effect on how people enact and read masculinity or femininity, or preferably – masculinities and femininities in the plural. Thus, gender roles are not given, static attributes but recursive, dynamic patterns of *being* and *doing*.

One resource that people have available to them to construct gender identities is, of course, *gendered speech*. Cameron examines how the students in her study enact their male, heterosexual identity by engaging in a disparaging exchange of opinions about other men as 'gays'. In this specific instance and frame of talk, references to 'gayness' are largely a ritualistic, boundary-marking activity, as the classification of people as 'gay' in their conversation has little to do with the known sexuality of the objects of their gossip. However, displaying hostility to gay men is a way for these students to establish their preferred version of masculinity in this particular context of an all-male peer group. In other contexts, for example, at a party with their girlfriends present, the heterosexual masculine identity of the same men could be enacted in totally different, possibly non-verbal ways.

Another interesting aspect of Cameron's chapter is the role of stereotypes and expectations in attributing meaning to the communicative strategies used by males and females. The five men engage in acts of asserting their solidarity and in-groupness through a stereotypically female verbal activity: gossip. However, their competent gossip is precisely used to allow them to dissociate themselves from the stereotypically non-masculine concerns (e.g., the alleged preoccupation of females and gays with their bodies). Besides, the men display certain conversational features (joint discourse production through interruptions and overlapping talk), which in female talk is associated with conversational co-operativity. In male talk, it seems more like competitiveness. Cameron shows how both these interpretations (co-operativity and competitiveness) may suit her data, and she warns against 'gender-stereotyping that causes us to miss or minimize the status-seeking element in women friends' talk, and the connection-making dimension of men's' (p. 428).

Deborah Cameron's second contribution, 'Styling the worker' (Chapter 30), deals with a number of current issues in sociolinguistics and discourse analysis. Most notably, she invokes 'style' and 'styling' and relates these notions to the discursive conditions of late-modern life (which is Anthony Giddens's term), globalised service-based industry (cf. Fairclough, Chapter 9). The term 'style' typically refers to how an individual speaker uses language differently in different social circumstances – 'the range of variation within the speech of an individual speaker' (Bell 1997: 240). The older term 'register' is used with the same meaning. Traditionally, style shifts have usually been thought to occur in accordance with varying degrees of situational formality/informality (Joos 1961) or the degree of attention paid to speech by the speaker (Labov 1972). In these approaches, style has been treated as a correlate of rather simple and stable types of situations, and speakers' demographic characteristics. However, in more 'dynamic' approaches, style is not so much a stable attribute of a particular type of speaker or situation, but a reflexively managed resource for performing 'acts of identity' (Le Page and Tabouret-Keller 1985). It is in this tradition that Coupland (2006) argues for style to be treated as a resource for strategic positioning of self and others in discourse. Style allows us to enact particular social personas, a form of self-identification with and self-differentiation from particular groups or group-orientations.

A related though narrower concept is *stylisation*, i.e., a knowing display of language style(s) deemed in a particular situation to be non-normative, unpredictable, or an 'as if' construction (Rampton 1995; Coupland 2001). Stylisation has its origins in the work of Mikhail Bakhtin on multiple voicing (Bakhtin 1981, 1986, Chapter 6) and in performative language use (Austin, Chapter 2; Bauman and Briggs 1990; Butler 1990, Chapter 34; Cameron, Chapter 29). According to Bakhtin, language is always dialogic, which presupposes a rich mixing and multiplicity of 'voices', or 'heteroglossia', in all texts. Thus, identities are not autonomous and separate but involved and intercorporeal, produced as a series of stylisations by appropriating, reworking and subverting different voices. We can talk of identities being actively 'styled' (see Bell 1997) and of people 'crossing' (Rampton 1995) from one identity format into another. Cameron finds telephone workers modifying their speech, not because they are able to make choices about their linguistic performance (*self*-styling in the traditional sense), but because they are given a script and a way of delivering this script by others. Their talk can be said to be stylised because they are involved in 'giving a performance, the "script" for which has been written by someone else' (p. 436). In this context, being scripted into stylised performance is a form of what Cameron calls 'verbal hygiene' (Cameron 1995), the imposition of a style complete with its commodification as a work-related skill or a lifestyle choice (Thurlow and Jaworski 2006).

Deborah Tannen's chapter on 'New York Jewish conversational style' (Chapter 31) is firmly rooted in the tradition of interactional sociolinguistics (see the general Introduction). The data come from a Thanksgiving dinner conversation in 1978, which brought together three New Yorkers of Jewish background and three non-New Yorkers from different parts of the English-speaking world. New York Jewish conversational style is described as displaying the following features: fast rate of speech and turn-taking, tolerance of overlapping speech, persistence in having one's turn acknowledged, marked shifts in pitch, preference for personal stories and abrupt topic shifts. Tannen demonstrates how the sharing of these features creates *involvement* between members of the same ethnic group, while non-New Yorkers react to some of these features with unease or downright opposition by intensifying opposing behaviour.

Again, notice the reflexivity of the discourse and the analysis – how the participants are (or are not) 'doing being New York Jews', how they apparently enjoy the shared construction of discourse and, consequently, their shared ethnic identity. On the other hand, the anxiety with which the non-members of the in-group react to this discourse reminds us of Giddens's observation that one of the sources of the 'tribulation of the self' comes from the tension brought about by globalisation. Note that this conversation was recorded in the home of one of the (category-labelled) 'New York Jews' in Oakland, California, and that the other participants came from other parts of the US and from the UK. This situation seems to provide a good illustration of Shotter's observation that

> as Gergen (1991) has described in detail, due to the way that our technologies of communication and travel have advanced, there is a quantum leap in our exposure to each other; we have become 'saturated' with the voices of others. We have become embroiled in (what Giddens 1991 calls) the dialectic of local and the global: Events distant from us in both space *and time*, transmitted to us through communication media, play an intimate part in who we feel we want or ought to be. No wonder

that *identity* has become the watchword of the times; for it provides the much needed vocabulary in terms of which we now define our loyalties and our commitments.

(Shotter 1993: 5–6)

As we have argued in this Introduction, the emergence and re-emergence of the self is a process that is a function of a number of situational, social, cultural and historical factors. The role of discourse, in its various multimodal guises, and its meaning-making capacity is paramount. Thus, the ways we speak (as males, females, doctors, patients, call centre operators, Jews, non-Jews, and so on) and the way we speak to and about others (the 'narrated self' in Young's chapter, or the 'gays' in Cameron's data) turns individuals into *subjective* selves. Even though we mistakenly treat our descriptive categories as 'natural' (cf. our general introduction), and our descriptions of self and other may be meant 'objectively', various private and institutional discourses are constitutive of us and others as *social* subjects. In other words, these discourses fabricate our subjectivities (Foucault 1972; see also Potter 1996; Mills 1997).

Deborah Cameron (1992: 161–2) gives one compelling example of how our gendered social subjectivities are fabricated discursively from the day we are born:

Recently a woman who had just had a baby told me that in the hospital nursery, each newborn's crib bore a label announcing its sex. The label said either 'I'm a boy' or 'It's a girl'. Obviously none of the infants was yet capable of speech. But on the day they were born, the culture hailed them differently: boys were hailed as active 'speaking subjects', unproblematically 'I'; girls were not. This is the order which, as they grow older, these children will be forced to enter.

Subjectivity is the site of our consciousness, but far from being a fully independent entity, it is bound up by the structures and discourses of institutional and interpersonal order, power and ideology.

References

Bakhtin, M.M. (1981) *The Dialogic Imagination: Four Essays*, edited by M. Holquist. Translated by Vern W. McGee. Austin, TX: University of Texas Press.
—— (1986) *Speech Genres and Other Late Essays*, translated by Vern W. McGee. Austin, TX: University of Texas Press.
Bauman, R. and Briggs, C. (1990) 'Poetics and performance as critical perspectives on language and social life', *Annual Review of Anthropology* 19: 59–88.
Bell, A. (1997) 'Language style as audience design', in N. Coupland and A. Jaworski (eds) *Sociolinguistics: A Reader and Coursebook*, Basingstoke: Macmillan. 240–50.
Butler, J. (1990) *Gender Trouble: Feminism and the Subversion of Identity*, New York: Routledge.
Cameron, D. (1992) *Feminism and Linguistic Theory*, 2nd edition, London: Macmillan.
—— (1995) *Verbal Hygiene*, London: Routledge.

Coupland, N. (2001) 'Dialect stylisation in radio talk', *Language in Society* 30: 345–75.

—— (2006) *Style: Language Variation, Identity and Social Meaning*, Cambridge: Cambridge University Press.

——, Nussbaum, J.F. and Grossman, A. (1993) 'Introduction: discourse, selfhood and the lifespan', in N. Coupland and J.F. Nussbaum (eds) *Discourse and Lifespan Identity*, Newbury Park, CA: Sage. x–xxviii.

Foucault, M. (1972) *The Archaeology of Knowledge*, translated by S. Smith, London: Tavistock.

Gergen, K.J. (1985) 'Social constructionist inquiry: context and implications', in K.J. Gergen and K.E. Davis (eds) *The Social Construction of the Person*, New York: Springer-Verlag.

Giddens, A. (1990) *The Consequences of Modernity*, Cambridge: Polity Press.

—— (1991) *Modernity and Self-identity: Self and Identity in the Late Modern Age*, Cambridge: Polity Press.

Goffman, E. (1959) *The Presentation of Self in Everyday Life*, New York: Anchor Books.

Joos, M. (1961) *The Five Clocks*, New York: Harcourt Brace.

Labov, W. (1972) *Sociolinguistic Patterns*, Philadelphia, PA: Pennsylvania University Press.

Le Page, R.B. and Tabouret-Keller, A. (1985) *Acts of Identity: Creole-based Approaches to Language and Ethnicity*, Cambridge: Cambridge University Press.

Mills, S. (1997) *Discourse*, London: Routledge.

Potter, J. (1996) *Representing Reality: Discourse, Rhetoric and Social Construction*, London: Sage.

—— and Wetherell, M. (1987) *Discourse and Social Psychology: Beyond Attitudes and Behaviour*, London: Sage.

Rampton, B. (1995) *Crossing: Language and Ethnicity among Adolescents*, London: Longman.

Shotter, J. (1993) 'Becoming someone', in N. Coupland and J.F. Nussbaum (eds) *Discourse and Lifespan Identity*, Newbury Park, CA: Sage. 5–27.

—— and Gergen, K.J. (eds) (1989) *Texts of Identity*, London: Sage.

Thurlow, C. and Jaworski, A. (2006) 'The alchemy of the upwardly mobile: symbolic capital and the stylization of elites in frequent-flyer programs', *Discourse & Society* 17: 131–67.

Chapter 27

Stuart Hall

THE WHITES OF
THEIR EYES

. . .

'**RACISM AND THE MEDIA**' touches directly the problem of *ideology*, since the media's main sphere of operations is the production and transformation of ideologies. An intervention in the media's construction of race is an intervention in the *ideological* terrain of struggle. Much murky water has flowed under the bridge provided by this concept of ideology in recent years; and this is not the place to develop the theoretical argument. I am using the term to refer to those images, concepts and premises which provide the frameworks through which we represent, interpret, understand and 'make sense' of some aspect of social existence. Language and ideology are not the same – since the same linguistic term ('democracy' for example, or 'freedom') can be deployed within different ideological discourses. But language, broadly conceived, is by definition the principal medium in which we find different ideological discourses elaborated.

Three important things need to be said about ideology in order to make what follows intelligible. First, ideologies do not consist of isolated and separate concepts, but in the articulation of different elements into a distinctive set or chain of meanings. In liberal ideology, 'freedom' is connected (articulated) with individualism and the free market; in socialist ideology, 'freedom' is a collective condition, dependent on, not counterposed to, 'equality of condition', as it is in liberal ideology. The same concept is differently positioned within the logic of different ideological discourses. One of the ways in which ideological struggle takes place and ideologies are transformed is by articulating the elements differently, thereby producing a different meaning: breaking the chain in which they are currently fixed (e.g. 'democratic' = the 'Free' West) and establishing a new articulation (e.g.

Source: Stuart Hall, 'The whites of their eyes', in George Bridges and Rosalind Brunt (eds) *Silver Lining*, London: Lawrence & Wishart, 1981, 28–52.

'democratic' = deepening the democratic content of political life). This 'breaking of the chain' is not, of course, confined to the head: it takes place through social practice and political struggle.

Second, ideological statements are made by individuals: but ideologies are not the product of individual consciousness or intention. Rather we formulate our intentions *within ideology*. They pre-date individuals, and form part of the determinate social formations and conditions in which individuals are born. We have to 'speak through' the ideologies which are active in our society and which provide us with the means of 'making sense' of social relations and our place in them. The transformation of ideologies is thus a collective process and practice, not an individual one. Largely, the processes work *unconsciously*, rather than by conscious intention. Ideologies produce different forms of social consciousness, rather than being produced by them. They work most effectively when we are not aware that how we formulate and construct a statement about the world is underpinned by ideological premises; when our formations seem to be simply descriptive statements about how things are (i.e. must be), or of what we can 'take-for-granted'. 'Little boys like playing rough games; little girls, however, are full of sugar and spice' is predicated on a whole set of ideological premises, though it seems to be an aphorism which is grounded, not in how masculinity and femininity have been historically and culturally constructed in society, but in Nature itself. Ideologies tend to disappear from view into the taken-for-granted 'naturalised' world of common sense. Since (like gender) race appears to be 'given' by Nature, racism is one of the most profoundly 'naturalised' of existing ideologies.

Third, ideologies 'work' by constructing for their subjects (individual and collective) positions of identification and knowledge which allow them to 'utter' ideological truths as if they were their authentic authors. This is not because they emanate from our innermost, authentic and unified experience, but because we find ourselves mirrored in the positions at the centre of the discourses from which the statements we formulate 'make sense'. Thus the same 'subjects' (e.g. economic classes or ethnic groups) can be differently constructed in different ideologies. When Mrs Thatcher says, 'We can't afford to pay ourselves higher wages without earning them through higher productivity', she is attempting to construct at the centre of her discourse an identification for workers who will cease to see themselves as opposed or *antagonistic* to the needs of capital, and begin to see themselves in terms of the *identity of interests* between themselves and capital. Again, this is not only in the head. Redundancies are a powerful material way of influencing 'hearts and minds'.

Ideologies therefore work by the transformation of discourses (the disarticulation and re-articulation of ideological elements) and the transformation (the fracturing and recomposition) of subjects-for-action. How we 'see' ourselves and our social relations *matters*, because it enters into and informs our actions and practices. Ideologies are therefore a site of a distinct type of social struggle. This site does not exist on its own, separate from other relations, since ideas are not free-floating in people's heads. The ideological construction of black people as a 'problem population' and the police practice of containment in the black communities mutually reinforce and support one another. Nevertheless, ideology is a practice. It has its own specific way of working. And it is generated, produced and reproduced in specific settings (sites) – especially, in the apparatuses of ideological production which 'produce' social meanings and distribute them throughout society, like the media. It is therefore the site of a particular kind of struggle, which cannot be simply reduced to or incorporated into some other level of struggle – for example, the economic class struggle, which is sometimes held to govern or determine it. It is the struggle over what Lenin once called 'ideological relations', which have their own tempo and specificity. It is located in specific practices. Ideological struggle, like any other form of struggle, therefore represents an intervention in an existing field of practices and institutions; those which sustain the dominant discourses of meaning of society.

. . .

Let us look, then, a little more closely at the apparatuses which generate and circulate ideologies. In modern societies, the different media are especially important sites for the production, reproduction and transformation of ideologies. Ideologies are, of course, worked on in many places in society, and not only in the head. . . . But institutions like the media are peculiarly central to the matter since they are, by definition, part of the dominant means of *ideological* production. What they 'produce' is, precisely, representations of the social world, images, descriptions, explanations and frames for understanding how the world is and why it works as it is said and shown to work. And, amongst other kinds of ideological labour, the media construct for us a definition of what *race* is, what meaning the imagery of race carries, and what the 'problem of race' is understood to be. They help to classify out the world in terms of the categories of race.

The media are not only a powerful source of ideas about race. They are also one place where these ideas are articulated, worked on, transformed and elaborated. We have said 'ideas' and 'ideologies' in the plural. For it would be wrong and misleading to see the media as uniformly and conspiratorially harnessed to a single, racist conception of the world. Liberal and humane ideas about 'good relations' between the races, based on open-mindedness and tolerance, operate inside the world of the media – among, for example, many television journalists and newspapers like the *Guardian* – alongside the more explicit racism of other journalists and newspapers like the *Express* or the *Mail*. In some respects, the line which separates the latter from the extreme right on policies, such as, for example, guided repatriation for blacks, is very thin indeed.

It would be simple and convenient if all the media were simply the ventriloquists of a unified and racist 'ruling class' conception of the world. But neither a unifiedly conspiratorial media nor indeed a unified racist 'ruling class' exist in anything like that simple way. I don't insist on complexity for its own sake. But if critics of the media subscribe to too simple or reductive a view of their operations, this inevitably lacks credibility and weakens the case they are making because the theories and critiques don't square with reality. They only begin to account for the real operation of racism in society by a process of gross abstraction and simplification.

. . .

Another important distinction is between what we might call 'overt' racism and 'inferential' racism. By *overt* racism, I mean those many occasions when open and favourable coverage is given to arguments, positions and spokespersons who are in the business of elaborating an openly racist argument or advancing a racist policy or view. Many such occasions exist; they have become more frequent in recent years more often in the press, which has become openly partisan to extremist right-wing arguments, than in television, where the regulations of 'balance', 'impartiality and neutrality' operate.

By *inferential* racism I mean those apparently naturalised representations of events and situations relating to race, whether 'factual' or 'fictional', which have racist premises and propositions inscribed in them as a set of *unquestioned assumptions*. These enable racist statements to be formulated without ever bringing into awareness the racist predicates on which the statements are grounded.

Both types of racism are to be found, in different combinations, in the British media. Open or overt racism is, of course, politically dangerous as well as socially offensive. The open partisanship of sections of the popular press on this front is an extremely serious development. It is not only that they circulate and popularise openly racist policies and ideas, and translate them into the vivid populist vernacular (e.g. in the tabloids, with their large working-class readership) it is the very fact that such things can now be openly said and advocated which *legitimates* their public expression and increases the threshold of the public acceptability of racism. Racism becomes 'acceptable' – and thus, not too long after, 'true' – just common sense: what everyone knows and is openly saying. But *inferential racism* is more widespread – and in many ways, more insidious, because it is largely *invisible* even to those who formulate the world in its terms.

An example of *this* type of racist ideology is the sort of television programme which deals with some 'problem' in race relations. It is probably made by a good and honest liberal broadcaster, who hopes to do some good in the world for 'race relations' and who maintains a scrupulous balance and neutrality when questioning people interviewed for the programme. The programme will end with a homily on how, if only the 'extremists' *on either side* would go away, 'normal blacks and whites' would be better able to get on with learning to live in harmony together. Yet every word and image of such programmes is impregnated with unconscious racism because they are all predicated on the unstated and unrecognised assumption that the *blacks* are the *source of the problem*. Yet virtually the whole of 'social problem' television about race and immigration – often made, no doubt, by well-intentioned and liberal-minded broadcasters – is precisely predicated on racist premises of this kind. This was the criticism we made in the CARM programme, *It Ain't Half Racist, Mum* and it was the one which most cut the broadcasters to their professional quick. It undermined their professional credentials by suggesting that they had been partisan where they are supposed to be balanced and impartial. It was an affront to the liberal consensus and self-image which prevails within broadcasting. Both responses were, in fact, founded on the profound misunderstanding that racism is, by definition, mutually exclusive of the liberal consensus – whereas, in inferential racism, the two can quite easily cohabit – and on the assumption that if the television discourse could be shown to be racist, it must be 'because the individual broadcasters were intentionally and deliberately racist'. In fact, an ideological discourse does *not* depend on the conscious intentions of those who formulate statements within it.

How, then, is race and its 'problems' constructed on British television? This is a complex topic in its own right, and I can only illustrate its dimensions briefly here by referring to some of the themes developed in the two programmes I was involved in. One of the things we tried to show in *The Whites Of Their Eyes* was the rich vocabulary and syntax of race on which the media have to draw. Racism has a long and distinguished history in British culture. It is grounded in the relations of slavery, colonial conquest, economic exploitation and imperialism in which the European races have stood in relation to the 'native peoples' of the colonised and exploited periphery.

Three characteristics provided the discursive and power-coordinates of the discourses in which these relations were historically constructed. (1) Their imagery and themes were polarised around fixed relations of subordination and domination. (2) Their stereotypes were grouped around the poles of 'superior' and 'inferior' natural species. (3) Both were displaced from the 'language' of history into the language of Nature. Natural physical signs and racial characteristics became the unalterable signifiers of inferiority. Subordinate ethnic groups and classes appeared, not as the objects of particular historical relations (the slave trade, European colonisation, the active underdevelopment of the 'underdeveloped' societies), but as the given qualities of an inferior *breed*. Relations, secured by economic, social, political and military domination were transformed and 'naturalised' into an order of *rank*, ascribed by Nature. Thus, Edward Long, an acute English observer of Jamaica in the period of slavery wrote (in his *History of Jamaica*, 1774) – much in the way the Elizabethans might have spoken of 'the Great Chain Of Being' – of 'Three ranks of men [*sic*], (white, mulatto and black), dependent on each other, and rising in a proper climax of subordination, in which the whites hold the highest place'.

One thing we wanted to illustrate in the programme was the 'forgotten' degree to which, in the period of slavery and imperialism popular literature is saturated with these fixed, negative attributes of the colonised races. We find them in the diaries, observations and accounts, the notebooks, ethnographic records and commentaries, of visitors, explorers, missionaries and administrators in Africa, India, the Far East and the Americas. And also something else: the 'absent' but imperialising 'white eye'; the unmarked position from which all these 'observations' are made and from which, alone, they make sense. This is the history of slavery and conquest, written, seen, drawn and photographed by The Winners. They cannot be *read* and made sense of from any other position. The 'white eye' is always outside the frame but seeing and positioning everything within it.

Some of the most telling sequences we used were from early film of the British Raj in India – the source of endless radio 'reminiscences' and television historical show-pieces today. The assumption of effortless superiority structures every image – even the portioning in the frame: the foregrounding of colonial life (tea-time on the plantation), the background of native bearers. . . . In the later stages of High Imperialism, this discourse proliferates through the new media of popular culture and information – newspapers and journals, cartoons, drawings and advertisements and the popular novel. Recent critics of the literature of imperialism have argued that, if we simply extend our definition of nineteenth-century fiction from one branch of 'serious fiction' to embrace popular literature, we will find a second, powerful strand of the English literary imagination to set beside the *domestic* novel: the male-dominated world of imperial adventure, which takes *empire*, rather than *Middlemarch*, as its microcosm. I remember a graduate student, working on the construction of race in popular literature and culture at the end of the Nineteenth Century, coming to me in despair – racism was so ubiquitous, and at the same time, *so unconscious* – simply assumed to be the case – that it was impossible to get any critical purchase on it. In this period, the very idea of *adventure* became synonymous with the demonstration of the moral, social and physical mastery of the colonisers over the colonised.

Later, this concept of 'adventure' – one of the principal categories of modern *entertainment* – moved straight off the printed page into the literature of crime and espionage, children's books, the great Hollywood extravaganzas and comics. There, with recurring persistence, they still remain. Many of these older versions have had their edge somewhat blunted by time. They have been distanced from us, apparently, by our superior wisdom and liberalism. But they still reappear on the television screen, especially in the form of 'old movies' (some 'old movies', of course, continue to be made). But we can grasp their recurring resonance better if we identify some of the base-images of the 'grammar of race'.

There is, for example, the familiar *slave-figure*: dependable, loving in a simple, childlike way – the devoted 'Mammy' with the rolling eyes, or the faithful field-hand or retainer, attached and devoted to 'his' Master. The best-known extravaganza of all – *Gone With The Wind* – contains rich variants of both. The 'slave-figure' is by no means limited to films and programmes about *slavery*. Some 'Injuns' and many Asians have come on to the screen in this disguise. A deep and unconscious ambivalence pervades this stereotype. Devoted and childlike, the 'slave' is also unreliable, unpredictable and undependable – capable of 'turning nasty', or of plotting in a treacherous way, secretive, cunning, cut-throat once his or her Master's or Mistress's back is turned: and inexplicably given to running way into the bush at the slightest opportunity. The whites can never be sure that this childish simpleton – 'Sambo' – is not mocking his master's white manners behind his hand, even when giving an exaggerated caricature of white refinement.

Another base-image is that of the 'native'. The good side of this figure is portrayed in a certain primitive nobility and simple dignity. The bad side is portrayed in terms of cheating and cunning, and, further out, savagery and barbarism. Popular culture is still full today of countless savage and restless natives, and sound-tracks constantly repeat the threatening sound of drumming in the night, the hint of primitive rites and cults. Cannibals, whirling dervishes, Indian tribesmen, garishly got up, are constantly threatening to over-run the screen. They are likely to appear at any moment out of the darkness to decapitate the beautiful heroine, kidnap the children, burn the encampment or threatening to boil, cook and eat the innocent explorer or colonial administrator and his lady-wife. These 'natives' always move as an anonymous collective mass – in tribes or hordes. And against them is always counterposed the isolated white figure, alone 'out there', confronting his Destiny or shouldering his Burden in the 'heart of darkness', displaying coolness under fire and an unshakeable authority – exerting mastery over the rebellious natives or quelling the threatened uprising with a single glance of his steel-blue eyes.

A third variant is that of the 'clown' or 'entertainer'. This captures the 'innate' humour, as well as the physical grace of the licensed entertainer – putting on a show for The Others. It is never quite clear whether we are laughing with or at this figure: admiring the physical and rhythmic grace, the open expressivity and emotionality of the 'entertainer', or put off by the 'clown's' stupidity.

One noticeable fact about all these images is their deep *ambivalence* – the double vision of the white eye through which they are seen. The primitive nobility of the ageing tribesman or chief, and the native's rhythmic grace, always contain both a nostalgia for an innocence lost forever to the civilised, and the threat of civilisation being over-run or undermined by the recurrence of savagery, which is always lurking just below the surface; or by an untutored sexuality, threatening to 'break out'. Both are aspects – the good and the bad sides – of *primitivism*. In these images, 'primitivism' is defined by the fixed proximity of such people to Nature.

Is all this so far away as we sometimes suppose from the representation of race which fill the screens today? These *particular* versions may have faded. But their *traces* are still to be observed, reworked in many of the modern and up-dated images. And though they may appear to carry a different meaning, they are often still constructed on a very ancient grammar. Today's restless native hordes are still alive and well and living, as guerrilla armies and freedom fighters in the Angola, Zimbabwe or Namibian 'bush'. Blacks are still the most frightening, cunning and glamorous crooks (and policemen) in New York cop series. They are the fleet-footed, crazy-talking under-men who connect Starsky and Hutch to the drug-saturated ghetto. The scheming villains and their giant-sized bully boys in the world of James Bond and his progeny are still, unusually, recruited from 'out there' in Jamaica, where savagery lingers on. The sexually-available 'slave girl' is alive and kicking, smouldering away on some exotic TV set or on the covers of paper-backs, though she is now the centre of a special admiration, covered in a sequinned gown and supported by a white chorus line. Primitivism, savagery, guile and unreliability – all 'just below the surface' – can still be identified in the faces of black political leaders around the world, cunningly plotting the overthrow of 'civilisation': Mr Mugabe, for example, up to the point where he happened to win both a war and an election and became, temporarily at any rate, the best (because the most politically credible) friend Britain had left in that last outpost of the Edwardian dream.

The 'Old Country' – white version – is still often the subject of nostalgic documentaries: 'Old Rhodesia', whose reliable servants, as was only to be expected, plotted treason in the outhouse and silently stole away to join ZAPU in the bush . . . Tribal Man in green khaki. Black stand-up comics still ape their ambiguous incorporation into British entertainment by being the first to tell a racist joke. No Royal Tour is complete without its troupe of swaying bodies, or its mounted tribesmen, paying homage. Blacks are such 'good movers', so *rhythmic*, so *natural*. And the dependent peoples, who couldn't manage for a day without the protection and know-how of their white masters, reappear as the starving victims of the Third World, passive and waiting for the technology or the Aid to arrive, objects of our pity or of a *Blue Peter* appeal. They are not represented as the subjects of a continuing exploitation or dependency, or the global division of wealth and labour. They are the Victims of Fate.

These modern, glossed and up-dated images seem to have put the old world of Sambo behind them. Many of them, indeed, are the focus of a secret, illicit, pleasurable-but-taboo admiration. Many have a more active and energetic quality – some black athletes, for example, and of course the entertainers. But the connotations and echoes which they carry reverberate back a very long way. They continue to shape the ways whites see blacks today – even when the white adventurer sailing up the jungle stream is not *Sanders Of The River*, but historical drama-reconstructions of Stanley and Livingstone; and the intention is to show, not the savagery, but the serenity of African village life – ways of an ancient people 'unchanged even down to modern times' (in other words, still preserved in economic backwardness and frozen in history for our anthropological eye by forces unknown to them and, apparently, unshowable on the screen).

'Adventure' is one way in which we *encounter* race without having to *confront* the racism of the perspectives in use. Another, even more complex one is 'entertainment'. In television, there is a strong counterposition between 'serious', informational television, which we watch because it is good for us, and 'entertainment', which we watch because it is pleasurable. And the purest form of pleasure in entertainment television is *comedy*. By definition, comedy is a licensed zone, disconnected from the serious. It's all 'good, clean fun'. In the area of fun and pleasure it is forbidden to pose a serious question, partly because it seems so puritanical and destroys the pleasure by switching registers. Yet race is one of the most significant themes in situation comedies – from the early Alf Garnett to *Mind Your Language*, *On The Buses*, *Love Thy Neighbour* and *It Ain't Half Hot, Mum*. These are defended on good 'anti-racist' grounds: the appearance of blacks, alongside whites, in situation comedies, it is argued, will help to naturalise and normalise their presence in British society. And no doubt, in some examples, it does function in this way. But, if you examine these fun occasions more closely, you will often find, as we did in our two programmes, that the comedies do not simply include blacks: they are *about race*. That is, the same old categories of racially-defined characteristics and qualities, and the same relations of superior and inferior, provide the pivots on which the jokes actually turn, the tension-points which move and motivate the situations in situation comedies. The comic register in which they are set, however, protects and defends viewers from acknowledging their incipient racism. It creates disavowal.

This is even more so with the television stand-up comics, whose repertoire in recent years has come to be dominated, in about equal parts, by sexist and racist jokes. It's sometimes said, again in their defence, that this must be a sign of black acceptability. But it *may* just be that racism has become more normal: it's hard to tell. It's also said that the best tellers of anti-Jewish jokes are Jews themselves, just as blacks tell the best 'white' jokes against themselves. But this is to argue as if jokes exist in a vacuum separate from the contexts and situations of their telling. Jewish jokes told by Jews among themselves are part of the self-awareness of the community. They are unlikely to function by 'putting down' the race, because both teller and audience belong on equal terms to the same group. Telling racist jokes across the racial line, in conditions where relations of racial inferiority and superiority prevail, reinforces *the difference* and reproduces the unequal relations because, in those situations, the point of the joke depends on the existence of racism. Thus they reproduce the categories and relations of racism, even while normalizing them through laughter. The stated good intentions of the joke-makers do not resolve the problem here, because they are not in control of the circumstances – conditions of continuing racism in which their joke discourse will be read and heard. The time *may* come when blacks and whites can tell jokes about each other in ways which do not reproduce the racial categories of the world in which they are told. The time, in Britain, is certainly *not yet arrived*.

Two other arenas . . . relate to the 'harder' end of television production – news and current affairs. This is where race is constructed as *problem* and the site of *conflict* and debate. . . . The general tendency of the run of programmes in this area is to see blacks – especially the mere fact of their existence (their 'numbers') – as constituting a problem for English white society. They appear as law-breakers, prone to crime; as 'trouble'; as the collective agent of civil disorder. In the numerous incidents where black communities have reacted to racist provocation (as at Southall) or to police harrassment and provocation (as in Bristol), the media have tended to assume that 'right' lay on the side of the law, and have fallen into the language of 'riot' and 'race warfare' which simply feeds existing stereotypes and prejudices. The precipitating conditions of conflict are usually *absent* – the scandalous provocation of a National Front march through one of the biggest black areas, Southall, and the saturation police raiding of the last refuge for black youth which triggered off Bristol – to take only two examples. They are either missing, or introduced so late in the process of signification, that they fail to dislodge the dominant definition of these events. So they testify, once again, to the disruptive nature of black and Asian people *as such*.

. . .

A good example of how the real causes of racial conflict can be absorbed and transformed by the framework which the media employ can be found in the *Nationwide* coverage of Southall on the day following the events. Two interlocking frameworks of explanation governed this programme. In the first, conflict is seen in the conspiratorial terms of far-left against extreme-right – the Anti-Nazi League against the National Front. This is the classic logic of television, where the medium identifies itself with the moderate, consensual, middle-road, Average viewer, and sets off, in contrast, extremism on both sides, which it then equates with each other. In this particular exercise in 'balance', fascism and anti-fascism are represented as *the same* – both equally *bad*, because the Middle Way enshrines the Common Good under all circumstances. This balancing exercise provided an opportunity for Martin Webster of the National Front to gain access to the screen, to help set the terms of the debate, and to spread his smears across the screen under the freedom of the airwaves: 'Well,' he said, 'let's talk about Trotskyists, extreme Communists of various sorts, raving Marxists and other assorted left-wing cranks.' Good knockabout stuff. Then, after a linking passage – 'Southall, the day after' – to the second framework: rioting Asians *vs* the police. 'I watched television as well last night,' Mr Jardine argued, 'and I certainly didn't see any police throwing bricks

. . . So don't start making those arguments.' The growth of organised political racism and the circumstances which have precipitated it were simply not visible to *Nationwide* as an alternative way of setting up the problem.

In the CARM programme *It Ain't Half Racist, Mum*, we tried to illustrate the inferential logic at work in another area of programming: the BBC'S 'Great Debate' on Immigration. It was not necessary here to start with any preconceived notions, least of all speculation as to the personal views on race by the broadcasters involved. . . . You have simply to look at the programme with one set of questions in mind: Here is a problem, defined as 'the problem of immigration'. What is it? How is it defined and constructed through the programme? What logic governs its definition? And where does that logic derive from? I believe the answers are clear. The problem of immigration is that 'there are too many blacks over here', to put it crudely. It is *defined* in terms of *numbers of blacks* and what to do about them. The *logic* of the argument is 'immigrants = blacks = too many of them = send them home'. That is a racist logic. And it comes from a chain of reasoning whose representative, in respectable public debate and in person, on this occasion, was Enoch Powell. Powellism set the agenda for the media. Every time (and on many more occasions than the five or six we show in the programme) the presenter wanted to define the base-line of the programme which others should address, Mr Powell's views were indicated as representing it. And every time anyone strayed from the 'logic' to question the underlying premiss, it was back to 'as Mr Powell would say . . .' that they were drawn.

. . .

If the media function in a systematically racist manner, it is not because they are run and organised exclusively by active racists; this is a category mistake. This would be equivalent to saying that you could change the character of the capitalist state by replacing its personnel. Whereas the media, like the state, have a *structure*, a set of *practices* which are *not* reducible to the individuals who staff them. What defines how the media function is the result of a set of complex, often contradictory, social relations; not the personal inclinations of its members. What is significant is not that they produce a racist ideology, from some single-minded and unified conception of the world, but that they are so powerfully constrained − 'spoken by' − a particular set of ideological discourses. The power of this discourse is its capacity to constrain a very great variety of individuals: racist, anti-racist, liberals, radicals, conservatives, anarchists, know-nothings and silent majoritarians.

What we said, however, about the *discourse* of problem television was true, despite the hurt feelings of particular individuals: and demonstrably so. The premiss on which the Great Immigration Debate was built and the chain of reasoning it predicated was a racist one. The evidence for this is in what was said and how it was formulated − how the argument unfolded. If you establish the topic as 'the numbers of blacks are too high' or '*they* are breeding too fast', the opposition is obliged or constrained to argue that 'the numbers are not as high as they are repre-sented to be'. This view is opposed to the first two: but it is also imprisoned by the same logic – the logic of the 'numbers game'. Liberals, anti-racists, indeed raging revolutionaries can contribute 'freely' to this debate, and indeed are often obliged to do so, so as not to let the case go by default: without breaking for a moment the chain of assumptions which holds the racist proposition in place. However, changing the terms of the argument, questioning the assumptions and starting points, breaking the logic – this is a quite different, longer, more difficult task.

. . .

Chapter 28

Katharine Young

NARRATIVE EMBODIMENTS: ENCLAVES OF THE SELF IN THE REALM OF MEDICINE

To write the body.
Neither the skin, nor the muscles, nor the bones,
nor the nerves, but the rest: an awkward, fibrous,
shaggy, raveled thing, a clown's coat.

Roland Barthes

PERSONS ARE TENDER OF their bodies as if their selves inhered in its organs, vessels, tissues, bones and blood, as if they were embodied. For us, the body is the locus of the self, indistinguishable from it and expressive of it. As the phenomenologist, Maurice Natanson, writes,

> The immediacy of my experience of corporeality should be understood as an indication of the interior perspective I occupy with respect of 'my body'. I am neither 'in' my body nor 'attached to' it, it does not belong to me or go along with me. *I am my body*.
>
> (Natanson 1970: 12)

I experience myself as embodied, incorporated, incarnated in my body. To appear in my own person is to evidence this implication of my self in my body.

Medical examinations threaten this embodied self with untoward intimacies. The accoutrements of propriety are stripped away: I appear in nothing but my body. What follows has the structure of a transgression, an infringement, but one in which I am complicit. I disclose my body to the other, the stranger, the physician (see Berger and Mohr 1976: 68). To deflect this threat to the embodied self, medicine constitutes a separate realm in which the body as lodgement of the self is transformed into the body as object of scrutiny: persons become patients.

Source: Katharine Young, 'Narrative embodiments: enclaves of the self in the realm of medicine', in John Schotter and Kenneth J. Gergen (eds) *Texts of Identity*, London: Sage, 1989, 152–65.

This transformation is intended to protect the sensibilities of the social self from the trespasses of the examination. Whatever the medical business of the examination, its phenomenological business is to displace the self from the body. However, persons can perceive rendering the body an object as depersonalizing, dehumanizing or otherwise slighting to the self.[1] The disparity between the physician's intention and the patient's perception establishes the context for 'gaps', 'distortions' and 'misunderstandings' between patients and physicians (Mishler 1984: 171).

Because of their sense of the loss of self – a well-founded sense if also a well-intentioned loss – patients can have some impulse to reconstitute a self during medical examinations. This reconstitution can be undertaken by the patient in one of two moves: either by breaking the framework of the realm of medicine by disattending, misunderstanding or flouting its conventions or by maintaining the framework but inserting into the realm of medicine an enclave of another ontological status, specifically, a narrative enclave.

Rules for producing narratives on ordinary occasions require that they be set off by their frames from the discourses in which they are embedded (see Young 1982). Narrative frames – prefaces, openings, beginnings, endings, closings, codas – create an enclosure for stories within medical discourse. The discourse within the frames is understood to be of a different ontological status from the discourse without. In particular, the *storyrealm*, the realm of narrative discourse, conjures up another realm of events, or *taleworld*, in which the events the story recounts are understood to transpire (see Young 1987: 15–18). It is in this alternate reality that the patient reappears as a person. This move depends on the existence of what Alfred Schutz calls 'multiple realities' (1967: 245–62), the different realms of being, each with its own 'metaphysical constants' (Natanson 1970: 198), which individuals conjure up and enter into by turning their attention to them.

Embodying the self in a narrative enclave respects the conventions of the realm of medicine and at the same time manages the presentation of a self, but of one who is sealed inside a story. An inverse relationship develops between the uniquely constituted narrative enclosure in which a patient presents a self and the jointly constituted enclosing realm in which the patient undergoes a loss of self. Stories become enclaves of self over the course of an occasion on which medicine inhabits the realm of the body.

Erving Goffman argues that persons are in the way of presenting themselves, guiding controlled impressions, not necessarily to deceive, but to sustain a reality, an event, a self. Structurally, the self is divided into two aspects: (1) the performer who fabricates these impressions, and (2) the character who is the impression fabricated by an ongoing performance which entails them both (Goffman 1959: 252). On ordinary occasions, then, persons do not provide information to recipients but present dramas to an audience (Goffman 1974: 508). It is here that the theatrical metaphor for which Goffman is famous takes hold: talk about the self is not so far removed from enactment. We do not have behaviours and descriptions of them but a modulation from embodied to disembodied performances. Storytelling is a special instance of the social construction of the self in which 'what the individual presents is not himself but a story containing a protagonist who may happen also to be himself' (Goffman 1974: 541). On the occasion investigated here, embodying the self in stories occurs in circumstances in which the self is being disembodied, a complication of the matter Goffman has called 'multiple selfing', that is, the evolving or exuding of a second self or several selves over the course of an occasion on which the self is being presented (Goffman 1974: 521 fn.).

The natural occurrence of these 'texts of identity' in the course of a medical examination suggests implications about the uses of narrativity in social scientific discourse. Kenneth and Mary Gergen write that 'rules for narrative construction guide our attempt to account for human actions across time', both in making ourselves intelligible informally and in social scientific discourse (Gergen and Gergen 1986: 6). Individuals use narratives, they argue, to reflexively reconstruct a sense of self. 'The fact that people believe they possess identities fundamentally depends on their capacity to relate fragmentary occurrences across temporal boundaries' (Gergen and Gergen 1983: 255). What the Gergens call 'self-narratives' then 'refer to the individual's account of the relationship among self-relevant events across time' (p. 255). Kenneth Gergen's speculation that 'lives are constructed around pervading literary figures or tropes' (Gergen 1986: 3) is an instance of his more general claim 'that scientific theory is governed in substantial degree by what are essentially aesthetic forms' (Gergen and Gergen 1986: 20).

Note that two claims are being made here: that individuals use stories to make sense of events, and that so, in the same vein, do social scientists. The narrativity of social scientific discourse, then, takes its legitimation from storytelling in everyday life. This in turn warrants the application of narrative theory to social scientific discourse. However, discovering the structures of narrative in discourses about the self must be distinguished from imputing narrative structures to discourses about the self. The first is an ethnographic enterprise; the second an analytic one. To regard social scientific discourse as narrative is to treat it under a metaphor, in the same way that it is to regard cultures as texts or minds as cybernetic systems or reality as mechanistic. Analysts' uses of the devices of narrative to structure their approaches to discourses about the self render problematic the conventions that narrativity imports into the social sciences. My concern as a narratologist is to distinguish these approaches from persons' presentations of self in narrative modes. It is crucial to return to the social disposition of stories, to their linguistic coding, their contexts of use, to see how they illuminate the way individuals construe their lives. Doing so lays the groundwork for pursuing enquiries into narrativity as an interpretive structure for social scientific discourses about the self.

This is an analysis of a medical examination in the course of which the patient tells three stories in which he appears as a character. The links and splits between the realm of medicine and the realm of narrative illuminate the nature of narrative, the nature of medicine, and the nature of the self.

Medical examinations are divided into two parts: the history-taking, and the physical examination. These internal constituents of the realm of medicine are bounded by greetings and farewells which mark the transition between the realm of the ordinary and the realm of medicine. The shift from greetings, in which the physician emerges from his professional role to speak to his patient as a social person, to history-taking, in which the physician elicits information from the patient about his body, is the first move towards dislodging the self from the body. The patient's social person is set aside to attend to his physical body.

The patient on this occasion is Dr Michael Malinowski, a seventy-eight-year-old professor of Jewish history and literature. He has come to University Hospital to consult an internist, Dr Mathew Silverberg. Dr Silverberg shakes hands with the professor and his son in the waiting room, escorts them to his office, and there begins to take the patient's history. The shift from the waiting room to the office reifies the transition between realms. The history-taking reorientates the person's attitude towards his body in two respects: it invites him to regard his body from outside instead of from inside, and it invites him to see it in parts instead of as a whole. Dr Silverberg's enquiries direct the patient to attend to his body as an object with its own vicissitudes which he recounts with the detachment of an outsider. In so doing, Dr Malinowski suffers a slight estrangement from his own body. In making these enquiries, Dr Silverberg asks about the parts of the body separately, disarticulating it into segments. So Dr Malinowski's body undergoes a fragmentation. Since the self is felt to inhere in the body as a whole from the inside, these shifts of perspective tend to separate the self from the body. It is against the thrust of this ongoing estrangement and fragmentation that the professor sets his first story, the story of the liberation. Dr Silverberg has shifted from general enquiries about the whole body – height, weight, age, health – to specific enquiries about the eyes, the throat and the blood. He continues:

Story 1
The liberation
    Dr S: Have you ever had any problems with your heart?
    Dr M: No.
    Dr S: No heart attacks?
    Dr M: Pardon me?
    Dr S: Heart attacks?
    Dr M: No.
    Dr S: No pain in the chest?
    Dr M: No pain in the chest.
    Dr S: I
            noticed that =
    Dr M: I am a graduate from Auschwitz.
    Dr S: I know— I heard already =
    Dr M: Yeah.
            I went there when— I tell Dr Young about this
            and
            after Auschwitz
            I went through a lot of— I lost this
    Dr S: Umhm.
    Dr M: top finger there
            and
            I was in a—
            after the liberation we were under supervision of
            American doctors.
    Dr S: Yeah?
    Dr M: American doctors.

Dr S: Right.
Dr M: And it uh
        I was sick of course after two years in Auschwitz I was
            quite uh uh exhausted.
        And later I went through
        medical examination
        in the American Consul
        in Munich
Dr S: Yeah?
Dr M: and I came to the United States.
Dr S: Right?
Dr M: In nineteen hundred forty-seven.
        Nineteen forty-six—
        about nineteen forty-seven.
        One day—
        I lived on Fairfield Avenue
        I started to spit
        blood.
Dr S: Right?
Dr M: Yeah?
        And I called the doctor
        and he found that something here ((*gestures to his chest*))
Dr S: Tuberculosis?
Dr M: Somethin— yeah.
        And I was in the Deborah
        Sanitorium for a year.
Dr S: In nineteen forty-seven.
Dr M·   I would say forty-seven and about
        month of forty-eight.
            . . .
Dr S: Back
        to your heart.

The story conjures up a *taleworld*, the realm of Auschwitz, which is juxtaposed to the ongoing history-taking. The preface, 'I am a graduate from Auschwitz', opens onto the other realm. Prefaces are a conventional way of eliciting permission to take an extended turn at talk in order to tell a story (Sacks 1970: II: 10). In response to what he perceives as a divagation from the realm of medicine, Dr Silverberg says, 'I know – I heard already.' Having heard a story is grounds for refusing permission to tell it again (Goffman 1974: 508). Dr Malinowski persists in spite of this refusal, thus overriding one of the devices available to physicians for controlling the course of an examination, namely, a relevancy rule: that the discourse stay within the realm of medicine. To insert the realm of narrative into the realm of medicine, the professor initially breaks its frame. But in so doing, he substitutes another relevancy rule: topical continuity. Like the history-taking, the *taleworld* focuses on a part of the body, the chest. It is this part of the body that the professor uses to produce topical continuity between the history-taking and the story.

However, it is not the chest but the heart on which the physician is focusing. When he returns talk to the realm of medicine with the remark, 'Back to your heart', he is at the same time protesting the irrelevance of the excursion. As is apparent from this, the rule for topical continuity, the selection of a next discourse event which shares at least one element with a previous discourse event, permits trivial connections between discourses and, by extension, between realms. But there is a deeper continuity here. Both the realm of Auschwitz and the realm of medicine address the body.

In the realm of medicine, the dismantling of the body continues with Dr Silverberg's enquiries about the heart, breath, ankles and back; he recurs to whole body concerns with enquiries about allergies, habits and relatives; then he goes on to segment the body into the skin, head, eyes again, nose, throat again, excretory organs, stomach again, muscles, bones and joints. Into this discourse, the professor inserts his second story, the story of the torture. This story is also about a part of the body, the finger, and so again maintains a parallel with the realm in which it is embedded, although not the strict tie of topical continuity. Having created an enclosure in medical discourse for the Auschwitz stories earlier on, Dr Malinowski now feels entitled to extend or elaborate that Taleworld (see Young, 1987, pp. 80–99). This story is tied not to the discourse that preceded it but to the previous story in which he mentions his finger. As if in acknowledgement of the establishment of this enclosure, Dr Malinowski's preface, 'I was not sick except this finger', elicits an invitation from Dr Silverberg to tell the story: 'What happened to that finger.' The Taleworld is becoming a realm of its own.

Story 2
The torture

Dr M: No.
       I don't know.
       I tell you— I told you Dr ((*to me*)) I don't—
       during the twenty-three months in Auschwitz
Dr S: Yeah?
Dr M: I was not sick except this finger.
Dr S: What happened to that finger?
Dr M: I wa—
       I tell Dr Young
       I was sitting
       ((*coughs*)) you have something to drink
Dr S: Yeah.
       I have for you.
Dr M: Yeah.
       I was sitting at the press—
       the machine
       I don't know how to say in English
       [— a machine or]
Dr S: [I understand.]
Dr M: Anyway I had to put in this was
       iron

and I had to put in— in here with the right hand to put
    this which made a hole or whatever it did.
Dr S: Made a hole in your finger.
Dr M: No.
    Made a hole here. ((*in the piece of iron*))
    My finger got it.
    And behind me was an SS man.
    And he stood behind me
    and at one moment he pushed me.
    Just— this was a— a— a—
    daily sport.
    And instead to put the iron in I put my finger in.
    /
    But otherwise I wasn't sick.

The shift from taking the history to giving the physical examination involves moving to another space, the examining room, which is an even more narrowly medical realm. Dr Silverberg closes the history-taking by saying:

Dr S: I would like to examine you.
Dr M: For this I came.
Dr S: I will lead you into the examining room?
Dr M: All right.
Dr S: I would like you to
    take everything off
    Down to your undershorts.
    And have a seat on the table.

Dr Silverberg then takes his patient to the examining room down the hall and leaves him to take off his clothes. Clothes are the insignia of the social self. Their removal separates the body from its social accoutrements. This reduction of the social self along with the enhancement of the medical realm completes the dislodgement of the self. What remains is the dispirited, unpersoned, or dehumanized body.

During the physical examination, the body is handled as an object. When Dr Silverberg returns he finds the professor lying on the examining table in old-fashioned long white shorts that button at the top, with his arms folded across his chest. They speak to each other and then Dr Silverberg comes up to the examining table, picks the patient's right hand up off his chest, holds it in his right hand, and feels the pulse with his left fingertips. Here is the inversion of the initial handshake which enacted a symmetry between social selves; the physician touches the patient's hand as if it were inanimate. The examination is the rendering in a physical medium of the estrangement of the self and the fragmentation of the body. The external perspective is substituted for the internal perspective and the whole is disarticulated into parts. Of course, there is still talk – questions, comments, instructions; but now such remarks are inserted into interstices between the acts, the investigations, the physical manipulations that structure the examination.

Henceforth, for the course of the physical examination, the patient's body is touched, lifted, probed, burned, bent, tapped, disarranged and recomposed by the physician. It is here that the absence of the self from the body can be intended as a protection: the social self is thereby preserved from the trespasses of the examination. These are committed only on an object.

The physical examination proceeds from the hands up the arms; then Dr Silverberg sits the patient up, looks at his head, ears, eyes, nose, mouth, throat, back, chest and heart; then he lays the patient back down on the table, tucks down the top of his shorts, examines his genitals, and folds the shorts back together at the top. He continues down the legs to the feet, then sits him up again and returns to the arms and hands. At this point, Dr Silverberg asks the patient to touch his nose with the tips of his fingers and as he does so the patient alludes to a bump on his skull: 'I have to tell you how I got that.' And the physician responds, 'How.' Despite this invitation, Dr Malinowski appears uncertain about the propriety of inserting a story into this realm.

Story 3
The capture

    Dr M: I have to tell you how I got that. ((*the bump*))
    Dr S: How.
    Dr M: Should I talk here?
    Dr S: You
    Dr M: Can I talk here?
    Dr S: Sure.
               /
    Dr M: You already know. ((*to me*))
               When I (s— try) to go the border
               between Poland and Germany
    Dr S: Yeah?
    Dr M: I wanted to escape
               to the border over Switzerland=
    Dr S: Umhm.
    Dr M: as a Gentile.
    Dr S: Yeah?
    Dr M: When they caught me
               they wanted investigation.
               /
    Dr S: That it?
    Dr M: (At)
               the table was (sitting) near me
               and (his arm) was extending behind me
               with— how the police ha— how do you call it.
               A police club?
    Dr S: Nightstick.
    Dr M: Nightstick.
    Dr S: Umhm.
    Dr M: And they—

> I had to count
> and they hit me twenty
> times over the head.
> And er— he told me zählen
> zähle means you count.
> And after the war—
> after the liberation shortly about two three days
> American Jewish doctors came
> they (examined us)
> and he told me
> that I have
> a nerve splint here?

Dr S: Yeah.

Dr M: And this made me be deaf.

The physician then examines the patient's ears, and finally his prostate and rectum. So here, suspended between the genital and rectal examinations, the two procedures towards which the displacement of the self from the body are primarily orientated, is the professor's third and last story. Once again, the story is about a part of the body, the ears, which maintains a continuity with the realm of medicine. But it is also about another part of the body, the genitals. As he mentions, Dr Malinowski has already told me this story when I talked to him in the waiting room to get his permission to observe and tape-record his examination. He told me that he and a friend had decided, boldly, to cross the border out of Poland into Germany and work their way across Germany to the Swiss border. They carried forged papers. He himself got through the border and was already on the other side when something about his friend aroused the border guard's suspicion and they called him back. To check their suspicions, the guards pulled down his pants and exposed his genitals. Jews were circumcised. This story is concealed as a subtext directed to me within a text directed to the physician. On this understanding, the positioning of the story between the genital and rectal examinations has a tighter topical continuity than is apparent on the surface.

Stories are sealed off from the occasions on which they occur – here, the realm of medicine – as events of a different ontological status. For that reason they can be used to reinsert into that realm an alternate reality in which the patient can reappear in his own person without disrupting the ontological conditions of the realm of medicine. Stories about the realm in which he appears, the world of Auschwitz, might be supposed to be inherently theatrical, on the order of high tragedy. But the boundary between realms insulates medicine in some measure from the tragic passion. The apertures along the boundary through which the realms are connected are here restricted to parts of the body. In telling these stories, Michael Malinowski is not intending to play on his hearers' emotions. He is rather reconstituting for them the ontological conditions of his world and, having done so, inserting himself into that realm as a character. Besides creating a separate reality, telling stories during a medical examination creates a continuity between the two realms which converts the ontological conditions of the realm of medicine precisely along the dimensions of the body.

The stories are tokens of the man, talismans of the salient and defining history which has shaped him. They are not, on that account, unique to this occasion, but are invoked as touchstones of his presence (as they were, for instance, for me when we talked before the examination). They present a person whose life is wrought around an event of existential proportions. Auschwitz was a life-pivoting, world-splitting event: time is reckoned before-Auschwitz and after-Auschwitz; space is divided by it. Not only has he lost a country, a language and a childhood, but he has also lost a life-form. Before Auschwitz, he had a wife and child in Poland; the son who has brought him today is the only child of a second marriage made in the USA after the war. Dr Malinowski mentions once that he had two sisters: one perished, the other died a few years ago of cancer.

The sequential order of events in a story replicates the temporal unfolding of events in the realm it represents (Labov 1972: 359–60; [see Chapter 14]). This replication is supposed by social scientists to extend to the sets of stories which are strung together to make a life history. In this instance, the sequential order in which these stories are told does not replicate the temporal order in which the events they recount occurred. He tells about the liberation first, then the torture, and finally the capture. There are of course clear contextual reasons for this which have been detailed here in terms of topical continuity. But I would like to suggest a deeper reason for their array. These stories cluster around Michael Malinowski's sense of self. Auschwitz provides what I would like to call centration: life is anchored here, everything else unfolds around this. The set of stories that make up the Auschwitz experience could be told in any order. There is an implication here for the use of narrativity in the social sciences. In insisting either on the notion that temporally ordered events are presented sequentially in stories or on re-ordering stories to present them so, social scientists have misunderstood the shape of experience: a life is not always grasped as a linear pattern. Serious attention to narrativity in stories of the self will not force the sense of self into the pattern of narrative, but will deploy narrative to discover the sense of self.

In so presenting the man and reconstituting the ontological conditions of his world, these stories attain the status of moral fables and lend the medical examination a delineation which renders the etiquette of touch an ethical condition. Not that the stories are warnings to the physician against similar transgressions. Rather, in the existential context of these stories, what might otherwise be seen as indignities to the body are transmuted into honours: the physician is a man whose touch preserves just those proprieties of the body that are infringed at Auschwitz.

The body in the *taleworld* is the analogue of the body in the realm of the examination, connected to it part for part, but inverted. The stories spin out existential situations in which the self is constrained to the body. In the first story, 'The liberation', the part of the body is the chest and the mode of insertion of the self in the body is sickness. The self cannot transcend its absorption in its bodily discomforts: its sensibilities are sealed in its skin. In the second story, 'The torture', the part of the body is the finger and the mode of insertion of the self in the body is pain. The self is jolted into the body, its sensibilities concentrated in its minutest part, the tip of a finger. In the third story, 'The capture', the parts of the body are the head and the genitals, and the mode of insertion is humiliation.

Here the body is emblematic of the man, literally inscribed with his identity. Its degradations are his.

The phenomenological cast of the *taleworld* is set against the phenomenological cast of the realm of the examination in which the self is extricated from the body. The medical history of the tuberculosis, the severed fingertip, the deafness, which could be detached, is instead enfolded in the personal history of the concentration camp and recounted as a story. So Auschwitz is invoked not as the cause of these dissolutions of the flesh, but as the frame in terms of which we are to understand what has befallen the body and, it transpires, the frame in terms of which we are to understand what has become of the man. To see the fact that both the realm of medicine and the realm of narrative are about the body as topical continuity is a trivial rendering. The stories are transforms of the ontological problem that is central to the examination: the fragile, stubborn, precarious, insistent insertion of a self in the body.

Transcription conventions

Line-ends	Pauses
From Tedlock, 1978:	
=	Absence of obligatory end-pause
/	One turn pause
Capital letters	Start of utterance
.	Down intonation at end of utterance
?	Up intonation at end of utterance
—	Correction phenomena
( )	Doubtful hearings
(( ))	Editorial comments
[[	Simultaneous speech
[ ]	Extent of simultaneity

Adapted by Malcah Yeager from Schenkein, 1972:

. . .	Elisions

Initials before turns are abbreviations of speakers
English spelling indicates English speaking

Note

This paper was first given in 1985 at the American Folklore Society Meetings in Cincinnati, Ohio. The present version was clarified by a critical reading by Kenneth Gergen. The data were collected in 1984 during my research on the phenomenology of the body in medicine.

1   This sense of dehumanization is well attested to in both popular and social scientific literature. Elliot Mishler locates dehumanization in the discourse of medicine, where he describes it as the conflict between the voice of medicine, which is understood to dominate during medical examinations, and the voice of the life-world, which is suppressed in a way, he argues, that leads to an 'objectification of the patient, to a

stripping away of the life-world contexts of patient problems' (Mishler 1984: 128). To protect confidentiality, the names of the patient, the physician and the hospital are fictitious.

References

Barthes, R. (1977) *Roland Barthes*, New York: Hill and Way.

Berger, J. and Mohr, J. (1976) *A Fortunate Man: The Story of a Country Doctor*, New York: Pantheon.

Gergen, K. (1986) *If Persons are Texts*, New Brunswick, NJ: Rutgers University Press.

—— and Gergen, M. (1983) 'Narratives of the self', in Sarbin, T.R. and Scheibe, K.E. (eds) *Studies in Social identity*, New York: Praeger.

—— and —— (1986) 'Narrative form and the construction of psychological theory', unpublished paper, Swarthmore College/Pennsylvania State University.

Goffman, E. (1959) *The Presentation of Self in Everyday Life*, New York: Doubleday.

—— (1974) *Frame Analysis*, New York: Harper & Row.

Labov, W. (1972) 'The transformation of experience in narrative syntax', in *Language in the Inner City*, Philadelphia, PA: University of Pennsylvania Press.

Mishler, E.G. (1984) *The Discourse of Medicine: Dialectics of Medical Interviews*, Norwood, NJ: Ablex.

Natanson, M. (1970) *The Journeying Self: A Study in Philosophy and Social Role*, Reading, MA: Addison Wesley.

Sacks, H. (1968) Unpublished lecture notes, University of California, Irvine, 17 April 1968.

—— (1970) Unpublished lecture notes, University of California, Irvine, 17 April 1970.

Schenkein, J. (1972) *Foundations in Sociolinguistics*, Philadelphia, PA: University of Pennsylvania Press.

Schutz, A. (1967) *On Phenomenology and Social Relations*, Chicago and London: University of Chicago Press.

Tedlock, D. (1978) *Finding the Center: Narrative Poetry of the Zuni Indians*, Lincoln and London: University of Nebraska Press.

Young, K. (1982) 'Edgework: frame and boundary in the phenomenology of narrative communication', *Semiotica* 41(1.4): 277–315.

—— (1987) *Taleworlds and Storyrealms: The Phenomenology of Narrative*, Dordrecht: Martinus Nijhoff.

Chapter 29

Deborah Cameron

PERFORMING GENDER IDENTITY: YOUNG MEN'S TALK AND THE CONSTRUCTION OF HETEROSEXUAL MASCULINITY

Introduction

IN 1990, A 21-YEAR-OLD STUDENT in a language and gender class I was teaching at a college in the southern USA tape-recorded a sequence of casual conversation among five men; himself and four friends. This young man, whom I will call 'Danny',[1] had decided to investigate whether the informal talk of male friends would bear out generalizations about 'men's talk' that are often encountered in discussions of gender differences in conversational style – for example that it is competitive, hierarchically organized, centres on 'impersonal' topics and the exchange of information, and foregrounds speech genres such as joking, trading insults and sports statistics [cf. Holmes, Chapter 23].

Danny reported that the stereotype of all-male interaction was borne out by the data he recorded. He gave his paper the title 'Wine, women, and sports'. Yet although I could agree that the data did contain the stereotypical features he reported, the more I looked at it, the more I saw other things in it too. Danny's analysis was not inaccurate, his conclusions were not unwarranted, but his description of the data was (in both senses) *partial*: it was shaped by expectations that caused some things to leap out of the record as 'significant', while other things went unremarked.

I am interested in the possibility that Danny's selective reading of his data was not just the understandable error of an inexperienced analyst. Analysis is never done without preconceptions, we can never be absolutely non-selective in our observations, and where the object of observation and analysis has to do with gender it is extraordinarily difficult to subdue certain expectations.

Source: Deborah Cameron, 'Performing gender identity: young men's talk and the construction of heterosexual identity', in Sally Johnson and Ulrike Hanna Meinhof (eds) *Language and Masculinity*, Oxford: Blackwell, 1997, 47–64.

One might speculate, for example, on why the vignettes of 'typical' masculine and feminine behaviour presented in popular books like Deborah Tannen's *You Just Don't Understand* (1990) are so often apprehended as immediately *recognizable*.[2] Is it because we have actually witnessed these scenarios occurring in real life, or is it because we can so readily supply the cultural script that makes them meaningful and 'typical'? One argument for the latter possibility is that if you *reverse* the genders in Tannen's anecdotes, it is still possible to supply a script which makes sense of the alleged gender difference. For example, Tannen remarks on men's reluctance to ask for directions while driving, and attributes it to men's greater concern for status (asking for help suggests helplessness). But if, as an experiment, you tell people it is women rather than men who are more reluctant to ask for directions, they will have no difficulty coming up with a different and equally plausible explanation – for instance that the reluctance reflects a typically feminine desire to avoid imposing on others, or perhaps a well-founded fear of stopping to talk to strangers.[3]

What this suggests is that the behaviour of men and women, whatever its substance may happen to be in any specific instance, is invariably read through a more general discourse on gender difference itself. That discourse is subsequently invoked to *explain* the pattern of gender differentiation in people's behaviour; whereas it might be more enlightening to say the discourse *constructs* the differentiation, makes it visible *as* differentiation.

I want to propose that conversationalists themselves often do the same thing I have just suggested analysts do. Analysts construct stories about other people's behaviour, with a view to making it exemplify certain patterns of gender difference; conversationalists construct stories about themselves and others, with a view to performing certain kinds of gender identity.

Identity and performativity

In 1990, the philosopher Judith Butler published an influential book called *Gender Trouble: Feminism and the Subversion of Identity*. Butler's essay is a postmodernist reconceptualization of gender, and it makes use of a concept familiar to linguists and discourse analysts from speech-act theory: *performativity*. For Butler, gender is *performative* – in her suggestive phrase 'constituting the identity it is purported to be'. Just as J.L. Austin [Chapter 2] maintained that illocutions like 'I promise' do not describe a pre-existing state of affairs but actually bring one into being, so Butler claims that 'feminine' and 'masculine' are not what we are, nor traits we *have*, but effects we produce by way of particular things we *do*: 'Gender is the repeated stylization of the body, a set of repeated acts within a rigid regulatory frame which congeal over time to produce the appearance of substance, of a "natural" kind of being' (p. 33).

This extends the traditional feminist account whereby gender is socially constructed rather than 'natural;', famously expressed in Simone de Beauvoir's dictum that 'one is not born, but rather becomes a woman'. Butler is saying that 'becoming a woman' (or a man) is not something you accomplish once and for all at an early stage of life. Gender has constantly to be reaffirmed and publicly displayed by repeatedly performing particular acts in accordance with the cultural norms (themselves historically and socially constructed, and consequently variable) which define 'masculinity' and 'femininity'.

This 'peformative' model sheds an interesting light on the phenomenon of gendered *speech*. Speech too is a 'repeated stylization of the body'; the 'masculine' and 'feminine' styles of talking identified by researchers might be thought of as the 'congealed' result of repeated acts by social actors who are striving to constitute themselves as 'proper' men and women. Whereas sociolinguistics traditionally assumes that people talk the way they do because of who they (already) are, the postmodernist approach suggests that people are who they are because of (among other things) the way they talk. This shifts the focus away from a simple cataloguing of differences between men and women to a subtler and more complex inquiry into how people use linguistic resources to produce gender differentiation. It also obliges us to attend to the 'rigid regulatory frame' within which people must make their choices – the norms that define what kinds of language are possible, intelligible and appropriate resources for performing masculinity or femininity.

A further advantage of this approach is that it acknowledges the instability and variability of gender identities, and therefore of the behaviour in which those identities are performed. While Judith Butler rightly insists that gender is regulated and policed by rather rigid social norms, she does not reduce men and women to automata, programmed by their early socialization to repeat forever the appropriate gendered behaviour, but treats them as conscious agents who may – albeit often at some social cost – engage in acts of transgression, subversion and resistance. As active producers rather than passive reproducers of gendered behaviour, men and women may use their awareness of the gendered meanings that attach to particular ways of speaking and acting to produce a variety of effects. This is important, because few, if any, analysts of data on men's and women's speech would maintain that the differences are as clear-cut and invariant as one might gather from such oft-cited dichotomies as 'competitive/cooperative' and 'report talk/rapport talk'. People *do* perform gender differently in different contexts, and do sometimes behave in ways we would normally associate with the 'other' gender. The conversation to which we now turn is a notable case in point.

The conversation: wine, women, sports . . . and other men

The five men who took part in the conversation, and to whom I will give the pseudonyms Al, Bryan, Carl, Danny and Ed, were demographically a homogeneous group: white, middle-class American suburbanites aged 21, who attended the same university and belonged to the same social network on campus. This particular conversation occurred in the context of one of their commonest shared leisure activities: watching sports at home on television.

Throughout the period covered by the tape-recording there is a basketball game on screen, and participants regularly make reference to what is going on in the game. Sometimes these references are just brief interpolated comments, which do not disrupt the flow of ongoing talk on some other topic; sometimes they lead to extended discussion. At all times, however, it is a legitimate conversational move to comment on the basketball game. The student who collected the data drew attention to the status of sport as a resource for talk available to North American men of all classes and racial/ethnic groups, to strangers as well as friends, suggesting that 'sports talk' is a typically 'masculine' conversational genre in the US, something all culturally competent males know how to do.

But 'sports talk' is by no means the only kind of talk being done. The men also recount the events of their day – what classes they had and how these went; they discuss mundane details of their domestic arrangements, such as who is going to pick up groceries; there is a debate about the merits of a certain kind of wine; there are a couple of longer narratives, notably one about an incident when two men sharing a room each invited a girlfriend back without their room-mate's knowledge – and discovered this at the most embarrassing moment possible. Danny's title 'Wine, women and sports' is accurate insofar as all these subjects are discussed at some length.

When one examines the data, however, it becomes clear there is one very significant omission in Danny's title. Apart from basketball, the single most prominent theme in the recorded conversation, as measured by the amount of time devoted to it, is 'gossip': discussion of several persons not present but known to the participants, with a strong focus on critically examining these individuals' appearance, dress, social behaviour and sexual mores. Like the conversationalists themselves, the individuals under discussion are all men. Unlike the conversationalists, however, the individuals under discussion are identified as 'gay'.

The topic of 'gays' is raised by Ed, only a few seconds into the tape-recorded conversation:

> ED: Mugsy Bogues (.) my name is Lloyd Gompers I am a homo-
> sexual (.) you know what the (.) I saw the new Remnant I
> should have grabbed you know the title? Like the head thing?

'Mugsy Bogues' (the name of a basketball player) is an acknowledgement of the previous turn, which concerned the on-screen game. Ed's next comment appears off-topic, but he immediately supplies a rationale for it, explaining that he 'saw the new Remnant' – *The Remnant* being a deliberately provocative right-wing campus newspaper whose main story that week had been an attack on the 'Gay Ball', a dance sponsored by the college's Gay Society.

The next few turns are devoted to establishing a shared view of the Gay Ball and of homosexuality generally. Three of the men, Al, Bryan and Ed, are actively involved in this exchange. A typical sequence is the following:

> AL: gays=
> ED: =gays w[hy? that's what it should read [gays why?
> BRYAN: [gays]   [I know]

What is being established as 'shared' here is a view of gays as alien (that is, the group defines itself as heterosexual and puzzled by homosexuality ('gays, why?'), and also to some extent comical. Danny comments at one point, 'it's hilarious', and Ed caps the sequence discussing the Gay Ball with the witticism:

ED: the question is who wears the boutonnière and who wears the corsage, flip for it? or do they both just wear flowers coz they're fruits

It is at this point that Danny introduces the theme that will dominate the conversation for some time: gossip about individual men who are said to be gay. Referring to the only other man in his language and gender class, Danny begins

DANNY: My boy Ronnie was uh speaking up on the male perspective today (.) way too much

The section following this contribution is structured around a series of references to other 'gay' individuals known to the participants as classmates. Bryan mentions 'the most effeminate guy I've ever met' and 'that really gay guy in our Age of Revolution class'. Ed remarks that 'you have never seen more homos than we have in our class. Homos, dykes, homos, dykes, everybody is a homo or a dyke'. He then focuses on a 'fat, queer, goofy guy . . . [who's] as gay as night' [sic], and on a 'blond hair, snide little queer weird shit', who is further described as a 'butt pirate'. Some of these references, but not all, initiate an extended discussion of the individual concerned. The content of these discussions will bear closer examination.

'The antithesis of man'

One of the things I initially found most puzzling about the whole 'gays' sequence was that the group's criteria for categorizing people as gay appeared to have little to do with those people's known or suspected sexual preferences or practices. The terms 'butt pirate' and 'butt cutter' were used, but surprisingly seldom; it was unclear to me that the individuals referred to really were homosexual, and in one case where I actually knew the subject of discussion, I seriously doubted it.

Most puzzling is an exchange between Bryan and Ed about the class where 'everybody is a homo or a dyke', in which they complain that 'four homos' are continually 'hitting on' [making sexual overtures to] one of the women, described as 'the ugliest-ass bitch in the history of the world'. One might have thought that a defining feature of a 'homo' would be his lack of interest in 'hitting on' women. Yet no one seems aware of any contradiction in this exchange.

I think this is because the deviance indicated for this group by the term 'gay' is not so much *sexual* deviance as *gender* deviance. Being 'gay' means failing to measure up to the group's standards of masculinity or femininity. This is why it makes sense to call someone '*really* gay': unlike same- versus other-sex preference, conformity to gender norms can be a matter of degree. It is also why hitting on an 'ugly-ass bitch' can be classed as 'homosexual' behaviour – proper masculinity requires that the object of public sexual interest be not just female, but minimally attractive.

Applied by the group to men, 'gay' refers in particular to insufficiently masculine appearance, clothing and speech. To illustrate this I will reproduce a longer sequence of conversation about the 'really gay guy in our Age of Revolution class', which ends with Ed declaring: 'he's the antithesis of man'.

BRYAN: uh you know that really gay guy in our Age of Revolution
    class who sits in front of us? he wore shorts again, by
    the way, it's like 42 degrees out he wore shorts again
    [laughter] [Ed: That guy] it's like a speedo, he wears a
    speedo to class (.) he's got incredibly skinny legs [Ed:
    it's worse] you know=

ED: =you know
    like those shorts women volleyball players wear? it's like those (.)
    it's l[ike

BRYAN: [you know what's even more ridicu[lous? When
ED: [French cut spandex]
BRYAN: you wear those shorts and like a parka on . . .
(5 lines omitted)
BRYAN: he's either got some condition that he's got to like have
    his legs exposed at all times or else he's got really good
    legs=

ED: =he's probably he'[s like
CARL: [he really likes
BRYAN: =he
ED: =he's like at home combing his leg hairs=
CARL: his legs =
BRYAN: he doesn't have any leg hair though=   [yes and oh
ED: =he real[ly likes
ED: his legs =
AL: =very long very white and very skinny
BRYAN: those ridiculous Reeboks that are always (indeciph)
    and goofy white socks always striped=   [tube socks
ED: =that's [right
ED: he's the antithesis of man

In order to demonstrate that certain individuals are 'the antithesis of man', the group engages in a kind of conversation that might well strike us as the antithesis of 'men's talk'. It is unlike the 'wine, women, and sports' stereotype of men's talk – indeed, rather closer to the stereotype of 'women's talk' – in various ways, some obvious, and some less so.

The obvious ways in which this sequence resembles conventional notions of 'women's talk' concern its purpose and subject-matter. This is talk about people, not things, and 'rapport talk' rather than 'report talk' – the main point is clearly not to exchange information. It is 'gossip', and serves one of the most common purposes of gossip, namely affirming the solidarity of an in-group by constructing absent others as an out-group, whose behaviour is minutely examined and found wanting.

The specific subjects on which the talk dwells are conventionally 'feminine' ones: clothing and bodily appearance. The men are caught up in a contradiction: their criticism of the 'gays' centres on their unmanly interest in displaying their bodies, and the inappropriate garments they choose for this purpose (bathing costumes worn to class, shorts worn in cold weather with parkas which render the effect ludicrous, clothing which resembles the outfits of 'women volleyball players'). The implication is that real men just pull on their jeans and leave it at that. But in order to pursue this line of criticism, the conversationalists themselves must show an acute awareness of such 'unmanly' concerns as styles and materials. ('French cut spandex', 'tube socks'), what kind of clothes go together, and which men have 'good legs'. They are impelled, paradoxically, to talk about men's bodies as a way of demonstrating their own total lack of sexual interest in those bodies.

The less obvious ways in which this conversation departs from stereotypical notions of 'men's talk' concern its *formal* features. Analyses of men's and women's speech style are commonly organized around a series of global oppositions, e.g. men's talk is 'competitive', whereas women's is 'cooperative'; men talk to gain 'status', whereas women talk to forge 'intimacy' and 'connection'; men do 'report talk' and women 'rapport talk'. Analysts working with these oppositions typically identify certain formal or organizational features of talk as markers of 'competition' and 'cooperation' etc. The analyst then examines which kinds of features predominate in a set of conversational data, and how they are being used.

In the following discussion, I too will make use of the conventional oppositions as tools for describing data, but I will be trying to build up an argument that their use is problematic. The problem is not merely that the men in my data fail to fit their gender stereotype perfectly. More importantly, I think it is often the stereotype itself that underpins analytic judgements that a certain form is cooperative rather than competitive, or that people are seeking status rather than connection in their talk. As I observed about Deborah Tannen's vignettes, many instances of behaviour will support either interpretation, or both; we use the speaker's gender, and our beliefs about what sort of behaviour makes sense for members of that gender, to rule some interpretations in and others out.

Cooperation

Various scholars, notably Jennifer Coates (1989), have remarked on the 'cooperative' nature of informal talk among female friends, drawing attention to a number of linguistic features which are prominent in data on all-female groups. Some of these, like hedging and the use of epistemic modals, are signs of attention to others' face, aimed at minimizing conflict and securing agreement [cf. Holmes, Chapter 23]. Others, such as latching of turns, simultaneous speech where this is not interpreted by participants as a violation of turn-taking rights (cf. Edelsky 1981), and the repetition or recycling of lexical items and phrases across turns, are signals that a conversation is a 'joint production': that participants are building on one another's contributions so that ideas are felt to be group property rather than the property of a single speaker.

On these criteria, the conversation here must be judged as highly cooperative. For example, in the extract reproduced above, a strikingly large number of turns (around half) begin with 'you know' and/or contain the marker 'like' ('you know like those shorts women volleyball players wear?'). The functions of these items (especially 'like') in younger Americans' English are complex and multiple, and may include the cooperative, mitigating/face-protecting functions that Coates and Janet Holmes (1984) associate with hedging. Even where they are not clearly hedges, however, in this interaction they function in ways that relate to the building of group involvement and consensus. They often seem to mark information as 'given' within the group's discourse (that is, 'you know', 'like', 'X' presupposes that the addressee is indeed familiar with X); 'you know' has the kind of hearer-orientated affective function (taking others into account or inviting their agreement) which Holmes attributes to certain tag-questions; while 'like' in addition seems to function for these speakers as a marker of high involvement. It appears most frequently at moments when the interactants are, by other criteria such as intonation, pitch, loudness, speech rate, incidence of simultaneous speech, and of 'strong' or taboo language, noticeably excited, such as the following:

> ED: he's I mean he **like** a real artsy fartsy fag he's **like** (indeciph)
>   he's so gay he's got this **like** really high voice and wire rim
>   glasses and he sits next to the ugliest-ass bitch in the history
>   of the world
> ED: [and
> BRYAN: [and they're all hitting on her too, **like** four
> ED: [I know it's **like** four homos hitting on her
> BRYAN: guys [hitting on her

It is also noticeable throughout the long extract reproduced earlier how much latching and simultaneous speech there is, as compared to other forms of turn transition involving either short or long pauses and gaps, or interruptions which silence the interruptee. Latching – turn transition without pause or overlap – is often taken as a mark of cooperation because in order to latch a turn so precisely onto the preceding turn, the speaker has to attend closely to others' contributions.

The last part of the reproduced extract, discussing the 'really gay' guy's legs, is an excellent example of jointly produced discourse, as the speakers cooperate to build a detailed picture of the legs and what is worn on them, a picture which overall could not be attributed to any single speaker. This sequence contains many instances of latching, repetition of one speaker's words by another speaker (Ed recycles Carl's whole turn, 'he really likes his legs', with added emphasis), and it also contains something that is relatively rare in the conversation as a whole, repeated tokens of hearer support like 'yes' and 'that's right'.[4]

There are, then, points of resemblance worth remarking on between these men's talk and similar talk among women as reported by previous studies. The question does arise, however, whether this male conversation has the other important hallmark of women's gossip, namely an egalitarian or non-hierarchical organization of the floor.

Competition

In purely quantitative terms, this conversation cannot be said to be egalitarian. The extracts reproduced so far are representative of the whole insofar as they show Ed and Bryan as the dominant speakers, while Al and Carl contribute fewer and shorter turns (Danny is variable; there are sequences where he contributes very little, but when he talks he often contributes turns as long as Ed's and Bryan's, and he also initiates topics). Evidence thus exists to support an argument that there is a hierarchy in this conversation, and there is competition, particularly between the two dominant speakers, Bryan and Ed (and to a lesser extent Ed and Danny). Let us pursue this by looking more closely at Ed's behaviour.

Ed introduces the topic of homosexuality, and initially attempts to keep 'owner-ship' of it. He cuts off Danny's first remark on the subject with a reference to *The Remnant*: 'what was the article? cause you know they bashed them they were like'. At this point Danny interrupts: it is clearly an interruption because in this context the preferred interpretation of 'like' is quotative – Ed is about to repeat what the gay-bashing article in *The Remnant* said. In addition to interrupting so that Ed falls silent, Danny contradicts Ed, saying 'they didn't actually (.) cut into them big'. A little later on during the discussion of the Gay Ball, Ed makes use of a common competitive strategy, the joke or witty remark which 'caps' other contri-butions (the 'flowers and fruits' joke quoted above). This, however, elicits no laughter, no matching jokes and indeed no take-up of any kind. It is followed by a pause and a change of direction if not of subject, as Danny begins the gossip that will dominate talk for several minutes.

This immediately elicits a matching contribution from Bryan. As he and Danny talk, Ed makes two unsuccessful attempts to regain the floor. One, where he utters the prefatory remark 'I'm gonna be very honest', is simply ignored. His second strategy is to ask (about the person Bryan and Danny are discussing) 'what's this guy's last name?'. First Bryan asks him to repeat the question, then Danny replies 'I don't know what the hell it is'.

A similar pattern is seen in the long extract reproduced above, where Ed makes two attempts to interrupt Bryan's first turn ('That guy' and 'it's worse'), neither of which succeeds. He gets the floor eventually by using the 'you know, like' strategy. And from that point, Ed does orient more to the norms of joint produc-tion; he overlaps others to produce simultaneous speech but does not interrupt; he produces more latched turns, recyclings and support tokens.

So far I have been arguing that even if the speakers, or some of them, compete, they are basically engaged in a collaborative and solidary enterprise (reinforcing the bonds within the group by denigrating people outside it), an activity in which all speakers participate, even if some are more active than others. Therefore I have drawn attention to the presence of 'cooperative' features, and have argued that more extreme forms of hierarchical and competitive behaviour are not rewarded by the group. I could, indeed, have argued that by the end, Ed and Bryan are not so much 'competing' – after all, their contributions are not antagonistic to one another but tend to reinforce one another – as engaging in a version of the 'joint production of discourse'.

Yet the data might also support a different analysis in which Ed and Bryan are simply *using* the collaborative enterprise of putting down gay men as an occasion to engage in verbal duelling where points are scored – against fellow group members rather than against the absent gay men – by dominating the floor and coming up with more and more extravagant put-downs. In this alternative analysis, Ed does not so much modify his behaviour as 'lose' his duel with Bryan. 'Joint production' or 'verbal duelling' – how do we decide?

Deconstructing oppositions

One response to the problem of competing interpretations raised above might be that the opposition I have been working with – 'competitive' versus 'cooperative' behaviour – is inherently problematic, particularly if one is taken to exclude the other. Conversation can and usually does contain both cooperative and competitive elements: one could argue (along with Grice [Chapter 3]) that talk must by defin-ition involve a certain minimum of cooperation, and also that there will usually be some degree of competition among speakers, if not for the floor itself then for the attention or the approval of others (see also Hewitt 1997).

The global competitive/cooperative opposition also encourages the lumping together under one heading or the other of things that could in principle be distin-guished. 'Cooperation' might refer to agreement on the aims of talk, respect for other speakers' rights or support for their contributions; but there is not always perfect co-occurrence among these aspects, and the presence of any one of them need not rule out a 'competitive' element. Participants in a conversation or other speech event may compete with each other and at the same time be pursuing a shared project or common agenda (as in ritual insult sessions); they may be in severe disagreement but punctiliously observant of one another's speaking rights (as in a formal debate, say); they may be overtly supportive, and at the same time covertly hoping to score points for their supportiveness.

This last point is strangely overlooked in some discussions of women's talk. Women who pay solicitous attention to one another's face are often said to be seeking connection or good social relations *rather than* status; yet one could surely argue that attending to others' face and attending to one's own are not mutually exclusive here. The 'egalitarian' norms of female friendship groups are, like all norms, to some degree coercive: the rewards and punishments precisely concern one's status within the group (among women, however, this status is called 'popu-larity' rather than 'dominance'). A woman may gain status by displaying the correct degree of concern for others, and lose status by displaying too little concern for others and too much for herself. Arguably, it is gender-stereotyping that causes us to miss or minimize the status-seeking element in women friends' talk, and the connection-making dimension of men's.

How to do gender with language

I hope it will be clear by now that my intention in analysing male gossip is not to suggest that the young men involved have adopted a 'feminine' conversational style. On the contrary, the main theoretical point I want to make concerns the folly of making any such claim. To characterize the conversation I have been considering as 'feminine' on the basis that it bears a significant resemblance to conversa-tions among women friends would be to miss the most important point about it, that it is not only *about* masculinity, it is a sustained performance *of* masculinity. What is important in gendering talk is the 'performative gender work' the talk is doing; its role in constituting people as gendered subjects.

To put matters in these terms is not to deny that there may be an empirically observable association between a certain genre or style of speech and speakers of a particular gender. In practice this is undeniable. But we do need to ask: in virtue of what does the association hold? Can we give an account that will not be vitiated by cases where it does *not* hold? For it seems to me that conversations like the one I have analysed leave, say, Deborah Tannen's contention that men do not do 'women's talk', because they simply *do not know how*, looking lame and unconvincing. If men rarely engage in a certain kind of talk, an explanation is called for; but if they do engage in it even very occasionally, an explanation in terms of pure ignorance will not do.

I suggest the following explanation. Men and women do not live on different planets, but are members of cultures in which a large amount of discourse about gender is constantly circulating. They do not only learn, and then mechanically reproduce, ways of speaking 'appropriate' to their own sex; they learn a much broader set of gendered meanings that attach in rather complex ways to different ways of speaking, and they produce their own behaviour in the light of those meanings.

This behaviour will vary. Even the individual who is most unambiguously committed to traditional notions of gender has a range of possible gender identities to draw on. Performing masculinity or femininity 'appropriately' cannot mean giving exactly the same performance regardless of the circumstances. It may involve different strategies in mixed and single-sex company, in private and in public settings, in the various social positions (parent, lover, professional, friend) that someone might regularly occupy in the course of everyday life.

Since gender is a relational term, and the minimal requirement for 'being a man' is 'not being a woman', we may find that in many circumstances, men are under pressure to constitute themselves as masculine linguistically by avoiding forms of talk whose primary association is with women/femininity. But this is not invariant, which begs the question: under what circumstances does the contrast with women lose its salience as a constraint on men's behaviour? When can men do so-called 'feminine' talk without threatening their constitution as men? Are there cases when it might actually be to their advantage to do this?

When and why do men gossip?

Many researchers have reported that both sexes engage in gossip, since its social functions (like affirming group solidarity and serving as an unofficial conduit for information) are of universal relevance, but its cultural meaning (for us) is undeniably 'feminine'. Therefore we might expect to find most men avoiding it, or disguising it as something else, especially in mixed settings where they are concerned to mark their difference from women (see Johnson and Finlay 1997). In the conversation discussed above, however, there are no women for the men to differentiate themselves from; whereas *there is* the perceived danger that so often accompanies western male homosociality: homosexuality. Under these circumstances perhaps it becomes acceptable to transgress one gender norm ('men don't gossip, gossip is for girls') in order to affirm what in this context is a more important norm ('men in all-male groups must unambiguously display their heterosexual orientation').

In these speakers' understanding of gender, gay men, like women, provide a contrast group against whom masculinity can be defined. This principle of contrast seems to set limits on the permissibility of gossip for these young men. Although they discuss other men besides the 'gays' – professional basketball players – they could not be said to gossip about them. They talk about the players' skills and their records, not their appearance, personal lives or sexual activities. Since the men admire the basketball players, identifying *with* them rather than *against* them, such talk would border dangerously on what for them is obviously taboo: desire for other men.

Ironically, it seems likely that the despised gay men are the *only* men about whom these male friends can legitimately talk among themselves in such intimate terms without compromising the heterosexual masculinity they are so anxious to display – though in a different context, say with their girlfriends, they might be able to discuss the basketball players differently. The presence of a woman, especially a heterosexual partner, displaces the dread spectre of homosexuality, and makes other kinds of talk possible; though by the same token her presence might make certain kinds of talk that take place among men *im*possible. What counts as acceptable talk for men is a complex matter in which all kinds of contextual variables play a part.

In this context – a private conversation among male friends – it could be argued that to gossip, either about your sexual exploits with women or about the repulsiveness of gay men (these speakers do both), is not just one way, but the most appropriate way to display heterosexual masculinity. In another context (in public, or with a larger and less close-knit group of men), the same objective might well be pursued through explicitly agonistic strategies, such as yelling abuse at women or gays in the street, or exchanging sexist and homophobic jokes. *Both* strategies could be said to do performative gender work: in terms of what they do for the speakers involved, one is not more 'masculine' than the other, they simply belong to different settings in which heterosexual masculinity may (or must) be put on display.

Conclusion

I hope that my discussion of the conversation I have analysed makes the point that it is unhelpful for linguists to continue to use models of gendered speech which imply that masculinity and femininity are monolithic constructs, automatically giving rise to predictable (and utterly different) patterns of verbal interaction. At the same time, I hope it might make us think twice about the sort of analysis that implicitly seeks the meaning (and sometimes the *value*) of an interaction among men or women primarily in the style, rather than the substance, of what is said. For although, as I noted earlier in relation to Judith Butler's work, it is possible for men and women to performatively subvert or resist the prevailing codes of gender, there can surely be no convincing argument that this is what Danny and his friends are doing. Their conversation is animated by entirely traditional anxieties about being seen at all times as red-blooded heterosexual males: not women and not queers. Their skill as performers does not alter the fact that what they perform is the same old gendered script.

Transcription conventions

=	latching
[	turn onset overlaps previous turn
[ ]	turn is completely contained within another speaker's turn
?	rising intonation on utterance
(.)	short pause
(indeciph)	indecipherable speech
italics	emphatic stress on italicized item

Notes

1   Because the student concerned is one of the speakers in the conversation I analyse, and the nature of the conversation makes it desirable to conceal participants' identities (indeed, this was one of the conditions on which the data were collected and subsequently passed on to me), I will not give his real name here, but I want to acknowledge his generosity in making his recording and transcript available to me, and to thank him for a number of insights I gained by discussing the data with him as well as by reading his paper. I am also grateful to the other young men who participated. All their names, and the names of other people they mention, have been changed, and all pseudonyms used are (I hope) entirely fictitious.
2   I base this assessment of reader response on my own research with readers of Tannen's book (see Cameron 1995: Chapter 5), on non-scholarly reviews of the book, and on reader studies of popular self-help generally (e.g., Lichterman 1992; Simonds 1992).
3   I am indebted to Penelope Eckert for describing this 'thought experiment', which she has used in her own teaching (though the specific details of the example are not an exact rendition of Eckert's observations).
4   It is a rather consistent research finding that men use such minimal responses significantly less often than women, and in this respect the present data conform to expectations – there are very few minimal responses of any kind. I would argue, however, that active listenership, involvement and support are not *absent* in the talk of this group; they are marked by other means such as high levels of latching/simultaneous speech, lexical recycling and the use of *like*.

References

Butler, J. (1990) *Gender Trouble: Feminism and the Subversion of Identity*, New York: Routledge.
Cameron, D. (1995) *Verbal Hygiene*, London: Routledge.
Coates, J. (1989) 'Gossip revisited: language in all-female groups' in Coates, J. and Cameron, D. (eds) *Women in their Speech Communities*, Harlow: Longman, 94–121.

Edelsky, C. (1981) 'Who's got the floor?' *Language in Society* 10 (3): 383–422.

Hewitt, R. (1997) '"Box-out" and "Taxing"', in Johnson, S. and Meinhof, U.H. (eds) *Language and Masculinity*, Oxford: Blackwell, 27–46.

Holmes, J. (1984) 'Hedging your bets and sitting on the fence: some evidence for hedges as support structures', *Te Reo* 27: 47–62.

Johnson, S. and Finlay, F. (1997) 'Do men gossip? An analysis of football talk on television', in Johnson, S. and Meinhof, U.H. (eds) *Language and Masculinity*, Oxford: Blackwell, 130–43.

Lichterman, P. (1992) 'Self-help reading as a thin culture', *Media, Culture and Society* 14: 421–47.

Simonds, W. (1992) *Women and Self-help Culture: Reading Between the Lines*, New Brunswick, NJ: Rutgers University Press.

Tannen, D. (1990) *You Just Don't Understand: Women and Men in Conversation*, New York: Ballantine Books.

Chapter 30

Deborah Cameron

STYLING THE WORKER: GENDER AND THE COMMODIFICATION OF LANGUAGE IN THE GLOBALIZED SERVICE ECONOMY[1]

Introduction

SOCIOLINGUISTS ARE INCREASINGLY recognizing that the phenomenon of globalization, a set of far-reaching, transnational, economic, social and cultural changes, has implications for patterns of language-use, linguistic variation and change (Cope and Kalantzis 2000; Fairclough 1992; Heller 1999). One aspect of globalization on which a number of researchers have focused is the 'new work order' (Gee *et al.* 1996) in which new ('post-Fordist') ways of working make new demands on the linguistic abilities of workers. Commentators on this subject (e.g. many contributors to Cope and Kalantzis 2000; Gee *et al.* 1996; Gee 2000) place emphasis on the new forms of linguistic and other agency that workers must in principle develop to meet the demands of the new capitalism. There is also an argument, however, that new linguistic demands on workers may in practice entail new (or at least, newly intensified) forms of *control* over their linguistic behaviour, and thus a diminution of their agency as language-users.

. . .

Here I examine the imposition on one group of English-speaking customer service workers (telephone call centre operators) of a particular speech style as the norm or 'standard' for interaction on the job. As well as discussing the means used by organizations seeking to exert control over the speech of their employees, I will discuss some of the sociolinguistic characteristics of the speech style that is prescribed as a 'standard'. I will argue that its most salient features are not markers of class, region, or nationality/ethnicity, but symbolic markers of feminine gender

Source: Deborah Cameron, 'Styling the worker: gender and the commodification of language in the globalized service economy', *Journal of Sociolinguistics*, 4 (3), 2000: 323–47.

(though they are not presented explicitly as gendered, and they are prescribed to workers of both sexes). The commodification of language in contemporary service workplaces is also in some sense the commodification of a quasi-feminine service persona.

Before I proceed, my use of certain terms requires clarification. When I talk about the imposition of a *standard* or about the *standardization* of speech within an organization, this is not intended to mean 'the imposition of the lexico-grammatical norms of a standard (national/international) language', but more abstractly, the practice of making and enforcing rules for language-use with the intention of reducing optional variation in performance (Milroy and Milroy 1998). As will be seen in more detail below, the rules in question tend not to target grammatical or phonological variation (these being the prototypical targets for language standardization in the less abstract sense). They are more concerned to prescribe features of interactive discourse such as prosody and voice quality, the way in which particular speech acts should be performed, the choice of address terms/salutations and the consistent use of certain politeness formulae. In this instance standardization is not prompted by the need to communicate across regional/national boundaries (though in the case of multinational companies it may operate across them), but rather by the need to subordinate individuals to a *corporate* norm. Employees' verbal behaviour, along with other aspects of their self-presentation such as bodily appearance and dress (cf. Witz *et al.* 1998), is treated as a commodity – part of what organizations are selling to their customers, an element of their 'branding' and corporate image. The significance organizations accord to the prescribed style of speaking is evident from the degree of effort they put into its production via training, regulation and surveillance of employees' speech.

Above I used the phrase 'prescribed style of speaking', and throughout this chapter I will refer to the object/product of linguistic regulation as a 'style'. At this point it is helpful to clarify what I mean by the term *style* and how the phenomena discussed below fit into ongoing discussions of style in sociolinguistics.

Style, styling, stylization

Classically in the variationist paradigm of sociolinguistics, 'styles' were defined along an axis of formality: an increase in the formality of the situation leads to increased self-monitoring by the speaker and therefore, in the typical case, to rising frequencies of prestige variants in that speaker's output (cf. Labov 1972). Over time, however, there has been a tendency to adopt a less monodimensional view of style and of the meanings or effects produced by stylistic variation. An example of the more multidimensional approach is Allan Bell's influential theory of style as 'audience design' (Bell 1984, 1997) in which it is argued that stylistic choices are primarily motivated by the speaker's assessment of the effect certain ways of speaking will have on particular addressees. Bell's account is informed by accommodation theory (e.g. Giles and Powesland 1975): audience design commonly takes the form of convergence towards the addressee's way of speaking (for empirical examples see Bell 1984; Coupland 1984). However, Bell also notes the existence of what he calls 'initiative' (as opposed to 'responsive') styleshift, and of cases in which 'the individual speaker makes creative use of language resources often from beyond the immediate speech community' (Bell 1997: 248). An instance which has attracted attention in recent sociolinguistic research is the phenomenon of 'crossing' (Rampton 1995) – appropriating linguistic features that index an identity which is in some salient way 'other' (as with the use of variants marked as Black by speakers who are themselves white; see Bucholtz 1999; Cutler 1999). Crossing is rarely a case of convergence towards the immediate addressee (more usually it reproduces features associated with an absent reference group – not uncommonly one whose speech lacks prestige by mainstream definitions). Allan Bell, following the literary theorist Bakhtin, puts this under the heading of 'stylization' – taking on a voice which is recognizably different from one's 'normal' or 'expected' voice (Bell 1997: 248).

The creative deployment of varied linguistic resources may also be manifested in linguistic behaviour that is not crossing, but rather involves some mixing of elements from different sources. Penelope Eckert suggests: 'The construction of a style is a process of bricolage: a stylistic agent appropriates resources from a broad sociolinguistic landscape, recombining them to make a distinctive style' (1996: 3). 'Style' in Eckert's usage can be a verb as well as a noun: the 'stylistic agent' who draws on the meanings made available by linguistic variation and combines these into a distinctive way of speaking can be seen as 'styling' her/himself. Eckert's particular interest is in the self-styling undertaken by adolescents and pre-adolescents as they experiment with various possible positionings within their newly significant peer groups and social networks.

My own use of the term *style* is broadly in the spirit of the post-Labovian work cited above, but there are some significant (and interesting) differences between the styling practices I am interested in and those studied by Bell, Rampton or Eckert. Their work focuses on practices of *self*-styling, where the speaker is also what Eckert calls the 'stylistic agent', the person who makes choices about her or his own linguistic performance. In the service workplaces investigated here, by contrast, the roles of speaker and stylistic agent are separated to a significant extent. It is of course true that any actual linguistic performance must, in the final analysis, be produced by the speaker her or himself. It is also true that *some* stylistic choices remain the prerogative of individual speakers, because they involve variables that have not become objects of institutional regulatory zeal (in the call centre case for example, accent is not normally a target for institutional regulation). In general, however, service styles are designed by one set of people (managers on site or at head office, or – not uncommonly – outside consultants) to be enacted in speech by a different set of people (frontline customer-service workers). Typically a third set of people (supervisors or 'team leaders', and sometimes also 'mystery shoppers', people employed by companies to carry out spot-checks on service while posing as genuine customers) are charged with ensuring compliance through monitoring, 'coaching' (the ongoing provision of critical feedback) and appraisal of workers' linguistic performance.

A further difference takes us back to the question of 'audience design'. Corporate style designers do, of course, make stylistic choices with an audience in mind, namely the customers with whom service workers interact. In this they resemble the radio presenters discussed by Bell (1984) in his chapter on style as audience design, who are obliged to imagine their target addressees as a collectivity, and to make guesses about the preferences of those addressees. But whereas the radio presenters do their own speaking, the corporate style designers' relationship to the audience is indirect, mediated by the workers who actually talk to customers. These workers effectively have a dual audience: they speak *to* the customer, but at the same time they are also using the prescribed style for the benefit of the supervisor or manager who enforces linguistic and other norms through surveillance. Some workers I interviewed, though clear that in theory their job was to serve the customer, not their supervisor, reported that in practice they prioritized the requirements of the 'in-house' audience, whose judgements on their performance had more direct and immediate consequences. This is an intriguing case where the demands of what Bell (1997: 246–7) refers to as 'auditors' and 'overhearers' appear capable of overriding those of the actual addressee.

In sum, 'styling' in contemporary service workplaces is less a community practice, generated from the bottom up, than a prescriptive or 'verbal hygiene' practice (Cameron 1995), imposed from the top down. For this reason, and despite some points of resemblance, it is not wholly comparable either to the self-styling practices of adolescents (Cutler 1999; Eckert 1996; Rampton 1995) or to the stylistic behaviour of workers modifying their speech (whether consciously or unconsciously) to advance their own interests in business transactions (Coupland 1984; Hall 1995; Johnstone 1999). It might be considered a case of 'stylization', since it involves speakers giving a performance, the 'script' for which has been written by someone else (literally in some instances, as will be discussed further below). Yet it lacks what might be seen as a defining feature of stylized utterance, namely the quality of calling attention to itself (however subtly) *as* a performance, of pointing to some kind of separation between the speaker's self and her/his speech at that moment. Though they may vary in their ability to bring it off, service workers performing standard routines are typically instructed to aim for a 'natural' and 'authentic' performance.

. . .

What follows, then , is a description and analysis of a stylistic *ideal*, or in corporate language the 'brand': a normative construct which shapes, even if it cannot wholly determine, the behaviour of those language-users to whom it is prescribed.[2]

The data

My data were collected for a larger project (Cameron 2000) which looked at some range of service workplaces, but for the purposes of this chapter I concentrate on a single type of workplace, namely the 'call centre', an institution in which people are employed to make or take telephone calls. (The 'make or take' distinction is captured in the industry terms 'outbound' and 'inbound' to refer to call centres where employees either initiate or receive calls. The centres I looked at were exclusively 'inbound', i.e. calls were initiated by customers. Outbound call centres typically have sales rather than service as their prime function, whereas I was most interested in the provision of customer services.)

I chose to study call centres, in particular, for two reasons. First, they provide a prototypical example of a 'new' service workplace: the vast majority have existed for less than ten years, and their institutional culture has always incorporated the disciplines of globalized capitalism. Call centres as we now know them came into existence when it was recognized that advances in telephony and computing enabled customer service functions traditionally performed locally (e.g. in each branch of a bank or travel agency) to be concentrated in a single 'remote' location with access to a central computer database. Companies can cut costs by routing all customer enquiries to one point, and since its physical location is irrelevant – customers do not have to go there – it can be put where rents and labour costs are low. In addition, since call centre operators, unlike more traditional clerical workers, perform only one function, the work itself can be organized to maximize productivity. Again, this goal is pursued with the aid of technology. Many centres use an Automated Call Distribution (ACD) system which ensures that incoming calls are passed to operators as soon as they become available, meaning that at busy times operators handle calls continuously, with no more than seconds in between. The work of call centre operators is notoriously stressful, being both extremely repetitive and subject to demanding performance targets, and this is reflected in high rates of employee turnover in the industry (Carter 1998; Reardon 1996). Media coverage of call centres has been both copious and generally critical, often suggesting that they are the sweatshops of the twenty-first century (Wazir 1999).

Second, language has a special significance in call centre work. The operator's job consists of little else but language-using – talking to customers on the phone and inputting/retrieving data using a computer – and her/his professional persona must be created entirely through speech. Typically, the speech of call centre operators is subject to intensive regulation and constant surveillance. Supervisors can covertly listen in on any call (known in the industry as 'silent listening'), while in some centres every call is recorded and may become the subject of 'counselling' (a worker and a supervisor or manager listen together to examples of the worker's performance and engage in critical assessment). Call centres, then, are a good example of service work as language work, and as such they are also a particularly rich source of insight into the commodification and regulation of language on the job.

I collected data relating to seven centres located in various parts of the U.K. (central Scotland, the north of England and London). The service functions performed in these centres were: providing directory assistance to telephone subscribers, logging faults in telecommunications equipment, dealing with auto insurance claims, processing personal banking transactions, authorizing credit requests, booking rail tickets and handling enquiries for a utility (gas) company. The data at my disposal take the form of notes on observations, tapes/transcripts of interviews, and copies of written materials including employee manuals, training packs, appraisal forms and lists of criteria for assessing performance, scripts and prompt sheets for standard work routines, and memos discussing linguistic issues.

The analysis in this chapter draws most heavily on the last-mentioned of these data-types, namely the textual materials. These provide the clearest and most detailed picture of what linguistic ideal a call centre 'officially' wants its operators to aim for, what it prescribes and what it proscribes. However, it should be noted here that I was able to obtain a suitable quantity and quality of texts from only four of the seven centres in my sample; these four therefore dominate the analysis presented below (it will be obvious which they are from my attribution of extracts). Of the other three centres, one did not as yet produce detailed written specifications for linguistic performance; in the remaining two cases I was not able to procure copies of the specifications from the sources available to me (see further below).

Some supplementary information comes from a set of interviews conducted between May and December 1998 (the main purpose of interviewing was to elicit insiders' perceptions of call centre work; since that is not the focus of the present chapter, the use made of interview data here is limited). I interviewed four call centre managers, two supervisors and six operators, employed in five different centres located in central Scotland, northern England and London (these are a subset of the seven mentioned above). All interviews were conducted individually, in most cases face to face but in two cases on the phone. (All but two took place 'off-site', for reasons explained below.) Interviews were semi-structured' – I had a schedule of questions, but I encouraged informants to respond at length where they had more to say, and to introduce additional concerns. Each interview lasted at least 30 minutes.

It will be evident from the details just given that different centres I had dealings with provided different kinds and quantities of information. This reflects some problems associated with researching commercial enterprises in general and call centres in particular. In cases where I undertook observation in a call centre I did so with the co-operation of the management, but there were often restrictive conditions attached. Because of the critical media coverage I have already mentioned, I found many managers concerned about negative publicity, which led some to want to control what I saw, heard and ultimately wrote in ways that could not be acceptable to an academic researcher. Others refused certain requests (e.g. to record on-site, see also note 4) to protect the privacy of their customers. More unexpectedly, documents such as training manuals and assessment criteria were commonly defined as confidential and not to be reproduced, on the grounds that such texts constitute commercial assets from which competitors might benefit if they were in the public domain. In addition it proved difficult to interview employees in their workplaces, both because their work routines left little time for it and because of reticence engendered by the culture of surveillance.

When I became aware of these problems I resorted to approaching employees of centres where I had *not* secured any official co-operation, and speaking to them outside their workplaces, without the knowledge of their employers. This approach precluded on-site observations in the centres concerned, but it gave me access to more textual material (employees were generally not troubled by the commercial implications of letting me see their manuals) as well as more extensive and candid interview data. Even so, many of my subjects feared disciplinary sanctions if it were discovered that they had spoken to me and passed on internal documents. I have therefore left them anonymous and used generic labels (e.g. 'directory assistance centre') for the centres they work in.

Standardizing speech in call centres: scripting and styling

The institutional regime of the call centre exemplifies the hyper-rationalizing tendency that the sociologist George Ritzer (1996) has dubbed 'McDonaldization'. For Ritzer this tendency is defined by its drive to maximize four things: efficiency (the most output for the least effort), calculability (the measurement of quality in terms of quantity), predictability (as little variation as possible) and control (of workers' activities by means of technology). Since explaining how these notions apply to the specific case of the call centre is also a useful way of describing the workings of call centres to readers who may not be familiar with them, I will examine them briefly in turn.

Efficiency is maximized in call centres by designing interactional routines so that they consist of the fewest moves needed to complete a given transaction success-fully. For example, in the directory assistance centre, the standard routine for processing a request for a phone number has the 'core' moves 'which name please', 'which town', 'which address'. This reflects the fact that the software used to retrieve phone numbers needs all and only the answers to these questions (prefer-ably in the order just given) to trigger a search. It is also specified in the manual that operators must repeat back to the customer the answer s/he gives to each 'core' question. This might appear inefficient, since it doubles the number of moves made by the operator, but it is intended to reduce the risk of incorrect details being input and preventing the successful completion of the call.

Calculability is maximized by setting targets for the time taken to process calls, and judging the quality of employees' work in terms of the number of calls handled in a given period (though as we will see, this is not the only measure of their performance). Operators in the directory assistance centre, for instance, are expected to process standard enquiries in 32 seconds or less. Operators in the rail reservation centre are given a target of four minutes per transaction. The use of standardized scripts for common routines enhances calculability as well as efficiency, since the duration of a pre-scripted routine can be estimated more accurately than if there is no script. Though the customer's moves are not scripted, it has been suggested that customers dealing with employees who follow scripts are apt to 'routinize' their own behaviour in response (Leidner 1993).

Not all call centre regimes use scripting proper ('scripting' being defined here as the provision of a full specification for every word uttered by the operator.) An alternative is to provide a 'prompt sheet', which specifies what interactional moves the operator should make in what order, but does not prescribe a standard form of words. Some centres do not even go that far, providing only general guidelines for the 'staging' of a transaction, leaving the exact number of moves in each stage to the operator's discretion. Others use some mixture of the strategies just described. These options exemplify differing degrees of emphasis placed on the *predictability* of call centre interaction. Scripting maximizes predictability, and during my fieldwork I saw indications that call centres are moving increasingly in this direction, mainly because it is thought to produce efficiency gains. For instance, one centre in my sample was in the process of introducing what it called a 'standard telephone speech' (a script). While operators were informed that the intention was to improve the quality of service, a memo addressed to supervisors expressed the hope and belief that standardization would reduce call-handling times. It should not be assumed, however, that the only motive for maximizing predictability is to improve efficiency. Predictability is often presented as a virtue in itself. Thus a section of the directory assistance centre's manual asks, 'why have salutations?'. ('Salutations' is this company's term for all the polite, interpersonally-oriented formulae that operators are required to insert at various points in the standard routine, such as 'thank you', 'sorry to keep you waiting' and 'just searching for you'.) The answer given is that the use of standard formulae meets customers' expectations of 'professional' service by giving them an experience which is 'consistent every time they call'.

Finally, technological *control* over human operators is seen in various aspects of the call centre regime. Automated call distribution systems dictate the pace of work, while the software used for functions like retrieving telephone numbers, bank account details and rail timetables shapes the sequence and content of many routines. Perhaps the most striking instance of technological control in call centres, however, is hi-tech surveillance. Supervisors can see at the click of a mouse how all members of their team are occupied (in some centres operators who propose to visit the bathroom must key a special code in on their computers so their supervisor can assess whether the time they spend there is reasonable), and they can constantly monitor performance statistics (e.g. how many calls a given operator has taken during a shift and what their average duration has been). In addition, as I noted earlier, the phone system is typically set up to permit 'silent listening' by supervisors to calls in progress, and taping of calls for retrospective assessment. These surveillance practices focus more specifically on the operator's handling of the *interactional* task, rather than simply on her/his performance as measured by statistics. If a script is in use, for example, silent listening and taping will be used to monitor operators' compliance with the prescribed wording. But even when there is no script, surveillance is used to monitor various aspects of operators' verbal behaviour. Whether call-handling routines are fully scripted, partially scripted or unscripted, their performance is usually subject to detailed specifications of the manner or *style* in which the operator should interact with callers. This is the approach that I refer to as 'styling'.

Styling is used – either on its own or in combination with scripting – because specifying a standard form of words does not on its own ensure the kind and degree of standardization many service organizations, including many call centres, are trying to achieve. Scripting standardizes *what* is said, but styling is an attempt to standardize *how* it is said, addressing the many aspects of spoken interaction that are not readily represented in a written script.

. . .

From a linguist's point of view the concerns embodied in styling rules fall into two main categories. Firstly, . . . attention is given to the operator's use of her/his voice, with a particular focus on supra-segmental phenomena such as voice quality and intonation. Secondly, emphasis is placed on various aspects of the management of interactive spoken discourse. Operators may be reminded for instance to avoid gap and overlap in turn transitions, to use minimal responses frequently, to ask 'open' questions and to pause so that callers can assimilate important information. Some of these considerations (e.g. the phrasing of questions) can be incorporated into a pre-written script, but many cannot (e.g. the placement of minimal responses and turn transitions, which depends on the behaviour of the caller).

Probably the most important instruments of styling are the checklists used in many centres for purposes of assessment by supervisors, managers and 'mystery callers' (that is, outsiders employed to perform 'spot checks' by posing as real callers and then logging their assessment of the operator's performance). Here, for example, is a selection of the contents of a 12-point checklist used in the assessment of operators at the credit authorization centre in my sample (a centre, incidentally, which also scripts call routines exhaustively):

- Smiling. Does the member of staff answer the phone with a smile?
- Pitch. The depth of pitch in the staff's voice will determine the degree of sincerity and confidence associated with the message that they are giving the caller.
- Volume. Ensure staff are not shouting or hardly audible.
- Pace. Ensure the member of staff is not dragging out the sentences nor speeding through it [*sic*].
- Acknowledge. Staff can let the caller know they have understood them by making simple acknowledgement sounds, if the caller is not acknowledged in this way they will presume they have not been understood and repeat themselves.

This is hardly a sophisticated instrument of assessment (it is unclear for example what 'depth of pitch' the assessor is meant to be looking for, even if one understands what 'depth of pitch' refers to), but it does at least specify which aspects of performance operators and assessors are expected to be attentive to. (Lists like this one are typically used in both formal appraisal and more informal regular coaching of individual operators by their supervisors. They also inform the preliminary training of operators.)

Having established what I mean by 'styling' and how it is embedded in the call centre regime, I now turn to a more detailed examination of the linguistic characteristics of the preferred style. I will seek to show that the style is *gendered*, produced through a consistent and deliberate preference for ways of speaking that are symbolically coded as 'feminine' (and that in some cases are also empirically associated with women speakers).

Call centre style and 'women's language'

As is well known, . . . Robin Lakoff (1975) elaborated a notion of 'women's language' (WL), a register or, in Eckert's sense, a 'style' characterized by linguistic features such as the use of 'weak' expletives and lexical items like *charming*, *divine*, rising intonation on declaratives, tag-questions in contexts where the speaker is not checking information, etc. Subsequent empirical investigations of the 'Lakoff hypothesis' produced a copious literature, the import of which is perhaps most succinctly summarized by saying that not all women use WL and not all WL-users are women. This however did not deter scholars from advancing alternative proposals about women's style of speaking and how it differs, on average, from men's. For example, one general claim widely canvassed in the 1980s and 1990s was that women are more cooperative conversationalists and more sensitive to the face-wants of others (Coates 1996; Holmes 1995 [Chapter 23]; Tannen 1990). This difference has been invoked to explain women's use of an array of discourse features such as supportive simultaneous speech, precision-timed minimal responses and questions whose function is to show interest in or engage the participation of others, hedging and indirectness used to mitigate face-threat, and so on.

This brief excursion into the history of language and gender studies is relevant here, because it is evident that the products of the research tradition inaugurated by Lakoff have filtered steadily, though selectively, into popular consciousness. This process has produced a lay notion of 'women's language' that is an amalgam of long-established folk-beliefs, elements of the early Lakoff hypothesis, popularized accounts of more recent findings, and new, or at least reworked, stereotypes disseminated via popular psychology and self-help texts. However inaccurate it may be as an *empirical* description of the way women 'really' speak, and however unsatisfactory it may appear from the perspective of academic scholarship, this notion of 'women's language' provides a powerful *symbolic* 'meaning resource' for 'stylistic agents' to draw on. In the following discussion I will seek to show in more detail how various elements of the symbolic construct 'women's language' are appropriated and recombined in the call centre context to produce a particular service style. The discussion is based on materials (e.g. training manuals and appraisal criteria) I collected from four call centres in my sample, and it focuses on concerns that recur across those materials.

One concern that is highlighted in all the materials I collected is with the styling of the operator's *voice*. Two instructions on vocal performance are invariably given: that operators should smile — even though, obviously, they are invisible to their interlocutors — and that they should use an 'expressive' intonation. What the instruction to smile actually means is that the routine (or sometimes just part of it, e.g. the opening) should be performed with the lips in a smile posture. 'Expressive' intonation means *emotionally* expressive, and is explicitly contrasted to intonation which will be heard as monotonous or uninvolved.

Smiling

Does the member of staff answer the phone with a smile?
(credit authorization centre appraisal checklist)

Remember, smiling can be heard as well as seen
(directory assistance centre employee manual)

Have a smile in your voice and avoid sounding abrupt
(performance guidelines, auto insurance centre)

'Expressive' intonation projecting attitudes/emotional states

> Our commitment is to give the caller an impression of excitement, friendliness, helpfulness and courtesy. Your telephone manner should sound as if you have been waiting for that particular call all day. You must never sound bored on a call
>
>   (directory assistance centre employee manual)

> The objective at the beginning of a call is to demonstrate sincerity and warmth. Try to make the caller feel you are there for them . . . [avoid] a disinterested, monotonous tone to voice
>
>   (performance guidelines, auto insurance centre)

It has been argued that both smiling and using expressive intonation are symbolically feminine behaviours. In the case of smiling, nonverbal communication researchers point out that it is not simply a spontaneous expression of pleasure but often functions, especially with non-intimates, to signal deference or appeasement. In the words of Nancy Henley, the smile is 'understood as a gesture offered upward in the status hierarchy' (1986: 171). This analysis of what smiling means has in turn been linked with findings suggesting that women smile more than men and that they are more likely to return smiles than men (Henley 1986: 175–8). It has also been linked with the observation that women are routinely expected to smile, and sometimes publicly castigated by complete strangers if they do not smile. Shulamith Firestone (1970: 90) once proposed a 'smile boycott' as a form of feminist political action; in 1999 female flight attendants employed by Cathay Pacific airlines threatened to take industrial action in a dispute on pay and conditions by refusing to smile at passengers for one hour of every flight. Such actions are meaningful precisely because of the existence of strong symbolic links between smiling, femininity and subordinate status.[3]

As for expressive intonation, it is both a stereotype and in some cases an empirical finding that female speakers exploit a broader pitch range, in other words tend less to monotony. This characteristic has been used in the past to label women as over-emotional and lacking in authority, tempting women like Margaret Thatcher to deliberately reduce the pitch range they use. The fact that vocal expressiveness is valued in service-work might suggest that authority is not among the qualities workers are expected to display.

If we consider the sorts of emotional or attitudinal states operators are instructed to project through their intonation, we see references in the above examples to *warmth*, *sincerity*, *excitement*, *friendliness*, *helpfulness*, *confidence*. These are not inherently gendered qualities, but overall they produce a style of service which is strongly *affective* – that is, not just neutrally polite and efficient, but based on the expression of positive feelings towards the customer. Again, it has been argued that overt displays of positive affect, or of any emotion other than anger, are culturally coded as 'feminine' rather than 'masculine' (Gervasio and Crawford 1989).

Other recurrent styling concerns are to do with the management of interpersonal relationships through strategic choices at the level of discourse. One common instruction, for example, is to *create rapport* with callers, while another is to display *empathy* with them. In this example these (related) concerns are combined in the following, quite lengthy recommendation:

Rapport/empathy

> Creating a rapport and showing empathy is about adding the human touch to a business call relationship . . . This means treating the caller as a person, recognizing their situation and building a genuine conversation to reflect this. . . . Use language which conveys understanding of and empathy for the caller's individual situation, e.g. 'are you OK?' 'was anyone hurt?' 'that must have been very distressing for you'
>
> (performance guidelines, auto insurance centre)

Here, two main discourse strategies are suggested. One is asking questions to show concern for the caller and encourage her/him to air her/his feelings about the incident that prompted the call (in this context, a traffic accident). The other is the technique known to communication trainers as 'mirroring', which means trying to demonstrate awareness of the interlocutor's mood and reflect it back to her/him in your own verbal and nonverbal behaviour. It is, of course, a common stereotype that women are better than men at inferring others' feelings from their outward behaviour, which is a precondition for successfully displaying empathy. The association of rapport-building with women's talk appears in many sources, notably Deborah Tannen's (1990) aphorism that men do 'report talk' and women do 'rapport talk'.

Another issue that is often addressed in call centre styling materials is the use of minimal responses. Concern about this aspect of interaction might seem to be motivated primarily by the need to make operators aware of specific constraints affecting telephone talk – that is, since there are no visual cues, verbal back-channelling is necessary to reassure the caller that the operator is still present and listening actively. However, the following example shows that the writer realizes there is more to the use of minimal responses than simply keeping the channel of communication open.

Minimal responses

> Use words of acknowledgement: yes, OK, thank you, I understand, I see. . . . [avoid] disruptive, disinterested or challenging use of listening acknowledgements, and using the same listening acknowledgement throughout the call
>
> (performance guidelines, auto insurance centre)

This is a recommendation to use minimal responses *supportively*: they should not be inserted where they will disrupt interaction, connote lack of interest or disagreement. It may be recalled here that some researchers (Fishman 1983; Reid 1995) have found women not only using more minimal responses than men, but also timing them more precisely, to coincide with or immediately follow the completion of the point they are responding to. The use of delayed minimal responses, which may suggest inattention, lack of interest or disagreement, has been associated more with male speakers. Once again, what is being recommended here would seem to be gendered, matching what is believed and what in some cases has been found to be women's rather than men's behaviour.

It is not surprising that service workers should receive instructions on the subject of asking questions, since question-answer routines are characteristic of institutional talk (Drew and Heritage 1992). What is more interesting, however, is the stress placed on using questions not merely to elicit information (the function that makes questioning so central to institutional discourse), but to display interest in the customer as a person, to make the interaction a more 'genuine' dialogue, and to give the customer 'space' to speak freely and at length. This concern (facilitating extended talk) is observable in advice on the *kinds* of questions workers are told they should prefer. Typically they are advised to avoid what linguists would call 'conducive' questions, those which strongly favour a predetermined answer, and select instead the kinds of questions that encourage extended talk by the addressee. (In training materials these are usually called 'open questions' and usually equated with WH-syntax, though some materials do distinguish 'how' and 'why' questions from the rest.) According to gender researchers like Pamela Fishman (1983) and Janet Holmes (1984), using questions to facilitate talk – an 'interpersonal' rather than purely 'informational' use of language – is a strategy associated in particular with women speakers.

Asking questions

Ask questions – don't demand information!
(guidance for operators, utility company centre)

Staff must give the caller space . . . by . . . asking questions
(credit authorization appraisal checklist)

Varying the type of questions gives a rounded and interesting communication
(performance guidelines, auto insurance centre)

With the foregoing examples I hope I have shown that the ways of interacting recommended in training and appraisal materials for call centre operators bear a striking resemblance to ways of speaking that are associated, in the popular imagination and also in some instances by empirical research, with women speakers rather than men. This might prompt the question: do the style designers themselves make the connection?

In my view, the answer to this question is 'yes and no'. On one hand, there is evidence that many call centre managers regard young women, in particular, as 'naturally' suited to the work (Reardon 1996). . . .

On the other hand, organizations do not present the ideal speech style explicitly as a gendered style: women may be considered 'naturally good at that sort of thing', but the 'thing' in question is not just (tautologically) 'being women', and the same style is also expected of men. What the preferred style of communication overtly signifies is not 'femininity' but 'good customer service'. This raises the question: why should performing 'good customer service' involve so many of the same linguistic strategies as performing 'femininity'? What is the nature of the connection between the two?

To answer this question it is necessary to consider the question of symbolic meaning. In an influential paper, Elinor Ochs (1992) argued that the linguistic indexing of gender is not usually direct – in other words, there are few verbal markers whose exclusive and unambiguous meaning is 'this speaker is a woman/ a man'. More commonly gender is indexed by using language that signifies a role (e.g. 'mother') or a quality (e.g. 'modesty') which is linked in turn by cultural convention to femininity or masculinity. In a similar vein, one might suggest that the practice of styling in call centres recruits a linguistic style already convention-ally coded as 'feminine' to index the meaning 'good customer service'. What enables this connection to be made is not simply the common-sense belief 'customer service is a woman's role' (that would just beg the original question of *why* serving customers is regarded as a woman's role), but rather the congruence between the meanings and values attached to 'femininity' and those attached to 'good service'.

Some degree of congruence between the two sets of meanings may well have existed for a long time, but the connection has become more compelling as a result of recent developments in the culture of business. What is entailed by 'customer service' has been redefined as part of organizations' response to globalization. A particular philosophy of service has come to dominate organizational thinking and practice, and it is this, I will argue, that has given the meanings attached to 'women's language' new relevance and value for the service sector.

Revaluing 'women's language': customer service as emotional labour

It is frequently noted that globalization involves a shift away from industrial pro-duction. In his influential book *The Work of Nations*, former U.S. Labour secretary Robert Reich (1992) popularized the notion of two major categories of post-industrial workers, 'symbolic analysts' (a knowledge-producing elite) and 'in-person servers' (a larger and less privileged group servicing the needs of others). Of this second group, which includes call centre operators, Gee *et al.* (1996: 46–7) observe that their work 'tends to call primarily for reliability, loyalty . . . the capacity to take direction and . . . "a pleasant demeanour"'. And indeed, the issue of service workers' 'demeanour' has become increasingly salient as large numbers of organizations have adopted the philosophy known as 'customer care'. The idea is to make customers feel they are not merely being served but actively and individually 'cared for': it is believed that this close attention to each customer's needs and feelings promotes loyalty to the company and thus enhances its 'compet-itive advantage' in the market.

For service workers the upshot of all this is that they find themselves performing more and more of what sociologists of work call 'emotional labour' (Hochschild 1983) – the management of feelings. This has consequences for the language of customer service, which becomes a more 'expressive' language, a language of feeling and a language of caring. The ability, not merely to sound polite and professional but to project *positive* emotions towards customers using the resources of language and voice, is highly valued. Recall the instruction in the directory assistance centre's manual for employees, quoted above: 'your telephone manner should sound as if you have been waiting for that particular call all day' (this in relation to a service encounter lasting 32 seconds or less); or the auto insurance centre's exhortation about beginning a call, 'try to make the customer feel you are there for them'.

. . .

The point has often been made that emotion in general is discursively constructed (certainly in anglophone cultures) as a 'feminine' domain (Lutz 1990); both 'emotional expressiveness' and 'caring' are salient symbolic meanings of 'women's language'. If, as I have suggested, these are also key values in new regimes of customer care, that provides a rationale for making a 'feminine' or feminized linguistic style the norm in service contexts.

It should not be overlooked, though, that emotional labour, and indeed service work in general, is not performed only by women. Women still represent the majority of rank-and-file employees in many service workplaces (including most call centres), but the relentless rise of the service sector and the concurrent decline of manufacturing industry mean that increasingly, men are also finding employment in routine customer service positions. Talk of 'changing gender roles at work' may conjure up the familiar icon of Rosie the Riveter, but in today's reality it is more likely to mean Charlie the checkout clerk and Kevin the call centre operator. Charlie and Kevin are subject to exactly the same communicational demands and linguistic styling practices as their female colleagues; it is of interest to ask how they negotiate the expectation that they will interact with customers in what is, covertly if not overtly, a 'feminine' linguistic persona.

The male call centre operators I interviewed in the course of my research in Britain did not consider their gender to be an issue. Where they were critical of the call centre regime, the main issue, for them as for female operators, was the artificiality, inauthenticity, and in some cases extreme subservience, of the persona imposed on them by scripts and styling rules. These informants seemed to orient more to the overt meaning of the preferred style – 'good service' – than to its covertly gendered meaning. (Of course, I cannot claim that my own small group of male informants constitute a representative sample for the country as a whole.) In the USA, on the other hand, although I did no systematic fieldwork, I did meet men, and hear stories about men, who perceived the behaviour they were required to produce in customer service contexts (such as shops, restaurants and call centres) as 'feminizing' and for that reason problematic. For instance, one woman told me a story about her son's experience working for a chain of Mexican restaurants. Employees were required to send diners on their way with a scripted farewell sequence that included a cheery wave. No one liked performing this embarrassingly phony routine, but the men found the wave especially problematic, since they regarded the gesture as 'effeminate'. Eventually they solved the problem by rendering it as a quasi-salute.[4]

Although the evidence given above is anecdotal, it does suggest that some of the risks involved in adopting a prescribed service style may be different for women and men. At least some men find aspects of the style threatening to their gender and/or sexual identity. For women on the other hand a recurrent complaint concerns the risk of being exposed to sexual harassment. Here the evidence is not just anecdotal. In 1998, a group of female Safeway supermarket workers in California complained at a union conference about the company's 'superior service' programme. The friendliness, personal interest and eagerness to please that employees had to display were treated by many male customers, the workers claimed, as signs of 'romantic interest' and invitations to 'lewd behaviour' (Grimsley 1998). If one accepts the feminist argument that sexual harassment is a way of asserting power over the target rather than simply a display of erotic interest in her (sex may be the means but domination is the end), this might well remind us of another symbolic meaning attached to 'women's language': powerlessness or subservience. In the culture of customer care, the old maxim 'the customer is king' is taken to new extremes; this too may be a factor in the appropriation of WL as the preferred style for customer service.

Conclusion

In this chapter I have explored some issues relating to the regulation of spoken language used by workers in contemporary service environments. I will conclude by trying to gather the main threads of the argument, briefly taking up a few outstanding questions, and suggesting reasons why the phenomena discussed here should be of interest to students of language and society.

One theme of the analysis presented above is the linguistic consequences of globalization. I have suggested that present-day corporate verbal hygiene practices may be analysed as part of a strategic attempt by organizations to maximize their advantages in a hyper-competitive globalized economy which is increasingly dominated by the provision of services. Yet it might well be asked whether current practices have precedents in the pre-globalization era. I certainly would not wish to argue that until the late 1980s (the moment of financial deregulation which is generally taken to have inaugurated the shift to today's global economy) workers spoke exactly as they liked, without norms or constraints. Clearly, for as long as 'work' has been a distinct domain of social practice, people have developed ways of acting and speaking peculiar to that domain, undergoing within particular workplaces processes of linguistic and other acculturation. It is also evident that what I have described here can be related to much older practices such as the scripting of sales encounters (Leidner 1993) and – an example with particular relevance to the call centre case – the regulation of telephone operators' speech in the period before direct dialling.

However, I would argue that there has been significant intensification, both of the desire of organizations to control employees' language-use and of their ability to do it with some degree of effectiveness (in the case of call centres, by using hi-tech surveillance). Linguistic regulation is part of the general trend that George Ritzer (1996) has dubbed 'McDonaldization', and about which he has observed that its goal is to pre-empt any choice of means to ends by the people actually engaged in a given activity. Instead, decisions on what to do, how and when are reserved to people at the top of the organizational hierarchy. That, of course, is the very opposite of what is usually claimed about the new global economy, which is frequently said to require highly skilled, self-motivating decision-makers and problem-solvers. Research like that reported here might suggest, however, that accounts such as Ritzer's, and Gee, Hull and Lankshear's description of 'in-person servers' (quoted above) are closer to the reality of much contemporary service work.

Another field of scholarship to which the analysis of service styling is relevant is the study of institutional, and more particularly workplace, talk. The spread of 'McDonaldizing' practices in what might seem the rather unlikely domain of language-use arguably poses a challenge to what is perhaps the best-established approach to the study of talk at work, that of conversation analysis (e.g. Boden 1994; Drew and Heritage 1992). Ian Hutchby summarises the orthodox conversation analyst's position: 'Institutions do not define the kind of talk produced within them: rather participants' ways of designing their talk actually constructs the "institutionality" of such settings' (Hutchby 1999: 41). 'Interaction', say Drew and Heritage, 'is institutional insofar as participants' institutional or professional identities are somehow made relevant to the work activities in which they are engaged' (1992: 4). But while anything that goes on in talk has in the final analysis to be accomplished by the participants, in my view these formulations fail to capture the extent to which institutions like the ones discussed in this article (or more exactly, agents with authority in those institutions) *do* increasingly define the kind of talk produced in institutional contexts. Practices of scripting, styling and surveillance cannot entirely override the necessity for interaction to be locally managed, but they can and do place constraints on the freedom of participants to 'design their talk' or to choose how they will make their institutional identities 'relevant'. True, the practices discussed above were still marginal in the early 1990s when Drew and Heritage were writing, and they still have little purchase on the high-status professionals (e.g. doctors) whose interactions have always featured heavily in the literature on institutional talk. They are nevertheless increasingly common realities, which the study of talk at work must have something to say about in future.

Finally, the verbal hygiene practices which are the subject of this article are of interest for what they tell us about the relationship between language and gender. I have argued that the regulation and commodification of language in service workplaces has resulted in the valorization of a speech style whose characteristics include expressiveness, caring, empathy and sincerity – characteristics popularly associated with the speech of women (if anyone doubts this, let them consult any example of the 'Mars and Venus' genre originated by Gray 1992, whose tenets have subsequently pervaded popular culture (cf. Cameron 1999; Talbot 2000)). However, I hope it will be obvious that I do not regard the value attached to 'women's language' in service work as a cause for feminist celebration. Whether it benefits women in any way whatever is open to question; the advantage they currently enjoy over men in terms of numbers employed in the service sector may arise in part from discrimination in their favour, but it also reflects the continuing disdain of many men for service work. Though commentators have been warning for a decade that this contempt is a luxury men cannot afford – globalization is destroying alternative sources of employment for low-skilled workers – resistance is still pronounced among school-age boys, especially those from the white working class (Mahony 1998).

In time, it is possible that men will serve in equal numbers alongside women. If that happens, it raises the intriguing question whether the linguistic style I have described will become 'de-gendered', associated in the popular imagination less with the supposed dispositions of a particular social group (women), and more with a social domain in which individuals play a particular social role (customer service). I do not of course suggest that the de-gendering of a particular style would put an end to the linguistic construction of gender in any form. For as long as gender remains a salient social category, linguistic behaviour will doubtless continue to be one site for its production and reproduction. But the meaning of 'gender' is not fixed for all time, and there is no reason either to suppose that its linguistic instantiations must remain forever the same.

Globalization is changing, or has the potential to change, many of the social realities that preoccupy social scientists, among them 'class', 'ethnicity', 'nation', 'gender', 'work' and indeed 'language'. These developments are as significant for sociolinguistics as for any other social science discipline, and sociolinguists should be prepared to follow them wherever they may lead.

Notes

1   I am indebted to the editors of the *Journal of Sociolinguistics* and two anonymous reviewers for helpful comments on an earlier version of this chapter, and to audiences at the 1999 ILA and NWAVE conferences who commented on oral presentations of the material. I am grateful also to Sylvie Roy, Steve Taylor, Jack Whalen and Anne Witz for making unpublished work available to me. Last but not least, I thank the call centre operators, supervisors and managers (their names withheld at their own request) who provided me with the information and many of the insights on which this chapter is based.

2   One reason why I offer no observations on how far the actual performance of service routines matches the norms laid down for that performance is that the call centres to which I gained access would not permit me to use audio-recordings of routine transactions. This might seem curious given that many call centres record such transactions themselves for purposes of training and appraisal. In Britain, however, recording of calls is subject to conditions laid down by the telecommunications regulator Oftel, and in some cases also to agreements with trades unions about the use of recorded data. My own and others' observations (e.g. Tyler and Taylor 1997) suggest that compliance with style rules is variable, but workers are likely to display a higher degree of compliance when they assume they are being monitored – this being in most cases the default or 'safe' assumption.

3   The Cathay Pacific action was reported in *The Scotsman* (7 January 1999). The report quoted a company spokesman who described attendants' smiles as 'sincere', 'genuine' and an expression of the 'warmth and superior service' for which Asian carriers are renowned. The racial stereotyping here is overt, but covertly there is also gender

stereotyping. 'Superior service' in the past and present advertising of several Asian airlines (e.g. Singapore as well as Cathay Pacific) is invariably personified by a smiling Asian *woman*. A smiling Asian man would be a much less 'natural' and more problematic image with which to convey the desired meaning.

4   This story does not necessarily indicate a greater sensitivity about gender/sexual identity among American male workers than among their British counterparts. Rather it probably reflects the greater willingness of American businesses to prescribe this sort of behaviour. While British service cultures are changing (and arguably they are changing in the direction of 'Americanization'), routines like the one described in the anecdote would still be considered 'over the top' in the British context. In my UK-based research I came across several attempts to introduce American service customs, which had foundered on the rock of British customers' bafflement, contempt or ridicule. (One example: the stationing at the entrance to a Scottish supermarket of a 'greeter' who exhorted customers to 'enjoy your shopping experience' while handing them a basket. Both staff and customers reportedly found this innovation embarrassing and ludicrous.)

References

Bell, Allan (1984) 'Language style as audience design', *Language in Society* 13: 145–204.
—— (1997) 'Style as audience design', in Nikolas Coupland and Adam Jaworski (eds) *Sociolinguistics: A Reader and Coursebook*, London: Macmillan. 240–9.
Boden, Deirdre (1994) *The Business of Talk: Organizations in Action*, Cambridge: Polity Press.
Bucholtz, Mary (1999) 'You da man: Narrating the racial other in the production of white masculinity', *Journal of Sociolinguistics* 3: 443–60.
Cameron, Deborah (1995) *Verbal Hygiene*, London: Routledge.
—— (1999) 'Better conversations: a morality play in twelve tapes', *Feminism and Psychology* 9: 315–33.
—— (2000) *Good to Talk? Living and Working in a Communication Culture*, London: Sage Publications.
Carter, Meg (1998) 'Despite the palm trees, working in a call centre can be far from paradise', *Independent on Sunday* 17 May: 9.
Coates, Jennifer (1996) *Women Talk: Conversation between Women Friends*, Oxford: Blackwell.
Cope, Bill and Kalantzis, Mary (eds) (2000) *Multiliteracies: Literacy Learning and the Design of Social Futures*, London: Routledge.
Coupland, Nikolas (1984) 'Accommodation at work: some phonological data and their implications', *International Journal of the Sociology of Language* 46: 49–70.
Cutler, Cecilia (1999) 'Yorkville Crossing: white teens, hip hop and African American English', *Journal of Sociolinguistics* 3: 428–42.
Drew, Paul and Heritage, John (eds) (1992) *Talk at Work: Interaction in Institutional Settings*, Cambridge: Cambridge University Press.
Eckert, Penelope (1996) 'Vowels and nail polish: The emergence of linguistic style in the preadolescent heterosexual marketplace', Stanford University/Institute for Research on Learning.
Fairclough, Norman (1992) *Discourse and Social Change*, Cambridge: Polity Press.
Firestone, Shulamith (1970) *The Dialectic of Sex*, New York: Bantam.
Fishman, Pamela (1983) 'Interaction: the work women do', in Barrie Thorne, Cheris Kramarae and Nancy Henley (eds) *Language, Gender and Society*, Rowley, MA: Newbury House. 89–102.

Gee, James Paul (2000) 'The New Literacy Studies: from "socially situated" to the work of the social', in David Barton, Mary Hamilton and Roz Ivanic (eds) *Situated Literacies: Reading and Writing in Context*, London: Routledge. 180–96.

——— , Hull, Glynda and Lankshear, Colin (1996) *The New Work Order: Behind the Language of the New Capitalism*, Boulder, CO: Westview.

Gervasio, Amy and Crawford, Mary (1989) 'Social evaluations of assertiveness: a critique and speech act reformulation', *Psychology of Women Quarterly* 13: 1–25.

Giles, Howard and Powesland, Peter (1975) *Speech Style and Social Evaluation*, London: Academic Press.

Gray, John (1992) *Men are from Mars, Women are from Venus*, New York: HarperCollins.

Grimsley, Kirsten Downey (1998) 'Service with a forced smile: Safeway's courtesy campaign also elicits some frowns', *Washington Post* 18 October: A1.

Hall, Kira (1995) 'Lip service on the fantasy lines', in Kira Hall and Mary Bucholtz (eds) *Gender Articulated: Language and the Socially Constructed Self*, London: Routledge. 183–216.

Heller, Monica (1999) 'Alternative ideologies of la *francophonie*', *Journal of Sociolinguistics* 3: 336–59.

Henley, Nancy (1986) *Body Politics: Power, Sex and Nonverbal Communication*, New York: Simon & Schuster.

Hochschild, Arlie (1983) *The Managed Heart: The Commercialization of Human Feeling*, Berkeley, CA: University of California Press.

Holmes, Janet (1984) 'Hedging your bets and sitting on the fence: some evidence for tag questions as support structures', *Te Reo* 27: 47–62.

——— (1995) *Women, Men and Politeness*, London: Longman.

Hutchby, Ian (1999) 'Frame alignment and footing in the organisation of talk radio openings', *Journal of Sociolinguistics* 3: 41–63.

Johnstone, Barbara (1999) 'Uses of southern-sounding speech by contemporary Texas women', *Journal of Sociolinguistics* 3: 505–22.

Labov, William (1972) *Sociolinguistic Patterns*, Philadelphia, PA: University of Pennsylvania Press.

Lakoff, Robin (1975) *Language and Woman's Place*, New York: Harper & Row.

Leidner, Robin (1993) *Fast Food, Fast Talk: Service Work and the Routinization of Everyday Life*, Berkeley, CA: University of California Press.

Lutz, Catherine A. (1990) 'Engendered emotion: gender, power and the rhetoric of emotional control in American discourse', in Catherine A. Lutz and Lila Abu-Lughod (eds) *Language and the Politics of Emotion*, Cambridge and New York: Cambridge University Press. 69–91.

Mahony, Pat (1998) 'Girls will be girls and boys will be first', in Debbie Epstein, Janette Elwood, Valerie Hey and Janet Maw (eds) *Failing Boys: Issues in Gender and Achievement*, Buckingham: Open University Press. 37–55.

Milroy, James and Milroy, Lesley (1998) *Authority in Language*, 3rd edition, Oxford: Blackwell.

Ochs, Elinor (1992) 'Indexing gender', in Alessandro Duranti and Charles Goodwin (eds) *Rethinking Context: Language as an Interactive Phenomenon*, Cambridge: Cambridge University Press. 335–59.

Rampton, Ben (1995) *Crossing: Language and Ethnicity among Adolescents*, London: Longman.

Reardon, Geraldine (1996) *Dialling the Future? Phone Banking and Insurance*, London: Banking, Insurance and Finance Union.

Reich, Robert (1992) *The Work of Nations*, New York: Vintage.

Reid, Julie (1995) 'A study of gender differences in minimal responses', *Journal of Pragmatics* 24: 489–512.

Ritzer, George (1996) *The McDonaldization of Society: An Investigation into the Changing Character of Contemporary Social Life*, revised edition, Thousand Oaks, CA: Pine Forge Press.

Talbot, Mary (2000) ' "It's good to talk?" The undermining of feminism in a British Telecom advertisement', *Journal of Sociolinguistics* 4: 108–19.

Tannen, Deborah (1990) *You Just Don't Understand: Men and Women in Conversation*, New York: Ballantine Books.

Tyler, Melissa and Taylor, Steve (1997) 'Come fly with us: emotional labour and the commodification of difference in the airline industry', paper presented to the Annual International Labour Process Conference, University of Edinburgh.

Wazir, Burhan (1999) 'Life at the end of the line. Focus: Sweatshop Britain', *Observer* 21 November: 17.

Witz, Anne, Warhurst, Chris, Nickson, Dennis and Cullen, Anne-Marie (1998) 'Human hardware? Aesthetic labour, the labour of aesthetics and the aesthetics of organisation', paper presented to the Work, Employment and Society Conference, University of Cambridge.

Chapter 31

Deborah Tannen

NEW YORK JEWISH CONVERSATIONAL STYLE[1]

A pause in the wrong place, an intonation misunderstood, and a whole conversation went awry.

E.M. Forster, *A Passage to India*

Conversation, New York's biggest cottage industry, doesn't exist in San Francisco in the sense of sustained discourse and friendly contentiousness.

Edmund White, *States of Desire*[2]

TAKE FOR EXAMPLE, the following conversation.[3]

F: How often does your acting group work?
M: Do you mean how often we rehearse or how often we perform.⌐
F: └Both.
M: [Laughs uneasily.]
F: Why are you laughing?
M: Because of the way you said that. It was like a bullet. Is that why your marriage broke?
F: What?
M: Because of your aggressiveness.

Of the many observations that could be made based on this interchange, I would like to focus on two: the general tendency to extrapolate personality from conversational style, and the specific attribution of aggressiveness to a speaker who uses

Source: Deborah Tannen, 'New York Jewish conversational style', *International Journal of Sociology of Language*, 30: 133–49, 1981.

fast pacing in conversation. In the discussion that follows, I will suggest that the stereotype of the 'pushy New York Jew' may result in part from discourse conventions practiced by some native New Yorkers of East European Jewish background. After examining some evidence for the existence of such a stereotype, I will (1) briefly present my notion of conversational style, (2) outline the linguistic and paralinguistic features that make up New York Jewish style and (3) demonstrate their use in cross-stylistic and co-stylistic interaction. In conclusion, I will (4) discuss the personal and social uses of conversational style.

The negative stereotype

Evidence abounds of the negative stereotype of New York speech in general and New York Jewish speech in particular. The most widely recognized component of this speech is, of course, phonology. An Associated Press release (Boyer 1979) reports on California therapists who help cure New York accents. One such therapist is quoted: 'It's really a drag listening to people from New York talk. It upsets me when I hear a New York accent. . . . We're here to offer a service to newcomers, they alienate everyone. We're here to help them adjust to life in Marin County.'

A third-grade teacher in Brooklyn wrote to Ann Landers complaining of native-born children who say, for example, 'Vot's the kvestion?', 'It's vorm ottside', and 'heppy as a boid'. Ann Landers advised the teacher, 'With consistent effort, bad speech habits can be unlearned. I hope you will have the patience to work with these students. It's a real challenge.'

Teachers in New York City have been rising to the challenge for a long time. Not so long ago one of the requirements for a license to teach in the New York City public schools was passing a speech exam, which entailed proving that one did not speak with the indigenous 'accent'. I myself recall being given a shockingly low midterm grade by a speech teacher in a Manhattan high school who promised that it would not be raised until I stopped 'dentalizing'. I am not aware of any other group whose members feel that their pronunciation is wrong, even when they are comfortably surrounded by others from the same group and have never lived anywhere else. Labov (1970) has documented the hypercorrection that results from the linguistic insecurity of middle-class Jewish New York women. I confronted this myself each time I recognized a fellow New Yorker in California by her or his accent. The most common response was, 'Oh is it THAT obvious?' or 'Gee, I thought I'd gotten rid of that'.

. . .

Background of the study

My own findings on New York Jewish conversational style were in a way serendipitous as well. I had begun with the goal of discovering the features that made up the styles of each participant in two-and-a-half hours of naturally occurring conversation at dinner on Thanksgiving 1978. Analysis revealed, however, that three of the participants, all natives of New York of East European Jewish background, shared many stylistic features which could be seen to have a positive effect when used with each other and a negative effect when used with the three others. Moreover, the evening's interaction was later characterized by three of the participants (independently) as 'New York Jewish' or 'New York'. Finally, whereas the tapes contained many examples of interchanges between two or three of the New Yorkers, it had no examples of talk among non-New Yorkers in which the New Yorkers did not participate. Thus, what began as a general study of conversation style ended by becoming an analysis of New York Jewish conversational style (Tannen 1984).

The dinner at which this conversation was taped took place in the home of Kurt, a native New Yorker living in Oakland, California. The guests, who were also New Yorkers living in California, were Kurt's brother, Peter, and myself.[4] The three other guests were Kurt's friend David, a native of Los Angeles of Irish, Scotch and English parents from Iowa and North Dakota; David's friend Chad, a native and resident of Los Angeles whose father was of Scotch/English extraction and whose mother was from New York, of Italian background; and Sally, born and raised in England, of a Jewish father and American mother. Complex as these ethnic backgrounds are, the group split into two when looked at on the basis of conversational style.

Theoretical background

My notion of conversational style grows out of R. Lakoff's (1973; 1979) work on communicative style and Gumperz's (1982 [Chapter 14]) on conversational inference. 'Style' is not something extra, added on like frosting on a cake. It is the stuff of which the linguistic cake is made: pitch, amplitude, intonation, voice quality, lexical and syntactic choice, rate of speech and turntaking, as well as what is said and how discourse cohesion is achieved. In other words, style refers to all the ways speakers encode meaning in language and convey how they intend their talk to be understood. Insofar as speakers from similar speech communities share such linguistic conventions, style is a social phenomenon. Insofar as speakers use particular features in particular combinations and in various settings, to that extent style is an individual phenomenon. (See Gumperz and Tannen 1979, for a discussion of individual vs. social differences.)

Lakoff (1973) observes that speakers regularly avoid saying precisely what they mean in the interest of social goals which they pursue by adhering to one of three *rules of politeness*, later renamed *rules of rapport* (Lakoff 1979). Each rule is associated with a communicative style growing out of habitual application of that rule:

1   Don't impose (distance).
2   Give options (deference).
3   Be friendly (camaraderie).

To illustrate (with my own examples), if a guest responds to an offer of something to drink by saying, 'No thank you; I'm not thirsty', s/he is applying R1. If s/he says, 'Oh, I'll have whatever you're having', s/he is applying R2. If s/he marches into the kitchen, throws open the refrigerator, and says, 'I'm thirsty. Got any juice?' s/he is applying R3. Individuals differ with regard to which sense of politeness they tend to observe, and cultural differences are reflected by the tendency of members of a group to observe one or the other sense of politeness in conventionalized ways.

. . .

Another deeply related strand of research in sociology is brilliantly elaborated by Goffman, building on the work of Durkheim. Durkheim (1915) distinguished between negative and positive religious rites. Negative rites are 'a system of abstentions' which prepares one for 'access to the positive cult'. Goffman (1967: 72–3) builds upon this dichotomy in his notion of *deference*, 'the appreciation an individual shows of another to that other, whether through avoidance rituals or presentational rituals'. Presentational rituals include 'salutations, invitations, compliments, and minor services. Through all of these the recipient is told that he is not an island unto himself and that others are, or seek to be, involved with him . . .'. Avoidance rituals 'lead the actor to keep at a distance from the recipient' (Goffman 1967: 62) and include 'rules regarding privacy and separateness' (Goffman 1967: 67). Following Lakoff and Goffman, Brown and Levinson (1987 [Chapter 22]) refer to two overriding goals motivating linguistic forms of politeness: negative face, 'the want of every adult member that his actions be unimpeded by others', and positive face, 'the want of every adult member that his actions be desirable to at least some others'.

All these schemata for understanding human interaction recognize two basic but conflicting needs: to be involved with others and to be left alone. Linguistic systems, like other cultural systems, represent conventionalized ways of honoring these needs. I would like to suggest that the conversational style of the New Yorkers at Thanksgiving dinner can be seen as conventionalized strategies serving the need for involvement, whereas the non-New York participants expected strategies serving the need for independence.

Features of New York Jewish conversational style

Following are the main features found in the talk of three of the six Thanksgiving celebrants.

1   *Topic* (a) prefer personal topics, (b) shift topics abruptly, (c) introduce topics without hesitance, (d) persistence (if a new topic is not immediately picked up, reintroduce it, repeatedly if necessary).
2   *Genre* (a) tell more stories, (b) tell stories in rounds, (c) internal evaluation (Labov 1970 [Chapter 14]) is preferred over external (i.e., the point of a story is dramatized rather than lexicalized), (d) preferred point of a story is teller's emotional experience.

3   *Pacing* (a) faster rate of speech, (b) inter-turn pauses avoided (silence is evidence of lack of rapport), (c) faster turntaking, (d) cooperative overlap and participatory listenership.

4   *Expressive paralinguistics* (a) expressive phonology, (b) pitch and amplitude shifts, (c) marked voice quality, (d) strategic within-turn pauses.

All of these marked features were combined to create linguistic devices which enhanced conversational flow when used among the New Yorkers, but they had an obstructive effect on conversation with those who were not from New York. Comments by all participants upon listening to the tape indicated that they misunderstood the intentions of members of the other group.

Perhaps the most easily perceived and characteristic feature of this style is the fast rate of speech and tendency to overlap (speak simultaneously) and latch (Sacks's term for allowing no pause before turntaking). Overlap is used cooperatively by the New Yorkers, as a way of showing enthusiasm and interest, but it is interpreted by non-New Yorkers as just the opposite: evidence of lack of attention. The tendency to use fast pace and overlap often combines, moreover, with preference for personal topics, focusing attention on another in a personal way. Both the pacing and the personal focus can be seen repeatedly to cause Sally, Chad and David to become more hesitant in their speech as they respond in classic complementary schismogenetic fashion (Bateson 1972). That is, the verbal devices used by one group cause speakers of the other group to react by intensifying the opposing behavior, and vice versa.

Cross-stylistic interchange

The following conversation illustrates how both Peter and I use fast pacing and personal focus to show interest in David's discourse, with the result that he feels 'caught off guard' and 'on the spot'. (This is only one of many such examples.) David, a professional sign interpreter, has been talking about American Sign Language.

(1)   D: So: and thís is the one that's Bèrkeley. This is the Bérkeley
. . . sign for . . . for ⌈Christmas
⌊Do you figure oút those . . those
(2)   T: um correspòndences? Or do? when you learn the signs,
/does/ somebody télls you.
(3)   D: Oh you mean ⌈watching it? like
(4)   T: ⌊ Cause I can imagine knòwing that sìgn, . . .
and not . . figuring out that it had anything to do with
the decorations.
. . . .
(5)   D: No. Y You knòw that it has to do with the

decorations.┐
(6)   T: └Cause somebody télls you? Or you figure it oút.
      D: ⌊No ⌋
(7)   D: Oh. . . . You you talking about mé, or a deáf person.┐
(8)   T: ⌊Yeah.⌋   └You. You.
(9)   D: Me? uh: someone télls me, ùsually. . . . But a lót of em I can
           téll. I mean they're óbvious. . . . . the bétter I get the móre
           I can tell. The lónger I do it the mòre I can tell what they're
           talking about. . . . . . Withoút knowing what the sign is.┐
(10) T: ⌊Huh.⌋   ⌊That's interesting.⌋ │
(11) P: └ But
           how do you learn a new sign.
           . . . . .
(12) D: How do I learn a new sign?┐
(13) P: └ Yeah. I mean supposing . . .
           Victor's talking and all of a sudden he uses a sign for
           Thanksgiving, and you've never séen it before.

My questions (2) (4) and (6) and Peter's Questions (11) and (13) overlap or latch onto David's preceding comments. In contrast, David's comments follow out questions after 'normal' or even noticeable (5, 12) pauses.

My question (2) about how David learns about the symbolism behind the signs not only is latched onto David's fading comment (1) but is spoken loudly and shifts the focus from a general discourse about signs to focus on David personally. The abrupt question catches him off guard, and he hesitates by rephrasing the question. I then interrupt David's rephrasing to supply more information (4), interpreting his hesitation as indication that I had been unclear. The real trouble, however, was the suddenness of my question and its shift from general to personal. Thus, I hoped to make David comfortable by acknowledging the fault had been mine and rectifying the matter by supplying more information right away, but the second interruption could only make him more uncomfortable; hence, the pause.

David answers my question (4) by commenting (5) 'You know that it has to do with the decorations', but he avoids the more personal focus of my question (2) and *how* he knows. I therefore become more specific (6) and again latch my question. David stalls again, this time by asking (7) for clarification. His question comes after a filler, a pause, a slight stutter: 'Oh. . . . You you talking about me . . .'. He expresses his surprise at the shift in focus. Yet again, I clarify in machine-gun fashion: (8) 'Yeah. You. You.' David then answers the question and my response (10) overlaps his answer.

Just as this interchange between David and me is settled, Peter uses precisely the strategy that I was using, with the same results. Latching onto David's answer (9), Peter asks another question focusing on David (11); David hesitates by rephrasing the question after a pause (12); Peter barely waits for the rephrasing to finish before he makes his question more specific (13).

The rhythm of this segment is most peculiar. Normally, a question–answer are seen as an 'adjacency pair' (Sacks, Schegloff and Jefferson 1974), and in a smooth conversation they are rhythmically paired as well. The differences in David's pacing on the one hand and Peter's and mine on the other, however, create pauses between our questions and his delayed answers, so that the resultant rhythmic pairs are made up of an answer and the next question. This is typical of how stylistic differences obstruct conversational rhythm. While participants in this conversation were friends and disposed to think well of each other, the operation of such differences in other settings can leave participants with the conviction that the other was uncooperative or odd.

Co-stylistic interchange

In the previous example, Peter and I directed similar questions to David, with unexpected results. The following segment shows how the same device serves to enhance conversational flow when used with each other. This segment begins when I turn to Peter suddenly and address a question to him.

(1)   T: Do you réad?
          . . . .
(2)   P: Do I | réad?
          . . .
(3)   T: Do you reàd things just for fún?
          . . . .
(4)   P: Yeah. . . . . Right now I'm reading Norma Jean the Térmite
          Queen. [Laughs]
(5)   T: ⌈Whàt's thát? . . . . Norma Jean like uh: . . . . Marilyn
          f
          Mon | róe?
(6)   P: It's . . ⌐No: It's a book about . . . . . . a housewife /??/
(7)   T: Is it a ⌐nóvel or whàt.
                  dec
(8)   P: | It's a | nóvel.
(9)   T: | Yeah?
(10) P: Before that . . . I read the French Lieutenant's Woman?
          ⌈Have you ⌈read that?
(11) T: ⌊ ⌈Oh yeah? No. Whó wrote that?
(12) P: John Fowles.
(13) T: Yeah I've heárd that he's good.
(14) P: | Hé's a ⌐gréat writer. | Í think he's one of the ⌐bést writers.
                                                          T: hm
(15) T: /?/
(16) P: | Hé's really ⌐goòd.
(17) T: /?/
          . . . . ⌐. . . .
(18) P: But Ì get very busy. . . . ⌈Y know?
(19) T: ⌊Yeah. Í? . . hardly éver read.
          . . . .

(20) P: What I've been doing is cutting down on my sleep.

(21) T: Oy! ⌐ [sighs]

(22) P: ⌊ And I've been   . . . . . and I ⌐ s

                    [K laughs]

(23) T: ⌊Í do that tòo

      but it's páinful. ⌐

(24) P: ⌊ Yeah, Fi:ve, six hours a |níght, and ⌐

(25) T: ⌊Oh

      Gód, hòw can you dó it. You survíve?

      . . . .

(26) P: Yeah làte afternoon méetings are hàrd. . . . . . But outside
          of thát I

      T: mmm

      can keep ⌐gòing pretty well.

(27) T: ⌊Not sleeping enough is térrible. . . . . I'd múch rather

      not eàt than not sleèp.

          [S laughs]
            P

(28) P: I próbably should not eàt so much, it would . . it would
          uh . . . sáve a lot of time.

(29) T: If I'm /like really/ busy I don't I don't I don't eat. I don't
          yeah I just don't eat but ⌐I

(30) P: ⌊I ?I tend to spend a lòt of time

      eáting and prepáring and ⌐/?/

(31) T: ⌊Oh: I néver prepare foòd. . . .

      . . . I eat whatéver I can get my hánds on. ⌐

(32) P: ⌊ Yeah.

This interchange exhibits many features of New York Jewish conversational style. In addition to the characteristic use of overlap, fast pacing and personal focus, it exhibits devises I have called (Tannen 1984) persistence, mutual revelation and expressive paralinguistics.

Both Peter and I use overlap and latching in this segment: Peter's (22) (24) and (30) and my (19) (23) (25) (27) and (31). The interchange begins with a sudden focus of attention on him by my question (1). Like David, Peter is initially 'caught off guard', so he repeats the question after a pause. But then he not only answers the question but supplies specific information (4) about the book he is reading. A common feature of participatory listenership is seen in (5) and (6). While (6) is ostensibly an answer to my question (5), it is clear that Peter would have gone to give that information in any case. He begins, 'It's . . .', has to stop in order to answer my question with 'No', and then repeats the beginning and continues, 'It's a book about a housewife'.

Persistence refers to the pattern by which speakers continue trying to say something despite lack of attention or interruption. In this example it can be seen in (22) and (24), in which Peter makes three attempts to say that he sleeps only five or six hours a night. Persistence is a necessary concomitant to overlap. It reflects a conversational economy in which it is not the business of a listener to make room for another speaker to speak. Rather, it is the business of the listener to show enthusiasm; the speaker, in this system, can be counted on to find room to speak. The conversational burden, in other words, is to serve the need for involvement at the risk of violating independence.

The mutual revelation device can be seen in the series of observations Peter and I make about our own habits. In (19) I state that I hardly ever read as a way of showing understanding of Peter's tight schedule (18). (23) is a similar response to his statement that he cuts down on sleep. (27) is a statement of my preference to balance his statement (26) about sleeping. In (28) Peter makes a statement about his eating habits; in (29) I describe mine; in (30) he reiterates his, and in (31) I reiterate mine. It might seem to some observers that we are not 'communicating' at all, since we both talk only about ourselves. But the juxtaposition of comments and the relationship of topics constitutes thematic cohesion and establishes rapport. In this system, the offer of personal information is encouragement to the other to volunteer the same, and volunteered information is highly valued.

Throughout the Thanksgiving conversation, Peter, Kurt and I use exaggerated phonological and paralinguistic cues. For example, my question (5) 'What's that?' is loud and high pitched. When any of the New Yorkers uses such features with Chad or David, the result is that they stop talking in surprise, wondering what caused the outburst. When used in talk among the New Yorkers, introduction of exaggerated paralinguistics spurs the others to follow suit, in a mutually escalating way such as Bateson (1972) has characterized as symmetrical. In the present segment, many of the words and phrases are uttered with extra high or low pitch as well as heavily colored voice quality.

It seems likely that my use of high pitch on 'What's that?' as well as on the last syllable of 'Monroe' in (5) was triggered by Peter's laughter while uttering the book title. In any case, Peter's response (6) uses sharp contrasts in pitch and pacing to signal the message, 'I know this is a silly book'. The pitch on 'No' is very low, the vowel is drawn out, the sentence is uttered slowly, and it contains a very long pause before the key work 'housewife' is uttered. Similar sharp shifts from high to low pitch can be seen repeatedly:

> (8)   P: |It's a ˌnovel.
> (14)   P: |He's a ˌgreat writer. |I think he's one of the ˌbest writers.
> (16)   P: |He's really ˌgood.

These pitch shifts, together with voice quality, signal in (8) denigration of the book discussed and in (14) and (16) great earnestness.

Exaggerated paralinguistics can be seen as well in my expressions of concern for Peter's loss of sleep in (23) (25) and (27). These are all uttered with marked stress and breathy voice quality that demonstrate exaggerated and stylized concern.

Yet another stylized response to Peter's assertion that he doesn't sleep enough is a Yiddish non-verbal 'response cry' (Goffman 1978), 'Oy!'. This utterance is rapport-building in a number of ways. Obviously, the choice of a Yiddish expression signals our shared ethnic background. At the same time, the exaggerated nature of my response – the utterance of a great sigh along with 'oy' – is a way of mocking my own usage, making the exclamation ironic in much the way Peter was mocking his own reading material while telling about it. (In a similar way, Kurt often mocks his own hosting behavior by offering food in an exaggerated Yiddish accent.) Finally, I utter this cry as if it were an expression of my own feeling, thus taking Peter's point of view as a show of empathy.

The interchange between Peter and me ends with another cooperative use of overlap and repetition. The conversation has turned to dating, and it has continued to be characterized by the features seen in the earlier segment. It ends this way:

(1) P: And you just cán't get to know . . . . ten   people <u>really</u> <u>well</u>.
                                                          [breathy]
            ⌈You can't dó it.
            ⌊P
(2) T: ⌊Yeah right. Y'have to there's no? Yeah there's ⌈no tíme.
(3) P: ⌊There's

      not tíme.
(4) T: Yeah . . . . 'strue.

Peter's statements (1) and (3) flow in a continuous stream, ending with 'You can't do it. There's not time'. However the last phrase echoes my words in (2). The end of the talk is signaled by a quieting down of voices as well as the pattern of blended voices and phrases.

The coherence of conversational style

As Reisman (1974: 110) points out, 'The conventions which order speech inter-action are meaningful not only in that they order and mediate verbal expression, but in that they participate in and express larger meanings in the society which uses them'. Becker (1979a: 18) explains, 'The figure a sentence makes is a strategy of interpretation' which 'helps the people it is used by understand and feel coherent in their worlds'. The structure and habits of language which seem self-evidently natural, serve not only as a way to communicate meaning but also to reestablish and ratify one's way of being in the world. In another paper, Becker (1979b: 241) explains:

> The universal source of language pathology is that people appear to say one thing and 'mean' another. It drives people mad (the closer it gets to home). An aesthetic response is quite simply the opposite of this pathology. . . . Schizophrenia, foreign language learning, and artistic expression in language all operate under the same set of linguistic variables – constraints on coherence, invention, intentionality, and reference. The difference is that in madness (and in the temporary madness of learning a new language or a new text) these constraints are misunderstood and often appear contradictory, while in an aesthetic response they are understood as a coherent integrated whole. . . . The integration of communication (art) is, hence, as essential to a sane community as clean air, good food, and, to cure errors, medicine.

The emotional/aesthetic experience of a perfectly tuned conversation is as ecstatic as an artistic experience. The satisfaction of having communicated successfully goes beyond the pleasure of being understood in the narrow sense. It is a ratification of one's place in the world and one's way of being human. It is, as Becker calls a well-performed shadow play, 'a vision of sanity'.

To some extent there is for everyone a discontinuity between the private code, i.e., communicative habits learned at home and on the block (or in the fields) around one's home, and the public code, i.e., the form of language used in formal settings. Hence the anxiety most people feel about communicating with strangers. But the degree of discontinuity may be greater or lesser. Those who learned and have reinforced at home norms of interaction which are relatively similar to those which are widely accepted in society at large have a certainty about their linguistic convictions. If they proclaim that it is rude to interrupt or that one ought to state the point of a story outright, it is without ambivalence. But those who have grown up hearing and using norms of interaction which differ significantly from more widely accepted ones may feel ambivalent about their own styles. Thus New Yorkers of Jewish background cannot complain 'Why don't you interrupt?'. On hearing a taperecording of a conversation they thoroughly enjoyed in the process, they often feel critical of themselves and slightly embarrassed. They, too, believe that it is rude to interrupt, to talk loudly, to talk too much. The 'interruption' may actually be the creation of the interlocutor who stopped when s/he was expected to continue talking over the overlap, but the cooperative overlapper is no more likely to realize this than the overlap-resistant speaker.

The greater the discontinuity between ingroup style and public expectations, the more difficult it is for one to feel sane in both worlds. Hence it is not surprising that many speakers reject one or the other style, and New York Jews who have moved away from New York may be heard to proclaim that they hate New York accents, hate to go back to New York or hate to go home, because 'no one listens to anyone else' to 'it's so loud' or 'people are so rude'. There are probably few speakers of this background who have not at times felt uncomfortable upon seeing through public eyes someone from their own background talking in a way that is attracting attention in an alien setting, just as American travelers may feel embarrassed on seeing another American tourist who fits too neatly the stereotype of the ugly American abroad. In contrast, the comfort of interaction in a setting in which one's home style predominates goes far to explain what often appears as clannishness – the preference for the company of those of similar ethnic background. The coherence principles (to borrow a term from Becker) that create conversational style operate on every level of discourse and contribute to, at the same time that they grow out of, people's attempts to achieve coherence in the world.

Notes

1   My thanks to Stephen Murray for this reference.
2   This conversation was reconstructed from memory. Other presented are transcribed from tape recordings. The following transcription conventions are used, as gleaned from Schenkein (1978) and from those developed at the University of California, Berkeley, by Gumperz and Chafe and their respective collaborators.

. . .   half second pause. Each extra dot represents another half second of pause.

ʹ   marks primary stress

ˋ   marks secondary stress

<u>underline</u> indicates emphatic stress

| marks high pitch on word

⌈   marks high pitch on phrase, continuing until punctuation

| marks low pitch on word

.   sentence-final falling intonation

,   clause-final intonation (more to come)

?   yes/no question rising intonation

ʔ   glottal stop

:   lengthened vowel sound

p   spoken softly (piano)

f   spoken loudly (forte)

dec   spoken slowly

/?/   inaudible segment

⌈Brackets connecting lines show overlapping speech.
⌊Two people talking at the same time.

Brackets with reversed flaps ⌉
⌋ indicate latching (no intraturn
pause)

3   Thus I was both perpetrator and object of my analysis, making me not a participant observer (an observer who becomes a participant) but a participant who is also an observer. At the time of taping, I was in the habit of taping many interactions and had not decided to use this one, let alone what I would look for in analysis. Nonetheless there is a problem of objectivity which I have tried to correct for by painstaking review of the analysis with participants as well as others. I believe that the loss of objectivity is a disadvantage outweighed by the advantage of insight into what was going on which is impossible for a nonparticipant to recover, and that only by taping an event in which one is a natural participant can one gather data not distorted by the presence of an alien observer.

4   With the exception of my own, names have been changed. Now, as always, I want to express my gratitude to these friends who became my data, for their willingness and insight during taping and later during playback. The transcripts will reflect initials of these pseudonyms, except for my own, which is rendered 'T' to avoid confusion with 'D' (David).

References

Bateson, Gregory (1972) *Steps to an Ecology of Mind*, New York: Ballantine.

Becker, A. (1979a) 'The figure a sentence makes', in Givon, T. (ed.) *Discourse and Syntax*, New York: Academic Press.

—— (1979b) 'Text-building, epistemology and aesthetics in Javanese Shadow Theatre', in Becker, A.L. and Yengoyan, A.A. (eds) *The Imagination of Reality: Essays in Southeast Asian Coherence Systems*, Norwood, NJ: Ablex.

Boyer, P.J. (1979) 'Therapists cure New York accents', *The Tribune*, 4 February: 6E.

Brown, P. and Levinson, S.C. (1987) *Politeness: Some Universals in Language Usage*, Cambridge: Cambridge University Press.

Durkheim, E. (1915) *The Elementary Forms of the Religious Life*, New York: The Free Press.

Forster, E.M. (1924) *A Passage to India*, New York: Harcourt Brace Jovanovich.

Goffman, E. (1967) *Interaction Ritual: Essays on Face-to-Face Behavior*, Garden City: Doubleday.

—— (1978) 'Response cries', *Language* 54(4): 787–815.

Gumperz, J. (1982) *Discourse Strategies*, Cambridge: Cambridge University Press.

Gumperz, J. and Tannen, D. (1979) 'Individual and social differences in language use', in Fillmore, C.J., Kempler, D. and Wang, W.S.-Y. (eds) *Individual Differences in Language Ability and Language Behavior*, New York: Academic Press.

Labov, W. (1970) 'The study of language in its social context', *Studium Generale* 23: 30–87.

Lakoff, R. (1973) 'The logic of politeness; or, minding your p's and q's', *Papers from the Ninth Regional Meeting of the Chicago Linguistics Society*, Chicago: University of Chicago Department of Linguistics.

—— (1979) 'Stylistic strategies within a grammar of style', in Oransanu, J., Slater, M. and Adler, L. (eds) *Language, Sex and Gender*, Annals of the New York Academy of Sciences.

Reisman, K. (1974) 'Contrapuntal conversations in an Antiguan village', in Bauman, R. and Sherzer, J. (eds) *Explorations in the Ethnography of Speaking*, Cambridge: Cambridge University Press, 110–24.

Sacks, H., Schegloff, E. and Gail, J. (1974) 'A simplest systematics for the organization of turn-taking for conversation', *Language* 50(4): 696–735.

Schenkein, J. (1978) *Studies in the Organization of Conversational Interaction*, New York: Academic Press.

Tannen, D. (1984) *Conversational Style*, Norwood, NJ: Ablex.

White, E. (1980) *States of Desire: Travels in Gay America*, New York: Dutton.

Discussion points
for Part Five

1   In our Introduction to Part Five we returned to the topic of Harvey Sacks's 'membership categorization device', and we discussed how social categories in discourse often seem to lock people into membership of groups that they may not feel they belong to. Choose an academic text that talks about social or cultural groups. (You could even choose our own Introduction to Part Five.) Mark the words and phrases used to refer to different groups – such as 'women' or 'students' in our own text. Consider the implications of using these 'category-bound' words and phrases. Do you recognise yourself in these categories, or them in you? Can we avoid using them? Try to formulate other ways of referring to the same or similar groups.

2   Collect ten magazine advertisements using non-'white' models. Are they represented in ways that stereotype their ethnic features through the choice of dress, hairstyle, pose, advertised product or any other means?

3   The source of this task and all the quotes below is Kira Hall (1995). The transcription conventions used are:

a – a   a hyphen between spaces before and after indicates a short pause, less than 0.2 seconds
sa-   a hyphen immediately following a letter indicates an abrupt cutoff in speaking
(( ))   double parentheses enclose nonverbal movements and extralinguistic commentary
[ ]   brackets enclose words added to clarify the meaning of the text
___   underlining indicates syllabic stress
CAPS   upper case indicates louder or shouted talk
.   a period indicates falling intonation
,   a comma indicates continuing intonation
?   a question mark indicates rising intonation at the end of a syllable or word
. . .   deletion of some portion of original talk.

Consider the following extracts from interviews with phone-sex workers, in which they describe the linguistic resources they use in meeting their clients' (heterosexual males) fantasies and expectations of an 'ideal woman'. In what ways do these extracts support the notion of (gender) identity being a performative act?

'Rachel':

I can describe myself now so that it lasts for about five minutes, by using lots of adjectives, spending a lot of time describing the shape of my tits. And that's both – it's not just wasting time, because they need to build up a mental picture in their minds about what you look like, and also it allows me to use words that are very feminine. I always wear peach, or apricot, or black lace- or charcoal-colored lace, not just black. I'll talk about how my hair feels, how curly it is. Yeah, I probably use more feminine words. Sometimes they'll ask me, 'What do you call it [female genitalia]?' And I'll say, well my favourite is the *snuggery* . . . And then they crack up, because it's such a feminine, funny word.

'Sheila':

Most of the guys who call are white, definitely, and for them talking to someone of a different race is exotic and a fetish, you know. So it's really weird. They have this stereotypical idea of how, like, a Black woman should sound and what she's gonna be like. So frequently, we'd have women who were actually Black and we'd hook them up, and they wouldn't believe the woman, that she was Black, because she didn't <u>sound</u> like the stereotype. So conversely, what we had to do- I remember there was this one woman who did calls and she had this sort of Black persona that she would do, which was like the total stereotype. I mean, it really bugged me when I would hear her do it. And the guys loved it. They <u>really</u> thought that this is what a Black woman was!

'Andy':

Believe it or not, it's important to them that you're basically in the same mood as they are, that you're enjoying it too. So if you can sound like you are, then that's the better, that's always the better. And the other thing I've found over the years is it's better to sound soft and quiet than loud and noisy . . . if you're a woman. . . . [It's] better to sound ((whispered)) soft, you know, softer. ((in natural voice)) You know, like whispering, rather than ((in loud voice)) OH HO HO HO, ((in natural voice)) really loud, you know, and screaming. 'Cause basically you're in their ear. And physically that's a very strange thing also. Because with the phone, you know, you are in somebody's ear.

4   In Chapter 30, Cameron discusses one example of a work context (call centres) in which communication is the basic skill and language undergoes commodification. Think of other domains of service- and information-based economy in which communication, language, and other semiotic modes, are the basis of economic exchange or in which they undergo commodification.

5   Make a list of features of style that would help anyone become a successful waiter, flight attendant, tour guide, lecturer, news correspondent, or politician. Which of these features standardise the form of words (*scripting*), and which refer to how they are to be uttered (*styling*) (cf. Chapter 30).

Reference

Hall, Kira (1995) 'Lip service on the fantasy lines', in Kira Hall and Mary Bucholtz (eds) *Gender Articulated: Language and the Socially Constructed Self*, London: Routledge. 183–216.

Power, ideology and control

Editors' introduction
to Part Six

CHAPTERS IN PART FOUR dealt expressly with issues of intimacy, involvement, detachment and other manifestations of interpersonal distance. In Part
Five the focus was mainly on identity work in discourse and the subjectivities of
selfness and groupness. Ever since the work of Roger Brown and his associates
(Brown and Gilman 1972 [1960]; Brown and Ford 1964) on pronouns and other
forms of address, *power*, and its relational counterpart *solidarity*, have remained
firmly at the centre of discourse analytic and sociolinguistic research into interpersonal and intergroup relations. So in this final Part of the *Reader*, we need to
focus closely on power, which is in many ways the primary concern of discourse
analysis, particularly in its critical (CDA) version.

A related concept, which the six chapters in this Part of the book explore, is
the belief systems or *ideologies* underlying different power relations, and the concept
of ideology has already been inescapably present in the volume. Following the work
of Michael Billig (e.g., 1990) in rhetoric and Van Dijk (e.g., 1998) in discourse
analysis itself, it is demonstrably the case that ideology is intimately related to
situated practices of day-to-day interaction. In fact, Van Dijk argues that it is
through discourse and other semiotic practices that ideologies are formulated,
reproduced and reinforced. Accomplishing ideology is an important end in political
(both with capital and small 'p') discourse because a discourse's acceptance by an
audience, especially mass media audiences, ensures the establishment of group
rapport. As Fowler (1985: 66) puts it, through the emergence of a 'community of
ideology', a shared system of beliefs about reality comes into being and creates
group identity.

We understand the term *ideology* as social (general and abstract) representations shared by members of a group and used by them to accomplish everyday
social practices, including communication (e.g., Van Dijk 1998; Billig *et al*. 1988;
Fowler 1985; see also Hall, Chapter 27). These representations are organised into

systems that are deployed by social classes and other groups 'in order to make sense of, figure out and render intelligible the way society works' (Hall 1996: 26). Billig *et al.* (1988) make a distinction between 'lived' and 'intellectual' ideology. Our definition above aligns with the idea of lived ideology. Intellectual ideology refers to an overall, coherent system of thought: political programmes or mani-festos, philosophical orientations or religious codifications. This distinction is useful because it reflects the workings of ideology on two levels: people's coherent, formal systems of belief (their intellectual ideologies) and the architecture of their everyday practices. This includes their objectives in self- and other-presentation, their expres-sions of opinions that represent and satisfy their own and their groups' preferred views of reality, constructed to suit local goals of interaction (see e.g., Jaworski and Galasiński 1998). One of the ideologically relevant discourse structures pointed to by Van Dijk (1988: 209) is interactional control, where ideologies get legit-imised. Who starts an interactional exchange, who ends it, who initiates new topics, who interrupts whom, and which address forms are used in the course of inter-action, may all be indicative of a person's power and as such it is ideologically charged, or to use Van Dijk's (1998: 209) term, has an 'ideological dimension'.

As we explained in the general Introduction (and see Fairclough, Chapter 9), CDA's social constructionist view of language prevents it from treating language as a mirror of social relations. Thus, CDA examines the structure of spoken and written texts in search of politically and ideologically salient features, which are constitutive of particular power relations, often without being evident to partici-pants. Some of the key linguistic/discursive features discussed by critical linguists include: nominalisation, passivisation and sequencing. They are used for ideolog-ical control as 'masking devices' (Ng and Bradac 1993) as they allow speakers or writers to withhold the identity of the actors and causality of events. For example, nominalisation, as in '*Failure* to display this notice will result in *prosecution*', and passivisation, as in 'John *was murdered*' (Fowler 1985: 71), remove the visible agents of verbal action and, consequently, deflect responsibility (compare: 'John was murdered by the police'). Exploitation of sequencing as in: 'Fords I find par-ticularly reliable' (Fowler 1985: 72), is a rhetorical device serving the purpose of manipulating the addressee's attention. The seemingly semantically equivalent sentences, 'Employers always quarrel with unions' and 'Unions always quarrel with employers' (Ng and Bradac 1993: 156), give varying impressions of importance as to who quarrels the most and who is responsible for conflict.

Another area of discourse analysis in which power, dominance and control have been major agenda-setting issues is one we have discussed briefly already – language and gender. Women have been shown to be linguistically dominated by men, whose assertive and aggressive communication strategies are not 'mere' cultural differ-ences between the sexes but manifestations of male dominance over females (Henley and Kramarae 1991). However, as Tannen (1993) argues, different discourse strat-egies do not uniformly create dominance or powerlessness. One has to look at their meaning in relation to context, the conversational styles of the participants and the interaction between different speakers' styles and strategies. Only then might it be possible to interpret such strategies as silence, interruption or indirectness as expressions of power, powerlessness, assertion, aggressiveness or co-operation (see also Holmes, Chapter 23; Cameron, Chapters 29, 30).

The first two chapters of this Part of the *Reader* represent seminal writing on discourse and power by two major social theorists: Pierre Bourdieu and Michel Foucault. As we have pointed out in the general Introduction, their interest in discourse is not so much in empirical examination of particular sequences of inter-actional data, but, as in the case of Giddens (see the Introduction to Part Five), in discourse as an abstract vehicle for social and political processes. Language in Bourdieu's (1986, 1991, 1993, Chapter 32) theory of social practice is related to his notion of *habitus*, the group norms or dispositions that people have internalised whose task is to regulate and generate their actions (practices), perceptions and representations of individuals, and to mediate the social structures that they inhabit. Two important and inter-related aspects of habitus are that it reflects the social structures in which it was acquired and also reproduces these structures. Thus, a person who was brought up in a working-class background will manifest a set of discursive dispositions that are different from those acquired by a person from a middle-class background. These differences will, in turn, reproduce the class divi-sions between individuals and their groups.

For Bourdieu, language is a locus of struggle for power and authority in that some types of language (styles, accents, dialects, codes, and so on) are presup-posed to be 'correct', 'distinguished' or 'legitimate' in opposition to those which are 'incorrect' or 'vulgar'. Those who use (in speaking or writing) linguistic vari-eties ranked as acceptable exert a degree of control over those with a dominated linguistic *habitus* (Bourdieu 1991: 60). The field of linguistic production, however, can be manipulated in that the symbolic capital claimed by the authority of 'legit-imate' language may be reclaimed in the process of negotiation 'by a metadiscourse concerning the conditions of use of discourse' (p. 482):

> The habitus ... provides individuals with a sense of how to act and respond in the course of their daily lives. It 'orients' their actions and inclinations without strictly determining them. It gives them a 'feel for the game', a sense of what is appropriate in the circumstances and what is not, a 'practical sense'
>
> (Thompson 1991: 13)

Foucault's model of power is 'productive' (Mills 1997). For Foucault, power is dispersed throughout all social relations as a force that prevents some actions and enables others. However, power is not confined to large-scale, macro processes of politics and society. It is a *potential* present in all everyday exchanges and social encounters. In Foucault's system, one of the significant influences of power is in constituting different versions of individuals' subjectivity (see the Introduction to Part Five). For example, in the extract from *The History of Sexuality* (Chapter 33) it transpires that in the Victorian era, children's sexuality was not 'simply' suppressed. Rather, children faced a hegemonic discourse of 'acceptable' sexuality constructed for them. Another important aspect of Foucault's (1997) view of power is that it is explicitly linked to *knowledge*. Sarah Mills illustrates this as follows, in an example that fits well alongside the one used by Deborah Cameron, at the end of our Introduction to Part Five:

> [W]hat is studied in schools and universities is the result of struggles over whose version of events is sanctioned. Knowledge is often the product of the subjugation of objects, or perhaps it can be seen as the process through which subjects are constituted as subjugated; for example, when consulting a university library catalogue, if you search under the term 'women', you will find a vast selection of books and articles discussing the oppression of women, the psychology of women, the physical ailments that women suffer from, and so on. If you search under the term 'men' you will not find the same wealth of information.
>
> (Mills 1997: 21)

Judith Butler's text (Chapter 34) completes a trilogy of theoretical readings at the start of this Part of the book. Her starting point is J.L. Austin's innocuous-seeming idea of performative speech acts (Chapter 2, see our Introduction to Part One) – acts that 'perform what they name'. Butler's own theory of performativity cuts much deeper, however. Her critical writing on gender (which we cited in our Introduction to Part Five) relies heavily on the notion of performativity, arguing that gender is an identity that women are called into performing as a pre-defined practice of social display. This argument de-essentialises gender and we might feel it 'releases' women from the burden of a determined social position. But in the present text, Butler entertains a philosophical argument about the politics of hate speech, and specifically about the action of burning a cross ('burning acts') in front of a black family's house in the US. One key issue is whether such actions, and by implication hate speech as a form of symbolic violence, is actually attributable to the person who perpetrates it. Is the speaker or should the speaker be, in a US context, protected by the First Amendment (guaranteeing freedom of speech)?

The moral case seems entirely clear – that cross-burning in these circumstances is racist, intimidating and, indeed, a form of violence. Butler accepts this, but she is then interested in the chain of events that, as an actual historical instance, followed when the burning event came to court and its perpetrator was formally prosecuted. She argues that legal arguments in defence of the perpetrator, based on the First Amendment, are themselves violent, injurious, racist acts. She shows how legal institutions are badly equipped to handle matters of intention, implication and context in the analysis of hateful actions. In short, they are deficient in their understanding of discourse.

Teun Van Dijk's contribution to this Part, Chapter 35, is an example of the sinister and twisted working of discursive processes which are involved in the legitimising of racist ideology in face-to-face conversation (for example in an interview) and in newspaper articles. The practices depend on the overt denial of the underlying ideology. It takes a fine-grained textual analysis of discourse for Van Dijk to demonstrate how socially unacceptable positions are overtly denied but covertly present in speakers' or writers' accounts of race and ethnic relations. The original article, too long for us to reproduce here in its entirety, offers a simple taxonomy of *denials of racism*:

1   act-denial ('I did not do/say that at all');
2   control-denial ('I did not do/say that on purpose', 'It was an accident');
3   intention-denial ('I did not mean that', 'You got me wrong');
4   goal-denial ('I did not do/say that, in order to . . .').

(Van Dijk 1992: 92)

Why do people put so much effort into disguising their racism? As we have already said, racism is an ideology which officially, in public discourse in a liberal democracy, does not find social approval. Therefore, denying racism (despite one's beliefs or one's 'lived' ideology) is an important aspect of positive self-presentation, whether one is a private individual, journalist, or Member of Parliament. (One part of the original article, not reproduced here, examines denials of racism in parliamentary debates.) On the other hand, maintaining racist ideology is an expression and reinforcement of white, middle-class power over ethnic minorities (again see Hall, Chapter 27).

Ian Hutchby (Chapter 36), in his analysis of locally produced patterns of power and resistance in argumentative talk of phone-in radio programmes, takes up Foucault's point about the potential for all talk to embed power relationships. His methodology is conversation analytic (see Part Three). But like Foucault, he defines power not as a set of attributes characterising any one person, but 'as a set of potentials which, while always present, can be variably exercised, resisted, shifted around and struggled over by social agents' (p. 530). Phone-ins are one sub-genre of media talk that have spawned their own normative structure, for example around who gets to decide what the agenda for talk is. Callers are positioned to make the first formulation of what might be a relevant topic for discussion. But Hutchby shows that the second position – allocated to the show's host – carries the power to challenge the first formulation of what the agenda is, and also to do this without the need for a detailed rationale or account. Although power in this instance isn't a particularly loaded social relation, Hutchby's analysis shows how institutions (such as radio broadcasting) generate power structures that we have to conform to.

Mehan's chapter, 'Oracular reasoning in a psychiatric exam' (Chapter 37), is a poignant and powerful demonstration of the power/knowledge interface in discourse. In his study, a panel of psychiatrists and a patient diagnosed as schizophrenic put forward their arguments to each other in order for the panel to decide whether the patient can be released from the mental hospital – a kind of negative gatekeeping exercise. As Mehan demonstrates, both sides come to the examination totally unprepared to accept the opposite (and conflicting) views of the other party. The patient claims he is ready to be released from the hospital, and the panel sees him as totally unfit to be released. Both sides engage in argument trying to sanction their own versions of reality. But in the end, it is the party that can command greater power, through institutional authority, i.e., the panel, whose version of 'the truth' about the patient comes to dominate. As Mehan (p. 532) aptly puts it: 'All people define situations as real; but when powerful people define situations as real, then they are real for everybody involved in their consequences.'

Overall, this Part offers a selection of readings that discuss power in and through discourse from a number of different positions and in several different social contexts. Principally, we see these chapters as conceptualising power in two basic ways. First, we have seen power functioning as an attribute of 'unequal' relations, defined to be unequal, pre-discursively, in institutional or other contexts (e.g., parent–child, teacher–pupil, officer–private, employer–employee). Second, we have seen power as an emergent, interactional quality, between 'equals' or 'non-equals', through the strategic deployment of strategies of language and other symbolic systems (cf. Fowler *et al.* 1979; Fairclough 1989).

References

Billig, M. (1990) 'Stacking the cards of ideology: the history of the Sun Royal Album', *Discourse & Society* 1: 17–37.
——, Condor, S., Edwards, D., Gane, M., Middleton, D. and Radley, A.R. (1988) *Ideological Dilemmas*, London: Sage.
Bourdieu, P. (1986) *Distinction: A Social Critique of the Judgement of Taste*, London: Routledge.
—— (1991) *Language and Symbolic Power*, Cambridge: Polity Press.
—— (1993) *The Field of Cultural Production: Essays on Art and Literature*, Cambridge: Polity Press.
Brown, R. and Ford, M. (1964) 'Address in American English', in D. Hymes (ed.) *Language in Culture and Society*, New York: Harper & Row. 234–44.
—— and Gilman, A. (1972) 'The pronouns of power and solidarity', in P.P. Giglioli (ed.) *Language and Social Context*, Harmondsworth: Penguin. 256–82 [first published in: T.A. Sebeok (ed.) *Style in Language*, Cambridge, MA: MIT Press. 253–77].
Fairclough, N. (1989) *Language and Power*, London: Longman.
Foucault, M. (1997) *Power/Knowledge*, Hemel Hempstead: Harvester.
Fowler, R. (1985) 'Power', in T. Van Dijk (ed.) *Handbook of Discourse Analysis*, vol. 4, London: Academic Press. 61–82.
——, Hodge, R., Kress, G.R. and Trew, T. (1979) *Language and Control*, London: Routledge & Kegan Paul.
Hall, S. (1996) 'The problem of ideology: Marxism without guarantees', in D. Morley and K.H. Chen (eds) *Stuart Hall: Critical Dialogues in Cultural Studies*, London: Routledge. 25–46.
Henley, N. and Kramarae, C. (1991) 'Miscommunication, gender, and power', in N. Coupland, J.M. Wiemann and H. Giles (eds) *'Miscommunication' and Problematic Talk*, Newbury Park, CA: Sage. 18–43.
Jaworski, A. and Galasiński, D. (1998) 'The last Romantic hero: Lech Wałesa's image-building in TV presidential debates', *TEXT* 18: 525–44.
Mills, S. (1997) *Discourse*, London: Routledge.
Ng, S.H. and Bradac, J.J. (1993) *Power in Language: Verbal Communication and Social Influence*, Newbury Park, CA: Sage.

Tannen, D. (1993) 'The relativity of linguistic strategies: rethinking power and solidarity in gen-
    der and dominance', in D. Tannen (ed.) *Gender and Conversational Interaction*, New York:
    Oxford University Press. 165–88.
Thompson , J.B. (1991) 'Editor's introduction', in P. Bourdieu, *Language and Symbolic Power*,
    Cambridge: Polity Press. 1–31.
Van Dijk, T.A. (1992) 'Discourse and the denial of racism', *Discourse & Society* 3: 87–118.
—— (1998) *Ideology*, London: Sage.

Chapter 32

Pierre Bourdieu

LANGUAGE AND SYMBOLIC POWER

. . .

L INGUISTIC EXCHANGE — a relation of communication between a sender and a receiver, based on enciphering and deciphering, and therefore on the implementation of a code or a generative competence — is also an economic exchange which is established within a particular symbolic relation of power between a producer, endowed with a certain linguistic capital, and a consumer (or a market), and which is capable of procuring a certain material or symbolic profit. In other words, utterances are not only (save in exceptional circumstances) signs to be understood and deciphered; they are also *signs of wealth*, intended to be evaluated and appreciated, and *signs of authority*, intended to be believed and obeyed. Quite apart from the literary (and especially poetic) uses of language, it is rare in everyday life for language to function as a pure instrument of communication. The pursuit of maximum informative efficiency is only exceptionally the exclusive goal of linguistic production and the distinctly instrumental use of language which it implies generally clashes with the often unconscious pursuit of symbolic profit. For in addition to the information expressly declared, linguistic practice inevitably communicates information about the (differential) manner of communicating, i.e., about the *expressive style*, which, being perceived and appreciated with reference to the universe of theoretically or practically competing styles, takes on a social value and a symbolic efficacy.

Source: Pierre Bourdieu, *Language and Symbolic Power*, translated by Gino Raymond and Matthew Adamson. Edited by John B. Thompson. Cambridge: Polity Press in association with Blackwell, 1991.

Capital, market and price

Utterances receive their value (and their sense) only in their relation to a market, characterized by a particular law of price formation. The value of the utterance depends on the relation of power that is concretely established between the speakers' linguistic competences, understood both as their capacity for production and as their capacity for appropriation and appreciation; it depends, in other words, on the capacity of the various agents involved in the exchange to impose the criteria of appreciation most favourable to their own products. This capacity is not determined in linguistic terms alone. It is certain that the relation between linguistic competences – which, as socially classified productive capacities, characterize socially classified linguistic units of production and, as capacities of appropriation and appreciation, define markets that are themselves socially classified – helps to determine the law of price formation that obtains in a particular exchange. But the linguistic relation of power is not completely determined by the prevailing linguistic forces alone: by virtue of the languages spoken, the speakers who use them and the groups defined by possession of the corresponding competence, the whole social structure is present in each interaction (and thereby in the discourse uttered). That is what is ignored by the interactionist perspective, which treats interaction as a closed world, forgetting that what happens between two persons – between an employer and an employee or, in a colonial situation, between a French speaker and an Arabic speaker or, in the post-colonial situation, between two members of the formerly colonized nation, one Arabic-speaking, one French-speaking – derives its particular form from the objective relation between the corresponding languages or usages, that is, between the groups who speak those languages.

The concern to return to the things themselves and to get a firmer grip on 'reality', a concern which often inspires the projects of 'micro-sociology', can lead one purely and simply to miss a 'reality' that does not yield to immediate intuition because it lies in structures transcending the interaction which they inform. There is no better example of this than that provided by *strategies of condescension*. Thus a French-language newspaper published in Béarn (a province of south-west France) wrote of the mayor of Pau who, in the course of a ceremony in honour of a Béarnais poet, had addressed the assembled company in Béarnais: 'The audience was greatly moved by this thoughtful gesture' [*La République des Pyrénées*, 9 September 1974]. In order for an audience of people whose mother tongue is Béarnais to perceive as a 'thoughtful gesture' the fact that a Béarnais mayor should speak to them in Béarnais, they must tacitly recognize the unwritten law which prescribes French as the only acceptable language for formal speeches in formal situations. The strategy of condescension consists in deriving *profit* from the objective relation of power between the languages that confront one another in practice (even and especially when French is absent) in the very act of symbolically negating that relation, namely, the hierarchy of the languages and of those who speak them. Such a strategy is possible whenever the objective disparity between the persons present (that is, between their social properties) is sufficiently known and recognized by everyone (particularly those involved in the interaction, as agents or spectators) so that the symbolic negation of the hierarchy (by using the 'common touch', for instance) enables the speaker to combine the profits linked to the undiminished hierarchy with those derived from the distinctly symbolic negation of the hierarchy – not the least of which is the strengthening of the hierarchy implied by the recognition accorded to the way of using the hierarchical relation. In reality, the Béarnais mayor can create this condescension effect only because, as mayor of a large town, attesting to his urbanity, he also possesses all the titles (he is a qualified professor) which guarantee his rightful participation in the 'superiority' of the 'superior' language (no one, and especially not a provincial journalist, would think of praising the mayor's French in the same way as his Béarnais, since he is a qualified, licensed speaker who speaks 'good quality' French by definition, *ex officio*). What is praised as 'good quality Béarnais', coming from the mouth of the legitimate speaker of the legitimate language, would be totally devoid of value – and furthermore would be sociologically impossible in a formal situation – coming from the mouth of a peasant, such as the man who, in order to explain why he did not dream of becoming mayor of his village even though he had obtained the biggest share of the vote, said (in French) that he 'didn't know how to speak' (meaning French), implying a definition of linguistic competence that is entirely sociological. One can see in passing that strategies for the subversion of objective hierarchies in the sphere of language, as in the sphere of culture, are *also* likely to be strategies of condescension, reserved for those who are sufficiently confident of their position in the objective hierarchies to be able to deny them without appearing to be ignorant or incapable of satisfying their demands. If Béarnais (or, elsewhere, Creole) is one day spoken on formal occasions, this will be by virtue of its takeover by speakers of the dominant language, who have enough claims to linguistic legitimacy (at least in the eyes of their interlocutors) to avoid being suspected of resorting to the stigmatized language *faute de mieux*.

The relations of power that obtain in the linguistic market, and whose variations determine the variations in the price that the same discourse may receive on different markets, are manifested and realized in the fact that certain agents are incapable of applying to the linguistic products offered, either by themselves or others, the criteria that are most favourable to their own products. This effect of the imposition of legitimacy is greater – and the laws of the market are more favourable to the products offered by the holders of the greatest linguistic competence – when the use of the legitimate language is more imperative, that is, when the situation is more formal (and when it is more favourable, therefore, to those who are more or less formally delegated to speak), and when consumers grant more complete recognition to the legitimate language and legitimate competence (but a recognition which is relatively independent of their knowledge of that language). In other words, the more formal the market is, the more practically congruent with the norms of the legitimate language, the more it is dominated by the dominant, i.e., by the holders of the legitimate competence, authorized to speak with authority.

. . .

It is true that the definition of the symbolic relation of power which is constitutive of the market can be the subject of *negotiation* and that the market can be manipulated, within certain limits, by a metadiscourse concerning the conditions of use of discourse. This includes, for example, the expressions which are used to introduce or excuse speech which is too free or shocking ('with your permission', 'if I may say so', 'if you'll pardon the expression', 'with all due respect', etc.) or those which reinforce, through explicit articulation, the candour enjoyed on a particular market ('off the record', 'strictly between ourselves', etc.). But it goes without saying that the capacity to manipulate is greater the more capital one possesses, as is shown by the strategies of condescension. It is also true that the unification of the market is never so complete as to prevent dominated individuals from finding, in the space provided by private life, among friends, markets where the laws of price formation which apply to more formal markets are suspended. In these private exchanges between homogeneous partners, the 'illegitimate' linguistic products are judged according to criteria which, since they are adjusted to their principles of production, free them from the necessarily comparative logic of distinction and of value. Despite this, the formal law, which is thus provisionally suspended rather than truly transgressed, remains valid, and it re-imposes itself on dominated individuals once they leave the unregulated areas where they can be outspoken (and where they can spend all their lives), as is shown by the fact that it governs the production of their spokespersons as soon as they are placed in a formal situation.

＊ ＊ ＊

The anticipation of profits

Since a discourse can only exist, in the form in which it exists, so long as it is not simply grammatically correct but also, and above all, socially acceptable, i.e., heard, believed, and therefore effective within a given state of relations of production and circulation, it follows that the scientific analysis of discourse must take into account the laws of price formation which characterize the market concerned or, in other words, the laws defining the social conditions of acceptability (which include the specifically linguistic laws of grammaticality). In reality, the conditions of reception envisaged are part of the conditions of production, and anticipation of the sanctions of the market helps to determine the production of the discourse. This anticipation, which bears no resemblance to a conscious calculation, is an aspect of the linguistic habitus which, being the product of a prolonged and primordial relation to the laws of a certain market, tends to function as a practical sense of the acceptability and the probable value of one's own linguistic productions and those of others on different markets. It is this sense of acceptability, and not some form of rational calculation oriented towards the maximization of symbolic profits, which, by encouraging one to take account of the probable value of discourse during the process of production, determines corrections and all forms of self-censorship – the concessions one makes to a social world by accepting to make oneself acceptable in it.

Since linguistic signs are also goods destined to be given a price by powers capable of providing credit (varying according to the laws of the market on which they are placed), linguistic production is inevitably affected by the anticipation of market sanctions: all verbal expressions – whether words exchanged between friends, the bureaucratic discourse of an authorized spokesperson or the academic discourse of a scientific paper – are marked by their conditions of reception and owe some of their properties (even at a grammatical level) to the fact that, on the basis of a practical anticipation of the laws of the market concerned, their authors, most often unwittingly, and without expressly seeking to do so, try to maximize the symbolic profit they can obtain – from practices which are, inseparably, oriented towards communication and exposed to evaluation. This means that the market fixes the price for a linguistic product, the nature, and therefore the objective value, of which the practical anticipation of this price helped to determine; and it means that the practical relation to the market (ease, timidity, tension, embarrassment, silence, etc.), which helps to establish the market sanction, thus provides an apparent justification for the sanction by which it is partly produced.

In the case of symbolic production, the constraint exercised by the market via the anticipation of possible profit naturally takes the form of an anticipated *censorship*, of a self-censorship which determines not only the manner of saying, that is, the choice of language – 'code switching' in situations of bilingualism – or the 'level' of language, but also what it will be possible or not possible to say.

. . .

What our social sense detects in a form which is a kind of symbolic expression of all the sociologically pertinent features of the market situation is precisely that which oriented the production of the discourse, namely, the entire set of characteristics of the social relation obtaining between the interlocutors and the expressive capacities which the speaker was able to invest in the process of euphemization. The interdependence between linguistic forms and the structure of the social relation within and for which it is produced can be seen clearly, in French, in the oscillations between the forms of address, *vous* and *tu*, which sometimes occur when the objective structure of the relation between two speakers (e.g., disparity in age or social status) conflicts with the length and continuity of their acquaintance, and therefore with the intimacy and familiarity of their interaction. It then seems as if they are feeling their way towards a readjustment of the mode of expression and of the social relation through spontaneous or calculated slips of the tongue and progressive lapses, which often culminate in a sort of linguistic contract designed to establish the new expressive order on an official basis: 'Let's use *tu*.' But the subordination of the form of discourse to the form of the social relationship in which it is used is most strikingly apparent in situations of *stylistic collision*, when the speaker is confronted with a socially heterogeneous audience or simply with two interlocutors socially and culturally so far apart that the sociologically exclusive modes of expression called for, which are normally produced through more or less conscious adjustment in separate social spaces, cannot be produced simultaneously.

What guides linguistic production is not the degree of tension of the market or, more precisely, its degree of formality, defined in the abstract, for any speaker, but rather the relation between a degree of 'average' objective tension and a linguistic habitus itself characterized by a particular degree of sensitivity to the tension of the market; or, in other words, it is the anticipation of profits, which can scarcely be called a subjective anticipation since it is the product of the encounter between an objective circumstance, that is, the average probability of success, and an incorporated objectivity, that is, the disposition towards a more or less rigorous evaluation of that probability. The practical anticipation of the potential rewards or penalties is a practical quasi-corporeal sense of the reality of the objective relation between a certain linguistic and social competence and a certain market, through which this relation is accomplished. It can range from the certainty of a positive sanction, which is the basis of *certitudo sui*, of *self-assurance*, to the certainty of a negative sanction, which induces surrender and silence, through all the intermediate forms of insecurity and timidity.

The linguistic habitus and bodily hexis

The definition of acceptability is found not in the situation but in the relationship between a market and a habitus, which itself is the product of the whole history of its relations with markets. The habitus is, indeed, linked to the market no less through its conditions of acquisition than through its conditions of use. We have not learned to speak simply by hearing a certain kind of speech spoken but also by speaking, thus by offering a determinate form of speech on a determinate market. This occurs through exchanges within a family occupying a particular position in the social space and thus presenting the child's imitative propensity with models and sanctions that diverge more or less from legitimate usage. And we have learned the value that the products offered on this primary market, together with the authority which it provides, receive on other markets (like that of the school). The system of successive reinforcements or refutations has thus constituted in each one of us a certain sense of the social value of linguistic usages and of the relation between the different usages and the different markets, which organizes all subsequent perceptions of linguistic products, tending to endow it with considerable stability. (We know, in general terms, that the effects that a new experience can have on the habitus depend on the relation of practical 'compatibility' between this experience and the experiences that have already been assimilated by the habitus, in the form of schemes of production and evaluation, and that, in the process of selective re-interpretation which results from this dialectic, the informative efficacy of all new experiences tends to diminish continuously.) This linguistic 'sense of place' governs the degree of constraint which a given field will bring to bear on the production of discourse, imposing silence or a hyper-controlled language on some people while allowing others the liberties of a language that is securely established. This means that competence, which is acquired in a social context and through practice, is inseparable from the practical mastery of a usage of language and the practical mastery of situations in which this usage of language is *socially acceptable*. The sense of the value of one's own linguistic products is a fundamental dimension of the sense of knowing the place which one occupies in the social space. One's original relation with different markets and the experience of the sanctions applied to one's own productions, together with the experience of the price attributed to one's own body, are doubtless some of the mediations which help to constitute that *sense of one's own social worth* which governs the practical relation to different markets (shyness, confidence, etc.) and, more generally, one's whole physical posture in the social world.

While every speaker is both a producer and a consumer of his own linguistic productions, not all speakers, as we have seen, are able to apply to their own products the schemes according to which they were produced. The unhappy relation which the petits bourgeois have to their own productions (and especially with regard to their pronunciation, which, as Labov shows, they judge with particular severity); their especially keen sensitivity to the tension of the market and, by the same token, to linguistic correction in themselves and in others, which pushes them to hyper-correction; their insecurity, which reaches a state of paroxysm on formal occasions, creating 'incorrectness' through hyper-correction or the embarrassingly rash utterances prompted by an artificial confidence – are all things that result from a divorce between the schemes of production and the schemes of evaluation. Divided against themselves, so to speak, the petits bourgeois are those who are both the most 'conscious' of the objective truth of their products (the one defined in the academic hypothesis of the perfectly unified market) and the most determined to reject it, deny it, and contradict it by their efforts. As is very evident in this case, what expresses itself through the linguistic habitus is the whole class habitus of which it is one dimension, which means in fact, the position that is occupied, synchronically and diachronically, in the social structure.

As we have seen, hyper-correction is inscribed in the logic of pretension which leads the petits bourgeois to attempt to appropriate prematurely, at the cost of constant tension, the properties of those who are dominant. The particular intensity of the insecurity and anxiety felt by women of the petite bourgeoisie with regard to language (and equally with regard to cosmetics or personal appearance) can be understood in the framework of the same logic: destined, by the division of labour between the sexes, to seek social mobility through their capacity for symbolic production and consumption, they are even more inclined to invest in the acquisition of legitimate competences. The linguistic practices of the petite bourgeoisie could not fail to strike those who, like Labov, observed them on the particularly tense markets created by linguistic investigation. Situated at the maximum point of subjective tension through their particular sensitivity to objective tension (which is the effect of an especially marked disparity between recognition and cognition), the petits bourgeois are distinct from members of the lower classes who, lacking the means to exercise the liberties of plain speaking, which they reserve for private usage, have no choice but to opt for the broken forms of a borrowed and clumsy language or to escape into abstention and silence. But the petits bourgeois are no less distinct from the members of the dominant class, whose linguistic habitus (especially if they were born in that class) is the *realization of the norm* and who can express all the self-confidence that is associated with a situation where the principles of evaluation and the principles of production coincide perfectly.

In this case, as, at the other extreme, in the case of popular outspokenness on the popular market, the demands of the market and the dispositions of the habitus are perfectly attuned; the law of the market does not need to be imposed by means of constraint or external censorship since it is accomplished through the relation to the market which is its incorporated form. When the objective structures which it confronts coincide with those which have produced it, the habitus anticipates the objective demands of the field. Such is the basis of the most frequent and best concealed form of censorship, the kind which is applied by placing, in positions which imply the right to speak, those agents who are endowed with expressive dispositions that are 'censored' in advance, since they coincide with the exigencies inscribed in those positions. As the principle underlying all the distinctive features of the dominant mode of expression, *relaxation in tension* is the expression of a relation to the market which can only be acquired through prolonged and precocious familiarity with markets that are characterized, even under ordinary circumstances, by a high level of control and by that constantly sustained attention to forms and formalities which defines the 'stylization of life'.

. . .

It is no coincidence that bourgeois distinction invests the same intention in its relation to language as it invests in its relation to the body. The sense of acceptability which orients linguistic practices is inscribed in the most deep-rooted of bodily dispositions: it is the whole body which responds by its posture, but also by its inner reactions or, more specifically, the articulatory ones, to the tension of the market. Language is a body technique, and specifically linguistic, especially phonetic, competence is a dimension of bodily hexis in which one's whole relation to the social world, and one's whole socially informed relation to the world, are expressed. There is every reason to think that, through the mediation of what Pierre Guiraud calls 'articulatory style', the bodily hexis characteristic of a social class determines the system of phonological features which characterizes a class pronunciation. The most frequent articulatory position is an element in an *overall way of using the mouth* (in talking but also in eating, drinking, laughing, etc.) and therefore a component of the bodily hexis, which implies a *systematic informing* of the whole phonological aspect of speech. This 'articulatory style', a life-style 'made flesh', like the whole bodily hexis, welds phonological features – which are often studied in isolation, each one (the phoneme 'r', for example) being compared with its equivalent in other class pronunciations – into an indivisible totality which must be treated as such.

Thus, in the case of the lower classes, articulatory style is quite clearly part of a relation to the body that is dominated by the refusal of 'airs and graces' (i.e., the refusal of stylization and the imposition of form) and by the valorization of virility – one aspect of a more general disposition to appreciate what is 'natural'. Labov is no doubt right when he ascribes the resistance of male speakers in New York to the imposition of the legitimate language to the fact that they associate the idea of virility with their way of speaking or, more precisely, their way of using the mouth and throat when speaking. In France, it is surely no accident that popular usage condenses the opposition between the bourgeois relation and the popular relation to language in the sexually over-determined opposition between two words for the mouth: *la bouche*, which is more closed, pinched, i.e., tense and censored, and therefore feminine, and *la gueule*, unashamedly wide open, as in 'split' (*fendue*, *se fendre la gueule*, 'split oneself laughing'), i.e., relaxed and free, and therefore masculine. Bourgeois dispositions, as they are envisaged in the popular mind, and in their most caricatured, petit-bourgeois form, convey in their physical postures of tension and exertion (*bouche fine, pincée, lèvres pincées, serrées, du bout des lèvres, bouche en cul-de-poule* — to be fastidious, supercilious, 'tight-lipped') the bodily indices of quite general dispositions towards the world and other people (and particularly, in the case of the mouth, towards food), such as haughtiness and disdain (*fare la fine bouche, la petite bouche* — to be fussy about food, difficult to please), and the conspicuous distance from the things of the body and those who are unable to mark that distance. *La gueule*, by contrast, is associated with the manly dispositions which, according to the popular ideal, are rooted in the calm certainty of strength which rules out censorships — prudence and deviousness as well as 'airs and graces' — and which make it possible to be 'natural' (*la gueule* is on the side of nature), to be 'open' and 'outspoken' (*jouer franc-jeu, avoir son franc-parler*) or simply to sulk (*faire la gueule*). It designates a capacity for verbal violence, identified with the sheer strength of the voice (*fort en gueule, coup de gueule, grande gueule, engueuler, s'engueuler, gueuler, aller gueuler* — 'loud-mouthed', a 'dressing-down', 'bawl', 'have a slanging match', 'mouth-off'). It also designates a capacity for the physical violence to which it alludes, especially in insults (*casser la gueule, mon poing sur la gueule, ferme ta gueule* — 'smash your face in', 'a punch in the mouth', 'shut your face'), which, through the *gueule*, regarded both as the 'seat' of personal identity (*bonne gueule, sale gueule* — 'nice guy', 'ugly mug') and as its main means of expression (consider the meaning of *ouvrir sa gueule*, or *l'ouvrir*, as opposed to *la fermer, la boucler, taire sa gueule, s'écraser* — 'say one's piece', as opposed to 'shut it', 'belt up', 'shut your mouth', 'pipe down'), aims at the very essence of the interlocutor's social identity and self-image. Applying the same 'intention' to the site of food intake and the site of speech output, the popular vision, which has a clear grasp of the unity of habitus and bodily hexis, also associates *la gueule* with the frank acceptance (*s'en foutre plein la gueule, se rincer la gueule* — stuffing oneself with food and drink) and frank manifestation (*se fendre la gueule*) of elementary pleasure.

On the one hand, domesticated language, censorship made natural, which proscribes 'gross' remarks, 'coarse' jokes and 'thick' accents, goes hand in hand with the domestication of the body which excludes all excessive manifestations of appetites or feelings (exclamations as much as tears or sweeping gestures), and which subjects the body to all kinds of discipline and censorship aimed at denaturalizing it. On the other hand, the 'relaxation of articulatory tension', which leads, as Bernard Laks has pointed out, to the dropping of the final 'r' and 'l' (and which is probably not so much an effect of *laisser-aller* as the expression of a refusal to 'overdo it' to conform too strictly on the points most strictly demanded by the dominant code, even if the effort is made in other areas), is associated with rejection of the censorship which propriety imposes, particularly on the tabooed body, and with the outspokenness whose daring is less innocent than it seems since, in reducing humanity to its common nature – belly, bum, bollocks, grub, guts and shit – it tends to turn the social world upside down, arse over head. Popular festivity as described by Bakhtin and especially revolutionary crisis highlight, through the verbal explosion which they facilitate, the pressure and repression which the everyday order imposes, particularly on the dominated class, through the seemingly insignificant constraints and controls of politeness which, by means of the stylistic variations in ways of talking (the formulae of politeness) or of bodily deportment in relation to the degree of objective tension of the market, exacts recognition of the hierarchical differences between the classes, the sexes and the generations.

It is not surprising that, from the standpoint of the dominated classes, the adoption of the dominant style is seen as a denial of social and sexual identity, a repudiation of the virile values which constitute class membership. That is why women can identify with the dominant culture without cutting themselves off from their class as radically as men. 'Opening one's big mouth' (*ouvrir sa grande gueule*) means refusing to submit, refusing to 'shut it' (*la fermer*) and to manifest the signs of docility that are the precondition of mobility. To adopt the dominant style, especially a feature as marked as the legitimate pronunciation, is in a sense doubly to negate one's virility because the very fact of acquiring it requires docility, a disposition imposed on women by the traditional sexual division of labour (and the traditional division of sexual labour), and because this docility leads one towards dispositions that are themselves perceived as effeminate.

In drawing attention to the articulatory features which, like the degree of 'aperture', sonority or rhythm, best express, in their own logic, the deep-rooted dispositions of the habitus and, more precisely, of the bodily hexis, spontaneous sociolinguistics demonstrates that a differential phonology should never fail to select and interpret the articulatory features characteristic of a class or class fraction in relation not only to the other systems with reference to which they take on their distinctive value, and therefore their social value, but also in relation to the synthetic unity of the bodily hexis from which they spring, and by virtue of which they represent the ethical or aesthetic expression of the necessity inscribed in a social condition.

> The linguist, who has developed an abnormally acute perception (particularly at the phonological level), may notice differences where ordinary speakers hear none. Moreover, because he has to concentrate on discrete criteria (such as the dropping of the final 'r' or 'l') for the purposes of statistical measurement, he is inclined towards an analytical perception very different in its logic from the ordinary perception which underlies the classificatory judgements and the delimitation of homogeneous groups in everyday life. Not only are linguistic features never clearly separated from the speaker's whole set of social properties (bodily hexis, physiognomy, cosmetics, clothing), but phonological (or lexical, or any other) features are never clearly separated from other levels of language; and the judgement which classifies a speech form as 'popular' or a person as 'vulgar' is based, like all practical predication,

on sets of indices which never impinge on consciousness in that form,
even if those which are designated by stereotypes (such as the 'peasant'
'r' or the southern *ceusse*) have greater weight.

The close correspondence between the uses of the body, of language and no doubt
also of time is due to the fact that it is essentially through bodily and linguistic
disciplines and censorships, which often imply a temporal rule, that groups inculcate
the virtues which are the transfigured form of their necessity, and to the fact that
the 'choices' constitutive of a relationship with the economic and social world are
incorporated in the form of durable frames that are partly beyond the grasp of
consciousness and will.

Chapter 33

Michel Foucault

THE INCITEMENT TO DISCOURSE

THE SEVENTEENTH CENTURY was the beginning of an age of repression emblematic of what we call the bourgeois societies, an age which perhaps we still have not completely left behind. Calling sex by its name thereafter became more difficult and more costly. As if in order to gain mastery over it in reality, it had first been necessary to subjugate it at the level of language, control its free circulation in speech, expunge it from the things that were said, and extinguish the words that rendered it too visibly present. And even these prohibitions, it seems, were afraid to name it. Without even having to pronounce the word, modern prudishness was able to ensure that one did not speak of sex, merely through the interplay of prohibitions that referred back to one another: instances of muteness which, by dint of saying nothing, imposed silence. Censorship.

Yet when one looks back over these last three centuries with their continual transformations, things appear in a very different light: around and apropos of sex, one sees a veritable discursive explosion. We must be clear on this point, however. It is quite possible that there was an expurgation – and a very rigorous one – of the authorized vocabulary. It may indeed be true that a whole rhetoric of allusion and metaphor was codified. Without question, new rules of propriety screened out some words: there was a policing of statements. A control over enunciations as well: where and when it was not possible to talk about such things became much more strictly defined; in which circumstances, among which speakers, and within which social relationships. Areas were thus established, if not of utter silence, at least of tact and discretion: between parents and children, for instance, or teachers and pupils, or masters and domestic servants. This almost certainly constituted a whole restrictive economy, one that was incorporated into that

Source: Michel Foucault, *The History of Sexuality: An Introduction*, translated by Robert Huxley, London: Penguin, 1978.

politics of language and speech – spontaneous on the one hand, concerted on the other – which accompanied the social redistributions of the classical period.

At the level of discourses and their domains, however, practically the opposite phenomenon occurred. There was a steady proliferation of discourses concerned with sex – specific discourses, different from one another both by their form and by their object: a discursive ferment that gathered momentum from the eighteenth century onward. Here I am thinking not so much of the probable increase in "illicit" discourses, that is, discourses of infraction that crudely named sex by way of insult or mockery of the new code of decency; the tightening up of the rules of decorum likely did produce, as a countereffect, a valorization and intensification of indecent speech. But more important was the multiplication of discourses concerning sex in the field of exercise of power itself: an institutional incitement to speak about it, and to do so more and more; a determination on the part of the agencies of power to hear it spoken about, and to cause it to speak through explicit articulation and endlessly accumulated detail.

. . .

It was here, perhaps, that the injunction, so peculiar to the West, was laid down for the first time, in the form of a general constraint. I am not talking about the obligation to admit to violations of the laws of sex, as required by traditional penance; but of the nearly infinite task of telling – telling oneself and another, as often as possible, everything that might concern the interplay of innumerable pleasures, sensations, and thoughts which, through the body and the soul, had some affinity with sex. This scheme for transforming sex into discourse had been devised long before in an ascetic and monastic setting. The seventeenth century made it into a rule for everyone. It would seem in actual fact that it could scarcely have applied to any but a tiny elite; the great majority of the faithful who only went to confession on rare occasions in the course of the year escaped such complex prescriptions. But the important point no doubt is that this obligation was decreed, as an ideal at least, for every good Christian. An imperative was established: not only will you confess to acts contravening the law, but you will seek to transform your desire, your every desire, into discourse. Insofar as possible, nothing was meant to elude this dictum, even if the words it employed had to be carefully neutralized. The Christian pastoral prescribed as a fundamental duty the task of passing everything having to do with sex through the endless mill of speech. The forbidding of certain words, the decency of expressions, all the censorings of vocabulary, might well have been only secondary devices compared to that great subjugation: ways of rendering it morally acceptable and technically useful.

One could plot a line going straight from the seventeenth-century pastoral to what became its projection in literature, "scandalous" literature at that. "Tell everything," the directors would say time and again: "not only consummated acts, but sensual touchings, all impure gazes, all obscene remarks . . . all consenting thoughts" (de'Liguori 1835: 5). Sade takes up the injunction in words that seem to have been retranscribed from the treatises of spiritual direction: "Your narrations must be decorated with the most numerous and searching details; the precise way and extent to which we may judge how the passion you describe relates to human manners and man's character is determined by your willingness to disguise no circumstance; and what is more, the least circumstance is apt to have an immense influence upon the procuring of that kind of sensory irritation we expect from your stories" (de Sade 1966: 271).

. . .

Toward the beginning of the eighteenth century, there emerged a political, economic, and technical incitement to talk about sex. And not so much in the form of sexuality as in the form of analysis, stocktaking, classification, and specification, of quantitative or causal studies. This need to take sex "into account," to pronounce a discourse on sex that would not derive from morality alone but from rationality as well, was sufficiently new that at first it wondered at itself and sought apologies for its own existence. How could a discourse based on reason speak of *that*? "Rarely have philosophers directed a steady gaze to these objects situated between disgust and ridicule, where one must avoid both hypocrisy and scandal" (Flandrin 1976). And nearly a century later, the medical establishments which one might have expected to be less surprised by what it was about to formulate, still stumbled at the moment of speaking: "The darkness that envelops these facts, the shame and disgust they inspire, have always repelled the observer's gaze. . . . For a long time I hesitated to introduce the loathsome picture into this study" (Tardieu 1857: 114). What is essential is not in all these scruples, in the "moralism" they betray, or in the hypocrisy one can suspect them of, but in the recognized necessity of overcoming this hesitation. One had to speak of sex; one had to speak publicly and in a manner that was not determined by the division between licit and illicit, even if the speaker maintained the distinction for himself (which is what these solemn and preliminary declarations were intended to show): one had to speak of it as of a thing to be not simply condemned or tolerated but managed, inserted into systems of utility, regulated for the greater good of all, made to function according to an optimum. Sex was not something one simply judged; it was a thing one administered. It was in the nature of a public potential; it called for management procedures; it had to be taken charge of by analytical discourses. In the eighteenth century, sex became a "police" matter – in the full and strict sense given the term at the time: not the repression of disorder, but an ordered maximization of collective and individual forces.

. . .

A policing of sex: that is, not the rigor of a taboo, but the necessity of regulating sex through useful and public discourses.

A few examples will suffice. One of the great innovations in the techniques of power in the eighteenth century was the emergence of "population" as an economic and political problem: population as wealth, population as manpower or labor capacity, population balanced between its own growth and the resources it commanded. Governments perceived that they were not dealing simply with subjects, or even with a "people," but with a "population," with its specific phenomena and its peculiar variables: birth and death rates, life expectancy, fertility, state of health, frequency of illnesses, patterns of diet and habitation. All these variables were situated at the point where the characteristic movements of life and the specific effects of institutions intersected.

. . .

At the heart of this economic and political problem of population was sex: it was necessary to analyze the birthrate, the age of marriage, the legitimate and illegitimate births, the precocity and frequency of sexual relations, the ways of making them fertile or sterile, the effects of unmarried life or of the prohibitions, the impact of contraceptive practices – of those notorious "deadly secrets" which demographers on the eve of the Revolution knew were already familiar to the inhabitants of the countryside.

Of course, it had long been asserted that a country had to be populated if it hoped to be rich and powerful; but this was the first time that a society had affirmed, in a constant way, that its future and its fortune were tied not only to the number and the uprightness of its citizens, to their marriage rules and family organization, but to the manner in which each individual made use of his sex. Things went from ritual lamenting over the unfruitful debauchery of the rich, bachelors, and libertines to a discourse in which the sexual conduct of the population was taken both as an object of analysis and as a target of intervention; there was a progression from the crudely populationist arguments of the mercantilist epoch to the much more subtle and calculated attempts at regulation that tended to favor or discourage – according to the objectives and exigencies of the moment – an increasing birthrate. Through the political economy of population there was formed a whole grid of observations regarding sex. There emerged the analysis of the modes of sexual conduct, their determinations and their effects, at the boundary line of the biological and the economic domains. There also appeared those systematic campaigns which, going beyond the traditional means – moral and religious exhortations, fiscal measures – tried to transform the sexual conduct of couples into a concerted economic and political behavior. In time these new measures would become anchorage points for the different varieties of racism of the nineteenth and twentieth centuries. It was essential that the state know what was happening with its citizens' sex, and the use they made of it, but also that each individual be capable of controlling the use he made of it. Between the state and the individual, sex became an issue, and a public issue no less; a whole web of discourses, special knowledges, analyses, and injunctions settled upon it.

The situation was similar in the case of children's sex. It is often said that the classical period consigned it to an obscurity from which it scarcely emerged before the *Three Essays* or the beneficent anxieties of Little Hans. It is true that a long-standing "freedom" of language between children and adults, or pupils and teachers, may have disappeared. No seventeenth-century pedagogue would have publicly advised his disciple, as did Erasmus in his *Dialogues*, on the choice of a good prostitute. And the boisterous laughter that had accompanied the precocious sexuality of children for so long – and in all social classes, it seems – was gradually stifled. But this was not a plain and simple imposition of silence. Rather, it was a new regime of discourses. Not any less was said about it; on the contrary.

But things were said in a different way; it was different people who said them, from different points of view, and in order to obtain different results. Silence itself – the things one declines to say, or is forbidden to name, the discretion that is required between different speakers – is less the absolute limit of discourse, the other side from which it is separated by a strict boundary, than an element that functions alongside the things said, with them and in relation to them within over-all strategies. There is no binary division to be made between what one says and what one does not say; we must try to determine the different ways of not saying such things, how those who can and those who cannot speak of them are distrib-uted, which type of discourse is authorized, or which form of discretion is required in either case. There is not one but many silences, and they are an integral part of the strategies that underlie and permeate discourses.

Take the secondary schools of the eighteenth century, for example. On the whole, one can have the impression that sex was hardly spoken of at all in these institutions. But one only has to glance over the architectural layout, the rules of discipline, and their whole internal organization: the question of sex was a constant preoccupation. The builders considered it explicitly. The organizers took it perma-nently into account. All who held a measure of authority were placed in a state of perpetual alert, which the fixtures, the precautions taken, the interplay of punish-ments and responsibilities, never ceased to reiterate. The space for classes, the shape of the tables, the planning of the recreation lessons, the distribution of the dormitories (with or without partitions, with or without curtains), the rules for monitoring bedtime and sleep periods – all this referred, in the most prolix manner, to the sexuality of children. What one might call the internal discourse of the institution – the one it employed to address itself, and which circulated among those who made it function – was largely based on the assumption that this sexuality existed, that it was precocious, active, and ever present. But this was not all: the sex of the schoolboy became in the course of the eighteenth century – and quite apart from that of adolescents in general – a public problem. Doctors counseled the directors and professors of educational establishments, but they also gave their opinions to families; educators designed projects which they submitted to the authorities; schoolmasters turned to students, made recommendations to them, and drafted for their benefit books of exhortation, full of moral and medical examples. Around the schoolboy and his sex there proliferated a whole literature of precepts, opinions, observations, medical advice, clinical cases, outlines for reform, and plans for ideal institutions. With Basedow and the German "philan-thropic" movement, this transformation of adolescent sex into discourse grew to considerable dimensions.

. . .

It would be less than exact to say that the pedagogical institution has imposed a ponderous silence on the sex of children and adolescents. On the contrary, since the eighteenth century it has multiplied the forms of discourse on the subject; it has established various points of implantation for sex; it has coded contents and qualified speakers. Speaking about children's sex, inducing educators, physicians, administrators, and parents to speak of it, or speaking to them about it, causing children themselves to talk about it, and enclosing them in a web of discourses which sometimes address them, sometimes speak about them, or impose canonical bits of knowledge on them, or use them as a basis for constructing a science that is beyond their grasp – all this together enables us to link an intensification of the interventions of power to a multiplication of discourse. The sex of children and adolescents has become, since the eighteenth century, an important area of contention around which innumerable institutional devices and discursive strategies have been deployed. It may well be true that adults and children themselves were deprived of a certain way of speaking about sex, a mode that was disallowed as being too direct, crude, or coarse. But this was only the counterpart of other discourses, and perhaps the condition necessary in order for them to function, discourses that were interlocking, hierarchized, and all highly articulated around a cluster of power relations.

One could mention many other centers which in the eighteenth or nineteenth century began to produce discourses on sex. First there was medicine, via the "nervous disorders"; next psychiatry, when it set out to discover the etiology of mental illnesses, focusing its gaze first on "excess," then onanism, then frustration, then "frauds against procreation," but especially when it annexed the whole of the sexual perversions as its own province; criminal justice, too, which had long been concerned with sexuality, particularly in the form of "heinous" crimes and crimes against nature, but which, toward the middle of the nineteenth century, broadened its jurisdiction to include petty offenses, minor indecencies, insignificant perversions; and lastly, all those social controls, cropping up at the end of the last century, which screened the sexuality of couples, parents and children, dangerous and endangered adolescents undertaking to protect, separate, and forewarn, signaling perils everywhere, awakening people's attention, calling for diagnoses, piling up reports, organizing therapies. These sites radiated discourses aimed at sex, intensifying people's awareness of it as a constant danger, and this in turn created a further incentive to talk about it.

. . .

Since the eighteenth century, sex has not ceased to provoke a kind of generalized discursive erethism. And these discourses on sex did not multiply apart from or against power, but in the very space and as the means of its exercise. Incitements to speak were orchestrated from all quarters, apparatuses everywhere for listening and recording, procedures for observing, questioning, and formulating. Sex was driven out of hiding and constrained to lead a discursive existence. From the singular imperialism that compels everyone to transform their sexuality into a perpetual discourse, to the manifold mechanisms which, in the areas of economy, pedagogy, medicine, and justice, incite, extract, distribute, and institutionalize the sexual discourse, an immense verbosity is what our civilization has required and organized. Surely no other type of society has ever accumulated – and in such a relatively short span of time – a similar quantity of discourses concerned with sex. It may well be that we talk about sex more than anything else; we set our minds to the task; we convince ourselves that we have never said enough on the subject, that, through inertia or submissiveness, we conceal from ourselves the blinding evidence, and that what is essential always eludes us, so that we must always start out once again in search of it. It is possible that where sex is concerned, the most long-winded, the most impatient of societies is our own.

But as this overview shows, we are dealing less with *a* discourse on sex than with a multiplicity of discourses produced by a whole series of mechanisms operating in different institutions. The Middle Ages had organized around the theme of the flesh and the practice of penance a discourse that was markedly unitary. In the course of recent centuries, this relative uniformity was broken apart, scattered, and multiplied in an explosion of distinct discursivities which took form in demography, biology, medicine, psychiatry, psychology, ethics, pedagogy, and political criticism. More precisely, the secure bond that held together the moral theology of concupiscence and the obligation of confession (equivalent to the theoretical discourse on sex and its first-person formulation) was, if not broken, at least loosened and diversified: between the objectification of sex in rational discourses, and the movement by which each individual was set to the task of recounting his own sex, there has occurred, since the eighteenth century, a whole series of tensions, conflicts, efforts at adjustment, and attempts at retranscription. So it is not simply in terms of a continual extension that we must speak of this discursive growth; it should be seen rather as a dispersion of centers from which discourses emanated, a diversification of their forms, and the complex deployment of the network connecting them. Rather than the uniform concern to hide sex, rather than a general prudishness of language, what distinguishes these last three centuries is the variety, the wide dispersion of devices that were invented for speaking about it, for having it be spoken about, for inducing it to speak of itself, for listening, recording, transcribing, and redistributing what is said about it: around sex, a whole network of varying, specific, and coercive transpositions into discourse. Rather than a massive censorship, beginning with the verbal proprieties imposed by the Age of Reason, what was involved was a regulated and polymorphous incitement to discourse.

The objection will doubtless be raised that if so many stimulations and constraining mechanisms were necessary in order to speak of sex, this was because there reigned over everyone a certain fundamental prohibition; only definite necessities — economic pressures, political requirements — were able to lift this prohibition and open a few approaches to the discourse on sex, but these were limited and carefully coded; so much talk about sex, so many insistent devices contrived for causing it to be talked about — but under strict conditions: does this not prove that it was an object of secrecy, and more important, that there is still an attempt to keep it that way? But this often-stated theme, that sex is outside of discourse and that only the removing of an obstacle, the breaking of a secret, can clear the way leading to it, is precisely what needs to be examined. Does it not partake of the injunction by which discourse is provoked? Is it not with the aim of inciting people to speak of sex that it is made to mirror, at the outer limit of every actual discourse, something akin to a secret whose discovery is imperative, a thing abusively reduced to silence, and at the same time difficult and necessary, dangerous and precious to divulge? We must not forget that by making sex into that which, above all else, had to be confessed, the Christian pastoral always presented it as the disquieting enigma: not a thing which stubbornly shows itself, but one which always hides, the insidious presence that speaks in a voice so muted and often disguised that one risks remaining deaf to it. Doubtless the secret does not reside in that basic reality in relation to which all the incitements to speak of sex are situated – whether they try to force the secret, or whether in some obscure way they reinforce it by the manner in which they speak of it. It is a question rather of a theme that forms part of the very mechanics of these incitements: a way of giving shape to the requirement to speak about the matter, a fable that is indispensable to the endlessly proliferating economy of the discourse on sex. What is peculiar to modern societies, in fact, is not that they consigned sex to a shadow existence, but that they dedicated themselves to speaking of it *ad infinitum*, while exploiting it as *the* secret.

References

Flandrin, J.-L. (1976) *Familles: parenté, maison, sexualité dans l'ancienne société*, Paris: Hachette.
De' Ligouri, A. (1835) *Préceptes sur le sixième commandement*, Trans., 5.
De Sade, D.-A. ([1931–5] 1966) *The 120 Days of Sodom*, Trans. Wainhouse, A. and Seaver, R., New York: Grove Press, 271.
Tardieu, A. (1857) *Étude médico-légale sur les attentats aux mœurs*, 114.

Chapter 34

Judith Butler

BURNING ACTS, INJURIOUS SPEECH

. . .

THAT WORDS WOUND SEEMS incontestably true, and that hateful, racist, misogynist, homophobic speech should be vehemently countered seems incontrovertibly right. But does understanding from where speech derives its power to wound alter our conception of what it might mean to counter that wounding power? Do we accept the notion that injurious speech is attributable to a singular subject and act? If we accept such a juridical constraint on thought – the grammatical requirements of accountability – as a point of departure, what is lost from the political analysis of injury? Indeed, when political discourse is fully collapsed into juridical discourse, the meaning of political opposition runs the risk of being reduced to the act of prosecution.

. . .

In two recent cases, the Supreme Court has reconsidered the distinction between protected and unprotected speech in relation to the phenomenon of "hate speech." Are certain forms of invidious speech to be construed as "fighting words:" and if so, are they appropriately considered to be a kind of speech unprotected by the first Amendment? In the first case, *R.A.V. v. St. Paul*, 112 S. Ct. 2538, 120 L. Ed. 2d 305 (1992), the ordinance in question was one passed by the St. Paul City Council in 1990, and read in part as follows:

> Whoever places on public or private property a symbol, object, appellation, characterization or graffiti, including, but not limited to, a burning

Source: Judith Butler, *Excitable Speech: A Politics of the Performative*, New York and London: Routledge, 1997.

cross or Nazi swastika, which one knows or has reasonable grounds to
know arouses anger, alarm, or resentment in others, on the basis of
race, color, creed, religion or gender commits disorderly conduct and
shall be guilty of a misdemeanor.

A white teenager was charged under this ordinance after burning a cross in
front of a black family's house. The charge was dismissed by the trial court but
reinstated by the Minnesota State Supreme Court; at stake was the question whether
the ordinance itself was "substantially overbroad and impermissably content
based." The defense contended that the burning of the cross in front of the black
family's house was to be construed as an example of protected speech. The State
Supreme Court overturned the decision of the trial court, arguing first that the
burning of the cross could not be construed as protected speech because it constituted "fighting words" as defined in *Chaplinsky v. New Hampshire*, 315 U.S. 568, 572
(1942), and second, that the reach of the ordinance was permissible considering
the "compelling government interest in protecting the community against bias –
motivated threats to public safety and order." *In Re Welfare of R.A.V.*, 464 N.W.2
507, 510 (Minn. 1991).
    The United States Supreme Court reversed the State Supreme Court decision,
reasoning first that the burning cross was not an instance of "fighting words:" but
a "viewpoint" within the "free marketplace of ideas" and that such "viewpoints" are
categorically protected by the first Amendment. The majority on the High Court
(Scalia, Rehnquist, Kennedy, Souter, Thomas) then offered a *second* reason for
declaring the ordinance unconstitutional, a judicially activist contribution which
took many jurists by surprise: the justices severely restricted the possible doctrinal
scope of "fighting words" by claiming it unconstitutional to impose prohibitions on
speech solely on the basis of the "content" or "subjects addressed" in that speech.
In order to determine whether words are fighting words, there can be no decisive
recourse to the content and the subject matter of what is said.
    One conclusion on which the justices appear to concur is that the ordinance
imposed overbroad restrictions on speech, given that forms of speech *not* considered to fall within the parameters of fighting words would nonetheless be banned
by the ordinance. But while the Minnesota ordinance proved too broad for all the
justices, Scalia, Thomas, Rehnquist, Kennedy, and Souter took the opportunity of
this review to severely restrict any future application of the fighting words doctrine.
At stake in the majority opinion is not only when and where "speech" constitutes
some component of an injurious act such that it loses its protected status under the
first Amendment, but what constitutes the domain of "speech" itself.
    According to a rhetorical reading of this decision – distinguished from a reading
that follows established conventions of legal interpretation – the court might be
understood as asserting its state-sanctioned linguistic power to determine what will
and will not count as "speech" and, in the process, enacting a potentially injurious
form of juridical speech. What follows, then, is a reading which considers not only
the account that the Court gives of how and when speech becomes injurious, but
considers as well the injurious potential of the account itself as "speech" considered
in a broad sense. Recalling Cover's claim that legal decisions can engage the nexus
of language and violence, consider that the adjudication of what will and will not

count as protected speech will itself be a kind of speech, one which implicates the state in the very problem of discursive power with which it is invested to regulate, sanction, and restrict such speech.

In the following, then, I will read the "speech" in which the decision is articulated against the version of "speech" officially circumscribed as protected content in the decision. The point of this kind of reading is not only to expose a contradictory set of rhetorical strategies at work in the decision, but to consider the power of that discursive domain which not only produces what will and will not count as "speech:" but which regulates the political field of contestation through the tactical manipulation of that very distinction. Furthermore, I want to argue that the very reasons that account for the injuriousness of such acts, construed as speech in a broad sense, are precisely what render difficult the prosecution of such acts. Lastly, I want to suggest that the court's speech carries with it its *own* violence, and that the very institution that is invested with the authority to adjudicate the problem of hate speech re-circulates and redirects that hatred in and as its own highly consequential speech, often by coopting the very language that it seeks to adjudicate.

The majority opinion, written by Scalia, begins with the construction of the act, the burning of the cross; and one question at issue is whether or not this act constitutes an injury, whether it can be construed as "fighting words" or whether it communicates a content which is, for better or worse, protected by first Amendment precedent. The figure of burning will be repeated throughout the opinion, first in the context in which the burning cross is construed as the free expression of a viewpoint within the marketplace of ideas, and, second, in the example of the burning of the flag, which could be held illegal were it to violate an ordinance prohibiting outside fires, but which could not be held to be illegal if it were the expression of an idea. Later Scalia will close the argument through recourse to yet another fire: "Let there be no mistake about our belief that burning a cross in someone's front yard is reprehensible." "But," Scalia continued, "St. Paul has sufficient means at its disposal to prevent such behavior without adding the first Amendment to the fire." *R.A.V. v. St. Paul*, 112 S. Ct. at 2550, 120 L. Ed. 2d at 326.

Significantly, Scalia here aligns the act of cross-burning with those who defend the ordinance, since both are producing fires, but whereas the cross-burner's fire is constitutionally protected speech, the ordinance-maker's language is figured as the incineration of free speech. The analogy suggests that the ordinance is itself a kind of cross-burning, and Scalia then draws on the very destructive implications of cross-burning to underscore his point that the ordinance itself is destructive. The figure thus affirms the destructiveness of the cross-burning that the decision itself effectively denies, the destructiveness of the act that it has just elevated to the status of protected verbal currency within the marketplace of ideas.

The Court thus transposes the place of the ordinance and the place of the cross-burning, but also figures the first Amendment in an analogous relation to the black family and its home which in the course of the writing has become reduced to "someone's front yard." The stripping of blackness and family from the figure of the complainant is significant, for it refuses the dimension of social power that constructs the so-called speaker and the addressee of the speech act in question, the burning cross. And it refuses as well the racist history of the convention of cross-burning by the Ku Klux Klan which marked, targeted, and, hence, portended a further violence against a given addressee. Scalia thus figures himself as quenching the fire which the ordinance has lit, and which is being stoked with the first Amendment, apparently in its totality. Indeed, compared with the admittedly "reprehensible" act of burning a cross in "someone's" front yard, the ordinance itself appears to conflagrate in much greater dimensions, threatening to burn the book which it is Scalia's duty to uphold; Scalia thus champions himself as an opponent of those who would set the constitution on fire, crossburners of a more dangerous order.

The lawyers arguing for the legality of the ordinance based their appeal on the fighting words doctrine. This doctrine, formulated in *Chaplinsky v. New Hampshire*, 315 U.S. 568, 572 (1942), argued that speech acts unprotected by the Constitution are those which are not essential to the communication of ideas: "such utterances are no essential part of any exposition of ideas, and are of such slight social value as a step to truth that any benefit that may be derived from them is clearly outweighed by the social interest in order and morality." Scalia takes this phrasing to legitimate the following claim: "the unprotected features of the words are, despite their verbal character, essentially a 'nonspeech' element of communication." *R.A.V. v. St. Paul*, 112 S. Ct. at 2545, 120 L. Ed. 2d at 319. In his efforts to protect all contents of communication from proscription, Scalia establishes a distinction between the content and the vehicle of that expression; it is the latter which is proscribable, and the former which is not. He continues, "fighting words are thus analogous to a noisy sound truck." *Id*. What is injurious, then, is the sound, but not the message, indeed, "the government may not regulate use based on hostility – or favoritism – towards the underlying message expressed." *Id*.

The connection between the signifying power of the burning cross and Scalia's regressive new critical distinction between what is and is not a speech element in communication is nowhere marked in the text.[1] Scalia assumes that the burning cross is a message, an expression of a viewpoint, a discussion of a "subject" or "content": in short, that the act of burning the cross is fully and exhaustively translatable into a *constative* act of speech; the burning of the cross which is, after all, on the black family's lawn, is thus made strictly analogous – and morally equivalent – to an individual speaking in public on whether or not there ought to be a fifty-cent tax on gasoline. Significantly, Scalia does not tell us what the cross would say if the cross could speak, but he does insist that what the burning cross is doing is expressing a viewpoint, discoursing on a content which is, admittedly, controversial, but for that very reason, ought not to be proscribed. Thus the defense of cross-burning as free speech rests on an unarticulated analogy between that act and a public constation. This speech is not a doing, an action or an injury, even as it is the enunciation of a set of "contents" that might offend. The injury is thus construed as one that is registered at the level of sensibility, which is to say that it is an offense that is one of the risks of free speech.

That the cross burns and thus constitutes an incendiary destruction is not considered as a sign of the intention to reproduce that incendiary destruction at the site of the house or the family; the historical correlation between cross-burning and marking a community, a family, or an individual for further violence is also ignored.

How much of that burning is translatable into a declarative or constative proposition? And how would one know exactly what constative claim is being made by the burning cross? If the cross is the expression of a viewpoint, is it a declaration as in, "I am of the opinion that black people ought not to live in this neighborhood" or even, "I am of the opinion that violence ought to be perpetrated against black people:" or is it a perlocutionary performative, as in imperatives and commands which take the form of "Burn!" or "Die!"? Is it an injunction that works its power metonymically not only in the sense that the fire recalls prior burnings which have served to mark black people as targets for violence, but also in the sense that the fire is understood to be transferable from the cross to the target that is marked by the cross? The relation between cross-burning and torchings of both persons and properties is historically established. Hence, from this perspective, the burning cross assumes the status of a direct address and a *threat* and, as such, is construed either as the incipient moment of injurious action *or* as the statement of an intention to injure.[2]

Although Justice Stevens agreed with the decision to strike down the Minnesota ordinance, he takes the occasion to rebuke Scalia for restricting the fighting words doctrine. Stevens reviews special cases in which conduct may be prohibited by special rules. Note in the following quotation how the cross-burning is nowhere mentioned, but the displacements of the figure of fire appear in a series of examples which effectively transfer the need for protection *from racist speech* to the need for protection *from public protest against racism*. Even within Stevens's defense of proscribing conduct, a phantasmatic figure of a menacing riot emerges:

> Lighting a fire near an ammunition dump or a gasoline storage tank is especially dangerous; such behavior may be punished more severely than burning trash in a vacant lot. Threatening someone because of her race or religious beliefs may cause particularly severe trauma or touch off a riot, and threatening a high public official may cause substantial social disruptions; such threats may be punished more severely than threats against someone based on, say, his support of a particular athletic team.
> (*R.A.V. v. St. Paul*, 112 S. Ct. at 2561, 120 L Ed. 2d at 340)

Absent from the list of fires above is the burning of the cross in question. In the place of that prior scene, we are asked first to imagine someone who would light a fire near a gas tank, and then to imagine a more innocuous fire in a vacant lot. But with the vacant lot, we enter the metaphor of poverty and property, which appears to effect the unstated transition to the matter of blackness introduced by the next line, "threatening someone because of her race or religious beliefs . . .": *because* of her race is not the same as "on the basis of" her race and leaves open the possibility that the race causally induces the threat. The threat appears to shift mid-sentence as Stevens continues to elaborate a second causality: this threat "may cause particularly severe trauma or touch off a riot" at which point it is no longer clear whether the threat which warrants the prohibition on conduct refers to the "threatening someone because of her race or religious beliefs" or to the riot that might result therefrom. What immediately follows suggests that the limitations on rioters has suddenly become more urgent to authorize than the limitation on those who would threaten this "her" "because of her race . . . ." After "or touch off a riot:" the sentence continues, "and threatening a high official may cause substantial social disruption . . . ," as if the racially marked trauma had already led to a riot and an attack on high officials.

This sudden implication of the justices themselves might be construed as a paranoid inversion of the original cross-burning narrative. That original narrative is nowhere mentioned, but its elements have been redistributed throughout the examples; the fire which was the original "threat" against the black family is re-located first as an incendiary move against industry, then as a location in a vacant lot, and then reappears tacitly in the riot which now appears to follow from the trauma and threaten public officials. The fire which initially constituted the threat against the black family becomes metaphorically transfigured as the threat that blacks in trauma now wield against high officials. And though Stevens is on record as endorsing a construction of "fighting words" that would include cross-burning as *un*protected speech, the language in which he articulates this view deflects the question to that of the state's right to circumscribe conduct to protect itself against a racially motivated riot.

The circumscription of content explicitly discussed in the decision appears to emerge through a production of semantic excess in and through the metonymic chain of anxious figuration. The separability of content from sound, for instance, or of content from context, is exemplified and illustrated through figures which signify in excess of the thesis which they are meant to support. Indeed, to the extent that, in the Scalia analysis, "content" is circumscribed and purified to estab-lish its protected status, that content is secured through the production and proliferation of "dangers" from which it calls to be protected. Hence, the question of whether or not the black family in Minnesota is entitled to protection from public displays such as cross-burnings is displaced onto the question of whether or not the "content" of free speech is to be protected from those who would burn it. The fire is thus displaced from the cross to the legal instrument wielded by those who would protect the family from the fire, but then to the black family itself, to blackness, to the vacant lot, to rioters in Los Angeles who explicitly oppose the decision of a court and who now represent the incendiary power of the trauma-tized rage of black people who would burn the judiciary itself. But, of course, that construal is already a reversal of the narrative in which a court delivers a decision of acquittal for the four policemen indicted for the brutal beating of Rodney King, a decision that might be said to "spark" a riot which calls into question whether the claim of having been injured can be heard and countenanced by a jury and a judge who are extremely susceptible to the suggestion that a black person is always and only endangering, but never endangered. And so the High Court might be understood in its decision of June 22, 1992, to be taking its revenge on Rodney King, protecting itself against the riots in Los Angeles and elsewhere which appeared to be attacking the system of justice itself. Hence, the justices identify with the black family who sees the cross burning and takes it as a threat, but they substi-tute themselves for that family, and reposition blackness as the agency behind the threat itself.

The decision enacts a set of metonymic displacements which might well be read as anxious deflections and reversals of the injurious action at hand; indeed, the original scene is successively reversed in the metonymic relation between figures such that the fire is lit by the ordinance, carried out by traumatized rioters on the streets of Los Angeles, and threatens to engulf the justices themselves.

Mari Matsuda and Charles Lawrence also write of this text as enacting a rhetorical reversal of crime and punishment: "The cross burners are portrayed as an unpopular minority that the Supreme Court must defend against the power of the state. The injury to the Jones family is appropriated and the cross burner is cast as the injured victim. The reality of ongoing racism and exclusion is erased and bigotry is redefined as majoritarian condemnation of racist views."

. . .

Notes

1   The lawyers defending the application of the ordinance to the cross burning episode made the following argument:

> . . . we ask the Court to reflect on the "content" of the "expressive conduct" represented by a "burning cross." It is no less than the first step in an act of racial violence. It was and unfortunately still is the equivalent of [the] waving of a knife before the thrust, the pointing of a gun before it is fired, the lighting of the match before the arson, the hanging of the noose before the lynching. It is not a political statement, or even a cowardly statement of hatred. It is the first step in an act of assault. It can be no more protected than holding a gun to a victim['s] head. It is perhaps the ultimate expression of "fighting words."
>
> _R.A.V. v. St. Paul_, 112 S. Ct. at 2569–70, fn. 8, 120 L.
> Ed. 2d at 320 (App. to Brief for Petitioner).

2   All of the justices concur that the St. Paul ordinance is overbroad because it isolates "subject-matter" as offensive, and (a) potentially prohibits discussion of such subject-matters even by those whose political sympathies are with the ordinance, and (b) fails to distinguish between the subject-matter's injuriousness and the context in which it is enunciated.

Chapter 35

Teun A. Van Dijk

DISCOURSE AND THE
DENIAL OF RACISM

· · ·

Discourse and racism

ONE OF THE CRUCIAL PROPERTIES of contemporary racism is its denial, typically illustrated in such well-known disclaimers as 'I have nothing against blacks, but . . .'. This article examines the discursive strategies, as well as the cognitive and social functions, of such and other forms of denial in different genres of text and talk about ethnic or racial affairs.

· · ·

The guiding idea behind this research is that ethnic and racial prejudices are prominently acquired and shared within the white dominant group through everyday conversation and institutional text and talk. Such discourse serves to express, convey, legitimate or indeed to conceal or deny such negative ethnic attitudes. Therefore, a systematic and subtle discourse analytical approach should be able to reconstruct such social cognitions about other groups.

It is further assumed in this research programme that talk and text about minorities, immigrants, refugees or, more generally, about people of colour or Third World peoples and nations, also have broader societal, political and cultural functions. Besides positive self-presentation and negative other-presentation, such discourse signals group membership, white ingroup allegiances and, more generally, the various conditions for the reproduction of the white group and their dominance in virtually all social, political and cultural domains.

Source: Teun A. Van Dijk, 'Discourse and the denial of racism', *Discourse & Society*, 3 (1), 1992: 87–118.

. . .

Political, media, academic, corporate and other elites play an important role in the reproduction of racism. They are the ones who control or have access to many types of public discourse, have the largest stake in maintaining white group dominance, and are usually also most proficient in persuasively formulating their ethnic opinions. Although there is of course a continuous interplay between elite and popular forms of racism, analysis of many forms of discourse suggests that the elites in many respects 'preformulate' the kind of ethnic beliefs of which, sometimes more blatant, versions may then get popular currency. Indeed, many of the more 'subtle', 'modern', 'everyday' or 'new' forms of cultural racism, or ethnicism, studied below, are taken from elite discourse. This hypothesis is not inconsistent with the possibility that (smaller, oppositional) elite groups also play a prominent role in the preformulation of anti-racist ideologies.

. . .

The denial of racism

The denial of racism is one of the moves that is part of the latter strategy of positive in-group presentation. General norms and values, if not the law, prohibit (blatant) forms of ethnic prejudice and discrimination, and many if not most white group members are both aware of such social constraints and, up to a point, even share and acknowledge them (Billig 1988). Therefore, even the most blatantly racist discourse in our data routinely features denials or at least mitigations of racism. Interestingly, we have found that precisely the more racist discourse tends to have disclaimers and other denials. This suggests that language users who say negative things about minorities are well aware of the fact that they may be understood as breaking the social norm of tolerance or acceptance.

Denials of racism, and similar forms of positive self-presentation, have both an *individual* and a *social* dimension. Not only do most white speakers individually resent being perceived as racists, [but] also, and even more importantly, such strategies may at the same time aim at defending the in-group as a whole: 'We are not racists', 'We are not a racist society'.

Whereas the first, individual, form of denial is characteristic of informal everyday conversations, the second is typical for public discourse, for instance in politics, the media, education, corporations and other organizations. Since public discourse potentially reaches a large audience, it is this latter, social form of denial that is most influential and, therefore, also most damaging: it is the social discourse of denial that persuasively helps construct the dominant white consensus. Few white group members would have reason or interest, to doubt let alone to oppose such a claim.

. . .

Conversation

Everyday conversation is at the heart of social life. Whether in informal situations, with family members or friends, or on the job with colleagues or clients or within a multitude of institutions, informal talk constitutes a crucial mode of social interaction. At the same time, conversations are a major conduit of social 'information-processing', and provide the context for the expression and persuasive conveyance of shared knowledge and beliefs.

In ethnically mixed societies, minority groups and ethnic relations are a major topic of everyday conversation. Whether through direct personal experience, or indirectly through the mass media, white people in Europe and North America learn about minorities or immigrants, formulate their own opinions and thus informally reproduce – and occasionally challenge – the dominant consensus on ethnic affairs through informal everyday talk.

Our extensive discourse analytical research into the nature of such everyday talk about ethnic affairs, based on some 170 interviews conducted in the Netherlands and California, shows that such informal talk has a number of rather consistent properties:

1   Topics are selected from a rather small range of subjects, and focus on socio-cultural differences, deviance and competition. Most topics explicitly or implicitly deal with interpersonal, social, cultural or economic 'threats' of the dominant white group, society or culture.
2   Storytelling is not, as would be usual, focused on entertaining, but takes place within an argumentative framework. Stories serve as the strong, while personally experienced, premises of a generally negative conclusion, such as 'We are not used to that here', 'They should learn the language' or 'The government should do something about that.'
3   Style, rhetoric and conversational interaction generally denote critical distance, if not negative attitudes towards minorities or immigration. However, current norms of tolerance control expressions of evaluations in such a way that discourse with strangers (such as interviewers) is generally rather mitigated. Strong verbal aggression tends to be avoided.
4   Overall, speakers follow a double strategy of positive self-presentation and negative other-presentation.

It is within this latter strategy also that disclaimers, such as 'I have nothing against Arabs, *but* . . .' have their specific functions. Such a denial may be called 'apparent', because the denial is not supported by evidence that the speaker does not have anything against 'them'. On the contrary, the denial often serves as the face-keeping move introducing a generally negative assertion, following the invariable *but*, sometimes stressed, as in the following example from a Dutch woman:

(1)   uhh . . . how they are and that is mostly just fine, people have their own religion have their own way of life, and I have abso*lutely* nothing against that, *but*, it *is* a fact that if their way of life begins to differ from mine to an *extent* that. . . .

Talking about the main topic of cultural difference, the denial here focuses on relative tolerance for such cultural differences, which, however, is clearly constrained. The differences should not be too great. So, on the one hand, the woman follows the norm of tolerance, but on the other hand, she feels justified to reject others when they 'go too far'. In other words, the denial here presupposes a form of limited social acceptance.

Speakers who are more aware of discrimination and racism, as is the case in California, are even more explicit about the possible inferences of their talk:

(2)   It sounds prejudiced, but I think if students only use English. . . .

The use of English, a prominent topic for 'ethnic' conversations in the USA, may be required for many practical reasons, but the speaker realizes that whatever the good arguments he or she may have, it may be heard as a form of prejudice against immigrants. Of course the use of 'It sounds' implies that the speaker does not think he is really prejudiced.

One major form of denial in everyday conversation is the denial of discrimination. Indeed, as also happens in the right-wing media (see below), we also find reversal in this case: we are the real victims of immigration and minorities. Here are some of the ways people in Amsterdam formulate their denials:

(3)   Yes, they have exploited them, that's what they say at least, you know, but well, I don't believe that either. . . .

(4)   Big cars, they are better off than we are. If anybody is being discriminated against, our children are. That's what I make of it.

(5)   And the only thing that came from her mouth was I am being discriminated against and the Dutch all have good housing, well it is a big lie, it is not true.

(6)   And they say that they are being dismi discri discriminated against. That is not true.

(7)   Listen, they always say that foreigners are being discriminated against here. No, *we* are being discriminated against. It is exactly the reverse.

In all these situations, the speakers talk about what they see as threats or lies by immigrants: a murder in (3), cheating on welfare in (4), a radio programme where a black woman says she is discriminated against in (5), and neighbourhood services in (6) and (7). In conversations such reversals may typically be heard in working-class neighbourhoods where crime is attributed to minorities, or where alleged favouritism (e.g., in housing) is resented. Poor whites thus feel that they are victims of inadequate social and urban policies, but instead of blaming the authorities or the politicians, they tend to blame the newcomers who, in their eyes, are so closely related to the changing, i.e., deteriorating, life in the inner city. And if *they* are defined as those who are responsible, such a role is inconsistent with the claim that *they* are discriminated against (Phizacklea and Miles 1979).

Note that this consensus is not universal. Negative behaviour may be observed, but without generalization and with relevant comparisons to Dutch youths:

(8)   And that was also, well I am sorry, but they were foreigners, they were apparently Moroccans who did that. But God, all young people are aggressive, whether it is Turkish youth, or Dutch youth, or Surinamese youth, is aggressive. Particularly because of discrimination uhh that we have here . . .

Here discrimination is not reversed, and the young immigrants are represented as victims of discrimination, which is used to explain and hence to excuse some of their 'aggressiveness'. Such talk, however, is rather exceptional.

The press

Many of the 'ethnic events' people talk about in everyday life are not known from personal experiences, but from the media. At least until recently, in many parts of Western Europe and even in some regions of North America, most white people had few face-to-face dealings with members of minority groups. Arguments in everyday talk, thus, may be about crime or cultural differences they read about in the press, and such reports are taken as 'proof' of the negative attitudes the speakers have about minorities.

Our analyses of thousands of reports in the press in Britain and the Netherlands (Van Dijk 1991), largely confirm the common-sense interpretations of the readers: a topical analysis shows that crime, cultural differences, violence ('riots'), social welfare and problematic immigration are among the major recurrent topics of ethnic affairs reporting. In other words, there are marked parallels between topics of talk and media topics.

Overall, with some changes over the last decade, the dominant picture of minorities and immigrants is that of *problems* (Hartmann and Husband 1974). Thus the conservative and right-wing press tends to focus on the problems minorities and immigrants are seen to create (in housing, schooling, unemployment, crime, etc.), whereas the more liberal press (also) focuses on the problems minorities have (poverty, discrimination), but which *we* (white liberals) do something about. On the other hand, many topics that are routine in the coverage of white people, groups or institutions tend to be ignored, such as their contribution to the economy, political organization, culture and in general all topics that characterize the everyday lives of minorities, and their own, active contributions to the society as a whole. Thus, in many respects, except when involved in conflicts or problems, minorities tend to be 'denied' by the press (Boskin 1980).

Practices of newsgathering as well as patterns of quotation also show that minorities and their institutions have literally little to say in the press. First of all, especially in Europe, there are virtually no minority journalists, so that the perspective, inside knowledge and experience, prevailing attitudes and necessary sources of journalists tend to be all white, as are also the government agencies, police and other institutions that are the main sources of news in the press (Van Dijk 1988a; 1988b). Even on ethnic events, minority spokespersons are less quoted, less credibly quoted, and if they are quoted their opinions are often 'balanced' by the more 'neutral' comments of white spokespersons. Especially on delicate topics, such as discrimination, prejudice and racism, minority representatives or experts are very seldom heard in a credible, authoritative way. If at all, such quotes are often presented as unwarranted or even ridiculous accusations.

It is at this point where the overall strategy of denial has one of its discursive manifestations in press reports. Of course, as may be expected, there is a difference between liberal, conservative and right-wing newspapers in this respect. Note, however, that there are virtually no explicitly anti-racist newspapers in Europe and North America. The official norm, even on the right, is that 'we are all against racism', and the overall message is, therefore, that serious accusations of racism are a figment of the imagination.

Liberal newspapers, however, do pay attention to stories of explicit discrimination, e.g., in employment (though *rarely* in their own newsrooms or news reports), whereas right-wing extremism is usually dealt with in critical terms, although such coverage may focus on violent or otherwise newsworthy incidents rather than on racist attitudes *per se*. By such means ethnic or racial inequality is redefined as marginal, that is, as individualized or outside the consensus. Thus, the Dutch liberal press extensively reports cases (accusations) of discrimination, and the same is true in the USA. In the right-wing press, discrimination is also covered, but from a different perspective. Here, it is usually covered as a preposterous accusation, preferably against 'ordinary' people, or embedded in explanations or excuses (the act was provoked).

Whereas discrimination gets rather wide attention in the press, racism does not. Indeed, discrimination is seldom qualified as a manifestation of racism. One of the reasons is that racism is still often understood as an ideology of white supremacy, or as the kind of practices of the extreme right. Since the large majority of the press does not identify with the extreme right, any qualification of everyday discriminatory practices as 'racism' is resolutely rejected.

For large sections of the press, only anti-racists see such everyday racism as racism, which results in the marginalization of anti-racists as a radical, 'loony' group. For much of the press, at least in Britain, the real enemies, therefore, are the anti-racists: they are intolerant, anti-British, busybodies, who see racism everywhere, even in 'innocent' children's books, and even in the press.

It is not surprising, therefore, that reports on general aspects of racism in one's own society or group tend to be rare, even in the liberal press. Anti-racist writers, researchers or action groups have less access to the media, and their activities or opinions tend to be more or less harshly scorned, if not ridiculed. For the right-wing press, moreover, they are the real source of the 'problems' attributed to a multi-cultural society, because they not only attack venerable institutions (such as the police, government or business), but also provide a competing but fully incompatible definition of the ethnic situation. It is this symbolic competition for the definition of the situation and the intellectual struggle over the definition of society's morals, that pitches the right-wing press against left-wing, anti-racist intellectuals, teachers, writers and action groups.

Let us examine in more detail how exactly the press engages in this denial of racism. Most of our examples are taken from the British press, but it would not be difficult to find similar examples in the Dutch, German and French press. Because of its long history of slavery and segregation, the notion of white racism is more broadly accepted in the USA, even when today's prevailing ideology is that, now minorities have equal rights, racism is largely a thing of the past.

Racism and the press

The denial of racism in and by the press is of course most vehement when the press itself is the target of accusations. Reflecting similar reactions by other editors of Dutch newspapers to our own research on racism in the press, the editor-in-chief of a major elite weekly, *Intermediair*, catering especially for social scientists and the business community, writes the following in a letter:

> (9)   In particular, what you state about the coverage of minorities remains unproven and an unacceptable caricature of reality. Your thesis 'that the tendency of most reports is that ethnic minorities cause problems for us' is in my opinion not only not proven, but simply incorrect.
>
> (Translated from the Dutch)

This reaction was inspired by a brief summary of mostly international research on the representation of minorities in the press. The editor's denial is not based on (other) research, but simply stated as a 'fact'.

. . .

Other editors take an even more furious stand, and challenge the very academic credentials of the researcher and the university, as is the case by the editor of the major conservative popular daily in the Netherlands, *De Telegraaf*, well known for its biased reporting on minorities, immigrants and refugees:

> (10)   Your so-called scientific research does not in any sense prove your slanderous insinuations regarding the contents of our newspaper, is completely irrelevant and raises doubt about the prevailing norms of scientific research and social prudence at the University of Amsterdam.
>
> (Translated from the Dutch)

We see that whatever 'proof' may be brought in one's painstaking analyses of news reports, the reaction is one of flat denial and counter-attack by discrediting the researcher. Examples like these may be multiplied at random. No newspaper, including (or especially) the more liberal ones, will accept even a moderate charge of being biased, while allegations of racism are rejected violently. Recall that these newspapers, especially in Europe, generally employ no, or only one or two token, minority journalists.

With such an editorial attitude towards racism, there is a general reluctance to identify racist events as such in society at large. Let us examine the principal modes of such denials in the press. Examples are taken from the British press coverage of ethnic affairs in 1985 (for analysis of other properties of these examples, see Van Dijk 1991). Brief summaries of the context of each fragment of news discourse are given between parentheses.

Positive self-presentation

The semantic basis of denial is 'truth' as the writer sees it. The denial of racism in the press, therefore, presupposes that the journalist or columnist believes that his or her own group or country is essentially 'tolerant' towards minorities or immigrants. Positive self-presentation, thus, is an important move in journalistic discourse, and should be seen as the argumentative denial of the accusations of anti-racists:

(11)   [Handsworth] Contrary to much doctrine, and acknowledging a small malevolent fascist fringe, this is a remarkably tolerant society. But tolerance would be stretched were it to be seen that enforcement of law adopted the principle of reverse discrimination.

(*Daily Telegraph*, editorial, 11 September)

(12)   [Racial attacks and policing] If the ordinary British taste for decency and tolerance is to come through, it will need positive and unmistakable action.

(*Daily Telegraph*, editorial, 13 August)

(13)   [Racial attacks against Asians] . . . Britain's record for absorbing people from different backgrounds, peacefully and with tolerance, is second to none. The descendants of Irish and Jewish immigrants will testify to that. It would be tragic to see that splendid reputation tarnished now.

(*Sun*, editorial, 14 August)

(14)   [Immigration] Our traditions of fairness and tolerance are being exploited by every terrorist, crook, screwball and scrounger who wants a free ride at our expense. . . . Then there are the criminals who sneak in as political refugees or as family members visiting a distant relative.

(*Mail*, 28 November)

(15)   We have racism too – and that is what is behind the plot. It is not white racism. It is black racism. . . . But who is there to protect the white majority? . . . Our tolerance is our strength, but we will not allow anyone to turn it into our weakness.

(*Sun*, 24 October)

These examples not only assert or presuppose white British 'tolerance' but at the same time define its boundaries. Tolerance might be interpreted as a position of weakness and, therefore, it should not be 'stretched' too far, lest 'every terrorist', 'criminal' or other immigrant, takes advantage of it. Affirmative action or liberal immigration laws, thus, can only be seen as a form of reverse discrimination, and hence as a form of self-destruction of white Britain. Ironically, therefore, these examples are self-defeating because of their internal contradictions. It is not toler- ance *per se* that is aimed at, but rather the limitations preventing its 'excesses'. Note that in example (15) positive self-presentation is at the same time combined with the well-known move of reversal. 'They are the real racists', 'We are the real victims.' We shall come back to such reversal moves below.

Denial and counter-attack

Having constructed a positive self-image of white Britain, the conservative and tabloid press especially engages in attacks against those who hold a different view, at the same time defending those who agree with its position, as was the case during the notorious Honeyford affair (Honeyford was headmaster of a Bradford school who was suspended, then reinstated and finally let go with a golden handshake, after having written articles on multicultural education which most of the parents of his mostly Asian students found racist). The attacks on the anti-racists often embody denials of racism:

> (16)   [Reaction of 'race lobby' against Honeyford] Why is it that this lobby have chosen to persecute this man. . . . It is not because he is a racist; it is precisely because he is not a racist, yet has dared to challenge the attitudes, behaviour and approach of the ethnic minority professionals.
>
> *(Daily Telegraph*, 6 September)

> (17)   [Honeyford and other cases] Nobody is less able to face the truth than the hysterical 'anti-racist' brigade. Their intolerance is such that they try to silence or sack anyone who doesn't toe their party-line.
>
> *(Sun*, 13 October, column by John Vincent)

> (18)   [Honeyford] For speaking commonsense he's been vilified; for being courageous he's been damned, for refusing to concede defeat his enemies can't forgive him. . . . I have interviewed him and I am utterly convinced that he hasn't an ounce of racism in his entire being.
>
> *(Mail*, 18 September, column by Lynda Lee-Potter)

> (19)   [Honeyford quits] Now we know who the true racists are.
>
> *(Sun* editorial, 30 November)

These examples illustrate several strategic moves in the press campaign against anti-racists. First, as we have seen above, denial is closely linked to the presupposition of 'truth': Honeyford is presented as defending the 'truth', namely the failure and the anti-British nature of multiculturalism. Second, consequent denials often lead to the strategic move of reversal: *we* are not the racists, *they* are the 'true racists'. This reversal also implies, thirdly, a reversal of the charges: Honeyford, and those who sympathize with him, are the victims, not his Asian students and their parents. Consequently, the anti-racists are the enemy: *they* are the ones who persecute innocent, ordinary British citizens, *they* are the ones who are intolerant. Therefore, victims who resist their attackers may be defined as folk heroes, who 'dare' the 'anti-racist brigade'.

Note also, in example (17), that the 'truth', as the supporters of Honeyford see it, is self-evident, and based on common sense. Truth and common sense are closely related notions in such counter-attacks, and reflect the power of the consensus, as well as the mobilization of popular support by 'ordinary' (white) British people. Apart from marginalizing Asian parents and other anti-racists by locating them outside of the consensus, and beyond the community of ordinary people like 'us', such appeals to common sense also have powerful ideological implications: self-evident truth is seen as 'natural', and hence the position of the others as 'unnatural' or even as 'crazy'. The anti-racist left, therefore, is often called 'crazy' or 'loony' in the right-wing British press.

Moral blackmail

One element that was very prominent in the Honeyford affair, as well as in similar cases, was the pretence of censorship: the anti-racists not only ignore the 'truth' about multicultural society, they also prevent others (us) from telling the truth. Repeatedly, thus, journalists and columnists argue that this 'taboo' and this 'censorship' must be broken in order to be able to tell the 'truth', as was the case after the disturbances in Tottenham:

> (20) [Tottenham] The time has come to state the truth without cant and without hypocrisy . . . the strength to face the facts without being silenced by the fear of being called racist.
> (*Mail*, 9 October, column by Lynda Lee-Potter)

Such examples also show that the authors feel morally blackmailed, while at the same time realizing that to 'state the truth', meaning 'to say negative things about minorities', may well be against the prevalent norms of tolerance and understanding. Clamouring for the 'truth', thus, expresses a dilemma, even if the dilemma is only apparent: the apparent dilemma is a rhetorical strategy to accuse the opponent of censorship or blackmail, not the result of moral soul-searching and a difficult decision. After all, the same newspapers extensively *do* write negative things about young blacks, and never hesitate to write what they see as the 'truth'. Nobody 'silences' them, and the taboo is only imaginary. On the contrary, the right-wing press in Britain reaches many millions of readers.

Thus, this strategic play of denial and reversal at the same time involves the construction of social roles in the world of ethnic strife, such as allies and enemies, victims, heroes and oppressors. In many respects, such discourse mimics the discourse of anti-racists by simply reversing the major roles: victims become oppressors, those who are in power become victims.

Subtle denials

Denials are not always explicit. There are many ways to express doubt, distance or non-acceptance of statements or accusations by others. When the official Commission for Racial Equality (CRE) in 1985 published a report on discrimination in the UK, outright denial of the facts would hardly be credible. Other discursive means, such as quotation marks, and the use of words like 'claim' or 'allege', presupposing doubt on the part of the writer, may be employed in accounting for the facts, as is the case in the following editorial from the *Daily Telegraph*:

> (21)   In its report which follows a detailed review of the operation of the 1976 Race Relations Act, the Commission claims that ethnic minorities continue to suffer high levels of discrimination and disadvantage.
>
> (*Daily Telegraph*, 1 August)

Such linguistic tricks do not go unnoticed, as we may see in the following reaction to this passage in a letter from Peter Newsam, then Director of the CRE.

> (22)   Of the Commission you say 'it claims that ethnic minorities continue to suffer high levels of discrimination and disadvantage'. This is like saying that someone 'claims' that July was wet. It was. And it is also a fact supported by the weight of independent research evidence that discrimination on racial grounds, in employment, housing and services, remains at a disconcertingly high level.
>
> (*Daily Telegraph*, 7 August)

Denials, thus, may be subtly conveyed by expressing doubt or distance. Therefore, the very notion of 'racism' usually appears between quotation marks, especially also in the headlines. Such scare quotes are not merely a journalistic device of reporting opinions or controversial points of view. If that were the case, also the opinions with which the newspaper happens to agree would have to be put between quotes, which is not always the case. Rather, apart from signalling journalistic doubt and distance, the quotes also connote 'unfounded accusation'. The use of quotes around the notion of 'racism' has become so much routine, that even in cases where the police or the courts themselves established that racism was involved in a particular case, the conservative press may maintain the quotes out of sheer habit.

Mitigation

Our conceptual analysis of denial already showed that denial may also be implied by various forms of mitigation, such as downtoning, using euphemisms or other circumlocutions that minimize the act itself or the responsibility of the accused. In the same editorial of the *Daily Telegraph* we quoted above, we find the following statement:

(23)   [CRE report] No one would deny the fragile nature of race relations in Britain today or that there is misunderstanding and distrust
between parts of the community.

(*Daily Telegraph*, editorial, 1 August)

Thus, instead of inequality or racism, race relations are assumed to be 'fragile', whereas 'misunderstanding and distrust' is also characteristic of these relations. Interestingly, this passage also explicitly denies the prevalence of denials and, therefore, might be read as a concession: there *are* problems. However, the way this concession is rhetorically presented by way of various forms of mitigation, suggests, in the context of the rest of the same editorial, that the concession is apparent. Such apparent concessions are another major form of disclaimer in discourse about ethnic relations, as we also have them in statements like: 'There are also intelligent blacks, but . . .', or 'I know that minorities sometimes have problems, but . . .'. Note also that in the example from the *Daily Telegraph* the mitigation not only appears in the use of euphemisms, but also in the *redistribu-tion of responsibility*, and hence in the denial of blame. Not we (whites) are mainly responsible for the tensions between the communities, but everybody is, as is suggested by the use of the impersonal existential phrase: '*There is* misunderstand-ing . . .'. Apparently, one effective move of denial is to either dispute responsible agency, or to conceal agency.

Defence and offence

On the other hand, in its attacks against the anti-racists, the right-wing press is not always that subtle. On the contrary, they may engage precisely in the 'diatribes' they direct at their opponents:

(24)   [Anti-fascist rally] The evening combined emotive reminders of
the rise of Nazism with diatribes against racial discrimination and
prejudice today.

(*Daily Telegraph*, 1 October)

(25)   [Black sections] In the more ideologically-blinkered sections of
his [Kinnock's] party . . . they seem to gain pleasure from identifying all difficulties experienced by immigrant groups, particularly
Afro-Caribbeans, as the result of racism . . .

(*Daily Telegraph*, editorial, 14 September)

(26)   [Worker accused of racism] . . . The really alarming thing is that
some of these pocket Hitlers of local government are moving into
national politics. It's time we set about exposing their antics while
we can. Forewarned is forearmed.

(*Mail*, editorial, 26 October)

These examples further illustrate that denial of discrimination, prejudice and
racism is not merely a form of self-defence or positive self-presentation. Rather,
it is at the same time an element of attack against what they define as 'ideologically blinkered' opponents, as we also have seen in the move of reversal in other
examples. Anti-racism is associated with the 'loony left', and attacking it therefore
also has important ideological and political implications, and not just moral ones.

'Difficulties' of the Afro-Caribbean community may be presupposed, though
not spelled out forcefully and in detail, but such presuppositions rather take the
form of an apparent concession. That is, whatever the causes of these 'difficulties',
as they are euphemistically called, they can not be the result of racism. Implicitly,
by attributing 'pleasure' to those who explain the situation of the blacks, the newspaper also suggests that the left has an interest in such explanations and, therefore,
even welcomes racism. This strategy is familiar in many other attacks against anti-
racists: 'If there were no racism, they would invent it'. It hardly needs to be spelled
out that such a claim again implies a denial of racism.

The amalgamation of comparisons and metaphors used in these attacks is quite
interesting. That is, in one example an ironic reference is made to the 'emotive
reminders' of Nazism, and in another these same opponents of Nazism are qualified as 'pocket Hitlers'. Yet, this apparent inconsistency in sociopolitical labelling
has a very precise function. By referring to their opponents in terms of 'pocket
Hitlers' the newspapers obviously distance themselves from the fascist opinions
and practices that are often part of the more radical accusations against the right.
At the same time, by way of the usual reversal, they categorize their opponents
precisely in terms of their own accusations, and thus put them in a role these
opponents most clearly would abhor.

Thus, the anti-racist left is associated with fascist practices, ideological blinkers
and antics. Apart from their anti-racist stance, it is, however, their (modest) political influence which particularly enrages the right-wing press – although virtually
powerless at the national level, and even within their own (Labour) party, some
of the anti-racists have made it into local councils, and therefore control (some)
money, funding and other forms of political influence. That is, they have at least
some counter-power, and it is this power and its underlying ideology that is challenged by a press which itself controls the news supply of millions of readers. What
the denial of racism and the concomitant attacks against the anti-racists in education or politics is all about, therefore, is a struggle over the definition of the ethnic
situation. Thus, their ideological and political opponents are seen as symbolic
competitors in the realm of moral influence. Whether directed at a headmaster or
against other ordinary white British or not, what the right-wing press is particularly concerned about is its own image: by attacking the anti-racists, it is in fact
defending itself.

. . .

Conclusions

Whether in the streets of the inner city, in the press or in parliament, dominant group members are often engaged in discourse about 'them': ethnic minority groups, immigrants or refugees, who have come to live in the country. Such discourses, as well as the social cognitions underlying them, are complex and full of contradictions. They may be inspired by general norms of tolerance and acceptance, but also, and sometimes at the same time, by feelings of distrust, resentment or frustration about those 'others'.

Topics, stories and argumentation may thus construct a largely negative picture of minorities or immigrants, e.g., in terms of cultural differences, deviance or competition, as a problem or as a threat to 'our' country, territory, space, housing, employment, education, norms, values, habits or language. Such talk and text, therefore, is not a form of individual discourse, but social, group discourse, and expresses not only individual opinions, but rather socially shared representations.

However, negative talk about minority groups or immigrants may be heard as biased, prejudiced or racist, and as inconsistent with general values of tolerance. This means that such discourse needs to be hedged, mitigated, excused, explained or otherwise managed in such a way that it will not 'count' against the speaker or writer. Face-keeping, positive self-presentation and impression management are the usual strategies that language users have recourse to in such a situation of possible 'loss of face': they have to make sure that they are not misunderstood and that no unwanted inferences are made from what they say.

One of the major strategic ways white speakers and writers engage in such a form of impression management is the denial of racism. They may simply claim they did not say anything negative, or focus on their intentions: it may have sounded negative, but was not intended that way. Similarly, they may mitigate their negative characterization of the others by using euphemisms, implications or vague allusions. They may make apparent concessions, on the one hand, and on the other hand support their negative discourse by arguments, stories or other supporting 'facts'.

Also, speakers and writers may abandon their position of positive self-presentation and self-defence and take a more active, aggressive counter-attack: the ones who levelled the accusations of racism are the real problem, if not the real racists. They are the ones who are intolerant, and they are against 'our' own people. We are the victims of immigration, and we are discriminated against.

It is interesting to note that despite the differences in style for different social groups, such discourse may be found at any social level, and in any social context. That is, both the 'ordinary' white citizens as well as the white elites need to protect their social self-image, and at the same time they have to manage the interpretation and the practices in an increasingly variegated social and cultural world. For the dominant group, this means that dominance relations must be reproduced, at the macro- as well as at the microlevel, both in action as well as in mind.

Negative representations of the dominated group are essential in such a reproduction process. However, such attitudes and ideologies are inconsistent with dominant democratic and humanitarian norms and ideals. This means that the dominant group must protect itself, cognitively and discursively, against the damaging charge of intolerance and racism. Cognitive balance may be restored only by actually being or becoming anti-racist, by accepting minorities and immigrants as equals, or else by denying racism. It is this choice that white groups in Europe and North America are facing. So far they have largely chosen the latter option.

References

Billig, M. (1988) 'The notion of "prejudice": some rhetorical and ideological aspects', *Text* 8: 91–110.
Boskin, J. (1980) 'Denials: the media view of dark skins and the city', in Rubin, B. (ed.) *Small Voices and Great Trumpets: Minorities and the Media*, New York: Praeger, 141–7.
Hartmann, P. and Husband, C. (1974) *Racism and the Mass Media*, London: Davis-Poynter.
Phizacklea, A. and Miles, R. (1979) 'Working-class racist beliefs in the inner city', in Miles, R. and Phizacklea, A. (eds) *Racism and Political Action in Britain*, London: Routledge & Kegan Paul, 93–123.
Van Dijk, T.A. (1988a) *News Analysis: Case Studies of International and National News in the Press*, Hillsdale, NJ: Erlbaum.
Van Dijk, T.A. (1988b) *News as Discourse*, Hillsdale, NJ: Erlbaum.
Van Dijk, T.A. (1991) *Racism and the Press*, London: Routledge.

Chapter 36

Ian Hutchby

POWER IN DISCOURSE: THE CASE OF ARGUMENTS ON A BRITISH TALK RADIO SHOW

. . .

I N THIS ARTICLE, I show how an approach informed by conversation analysis (CA) can provide an account of power as an integral feature of talk-in-interaction. CA has placed great emphasis on examining how participants in interaction display their orientation to phenomena that analysts claim are relevant (Schegloff 1991). This has proved a highly successful platform for analysing talk in institutional settings (e.g., Drew and Heritage 1992). What I show is that this approach, through focusing on such issues as how participants orient to features of a setting by designing their turns in specialized ways (e.g., restricting themselves either to asking questions or to giving answers), can be used to address how power is produced through oriented-to features of talk. One way in which this might be shown is by looking for occasions when participants actually topicalize or *formulate* the power relations between themselves (in the sense intended in Garfinkel and Sacks 1970). However, this clearly does not happen very often. An alternative possibility is this: the very ways in which participants design their interaction can have the effect of placing them in a relationship where discourse strategies of greater or lesser power are differentially available to each of them. In this sense, power can be viewed as an 'emergent feature' of oriented-to discourse practices in given settings. It is that possibility that I want to explore in the case of calls to a British talk radio show.

The data come from a collection of approximately 100 recorded calls to a British talk radio show. I began to study interaction on talk radio out of an interest in analysing argument and conflictual talk, and a recognition that this was a common occurrence on open-line talk radio shows. Observing the data, my interests rapidly

Source: Ian Hutchby, 'Power in discourse: the case of arguments on a British talk radio show', *Discourse & Society*, 1996, 7: 481–97.

turned to the question of how participation in talk radio disputes can be asymmetrical. In institutionalized settings for dispute, one of the things that may be of interest is the relationship between verbal patterns and resources used and the asymmetric social identities associated with the setting. In this article, I go further and argue that some of the asymmetrics we identify can be conceptualized in terms of the power of certain participants to engage in communicative actions not available (or not available in the same way) to others. This argument is based on a CA account of the ways in which arguments on talk radio articulate with, and are shaped and constrained by, the organizational and interactional parameters of the talk radio setting itself.

. . .

Analysing power: 'first' and 'second' positions

Talk radio represents a public context in which private citizens can articulate their opinions on social issues. In different shows, the space allotted to callers to forward their views is mapped out in different ways. For instance, some shows expressly address themselves to one issue per broadcast and the caller's role is to have a say on that issue while the host acts as a moderator, relating contributions together and drawing out differences and similarities between them. But in other shows, known as open-line, callers select their own issue to talk about and are given the floor at the beginning of calls in order to introduce their issue and express an opinion on it. In this sense, open-line talk radio shows enable callers to set the agenda for a discussion with the host.

However, agendas are not fixed things, nor are they established from one perspective only. In fact, agendas can become the contested arena for disputes focusing on what can relevantly be said within their terms. This leads to a paradox in talk radio disputes. While it may seem that the caller is in a position to control what will count as an acceptable or relevant contribution to his or her topic, in fact it is the host who tends to end up in that position. The very fact that introducing an agenda is the caller's prerogative on talk radio leads to a situation in which the argumentative initiative can rest with the host and the caller can relatively easily be put on the defensive.

How does this situation emerge? I suggest that it is an outcome of two factors. First, the way that arguments are sequentially organized and second, the way in which calls on talk radio themselves are organized. The principal sequential unit in an argument is the 'action–opposition' sequence (Hutchby 1996: 22–4), in which actions that can be construed as arguable are opposed, with the opposition itself subsequently open to being construed as arguable (Eisenberg and Garvey 1981; Maynard 1985). Within the organization of calls on talk radio, callers are required to begin by setting out their position (Hutchby 1991). This in turn situates the caller's opening turn as a possible first action in a potential action–opposition sequence. To put it another way, it is the host who has the first opportunity for opposition within each call. This turns out to be a powerful argumentative resource, which is not only linked to a particular kind of asymmetry between hosts and callers, but also has consequences for the shape and trajectory of disputes in the talk radio setting.

The asymmetry between first and second positions in arguments was first remarked on by Sacks in one of his lectures on conversation (1992: 2: 348–53). Sacks proposed that those who go first are in a weaker position than those who get to go second, since the latter can argue with the former's position simply by taking it apart. Going first means having to set your opinion on the line, whereas going second means being able to argue merely by challenging your opponent to expand on or account for his or her claims.

In many situations, first and second positions are open to strategic competition between participants. In such situations we can find speakers using systematic means to try and avoid first position, or to try and prompt or manoeuvre another into taking first position. For instance, Sacks (1992: 2: 344–7) discusses the following fragment of data:

Extract (1) GTS [From a conversation among teenagers]
1   Jim: Isn't the New Pike depressing?
2   Mike: hhh The Pike? ⟩ *neutral response to agreement*
                                                          pref
3   Jim: Yeah. Oh the place is disgusting. Any day of
4   the week.

In line 1, Jim indicates a position on the 'New Pike', a local amusement park. The way he states this position is designed to invite Mike's agreement that the New Pike is in fact 'depressing'.

In the next turn, however, Mike neither agrees nor disagrees with Jim. Rather, he produces a turn which on one level looks like an 'understanding check': a turn in which he initiates repair on Jim's prior turn, perhaps because he isn't sure he properly heard what Jim said. But there are features of Mike's turn which militate against that interpretation. For instance, he doesn't say: 'The what?' – which would be a straightforward way of indicating a possible mishearing or misunderstanding (Schegloff et al. 1977). Neither does he repeat Jim's naming of the place in full (i.e., 'The New Pike?'), which again might suggest a difficulty in locating the referent in his own stock of knowledge (Clark and Schaefer 1989). Rather, Mike 're-references' the amusement park, calling it 'The Pike' – an abbreviation which suggests he is in fact familiar with the place. Finally, Jim himself exhibits in his next turn that he does not take Mike's utterance to be initiating repair, by carrying on with and expanding his assessment (lines 3–4) instead of repairing his first turn by saying, for example: 'Yeah. You know, the amusement park?'.

Instead of an understanding check, Mike's turn can be treated as a move in an incipient argument: a manoeuvre by which the floor is thrown back to Jim with an invitation to go on and develop his position on the ways in which the New Pike is depressing. In other words, it is a manoeuvre which seeks to place Mike in second position with respect to Jim's opinion of the Pike. If he can succeed in manoeuvring Jim into first position, Mike would then be in a position to attack Jim's opinion by using what Jim said as a resource for disagreeing, rather than immediately focusing on building a defence for his own opinion.

In fact, this is precisely what happens as the conversation proceeds. Jim goes on to elaborate on his view of the Pike, which then places Mike in a position to attack that view merely by undermining its weaknesses rather than arguing for a particular counter-position:

Extract (2) GTS

```
1  Jim:   But you go down- dow- down to the New Pike
2         there's a buncha people, oh:: an' they're old,    } complain
3         an' they're pretending they're having fun, but
4         they're really not.
5  Mike:  How can you tell. Hm?   implicit disagreement
6  Jim:   They're- they're tryina make a living, but the
7         place is on the decline, 's like a degenerate
8         place . . .
```

In line 5 here, Mike takes up a critical stance *vis-à-vis* Jim's argument, not by putting forward a counter-position, but by <u>undermining</u> Jim's competence to make the claims he is making. This is done by using 'How can you tell' (line 5) to challenge Jim's grounds for the claim that people at the New Pike are 'really not' having fun. This turn does not give Jim much in the way of resources that will allow him to take up the offensive and challenge Mike. Rather, his options are either to account for how he can tell, or to attempt to change tack.

It is this situation which is at the root of the asymmetry between first and second positions in argument. While first-position arguers are required to build a defence for their stance, those in <u>second position</u> are able to <u>choose if and when they will set out their own argument</u>, as opposed to simply attacking the other's.

The point I want to make is that on talk radio, this asymmetry is one that is '<u>built into</u>' the overall structure of calls. Callers are expected, and may be constrained, to go first with their line, while the host systematically gets to go second, and thus to contest the caller's line by picking at its weaknesses. The fact that hosts systematically have the first opportunity for opposition within calls opens to them a collection of argumentative resources which are not available in the same way to callers.

In the following sections, I explore some of the uses and consequences of these second-position resources. In order to do this, I concentrate on episodes in which the participants argue about the dispute's agenda itself.

Agenda contests

One of the things that argument may be about is the struggle between participants over what can and cannot legitimately be said in a dispute: in other words, defining the <u>boundaries</u> of the dispute's agenda. I have already remarked that on talk radio, callers' agendas have an interesting status. While it is the role of the caller to set up an agenda for discussion, the agenda is not something that the caller necessarily maintains subsequent control of. By being in second position, the host is able to challenge the 'agenda-relatedness' of the caller's remarks: to question whether what the caller says is actually (relevant) within the terms of his or her own agenda.

One way in which this may be done is through the use of a class of utterances, including (So?) and 'What's that got to do with it?' which challenge a claim on the grounds of its validity or relevance to the matter in question. However, a significant aspect of such turns is that they need not make clear precisely on what terms the claim is being challenged. They may function purely as second position moves by which the first speaker is required to expand on or account for the challenged claim.

In the following extract the caller is complaining about the number of mailed requests for charitable donations she receives. Note that in line 7, the host responds simply by saying 'So?'

Extract (3) H:21.11.88:6:1

```
 1   Caller:  I: have got three appeals letters here this
 2            week.(0.4) All a:skin' for donations. (0.2) .hh
 3            Two: from tho:se that I: always contribute to
 4            anywa:y.
 5   Host:    Yes?←
 6   Caller:  .hh But I expect to get a lot mo:re.
 7   Host:    So? ←
 8   Caller:  .h Now the point is there is a limi ⌜t to (    )
 9   Host:                                        ⌞What's that ←
10            got to do- what's that got to do with telethons
11            though.
12   Caller:  hh Because telethons . . . ((Continues))
```

As an argumentative move, this (So?) achieves two things. First, it challenges the validity or relevance of the caller's complaint within the terms of her own agenda, which in this case is that charities represent a form of 'psychological blackmail'. Second, because it stands alone as a complete turn, 'So?' requires the caller to take the floor again and account for the relevance of her remark.

. . .

Another way in which the host may attempt to establish control over the agenda is by selectively *formulating* the gist or upshot of the caller's remarks. Heritage (1985: 100) describes the practice of formulating as: 'summarising, glossing, or developing the gist of an informant's earlier statements'. He adds: 'Although it is relatively rare in conversation, it is common in institutionalised, audience-directed interaction', that is, settings such as courtrooms, classrooms and news interviews, as well as other forms of broadcast talk.

Heritage also notes that in these institutional settings, formulating 'is most commonly undertaken by questioners' (1985: 100). This accords with the common finding in studies of institutional discourse that '[i]nstitutional incumbents (doctors, teachers, interviewers, family social workers, etc.) may strategically direct the talk through such means as their capacity to change topics and their selective formulations, in their "next questions," of the salient plants in the prior answers' (Drew and Heritage 1992: 49).

In Extract 4, we see a particular kind of strategic direction of talk, that is related to the argumentative uses of formulations in a setting such as talk radio. The host here uses two closely linked proposals of upshot to contentiously reconstruct the position being advanced by the caller. The caller has criticized the 'contradictions' of telethons, claiming that their rhetoric of concern in fact promotes a passive altruism which exacerbates the 'separateness' between donors and recipients. He goes on:

Extract (4) H:21.11.88:11:3

```
 1   Caller:  . . . but e:r, I- I think we should be working at
 2            breaking down that separateness I ┌ think ┐these
 3   Host:                                       └ Ho:w?┘
 4            (.)
 5   Caller:  these telethons actually increase it.
 6   Host:    Well, what you're saying is that charity does.
 7   Caller:  .h Charity do::es, ye ┌::s I mean-        ┐
 8   Host:                          └ Okay we- so you┘'re (.) so
 9            you're going back to that original argument we
10            shouldn't have charity.
11   Caller:  Well, no I um: I wouldn't go that fa:r, what I
12            would like to ┌ see is-
13   Host:                  └ Well how far are you going then.
14   Caller:  Well I: would- What I would like to see is . . .
```

In line 6, the host proposes that the caller's argument in fact embraces charities in general and not just telethons as one sort of charitable endeavour. This is similar to the 'inferentially elaborative' formulations that Heritage (1985) discusses. Note that although the caller has not made any such generalization himself in his prior talk, he assents to this in the next turn (line 7).

However, it turns out that the caller, by agreeing, provides the host with a resource for *reformulating* the agenda in play here. By linking a second formulation to the first, this time describing the 'upshot' of the caller's position, it is proposed that the caller is going back to an argument which the host had with a previous caller ('that earlier argument'), whose view had been that 'we shouldn't have charity' (lines 8–10).

The caller in fact rejects this further formulation (line 11). But the point is that the host is able to use the fact that the call is based on what the caller thinks about an issue to construct an argument without having to defend his own view. By relying on his ability to formulate the gist or upshot of the caller's remarks, the host can argumentatively define – and challenge – an underlying agenda in the caller's remarks.

In this sense, the 'agenda contests' which occur within calls begin to reveal significant aspects of the play of power in talk radio disputes. The fact that callers must begin by setting out a topical agenda means that argumentative resources are distributed asymmetrically between host and callers. The host is able to build opposition using basic second-position resources. The characteristic feature of these resources is that they require callers to defend or account for their claims, while enabling hosts to argue without constructing a defence for an alternative view. At the same time, as long as the host refrains from setting out his own position, such second-position resources are not available to the caller. Distinctive interactional prerogatives are thereby available to the host, by which he can exert a degree of control over the boundaries of an agenda which is ostensibly set by the caller.

Strategies for resistance

The implication so far has been that the way calls are set up provides the host with a natural incumbency in second position. This does not mean, however, that callers are incapable of offering resistance to the host's challenges. One way of doing this is to adopt the use of second-position resources on their own part. But as I have suggested, particular sequential environments are necessary for this. In particular, the host must have moved or been manoeuvred into adopting first position (that is, indicating an opinion in his or her own right). On talk radio, the host is able to choose when, or if, to express a view on the caller's issue: technically, the host is able to conduct a whole call simply by challenging and demanding justifications for the caller's claims. This, however, is very rare. And once the host has abandoned second position, that position then becomes available for the caller.

Extract 5 shows how a caller may succeed in turning the tables in this way. In this case the tables are turned only briefly because the host subsequently adopts a strategy for re-establishing himself in second position:

Extract (5) H:2.2.89:3:3

```
 1   Caller: But I still think a thousand pounds a night at a
 2           hotel:, .hhh a:nd the fact that she's going on
 3           to visit homeless peop [ le,
 4   Host:                          [ Where should sh- Where
 5           should she be staying in New York.
 6           (0.2)
 7   Caller: We:ll u-th- at a cheaper place I don't think the
 8           money-=.h WE'RE paying that money for her to
 9           stay there and I think it's ob°scene.
10   Host:   Well we're not actually paying the [ -e the money,
11   Caller:                                     [ Well
12           who:'s paying for it.
13   Host:   Well thee:: e:rm I imagine the the:r the money
14           the Royal Family has .h er is paying for it, .h
15           or indeed it may be paid for by somebody else, .h
16           erm but .h y'know if the Princess of Wales lives
17           in: (.) a palace in this country, w-w-why do
```

Agenda Shift

```
18          you think she should not live in something which
19          is comparable, .hh when she's visiting New York?
20  Caller: Well I should think that she could find
21          something comparable that- that- or- e-it could
22          be found for her that doesn't cost that money.
```

One thing to notice is the way the caller responds to the host's hostile questioning (which has been going on for some while) by suddenly attempting to shift the topical focus of her agenda (line 8). From the question of the price of the hotel suite, she shifts, by means of a self-interruption, to the more emotive issue of the ultimate responsibility of the tax-payer for footing the bill: '.h WE'RE paying that money for her to stay there' (lines 8–9).

The host's response to this, in line 10, is significant. By opposing the caller's assertion, he abandons his series of questioning challenges and instead asserts an opinion in his own right. It is this turn which allows the caller to move onto the offensive and produce a challenge of her own which, in a way characteristic of the second-position moves I have been discussing, requires the host to account for his assertion (lines 11–12).

At this stage, then, the local roles of challenger and defender of a position have been inverted. The host, from being in his customary challenger role, has suddenly been swung around into the role of defender. However, this inversion turns out to be only temporary. In the very next turn, the host manages to re-establish the prior state of affairs. He does this by not simply responding to the caller's challenge but also going on to produce a next challenge-bearing question of his own (lines 16–19). With this move, the host succeeds in doing two things. First, he re-establishes the agenda to which his earlier question, in the second turn of the extract, had been addressed and which the caller had attempted to shift away from. Second, he resituates the caller as the respondent to his challenging initiatives, rather than as the initiator of challenge-bearing moves herself.

The asymmetry between first and second positions is not, then, a straightforward, one-way feature of talk radio disputes. Although the organizational structure of calls situates callers in first position initially, they may subsequently find themselves with opportunities to move into the stronger second position. As the previous extract shows, the sequential space for this arises once the host has abandoned the second-position strategy of issuing challenges and made an assertion in his own right. However, the extract also shows that there are strategies available for turning the tables back again; and this suggests that the second position itself can become actively contested over a series of turns.

To illustrate this, finally, we can continue with this call and find that the caller subsequently adopts the host's strategy in order to retake the initiative in the argument. The following extract takes up towards the end of Extract 5:

Extract (6) H: 2.2.89:3:3
```
20  Caller: Well I should think that she could find
21          something comparable that- that- or- e-it could
22          be found for her that doesn't cost that money.
```

```
23              A⌐nd ⌐ you're only imagining that she's paying=
24   Host:      ⌊But⌋
25   Caller:  =for herself you don't know ei:ther do you.
26   Host:    E:rm, well . . .
```

The feature of interest here is in lines 22–5. In a similar way to the host in Extract 5, the caller moves from responding to a challenge to issuing a question. This requires the host in turn to respond and further account for his own position that 'she's paying for herself'. In part, the basis for this second challenge lies in the host's long turn in lines 13–19 of Extract 5, where he responded to the caller's first challenge. That is, the caller is not simply revisiting or revamping the earlier challenge, but developing a new line of attack which relies on the fact that the host's earlier response had been quite vague (see especially lines 13–15 of Extract 5).

To summarize: the call's initial stages situate the caller in first position and furnish the host with the power of second position. But that asymmetry is not an unchanging feature of the context. The more powerful argumentative resources attached to second position may also become available to the caller. Yet this is dependent upon the host expressing an opinion in his own right. Nonetheless, once the opportunity arises, determined and resourceful callers may challenge the host using second position tactics; although second position itself can then become the focus of a discursive struggle.

Discussion

In this article I have used the idea of a relationship between interactional activities and organizational structures as the basis for developing an account of the play of power in calls to a British talk radio show. In doing so, I have illustrated how power is a phenomenon brought into play through discourse. I focused on relatively small sequential details of arguments in order to show this. The upshot is that the sequential approach developed within CA has been applied to a question which has concerned critical linguists and discourse analysts – i.e., how power operates in and through language – by viewing power in terms of the relationships between turns (as actions) in sequences.

The analysis has detailed the relationship between the organization of activities within calls and the asymmetrical distribution of argument resources. On talk radio, the opening of the call is not only designed to set up an environment in which callers introduce the topic, but by virtue of that it also places the participants on significantly asymmetrical footings with respect to those topics. The fact that callers are required to go first by expressing a point of view on some issue means that hosts systematically get to go second. Going second, I have argued, represents a more powerful position in argumentative discourse than first position. Principally, the host is able to critique or attack the caller's line simply by exhibiting skepticism about its claims, challenging the agenda relevance of assertions, or taking the argument apart by identifying minor inaccuracies in its details (see also Hutchby 1992).

However, the fact that hosts may conduct arguments without expressing a counter-opinion or providing explanations and accounts for their own positions does not mean that they never do the latter. The asymmetry that I have noted is simply this: hosts are in a position to do this whereas callers, by virtue of the organization of the call, are not. At the same time, there are resources available for callers to resist the host's powerful strategies and sometimes to exercise powerful strategies themselves. Thus, power is not a monolithic feature of talk radio, with the corresponding simplistic claim that the host exercises power over the caller by virtue of his or her 'control of the mechanics of the radio program' (Moss and Higgins 1984: 373). Rather, in a detailed way, the power dynamics at work within calls are variable and shifting.

This argument results in a model of power which comes close to the theoretical conception outlined by Foucault (1977). Like Foucault, a CA approach seeks to view power not as a zero–sum game but as a set of potentials which, while always present, can be variably exercised, resisted, shifted around and struggled over by social agents. Foucault argued that power is not something that is possessed by one agent or collectivity and lacked by another, but a potential that has to be instantiated within a network equally including those who exercise power and those who accept or resist it. The network itself is viewed as a structure of possibilities and not as a concrete relationship between determinate social entities.

While Foucault's work is often pitched at the broadest theoretical level, the empirical analysis in this article goes some way towards demonstrating how two of his central ideas can be located in the analysis of power in the details of talk-in-interaction. These ideas are, first, that wherever there is power, there is resistance; and second, that power operates in the most mundane contexts of everyday life, not just at the macro-level of large processes (Foucault 1977).

On the first point, I have stressed that although hosts have a 'natural' incumbency in second position, and thereby have a set of powerful resources available for dealing skeptically with callers' contributions, there are ways in which callers may resist those strategies. They may do this by recognizing and attempting to forestall the effects of the powerful strategy being used by the host (as discussed, for example, by Hutchby 1992). Or they may resist by attempting to adopt the powerful strategies available to the host for themselves, by taking opportunities to move into second position.

The second point is perhaps the one with which this article resonates most strongly. There is a tendency in both mundane and social scientific discourse to conceive of power as a 'big' phenomenon, operating at the largest scale within social formations. Foucault, on the other hand, suggests that power is pervasive even at the smallest level of interpersonal relationships. The kind of power with which Foucault is mainly concerned exists in the form of the manifold 'discourses' by which we make sense of ourselves, others and the world in which we are situated. This tends to lead Foucault's analyses away from the detailed character of social interaction and towards the larger-scale historical trajectories of discursive formations that can be traced in archive documents. I have focused on a different kind of power, traced in a different level of discourse. By power, I have meant the interactional power that threads through the course and trajectory of an argument.

But in line with the conversation analytic approach, I have located that form of power in some of the smallest details of social life: the relationship between turns at talk-in-interaction.

References

Clark, H. and Schaefer, E. (1989) 'Contributing to discourse', *Cognitive Science* 13: 259–94.

Drew, P. and Heritage, J. (1992) *Talk at Work: Interaction in Institutional Settings*, Cambridge: Cambridge University Press.

Eisenberg, A. and Garvey, C. (1981) 'Children's use of verbal strategies in resolving conflicts', *Discourse Processes* 4: 149–70.

Foucault, M. (1977) *Power/Knowledge*, Hemel Hempstead: Harvester.

Garfinkel, H. and Sacks, H. (1970) 'On formal structures of practical actions', in McKinney, J.C. and Tiryakian, E.A. (eds) *Theoretical Sociology*, New York: Appleton Century Croft, 338–66.

Heritage, J. (1985) 'Analysing news interviews: aspects of the production of talk for an overhearing audience', in Van Dijk, T. (ed.) *Handbook of Discourse Analysis*, vol. 3, London: Academic Press, 95–119.

Hutchby, I. (1991) 'The organisation of talk on talk radio', in Scannell, P. (ed.) *Broadcast Talk*, London: Sage, 119–37.

—— (1992) 'The pursuit of controversy: routine skepticism in talk on talk radio', *Sociology* 26: 673–94.

—— (1996) *Confrontation Talk: Arguments, Asymmetries and Power on Talk Radio*, Hillsdale, NJ: Erlbaum.

Maynard, D.W. (1985) 'How children start arguments', *Language in Society* 14: 1–30.

Moss, P. and Higgins, C. (1984) 'Radio voices', *Media, Culture & Society* 6: 353–75.

Sacks, H. (1992) *Lectures on Conversation*, vols 1 and 2, Oxford: Blackwell.

Schegloff, E.A. (1991) 'Reflections on talk and social structure', in Boden, D. and Zimmerman, D. (eds) *Talk and Social Structure*, Cambridge: Polity Press, 44–70.

Schegloff, E.A., Jefferson, G. and Sacks, H. (1977) 'The preference for self-correction in the organisation of repair in conversation', *Language* 53: 361–82.

Chapter 37

Hugh Mehan

ORACULAR REASONING IN A PSYCHIATRIC EXAM: THE RESOLUTION OF CONFLICT IN LANGUAGE

> Men define situations as real and they are real in their consequences.
>
> (W.I. Thomas[1])

THE TWO MAJOR PURPOSES of this chapter are (1) to show how competing definitions of the situation are constructed and revealed in ongoing interaction within an institutionalized setting (a mental hospital), and (2) to show how institutionalized power is displayed and used to resolve disputes over conflicting definitions of the situation. In so doing, I will be commenting on the famous "Thomas Theorem." Parts of what I say will provide support for Thomas's idea that people define situations as real in and through their interaction. Other parts will stretch the limits of the theorem. Not all definitions of situations have equal authority. Competing definitions are resolved by imposing institutional definitions on lay persons' definitions. This "ironicizing of experience" (Pollner 1975) requires a modification in Thomas's consensual world view, which I have reformulated as follows:

> All people define situations as real; but when powerful people define situations as real, then they are real *for everybody involved* in their consequences.

My presentation will take a circuitous route. Before showing how institutionalized power is used to impose a certain definition on the situation, I will place the discussion in the context of debates about the thinking of "primitive" and "advanced" peoples. After introducing the notion of "oracular reasoning" (a concept which is central to the understanding of the events which follow), I will examine closely the interaction between a board of examining psychiatrists and a mental patient.

SOURCE Hugh Mehan, 'Oracular reasoning in a psychiatric exam: the resolution of conflict in language', in Allen D. Grimshaw (ed.) *Conflict Talk: Sociolinguistic Investigations of Arguments in Conversation*, Cambridge: Cambridge University Press, 1990, 160–77.

The thinking of primitive and advanced peoples

. . .

Oracular reasoning in a "primitive" society

The quintessential example of oracular reasoning is found in Evans-Pritchard's (1973) account of the Azande of Africa. When the Azande are faced with important decisions – decisions about where to build their homes, or whom to marry, or whether the sick will live, for example – they consult an oracle. They prepare for these consultations by following a strictly prescribed ritual. First, a substance is gathered from the bark of a certain type of tree. Then this substance is prepared in a special way in a séance-like ceremony. The Azande then poses a question to the oracle in a way that permits a simple yes or no answer and feeds the substance to a small chicken. The person consulting the oracle decides beforehand whether the death of the chicken will signal an affirmative or negative response, and so they always receive an unequivocal answer to their questions.

For monumental decisions, the Azande add a second step. They feed the substance to a second chicken, asking the same question, but reversing the importance of the chicken's death. If in the first consultation sparing the chicken's life meant the oracle said "yes," in the second reading, the oracle must now kill the chicken to once more reply in the affirmative and be consistent with the first response.

Seemingly, insuperable difficulties accrue to people who hold such beliefs, because the oracle could contradict itself. What if, for example, the first consultation of the oracle produces a positive answer and then the second produces a negative reply? Or, suppose that someone else consults the oracle about the same question, and contradictory answers occur? What if the oracle is contradicted by later events – the house site approved by the oracle, for example, is promptly flooded; or the wife the oracle selected dies or turns out to be infertile? How is it possible for the Azande to continue to believe in their oracle in the face of so many evident contradictions of their faith?

The answers to these questions are both simple and complex. Simple, because the Azande do not see the events just listed as contradictions, as threats to the oracle. Complex, because of the reasoning practices that are invoked to keep the efficacy of the oracle intact. The Azande know that an oracle exists. That is their beginning premise. All that subsequently happens is interpreted in terms of that "incorrigible proposition" – a proposition that one never admits to be false whatever happens; one that is compatible with any and every conceivable state of affairs (Gasking 1955: 432 as quoted in Pollner 1975). The Azande employ what Evans-Pritchard (1973: 330) calls "secondary elaborations of belief," practices which explain the failure of the oracle by retaining the unquestioned faith in oracles.

The culture provides the Azande with a number of ready-made explanations of the oracle's seeming contradictions. The secondary elaborations of belief that explain the failure of the oracle attribute the failure to other circumstances, some of this world, some of the spirit world – the wrong variety of poison being gathered, breach of taboo, witchcraft, the anger of the owners of the place where the poison plants grow, the age of the poison, the anger of ghosts, or sorcery.

By explaining away contradictions through these secondary elaborations of the belief in oracles, the reality of a world in which oracles are a basic feature is re-affirmed. Failures do not challenge the oracle. They are elaborated in such a way that they provide evidence for the constant success, the marvel, of oracles. Beginning with the incorrigible belief in oracles, all events reflexively become evidence for that belief.

Recent research suggests that maintaining belief by denying or repelling contra-dictory evidence is not limited to so-called primitives. Well-educated "modern" people also give evidence of oracular reasoning.

Oracular reasoning in modern form

EVERYDAY REASONING

Wason (1977) reviewed a set of delightful experiments that he and Johnson-Laird have conducted, with the same problems presented to subjects alternatively in abstract and concrete form. Again and again, the subjects of these ingenious exper-iments seemed to be influenced by the context and the content of the problems. When information was presented in semantically coherent form, such as stories, or with real-life manifestations, subjects performed consistently better than when information was presented in algebraic or symbolic form. When the totality of these studies is considered, we find that people do not employ problem-solving procedures that would challenge or falsify the hypothesis being tested nearly as often as they employ problem-solving procedures that confirm the hypothesis under consideration.

Pollner and McDonald-Wikler (1985) examined the routine transactions of a family with their severely mentally retarded child. They reported that the family employed practices which sustained the family's belief in the competence of the child in the face of overwhelming evidence to the contrary, i.e., a team of medical practitioners had diagnosed the child as severely mentally retarded. The authors' observations of video-taped family interaction revealed that family members pre-structured the child's environment to maximize the likelihood that whatever the child did could be seen as meaningful, intentional activity. The child's family would establish a definition of the situation and use it as a frame of reference for inter-preting and describing any and all of the child's subsequent behavior. They also tracked the child's ongoing behavior and developed physical or verbal contexts that could render the behavior intelligent and interactionally responsive.

RELIGIOUS REASONING

Millennial groups are organized around the prediction of some future events, for example, the second coming of Christ and the beginning of Christ's reign on earth, the destruction of the earth through a cataclysm – usually with a select group, the believers, slated for rescue from the disaster.

. . .

No millennial group is more fascinating than the Millerites. William Miller was a New England farmer who believed in literal fulfillment of biblical prophecy. In 1818, after a two-year study of the Bible, Miller reached the conclusion that the end of the world would occur in 1843. He slowly developed a following. The faithful took all the necessary precautions including dissolving relationships, settling debts, selling possessions – and waited together for the second coming of Christ. When the fateful day came – and went – the faithful were confronted with a devastating contradiction to their belief (and lives which were in total disrepair). Their response to this devastation was amazing: instead of turning away from their religious beliefs and spiritual leaders, they used the failure of prophecy as further proof of the wonder and mystery of God. The leaders, far from doubting their basic belief in the second coming, elaborated their belief by citing errors in calculation and weakness in faith as reasons why God did not reveal Himself at the time they predicted. Group leaders retreated to their texts and emerged some time later with new calculations. The number of believers increased – as if conviction was deepened by evidence which contradicted their beliefs. Alas, after three more specific predictions failed, the group disbanded in disbelief.

SCIENTIFIC REASONING

Oracular reasoning appears among scientists as well as among religious zealots, as Gould's (1981) chronicle of a long history of research conducted in defense of Caucasian racial superiority shows. Morton's craniology, Lombroso's criminal anthropology and Burt's intelligence testing start from the premise that whites are superior to blacks, native Americans and other racial or ethnic groups. Gould describes the methodological errors and outright fraud which arose, often unintentionally, when researchers held too dearly to that basic belief. For example, Gould's meticulous re-analysis of Morton's data uncovered a systematic pattern of distortion in the direction of the preferred hypothesis. Statistics were summed inappropriately across groups, and groups which seemed to counter the argument were excluded from statistical analysis. The overall effect of these practices was the production of data that confirmed the hypothesis of racial superiority, but did so by systematically manipulating or excluding potentially contradictory evidence.

Gould says that the recurrence of racist uses of IQ tests and other measurement techniques is aided by "unconscious bias." This concept liberates us from the suspicion that all racists are cynical plotters against the truth and it implies the existence of a coherent structure of expectations about the phenomena of the world which guides the thoughts of scientists and non-scientists alike. But "unconscious bias" is too limited an idea for such a pervasive intellectual practice (Greenwood 1984: 21). To the extent that unconscious biases are shared widely and perpetuated despite the use of empirical data and sound analytical procedures, they are not biases at all; they are collective conceptions about the structures and operation of the natural world.

Oracular reasoning in a psychiatric exam

These discussions have identified oracular reasoning in general terms. I want to show its practice concretely, in the detail of on-going discourse. To do so, I will discuss a "gatekeeping encounter" (Erickson 1975) between a board of psychiatrists and a mental patient. Unlike most gatekeeping encounters (in which the gatekeeper is judging whether the applicant is worthy of *entering* an institution – a place of business, a college, a medical care center) in this encounter the gatekeepers are deciding whether the applicant can *leave* the institution (the mental hospital).

The materials used in this analysis come from an unusual source, which requires some comment. During the course of making his documentary film on a mental hospital in the State of Massachusetts, *Titicut Follies*, Frederick Wiseman filmed a "psychiatric out-take interview." The edited version of this interview appearing in the film is the one I use for the analysis which follows. The use of edited documentary film for discourse analysis, of course, places me at a disadvantage: I neither have the background knowledge of the setting normally available to ethnographers nor am I privy to the film-editing process. Nevertheless, the language in the interview is so provocative that I can not resist analyzing it. It is my hope that readers of the analysis will forgive problems associated with the data in exchange for the heuristics with the analysis.

I approached the analysis of this film as I have others: I have watched the film numerous times – both in private viewings and in courses I teach. I constructed a transcript of the interview. The transcript and my memory of the audio and visual record served as the basis of my interpretation. After I completed the analysis which follows, I watched the film again, and made minor modifications – mostly concerning seating arrangements and the physical movements of the participants.[2]

The basis of the conflict

The interview starts with the patient, Vladimir, being led into the examining room. He stands before a table, behind which are seated four members of the examining board. The head psychiatrist begins questioning the patient, but the interrogation quickly breaks down into an argument about the quantity and quality of the patient's treatment. After a number of exchanges, the head psychiatrist abruptly orders the patient to be taken away. At this point, the film is edited; we see the members of the examining board give their interpretation of the case, and reach a conclusion about the patient's status.

The status of a patient's "career" in a hospital (Goffman 1959), indeed, about the patient's life, was established during the course of this gatekeeping encounter. He will remain in the hospital, diagnosed as a paranoid schizophrenic, and receive increased dosages of medicine.

At the outset, it is important to comment on the *social* nature of the outcome. The state of the patient's mental health was not the automatic result of a machine or a meter reading; the patient's mental state was determined by people, who participated in the assembly of an outcome. Here then we have a quintessential example of social construction (Berger 1968; Garfinkel 1967; Scheff 1966; Cicourel

1973; Mehan 1983a; 1983b): the medical fact of mental illness is constructed in social circumstances.

While this event is social in that a medical fact is assembled in interaction, it is not social in another sense. The event is not social in the sense that the participants failed to reach a mutually agreed-upon definition of the situation. Here we have a set of circumstances in which people, a group of doctors and a patient, have interacted with each other for a stretch of time; each has arrived at a definition of the situation, but the definitions are considerably different, indeed, in conflict with each other.

By looking at the interaction which takes place among the participants in this meeting closely, I will try to determine how it is that the doctors and the patient come to conflicting definitions of the situation. Putting the punch line up front, I will try to demonstrate that both the doctors and the patient were engaged in "oracular reasoning." Normally associated with the procedures used by so-called primitive, or poorly educated peoples when making decisions about life, both the psychiatrists (a presumably well-educated group of people in an "advanced" Western society) and a mental patient (not as well educated, nonetheless a member of an industrialized society) are engaged in this mode of discourse.

The practices of oracular reasoning which are visible in the out-take interview include the following:

> A basic premise or a fundamental proposition is presented which forms the basis of an argument.
>   When confronted with evidence which is potentially contradictory to a basic position, the evidence is ignored, repelled, or denied.
>   The presence of evidence which opposes a basic position is used reflexively as further support of the efficacy of the basic position.

I will now go through the transcript of the out-patient interview and show the presence of these features in both the doctors' *and* the patient's discourse. Doing so will enable us to understand how multiple and conflicting definitions of the situation were arrived at. The location of these features in the doctors' and not just the patient's discourse will illustrate the further point that oracular reasoning practices are not limited or confined to primitives or the uneducated; they make their appearance in the reasoning of highly educated thinkers. The persistent presence of oracular reasoning in a wide variety of domains recommends that we consider the possibility that oracular reasoning is a more widespread practice than often acknowledged.

The basic propositions

The basic premise or proposition which underlies the psychiatrists' definition of the situation concerns the health or rather, ill-health of the patient. From the doctors' point of view, the patient is mentally ill. The conclusion about this particular case is founded in even a more basic premise about a physician's expertise: the psychiatrist has access to a body of knowledge which is inaccessible to lay people. This premise gains ready empirical support: the patient is, after all, in a mental hospital.

People who are in mental hospitals are presumed to be mentally ill (Scheff 1966). The psychiatrists' commitment to this assumption is voiced by the head psychiatrist, who begins the hearing by saying:

> okay, now Vladimir, as I've promised you before, if I see enough improvement in you . . .

Although the patient, Vladimir, interrupts the psychiatrist before he finishes his introductory statement, the syntax of the psychiatrist's utterance enables us to infer the concluding phrase: (if you show improvement, then we will release you). The "need to show improvement" presupposes a prior mental state which is in need of improvement, i.e., mental illness. The fact of incarceration presupposes that same damaged mental state.

The psychiatrists' commitment to this assumption is reinforced throughout the hearing, especially as the head psychiatrist challenges the patient's arguments. He parries the patient's assertions of his mental health with questions about how he came to be a patient in the hospital ("what got you down here?") and his strange beliefs ("you felt the coffee was poison . . . you felt that people were mixing you up in your thinking").

The patient also has a basic premise from which he argues his definition of the situation. It is the exact opposite of the psychiatrists' definition: he is mentally healthy and does not deserve to be hospitalized. The patient's assertion of his mental health, argued in the face of underlying belief in psychiatric expertise, is to be found in virtually every one of his utterances during the hearing. Here are some quotes which give a sense of belief in his health and the depth of his commitment to this belief:

> my mind's perfect . . . I'm obviously logical, I know what I'm talking about. . . . everytime I come in here you call me I am crazy. Now, what's, if, if it's something you don't like about my face, that's I mean, that's another story. But that has nothing to do with my mental stability.

The incorrigibility of the propositions

The reasoning of the psychiatrists and of the patient share another feature: they both retain their belief in their basic premises and do so despite evidence which is presented to the contrary. The psychiatrists and the patient maintain the incorrigibility of their propositions by deflecting, ignoring, or reinterpreting evidence which is contrary to their basic beliefs.

The incorrigibility feature of oracular reasoning is present in virtually every exchange between the psychiatrists and the patient. I include some of these exchanges here to show how each uses the evidence presented by the other to retain their commitment to their original belief.

The head psychiatrist asks the patient about his participation in hospital activities, including work, sports, and therapy. The assumption underlying the doctor's line of questioning is that affirmative answers to these questions indicate a positive approach on the part of the patient — a patient who is making an effort to improve himself. The following exchanges indicate that the patient has a different attitude about these issues:

(1) HP: Are you working here Vladimir?
(2) Pt: No, there is no suitable work for me here. All I've got is, all I got is
(3)   the kitchen and all they do is throw cup cups around. In fact,
(4)   they got two television sets which are blaring, machines which
(5)   are going, everything which is against the mind. There is one
(6)   thing uh uh uh that a patient does need, and this is what I do
(7)   know, absolutely, is is quiet, if I have a mental problem or even
(8)   an emotional problem. I'm thrown in with over a hundred of
(9)   them and all they do is yell, walk around, televisions are blaring,
(10)   so that's doing my mind harm!
(11) HP: Are you involved in any sports here?
(12) Pt: There are no sports here. All I've got is a baseball and — and—a a
(13)   glove, and that's it! There's nothing else. Hum. There's nothing
(14)   else . . .
(15) HP: Are you in any group therapy here?
(16) Pt: No! There is no group, obviously I do not need group therapy, I
(17)   need peace and quiet. See me. This place is disturbing me! It's
(18)   harming me . . . I'm losing weight. Every, everything that's been
(19)   happening to me is bad. And all I got, all I get is: "well, why don't
(20)   you take medication?" Medication is disagreeable to me. There
(21)   are people to whom you may not give medication. Obviously,
(22)   and the medication that I got is hurting me, it's harming me!

The doctor has phrased his questions (1), (11), (15) in such a way that a "yes" or "no" is the expected reply. Instead of providing the canonical yes or no response to the doctor's questions about work, sports, and therapy, the patient denies the premise underlying the doctor's questioning (and by extension his professional expertise). There *is no* work, there *are no* sports, there *is no* therapy:

> I was supposed to only come down here for observation. What observa-
> tion did I get? You called me up a couple of times.

In denying the doctor's fundamental assumption, the patient articulates his commitment to his own belief — his health:

> I do not need group therapy, I need peace and quiet. . . . This place is
> disturbing me.

The doctors do not respond immediately to the patient. We must wait until the patient is removed from the room to hear them articulate their reaction to his position. In general, they do not accept the patient's assertion of his health;

in fact, they maintain the opposite – that "he's now falling apart", "reverting". "So he's not looking ready to be able to make it back to prison". The patient's assertions on his behalf contribute to the doctors' conclusion. By his own admission, he doesn't participate in hospital activities, sports, work and therapy. These are the very activities which have been established to help to rehabilitate the patient. The patient's calculated avoidance of these rehabilitative activities becomes further proof of his recalcitrance and contribute to his regression to a prior, unhealthy state of mind.

The attitude that the doctors and patient adopt toward medicine is a particularly telling example of how the same evidence can be used to support diametrically opposed positions. For the patient, medicine is for sick people; since he is healthy, he doesn't need it. In fact, to take medicine would be to admit that he *is* sick. Since he is healthy, he doesn't need the medicine. For the doctors, medicine is a part of a rehabilitation process; the patient's admitted reticence to take medicine is taken as a sign that the patient is both sick and unwilling to help in his own rehabilitation:

> Well I think what we have to do with him is, uh, put him on a higher
> dose of tranquilizers and see if we can bring the paranoid element under
> a little bit better control and see if we can get him back on medication.
> If he's taking it now, and I'm not even sure that he is.

Coulter (1979: 101) discusses how psychiatrists may engage in "strategic contextualization" to make sense out of what is manifestly disorderly or contradictory. In this instance, we seem to have the opposite set of circumstances: a strategic contextualization which undermines the ostensive rationality or logic of the patient's presentation. The patient's very logic becomes an expression of disorder. This strategic decontextualization through the selective invocation of background knowledge and the demand for literal (yes/no) answers to questions, simultaneously frames and undercuts the speaker and the power of his discourse. From the psychiatrists' point of view, even the patient's expressed emotion is symptomatic of his disorder (cf. Rosenhan 1973):

> the louder he shouts about going back the more frightened he indicates
> that he probably is.

The patient has presented himself to the doctors as agitated and unreasonable, which is further proof that he is mentally ill.

Of course, there is another perspective on the patient's presentation of himself. He feels unjustly treated, confined against his will. Given this one, brief opportunity to present his case, he does so forcefully, energetically. Anticipating the prospect of leaving the hospital, he is excited, which is an understandable emotion for a person who sees himself languishing in a cell:

> I have a perfect right to be excited. I've been here for a year and a half,
> hum, and this place is doing me harm.

With the patient's presentation of himself, as with the medicine and hospital activities, then, we have an instance in which the same state of affairs is interpreted differently from different perspectives. This perspectivally induced perception contributes to the maintenance of belief on the part of the physicians and on the part of the patient. Both cling to their basic assertions, denying the information presented which has the potential of undermining those basic beliefs.

One member of the board of examiners makes this belief-validating process visible for us during her contribution to the board's interpretation of the case:

> Dr 2: He argues in a perfectly paranoid pattern. If you accept his basic premise the rest of it is logical. But, the basic premise is not true.

She admits to the possibility of the patient's interpretation ("If you accept his basic premise"), entertains the viability of the patient's conclusions and the evidence he has presented in defense of his conclusions ("the rest is logical"), yet she does not change her opinion. She rejects the patient's line of reasoning and remains committed to her belief that the patient is mentally ill.

Competing languages of expression: the medical and the sociological

Two competing languages about the nature of mental illness have developed in the recent history of medicine. One, called the "medical model," treats the issue in biological terms. Because the body is an organism, its various parts are subject to pathologies. Mental illness has developed as an extension of this way of thinking. The mind is treated by analogy to an organ of the body; it, like the heart, liver or pancreas, is subject to disease. As an organ, it can be treated in the same way as disease to other organs, i.e., by medicine, confinement, operations to remove diseased tissues. The cause and the cure of mental illness, like physical illness, is to be found in the biological realm, a state or trait of the individual person.

The second, called the "sociological" or "deviance" model, treats the issue of mental illness in social and contextual terms. Denying the analogy between the mind and organs of the body, mental illness is talked about in terms of actions and rules. Mental illness is the label attached to people who break a certain set of society's rules. Its origins are to be found, therefore, not in biological pathologies, but in the social context of relationships between people, people who identify rule breakers, people who apply labels and in extreme cases, institutionalize the rule breakers (Scheff 1966; Kitsuse 1963; Becker 1963; Goffman 1959; Laing 1967; Szasz and Hollender 1956). Mental illness is eliminated by rearranging social contexts such that bizarre behavior is no longer necessary.

The participants in the meeting use these two languages during the course of their interaction. The medical language appears in most pronounced form during the discussion among the doctors after the patient was removed from the room. The cause of the patient's difficulties are talked about in terms of the patient's personal states. He is "paranoid," "schizophrenic", "depressed". That is, the cause of the problem is located within the patient. Increased doses of medicine are prescribed in order to gain better control of his paranoid state.

The patient voices the sociological model in virtually every one of his pronouncements. He blames the circumstances, focusing particular attention on the hospital and the treatment he has been getting (or rather, has not been getting) but *not* his mental state for his problems:

> I've been trying to tell you. I can tell you, day by day, I'm getting worse, because of the circumstances, because of the situation.

> So, it's obviously the treatment I'm getting or it's the situation or the place or or or the patients or the inmates or either of them. I don't know which.

His denial of the equation of mind to body, internal causes of illness, and the proposition that medicine can cure the mind, could have come from any of Thomas Szasz's or R.D. Laing's books:

> You say "well, take some medication." Medication for the mind? I am supposed to take medication for, if I have some bodily injury. Not for the mind. My mind's perfect.

A crucial exchange between the head psychiatrist and the patient highlights the patient's articulation of the sociological theory of mental illness with its emphasis on contextual causes:

> Pt: if you leave me here, that means that YOU want me to get harmed. Which is an absolute fact. That's plain logic. That goes without saying. Obviously.
>
> HP: That's interesting logic.
>
> Pt: Yes. It's absolutely perfect, because if I am, if I am at a point, it's as if I were in some kind of a hole or something, right, and if you keep me there, obviously you intend to do me harm.

By blaming the hospital and the doctors, the patient gives us a perfect rendition of the iatrogenic theory of illness; the locus of the patient's trouble is in the social context, not his own mental state.

Conclusions

We can draw the following conclusions from the doctor–patient exchange:

1 The psychiatrists and the patient differ in their definitions of the situation.
2 These differences are assembled because an array of behavioral particulars are bestowed with different meaning by participants operating from different theoretical perspectives and in different common sense systems of belief.
3 Within each system of belief, the participants marshal evidence to support a basic proposition and deflect evidence which has the potential to challenge the basic proposition.

If left here, the conclusion would be a (potentially interesting) demonstration of the Thomas theorem and would point to relativism played out in face-to-face interaction, i.e., that each perspective – that of doctor and patient – is equivalent.

While we can see that differences in perspective were visible in the interaction and maintained by a belief-validating process, there is another, important, dimension to the interaction that can not be overlooked. That dimension has to do with conflict and its resolution in language.

Conflict resolution in language: the politics of experience

While the physicians and the patient have conflicting definitions of the situation, these definitions are not equal. The patient's definition of his sanity is not on a par with the psychiatrists' definition of his insanity. The doctors' definition prevails. Despite the vehemence of his protestations and the admitted logic of his presentation, at the end of the meeting the patient is led from the examining room and returned to his lodgings, still convinced that he is healthy, there to await the decision and subsequent treatment recommended by the examining board.

So, although there is evidence of the socially negotiated construction of a medical fact here, the constituent negotiation is not evenly balanced. Instead, we have an example of what R.D. Laing (1967) has called "the politics of experience." Some persons, by virtue of their institutional authority, have the power to impose their definitions of the situation on others, thereby negating the others' experience. Speaking with the authority of the medical profession, in particular psychiatry, and, by extension, the legal institution, the definition voiced by members of the board is imposed on the definition voiced by the patient. The conflict between the patient and the psychiatrists is resolved by the imposition of an institutional definition of the situation on top of an everyday or lay definition of the situation. This imposition negates the patient's definition, relegating his experience to an inferior status.

The process by which the patient's experience is ironicized demonstrates how institutionalized power is manifested in language, making it necessary to fashion the corollary of the Thomas theorem that I proposed at the outset of this chapter.

> All people define situations as real; but when powerful people define situations as real, then they are real *for everybody involved* in their consequences.

The logical status of oracular reasoning

In closing, I'd like to make some final comments on the status of the logic of oracular reasoning. These comments are admittedly speculative, requiring further specification.

The parties in the conflict that I examined each operated within a certain frame of knowledge. They adhered to statements about the world whose validity could neither be confirmed nor disconfirmed (Shweder 1984: 39–40). The doctors maintained the absoluteness of their belief in the patient's mental illness by denying, repelling and transforming evidence which was contrary to their basic belief. The patient, too, used evidence presented in opposition to his argument as further support for the efficacy of his position. Thus, both a poorly educated, hospitalized patient and professionally educated physicians engaged in similar reasoning process. They admit to no universal standard (i.e., one that is outside both frames or in some frame acceptable by the people in the two frames) for judging the adequacy of ideas. As a result, no evidence or experience was allowed to count as disproof by either party.

. . .

The widespread appearance of belief-validating practices should lead us to realize that oracular reasoning is not limited to primitives, ancients, children or the uneducated, and to consider the possibility that it is a more extensive feature of reasoning. Since the appearance of oracular reasoning is not universal but variable, a productive next step would be to investigate how belief-validating practices operate in detail. If such practices can be found in any group, in any belief system, then it becomes important to determine when protection against discrediting evidence becomes so extensive that disconfirmation becomes virtually impossible and how potentially contradictory evidence is sufficient to change the structure and practice of belief.

Acknowledgements

This chapter was prepared for presentation at the Eleventh World Congress of the International Sociological Association, New Delhi, India, 18–24 August 1986.

A number of colleagues have commented on earlier drafts of the chapter. I wish to thank Dede Boden, Aaron Cicourel, Roy D'Andrade, Allen Grimshaw, Ed Hutchins, Jean Lave, Jim Levin, Tom Scheff, Ron Ryno, Alexandra Todd, Jim Wertsch – and especially Mell Pollner for penetrating criticisms and helpful suggestions.

Permission to quote from Frederick Wiseman's film, *Titicut Follies*, was kindly granted by *Zipporah Films*, Cambridge, Mass.

Notes

1   Thomas, W.I. and Thomas, D.S. (1928) *The Child In America*, New York: Alfred Knopf, 81.
2   [Excerpts from the transcript are used as examples in the text of the article. Pt is Patient (Vladimir), HP is head psychiatrist and Dr 2 is the Second doctor.]

References

Becker, H. (1963) *Outsiders*, New York: The Free Press.
Berger, P. (1968) *The Sacred Canopy*, Garden City, NY: Doubleday.
Cicourel, A.V. (1973) *Cognitive Sociology: Language and Meaning in Social Interaction*, New York: The Free Press.
Coulter, J. (1979) *Social Construction of Mind: Studies in Ethnomethodology and Linguistic Philosophy*, London: Macmillan.

Erickson, F. (1975) 'Gatekeeping and the melting pot: interaction in counseling encounters', *Harvard Educational Review* 45: 44–70.

Evans-Pritchard, E.E. (1937) *Witchcraft, Oracles and Magic Among the Azande*, Oxford: Clarendon Press.

Garfinkel, H. (1967) *Studies in Ethnomethodology*, Englewood Cliffs, NJ: Prentice-Hall.

Gasking, D. (1955) 'Mathematics: another world', in Flew, A. (ed.) *Logic and Language*, Garden City, NY: Anchor Books.

Goffman, E. (1959) 'The moral career of the mental patient', *Psychiatry* 22: 123–42.

Gould, S.J. (1981) *The Mismeasure of Man*, New York: W.W. Norton.

Greenwood, D.J. (1984) *The Taming of Evolution*, Ithaca: Cornell University Press.

Kitsuse, J. (1963) 'Societal reaction to deviant behavior', in Becker, H.S. (ed.) *The Other Side: Perspective on Deviance*, New York: Free Press.

Laing, R.D. (1967) *The Politics of Experience*, New York: Pantheon.

Mehan, H. (1983a) 'Le constructivism social en psychologie et sociologie', *Sociologie et Societés* XIV (2): 77–96.

—— (1983b) 'The role of language and the language of role in practical decision making', *Language in Society* 12: 1–39.

Pollner, M. (1975) '"The very coinage of your brain": the anatomy of reality disjunctures', *Philosophy of Social Science* 5: 411–30.

Pollner, M. and McDonald-Wikler, L. (1985) 'The social construction of unreality', *Family Process* 24: 241–54.

Rosenhan, D.L. (1973) 'On being sane in insane places', *Science* 179: 250–8.

Scheff, T.J. (1966) *Being Mentally Ill: A Sociological Theory*, Chicago: Aldine Publishing Company.

Shweder, R.A. (1984) 'Anthropology's romantic rebellion against the enlightenment, as there's more to thinking than reasoning and evidence', in Shweder, R.A. and LeVine, R.A. (eds) *Cultural Theory, Essays on Mind, Self and Emotion*, Cambridge: Cambridge University Press, 27–66.

Szasz, T. and Hollender, M.H. (1956) 'A contribution to the philosophy of medicine: the basic models of doctor–patient relationship', *AMA Archives of Internal Medicine* 97: 585–92.

Wason, P.C. (1977) 'The theory of formal operations: a critique', in Gerber, B.A. (ed.) *Piaget and Knowing*, London: Routledge & Kegan Paul, 119–35.

Discussion points
for Part Six

1   In Pierre Bourdieu's (Chapter 32) model of communication, linguistic exchange is likened to a 'market' where different languages and language varieties have different value and their use is associated with gaining (or not) specific 'profits'. Make a list of languages, accents, dialects, styles, etc. which enjoy a high prestige and those associated with low status. Are these values uniformly positive or negative? For example, English may be viewed as a highly desirable international, globalising language (widely used in popular culture, advertising, and so on), or as an undesirable tool and manifestation of westernisation, homogenisation and displacement of local languages and values. Likewise, rap and hip-hop may be dismissed by some as distinctly corrupt musical styles, while for others they constitute the epitome of a highly desirable lifestyle.

2   Most chapters in Part Six demonstrate the idea that to control discourse is to have power. According to Michel Foucault (Chapter 33), the proliferation of medical, educational, criminal justice and other institutionally-controlled discourses about sex in Europe in the eighteenth and nineteenth centuries constituted a manifestation of the state's control over the individual. Do contemporary institutions, including the mass media, control public discourses (knowledge) on sex, politics, wealth and poverty, globalisation, the environment, and so on? Can you find examples of 'alternative' discourses on such topics? What are the outlets for these voices to be heard? What are the possible sanctions for raising them?

3   'Free' speech or 'hate' speech? Find current examples of hate speech aimed at particular nations, ethnic minorities, refugees/asylum seekers, women, gay people, children, older people, disabled people, religious or any other groups. These may be openly aggressive (e.g., on the websites of right-wing, neo-nazi organisations), or veiled as political speeches endorsing war in the interest of national security, proselytising sermons, jokes, song lyrics, stand-up comedy acts, etc. Should they be always censored, or allowed without any restrictions? (Note: It is advisable to negotiate access to political and socially sensitive websites with your webmaster.)

4   Record and transcribe several interactions on a radio phone-in programme. Following the analyses in Ian Hutchby's study (Chapter 36), examine how patterns of conversational dominance are manifested and sequentially marked in your examples.

INDEX

Pages containing relevant illustrations are indicated in *italic* type.